Employment Termination

Rights and Remedies

Employment Termination
Rights and Remedies

William J. Holloway
Michael J. Leech

Partners
Hinshaw, Culbertson, Moelmann, Hoban & Fuller
Chicago, Illinois

BNA
BOOKS

The Bureau of National Affairs, Inc., Washington, D.C.

Library of Congress Cataloging in Publication Data

Holloway, William J.
  Employment termination.

  Includes index.
  1. Employees, Dismissal—Law and legislation—
United States. I. Leech, Michael J.
II. Title.
KF3471.H64 1985   344.73′012596   85-3830
                         347.30412596

International Standard Book Number: 0-87179-436-5
Printed in the United States of America

Foreword

This book covers a most significant area of the law which, for all practical purposes, didn't exist until only a few years ago.

The black-letter rule used to be—and some employers, employees, and their lawyers believe it still is the law—that the "at will" employee could be fired "for any reason, for an improper reason, or for no reason at all." The rule had been handed down and repeated virtually without question or exception from medieval times—seemingly since the beginning of time.

The age-old rule of law relating to the employer's right to fire the employee may have been harsh but it did have the advantage of all absolute rules. It was easily stated, comprehended, and applied. But as this book demonstrates, that is not true anymore. The employer's "absolute" right of discharge is now riddled with exceptions and limitations.

To say that these exceptions have now grown to the point where they have swallowed the traditional rule would be an overstatement. But it is not an overstatement to say that employers face very significant risks if they are not aware of these newly developing exceptions and instead continue to assume that the law still gives them an unlimited right to discharge any nonunion employee.

Protecting an individual's rights and freedom from the excesses of governmental power has always been a basic, ongoing concern in this country. That is not so with the excesses of employer power. Employee unions, it is true, came into existence for the ostensible purpose of protecting employees from some of the abuses of employer power. But more than three-fourths of this country's employees are not unionized. And many employees simply don't want to surrender their individuality to unions in order to have their individuality protected from employer excesses. Only as it has come to be realized that we are a nation of employees in a highly industrialized corporate society, where large corporations possess and wield power comparable to the power of governments, has it also come to be realized that there may be a need for the law to protect individual employees from the abuses of employer power.

I was asked to write this foreword apparently because, almost 20 years ago, I wrote what some commentators have regarded as a seminal article on the subject of limiting the employer's power over employees. I like to think I may at least have lighted a candle which might have illuminated, albeit in a crude and imperfect way, some of the potential abuses of employer power and some of the ways in which the law might step in and effectively deal with those abuses. My central thesis in that *Columbia Law Review* article was that there should be legally enforceable limitations on an employer's power to control an employee's life and freedom as to matters which should be none of an employer's business. But even as I wrote that article and attempted to elaborate on that thesis, I was concerned about suggesting a cure that might turn out to be worse than the problem itself. More specifically, I have been concerned about some of the dangers of having the law intrude with too heavy a hand upon the employer-employee relationship. What has always troubled me most about imposing legal limitations on the employer's otherwise absolute right to hire and fire is the danger of stifling the employer's freedom to build and go forward with an enterprise comprised of employees of the employer's own choice. The worst thing, I have thought, would be to come up with laws which would give unintended aid to those who look upon the employer-employee relationship strictly from an adversarial point of view, or even in terms of a perpetual class struggle.

In any event, numerous and sundry exceptions to this traditional rule have been developing over the last decade or so. This book is about these relatively new and rapidly developing exceptions.

No one has—until this book—treated all the exceptions to the employer's absolute right of discharge, probably because of the obvious difficulty of getting a handle on the great number of these exceptions that have gained and still others that appear to be gaining a foothold in the law. It isn't easy to take steady aim at so many fast-moving targets. But this is just what the authors have done here. They have zeroed in on these numerous and newly developing limitations on the employer's right of discharge and then dealt with each of them in a thorough and readily understandable fashion.

Without doubt, this book represents a major accomplishment in the field of law dealing with employer-employee relationships. In many ways it is light years ahead of other works that are now appearing, both in the analytical insights it offers and the comprehensive research it reflects.

Over the past 10 years or so I have been consulted many times about claims of unfair treatment of nonunion employees by their employers. Too often these consultations involved groping around for some imaginative ideas to help people escape the harshness of the traditional rule. From now on I don't think there will be any such groping. From now on my first reflex will be to reach to my shelf with sure-handed confidence for this book.

LAWRENCE E. BLADES

Iowa City, Iowa
January 1985

Preface

In 1975, *American Law Reports* could safely observe that in an employment for an indefinite term, the right to discharge without cause or notice and for any reason was perhaps the most settled rule of law in American jurisprudence.[1] Scarcely a decade later, the employment-at-will rule is riddled with exceptions; employees are winning six-figure judgments for wrongful discharge; and legislatures are considering and adopting a patchwork quilt of restrictions on the power to fire at will.

The employment relationship—the exchange of directed services for monetary compensation—is the dominant business arrangement in industrial society, necessitated by the economies of scale and demands of specialization. It results from the need of human enterprise for centralized direction by an organizational hierarchy which assigns work functions and maintains its control by a system of rewards and punishments.

Employment is both an economic and a social relationship. Economically, the employee has a serious stake in the direction and success of the employer's business, just as the employer's most important concern in business is the efficiency and cost effectiveness of the work force. But as organized labor is fond of pointing out, the employer is rarely dependent on any single employee, for in the economic sense employees are fungible items. The employee, by contrast, is dependent on the job for survival, for maintaining his family's standard of living, for meeting future hopes and expectations, and ultimately for security in retirement. The employee's perspective was simply and eloquently stated in Willie Loman's protest against his discharge in *Death of a Salesman*: "I put thirty-four years into this

---

[1]Annot., 62 A.L.R.3d 271, 274 (1975).

firm * * * . You can't eat the orange and throw the peel away—a man is not a piece of fruit."[2]

The social component of the employment relationship is as important as its economic component. Every work place develops its own social atmosphere and relationships, a necessary by-product of the fact that employees spend half their waking hours on the job. Employees may derive personal satisfaction from their work and often find meaning and identity in it. The psychological attachment to the society of the work place and to the friendships and rivalries that develop there is so strong that discharge from employment ranks second only to divorce or loss of spouse as a traumatic psychological event of adult life. Just as status and recognition at work and in the community are created by the job, they are destroyed by a discharge.

The recent change of judicial attitude toward the employee and his job results not from the rejection of laissez-faire principles, as some have suggested; that development took place during the New Deal. Rather, recent changes in the law favoring employee rights reflect a rejection of the conventional wisdom that replaced the principles of laissez-faire: the notion that social justice is best served by an economic balance of power between big business, government regulation, and organized labor. The latter view, which has been seriously eroded in the past 20 years, was consistent with the survival of the terminable-at-will rule and permitted it to continue in force as legal doctrine and social policy until recently.

Herbert Crowley's *The Promise of American Life*, the influential statement of liberal-progressive thought first published in 1909, conceded that "[t]o recognize the labor union, and incorporate it into the American legal system, is equivalent to the desertion by the state of the non-union laborer." This goal, however, was heartily endorsed:

> "[T]he non-union laborer is a species of industrial derelict. He is the laborer who has gone astray and who either from apathy, unintelligence, incompetence, or some immediately pressing need prefers his own individual interest to the joint interest of himself and his fellow laborers. * * * [He] should, in the interest of a genuinely democratic organization of labor, be rejected; and he should be rejected as emphatically, if not as ruthlessly, as the gardener rejects the weeds in his garden for the benefit of fruit- and flower-bearing plants."[3]

In the 1930's, labor unions obtained legal recognition and thereafter enjoyed success in organizing not just the skilled trades, but also industrial workers generally. Organized labor appeared well on its way to what Crowley had foreseen: "Every battle the unions win is a clear gain. Every fight which they lose merely means a temporary suspension of their aggressive tactics. * * * A few generations more of this sort of warfare will leave the unions in substantial possession of the whole area of conflict. * * *"[4]

---

[2]A. Miller, DEATH OF A SALESMAN, Act II.
[3]H. Crowley, THE PROMISE OF AMERICAN LIFE, 386-387 (Bobbs-Merrill ed., 1965).
[4]*Id.* at 389-390.

Between 1930 and 1960, social, and hence judicial, interest in the employment relationship focused on federal economic programs and organized labor. Lawsuits that sought protection for the individual employee from arbitrary discharge were consistently rejected. Judges whose sense of fairness and progressive views might have inclined them to create employee rights embraced the terminable-at-will rule because the social alternatives of government regulation and union organization were available to protect employees. New Deal programs like unemployment compensation, wage and hour regulation, and Social Security filled pressing needs of employees. Collective bargaining promised meaningful protection against wrongful discharge and an opportunity to deal with the employer on an equal basis through an elected representative. As a matter of national policy and conventional wisdom, there was no need for the courts to provide protection for the individual employee. It was not a proper part of the judicial function to deal with such matters.

But Crowley's prediction of the universal collectivization of American labor fell far short of the mark. By the 1960's, union organizers were on the defensive, and the past two decades have seen a slow but steady decline in union membership. That decline is at least in part the consequence of a resurgence of the native American individualism belittled by Crowley and his progressive followers and discredited in its economic aspect by the demise of Hoover's "rugged individualism" and the success of the New Deal. Growing prosperity after World War II, the upward mobility of the children of union families, and the growth of service industries and white collar labor fostered this individualism in the employment setting. The revolution in individual rights brought about by the Warren Court and the ideological influence of the civil rights and women's movements both reflected and encouraged this individualist trend, which has spawned legal protection for individuals in their dealings with manufacturers, utilities, government agencies, insurance companies, merchants, creditors, and landlords. The newly developed judicial protection of the individual employee's interest in his relationship with the employer also reflects this public distrust of institutions in general.

The terminable-at-will rule, as a rule whose essential mission was to deny judicial review of the exercise of employer discretion to discharge, is already dead. If even a single exception to the at-will rule is recognized, judicial review becomes available at least to determine whether that exception applies. Employer discretion is no longer absolute. As statutory and common law limits on employer discretion grow, the courts play an increasingly important role in employment discharge decisions; and juries made up of employees more frequently become the ultimate limitation on employer discretion.

We do not mean to suggest that litigation of discharge cases is an efficient or even desirable means of resolving employment controversies. It is not. Lawsuits, in this area as in others, often have a

cost far out of proportion to the injury sustained or the social importance of the injury. As one respected jurist lamented in the context
of a discharge case premised on discrimination laws and employee
statutory rights:

> "This decision is reached with a considerable sense of frustration.
> The tangled relationship between one employee and his employer, re-
> lating solely to the continued employment relationship, has been the
> subject of [a succession of administrative and legal proceedings]. And,
> years later, we have only resolved the pleading questions.
> "We have created an administrative, legislative and judicial lab-
> yrinth which serves no one well. During a period when employment
> relationships gave rise, for different reasons, to passionate disputes,
> private arbitration and administrative resolution through the National
> Labor Relations Board arose as a reasonably expeditious means of re-
> solving those disputes with justice and finality.
> "Those means do not exist here. The aggrieved employee has mul-
> tiple avenues to pursue, all strewn with technical obstacles, and all of
> which may postpone any possible relief into the indefinite future. The
> result is a festering sense of injustice. The employer settles one claim
> and finds itself faced with a variety of others, all requiring it to employ
> professional help to guide it through, and to preserve its rights, in the
> various proceedings in which it finds itself a target. Society one way
> or another, provides the resources for both sides until the grievances
> are ultimately resolved. This court is in the uncomfortable position of
> being a necessary participant."[5]

Nonetheless, at present and for the foreseeable future, the courts
are the one place where the employee can seek relief, and that is
where the employee goes. Loss of a job is not inherently less compelling and appropriate a subject for judicial resolution than loss of
a limb, an investment, a home, or a tax exemption. As is true in
other civil cases, the judiciary is the one institution that is empowered
to provide relief with rules that ensure an opportunity to be heard.
The expense and delay of litigation may be denounced by both sides,
but until alternative procedures are adopted by the legislature, employee discharge cases will continue to appear on the court calendar.

In 1978, we represented a discharged executive in *McGrath v.
Zenith Radio Corp.*, a case which, to our knowledge, still holds the
record for recovery in a single-employee discharge case: a $2 million
verdict, reduced to $1.3 million on appeal and ultimately paid with
interest.* Being trial lawyers in what we viewed as primarily a fraud
case, we had little appreciation at the outset for the sanctity of the
terminable-at-will rule. As a consequence of that case, we became
involved in a substantial number of discharge cases, representing
both employer and employee. We naturally sought a legal treatise
that would detail the existing case law, and were astonished to learn
that the most recent comprehensive treatise was the second edition

---

[5]*Aponte v. National Steel Serv. Center*, 500 F. Supp. 198, 204 (N.D. Ill. 1980) (Moran, J.).
*Editor's note: On May 30, 1985, the authors obtained a $3.2 million jury verdict in *Green
v. Advance Ross Corp.*, No. 79 CH 591 (Cook Co. Cir. Ct.) (executive with written contract
discharged for giving severance pay to his own father after being ordered to fire him).

of Labatt's *Master and Servant*,[6] published in 1913 (just four years after Crowley's *The Promise of American Life*). Two years later, we represented the defendant in *Kurle v. Evangelical Hospital Association*, in which an equitable remedy was granted to a discharged nurse by the trial court and disallowed by the appellate court. In that case, we encountered the extensive law of private associations and its application to the hospital setting, the still growing contract law on the enforceability of employee manuals, and the phenomenon of state statutory protection of employees. From our legal research in cases like these, we developed materials for our own use in handling wrongful discharge cases brought under a variety of theories.

In 1981, we began work on this book for The Bureau of National Affairs, Inc. We soon learned that the task of researching and compiling the law in this area would be far more formidable than we had imagined. As the work progressed, we repeatedly encountered new topics and legal theories. The present volume represents the first serious effort since Labatt to provide a thorough and comprehensive treatment of the law governing employee termination.

Since Labatt wrote, statutory regulatory programs have been adopted which we chose not to cover because comprehensive material was already available in such works as *Employment Discrimination Law*[7] and *The Developing Labor Law*.[8]

This book is intended for lawyers and others having an interest in the legal consequences of the termination of an employment relationship, whether as scholars, practitioners, or students. Chapter 1 examines the origins and development of the employment-at-will doctrine in the United States and England. Chapters 2, 3, and 4 are devoted to a contract analysis of employment termination issues. Chapter 5 concerns the preclusion doctrines which may foreclose claims, defenses, or specific issues within claims and defenses. Chapter 6 summarizes the leading cases governing the discharge of public officials. In Chapter 7, eight common law tort and statutory actions that may stem from an employment discharge are examined. Chapter 8 is devoted to retaliatory discharge in violation of public policy, a cause of action which has developed in the last decade and is still in its infancy. Chapter 9 is devoted to claims of defamation, which are a common companion to wrongful discharge claims. Chapter 10 examines self-employment and employment in the service of another, since they are often conditioned upon membership in voluntary organizations such as a labor union, a hospital medical staff, a professional society, or a trade organization. Although few commentators have yet recognized its implications for employee termination cases,

---

[6]C. B. Labatt, COMMENTARIES ON THE LAW OF MASTER AND SERVANT (2d ed., Lawyer's Cooperative, 1913).

[7]B. Schlei and P. Grossman, EMPLOYMENT DISCRIMINATION LAW (2d ed., BNA Books, 1983).

[8]C. Morris ed., THE DEVELOPING LABOR LAW (2d ed., BNA Books, 1983).

principles established by the extensive case law in this area could represent the next wave of employee protection doctrine. Chapter 11 concerns a topic that has received scant attention in legal periodicals but may be the most important issue for trial lawyers representing employer and employee—the legal and equitable remedies that may ultimately be afforded if the employee prevails on any one of the contract, statutory, constitutional, status, or tort theories discussed in this text. Two appendixes compile current authorities on the common law rule of employment-at-will. Appendix A provides a list of state and federal statutes, and Appendix B gives the text of the three state "whistleblowers' protection" laws. Appendix C examines how to measure pecuniary damages in employment actions. In addition, the text in every chapter is abundantly footnoted so that counsel can easily bring research up to date and identify additional authorities through computer and orthodox legal research techniques.

Finally, we invite comments from readers concerning the topics and authorities included here.

WILLIAM J. HOLLOWAY
MICHAEL J. LEECH

Chicago
January 1985

Acknowledgments

This book would not have been possible but for the generous commitment of talent by our law firm, Hinshaw, Culbertson, Moelmann, Hoban & Fuller. Our partners were supportive over the five years it took to finish the manuscript. We remember with particular affection Tom Weithers who died in the prime of his career in 1982. He is remembered by his colleagues as a skilled advocate, inspired leader of our law firm, legal scholar and gentleman. George Hoban, Perry Fuller, Jerry Frazel, John Kirkland, Doug Reimer, and Dennis Horan were particularly helpful in assuring us cooperation until the project was completed.

The Bureau of National Affairs, Inc., assigned Andrea Posner, a talented copy editor, and Louise Rosenblatt, an experienced senior editor, to prepare the manuscript for publication. Don Farwell, a lawyer with thirty years experience in producing legal text books for BNA, contributed his considerable talent. We worked through the years of writing with Mary Green Miner, the editor in charge of the project. She assembled the team at BNA which greatly facilitated completion of the book.

Our friend Bob Falkner, an experienced labor lawyer, vice president, and legal counsel for Motorola Corporation, encouraged us to undertake a comprehensive study and helped draft the original outlines for the book.

Sanford M. Jacoby contributed the first chapter analyzing the history and development of the employment-at-will doctrine. He received an A.B. from the University of Pennsylvania and a Ph.D. in economics from the University of California at Berkeley. He presently serves as an assistant professor of Industrial Relations at the Graduate School of Management, UCLA. He is the author of numerous articles on economic history, industrial relations, and labor economics, and is the author of the book *Employing Bureaucracy: Managers, Unions, and the Transformation of Work in American Industry, 1900– 1945* (New York: Columbia University Press, 1984).

D. Jan Duffy contributed the portion on employment privacy issues that appears in Chapter 7. Ms. Duffy received an A.B. from Stanford University and a J.D. from Case Western Reserve Univer-

xiv *Employment Termination*

sity. She was chairman of the Minimum Wage Board of the State of California for 1984 and co-chairperson of the Subcommittee on Privacy in the Workplace of the American Bar Association Committee on the Law of Individual Rights and Responsibilities in the Workplace. She is presently a professor of Business and Labor Law at California Polytechnic State University at San Luis Obispo, and is a practicing lawyer with the firm of Sinsheimer, Schiebelhut & Baggett, specializing in labor and employment matters.

Professors of Finance at the University of Illinois Charles M. Linke and William R. Bryan assisted generously in the area of economic analysis. Their elegant review of the calculation of damages in employment cases comprises Appendix C. Both Drs. Linke and Bryan serve as economic counselors to business corporations and expert witnesses in litigation measuring the value of lost employment income.

Professor Jack Stieber of the School of Labor & Industrial Relations at Michigan State University is a pioneer in the search for a remedy for unjust discharge. His extensive research on the impact of a discharge upon future employment has broadened our thinking on the subject and is cited in Chapter 11.

Our colleagues in the firm prepared original drafts of portions of the manuscript. The contributors and their subjects are: Pamela Hollis, credentialing by voluntary associations; Paul Estes, damages; John Williamson, public employment; Gary Leydig and William Caputo, just cause for discharge; James Latta, defamation.

Our law clerks included Lee Perres, Sarah Davis, Leslie Lutz, Tim Trinka, Nick Kritikos, and B. J. Kelly. They each devoted many hours to library research.

Continual updating of research, completion of citations, and correction of case names was done by many paralegal assistants. Those chiefly responsible were Rosann Miller, Ann Reilly, Carol Day, and Kathy Woods.

Juanda Tate, Renee Ray, Bridget Marren, Linda Kozeluh, and Claudia Stroner finished revision after revision of the manuscript. Doubtless they were more pleased than anyone to see the last change to the last revision placed in its envelope and mailed to the publisher.

Finally, we owe a lasting debt of gratitude to our respective wives, Mary and Barbara, for their patience, encouragement and sacrifices during the long life of this project.

WILLIAM J. HOLLOWAY
MICHAEL J. LEECH

Summary Contents

Detailed Contents

II. PROCEDURAL CONSIDERATIONS AND ALTERNATE REMEDIES FOR DISCHARGE

III. STATUS ANALYSIS

IV. REMEDIES

APPENDIX B

APPENDIX C

I

Contract Analysis

1

An Historical Analysis*

Unless the duration of employment is fixed by an employment contract, private employers in almost every jurisdiction in the United States can dismiss a nonunionized employee without notice or cause. In England, however, the courts presume that an indefinite employment contract may be terminated only upon reasonable notice by the employer. The American courts originally adopted the rules of English law for determining the duration of employment contracts. But toward the end of the nineteenth century, English and American law diverged, and the American courts began to apply a presumption of terminability-at-will.

The creation of the employment-at-will rule has been attributed to laissez-faire contract doctrines that were prominent at the end of the nineteenth century or to changes in private employment practices, which placed a premium on industrial flexibility of response to economic fluctuations. These explanations are sound if applied to manual workers. The American courts' presumption of terminability-at-will accurately reflected employment practices for manual workers. In England too, long-term contracts for manual workers were replaced by contracts that were effectively terminable at will, although the English courts stopped short of a strict presumption of at-will terminabililty.

But unlike manual workers, white collar employees often were hired with fixed contracts of at least a year's duration. The English courts recognized this fact by presuming long-term hirings or by requiring lengthy notice of termination in cases involving salaried employees with indefinite contracts. Yet in the United States most courts extended the at-will presumption to salaried employees. It will

---

*This chapter originally appeared under the title "The Duration of Indefinite Employment Contracts in the United States and England: An Historical Analysis" in *Comparative Labor Law*, vol. 5, pp. 85–128 (1982). It is reproduced here with the permission of the author, Sanford M. Jacoby, and the publisher, International Society for Labor Law and the UCLA Law School.

be argued that this development was due to the absence of strong status distinctions between blue and white collar workers in the United States and, paradoxically, to the relative weakness of the American trade union movement.

Master and Servant Before the Industrial Revolution

The Statute of Artificers was the source for much of the common law of master and servant during the two centuries after its passage in 1563.[1] The law was enacted during a period of labor scarcity that saw England's population decline by at least five percent as a result of an epidemic.[2] Labor scarcity also had brought the passage of the law's predecessor, the Statute of Labourers (1351), which was enacted after the Black Death had depopulated the English countryside.[3] The statutes checked what might otherwise have been an unsettling situation for those who employed wage labor. Strict controls were placed on labor mobility and wages in an attempt to lessen the impact of labor shortages. The statutes thus helped to preserve quasi-feudal servility and stability long after labor nominally had been freed.[4]

The English statutes and the common law that grew up around them became a model for the American colonies. The colonies found the English law well-suited to their relative dearth of labor and, at least in the tobacco colonies, to their quasi-feudal employment relations. However, the free worker in the colonies enjoyed somewhat greater liberty than his contemporaries in the home country.[5]

The Statute of Artificers gave local justices of the peace the authority to annually fix maximum wage scales according to "the plenty or scarcity of the time." English employers who paid more than the maximum, an unlikely occurrence, could be fined. Workers who refused to labor at the maximum could be imprisoned for up to three months. The colonies never adopted the extensive English system of wage regulation, although colonial licensing bodies fixed wages in certain service occupations. In addition, the colonial courts punished those who, by the offer of higher wages or other terms, enticed a worker to quit his master's service before his contract had expired.[6]

Enticement was a crime recognized by the Statute of Artificers. No servant was to leave his parish without a testimonial from his master that he was allowed to depart; otherwise he would be imprisoned and any master who hired him could be fined.[7] In the col-

---

[1] 5 Eliz., ch. 4.
[2] E.A. Wrigley, POPULATION AND HISTORY (New York, 1969), 74–75.
[3] 23 Edw. 3 ch. 1.
[4] Carlo M. Cipolla, BEFORE THE INDUSTRIAL REVOLUTION (New York, 1976), 146–157; Maurice Dobb, STUDIES IN THE DEVELOPMENT OF CAPITALISM (New York, 1947), 48–70.
[5] Richard B. Morris, GOVERNMENT AND LABOR IN EARLY AMERICA (New York, 1946), 3, 483.
[6] W.S. Holdsworth, A HISTORY OF ENGLISH LAW (London, 1924), 382 of vol. 4; Bertha H. Putnam, THE ENFORCEMENT OF THE STATUTES OF LABOURERS (New York, 1908), 220–221; Morris, *op. cit.*, 18–21.
[7] Holdsworth, *op. cit.*, 383–384.

onies, an action for enticement would lie when a servant or apprentice had been persuaded to leave before the end of his contractual term of service. Suits against enticers were based on the master's property interest in his servants. Until the nineteenth century, the law treated enticement as a trespass of the master's property.[8]

This view of the servant as property allowed masters to obtain orders compelling specific performance of a labor contract. That is, a servant who left his master's employ before the end of his term could be compelled to return and work out the remainder of his service. Enticement penalties and decrees of specific performance blurred the line between slavery and free labor, as did the statutory compulsion to labor.[9]

The Statute of Artificers maintained compulsory labor for able-bodied, propertyless adults. English agricultural laborers were forbidden from apprenticing themselves to a trade and youths could be punished for refusing to enter apprenticeships.[10] Scarcity of labor and a deep resentment of idleness led colonial authorities also to favor compulsory labor. Idleness or unemployment was punished in the colonies by whipping, fines, or imprisonment in the workhouse. Even the employed could be impressed to labor on public works projects such as road construction.[11]

Compulsory labor and the meager standard of living of most workers made poor relief an important factor shaping the law of master and servant. The parish had become the unit of poor relief thirty years before the passage of the Statute of Artificers.[12] Parishes were given the responsibility of relieving the poor and unemployable with funds raised by a tax on local property; in the colonies this responsibility fell to the towns. The Settlement Law of 1662,[13] which was imitated by the colonies,[14] gave local poor law authorities the power to expel anyone thought likely to become impoverished and transport him back to his parish of settlement. The parish authorities' quest to hold down poor rates was aided by various provisions of the law of master and servant. These provisions proved beneficial to the worker, although this was an unintended consequence of the law.

The Statute of Artificers forbade dismissals before the end of a servant's term unless sufficient cause had been shown before two

---

[8]"If a servant be taken away from his service, his remedy is trespass *vi et armis*, with a *per quod*." Tapping Reeve, THE LAW OF BARON AND FEMME, OF PARENT AND CHILD, GUARDIAN AND WARD, MASTER AND SERVANT (New Haven, 1816), 376. Also see Morris, *op. cit.*, 414–434, 519; William E. Nelson, AMERICANIZATION OF THE COMMON LAW: THE IMPACT OF LEGAL CHANGE IN MASSACHUSETTS SOCIETY, 1760–1830 (Cambridge, 1975), 51, 225; Francis B. Sayre, *Inducing Breach of Contract*, 36 HARV. L. REV. 663 (1923); Note, *Tortious Interference with Contractual Relations in the Nineteenth Century*, 93 HARV. L. REV. 1511–1514 (1980).
[9]Morris, *op. cit.*, 221–222, 529.
[10]Holdsworth, *op. cit.*, 462–464 of vol. 2; 380–381 of vol. 4.
[11]Morris, *op. cit.*, 6–13.
[12]27 Henry 8 ch. 25 (1536).
[13]13 and 14 Car. 2 ch. 12 (1662).
[14]Benjamin J. Klebaner, PUBLIC POOR RELIEF IN AMERICA, 1790–1860 (New York, 1976), Chap. 4; Morris, *op. cit.*, 15–16.

justices of the peace.[15] The grounds justifying summary dismissal were broad, including misconduct, immorality, neglect, incompetence, and dishonesty, although a business downturn was not considered a reasonable cause for dismissal.[16] By requiring judicial oversight of dismissals, the law prevented a trade depression from becoming the source of a drain on parochial relief funds.[17] Judicial oversight also gave the servant some protection against an unreasonable dismissal, although the scales of justice were weighted in the employer's favor. If the servant challenged his dismissal, it was his word against his master's. The justices were likely to be friends of the master or sympathetic to his claims.[18]

The colonies, which equally were concerned with their poor rates, followed the English law on dismissals. In colonial Rhode Island a servant could not be dismissed without "reasonable and sufficient cause"; such dismissals had to be approved by the town's chief officer and three men from the Common Council. As in England, a servant dismissed without cause during the winter months might receive an award from his employer.[19]

Colonial law also compelled masters to care for their servants so as to keep them from becoming public charges. A master could not dismiss his servant for incurable illness and he was required to provide medical care to his servants if they became ill or injured. In Massachusetts employers had to provide "Suitable Meat Drinking Lodging and Apparel" to their servants and apprentices.[20]

Minimizing the cost of poor relief was not the only source of the law's obligatory paternalism. The common law conceived of the master as having an *in loco parentis* obligation to provide medical care, moral guidance, and instruction in literacy to his servants. Legal treatises typically classified master and servant as a domestic relation, along with marriage and parenthood. This domestic model was especially appropriate to apprentices and some domestic servants who lived and worked within the walls (*intra moenia*, hence "menial") of their master's home. Like a husband or father, the master was expected to provide for the physical and moral well-being of those dependent upon him.[21]

---

[15]5 Eliz., ch. 4, §5.

[16]F.R. Batt, THE LAW OF MASTER AND SERVANT (4th ed. London, 1950), 60–69.

[17]But the actions of the Privy Council in the seventeenth century suggest that the law was weakly enforced, possibly because of the justices' sympathies for the master. On four separate occasions after the Statute's enactment, the Council, which supervised the Poor Laws, was forced to take special actions requiring manufacturers to retain their workers when there was no market for their goods. Holdsworth, *op. cit.*, 381, 400–401 of vol. 4; Morris, *op. cit.*, 17.

[18]Daphne Simon, *Master and Servant* in John Saville (ed.), DEMOCRACY AND THE LABOUR MOVEMENT (London, 1954), 170. Yet relatively few servants sued their masters. Most dismissal cases involved suits between parishes over settlement rather than suits between master and servant. See text at notes 29–33, *infra*.

[19]Morris, *op. cit.*, 17–18, 526

[20]Nelson, *op. cit.*, 48, 52; Morris, *op. cit.*, 18, 520

[21]Reeve, *op. cit.*, 374; Morris, *op. cit.*, 376–382; Philip Selznick, LAW, SOCIETY AND INDUSTRIAL JUSTICE (New York, 1969), 128–129.

One should be wary of romanticizing this aspect of the relation. The master's quasi-parental duties included the administration of discipline, even corporal punishment, so long as this was rendered with moderation. Yet the colonial court records show that masters often treated their bound servants and apprentices with great cruelty. Cases of murder, manslaughter, and starvation of servants were not uncommon. The courts generally penalized an oppressive master merely by allowing the abused servant to terminate his contract. Masters in the tobacco colonies rarely were convicted even for murder or manslaughter.[22]

The duration of the employment contract was among the most important issues adjudicated by the colonial and English courts. Enforcing the contract was a relatively simple matter when its duration was clearly specified. A master might bring a criminal action or seek either specific performance or damages if a worker failed to complete his contractual term of service. Workers usually sought to recover any unpaid wages if they were dismissed prematurely. But problems arose when there was no written contract, as was often the case before mass literacy, or when the contract was of indefinite or uncertain duration.[23]

In England, a presumption at common law had grown up that a hiring of indefinite duration was a yearly hiring. Blackstone attributed the presumption to "a principle of natural equity, that the servant shall serve, and the master maintain him, throughout all the revolutions of the respective seasons, as well when there is work to be done as when there is not."[24] The presumption meant that a worker who had been supported during the winter could not quit during the growing season, and a master had to support through winter a servant who had helped him with his sowing and harvesting. But the presumption owed its origins less to equity between servant and master than to the two foundations of early employment law: the alleviation of the effects of labor scarcity and the imperatives of a parochial system of poor relief.

The Statute of Artificers had required that no hirings were to be for less than one year and could be terminated only by a quarter's warning from either party.[25] This requirement was designed to compel labor and to control labor competition by restricting a worker's mobility for annual periods. It had little to do with natural equity, as may be seen from the statute's penalties. A servant who quit before the end of the year or who failed to give proper notice was to be imprisoned by the justices of the peace. A master who dismissed prematurely or without warning was liable only for a fine of forty

---

[22]Morris, *op. cit.*, 461–500.
[23]Simon, *op. cit.*, 160, 165–166; Morris, *op. cit.*, 221, 523.
[24]William Blackstone, COMMENTARIES (Chicago, 1872), 425.
[25]5 Eliz., ch. 4, §§1, 4, 9, and 10.

shillings.[26] Thus, a worker might lose an entire year's wages if the dismissal could be justified.[27]

An annual hiring requirement also minimized parochial relief rates by forcing the master to retain his servants during the months when they were unlikely to find alternative employment. But the Statute of Artificers had become somewhat of an anachronism by the late seventeenth century.[28] Annual hiring might have slipped into obscurity had it not been for a 1691 amendment to the Settlement Laws that caused the presumption of annual hiring to become standard judicial practice during the eighteenth century.

The amendment[29] changed the laws so as to permit a person to obtain settlement in a parish by showing that he had been hired to serve and had served for one year. The determination of hiring duration thus became a key issue in the eighteenth century's "endless litigation" between parishes to determine which one was liable for a pauper's relief.[30] The presumption that an indefinite hiring was annual greatly eased the judicial task of resolving these cases.

Natural equity usually was far from the court's mind. A parish could avoid paying relief if it could prove to the court that a servant had not worked for twelve consecutive months. An author writing at the same time as Blackstone reported that overseers of the poor advised local employers to "pick a quarrel with them before the year's end, and to get rid of them."[31]

The colonies followed English usage. The requirement that three months notice be given was widely, though not uniformly, observed. Contracts for annual employment were customary for domestic servants and agricultural laborers, although artisans often were hired by the day or month.[32] Massachusetts, New York, Pennsylvania, and several other colonies allowed a person to obtain settlement in a town by proving that he had been hired to serve and had served for one year. There was a heavy volume of litigation over this issue, as in England. This suggests that colonial courts were willing to presume that an indefinite hiring was annual, at least in those occupations where it was customary.[33]

But the customary occupational structure became increasingly complex after the mid-eighteenth century. The rapid expansion of trade and industry shifted employment into occupations that did not

---

[26]5 Eliz., ch. 4, §§8 and 9. The annual hiring requirement was followed by a provision allowing the whipping and imprisonment of workers who left their parish without a testimonial from their masters.

[27]E.g., *Spain v. Arnott*, 2 Starkie 256 (1817).

[28]Simon, *op.cit.*, 197.

[29]3 W. & M., ch. 11 (1691).

[30]J.L. and B. Hammond, THE VILLAGE LABOURER, 1760–1832 (London, 1920), 88.

[31]Richard Burn, THE HISTORY OF THE POOR LAWS (London, 1764), 211, cited in Morris, *op. cit.*, 219.

[32]Morris, *op. cit.*, 219. This also reflected English usage, since the annual hiring provision of the Statute of Artificers had exempted workers hired by the day or week, or to do a particular piece of work. 5 Eliz., ch. 4, §§9 and 10.

[33]Nelson, *op. cit.*, 187–188; Klebaner, *op. cit.*, ch. 4.

easily fit the traditional categories of master and servant law.[34] The law slowly accommodated itself to the economic and ideological changes wrought by the industrial revolution.

Master and Servant in the Age of Contract

England and the United States entered the nineteenth century under the sway of new economic and legal philosophies. The elaborate mercantilist system of governmental controls and regulations now was viewed as an anachronistic impediment on the economy. Prosperity and personal liberty were thought to depend on the elimination of all barriers to the process of free exchange, including the exchange of labor for wages. In both nations, the labor market restraints of the Statute of Artificers and the common law were loosened so as to enlarge the realm of contractual freedom.

The English system of wage-fixing by justices of the peace largely disappeared by the mid-eighteenth century, although the Statute of Artificers still was in effect. Groups of industrial workers sought to activate the law at the end of the century so as to shield themselves from wage reductions. As a result, the clause of the statute that allowed the justices to fix wages was repealed in 1813. In the United States, wage controls briefly were applied during the Revolutionary War and then quickly died out. This left English and American employers free to set wages without judicial interference.[35]

Judicial intervention also was checked in the area of dismissals. In 1777, the English courts recognized the right of a master to summarily dismiss a servant without the prior approval of the justices of the peace, at least in cases where the servant had committed a "moral offense."[36] By 1817, the master's right to summarily rescind the contract was widely accepted in England; judicial intervention already had disappeared in the United States.[37] A servant with a fixed contract still had recourse to the courts if he believed a summary dismissal was unfair, but the courts refused to impose prior restraint.

The disappearance of wage-fixing and dismissal restraints reflected the growing reluctance of the courts to supervise the fairness of commercial and labor contracts. During the seventeenth and eighteenth centuries, colonial and English courts were willing to impose

---

[34]Blackstone's four categories of servants included domestic servants, apprentices, laborers hired by the day or week, and "superior" servants such as stewards and bailiffs. These categories continued to appear in nineteenth century legal treatises even though they already were an inaccurate portrayal of the English occupational structure when Blackstone devised them in the mid-eighteenth century. Kahn-Freund called Blackstone's categories "a portrait of a society which had long ceased to exist." Otto Kahn-Freund, *Blackstone's Neglected Child: The Contract of Employment*, 93 L.Q.R. 520 (1977).

[35]Simon, *op. cit.*, 197; Paul Mantoux, THE INDUSTRIAL REVOLUTION IN THE EIGHTEENTH CENTURY (London, 1961), 92–133; Morris, *op. cit.*, 92–133.

[36]*Rex v. Brampton*, Cald. Wag. Cas. 11 (1777).

[37]*Supra* note 27. Reeve's 1816 treatise made no mention of prior judicial restraint in the United States. Reeve, *op. cit.*, 339–380.

customary standards of fairness on the parties to a contractual agreement in order to "compel the performance of a legal and a moral duty."[38] These moral obligations included the master's duty to care for his servant, a duty that the master couldn't shirk by exercising superior bargaining power. But the imposition of moral obligations was repugnant to the concept of contract held by the courts after 1800. The courts, under the influence of laissez-faire ideologies, would enforce only those terms of the contract that the parties voluntarily had agreed to. The parties were free to design their own relation without interference from the state or traditional moral authority. The law no longer would supply obligations except where these had been intended by the parties. The primary function of the courts was the identification and enforcement of the parties' manifest intentions. This marked the initiation of a formalistic approach to contract interpretation.[39]

One result of this formal approach to the employment contract was the demise of the familial model in master and servant law. The courts developed a new common law rule that masters did not have to provide medical or surgical care for their servants. The courts held that an employer had to care for an injured servant only if the contract specifically provided for this.[40] The only standard of justice was the parties' own agreement, a position that gave rise to the laissez-faire doctrine of "assumption of risk" in workmen's injury cases.[41] The other obligations of the master, such as moral indoctrination and Christian training, were "increasingly neglected" by employers and the courts, since these now were viewed as "encumbrances upon a contractual arrangement of limited purpose."[42]

The demise of the familial model was not entirely injurious to the servant, for the master no longer had the right to administer corporal punishment. An 1816 legal treatise said that corporal "correction" only could be given to apprentices and menial servants; other servants were free to terminate their contracts if struck by a master.

---

[38]Theron Metcalf, PRINCIPLES OF THE LAW OF CONTRACTS (1867), 4 in Morton J. Horwitz, THE TRANSFORMATION OF AMERICAN LAW, 1780–1860 (Cambridge, 1977), 185.

[39]On the rise of a laissez-faire, formal approach to contracts, see Horwitz, *ibid.*, 3–30, 161–210, 256–266; Nelson, *op. cit.*, 137–144; Selznick, *op. cit.*, 131–137.

[40]*Clark v. Waterman*, 7 Vt. 76 (1835); 18 RULING CASE LAW (hereafter cited as R.C.L.) 506 (1917).

[41]A. Larson, WORKMEN'S COMPENSATION FOR OCCUPATIONAL INJURIES AND DEATH (desk ed. New York, 1980), 2-3–2-10 of vol. 1. The first cases of employees suing their employers for compensation for on-the-job injuries occurred at roughly the same time in England (1837) and the United States (1842). Thus the demise of the familial model in law corresponded to its dissolution in the private sector. Horwitz, *op. cit.*, 209–210.

[42]B. Bailyn, EDUCATION IN THE FORMING OF AMERICAN SOCIETY (1960), 17 in Horwitz, *ibid.*, 208. However, these obligations did not immediately disappear. The paternalism of Lowell's mill owners between 1820 and 1850 was one instance of the preservation of a pre-industrial ethic, as was Schouler's claim in 1870 that a master had a "moral obligation" to "exert a good influence on his servant." Norman Ware, THE INDUSTRIAL WORKER, 1840–1860 (Boston, 1924), 69–100; James Schouler, A TREATISE ON THE LAW OF DOMESTIC RELATIONS; EMBRACING HUSBAND AND WIFE, PARENT AND CHILD, GUARDIAN AND WARD, INFANCY, AND MASTER AND SERVANT (Boston, 1870), 615.

An 1846 edition of this work noted that "better opinion" now had it that only minors could be struck. By 1870 another treatise flatly ruled out corporal punishment of any employee.[43]

Despite this seeming mutuality, English and American courts in the nineteenth century were not evenhanded in their new approach to contracts. They took an older, more flexible approach to suits on a *quantum meruit* in which a builder sought partial payment for partial performance of a building contract. Builders were allowed to recover "off the contract" when they had breached an express contract by failing to complete a building. The courts were willing to rely on an external standard of fairness—that it was unjust for the beneficiary of a building contract to get something for nothing—even though this overrode the express terms of the contract.[44] But when a worker sued on a *quantum meruit*, the courts were quite formal and rigid.

A worker with a fixed contract might sue on a *quantum meruit* if he had quit or been dismissed without receiving compensation for services rendered. Like a building contractor, he sought payment for services rendered under a partially performed contract. But in nearly every nineteenth century case, both English[45] and American[46] courts refused to allow a worker to recover if he had quit or been dismissed for cause.[47] In contrast to building contracts, the courts held that "full performance must precede a right of recovery."[48] To allow a worker to recover the reasonable value of his labor violated the canons of contract, for it allowed the worker to "rewrite" an express contract.[49] In cases where the contract was of indefinite duration, an employer who convinced the court to infer an annual contract could bar his servant from any recovery.[50]

The harsh results produced by this formalism led one New Hampshire court to argue in 1834 that the rule barring recovery was "unequal" and "unjust." The court said that the employee should be allowed to recover the difference between the benefit the employer had received and the damages he had incurred as a result of the premature termination.[51] But this argument "did not meet with gen-

---

[43]Reeve, *op. cit.*, 374; *Reeve*, 2d ed. (New York, 1846), 374; Schouler, *op. cit.*, 616
[44]Batt, *op. cit.*, 206; Horwitz, *op. cit.*, 187–188.
[45]*Huttman v. Boulnois*, 2 Car. & P. 510 (1826); *Turner v. Robinson*, 5 Barn. & Ad. 789 (1833).
[46]*McMillan v. Vanderlip*, 12 Johns. 165 (1815); *Reab v. Moor*, 19 Johns. 337 (1822); *Stark v. Parker*, 19 Mass. 267 (1824); *Thayer v. Wadsworth*, 36 Mass. 349 (1837); *Eldridge v. Rowe*, 7 Ill. 91 (1845); *Hutchinson v. Wetmore*, 2 Cal. 310 (1852); *Hogan v. Titlow*, 14 Cal. 255 (1859); *Beach v. Mullin*, 34 N.J.L. 344 (1870).
[47]However, a worker dismissed without cause could recover in the United States (e.g., *Webster v. Wade*, 19 Cal. 291 (1861)) but not in England (e.g., *Smith v. Hayward*, 7 Ald. & El. 544 (1837); *Wood v. Moyes*, 1 W.R. 166 (1853)).
[48]H.G. Wood, A Treatise on the Law of Master and Servant (Albany, 1877), 169, 252.
[49]19 Am. Dec. 272 (1880) in Horwitz, *op. cit.*, 186.
[50]In one such case, a foreman with an indefinite contract was dismissed and failed to recover on a *quantum meruit* when the court held the contract to be annual. On top of this, he was sued by his employer for breach of contract. *Turner v. Robinson*, note 45, *supra*.
[51]*Britton v. Turner*, 6 N.H. 481 (1834).

eral favor"[52] and by 1859 the rule was said to be "well established" in England and the United States.[53]

Thus, England and the United States by the mid-nineteenth century had rolled back various statutory and common law restraints on the employment relation. Freedom of choice and the discipline of the market replaced the extra-economic compulsion of the law. The focus of the law shifted from the prescriptive regulation of the relation to the enforcement of the contractual terms the parties freely had agreed to. Issues related to the duration, termination, and breach of the employment contract became the primary concern of the law. Yet the courts interpreted these issues rather differently in England and the United States.

England

The English courts of the early nineteenth century continued to apply the rule that an employment contract of indefinite duration was an annual hiring terminable only by notice. We have seen that the rule was an accommodation to the scarce labor conditions and seasonally unstable employment found in preindustrial England. But by the early nineteenth century, labor no longer was scarce in England and industry rapidly was supplanting agriculture as the nation's primary source of employment.[54] Labor markets were becoming more extensive and fluid, as evidenced by a rise in geographic mobility rates.[55] Nevertheless, the rule was extended to include new urban industrial occupations, manual[56] as well as nonmanual.[57] The extension of the rule was peculiar given the change in labor markets, the dissimilarity between preindustrial and industrial occupations, and the new judicial approach to employment contracts. The courts would have been more consistent had they examined what the parties intended as to duration. Instead they seemed inflexibly to be applying a legal atavism.

One explanation of the court's adherence to the rule was the persistence of settlement cases in which a pauper claimed settlement by hiring. The volume of settlement cases remained high throughout the early nineteenth century. The cases now involved litigation between industrial and rural parishes over the settlement of indigent industrial workers who had migrated from the countryside.[58] Consequently, the rule was extended to encompass all types of servants, not just domestics or those in agriculture, because, as J. Abbott noted

---

[52]Wood, *op, cit.*, 280.

[53]Joseph Chitty, A TREATISE ON THE LAW OF CONTRACTS (10th ed. Springfield, 1859), 619. But see *note 47, supra.*

[54]Phyllis Deane, THE FIRST INDUSTRIAL REVOLUTION (Cambridge, 1965), 254–257; H.J. Habakkuk, AMERICAN AND BRITISH TECHNOLOGY IN THE NINETEENTH CENTURY (Cambridge, 1962), 136–137.

[55]Arthur Redford, LABOUR MIGRATION IN ENGLAND, 1800–1850 (Manchester, 1926), 62–80

[56]*Turner v. Robinson*, note 45, *supra.*

[57]*Beeston v. Collier*, 4 Bing. 309 (1827); *Fawcett v. Cash*, 5 Barn. & Ad. 904 (1834).

[58]Hammonds, *op. cit.*, 155; Redford, *op. cit.*, 81–96.

in 1826, "it is on that ground that many of our settlement cases are decided."[59]

Another reason for the rule's extension was the prevalence of long-term, fixed contracts in some branches of industry. For example, annual employment contracts were customary in the pottery trades through the 1830s and in some coal-mining regions as late as the 1860s. Workers derisively termed these contracts the "annual bond" or the "pit-bond."[60] There even were cases of multiyear fixed contracts that resembled apprenticeship contracts—four years for a mill worker or seven years for a glassblower.[61]

Long-term contracts, either express or presumed by the courts, tended to benefit the employer. As noted, the presence of a long-term contract barred a worker from recovering on a *quantum meruit*. This inhibited quits by the worker but left his employer relatively free to get rid of him because of the broad grounds justifying summary dismissal.[62] The annual contract offered little employment security to the worker since the courts were quick to side with the employer. Even if a worker proved his case he was awarded only very slight damages for an unjust, premature dismissal.[63]

Long-term contracts also permitted the suppression of trade union activities. A worker under an extended hiring had to obey his master's interpretation of the contract for one year or more.[64] If a worker disobeyed his master by following a union working rule, or if he sought higher wages, he could be imprisoned[65] for breach of contract under the various Master and Servant Acts in effect until 1875.[66] Long-term contracts were incompatible with collective bargaining over wages since the contracts of different workers expired at different dates. For these reasons, the trade unions in the coal, pottery, and other industries fought hard to get rid of the "annual bond."

A final reason for the rule's application was that it helped the courts to maintain status distinctions in a highly status-conscious society. Nineteenth century clerks and domestic servants, despite their different social standings, both had quasi-filial relations to their employer and came into close personal contact with him. Some clerks and shop assistants even lived in their employer's home.[67] However, by the end of the eighteenth century a legally recognized custom had

---

[59]*Huttman v. Boulnois*, note 45, *supra*.

[60]Simon, *op. cit.*, 190–195; Sidney and Beatrice Webb, INDUSTRIAL DEMOCRACY (London, 1920), 432–433; REPORT FROM THE SELECT COMMITTEE APPOINTED TO INQUIRE INTO THE STATE OF THE LAW AS REGARDS CONTRACTS OF SERVICE BETWEEN MASTER AND SERVANT (COMMONS), 1865, vol. 8, 370, and 1866, vol. 13, 449.

[61]*Rex v. St. John Devizes*, 9 B. & C. 896 (1829); *Hartley v. Cummings*, 5 C.B. 247 (1847).

[62]*Tortious Interference*, 1515–1516, note 8, *supra*; Simon, *op. cit.*, 165–168.

[63]Simon, *op. cit.*, 161–163.

[64]Webbs, *op. cit.*, 432; Simon, *op. cit.*, 171–173.

[65]A worker convicted of breach of contract could be punished either by discharge, imprisonment, or an abatement of wages. 20 Geo. 4, ch. 34, §3 (1823).

[66]These acts included 20 Geo. 2, ch. 19 (1747), 6 Geo. 3, ch. 25 (1766), and, especially, 4 Geo. 4, ch. 34 (1823). See C.B. Labatt, COMMENTARIES ON THE LAW OF MASTER AND SERVANT (Rochester, 1913), 981 of vol. 1.

[67]David Lockwood, THE BLACKCOATED WORKER (London, 1958), 20, 30.

developed by which a master could terminate his domestic servant by giving one month's notice or a month's pay in lieu of notice.[68] This was supposed to protect the master from the displeasure of having to come into daily contact with a servant he no longer wished to retain. The courts still presumed that domestic servants had annual contracts, although these now were said to be "defeasible yearly hirings."[69] Yet until the middle of the nineteenth century, the courts refused to extend defeasible contracts to clerical and managerial employees, undoubtedly in recognition of their superior status. As one justice said of a clerk in 1828, "it would be, indeed, extraordinary, if a party in his station of life could be turned off at a month's notice, like a cook or scullion."[70]

A second notable exception to the annual hiring rule appeared in some late eighteenth and early nineteenth century settlement cases, usually involving agricultural laborers. The courts refused to presume an annual contract and allow a settlement by hiring when the only evidence of intended duration was the daily or weekly receipt of wages.[71] Instead, the courts held these hirings to be for a day or week. However, this rule—that the rate of payment determined the duration of an indefinite hiring—was not uniformly applied and could be rebutted by any evidence of alternative customs or intentions.[72]

Decline of the Rule: Manual Workers

The annual hiring presumption became relatively unimportant after the middle of the century in cases involving manual, industrial workers. This reflected actual industrial contracting practices and, possibly, the demise of settlement by hiring.[73] Industrial employers, particularly in large firms, came to prefer the short-term contract because of the flexibility it gave them to adjust employment to fluctuations in demand. Trade unions and their members accepted shorter contracts since this made prosecution for breach less likely and facilitated collective bargaining. The unions in some industries initiated the move to shorter contracts. They forbade members from entering contracts longer than "pay to pay" and insisted that members be paid weekly rather than monthly.[74]

Other unions and employers went so far as to adopt the so-called "minute contract." Either party was free to terminate the relation "at a minute's notice," usually at the end of the day. By 1870 minute

---

[68]*Robinson v. Hindman*, 3 Esp. 235 (1800); *Beeston v. Collier*, 4 Bing. 309, 313 (1827).

[69]William W. Story, A Treatise on the Law of Contracts (4th ed. Boston, 1856), 508 of vol. 2; C.G. Addison, A Treatise on the Law of Contracts (3rd ed., New York, 1875), 578 of vol. 2.

[70]*Beeston v. Collier*, 4 Bing. 309, 311 (1827).

[71]*Rex v. Newton Toney*, 2 T.R. 453 (1788); *Rex v. Pucklechurch*, 5 East 382 (1804); *Rex v. Mitcham*, 12 East 351 (1810).

[72]Charles M. Smith, A Treatise on the Law of Master and Servant (Philadelphia, 1852), 56.

[73]Settlement by hiring was abolished by the Poor Law Amendment Act of 1834.

[74]Webbs, *op. cit.*, 431–435.

contracts were used in many of the building trades and much of the mining, iron, and engineering industries.[75] The minute contract essentially made employment terminable at will. During World War I, the contracts of munitions workers were held to be terminable at will.[76]

Minute contracts represented the extreme end of the movement toward short-term contracts. Most industrial employers stopped short of the minute contract and instead hired by the week, fortnight, or month. Workers still had to give at least a week's notice to terminate their contracts.[77] This made the determination of the notice period the key duration issue to be settled by the courts. The duration of the hiring period became relatively unimportant except as a guide to determining the period of notice.[78] Moreover, the annual presumption now was nearly irrelevant. In 1862 the courts ruled that they no longer would presume annual hiring in cases involving industrial workers.[79]

Minute contracts were not adopted by most English employers because of the crucial role the notice period played in determining the legality of a strike. Under the Master and Servant Acts, a worker could be imprisoned for breach of contract if he quit without giving proper notice; this was a common nineteenth century method for prosecuting strikers.[80] In addition, trade union leaders or members could be sued for calling a strike if they had enticed workers to breach their contracts by quitting without giving proper notice. The courts after 1853 held such enticement to be a tortious interference with contract,[81] or even a form of criminal conspiracy.[82] Much of the energy of the trade union movement in the latter half of the nineteenth century was directed toward reducing the legal consequences of a quit without notice, both through collective bargaining and what the Webbs called "the method of legal enactment." The minute contract

---

[75]REPORT, *supra* note 60, vol. 13, Q. 79–82, 383–392, 703–704, 2113–2128.

[76]Frank Tillyard, THE WORKER AND THE STATE (London, 1923), 9–11; *Hulme v. Ferranti Ltd.*, 2 K.B. 426 (1918).

[77]REPORT, *supra* note 60, vol. 13, Q. 1457–1466, 1577–1580, 2496–2498.

[78]In some cases involving manual workers, the courts equated the "reasonable notice" period with the period for the payment of wages, which also determined the hiring period. Said Pollock, C.B., "No doubt the general rule is, that notice need not be more extensive than the period of payment." *Davis v. Marshall*, 4 L.T. 216 (1861). Also see Smith (1852), *op. cit.*, 56; *Evans v. Roe*, 7 C.P. 138 (1872); Batt, *op. cit.*, 58.

[79]*Taylor v. Carr & Porter*, 2 B.&S. 335 (1862), cited in M.R. Freedland, THE CONTRACT OF EMPLOYMENT (Oxford, 1976), 144.

[80]Simon, *op. cit.*, 171–172. Strikes called without proper notice also could be prosecuted as criminal conspiracies. E.g., *R. v. Bunn*, 12 Cox C.C. 316 (1872), in which a group of gas-stokers who simultaneously breached their contracts by striking without notice were sentenced to twelve months' hard labor.

[81]Breach procurement was given a modern contractual interpretation after *Lumley v. Gye*, 2 El. & Bl. 216 (1853), in which enticement was held to be tortious interference with any contractual relation. Previously, enticement only had applied to personal service contracts such as those of domestic servants; the master did not even have to prove the existence of a contract. Note 8, *supra*; Labatt, *op. cit.*, 8016, 8020–8021 of vol. 7; Morris, *op. cit.*, 433; *Tortious Interference*, note 8, *supra*, 1522–1524; Francis B. Sayre, *Inducing Breach of Contract*, 36 HARV. L. REV. 663 (1923).

[82]E.g., *R. v. Duffield*, 5 Cox C.C. 404 (1851); Simon, *op. cit.*, 172.

was one solution to this problem; the movement to reform the law was another.[83]

In 1867 and 1875, largely due to political pressure from the trade unions, the law was changed so that workers who breached their contracts, and trade union leaders who procured these breaches, were liable only for civil actions.[84] Yet even though the legal penalties were reduced, the notice period continued to be a potent device for discouraging strikes. Between 1875 and 1909[85] employers regularly sued trade union leaders and members when a strike involved either a breach, or procurement of a breach, of the employment contract. Both could be prosecuted as a civil conspiracy if held to be malicious.[86] Hence most employers stopped short of at-will terminability, despite the flexibility this might have given them, because it would have reduced the cost to the trade union of a strike,[87] especially the "quickie" called at a moment's notice.[88]

Nonmanual Employees

Until the 1840s the courts continued to presume that nonmanual employees were hired annually. In cases involving clerks,[89] managers,[90] and other white collar employees,[91] the courts explicitly recognized the superior status of these employees and held that their annual contracts could not be defeased by notice.

Then, in an 1844 case[92] involving an editor, the court declared that there was no inflexible rule that an indefinite hiring was annual but that it was a question of fact depending on the circumstances of each case. This opened the way to a series of cases involving white collar employees in which the courts weakened the rule by allowing an annual hiring to be defeased by notice. Nearly all of the cases involved a dismissed employee suing for the salary he would have

---

[83]Sidney and Beatrice Webb, THE HISTORY OF TRADE UNIONISM (London, 1920), 185–186, 249–253, 284–286; Simon, *op. cit.*, 173–189, 199.

[84]Masters and Servants Act, 30 & 31 Vict. ch. 141 (1867); Conspiracy and Protection of Property Act, 38 & 39 Vict. ch. 86 (1875); Employers and Workmen Act, 38 & 39 Vict. ch. 90 (1875).

[85]The 1906 Trade Disputes Act (6 Edw. 6 ch. 47) gave trade union officials and members immunity from liability for procuring breaches during the course of a labor dispute. The Act was the first major victory of the new Labour Party. Webbs, HISTORY, *op. cit.*, 604 *et seq.*; H. Vester and A. Gardner, TRADE UNION LAW AND PRACTICE (London, 1958), 133.

[86]E.g., *South Wales Miners' Fed. v. Glamorgan Coal Co.*, A.C. 239 (1905). Also see Otto Kahn-Freund, LABOUR AND THE LAW (London, 1972), 231–232; *Tortious Interference*, note 8, *supra*, 1527–1528; Labatt, *op. cit.*, 8029–8036 of vol. 7 and cases cited therein.

[87]In *Allen v. Flood*, A.C. 1 (1898), a union official avoided conviction for conspiracy to induce tortious breach of contract because the contracts in question were on a daily basis. Also see *Quinn v. Leathem*, A.C. 495, 518 (1901).

[88]After 1906 employers still could and did initiate damage suits against workers who breached their contracts by ceasing work without giving proper notice. However, these suits have become relatively rare today because modern employers believe that they lead to low morale after a strike and because they are costly. A separate suit must be filed against each striker. Webbs, HISTORY, *op. cit.*, 858; K.W. Wedderburn and P.L. Davies, EMPLOYMENT GRIEVANCES AND DISPUTES PROCEDURES IN BRITAIN (Berkeley, 1969), 29-30.

[89]*Beeston v. Collier*, 4 Bing. 309 (1827).

[90]*Fawcett v. Cash*, 5 Barn. & Ad. 904 (1834).

[91]Story, *op. cit.*, 527 of vol. 2.

[92]*Baxter v. Nurse*, 6 M. & G. 935 (1844).

received through the end of his annual hiring period.[93] The practice of allowing annual contracts to be defeased by notice at any time reduced the amount an employee might recover. As one authority noted,

> "The practical result of implying, in any given case, an obligation to give notice is to abridge *pro tanto* the rights of the party—usually the servant—whose claim is dependent upon his ability to establish a contract for a year."[94]

After 1850 a judicially recognized custom grew up of allowing a clerk's annual contract to be terminated by three months' notice at any time.[95] But in cases where no well-established custom existed, the courts were inconsistent. In some cases involving white collar employees, especially those of the highest rank such as executives and professionals, an indefinite contract still was held to be annual and terminable only at the end of the annual hiring period.[96] In other cases the courts allowed an implied annual contract to be terminated at any time by "reasonable notice," sometimes as little as one week's notice for a salesman paid an annual salary.[97] By the last quarter of the nineteenth century, most cases involving nonmanual employees turned on the question of what constituted reasonable notice. The annual presumption grew less important and in 1969 finally was replaced by the presumption of terminability upon reasonable notice.[98] As with manual workers, the length of notice, rather than the duration of hiring, had become the principal issue to be settled by the courts.

It is not clear why the courts dropped the annual presumption in favor of reasonable notice, although the answer may lie in the changing character of salaried employment. The salaried clerk or assistant now worked in a large corporation rather than a small, owner-operated enterprise. The familial model no longer was appropriate to clerical employment, nor did the occupation command the same prestige and perquisites as before.[99] Once the courts had established the principle of defeasible contracts for clerks, it was but a short step to extend this to other salaried occupations.[100] This had the virtue of consistency, yet the courts did not lose their sensitivity to the status claims of high-ranking salaried employees.

The reasonable notice period was a vestige of the employment

---

[93]See cases cited in Charles M. Smith, TREATISE ON THE LAW OF MASTER AND SERVANT (2d ed., London, 1860), 64–70.

[94]Labatt, *op. cit.*, 654 of vol. 1.

[95]*Metzner v. Bolton*, 9 Ex. 518 (1854); *Fairman v. Oakford*, 5 H.&N. 635 (1860); *Foxall v. International Land Credit Co.*, 16 L.T. 637 (1867); Joseph Chitty, A TREATISE ON THE LAW OF CONTRACTS (11th ed., Cambridge, Mass., 1881), 841.

[96]*Buckingham v. Surrey Canal Co.*, 46 L.T. 885 (1882); *Cayme v. Allan Jones & Co.*, 35 T.L.R. 453 (1919).

[97]*Levy v. Electrical Wonder Co.*, 9 T.L.R. 495 (1893).

[98]*Richardson v. Koefod*, 1 W.L.R. 1812 (1969). See Charles Drake, *The Deserted Village*, 23 M.L.R. 325 (1970).

[99]Lockwood, *op. cit.*, 30–34; Gregory Anderson, VICTORIAN CLERKS (Manchester, 1976), 30–49, 129–133.

[100]Freedland, *op. cit.*, 152.

security salaried employees had enjoyed under an annual contract. The courts preserved some of this security by requiring that the notice period be related not only to the period for payment of compensation,[101] but also to the nature of the employment and the ease with which a dismissed employee might find another job. In applying these criteria the courts made employment security, in the form of reasonable notice, a function of the employee's status and income. An examination of decided cases shows the length of reasonable notice to have been: managers—twelve months; editors—twelve months; subeditors—six months; traveling salesmen—three months; film editors—one month; journalists—one month; and foremen—one week.[102] This indicates that some salaried employees of relatively high status still had as much security as an annual contract would have provided, although this was not true for those in lower positions.

Reasonable notice periods were quite short for manual employees, usually one month or less. But the notice period had a completely different meaning for the manual worker. Long notice periods did not represent a form of security but were a vestige of servility that could be used to weaken trade unionism. The manual worker's security was determined by the strength of the closed shop in his trade. He did not have to depend on the courts for employment security, nor were the courts very dependable, as they awarded only very slight damages to a worker dismissed without notice.[103] Only workers in unorganized or weakly organized trades had to rely exclusively on notice periods to cushion the impact of dismissal.[104]

Thus, the courts mirrored private employment practices in their approach to contract interpretation. The annual presumption declined in importance as trade unions and employers moved toward shorter contracts and greater flexibility in terminations. Termination by notice replaced the annual presumption in the contracts of manual and white collar employees, although it had different implications for each group. Notice functioned as a form of status-derived security for white collar employees, whereas it was the link between the strike and the law for manual workers. If there had been a greater variety of tools to suppress strikes than notice periods, it is possible that employment-at-will would have become the norm for English workers. And had English courts been less concerned with status distinctions, the same may have become true of salaried employment.

Finally, it is important to note an irony of English law. The repeal of the Master and Servant Acts put breaches by the employee on an equal footing with breaches by his employer. This made employment

---

[101]Note 78, *supra*, Chitty (1881), *op. cit.*, 841.

[102]Drawn from cases cited in Smith (1860), *op. cit.*, 64–70; Batt, *op. cit.*, 57–58. Also see B.A. Hepple and P. O'Higgins, INDIVIDUAL EMPLOYMENT LAW (London, 1971), 127.

[103]Simon, *op. cit.*, 163.

[104]This may have been a reason for the 1897 attempt by a general union of railway workers to have enacted a statutory minimum period of notice. Webbs, INDUSTRIAL, *op. cit.*, 435; H.A. Clegg et al. A HISTORY OF BRITISH TRADE UNIONS SINCE 1889 (Oxford, 1964), 230, 234–235 of vol. 1.

a contractual relation like any other and removed the last penal traces of the Statute of Artificers. But this development did not result from any new philosophical stance by the courts. The courts were quite willing to be rigid contractarians on some occasions (e.g., *quantum meruit* suits) and rather feudal on others (e.g., imprisonment for breach). Their class bias often was their only form of consistency. Rather, the repeal of the Acts and the move toward true freedom of contract was the result of a trade union movement more deeply committed to the liberal ideal of contract than were the courts.[105]

United States

The nineteenth century American courts followed English common law rules when enforcing employment contracts of fixed duration. These contracts could not be terminated prematurely except for cause.[106] The employee's duties and rights as well as the grounds justifying summary dismissal were similar in both nations.[107] So long as the employer dismissed the servant with cause and in good faith, the courts upheld a summary dismissal.[108] An implied or express contract of definite duration was renewed for an identical period if the relation continued after its expiration.[109] However, the American and English courts diverged when it came to the rules governing contracts of indefinite duration.

Many scholars are convinced that the American rules took a sharp turn after 1877.[110] In that year Horace G. Wood, an author of legal textbooks, published his *Treatise on the Law of Master and Servant*, which frequently was cited as an authority for the presumption that an indefinite contract was terminable at will and without notice in the United States.[111] Because Wood has been criticized for his legal scholarship,[112] it is useful to survey the development of employment law prior to 1877 so as to better judge the legitimacy of his claims.

---

[105]Webbs, HISTORY, *op. cit.*, 291–292.

[106]*King v. Steiren*, 44 Pa. St. 99 (1862); *Trustees of Soldiers' Orphan Home v. Shaffer*, 63 Ill. 243 (1872).

[107]Compare Labatt, *op. cit.*, chs. 6 and 9 of vol. 1 to Batt, *op. cit.*, chs. 4 and 7.

[108]*Payne v. Western & Atl. Ry.*, 81 Tenn. 507 (1884); *Alexis Stoneware Mfg. Co. v. Young*, 59 Ill. App. 226 (1894); Labatt, *op. cit.*, 594–638 of vol. 1.

[109]Implied: *Tatterson v. Suffolk Mfg. Co.*, 106 Mass. 56 (1870); *Capron v. Strout*, 11 Nev. 304 (1876); *Greer v. People's T. & T. Co.*, 18 Jones & S. 517 (1884); *Kellogg v. Citizens Ins. Co. of Pittsburgh*, 94 Wis. 554 (1896). Express: *Huntington v. Claffin*, 38 N.Y. 182 (1868); *Hodge v. Newton*, 13 N.Y.S.R. 139 (1888); *Hermann v. Littlefield*, 109 Cal. 430 (1895).

[110]E.g., Lawrence E. Blades, *Employment At Will vs. Individual Freedom: On Limiting the Abusive Exercise of Employer Power*, 67 COLUM. L. REV. 1404 (1967); Note, *Implied Contract Rights to Job Security*, 26 STAN. L. REV. 335 (1974); Theodore J. St. Antoine, "Protection Against Unjust Discipline: An Idea Whose Time Has Come," Paper delivered to the Thirty-fourth Annual Meeting of the National Academy of Arbitrators (1981).

[111]Note 48, *supra*.

[112]E.g., Jay M. Feinman, *The Development of the Employment At Will Rule*, 20 AM. J. LEGAL HIST. 118, 126 (1976).

Pre-1877

Litigation involving contracts appears to have been less widespread in the United States than in England, especially for manual workers.[113] There are several reasons for this difference. First, the early American courts heard fewer settlement cases involving issues related to the employment contract. This was because by 1810 over half of the original thirteen states no longer permitted settlement by hiring.[114]

Second, breach of the employment contract rarely was subject to criminal penalties in the United States.[115] Even before the Revolution, several of the colonies were reluctant to allow masters to bring a criminal action against their free workers. After the Revolution, the concept of criminal proceedings to enforce the contract was repugnant to the doctrines of personal liberty and equality under the law, at least in the northern states.[116] The United States never enacted its own version of the Master and Servant Acts; in 1853 the New York courts could claim that they never had invoked criminal procedures to enforce an employment contract.[117] Yet in England and Wales, even during the last eighteen years of these Acts (1858–1875), there was an average of 10,000 criminal prosecutions for breach of contract each year.[118]

The factors explaining the difference in the volume of contract litigation in turn help to explain the weakness of the annual presumption in the United States. Since there were relatively few settlement cases in which a pauper claimed settlement by annual hiring, the presumption was not as strongly established in the United States. An 1816 treatise noted that the annual hiring rule was not recognized in Connecticut, a state that had abolished settlement by hiring several years earlier.[119] Occasionally a settlement case invoked the annual hiring rule, but these cases were relatively rare.[120]

Only a handful of pre-1877 cases could be found in which a court ruled that an indefinite hiring was annual. A few involved farm laborers or noted that the rule applied only to domestic and husban-

---

[113]A survey of Wisconsin contract cases during the antebellum (1836-1861) and industrialization (1905-1915) periods found only a handful that involved the employment contracts of manual workers. Yet the single English county of Staffordshire produced a total of ten thousand prosecutions under the Master and Servant Acts between 1858 and 1867. Lawrence M. Friedman, CONTRACT LAW IN AMERICA (Madison, 1965), 42–46; Simon, *op. cit.*, 195.

[114]Massachusetts abolished settlement by hiring in 1767, followed by New Hampshire (1796), Rhode Island (1798), and Connecticut (1810). Maine's law applied only to apprentices, while Georgia and Maryland did not have state settlement laws. Klebaner, *op. cit.*, ch. 4.

[115]There were some exceptions, such as statutes permitting the criminal prosecution of deserting seamen or of railway workers who endangered public safety by abandoning a train. J.R. Commons and J.B. Andrews, PRINCIPLES OF LABOR LEGISLATION (New York, 1916), 44–46.

[116]Morris, *op. cit.*, 523; Commons and Andrews, *ibid.*, 38–40.

[117]*Haight v. Badgeley*, 15 Barb. 499 (1853).

[118]Simon, *op.cit.*, 190.

[119]Reeve (1816), *op. cit.*, 347.

[120]E.g., *Heidleberg v. Lynn*, 5 Whart. 430 (1840).

dry servants.[121] This reflected colonial customs[122] and Blackstone's "natural equity" rationale for the rule. Only one case unambiguously stated that "the English rule is accepted as the law in this country."[123] In the remaining cases, the courts did not presume an annual hiring but instead looked at the facts and circumstances surrounding each case to determine if the parties had intended an annual hiring.[124] These cases really were not instances of the annual hiring rule. Instead they should be classified with cases that followed the newer English rule that the hiring period was identical to the period of payment, since the most significant fact the courts looked to in these cases was the payment of an annual salary.

Industrial workers were not involved in any of these pre-1877 cases. This may have been a throwback to the colonial period, when artisans and laborers were not presumed to be hired annually. Reeve's 1816 treatise noted that the presumption did not apply to laborers,[125] a distinction that the courts in some of these cases also made.[126] This also may have reflected American industrial contracting practices, which differed from those in England partly because of the lack of criminal penalties for breach in the United States.

Long-term contracts made it easier for the English employer to rely on the law for assistance in disciplining his workers, since the possibility of a criminal breach was greater when contracts were of extended duration. But employers in the United States only had the remedy of a civil suit for damages against employees who breached their contracts. These suits were not an effective deterrent to employee breaches since most workers had little savings and imprisonment for debt was on the way out after the 1830s.[127] One would expect American employers to have been less likely than their English counterparts to rely on long-term contracts, or on the courts. Evidence of contracting practices in the textile industry of New England, where the courts were reluctant to apply criminal penalties for breach of contract,[128] provides some support for this hypothesis.

Between 1820 and 1850, textile mill employers were faced by high labor turnover rates and serious labor shortages, a problem that never was as severe in industrial England.[129] During this period the mills had a requirement that employees had to work one full year before they could receive an "honorable discharge," and had to give

---

[121]*Davis v. Gorton*, 16 N.Y. 255 (1857); *Hobbs v. Davis*, 30 Ga. 423 (1860); *Coffin v. Landis*, 46 Pa. 426 (1864), in which the court said that the rule applied only to menial servants.

[122]Note 32, *supra*.

[123]*Bleeker v. Johnson*, 51 How. Pr. 380 (1876).

[124]*Kirk v. Hartman & Co.*, 63 Pa. 97 (1869); *Tatterson v. Suffolk Mfg. Co.*, 106 Mass. 56 (1870); *Franklin Mining Co. v. Harris*, 24 Mich. 115 (1871); *Tarbox v. Hartenstein*, 63 Tenn. 78 (1875); *Horn v. Western Land Ass'n*, 22 Minn. 233 (1875).

[125]Reeve (1816), *op. cit.*, 347.

[126]A slave hired from her owner to raise crops was presumptively hired for a year, but not a slave hired to build a house or chimney. *Hobbs v. Davis*, 30 Ga. 423 (1860).

[127]Commons and Andrews, *op. cit.*, 31, 47.

[128]Nelson, *op. cit.*, 126.

[129]Norman Ware, THE INDUSTRIAL WORKER, 1840-1860 (New York, 1924), 150; note 54, *supra*.

from two to four weeks' notice of intention to leave.[130] But the employer did not have to give notice of dismissal. His power of dismissal was absolute and *de facto* at will. Employers discharged employees "for any reason under the sun."[131]

The annual contract, which was intended to prevent labor turnover, rarely found its way into the courts. Employees didn't sue for breach since the mills accepted no responsibility as to length of employment and reserved the right to change wages and working conditions at will.[132] Employers relied on extrajudicial means to penalize breaches of contract. A worker who quit prematurely or otherwise breached the contract was blacklisted by the mill and could not find employment elsewhere. Names of workers who had not received honorable discharges circulated throughout the industry.[133] But the primary deterrent to breaches of contract was a system of wage withholding that was customary in New England. If a worker was dismissed or quit without notice, the employer withheld either all unpaid wages or wages equal to the notice period.[134] Since workers were paid quarterly or monthly, it was easy for an employer to retain the wages of a worker who quit or was dismissed.[135]

The system was open to many abuses. Workers who gave proper notice might immediately be discharged and thus barred from recovering on a *quantum meruit*. One worker, dismissed after a week, sought his back wages and was told he couldn't have them because he had left without giving proper notice.[136]

Prior to 1850, the annual contract gave the textile worker little or no security but gave the employer a means to encourage labor stability. But the annual hiring did not have the same legal significance as in England because employers relied on blacklists and wage withholding, rather than the courts, to enforce the contract.

After 1850, possibly due to the easing of labor shortages,[137] fixed annual contracts were discarded and the New England courts first recognized that an indefinite contract was terminable at will.[138] By the 1870s, most employment contracts in the industry were indefinite. Employers in Fall River could dismiss "at a moment's notice." In Lowell, "practically all discharges of operatives are without no-

[130]Ware, *ibid.*, 107; Caroline Ware, THE EARLY NEW ENGLAND COTTON MANUFACTURE (Boston, 1931), 264; *Stevens v. Reeves*, 9 Pick. 198 (1829); *Harmon v. Salmon Falls Mfg. Co.*, 35 Me. 447 (1853); *Hunt v. Otis*, 45 Mass. 464 (1862).
[131]N. Ware, *op. cit.*, 109; C. Ware, *op. cit.*, 264, 291.
[132]N. Ware, *op. cit.*, 107. The only cases in which the annual contract appeared in court were *quantum meruit* suits in which a worker was barred from recovering back wages. E.g., *Stark v. Parker*, 19 Mass. 267 (1824); *Thayer v. Wadsworth*, 36 Mass. 349 (1837).
[133]N. Ware, *op. cit.*, 109.
[134]*Thayer v. Wadsworth*, note 132, *supra*; *Hunt v. Otis*, note 130, *supra*; Ray Ginger, *Labor in a Massachusetts Cotton Mill: 1853-1860*, 28 BUS. HIST. REV. 88 (1954).
[135]C. Ware, *op. cit.*, 246–247; *Dodge v. Favor*, 81 Mass. 83 (1860).
[136]C. Ware, *op. cit.*, 266; Massachusetts Bureau of Statistics of Labor, THIRTEENTH ANNUAL REPORT (hereinafter cited as MBSL) (Boston, 1881), 329.
[137]Howard M. Gitelman, *The Waltham System and the Coming of the Irish*, 8 LAB. HIST. 225 (1967).
[138]*Blaisdell v. Lewis*, 32 Me. 515 (1851).

tice."[139] Yet employees still were required to give notice before they quit or be liable for back wages.[140] The basic inequity of the system continued. In the late 1870s a Lowell clergyman complained, "It is not fair in the abstract to demand notice and not to give it."[141]

Unlike England, notice was not required by law in the United States unless the employer had inserted it into the contract, usually by making it a rule of the establishment.[142] The courts treated the employer's rules as implied terms of the employment contract, although they sometimes required evidence that a worker was aware of a notice rule before they would enforce it.[143] Yet the courts refused to remedy the system's glaring lack of mutuality, possibly because notice was the employer's chief strike weapon in the era before the labor injunction. In an 1853 case involving a Maine weaver who quit without notice, the court observed,

> "The only valuable protection which the manufacturer can provide against such liability to loss and against what are in these days denominated 'strikes', is to make an agreement with his laborers that if they willfully leave their machines and his employment without notice, all or a certain amount of wages that may be due to them shall be forfeited."[144]

The inequity finally was relieved in 1875 when Massachusetts passed a law making employers who withheld wages for quits without notice liable for a like forfeiture if they dismissed without notice. Six other states enacted statutes modeled after this law.[145]

Thus, the absence of criminal penalties for breach of contract forced New England employers to rely on contractual notice periods and wage withholding to deter breaches. Long-duration contracts offered the employer little additional protection from breach of contract and rarely were presented to the courts. This may explain the absence of cases involving manual workers in which the annual presumption was applied. The shift to indefinite contracts after 1850 did not represent a major change in contracting practices. As before, employers could dismiss at will. A judicial presumption of annual hiring would have aided neither employee nor employer, nor expressed their intentions.

---

[139]MBSL, *op. cit.*, 338, 405.

[140]*Ibid.*, 328; *Hunt v. Otis*, note 130, *supra*; *Collins v. New England Iron Co.*, 115 Mass. 23 (1874).

[141]MBSL, *op. cit.*, 406.

[142]There are no pre-1877 cases of either party suing for failure to give other than contractual notice, although a few cases mentioned a requirement that "reasonable notice" be given to terminate a contract. (E.g., *Harper v. Hassard*, 113 Mass. 187 (1873). *Nichols v. Coolahan*, 51 Mass. 449 (1845).) The only mention of notice in pre-1877 American treatises is the observation that the custom of a month's notice for domestic servants "does not appear to exist, if at all, in the United States." (J. Chitty, CONTRACTS (10th ed., Springfield, Mass., 1859), 627; T. Parsons, CONTRACTS (2d ed., Boston, 1855), 518 of vol. 2.) Neither Schouler nor Reeve, the two American authors of pre-1877 treatises on master and servant, mentions notice, nor does the Field Code. (note 161, *infra*.)

[143]*Stevens v. Reeves*, 9 Pick. 198 (1829); *Hunt v. Otis*, 45 Mass. 464 (1862); *Collins v. New England Iron Co.*, 115 Mass. 23 (1874).

[144]*Harmon v. Salmon Falls Mfg. Co.*, 35 Me. 447, 450 (1853).

[145]Labatt, *op. cit.*, 2320–2321 of vol. 2.

If the courts rarely invoked the annual hiring presumption, what did they do when forced to determine the duration of an indefinite hiring contract? First, there was a group of cases in which the courts subscribed to the recent English rule—that a hiring at so much per week, month, or year, in the absence of other evidence, was a definite hiring for the period named.[146] As noted, in some cases involving employees paid an annual salary, the courts determined that the hiring was for a year.[147] In others, the courts held that monthly or weekly receipt of wages implied a hiring for a month or a week.[148] None made reference to the annual hiring rule except for a case involving a miner, which noted that, "In this country the English rule does not prevail even in regard to the hiring of domestic servants."[149]

In a second group of cases, the courts rejected both the annual hiring and the rate-of-pay rules in favor of allowing a termination at will. Two cases explicitly rejected the annual hiring rule as inconsistent with American customs and usages.[150] In several other cases, all involving employees paid an annual salary, the courts rejected the rate-of-pay rule in favor of a strict interpretation of the contract.[151] The employee's annual salary was held to be insufficient evidence of the parties' intentions. It merely was a rate of pay and to treat it as anything more would be to add liabilities to the contract that neither party had intended. "We are to judge of the contract by what it contains," said an Illinois court.[152] Other courts arrived at the at-will conclusion based on the facts surrounding the contract[153] or the language used in it.[154] Yet none mechanically applied a presumption that the relation was terminable at will.

The outcome of these cases sometimes was beneficial to the employee. In two such cases, the rejection of the annual hiring presumption allowed a worker to quit without liability for breach.[155] In another case an employee was allowed to recover on a *quantum meruit* after the court found that he had not breached his contract by a quit.[156]

The law was rather confused. Different courts might rule that

---

[146]Note 71, *supra*; see cases cited in 11 A.L.R. 471–475 (1921).
[147]Note 124, *supra*.
[148]*Nichols v. Coolahan*, 51 Mass. 449 (1845); *The Hudson*, 12 F. Cas. 805 (1846); *Young v. Lewis*, 9 Tex. 73 (1852); *Beach v. Mullin*, 34 N.J.L. 344 (1870); *Capron v. Strout*, 11 Nev. 304 (1876).
[149]*Capron v. Strout, ibid.*, 311.
[150]*Coffin v. Landis*, 46 Pa. 426 (1864); *Kansas Pac. Ry. v. Roberson*, 3 Colo. 142, 146 (1876), in which the court said, "As to the English rule that a general hiring shall be taken to be a hiring for a year, we have not found any American case which recognizes it, and we think it has not been adopted in this country."
[151]*Wyngert v. Norton*, 4 Mich. 286 (1856); *Pfund v. Zimmerman*, 29 Ill. 269 (1862); *Prentiss v. Ledyard*, 28 Wis. 131 (1871); *Orr v. Ward*, 73 Il. 318 (1874); *Kansas Pac. Ry. v. Roberson*, 3 Colo. 142 (1876).
[152]*Orr v. Ward*, 73 Ill. 318 (1874).
[153]*Coffin v. Landis*, 46 Pa. 426 (1864).
[154]*Durgin v. Baker*, 32 Me. 273 (1850); *Peacock v. Cummings*, 46 Pa. 434 (1864); *Harper v. Hassard*, 113 Mass. 187 (1873).
[155]*Durgin v. Baker*, 32 Me. 273 (1850); *Pfund v. Zimmerman*, 29 Ill. 269 (1862).
[156]*Wyngert v. Norton*, 4 Mich. 286 (1856).

an identical, indefinite contract was either presumptively annual, terminable at will, or terminable at the end of a payment period. The textbooks of the period demonstrated the confused state of the law. Some mentioned only the annual hiring rule[157] and others only the rate-of-pay rule,[158] while most referred to both.[159] The cases cited to support the annual hiring rule either were English or irrelevant American cases.[160]

The confused state of the law was nowhere more evident than in the proposed New York Civil Code, drawn up in 1862 by David Dudley Field and Alexander W. Bradford. The code attempted to systematize the entire common law, including the law of master and servant. This makes it an interesting commentary on how the vagaries of the law were reconciled by men who placed a premium on legal consistency.[161] Although the New York legislature never approved the Code, it was adopted by Georgia (1863), the Dakota Territories (1866), California (1872), and several other Western states.[162] I only will discuss the California Civil Code, which included Field's master and servant sections with minor revisions.[163]

Section 1999 of the California Code stated that "an employment having no specified term may be terminated at the will of either party, on notice to the other, except where otherwise provided by this title." This section suggested, *ceteris paribus*, a presumption that employment was terminable at will. This was a rather bold claim, although it followed industrial practices and an emerging judicial line of thought. Yet none of the cases cited in the Code supported the at-will presumption.[164]

But in Section 2010, the Code stated the rule that a "servant is presumed to have been hired for such length of time as the parties adopt for the estimation of wages," either yearly or daily. One of the cases cited was an English case in which a clerk paid an annual

---

[157]Reeve, note 8, *supra* (2d ed., New York, 1846), 347, and Reeve (3d ed., Albany, 1862), 347; Chitty, *op. cit.*, 626–627.

[158]Parsons (1855), *op. cit.*, 519; T. Parsons, CONTRACTS (6th ed., Boston, 1872), 32 *et seq.* of vol. 2.

[159]Story (1856), *op. cit.*, 506–507 of vol. 2; Smith (1852), *op. cit.*, 53, 56; Addison (1875), *op. cit.*, 576 of vol. 2; Schouler (1870), *op. cit.*, 606–607.

[160]Smith, *ibid.*, 53.

[161]David D. Field and Alexander W. Bradford, THE CIVIL CODE OF THE STATE OF NEW YORK (Albany, 1865), vii (hereinafter cited as FIELD CODE); Spencer L. Kimball, HISTORICAL INTRODUCTION TO THE LEGAL SYSTEM (St. Paul, 1954), 6; Lawrence Friedman, A HISTORY OF AMERICAN LAW (New York, 1973), 351–358.

[162]A. Van Alstyne, *The California Civil Code*, in WEST'S ANNOTATED CALIFORNIA CODES: CIVIL (St. Paul, 1954), 6; S. Williston, THE LAW OF CONTRACTS (New York, 1920), 63 of vol. 1. These other states included Idaho, Montana, and Oklahoma.

[163]The California Master and Servant sections are from THE CIVIL CODE OF THE STATE OF CALIFORNIA, annotated by Creed Haymond and John C. Burch (San Francisco, 1874). All of these sections except for Section 1999 (later Section 2922 of the Labor Code) were repealed in 1969. *Cal. Stat.* ch. 1537 p. 3132.

[164]Three of the citations concern agents, not servants. The fourth is an English case in which the courts presumed an annual hiring. *Hathaway v. Bennett*, 10 N.Y. 108 (1854); *Ward v. Ruckman*, 34 Barb. 419 (1861); J. Story, COMMENTARIES ON THE LAW OF AGENCY (Boston, 1857), §§462, 476–477; *Beeston v. Collier*, 4 Bing. 309 (1827).

salary was held to have a yearly hiring.[165] This would suggest a presumption of annual hiring for salaried employees, which indeed was how the California courts interpreted this section in some later cases.[166] Field apparently had it in mind that employment would be presumed at will if no mention was made of the rate of payment.

The final section of interest was the most confusing. Field originally wrote that in the absence of any agreement as to payment, domestic servants were presumed to be hired by the month; a clerk "or other servant not merely mechanical or agricultural" by the year; and all other servants "for no specified term," that is, at will. Here he drew back from the at-will presumption and sought to provide special protection for domestic servants and white collar employees whose compensation was irregular or uncertain.[167] The California version of this section removed all mention of specific occupations and simply said that in the absence of any mention of rate of pay, "a servant is presumed to be hired by the month, at a monthly rate of reasonable wages, to be paid when service is performed."[168] The meaning of this section was unclear, for it conflicted directly with Section 1999. The California Code cited cases in which an employee was allowed to recover on a *quantum meruit* only when service was performed,[169] so the code's framers apparently meant to emphasize only the last clause of the section.

The situation in the United States in 1877 strongly resembled that in England. Both nations had moved away from the annual presumption while preserving distinctions along occupational lines. For manual workers in the United States, the most security the courts would provide was a finding of a monthly or weekly contract based on rate of pay. However, industrial practices, the Field Code, and some cases suggested a movement toward at-will employment, either by presumption or the daily receipt of wages. In England, where notice periods were implied-in-law, the courts stopped short of finding employment at will except where minute contracts had become customary.

Salaried, nonmanual employees still were protected by the annual presumption in some cases in England, or by lengthy periods of notice. But in the United States, the salaried employee was in an uncertain position. The strict presumption of annual hiring was a rarity, although the courts, the texts, and the codes allowed the same effect through the rate-of-pay rule. But some courts were beginning to reject this rule based on a strict reading of the contract. Since there

---

[165]*Davis v. Marshall*, 4 L.T. 216 (1861). The other cases cited to support the section are wholly irrelevant. *Cany v. Halleck*, 9 Cal. 198 (1858); *Angulo v. Sunol*, 14 Cal. 402 (1859).

[166]*Luce v. San Diego Land and Town Co.*, 4 Cal. Unrep. 726 (1894); *Rosenberger v. Pacific Coast Ry.*, 111 Cal. 313 (1896); *Gabriel v. Bank of Suisun*, 145 Cal. 266 (1904). In other cases, California courts looked at the rate of payment and found weekly or monthly hirings. *Standing v. Morosco*, 43 Cal. App. 244 (1919) (weekly); *Shuler v. Corl*, 39 Cal. App. 195 (1918) (monthy).

[167]FIELD CODE, *op. cit.*, §1036.

[168]CAL. CIVIL CODE, *op. cit.*, §2011.

[169]*Hutchinson v. Wetmore*, 2 Cal. 310 (1852); *Hogan v. Titlow*, 14 Cal. 255 (1859); *Webster v. Wade*, 19 Cal. 291 (1861).

was no legal requirement for notice, this left the American salaried employee in danger of losing his special status in the eyes of the law.

Wood's Rule

Horace Wood's 1877 treatise, like Field's Code, sought to "harmonize apparent conflicts" in the law and to distinguish American decisions from those of the English courts.[170] In an oft-quoted section of his treatise, Wood supposedly resolved the contradictions of American law by declaiming:

> "With us the rule is inflexible, that a general or indefinite hiring is *prima facie* a hiring at will, and if the servant seeks to make it out a yearly hiring, the burden is upon him to establish it by proof. A hiring at so much a day, week, month or year, no time being specified, is an indefinite hiring, and no presumption attaches that it was for a day even, but only at the rate fixed for whatever time the party may serve."[171]

The first sentence of this section has drawn the most attention, for Wood here was suggesting a mechanical presumption that indefinite contracts were terminable at will. Critics have pointed out that none of the cases cited by Wood supported this presumption, which is true, but Wood was neither as foolish nor disingenuous as his critics have made him out to be.

Earlier in the treatise Wood had noted that in England the annual presumption applied to an indefinite contract whereas these contracts were "a mere hiring at will" in the United States. Here the cases cited by Wood supported his claim. One case explicitly rejected the English rule. In the others the courts held, although they did not presume, that an indefinite hiring was terminable at will.[172]

Wood did not intend the at-will rule to be applied mechanically. He noted that the rule applied "unless from the language of the contract itself it is evident that the intent of the parties was that it should, at all events, continue for a certain period, or until the happening of a certain contingency."[173] Here he left room for a rebuttal of the presumption by inferring the parties' intention from a close reading of the contract.[174]

Wood had said nothing especially radical. He hedged the rule more carefully than had Field. It was in harmony with a line of American cases and the laws of those states that had adopted the Field Code. About the only radical thing Wood had done was to reject

---

[170]Wood, *op. cit.*, iii. Some courts felt Wood was more authoritative than other treatise authors because of his sensitivity to Anglo-American differences. E.g., *Greer v. Arlington Mills*, 1 Penn. (Del.) 581 (1899).

[171]Wood, *op. cit.*, 272.

[172]*Ibid.*, 265. The cases were *Coffin v. Landis*, 46 Pa. 426 (1864); *Harper v. Hassard*, 113 Mass. 187 (1873); *Peacock v. Cummings*, 46 Pa. 434 (1864). Note that other treatises which supported the alternative English rule usually failed to cite relevant American cases. Note 160, *supra*.

[173]Wood, *op. cit.*, 265-266.

[174]However, Wood placed the burden of proof on the employee since the hiring was "*prima facie* a hiring at will." *Ibid.*, 272.

the annual hiring rule, which he believed had not been approved by any American court in recent years.[175] Here Wood was wrong, but he may genuinely have overlooked the handful of American cases in which the courts had applied the annual presumption.

But what of the rate-of-pay rule, which was supported by the codes, the courts, and other treatises? Wood was somewhat ambivalent on this issue. The language of the criticized section ("but only at the rate fixed for whatever time the party may serve") appeared to support the rate-of-pay rule. So did three of the four American cases cited by Wood in this section, the cases that his critics have thought were a reference to the at-will rule.[176] Wood backed away from a mechanical application of the pay rule and argued that the parties had to show a "mutual understanding" that the rate of payment implied a definite hiring for the pay period, an understanding to be proved by "the facts and circumstances surrounding the parties and the transaction."[177] This seemed to leave room for inferring duration from the rate of payment.

Nevertheless, further in the section Wood changed his moderate line of reasoning and bluntly rejected any form of the rule: "But a contract to pay one $800 a year for services is not a contract for a year, but a contract to pay at the rate of $800 a year for services actually rendered, and is determinable at will by either party."[178] This was quite radical, for it undercut any claim to an annual hiring by salaried employees. But Wood did not invent this harsh rejection of the rate-of-payment rule. The rule already had been rejected by several courts that took a strict approach to the contract.[179] Wood was consistent with the contractarian logic of some of the contemporary courts in his handling both of this rule and the at-will presumption.

Post-1877

The courts after 1877 had four alternatives when faced with an indefinite contract: (1) the annual presumption; (2) the analysis of the facts and circumstances of each case to determine intended duration; (3) the rate-of-payment rule; and (4) the at-will presumption. Many courts continued to accept the rate-of-pay rule. However, the major development of the period was the widespread rejection of that

---

[175]*Ibid.*, 272.

[176]*De Briar v. Minturn*, 1 Cal. 450 (1851) (monthly pay implied a monthly hiring); *Tatterson v. Suffolk Mfg. Co.*, 1106 Mass. 56 (1870) (annual salary implied an annual hiring); *Franklin Mining Co. v. Harris*, 24 Mich. 115 (1871) (annual salary implied an annual hiring); *Wilder v. United States*, 5 Ct. Cl. 462 (1869) (irrelevant). In 1888 Wood edited the eighth American edition of Addison's *Contracts* and let stand Addison's statement of the rate-of-pay rule. C.G. Addison, CONTRACTS (Boston, 1888), 629-635 of vol. 1.

[177]Wood, *op. cit.*, 272. But see *Resener v. Watts*, 73 W. Va. 342 (1913), where Wood was cited as an authority for a rejection of the rate-of-pay rule as lacking in mutuality.

[178]Wood, *op. cit.*, 273.

[179]Note 151, *supra*.

rule in favor of a strict presumption of terminability-at-will, often based solely on Wood's authority.

(1) As before, few courts entertained the annual presumption after 1877. Nearly all cases[180] that mentioned this rule rejected it in favor of the presumption that employment was terminable at will. The courts rarely gave a reason for rejecting the annual hiring rule except to cite Wood or cases citing him.[181] But one court did provide a sound explanation for favoring the at-will over the annual hiring rule: It allowed workers to sue on a *quantum meruit* and barred employers from seeking damages when a worker quit.[182] Pre-1877 courts also had been reluctant to apply the annual rule in such cases[183] and there is little reason to mourn its demise after 1877.

(2) Some courts after 1877 reached decisions favorable to the employee by examining the facts and circumstances surrounding a contract. A definite contract was inferred by such facts as an employee selling his home and moving to take the job in question,[184] by contractual provisions for annual pay increases[185] or annual profit sharing,[186] or by peculiar contract language that suggested an annual employment.[187] Most of these cases involved salaried employees and the courts also looked to the payment of an annual salary as a guide to intended duration.[188]

(3) The rate-of-payment rule continued to be accepted by the courts in a majority of states, even as late as 1942.[189] Some of these cases involved employees paid a weekly or monthly salary, which the courts held to be weekly[190] or monthly[191] hirings. But most of these cases were won by employees paid an annual salary, which the courts viewed as proof of a yearly hiring.[192]

---

[180]English rule supported in *Adams v. Fitzpatrick*, 125 N.Y. 124 (1891).
[181]E.g., *Watson v. Gugino*, 204 N.Y. 535 (1912).
[182]The worker is "thus relieved from the injustice of the English rule." *Boogher v. Maryland Life Ins. Co.*, 8 Mo. App. 533 (1880).
[183]Notes 155–156, *supra.*
[184]*Smith v. Theobald*, 86 Ky. 141 (1887); *Woods v. M.A. Shummard*, 114 La. 451 (1905); *Holcomb & Hoke Mfg. Co. v. Younge*, 103 Ind. App. 439 (1937).
[185]*Maynard v. Royal Worcester Corset Co.*, 200 Mass. 1 (1908).
[186]*Koehler v. Buhl*, 94 Mich. 496 (1893).
[187]*Babcock & W. Co. v. Moore*, 61 Md. 161 (1884); *Norton v. Cowell*, 65 Md. 359 (1886); *Kelly v. Carthage Wheel Co.*, 62 Ohio St. 598 (1900); *Heminway & Sons Silk Co. v. Porter*, 94 Ill. App. 609 (1900); *Hotchkiss v. Godkin*, 71 N.Y. Supp. 629 (1901); *Gabriel v. Opoznauer*, 153 N.Y. Supp. 999 (1915).
[188]E.g., *Smith v. Theobald*, 86 Ky. 141 (1887).
[189]Note, *Employment Contracts of Unspecified Duration*, 41 COLUM. L. REV. 107, 108 (1942).
[190]*Webb v. McCranie*, 12 Ga. App. 269 (1913); *Standing v. Morosco*, 43 Cal. App. 244 (1919).
[191]*Jones v. Trinity Parish*, 19 Fed. 59 (1883); *Magarahan v. Wright*, 83 Ga. 773 (1889); *San Antonio & A.P. Ry. v. Sale*, 31 S.W. 325 (1895); *Great Northern Hotel Co. v. Leopold*, 72 Ill. App. 1108 (1897); *White v. City of Alameda*, 124 Cal. 95 (1899); *Cronemillar v. Duluth*, 134 Wis. 248 (1908); *National Life Ins. Co. v. Ferguson*, 69 Ala. 823 (1915).
[192]*Bascom v. Shillito*, 37 Ohio St. 431 (1882); *Liddell v. Chidester*, 84 Ala. 508 (1887); *Smith v. Theobald*, 86 Ky. 141 (1887); *Howard v. Eastern Tenn. etc. Ry.*, 91 Ala. 268 (1890); *Douglas v. Merchants' Ins. Co. of N.Y.*, 118 N.Y. 484 (1890); *Adams v. Fitzpatrick*, 125 N.Y. 124 (1891); *Philadelphia Packing & Prov. Co.*, 4 Pa. Dist. R. 57 (1893); *Luce v. San Diego Land and Town Co.*, 4 Cal. Unrep. 726 (1894); *Chamberlain v. Detroit Stove Works*, 103 Mich. 124 (1894); *Rosenberger v. Pacific Coast Ry.*, 111 Cal. 313 (1896); *Kellogg v. Citizens Ins. Co. of Pittsburgh*, 94 Wis. 554 (1896); *Heminway and Sons Silk Co. v. Porter*, 94 Ill. App. 609 (1900); *Gabriel v. Bank of Suisun*, 145 Cal. 266 (1904); *Maynard v. Royal Worcester Corset Co.*, 200 Mass. 1 (1908); *Gabriel v. Opoznauer*, 153 N.Y. Supp. 999 (1915); *Moline Lumber Co. v. Harrison*, 128 Ark. 260 (1917); *Holcomb & Hoke Mfg. Co. v. Younge*, 103 Ind. App. 439 (1937).

One reason for the rule's persistence was that it protected the employment security of relatively high-paid, high-status employees. The courts were sensitive to the occupational status of the salaried employee and occasionally were explicit about their bias. One court noted that the word "salary" was "more frequently applied to annual employment than to any other, and its use may impart a factor of permanency."[193] Other courts buttressed the rule by referring to "the character of the employment"[194] or the fact that "the employment was an important one."[195] In states that accepted the rule, the burden of proof was on the person, usually the employer, seeking to prove an indefinite hiring.[196]

Also, the rule was kept alive by the courts of those states that had enacted Field's codification of the rule. These tended to be the states that applied the rule to low-status workers paid by the week or month.[197]

(4) Most[198] of the cases that asserted terminability-at-will involved a rejection of the rate-of-pay rule. The plaintiffs usually[199] were employees seeking to prove a yearly hiring based on their annual salaries. The courts rarely offered an explanation for their embrace of the at-will presumption. A few noted that an annual salary merely was a rate of compensation rather than a mutual specification of duration.[200] But most simply cited Wood or cases citing him to support the presumption.[201]

The strict application of the at-will presumption forced the courts to ignore other evidence that supported or undermined the employee's claims. Employees who had moved long distances[202] or who had ten or more years employment[203] were held to have indefinite contracts by virtue of the at-will rule. In some cases the courts upheld dismissals by using the at-will rule when the same result could have been reached by recognizing a good cause for dismissal.[204]

It is doubtful that the rigid application of the at-will doctrine

---

[193]*Maynard v. Royal Worcester Corset Co.*, 200 Mass. 1 (1908).
[194]*Bascom v. Shillito*, 37 Ohio St. 431, 433 (1882).
[195]*Holcomb & Hoke Mfg. Co. v. Younge*, 103 Ind. App. 439 (1937).
[196]Note, 1 CORNELL L.Q. 194, 195 (1915).
[197]See California and Georgia cases in notes 190–191, *supra*.
[198]But see text at note 243 *et seq.*, *infra*.
[199]The courts also rejected the rate-of-pay rule in cases involving employees paid on a weekly (*Watson v. Gugino*, 204 N.Y. 535 (1912)) or monthly basis (*Evans v. St. Louis etc. Ry.* 24 Mo. App. 114 (1887); *Kosloski v. Kelly*, 122 Wis. 365 (1904)). In one case the at-will result was reached by applying the rate-of-pay rule to a worker paid on a daily basis. *Davis v. Barr*, 12 N.Y.S.R. 111 (1887).
[200]*Tyng v. Theological Seminary*, 14 Jones & S. 250 (1880); *Norton v. Cowell*, 65 Md. 359 (1886); *Lynch v. Eimer*, 24 Ill. App. 185 (1887); *Resener v. Watts*, 73 W. Va. 342 (1913). Also see note 182, *supra*.
[201]*Finger v. Koch and Schilling Brewing Co.*, 13 Mo. App. 114 (1883); *McCullough Iron Co. v. Carpenter*, 67 Md. 554 (1887); *Martin v. New York Life Ins. Co.*, 148 N.Y. 117 (1895); *Copp v. Colorado Coal and Iron Co.*, 46 N.Y.S. 542 (1897); *Greer v. Arlington Mills Mfg. Co.*, 1 Penn. (Del.) 581 (1899); *Granger v. American Brewing Co.*, 55 N.Y.S. 695 (1899); *Watson v. Gugino*, 204 N.Y. 535 (1912).
[202]*Odom v. Bush*, 125 Ga. 184 (1906).
[203]*Martin v. New York Life Ins. Co.*, 148 N.Y. 117 (1895); *Greer v. Arlington Mills Mfg. Co.*, 1 Penn. (Del.) 581 (1899).
[204]Note, *Implied Contract Rights to Job Security*, 26 STAN. L. REV. 335, 344–345 (1974).

was due solely to Wood's influence upon the courts. Wood, after all, had drawn on existing tendencies in the law; he did not invent the doctrine.[205] Moreover, the courts after 1877 cited Wood to fit their own predilections. His formulation of the doctrine left room for consideration of the circumstances surrounding a case, an option that courts applying the doctrine chose to ignore.[206] Wood apparently rejected the rate-of-pay rule, yet courts that supported the rule nevertheless cited him as an authority on other aspects of a case.[207] Finally, other American treatises did not agree with Wood but the courts chose to ignore these as well.[208] Wood merely lent legitimacy to those who thought the alternatives to the at-will doctrine were inappropriate or ill-conceived.

The chief alternative to the at-will doctrine was the rate-of-pay rule. Many states were as ambivalent as Wood in choosing between these alternatives. Their courts applied the rate-of-pay rule in some cases and cited Wood to support the at-will presumption in others.[209] But by 1917 one authority noted that the "drift of modern judicial thought" was in the direction of favoring the at-will doctrine over the rate-of-pay rule.[210] We must go beyond Mr. Wood to understand the doctrine's triumph.

Contractarian Logic

Perhaps the most common explanation for the courts' embrace of the at-will doctrine was the rise of a formalistic approach to contract interpretation.[211] The law focused narrowly on the contract to determine what the parties had intended. According to this logic, if the parties had intended the employment to last for a definite period they would have made that an express term of the contract. The at-will rule was the apotheosis of the laissez-faire conception of a contractual relation: The parties had a limited commitment to each other; they were free to enter or end a relation and define its terms without judicial interference.[212] The period from 1890 to 1910, when the at-will rule became preeminent, marked the zenith of laissez-faire reasoning by the courts.[213] However, the explanation is not entirely convincing, since the at-will doctrine was at variance with the contractarian principle that the courts were supposed to give effect to the parties' manifest intentions.[214]

---

[205]See text at notes 170–179, *supra.*

[206]E.g., *Odom v. Bush*, 125 Ga. 184 (1906). Also see text at notes 217–221, *infra.*

[207]*Adams v. Fitzpatrick*, 125 N.Y. 124 (1891); *Philadelphia Packing and Prov. Co.*, 4 Pa. D. 57 (1893); *Mondon v. Western Union Tel. Co.*, 96 Ga. 499 (1895).

[208]See notes 157–159, *supra.*

[209]11 A.L.R. 469, 479–480; Labatt, *op. cit.*, 527–528 of vol. 1.

[210]18 R.C.L. 509 (1917); Labatt, *op. cit.*, 519 of vol. 1.

[211]Note, *Protecting At Will Employees Against Wrongful Discharge: The Duty To Terminate Only in Good Faith*, 93 HARV. L. REV. 1816, 1825-1826 (1980); Note, *Implied Rights*, note 204, *supra*, 343–345; Selznick, *op. cit.*, 130–137.

[212]*Ibid.*, 131; Horwitz, *op. cit.*, 256–265; see text at notes 45–53, *supra.*

[213]Clyde E. Jacobs, LAW WRITERS AND THE COURTS (Berkeley, 1954), 70, 93–97.

[214]Feinman, *op. cit.*, 130.

The rigid presumption of terminability-at-will forced the courts to ignore evidence of the parties' intentions.[215] In cases where the contract specified a rate of payment, a presumption of at-will terminability contradicted the parties' intentions that the relation should last as long as the period of payment. Strict contractarians like Williston argued that by ignoring the payment period, the

> "* * *courts had failed to observe that such a construction should, if possible, be put upon the language of the parties who enter into an agreement as will give rise to a legal obligation. [I]t seems a fair presumption that the parties intended the employment to last for at least one such period. * * * And should the parties continue their relation after the expiration of the first period, another contract by implication of fact would arise for another similar period."[216]

Also, the at-will doctrine flatly contradicted contractarian logic in cases involving permanent employment contracts. The courts in most jurisdictions after 1890 held that contracts for "permanent" or "lifetime" employment were indefinite as to duration and thus terminable at will.[217] Often the plaintiff had been promised permanent employment in return for dropping an injury claim against his employer.[218] The parties clearly had intended that employment should continue as long as the employee remained able to perform his job. Holding such contracts to be indefinite and terminable at will was a negation of these intentions, an outcome that Williston also found unacceptable.[219] English courts in the late nineteenth century considered these contracts to be perpetual in duration and enforceable,[220] as did some American courts.[221] But most American courts refused to enforce these contracts, which weakens the contractarian explanation for the doctrine.

Contract Duration

A second explanation for the at-will doctrine is that it was a reflection of a trend toward employment contracts of relatively short duration. The evidence for New England textile operatives indicates

---

[215]Notes 202–203, *supra.*

[216]Williston, *op. cit.,* 62.

[217]E.g., *Perry v. Wheeler,* 75 Ky. 541 (1871); *Lord v. Goldberg,* 81 Cal. 596 (1889); *Speeder Cycle Co. v. Teeters,* 18 Ind. App. 474 (1897); *Davidson v. Laughlin,* 6 Cal. Unrep. 878 (1902); *Faulkner v. Des Moines Drug Co.,* 117 Iowa 120 (1902); *Shuler v. Corl,* 39 Cal. App. 195 (1918). Also see 35 A.L.R. 1432 (1924).

[218]E.g., *East Line & R.R. Ry. v. Scott,* 72 Tex. 70 (1888); *Pennsylvania Co. v. Dolan,* 6 Ind. App. 109 (1892); *Harrington v. Kansas City Cable R. Co.,* 60 Mo. App. 223 (1895); *Louisville & Nashville R.R. v. Offutt,* 99 Ky. 427 (1896); *Sullivan v. Detroit, Y. & A.A. Ry.,* 135 Mich. 661 (1904); *Louisville & Nashville R.R. v. Cox,* 145 Ky. 667 (1911); *St. Louis, I.M. & S. Ry. v. Morgan,* 107 Ark. 202 (1913).

[219]Williston, *op. cit.,* 64.

[220]Freedland, *op. cit.,* 154–155.

[221]*Revere v. Boston Copper Co.,* 32 Mass. 351 (1834); *Roddy v. McGetrick,* 49 Ala. 159 (1873); *Carnig v. Carr,* 167 Mass. 544 (1897); *Sax v. Detroit, G.H. & M. Ry. Co.,* 125 Mich. 252 (1900). In *Carnig* the court said of a permanent employment promise, "consider the circumstances surrounding the making of the contract, its subject, the situation and relation of the parties, and the sense in which, taking these things into account, the words would be commonly understood." Also see 35 A.L.R. 1432, 1434–1437 (1924).

that contracts were terminable at will by the 1870s and possibly earlier, since employers enjoyed a de facto power to dismiss at will even when contracts were for definite periods.[222] The dearth of cases involving laborers or industrial workers suing for breach of contract[223] suggests that these workers accepted the employer's right to dismiss them at will.

However, the cases in which the rule was applied did not usually involve manual workers but well-paid professionals, clerks, and managers. It was not likely that these employees generally had contracts terminable at will. The contracts of these employees during the 1880s and later often were for definite periods, usually a year.[224] Moreover, the fact that many courts as well as juries[225] were willing to infer yearly hirings from the payment of an annual salary indicates a lack of a general perception that salaried employees were terminable at will.

New Middle Class

Feinman's Marxist explanation[226] for the at-will doctrine is that it was promulgated to prevent a new middle class of salaried employees from establishing interests in their jobs. The complexity and size of business organizations in the late nineteenth century brought about an increase in the number of educated middle managers and professionals. Employers were determined to assert their authority over these new employees and disabuse them of any expectation of a right to management and profits. An effective way for owners to assert control was to declare that these employees had no claims on the firm in the form of employment tenure, and were employed at the will of its owners. The courts supported the objectives of capital. They ignored traditional employment practices and held these employees' contracts to be terminable at will.

The courts may have been influenced by the changing character of salaried employment, but Feinman's explanation is not satisfactory. True, the salaried clerk or middle manager no longer had close personal ties to his employer, which reduced the familial or paternal character of salaried employment.[227] Employers felt less obligated to protect these employees from dismissal and the courts may have sensed this. This could explain the decline of the annual presumption in English and American cases involving salaried employees. But Feinman's explanation forces us to assume that the courts were un-

---

[222]See text at notes 131–141, *supra*.

[223]Note 113, *supra*.

[224]E.g., *Pullan v. Cochran*, 6 Ohio L.J. 390 (1881); *Soule v. Soule*, 157 Mass. 451 (1892); *Alexis Stoneware Mfg. Co. v. Young*, 59 Ill. App. 226 (1894); *Mason v. Produce Exch.*, 111 N.Y.S. 163 (1908).

[225]E.g., *Greer v. People's T. & T. Co.*, 18 Jones & S. 517 (1884); *McCullough Iron Co. v. Carpenter*, 67 Md. 554 (1887); Feinman, *op. cit.*, 128–129.

[226]*Ibid*, 131–134.

[227]Note 99, *supra*.

sympathetic to the status of white collar employees. This was not true, especially in England.

The English courts in the late nineteenth century protected the claims of white collar employees by requiring termination with fairly long periods of notice, often as long as a year for those in higher positions.[228] English employers no doubt were motivated by the same impulses as their American counterparts yet the courts refused to presume terminability-at-will.

The courts of many American states continued to apply the rate-of-pay rule long after the appearance of the at-will doctrine. As noted, this usually was for the benefit of high-status employees; some courts even argued that salaried employment connoted an expectation of permanence.[229] American commentators such as Labatt recognized that the at-will presumption would be prejudicial to the salaried employee since,

> " * * * the higher the position to which the contract relates the more certainly may it be inferred that the employer and the employed expect their relationship to continue for a considerable period."[230]

But by the 1910s the American courts were tending to favor the at-will doctrine over the rate-of-pay rule. They were increasingly reluctant to protect white collar employees, something that the English courts were quite willing to do via reasonable notice periods.

The Collar Line

One explanation of divergent developments in the United States and England may lie in the relative strength of the "collar line" in England. The collar line is the status difference a society perceives between white collar and blue collar occupations, which may be measured by comparing differences in income, privileges, and prestige between the two occupational groups. A recent comparative study found relatively indistinct cleavages between white and blue collar workers in the United States between 1890 and 1920. Class polarization was not pronounced in the United States, where

> " * * * contemporary public opinion, in fact, hardly seemed aware of a status distinction between skilled workers and lower and middle level white collar workers. They were usually mentioned in one breath, and jointly distinguished from the new immigrants who made up the mass of unskilled workers."[231]

In contrast to the United States, the collar line was much more distinct in England. There "the difference in status and esteem between the respectable black-coated worker and manual workers was quite

---

[228]See text at notes 101–102, *supra.*
[229]See text at notes 193–195, *supra.*
[230]Labatt, *op. cit.*, 519 of vol. 1.
[231]Jurgen Kocka, White Collar Workers in America, 1890–1940: A Social-Political History in International Perspective (Beverly Hills, 1980), 135–136.

visible."[232] The sharply drawn collar line in prewar England stamped social and political relationships far more strongly than in the United States.[233]

We only may speculate on the relation between the collar line and the law. But it seems plausible that the English courts were willing to require long notice periods for white collar employees because this corresponded to societal perceptions of class privilege and helped to preserve status distinctions in employment. The American courts failed to maintain distinctions between manual workers paid an hourly wage and white collar employees paid a monthly or annual salary because the collar line was less sharply drawn. Had there been greater stratification between these groups, the courts might have been willing to accord special privileges to salaried employees. The fact that the rate-of-pay rule still was recognized as late as World War II suggests that some courts *were* willing to grant the salaried an exemption from the at-will doctrine.[234] Yet most courts by 1917 refused to adhere to the rate-of-pay rule and treated the contracts of salaried employees in the same manner as manual workers' contracts.[235] The alacrity with which the courts erased any status distinctions also may have been due to the salience of the at-will doctrine in other areas after 1890.

Trade Unions and the Law

A second explanation for divergent developments in the law is based on the different methods used by English and American unions to limit the employer's power to dismiss. English trade unions, as we have seen, fought hard to establish contractual equality between the employer and worker. One outcome of this struggle was the practice of allowing quits on very short notice, which protected strikers and their unions from legal liability. But the liberal English unions never sought extensive limitations on the employer's power to dismiss. The right of the English employer to dismiss "has been remarkably little challenged * * * in the practice of British collective bargaining" and most collective agreements do not question the employer's right to dismiss.[236] Neither did the unions, until recently,[237] seek statutory restrictions on the employer's power to dismiss. Instead they relied on the institutions that epitomized their strength and solidarity—

---

[232]*Ibid.*, 269.

[233]*Ibid.*, 139–141, 268.

[234]Note 189, *supra*.

[235]18 R.C.L. 508–509 (1917).

[236]Wedderburn and Davies, *op. cit.*, 33; Frederic Meyers, OWNERSHIP OF JOBS: A COMPARATIVE STUDY (Los Angeles, 1964), 24. English trade unions provided for arbitration of grievances by joint committees and other bodies but these bodies rarely concerned themselves with dismissals. Handling dismissals through disputes procedures was a more recent development. Webbs, INDUSTRIAL DEMOCRACY, *op. cit.*, 175–195, 223–238; Wedderburn and Davies, *op. cit.*, 57–75, 129–152.

[237]B.A. Hepple and P. O'Higgins, ENCYCLOPAEDIA OF LABOUR RELATIONS LAW (London, 1972), 1012–1015.

the closed shop and the lightning strike—to protect their members against redundancies and what they viewed as unjust dismissals.[238] The typical link between union control over dismissals and the law was the protest strike called without proper notice. The mutual notice period, in turn, kept the courts from espousing any grand doctrine of terminability-at-will.[239]

American unions, for a variety of reasons, were relatively weak[240] and remedied their weakness by seeking both statutory and contractual restraints on dismissals. During the thirty-year period after 1885, the unions repeatedly turned to the legislatures for protection against discriminatory dismissals by employers. This period also saw the initiation of collective bargaining, whereby the unions pursued contractual limitations on the employer's power to dismiss. Both developments met with great hostility from the courts, which checked the unions by asserting the employer's right to terminate employment at will.

New York in 1887 was the first state to enact legislation making it a criminal offense to discharge an employee for being a union member, or to require a verbal or written ("yellow-dog") agreement making nonmembership in a union a condition for employment. The New York law was imitated by a succession of states during the 1890s and early 1900s. A total of twenty two states at one time had laws outlawing discrimination against union members.[241] In addition, Congress passed the Erdman Act in 1898, which, among other things, made it a misdemeanor for a railway to discharge or refuse to hire a worker because of union membership.[242]

The state supreme courts in nearly a dozen states held these laws to be unconstitutional in a series of cases that stretched from 1895

---

[238]Wedderburn and Davies, *op. cit.*, 115–117; P. Davies and M. Freedland, LABOUR LAW: TEXTS AND MATERIALS (London, 1979), 489–512.

[239]Notice periods were used in the United States but they were not implied-in-law unless they were part of the rules of the establishment. Hence American courts could allow at-will dismissals while enforcing contractual notice periods, as in New England. Yet American employers did not rely as heavily on contractual notice periods to discourage strikes because they had a more potent, and cheaper, deterrent in the labor injunction. The injunction became the preeminent American strike breaking device after 1880. English courts, however, consistently refused to issue injunctions against labor unions whose conduct harmed only intangible economic interests. Ken Foster, *Strikes and Employment Contracts*, 34 M.L.R. 275, 277–279 (1971); Charles O. Gregory, LABOR AND THE LAW (2d ed. New York, 1961), 95–104; Edwin E. Witte, THE GOVERNMENT IN LABOR DISPUTES (New York, 1932), 83–84; note 266, *infra*.

[240]The relative weakness of the trade union movement in the United States has been attributed to such factors as a more hostile political and legal environment, the heterogenous ethnic character of the American labor force, greater employer strength and hostility to trade unions, the youth of the labor movement, and the absence of ideologies supporting rank-and-file militance. In addition, this relative weakness may have been related to the permeability of the collar line in the United States. See note 270, *infra*; David Brody, *Radical Labor History and Rank-and-File Militancy*, 16 LAB. HIST. 117–126 (1975); James Hold, *Trade Unionism in the British and U.S. Steel Industries, 1888–1912: A Comparative Study*, 18 LAB. HIST. 5–35 (1977). On the political activities of organized labor, see Marc Karson, AMERICAN LABOR UNIONS AND POLITICS, 1900–1918 (Boston, 1965), 29–32, 51–54.

[241]Witte, *op.cit.*, 212; F.J. Stimson, HANDBOOK TO THE LABOR LAW OF THE UNITED STATES (New York, 1896), 181.

[242]U.S., Laws 1898, ch. 370.

to 1924.[243] The remaining laws were rendered nugatory by the Supreme Court's 1908 *Adair* decision, which held the discharge provisions of the Erdman Act to be unconstitutional, and by its 1915 *Coppage* decision, which held a state anti-yellow-dog law to be unconstitutional.[244] The various courts used similar laissez-faire arguments that sanctified the freedom of contract. The laws were held to be coercive class legislation that interfered with the employer's freedom to make or not to make contracts, a property right guaranteed by the Constitution.[245] The courts argued that the laws restricted the liberty of either party to terminate a contract by quitting or dismissing at will. In *Adair*, the court expressed this mutuality by noting that,

> "It was the legal right of the defendant Adair—however unwise such a course might have been—to discharge Coppage because of his being a member of a labor organization, as it was the legal right of Coppage, if he saw fit to do so—however unwise such a course on his part might have been—to quit the service in which he was engaged because the defendant employed some persons who were not members of a labor organization. In all such particulars the employer and the employee have equality of right, and any legislation that disturbs that equality is an arbitrary interference with the liberty of contract which no government can legally justify in a free land.[246]

The Wisconsin Supreme Court linked the parties' civil rights to the preservation of employment-at-will:

> "As each morning comes, the employee is free to decide not to work, the employer to decide not to receive him, but for this statute. That the act in question invades the liberty of the employer in an extreme degree, and in a respect entitled to be held sacred, except for the most cogent and countervailing considerations, we have pointed out. Hardly any of the personal civil rights is higher than that of free will in forming and continuing the relation of master and servant."[247]

The principle of mutuality—that if the employee was free to terminate at will then so was his employer—implied that any contract lacking a restriction on quits could be terminated at will by the employer. Although none of the courts explicitly ruled that an indefinite employment contract was presumptively terminable at will, this conclusion was easily drawn from the courts' arguments.

Trade union members also were protected by statutes in twenty five states that forbade blacklisting; six of these states penalized employers who refused to give discharged employees on demand a

---

[243]*State v. Julow*, 129 Mo. 163 (1895); *Gillespie v. People*, 188 Ill. 176 (1900); *Commonwealth v. Clark*, 14 Pa. Sup. Ct. 435 (1900); *State v. Kreutzberg*, 114 Wis. 530 (1903); *Coffeyville Brick & Tile Co. v. Perry*, 69 Kan. 297 (1904); *People v. Marcus* 185 N.Y. 257 (1906); *Goldfield Consol. Mines Co. v. Goldfield Miners' Union*, 159 F. 500 (1908); *State v. Daniels*, 118 Minn. 155 (1912); *Jackson v. Berger*, 92 Ohio 130 (1915); *Bemis v. State*, 12 Okla. Crim. 114 (1915); *People v. Western Union Tel. Co.*, 70 Colo. 90 (1924).
[244]*Adair v. United States*, 208 U.S. 161 (1908); *Coppage v. Kansas*, 136 U.S. 1 (1915).
[245]E.g., see Labatt, *op. cit.*, 8938–8944 of vol. 8; Jacobs, *op. cit.*, 76–78.
[246]*Adair, op. cit.*, 175.
[247]*State v. Kreutzberg*, 114 Wis. 530, 546 (1903).

truthful statement of the reasons for their discharge.[248] The blacklist statutes were usually held to be constitutional[249] but state courts rejected the discharge statement laws on constitutional and other grounds.[250] In one such case the court argued that the Texas law was unconstitutional because it interfered with "the liberty to make contracts." The court went on to note that since the employee's contract was indefinite as to duration, both parties had the right to terminate the contract "at any time without cause or notice." To support this claim, the court cited several classic at-will cases as well as Wood's treatise.[251]

Even though most states held their blacklisting laws to be constitutional, there were few cases in which blacklisted workers successfully sued for damages when dismissed.[252] Here too, the at-will doctrine was used to protect employers who blacklisted or discharged blacklisted union members. In one case the court upheld the dismissals of several blacklisted workers by noting that,

> "In a free country like ours, every employee, in the absence of contractual relations binding him to work for his employer a given length of time, has the legal right to quit the service of his employer without notice, and either with or without cause, at any time; and in the absence of such contractual relations, any employer may legally discharge his employee with or without notice, at any time."[253]

The at-will doctrine was well-suited to protect discriminatory discharges and blacklisting since it prevented any inquiry into the issue of just or good cause for dismissal. A Tennessee court that upheld the retaliatory dismissals of a group of railway workers observed that,

> "Obviously the law can adopt and maintain no such standards for judging human conduct. * * * All may dismiss their employees at will, be they many or few, for good cause, for no cause or even for cause morally wrong, without thereby being guilty of legal wrong."[254]

One commentator applauded the *Adair* decision for having closed off such inquiry since,

> "As soon as you begin to * * * introduce the element of motive and make that material, you have crossed the line that separates us from a state of society where the right of private property is not recognized."[255]

Finally, American unions sought protection from unjust or unfair dismissals through collective agreements negotiated with employers.

---

[248]Witte, *op. cit.*, 213.
[249]*Ibid.*, 213–214.
[250]*Wallace v. Georgia etc. R.R.*, 94 Ga. 732 (1894); *Crall v. T. & O.C. Ry.*, 7 Ohio C. C. 132 (1894); *Cleveland etc. Ry. v. Jenkins*, 174 Ill. 398 (1898); *Wabash Ry. v. Young*, 162 Ind. 102 (1904); *Atchison T. & S.F. Ry. v. Brown*, 80 Kan. 312 (1909).
[251]*St. Louis S.W. Ry. v. Griffin*, 106 Tex. 477, 483–484 (1914).
[252]Witte, *op. cit.*, 215–217.
[253]*Boyer v. Western Tel. Co.*, 124 Fed. 246, 248 (1903).
[254]*Payne v. Western A.R.R.*, 81 Tenn. 507, 518–519 (1884).
[255]Charles R. Darling, *The Adair Case*, 42 A.L.R. 884 (1908).

These agreements typically recognized the employer's right to dismiss but allowed a worker who believed his discharge to have been unjust to appeal to a joint committee or arbitration board, which had the power to reinstate him. Provisions for some form of arbitration of unjust dismissals were found before World War I in such industries as flint glass,[256] newspapers,[257] men's clothing,[258] and rail transportation.[259]

However, the enforceability of a collective agreement as well as its provisions to arbitrate disputes was in doubt at least until World War II.[260] The courts might enforce those terms of the collective agreement that could be read into an individual employment contract as customs or usages. An employer who failed to abide by an agreement to hear dismissal grievances then could be sued for breach of the aggrieved individual's employment contract. Yet the courts were reluctant to enforce in this manner a contract's just cause provisions.

The courts relied on the at-will doctrine to protect employers who had summarily dismissed a union member despite the existence of just cause provisions in a collective agreement. They held the collective agreement to be unenforceable either because it lacked mutuality or because the plaintiff had not ratified it. This left the individual's employment contract, which the courts found to be indefinite and terminable at will. Since the individual could be dismissed at will, this nullified any provisions for dismissal restraints.[261] As one court noted,

> "* * * there was no contract that he would serve, and that the appellant would employ him, for any stated time,—the agreement of both being necessary to fix the time of service,—and consequently, no violation of a contract by the discharge of appellee before the expiration of any particular time."[262]

When barring union or statutory restrictions on dismissals, the courts made heavy use of the contractual imagery that both employee and employer had equal liberty to terminate employment at will. One commentator praised the at-will doctrine since it meant that "In America, at any rate, the employee is on a plane with the employer."[263] Yet the at-will doctrine did not prevent the courts from granting injunctions to prevent "conspiratorial" quits during labor

---

[256]Harry A. Millis (ed.), How Collective Bargaining Works (New York, 1945), 702, 703.

[257]Harry A. Millis and Royal Montgomery, Organized Labor (New York, 1945), 710–711.

[258]J.M. Budish and George Soule, The New Unionism in the Clothing Industry (New York, 1920), 142–143.

[259]Robert F. Hoxie, Trade Unionism in the United States (New York, 1917), 105–109.

[260]T. Richard Witmer, *Collective Labor Agreements in the Courts*, 48 Yale L.J. 1917 (1938); Arthur Lenhoff, *The Present Status of Collective Agreements in the American Legal System*, 39 Mich. L. Rev. 1109 (1941); E.E. Witte, Historical Survey of Labor Arbitration (Philadelphia, 1952), 38–58.

[261]E.g., *Crotty v. Erie Ry.*, 133 N.Y.S. 697 (1912); *Hudson v. Cincinnati, N.O. & T.P. Ry.*, 152 Ky. 711 (1913); *Louisville & N.R.R. v. Bryant*, 263 Ky. 578 (1936).

[262]*St. Louis, I.M. & S. Ry. v. Matthews*, 64 Ark. 398, 406 (1897).

[263]18 R.C.L. 510–511 (1917).

disputes.[264] Neither did it prevent the courts from prosecuting union leaders for procuring breaches of contract in situations where workers were employed at will.[265] The *Hitchman* decision of 1917 let stand an injunction barring a union from organizing workers who had signed yellow-dogs despite the fact that they were employed at will.[266] The charge of enticement in cases where employment was terminable at will forced the courts to make absurd legal distinctions between enticement by another employer, which was lawful, and enticement by a union, which was malicious and unlawful.[267] Also, the courts had to strain to define the equity an employer held in a contract terminable at will.[268] These cases suggest that the strict at-will doctrine was based on an ideological bias against trade unionism rather than a principled commitment to contractual equality in employment.

The vigor with which the courts upheld the employer's "fundamental right"[269] to dismiss trade unionists at will was bound to have an effect on cases involving salaried employees. The courts upheld at-will dismissals of trade union members by reasoning that there was a mutual right to quit at will. It would have been inconsistent for the courts to argue that white collar employees, who could quit at will, still should be permitted to sue for their salaries when unfairly dismissed. It also would have been inconsistent to allow that a salaried employee was unfairly dismissed while refusing to recognize any unfairness in the discharge of a competent worker simply because he belonged to a trade union. These inconsistencies, when combined with a relatively indistinct collar line, weakened the rate-of-pay rule and other alternatives to the at-will doctrine.

Thus, we may speculate that if American trade unions had been stronger, they might have taken a more voluntarist approach to limiting unjust dismissals, such as the English trade unions followed. The at-will doctrine would not have become as salient an issue in the courts and, ironically, might not have been so readily extended to the "higher positions." Also, the rate-of-pay rule might have been retained had status distinctions been as sharp as those in England. But these two conditions—the relative weakness of the trade unions and of the collar line—were not independent and may have reinforced

---

[264]E.g., *Arthur v. Oakes*, 63 F. 310 (1894); *Southern Ry. v. Machinists Local Union*, 111 F. 49 (1901); Labatt, *op. cit.*, 8065–8066 of vol. 7.

[265]*Walker v. Cronin*, 107 Mass. 555 (1871); *Perkins v. Pendleton*, 90 Me. 166 (1897); *Brennan v. United Hatters*, 73 N.J.L. 729 (1906); *George Jonas Glass Co. v. Glass Bottle Blowers Ass'n*, 77 N.J. Eq. 219 (1911); *Patterson Glass Co. v. Thomas*, 41 Cal. App. 559, 566 (1919).

[266]*Hitchman Coal & Coke Co. v. Mitchell*, 245 U.S. 229 (1917). The court found justification for its decision in the Statute of Labourers. *Ibid.*, 252. Also see Gregory, *op. cit.*, 179–180. The League for Industrial Rights, an employers' association, worried that yellow-dog contracts were too blatant an exercise of employer power and might be used by radicals to turn public opinion against the employing class. The League suggested that employers rely instead on contractual notice provisions to deter strikes, much as nineteenth century New England employers had done. 2 LAW AND LAB. 166, 188–192 (1920); Witte, *op. cit.*, 230.

[267]Witte, *op. cit.*, 48–60.

[268]This usually was defined as the good will of the employees, something that the courts believed had a pecuniary value and could be protected by injunction. E.g., *Hitchman*, note 266, *supra*, 252; *Patterson Glass*, note 265, *supra*, 566–567.

[269]*Adair*, note 244, *supra*, 176.

each other. It is likely that the weakness of the trade union movement was related to the permeability of the collar line in the United States.[270]

Conclusion

Throughout most of the nineteenth century, English and American courts protected salaried employees without fixed contracts. The courts applied various rules that gave these employees the benefits of a fixed, long-term contract. For much of the twentieth century, the English courts continued to shield salaried employees from the effects of dismissal, either by presuming an annual contract or by requiring that notice be given to terminate the relation. But salaried employees in the United States lost their special status when the courts began to apply a strict presumption of terminability-at-will in the late nineteenth century.

The uniform application of the at-will presumption placed salaried employees on the same legal footing as manual workers, a development that vexed some contemporary observers. The presumption may have corresponded to contracting practices for manual workers but the same could not easily be claimed for salaried employees.

Today, the average American white collar worker employed in the private sector[271] enjoys less protection from wrongful discharge than a blue collar worker. Blue collar workers are more than four times as likely to be covered by a collective bargaining agreement that usually permits discharges only for just cause.[272] The spread of unionization among blue collar workers since the 1930s has left the salaried employee relatively deprived with respect to legal remedies available for wrongful discharge.

In England, all employees now are protected by statutory minimum periods of notice as well as statutory procedures to remedy an unfair dismissal.[273] The question remains open whether unorganized employees in the United States, most of whom are in white collar occupations, can best be protected against wrongful discharge by a

---

[270]The converse is not true. If British unions had been weaker, English law still might have stopped short of the at-will presumption because of the crucial role that notice periods played in determining strike legality. See note 241, *supra*. Note that the permeability of the collar line need not imply that there was greater social mobility in the United States than England. Instead, American workers may have failed to join trade unions and labor parties to the same extent as English workers because they did not think of themselves as members of a working class collectivity. However, recent comparative research on social mobility indicates that there *was* greater opportunity for individual advancement in the United States than in most European nations in the late nineteenth century. Stephen Thernstrom, THE OTHER BOSTONIANS: POVERTY AND PROGRESS IN THE AMERICAN METROPOLIS. 1880–1970 (Cambridge, 1973), 258–260.

[271]The Civil Service Reform Act of 1978 protects Federal civil service employees from wrongful dismissal; many state employees enjoy similar civil service and constitutional protections. Bureau of National Affairs, *Provisions of the Civil Service Reform Act of 1978*, GOV'T. EMPL. REL. REP. 781 (October 16, 1978), 73–78; Joan B. Lowy, *Constitutional Limitations on the Dismissal of Public Employees*, 43 BROOKLYN L. REV. 1 (1976).

[272]Neil W. Chamberlain et al, THE LABOR SECTOR (3d ed., New York, 1980), 134.

[273]See the discussion of the Employment Protection (Consolidation) Act in Hepple and O'Higgins, ENCYCLOPAEDIA, *op. cit.*, 1262–1292.

statute modeled along English lines, by self-help, or by some new remedy to be fashioned by the courts. The historical analysis presented in this paper suggests that the extension of the at-will doctrine to salaried employees in the United States was the result of particular social and political factors rather than any autonomous logic of the law. These are the sort of factors to which one must look to predict the outcome of recent attacks on the doctrine.

2

Contract Principles Applicable to Employment Relations

In addition to the employment-at-will doctrine reviewed in Chapter 1, an employee's legal claim to some form of job security is substantially governed by how the courts invoke one or more doctrines or rules of contract law: consideration, the exchange of something that turns a promise into an enforceable agreement; mutuality, the sometimes invoked condition that the employer is not bound to employ for a term unless the employee is bound to serve for a term; the statute of frauds, which requires that certain agreements be reduced to writing; and the covenant of good faith and fair dealing, which is a standard of conduct the court will read into a contract to make it fair whether the parties consciously intended the standard or not. Of course, these are not the only principles, rules, or standards that influence how the courts decide contract controversies between employer and employee. However, they are central to an understanding of how and why courts decide whether an employer can exercise an arbitrary right to discharge an employee or whether the employer's discretion must be tempered by some standard of fairness.

Consideration

The Requirement of Additional Consideration to Enforce a Promise of Job Security: The Formalist Approach

Blades' 1967 analysis of the employment-at-will rule[1] observed that "the technical difficulty of relaxing the rather rigid rules of

---

[1]Blades, *Employment at Will vs. Individual Freedom: On Limiting the Abusive Exercise of Employer Power*, 67 COLUM. L. REV. 1404 (1967).

consideration * * * makes it unlikely that the employer's right to terminate the at-will employment relationship can be limited under contract law."[2] A current commentator has expressed substantially the same opinion.[3] Although Blades correctly predicted the expansion of tort theories that have since substantially qualified the employer's assumed right of arbitrary discharge, he underestimated the capacity of contract theory to support claims of job security. This section will address the development of the contract theory of consideration in employment law. It is undergoing a transition from rigid rules that left little room for anything but employment-at-will to more flexible standards that accommodate the enforcement of express and implied contracts for job security even in the absence of an agreed term of employment.

The "rigid rules of consideration" referred to by Blades simply posit that the employment bargain is strictly and solely a pay-for-services exchange. Thus, without something more from the employee than employment services, there is a lack of consideration from the employee to support an employer promise of some form of job security. For example, if the employer and employee both agree that the employment will last two years, the consideration to support the employer's promise of a two-year job is the employee's promise to stay on the job for two years. The agreed term of employment removes the contract from the force of the employment-at-will doctrine. But if the employer promises a two-year job, or not to fire except for good cause, or to fire only after a notice of 60 days, or some other form of job security, without exacting a special promise from the employee, the formalist approach holds that there is no consideration to support the employer's promise. Without some special promise, property, or service by the employee in addition to his employment services, there is no consideration in the eyes of the law and the employer's promise is unenforceable. This refusal to enforce an employer promise that was honestly relied upon by the employee and made for the purpose of being relied upon is grounded upon an unstated presumption that job choice is made only in consideration of wages or salary.

It is the combination of the pay-for-services presumption of the formalist approach and the requirement that consideration have "legal value" that requires additional consideration to support a contractually enforceable promise of job security. The pay-for-services model views the employment contract as unilateral, with the employer promising to pay wages or salary as compensation for services after they are rendered. A promise of job security requires additional consideration because the employee is presumed to have made no

---

[2]*Id.* at 1421.
[3]"The continued force of the consideration requirements suggests * * * that the boundaries of traditional contract law will not accommodate the abolition of the employment at will doctrine." Association of the Bar of the City of New York, Comm. on Labor and Employment Law, *At-Will Employment and the Problem of Unjust Dismissal*, 36 RECORD 170, 175 (1981).

implied promise to work for even a day when accepting the job: the promise of services is thus illusory and lacking in legal value.

Applied to a case where there is something more than a strict pay-for-service bargain, as it has often been, the formalist approach is based on circular reasoning: the employee has given no consideration because the employment is terminable at will. The situation where pay *and* job security are promised in exchange for services could easily be construed as a unilateral contract in which the performance of services, once begun, serves as consideration for both pay and the promise to continue employment. The employment contract could also be viewed as bilateral in nature, with the customary employee notice of termination or an implied promise to work for a reasonable time serving as consideration to support a promise of job security. The formalist approach, however, simply refuses to recognize these possibilities. In so doing, it clashes with the traditional contract policies of not questioning the adequacy of consideration in a bargain, of enforcing the intent of the parties, and of finding an enforceable contract where the parties have exhibited an intent to create an agreement.

Courts today increasingly inquire into the question of what the parties intended in the way of job security. The pay-for-services bargain may, in particular cases, be the answer to that inquiry. But often there is more at work. The question thus narrows to what the parties themselves intended when the promise of job security was made. However consideration is defined, some courts allow the jury to decide if it exists.[4]

Criticism of the Rule Requiring Additional Consideration

Almost everyone today receives some form of deferred or indirect compensation. Deferred compensation includes bonuses and pensions. Indirect compensation includes "fringe benefits" such as group life and medical insurance, travel or merchandise discounts, paid vacations, choice of job assignments, and enhanced status by reason of seniority. It is only the employee's services that are exchanged for promised bonuses, pensions, group insurance, and paid vacations. No independent or additional consideration is required to support such so-called direct or indirect compensation or fringe benefits.[5] The courts find consideration for enforcement of promises of these benefits in the form of services rendered in reliance upon the promised benefits. Our research has not identified any court opinion that attempted to explain why a promise of a pension is enforceable but a promise of some kind of job security is not when both are in exchange for employment services.

---

[4]*Dickinson v. Auto Center Mfg. Co.*, 639 F.2d 250 (5th Cir. 1981).
[5]*Hurd v. Illinois Bell Tel. Co.*, 234 F.2d 942 (7th Cir. 1956); *Fries v. Mine Workers*, 30 Ill. App.3d 575, 333 N.E.2d 600 (1975).

A well-motivated, loyal, and experienced work force is generally assumed to result in higher productivity. An express or implied promise of job security or at least a promise of fair treatment by the employer is often an ingredient in the complex of benefits and salary that make up the environment of an efficient work place. Such promises are often a step in a strategy to discourage the organization of the work force into a collective bargaining unit. Although a time and motion study cannot positively relate the employee's performance to confidence in job security, fair treatment, pensions and bonuses, or accumulated experience on the job, it is reasonable to surmise that the employer at least believes that the encouragement of continuing employment and policies of job security and fairness have a favorable impact on productivity. There appears to be no justice in allowing the employer the benefit of such promises while at the same time refusing to enforce such promises.

Adoption of the Functional View of Consideration

Increasingly there is abandonment of the requirement of special or independent consideration for a promise of job security. Employment controversies are more frequently being judged by standards of conduct rather than by mechanical rules that owe more to history than to fairness and reasonableness. *Pugh v. See's Candies, Inc.*, concerned an alleged promise of job security where the employee was not bound to a specific term of employment. The case offers this evolution of the law of consideration:[6]

> "Moreover, while it has sometimes been said that a promise for continued employment subject to limitation upon the employer's power of termination must be supported by some 'independent consideration,' i.e., consideration other than the services to be rendered, such a rule is contrary to the general contract principle that courts should not inquire into the adequacy of consideration. (See *Calamari & Perillo*, CONTRACTS (2d ed. 1977) §4–3, p. 136.) 'A single and undivided consideration may be bargained for and given as the agreed equivalent of one promise or of two promises or of many promises.' (1 CORBIN ON CONTRACTS (1963) §125, pp. 535–536.) Thus there is no analytical reason why an employee's promise to render services, or his actual rendition of services over time, may not support an employer's promise both to pay a particular wage (for example) and to refrain from arbitrary

---

[6]116 Cal App.3d 311, 171 Cal. Rptr. 917 (1981). See also *Martin v. Federal Life Ins. Co.*, 109 Ill. App.3d 596, 440 N.E.2d 998 (1982). See generally Note, *Implied Contract Rights to Job Security*, 26 STAN. L. REV. 335, 351 (1974); *Cleary v. American Airlines*, 111 Cal. App.3d 443, 168 Cal. Rptr. 722 (1980); *Hepp v. Lockheed-California Co.*, 86 Cal. App.3d 714, 150 Cal. Rptr. 408 (1978); *Rabago-Alvarez v. Dart Indus., Inc.*, 55 Cal. App.3d 91, 127 Cal. Rptr. 222 (1976); *Drzewiecki v. H & R Block, Inc.*, 24 Cal. App.3d 695, 101 Cal. Rptr. 169 (1972); *Bussard v. College of St. Thomas, Inc.*, 294 Minn. 215, 223, 200 N.W.2d 155, 161 (1972) ("The rule of additional consideration is arguably too mechanical an answer to the more basic issue of ascertaining the real interest of the parties"); *Eilen v. Tappins, Inc.*, 14 N.J. Super. 162, 81 A.2d 500 (1951); *Eggers v. Armour & Co.*, 129 F.2d 729 (8th Cir. 1942); *Littell v. Evening Star Newspaper Co.*, 120 F.2d 36 (D.C. Cir. 1941); 9 WILLISTON ON CONTRACTS §1017 at 132 (1967).

dismissal. (See 1 CORBIN ON CONTRACTS, *op. cit. supra*, §125, p. 536, fn.68; 1A CORBIN ON CONTRACTS, *op. cit. supra*, §152, pp. 13–17.)

"The most likely explanation for the 'independent consideration' requirement is that it serves an evidentiary function: it is more probable that the parties intended a continuing relationship, with limitations upon the employer's dismissal authority, when the employee has provided some benefit to the employer or suffers some detriment, beyond the usual rendition of service. (See *Employment at Will and the Law of Contract* (1973) 23 BUFFALO L. REV. 211, 221–226) This functional view of 'independent consideration' in the employment context has acquired judicial recognition in other states (see *Littell v. Evening Star Newspaper Co.* (D.C. Cir. 1941) 120 F.2d 36, 37; *Bussard v. College of St. Thomas* (1972) 294 Minn. 215, 200 N.W.2d 155, 161; *Eilen v. Tappin's, Inc.* (Law Div. 1951) 16 N.J. Super. 53, 56–68, 83 A.2d 817, 818–819; cf. *Farmer v. Arabian American Oil Co.* (2d Cir. 1960) 277 F.2d 46 (applying New York law); *Stevens v. G.L. Rugo & Sons* (1st Cir. 1953) 209 F.2d 135 (applying Massachusetts law); *Garrett v. American Family Mutual Insurance Co.* (Mo. App. 1974) 520 S.W.2d 102, 110–112), and has been accepted in several recent cases by the California courts. 'It is fundamental that when construing contracts involving substantial employment rights, courts should avoid mechanical and arbitrary tests if at all possible; employment contracts, like other agreements, should be construed to give effect to the intention of the parties as demonstrated by the language used, the purpose to be accomplished and the circumstances under which the agreement was made.' [Citations omitted] *'We embrace the prevailing viewpoint that the general rule [requiring independent consideration] is a rule of construction, not of substance, and that a contract for permanent employment, whether or not it is based upon some consideration other than the employee's services, cannot be terminated at the will of the employer if it contains an express or implied condition to the contrary.'* (*Drzewiecki v. H & R Block, Inc., supra*, 24 Cal. App.3d 695, 703–704, 101 Cal. Rptr. 169, emphasis added.) Accordingly, '[i]t is settled that contracts of employment in California are terminable only for good cause if either of two conditions exist: (1) the contract was supported by consideration independent of the services to be performed by the employee for his prospective employer; or (2) the parties agree, expressly or impliedly, that that employee could be terminated only for good cause.' (*Rabago-Alvarez v. Dart Industries, Inc., supra*, 55 Cal. App.3d 91, 96, 127 Cal. Rptr. 222, emphasis added. *Accord, Cleary v. American Airlines, supra*, 111 Cal. App.3d 443, 452, 168 Cal. Rptr. 722.)"

Examples of Additional Consideration

If a jurisdiction still follows the formalist approach, the employee must have a contract that fulfills the requirement of additional consideration or it will not be enforced.

Release of Tort Claims

The most universally accepted independent consideration is the employee's release of a tort claim against the employer in return for a promise of permanent or lifetime employment.[7] These cases are not as numerous now as in the first few decades of this century. Workers' compensation acts have discouraged such exchanges by providing specific mandatory remedies for on-the-job injuries. After the advent of workers' compensation statutes, employers sometimes successfully argued that a promise of job security in exchange for release of a tort claim was not supported by consideration from the employee because the workers' compensation acts made such exchanges illegal.[8] This was certainly standing employee protectionism on its head. However, most jurisdictions when faced with the problem were unwilling to find a legislative intent to make the employer's promise unenforceable after the employee gave a release and allowed the statute of limitations to bar the tort claim.[9]

Giving Up Another Job

When an employee argues that giving up his former job is independent consideration for a promise of job security at the current work place, the outcome may be articulated in terms of consideration; but in most cases, it is governed largely by whether all the circumstances of the case establish the existence of a promise upon which the employee reasonably relied. The cases accepting and rejecting the giving up of the prior job as additional consideration address the employee's age, job security, and pay in his former position compared to the position he took in reliance upon some promise of job security in the succeeding job. The cases also consider any special value the employee's skills had to the new employer, recruitment efforts to persuade the employee to change jobs, employer knowledge of the sacrifice the employee would undertake in the course of changing jobs, and the extent to which such employee detriment or employer benefit was a factor in preemployment negotiations for the new job.[10]

---

[7]*Adkins v. Kelly's Creek R.R.*, 458 F.2d 26 (4th Cir. 1972); *Slabon v. St. Louis Car Co.*, 138 S.W.2d 673 (Mo. 1940); *Toni v. Kingman & Co.*, 214 Ind. 611, 15 N.E.2d 80 (1938); *Royster Guano Co. v. Hall*, 68 F.2d 533 (4th Cir. 1934); *Jones v. Stonewear Pipe Co.*, 277 Ill. App. 18 (1934); *Gerald B. Lambert Co. v. Fleming*, 169 Ark. 532, 275 S.W. 912 (1925); *Stevens v. Southern Ry.*, 187 N.C. 528, 122 S.E. 295 (1924); *Fisher v. John L. Roper Lumber Co.*, 183 N.C. 485, 111 S.E. 857 (1922); *St. Louis, Iron Mountain & S. Ry. v. Morgan*, 107 Ark. 202, 154 S.W. 518 (1913); *Rhoades v. Chesapeake & O. Ry.*, 49 W.Va. 494, 39 S.E. 209 (1901); *Sax v. Detroit, Grand Haven & Milwaukee Ry.*, 125 Mich. 252, 84 N.W. 314 (1901); *Jackowski v. Illinois Steel Co.*, 103 Wis. 448, 79 N.W. 314 (1899); *Stearns v. Lake Shore & Michigan S. Ry.*, 112 Mich. 651, 71 N.W. 148 (1897); *Pennsylvania Co. v. Dolan*, 6 Ind. App. 109, 32 N.E. 802 (1892).
[8]*James v. Vernan Calhoun Packing Co.*, 498 S.W.2d 160 (Tex. 1973); *Smith v. Sohio Petroleum Co.*, 163 So.2d 124 (La. Ct. App. 1964); *Gainey v. Coker's Pedigreed Seed Co.*, 227 S.C. 200, 87 S.E.2d 486 (1955).
[9]*Gainey v. Coker's Pedigreed Seed Co.*, 227 S.C. 200, 87 S.E.2d 486 (1955); *Oklahoma Portland Cement Co. v. Pollock*, 181 Okla. 266, 73 P.2d 427 (1937).
[10]*Change of jobs was consideration: Rowe v. Noren Pattern & Foundry Co.*, 91 Mich. App. 254, 283 N.W.2d 713 (1979); *Pursell v. Wolverine-Pentronix, Inc.*, 91 Mich. App. 700, 283 N.W.2d 833 (1979); *Rabago-Alvarez v. Dart Indus., Inc.*, 55 Cal. App.3d 91, 127 Cal. Rptr. 222 (1976); *Collins v. Parsons College*, 203 N.W.2d 594 (Iowa 1973); *Ward v. Consolidated Foods Corp.*, 480 S.W.2d 483 (Tex. Civ. App. 1972); *Lanier v. Alenco*, 459 F.2d 689 (5th Cir. 1972); *Molitor v. Chicago Title & Trust Co.*, 325 Ill. App. 124, 59 N.E.2d 695 (1945); *Millsap v. National Funding Corp.*, 57 Cal. App.2d 72, 135 P.2d 407 (1943); *Fletcher v. Agar Mfg. Corp.*, 45 F.

Moving to Take Another Job

Common sense indicates that a person does not move himself and his family from one city to another without some expectation of job security. Arguing this factor as independent consideration invokes the same comprehensive study of all the surrounding circumstances as appears in opinions considering whether leaving a former job is independent consideration.[11] Many cases exhibit both factors. The employee who has more than one basis to show detriment to himself and his family and benefit to the employer typically is received favorably by the courts.

Foregoing Another Job Opportunity and Longevity of Service

The employee who tries to enforce a job security promise made after hiring can argue that he remained in the job in reliance on the promise and consequently had to forego specific opportunities for alternative employment.[12] If the employee neither sought another job nor was recruited for another job, he can argue that simply continuing in the same employment or his longevity alone is independent consideration.[13]

Supp. 650 (W.D. Mo. 1942); *Jones v. Carolina Power & Light Co.*, 206 N.C. 862, 175 S.E. 167 (1934).

Change of jobs was not consideration: Parets v. Eaton Corp., 479 F. Supp. 512 (E.D. Mich. 1979); *Schoen v. Caterpillar Tractor Co.*, 103 Ill. App.2d 197, 243 N.E.2d 31 (1968); *Ferreyra v. E. & J. Gallo Winery*, 231 Cal. App.2d 426, 41 Cal. Rptr. 819 (1964); *Bryngelson v. Minnesota Valley Breeders Ass'n*, 262 Minn. 275, 114 N.W.2d 748 (1962); *McLaughlin v. Ford Motor Co.*, 269 F.2d 120 (6th Cir. 1959); *Pechon v. National Corp. Serv.*, 234 La. 398, 100 So.2d 213 (1958); *Roth v. Page's Pittsburgh Milk Co.*, 100 Pittsburgh Legal J. 246 (No. 757, March 13, 1952); *Lubrecht v. Laurel Stripping Co.*, 42 Luzerne Legal Reg. 203 (No. 1347, April 1952); *Orsini v. Trojan Steel Corp.*, 219 S.C. 272, 64 S.E.2d 878 (1951); *Thacker v. American Foundry*, 78 Cal. App.2d 76, 177 P.2d 322 (1947).

[11]*Moving was consideration: Hackett v. Foodmaker, Inc.*, 69 Mich. App. 591, 245 N.W.2d 140 (1976); *Brawthen v. H & R Block*, 52 Cal. App.3d 139, 124 Cal. Rptr. 845 (1975); *Ward v. Consolidated Foods Corp.*, 480 S.W.2d 483 (Tex. Civ. App. 1972); *Lanier v. Alenco*, 459 F.2d 689 (5th Cir. 1972); *Stecher v. Wollweber*, 85 York Legal Rec. 116 (No. 334, Sept. 22, 1971); *Miller v. Community Discount*, 83 Ill. App.2d 439, 228 N.E.2d 113 (1967); *Testard v. Penn-Jersey Auto Stores, Inc.*, 154 F. Supp. 160 (E.D. Pa. 1956); *Solomon v. Luria*, 45 Pa. D & C2d 291 (1967); *Fireboard Prods. v. Townsend*, 202 F.2d 180 (9th Cir. 1953).

Moving was not consideration: Cote v. Burroughs Wellcome Co., 558 F. Supp. 883 (E.D. Pa. 1982); *Smith v. Beloit Corp.*, 40 Wis.2d 550, 162 N.W.2d 585 (1968); *Ferreyra v. E. & J. Gallo Winery*, 231 Cal. App.2d 426, 41 Cal. Rptr. 819 (1964); *Levy v. Bellmar Enters.*, 241 Cal. App.2d 686, 50 Cal. Rptr. 842 (1966); *Witte v. Brasington*, 125 F. Supp. 784 (E.D.S.C. 1952); *Orsini v. Trojan Steel Corp.*, 219 S.C. 272, 64 S.E.2d 878 (1951); *Salvage v. Spur Distrib. Co.*, 33 Tenn. App. 20, 228 S.W.2d 122 (1949); *Saylor v. Marshall & Isley Bank*, 224 Wis. 511, 272 N.W. 369 (1937); *Rape v. Mobile & O.R.R.*, 136 Miss. 38, 100 So. 585 (1924).

[12]*Giving up another job opportunity was consideration: Fulton v. Tennessee Walking Horse Breeder's Ass'n*, 63 Tenn. App. 569, 476 S.W.2d 644 (1971); *Minyard v. Daking Mill, Inc.*, 599 S.W.2d 742 (Ark. 1980); *McNulty v. Borden, Inc.*, 474 F. Supp. 1111 (E.D. Pa. 1979).

Giving up another job opportunity was not consideration: Milligan v. Union Corp., 87 Mich. App. 179, 274 N.W.2d 10 (1978); *Roberts v. Atlantic Richfield Co.*, 88 Wash.2d 887, 568 P.2d 764 (1977); *Heuvelman v. Triplett Elec. Instrument Co.*, 23 Ill. App.2d 231, 161 N.E.2d 875 (1959); *Skagerberg v. Blandin Paper Co.*, 197 Minn. 291, 266 N.W. 872 (1936).

[13]*Continuing in the job or longevity in the job was consideration: Martin v. Federal Life Ins. Co.*, 109 Ill. App.3d 596, 440 N.E.2d 998 (1982); *Cleary v. American Airlines*, 111 Cal. App.3d 443, 168 Cal. Rptr. 722 (1980); *Toussaint v. Blue Cross & Blue Shield*, 408 Mich. 579, 292 N.W.2d 880 (1980); *Fries v. Mine Workers*, 30 Ill. App.3d 575, 333 N.E.2d 600 (1975); *Carter v. Kaskaskia Community Action Agency*, 24 Ill. App.3d 1056, 322 N.E.2d 574 (1974);

Special Detriment or Benefit as Additional Consideration

Some less frequently made arguments are that working during a strike,[14] selling a business,[15] giving up a professional practice, or even buying a used car[16] is independent consideration. Again, the outcome in each case rests on how persuasive the employee's claim is under all the circumstances.

Promissory Estoppel as a Substitute for Consideration

Professor Charles Fried has summed up the theory of promissory estoppel as follows:

> "There is a category of cases that has become famous in the law under the rubric of promissory estoppel or detrimental reliance. In these cases there has indeed generally been a promise, but the basis for *legal* redress is said to be plaintiff's detrimental reliance on the promise. Courts now tend to limit the amount of the redress in such cases to the detriment suffered through reliance. But these cases also do not show that reliance and harm are the general basis for contractual recovery. Rather, these cases should be seen for what they are: a belated attempt to plug a gap in the general regime of enforcement of promise, a gap left by the artificial and unfortunate doctrine of consideration."[17]

The promissory estoppel doctrine has been invoked in a variety of situations, but generally its use is triggered when a court is faced

---

Evatt v. Campbell, 234 S.C. 1, 106 S.E.2d 447 (1959); *Twohy v. Harris*, 194 Va. 69, 72 S.E.2d 329 (1952); *Chinn v. China Nat'l Aviation Corp.*, 138 Cal. App.2d 98, 291 P.2d 91 (1955).

Continuing on the job or longevity on the job was not consideration: *Degen v. Investors Diversified Servs., Inc.*, 260 Minn. 424, 110 N.W.2d 863 (1961); *Cummings v. Chicago, Aurora & Elgin Ry.*, 348 Ill. App. 537, 109 N.E.2d 378 (1953); *Roberts v. Atlantic Richfield Co.*, 88 Wash.2d 887, 568 P.2d 764 (1977); *Lewis v. Minnesota Mutual Life Ins. Co.*, 240 Iowa 1249, 37 N.W.2d 316 (1949).

[14]*Working during a strike was consideration*: *Baltimore & Ohio R.R. v. Foar*, 84 F.2d 67 (7th Cir. 1936); *Jones v. Carolina Power & Light Co.*, 206 N.C. 862, 175 S.E. 167 (1934).

Working during a strike was not consideration: *Albers v. Wilson & Co.*, 184 F. Supp. 812 (D. Minn. 1960); *Hope v. National Airlines*, 99 So.2d 244 (Fla. Dist. Ct. App. 1958).

[15]*Kevil v. Standard Oil Co.*, 8 Ohio N.P. 311 (1901) (liquidating a competing business as a step to prepare for employment was consideration); *Bussard v. College of St. Thomas, Inc.*, 294 Minn. 215, 200 N.W.2d 155 (1972) (sale of business to new employer consideration and evidence of implied agreement for job security). See also *Weidman v. United Cigar Stores Co.*, 223 Pa. 160, 72 A. 377 (1908), and *Corman Aircraft Corp. v. Weihmiller*, 78 F.2d 241 (7th Cir. 1935). But cf. *Lynas v. Maxwell Farm*, 279 Mich. 684, 273 N.W. 315 (1937) (sale of business that did not compete with new employer was not consideration for new job).

[16]*Seifert v. Arnold Bros.*, 138 Cal. App. 324, 31 P.2d 1059 (1934). See also *Klug v. Flambeau Plastics Corp.*, 62 Wis.2d 141, 214 N.W.2d 281 (1974) (salesman's agreement as independent contractor to maintain certain level of sales was consideration); *Warner v. Channell Chem. Co.*, 121 Wash. 237, 208 P. 1104 (1922) (increase in sales obligation of salesman was ample consideration for employer's covenant to continue salesman's employment even though salesman himself was not bound to continue); *Mayerson v. Washington Mfg. Co.*, 58 F.R.D. 377 (E.D. Pa. 1972) (salesman's guarantee of credit of new accounts was consideration); *McMullan v. Dickenson Co.*, 63 Minn. 405, 65 N.W. 661 (1896) (employee's promise to retain company stock and render efficient service was consideration). But see *Skagerberg v. Blandin Paper Co.*, 197 Minn. 291, 266 N.W. 872 (1936) (agreement to purchase employee's house if employee rejected job offer from another employer was not consideration); *Shealy v. Fowler*, 182 S.C. 81, 188 S.E. 499 (1936) (giving up plans to enter into a new business was not consideration). In *Lubrecht v. Laurel Stripping Co.*, 42 LUZERNE LEGAL REG. 203 (1952), the court noted that leaving employment to enter into a new employment contract is uniformly regarded as consideration, but the employer cannot be bound by elements of which it had no knowledge.

[17]C. Fried, CONTRACT AS PROMISE 25 (1981).

with outrageous or unjust results if a party's promise is not made binding.

Section 90 of the *Restatement (Second) of Contracts* states the generally accepted rule of promissory estoppel:

> "A promise which the promisor should reasonably expect to induce action or forebearance on the part of the promisee or a third person which does induce such action or forebearance is binding if injustice can be avoided only by enforcement of the promise."

Promissory estoppel has been identified by several courts as a "recognized species of consideration"[18] or as supporting contracts without any consideration.[19] However, the doctrine was not formulated in the Restatement as either a kind of consideration or as an element in the bargain type of contract. Most contracts are premised on the notion of a more or less bargained exchange. Promissory estoppel is often applied to situations where no bargained exchange took place, such as where a gratuitous promise was made.

The applicability of this doctrine still depends, however, on the presence of three elements:

(1) a clear and definite promise;
(2) reasonable reliance by the plaintiff on the promise;
(3) injustice that can be avoided only through enforcement of the promise.

Two cases show the difficulty of using the promissory estoppel rule as a substitute for consideration. In one of these, *Byerly v. Duke Power Co.*,[20] the employees had secured attractive fringe benefits by collective bargaining. The employer wished to sell the company and asked the employees to assist in the orderly transfer of control. The employees, however, were faced with the possible, though not certain, loss of the fringe benefits when the company was sold. The employer then promised that if the employees would aid in transferring the business, it would continue the fringe benefits in the event they were terminated. In reliance upon this promise, the employees continued to work for the employer. When the transfer was completed, the benefits were terminated and the original owner did not keep its promise.

The court acknowledged the promissory estoppel "exception" to the consideration requirement in simple contracts but held that the facts of this case did not fall within its terms. The court reasoned that the employer's promise was not given in exchange for any act, forebearance, or promise on the part of the employees but was voluntary and gratuitous. In addition, the fact that the employees continued to work was immaterial since they were fully paid for their

---

[18]*Porter v. Commissioner*, 60 F.2d 675 (2d Cir. 1932), and *Miller v. Lawlor*, 245 Iowa 1144, 1152, 66 N.W.2d 267, 272 (1954).
[19]*Feinberg v. Pfeiffer Co.*, 322 S.W.2d 163, 168 (Mo. Ct. App. 1959).
[20]217 F.2d 803 (4th Cir. 1954).

services. Most important, the court found that the situation lacked the "injustice" it deemed necessary to the application of the promissory estoppel rule. There was a dissent, which met with Professor Corbin's approval:

> "If the continuance in service was in fact bargained for and given in exchange for the new promise as might be inferred, it was a sufficient consideration satisfying the definition in the restatement, contract section 75. If not so bargained for, the continued service was definitely alleged to have been 'in reliance' and the defendant had reason to know that the promise would lead to that result. Service was rendered by them in exchange for both the promised wages and the promised increase or in reliance on both promises."[21]

Feinberg v. Pfeiffer Co.,[22] is a more persuasive case defining the scope of promisory estoppel in employment situations. An employee with 40 years of service retired when promised a pension. After paying the pension for two years, the employer revoked the pension and stopped sending the checks. The court found that although the pension was intended as a gift, the promise was made enforceable by plaintiff's reliance on it. The last clause of the promissory estoppel rule, "if injustice can be avoided only by enforcement of the promise," brought these facts within its purview.

When confronted with a promissory estoppel rationale, the courts have sometimes fallen back upon the bargain theory and declared promises void for lack of consideration. Consequently, the outlook for development of a promissory estoppel doctrine in employment cases is difficult to gauge. Where outrageously unjust results can be avoided only by enforcing a promise, such an argument may persuade the court to enforce the promise, at least to the extent of actual reliance. However, what is unjust to one court may seem nothing more than a bad bargain to another.[23]

Mutuality of Obligation

It is often said in employment cases that the employer is not bound to employ if the employee is not bound to continue his employment. This so-called "mutuality doctrine" is often invoked as a defense to the enforcement of express promises of job security.[24]

The mutuality doctrine has been repeatedly confused by the

---

[21]1A CORBIN ON CONTRACTS §206, at 257 n.73 (1963).

[22]322 S.W.2d 163, 163 (Mo. Ct. App. 1959). See also *Eby v. York-Division, Borg-Warner*, 455 N.E.2d 623 (Ind. App. 1983) (employee moved in reliance on promise to hire that was repudiated after he moved); *Kiely v. St. Germain*, 670 P.2d 764 (Colo. 1983); *Hedrick v. CCAT*, 7 Ohio App.3d 211, 454 N.E.2d 1343 (1982); *Pepsi-Cola Gen. Bottlers, Inc. v. Woods*, 440 N.E.2d 696 (Ind. App. 1982).

[23]See *Sanders v. Arkansas-Missouri Power Co.*, 593 S.W.2d 56 (Ark. Ct. App. 1980) (alleged promise to continue salary of permanently disabled worker enforced, where worker claimed to have purchased house in reliance on promise).

[24]There are a substantial number of decisions which have held that employers' promises to their employees to discharge them only for cause are not binding. See Annot., 60 A.L.R.3d 226 (1974).

courts.[25] This is, in part, because there are at least three discrete mutuality concepts: (1) mutuality of assent, (2) mutuality of remedy, and (3) mutuality of obligation.[26] Unfortunately, many cases have not kept the doctrines separate and by commingling their elements have distorted their purpose and meaning.

Confusion has resulted most frequently where one party is given an option, not accorded to the other, of discontinuing performance or of canceling a bilateral contract. If the option goes so far as to render illusory the promise of the party given the option, there is indeed no sufficient consideration and therefore no contract. But the mere fact that the option prevents the mutual promises from being coextensive does not prevent both promises from being binding according to their respective terms.[27]

It is quite possible that much of the attraction surrounding the mutuality of obligation doctrine is semantical.[28] The word "mutuality" connotes symmetry and fairness. However, there is nothing inherently fair about symmetry, and this is especially so when the parties have bargained for different promises. In the absence of fraud, mistake, or overreaching, the employer should not expect the court to step in, after services have been rendered in reliance on a promise of job security, and grant it the right to discharge an employee at will, a right for which it failed to bargain.[29]

Lack of symmetry has rarely troubled the law of contracts.[30] It

---

[25]Illinois provides an example of the confusion bred by the mutuality doctrine. In *Schoen v. Caterpillar Tractor Co.*, 103 Ill. App.2d 197, 243 N.E.2d 31 (1968), the plaintiff alleged that he had an oral agreement with the defendant's employment officers that he would have a job if he quit his then-current employment. No other terms appear in the opinion of the case. The court held that "in Illinois mutuality of obligation is essential to make an executory contract enforceable. Since the Caterpillar Company could not enforce it against Schoen, he cannot enforce it against the Company." *Id.* at 200, 243 N.E.2d at 330. Accord: *Vogel v. Pekoc*, 157 Ill. 339, 42 N.E. 386 (1895); *Meadows v. Radio Indus., Inc.*, 222 F.2d 347 (7th Cir. 1955); *Goodman v. Motor Prods. Corp.*, 9 Ill. App.2d 57, 132 N.E.2d 356 (1956); *Campbell v. Eli Lilly & Co.*, 413 N.E.2d 1054 (1980); *Kraftco Corp. v. Koblus*, 1 Ill. App.3d 634, 274 N.E.2d 153 (1971), holding mutuality of obligation is required in Illinois with respect to a controversy concerning termination of a distributorship agreement. However, none of these cases cites or attempts to distinguish *Armstrong Paint & Varnish Works v. Continental Can Co.*, 301 Ill. 102, 133 N.E. 711 (1921), which holds in no uncertain terms that mutuality of obligation is not necessary to the enforcement of a contract in Illinois. That case did not deal with an employment contract, however. Research has not disclosed any Illinois Supreme Court case that has addressed the contract law of employment except in dicta, *Palmateer v. International Harvester Corp.*, 85 Ill.2d 124, 421 N.E.2d 876 (1981), in which the Illinois Supreme Court expressed its disapproval of the doctrine of mutuality of obligation but did not cite *Armstrong Paint*. *Martin v. Federal Life Ins. Co.*, 109 Ill. App.3d 596, 440 N.E.2d 998 (1982), holds that mutuality of obligation does not prevent enforcement of an oral agreement for permanent employment.

[26]1 WILLISTON ON CONTRACTS §105A, at 424–425 (1957).

[27]See *id.* at 422 (1957). See also Corbin, *supra* note 21, §152 at 3, where Corbin lists a fourth category, mutuality of consideration.

[28]Austin, *Mutuality of Obligation: A Multi-Dimensional Doctrine for All Seasons*, 30 OHIO ST. L.J. 61 (1969).

[29]See generally *Littell v. Evening Star Newspaper Co.*, 120 F.2d 36, 37 (D.C. Cir. 1941), and *Drzewiecki v. H & R Block, Inc.*, 24 Cal. App.3d 695, 101 Cal. Rptr. 169 (1972).

[30]See G. Grismore, PRINCIPLES OF THE LAW OF CONTRACTS §68, at 113 (J. Murray rev. ed. 1965). See also L. Fuller & R. Braucher, BASIC CONTRACT LAW 228 (1964), and Williston, *Consideration in Bilateral Contracts*, 27 HARV. L. REV. 503, 528 (1914). Indeed, a promise that is not legally enforceable, e.g., a promise voidable because of infancy or insanity of the person promising, or because of fraud, duress, or illegality, can nevertheless be a sufficient consideration to make a counter promise binding and enforceable.

is universally admitted that the law will not inquire into the adequacy of the consideration to see if it is, in some rough fashion, equal on both sides of the bargain.[31] If the promissors intend to make a bargain where the consideration is unequal, there would seem little reason for refusing to sanction it, in the absence of fraud, mistake, or overreaching.[32]

The doctrine of mutuality of obligation cannot be sustained on the basis of symmetry because the law of contract has no symmetry requirement embodied in it. Insofar as it is taken to require additional consideration beyond services to support a promise of job security, the doctrine is in conflict with the prevailing view of consideration. A single and undivided consideration may be bargained for and given as the agreed equivalent of one promise or of two promises or of many promises. The fact that there are many promises given in exchange for the one consideration does not make it insufficient as to any of them.[33] Thus, in consideration of an employee's services, an employer may promise a salary and also promise not to discharge the employee except for cause. The employer's promises are supported by the employee's acceptance of the job.[34]

Accepting a job means coming to the employer's work place and leaving one's usual freedom at the door. From the first moment of the relation, the employee accepts and follows the instruction of the employer and performs tasks within a business hierarchy defined by the employer. This abandonment of liberty and acceptance of the express and implied duties that attach to one who accepts the status we call "employee" is one species of consideration given by every employee, even one free to leave at a moment's notice. Reliance in the form of giving up other jobs, being loyal and efficient, or giving two weeks' notice are in addition to this basic and universal form of employee consideration.

All of the commentators agree that it is consideration that is necessary to make the contract binding, not the requirement of mutuality, unless the want of mutuality would leave one party without a valid consideration for his promise.[35] Where the parties to a contract exchange promises, mutuality of obligation simply means that both must give consideration, in the form of a valid, legal, and binding promise.

The doctrine of mutuality of obligation appears, therefore, to be merely one aspect of the rule that mutual promises constitute con-

---

[31] RESTATEMENT (SECOND) OF CONTRACTS §79 (1981).
[32] *Id.*
[33] Corbin, *supra* note 21, §125 at 535.
[34] See generally J. Calamari & J. Perillo, CONTRACTS §75 at 1146 (1970).
[35] See Corbin, *supra* note 21, §152 at 5–6; Williston, *supra* note 30, at 525; RESTATEMENT (SECOND) OF CONTRACTS §79 (1981). Accord: *Meurer Steel Barrel Co. v. Martin,* 1 F.2d 687, 688 (3d Cir. 1924); *J.C. Millett Co. v. Park & Tilford Distillers Corp.,* 123 F. Supp. 484, 493 (N.D. Cal. 1954); *Jackson v. Pepper Gasoline Co.,* 280 Ky. 226, 133 S.W.2d 91, 93 (1939); *Standard Oil Co. v. Veland,* 207 Iowa 1340, 1343, 224 N.W. 467, 469 (1929). But see Case Note, 43 FORDHAM L. REV. 300, 302 (1974), where one commentator describes a modern rationale for the mutuality doctrine.

sideration for each other. Where there is no other consideration for a contract, mutual promises must be binding on both parties. But where there is any other consideration for the contract, mutuality of obligation is not essential.[36]

Accordingly, statements which in substance allege that "both parties to a contract must be bound or neither is bound" are erroneous to the extent that they mean anything more than that consideration must be given. Any further requirement of "mutuality" is surplusage.[37]

Statute of Frauds

The Statutory Requirement That Some Contracts Be in Writing

The gist of the statute of frauds is:

"[N]o action shall be brought upon any agreement that is not to be performed within the space of one year from the making thereof, unless the promise or agreement upon which such action shall be brought, or some memorandum or note thereof, shall be in writing * * *."[38]

Nearly identical language has been adopted by every American jurisdiction except Pennsylvania, North Carolina, and Louisiana.[39] The question occasionally arises whether an employment contract is governed by the law of a state with a statute of frauds or a state

---

[36]*Meurer Steel Barrel Co. v. Martin*, 1 F.2d 687, 688 (3d Cir. 1924); Grismore, *supra* note 30, at 116. The doctrine of mutuality of obligation has outlived any possible period of usefulness. *Weiner v. McGraw-Hill, Inc.*, 57 N.Y.2d 458, 443 N.E.2d 441, 457 N.Y.S.2d 193 (1982).

[37]Blades, *supra* note 1, at 1420:
"If the employee in addition to his services has given other 'good' consideration, such as foregoing a claim against the employer or giving up a business to accept the employment, the agreement will be enforced on behalf of the employee even though he is free to quit at anytime. Thus it seems clear that mutuality of obligation is not an inexorable requirement and the lack of mutuality is simply, as many courts have come to recognize, an imperfect way of referring to the real obstacle to enforcing any kind of contractual limitations on the employer's right of discharge—lack of consideration."

[38]Statute of Frauds, 29 Car. 2, ch. 3 (1677).

[39]ALA. CODE §8–9–2 (1975); ALASKA STAT. §09.25.010 (1973); ARIZ. REV. STAT. ANN. §44–101, (1967); ARK. STAT. ANN. §38–101 (1962); CAL. CIV. CODE §1624 (West 1973); COLO. REV. STAT. §38–10–112 (1982) CONN. GEN. STAT. §52–550 (1973); DEL. CODE ANN. tit. 6, §2714 (1974); D.C. CODE ANN. §28–3502 (1981); FLA. STAT. §725.01 (1969); GA. CODE §13–5–30 (1982) (except for contracts with an overseer); HAWAII REV. STAT. §656–1 (1976); IDAHO CODE §9–505 (1979); ILL. REV. STAT. ch. 59, § 1 (1972); IND. CODE §32–2–1–1 (1979); IOWA CODE §622.32 (1950); KAN. STAT. ANN. §33–106 (1981); KY. REV. STAT. §371.010 (1981); ME. REV. STAT. ANN. tit. 33, §51 (1964); MD. ANN. CODE art. 39 C, §1 (1957); MASS. GEN. LAWS ANN. ch. 259, §1 (West 1959); MICH. COMP. LAWS §566.132 (1967); MINN. STAT. §513.01 (1945); MISS. CODE ANN. §15–3–1 (1972); MO. REV. STAT. §432.010 (1952); MONT. CODE ANN. §13–606 (1979); NEB. REV. STAT. §36–202 (1978); NEV. REV. STAT. §111.220 (1979); N.H. REV. STAT. ANN. §506.2 (1968); N.J. REV. STAT. §25–1–5 (1940); New Mexico, by case law, *Childers v. Talbott*, 4 N.M. 168, 16 P. 275 (1888); N.Y. GEN. OBLIG. LAW §5–701 (McKinney 1977); N.D. CENT. CODE §9–06–04 (1975); OHIO REV. CODE ANN. §1335.05 (Page 1979); OKLA. STAT. tit. 15, §136 (1983); ORE. REV. STAT. §41.580 (1981); R.I. GEN. LAWS §9–1–4 (1956); S.C. CODE ANN. §32–3–10 (1976); S.D. COMP. LAWS ANN. §58–8–2 (1978); TENN. CODE ANN. §23–201 (1980); TEX. BUS. & COM. CODE ANN. §26.01 (Vernon 1968); UTAH CODE ANN. §25–5–4 (1953); VT. STAT. ANN. tit. 12, §181 (1973); V.I. CODE ANN. tit. 28, §244 (1976); VA. CODE §11–2 (1950); WASH. REV. CODE §19.36.010 (1974); W. VA. CODE §55–1–1 (1981); WIS. STAT. §241.02 (1981–82); WYO. STAT. §16–1–101 (1977).

without such legislation. The issue has been resolved by recourse to the usual conflict-of-laws rules.[40]

It is often said that the purpose of the statute is to prevent fraud by false swearing.[41] But there is nothing in the terms or operation of the statute that necessarily prevents fraud or false swearing. Indeed, the statute doubtless serves to motivate false swearing by some defendants to deny their promises to support a statute of frauds defense.[42]

Judicial recognition of the failure of the statute to serve any purpose other than encouraging parties to reduce agreements to writing has led the courts to apply the statute only to cases that inescapably fall within the language of the statute. Given the imagination of lawyers and the willingness of courts to find a way to enforce an honestly made agreement, it is difficult to begin to catalogue all the exceptions to the statute. Our task, however, is somewhat more manageable because we deal here only with oral agreements for employment security.

Application of the Statute to Employment Contracts

How is it determined whether a particular oral agreement is not "to be performed within the space of one year" within the meaning of the statute of frauds? The answer to this question determines whether the agreement is enforceable; that is, whether, if the agreement is breached, the injured party may recover damages or sometimes obtain equitable relief. Although the courts are far from uniform in their treatment of agreements that are on their face virtually identical, there are several common points for analysis.

Two situations can be described at the threshold. In the case of unilateral contracts—a promise in return for an act—it is sometimes argued that the promise is unenforceable if made more than a year before performance of the promise is due. For example, an employer may orally promise a stock option or dismissal only for good cause after one year of employment. By definition of a unilateral contract, the promise is not due until the act is fully performed. The courts consistently hold that the statute does not apply where the act has already been fully performed.[43] Similarly, in a bilateral contract, if one promise is within the statute but the other is not, the contract is held to be one not governed by the statute of frauds. An example of such a contract is an agreement in January to work from February through December in return for a bonus to be paid in March of the

---

[40]See, e.g., *Oakes v. Chicago Fire Brick Co.*, 388 Ill. 474, 58 N.E.2d 460 (1945) (where contract is to be performed in several states, law of place of making of contract governs interpretation and enforcement).

[41]Levin and Spak, *The Statute of Frauds and the One Year Rule—A Legal Illusion*, 68 Ill. B.J. 716 (1980).

[42]2 Corbin on Contracts §275 at 3 (1950).

[43]The statute of frauds does not make one party's promise unenforceable after full performance by the other party. See, e.g., *Hartung v. Billmeier*, 243 Minn. 148, 66 N.W.2d 784 (1954).

following year. The promise to pay the bonus on its face is not performable in less than one year. But the other promise is performable in less than one year. Thus the contract is not rendered unenforceable by the statute of frauds.[44]

If at the time the contract is made there is a possibility in law or in fact that the full performance the parties intended may be completed before the end of the year, the contract need not be in writing.[45] Examples of such agreements include an employee's agreeing to maintain a switch for as long as needed,[46] and a promise of employment for as long as the employer did business in Oklahoma.[47] Employment for life or permanent employment is likewise performable within one year.[48] But employment "until retirement" has been held subject to the statute.[49] In Michigan and other jurisdictions the contract is construed to be performable in less than a year if it can conclude "by any possibility," including death of the employer or the termination of the employer's business.

Some cases give less weight to a mere possibility that a contract may unexpectedly end. *Sinclair v. Sullivan Chevrolet Co.*[50] concerns the length of intended performance at the time of the making of the contract. It takes the position that even though a contract may be terminated by death or some other event, it is not thereby capable of performance within one year. *Gilliland v. Allstate Insurance Co.*[51] follows the approach of the *Sinclair* case. In *Gilliland* an employee claimed the company had agreed to employ him until the time of his retirement at age 62 as long as he complied with all lawful directions. He was terminated allegedly without good cause and without prior notice or warning. The court stated:

---

[44]*Marek v. Knab Co.*, 10 Wis.2d 390, 103 N.W.2d 31 (1960); *Miller v. Riata Cadillac Co.*, 517 S.W.2d 773 (Tex. 1974).

[45]3 WILLISTON ON CONTRACTS §495 (3d ed. 1960), citing *Warner v. Texas & Pac. Ry.*, 164 U.S. 418 (1896). See also, *Southwell v. Parker Plow Co.*, 234 Mich. 292, 207 N.W. 872 (1926); *Adolph v. Cookware Co. of Am.*, 283 Mich. 561, 278 N.W. 687 (1938); ·*Pierson v. Kingman Milling Co.*, 92 Kan. 468, 139 P. 394 (1914); *Rowe v. Noren Pattern & Foundry Co.*, 91 Mich. App. 254, 283 N.W.2d 713 (1979); *Bussard v. College of St. Thomas, Inc.*, 294 Minn. 215, 200 N.W.2d 155 (1972); *Bolstad v. Solem Mach. Co.*, 26 Ill. App.2d 419, 168 N.E.2d 732 (1960); *Hope v. National Air Lines*, 99 So.2d 244 (Fla. Dist. Ct. App. 1958).

[46]Williston, *supra* note 45, citing *Warner v. Texas & Pac. Ry.*, 164 U.S. 418 (1896).

[47]*Roxana Petroleum Co. v. Rice*, 109 Okla. 161, 165, 235 P. 502, 507 (1924). At 109 Okla. 166 the court said

"An oral agreement, the performance of which is dependent upon the happening of a certain contingency, is not within this statute of frauds. If the contingency is such as may occur within one year, and this is true, although the contingency may not in fact happen until after the expiration of the year, and although the parties may not have expected that it would occur within that period. It is sufficient if the possibility of performance within the prescribed time existed."

The court concluded that there was no question but that the defendant could have terminated its oil business in Oklahoma and Texas within a year and therefore the agreement would have been completed.

[48]*Sax v. Detroit, Grand Haven & Milwaukee Ry.*, 125 Mich. 252, 84 N.W. 314 (1900). See also *Fireboard Prods. v. Townsend*, 202 F.2d 180 (9th Cir. 1953); *Kitsos v. Mobile Gas Serv. Corp.*, 404 So.2d 40 (Ala. 1981).

[49]*McKinney v. National Dairy Council*, 491 F. Supp. 1108 (D. Mass. 1980) (applying New York law).

[50]31 Ill.2d 507, 202 N.E.2d 516 (1964).

[51]69 Ill. App.3d 630, 388 N.E.2d 68 (1979).

"The Statute of Frauds has been interpreted as rendering an oral contract unenforceable only if it is impossible of performance within one year from the time the contract is made. *Stein v. Malden Mills, Inc.* (1st Dist. 1972), 9 Ill.App.3d 266, 271–272, 292 N.E.2d 52.) To be outside the statute, the contract must be capable of being fully performed within one year and not simply terminated by some contingency such as death or bankruptcy. *Sinclair v. Sullivan Chevrolet Co.* (3d Dist. 1964), 45 Ill.App.2d 10, 195 N.E.2d 250 * * * ; *Osgood v. Skinner*, (1904), 111 Ill.App. 606 * * * .

"Plaintiff contends that the oral contract to employ him until age 62 could have been performed within one year because plaintiff could have quit or died or defendants could have terminated plaintiff's employment for a good cause within one year. Plaintiff cites *Balstad v. Solem Machine Co.* [citation omitted] * * * . Excepting plaintiff's contention to the contrary, we conclude that the oral contract was not of indefinite duration but was allegedly for a term of 36 years—plaintiff would be employed until he reached age 62, at which time he would receive certain benefits. The contract would not have been 'performed' had some contingency such as death or bankruptcy occured; rather the contract simply would have been terminated."[52]

The distinction made by the court in *Gilliland* between performance and termination of the contract within one year is questionable. If the reason for termination excuses further performance by the other party, it seems impossible to argue that the contract has not been fully performed on one side. To state that it has only been "terminated" and not fully performed is a play on words. If the termination constitutes a breach of the contract, or is unexcused, then perhaps performance has not taken place.

It would appear in a jurisdiction with authorities such as *Gilliland* that a plaintiff can attempt to insulate his cause of action from the statute of frauds by pleading the full and complete understanding of the parties to the oral agreement. The full and complete understanding would be, for example, that the alleged agreement would be fully performed in the event of the death of one party or the bankruptcy of the other. In another Illinois case, *Molitor v. Chicago Title & Trust Co.*,[53] the plaintiff recovered upon an oral agreement for permanent employment. The opinion does not mention the statute of frauds, but in *Heuvelman v. Triplett Electrical Instrument Co.*[54] the court expressly acknowledged that oral contracts for permanent employment were enforceable.[55] *Fireboard Products v. Townsend*,[56] decided under California law, holds that contracts for permanent employment and other employment agreements of indefinite duration do not come within the statute of frauds.

In Tennessee it appears that more weight is given to the intention of the parties that performance extend over a period of a year than

[52]*Id.* at 632, 633, 388 N.E.2d at 70.
[53]325 Ill. App. 124, 59 N.E.2d 695 (1945). See also *Martin v. Federal Life Ins. Co.*, 109 Ill. App.3d 596, 440 N.E.2d 998 (1982).
[54]23 Ill. App.2d 231, 161 N.E.2d 875 (1959).
[55]*Id.* at 235, 236, 161 N.E.2d at 877.
[56]202 F.2d 180 (9th Cir. 1953).

the fact that the contract may be fully performed by the intervention of extraordinary circumstances.[57] Further detail on a given jurisdiction's statute of frauds position might be found in the jurisdiction's nonemployment statute of frauds decisions.

Measuring the Year

A day's difference in the making of the contract can be the difference between an agreement that is enforceable and one that is not. It has been held that the day of the agreement itself is counted in measuring the year.[58] It has also been held that the day upon which the promise is made is not counted in measuring the year.[59] Where there is an agreement for a year's employment, the agreement may be enforceable only if made on the first day of employment. This is most likely what leads to cases in which it is testified that although there was an offer of employment sometime before the year began, the employee never decided to accept until the first day he reported for work.[60]

Sufficiency of a Writing

If the agreement is within the statute, the question narrows to whether there is a writing sufficient to comply with the statute. A letter is a sufficient memorandum if it has words fixing the term of employment,[61] but a letter has been held sufficient if the only reference to term of service is that salary is "$2,500.00 per year plus expenses."[62]

---

[57]See in this regard *Mobile, Jackson & Kansas City Railroad v. Hayden*, 116 Tenn. 672, 94 S.W. 940 (1906).

[58]*Brown v. Oneida Knitting Mills, Inc.*, 226 Wis. 662, 277 N.W. 653 (1938). The court stated, "The rule is well established, on an issue of limitation, where the time is to be computed from a certain date, that in the computation the day of the date is to be excluded, and, where the computation is from a certain event the date of that event must be included." See also *Alkire v. Alkire Orchid Co.*, 79 W. Va. 526, 91 S.E. 384 (1917).

[59]"The word 'year' as used in the statute, means a calendar year. In the computation of time within which any act is required to be done, there must be the exclusion of the first day and the inclusion of the last day. The reason for this rule is obvious. Such a rule would disregard fractions of the day, prevent injustices from arising, and favor the enforcement of contracts. The rule is based upon reason and justice and must prevail." *Holcomb & Hoke Mfg. Co. v. Younge*, 103 Ind. App. 439, 446, 8 N.E.2d 426, 429, 430 (1937).

[60]See *Mobile, Jackson & Kanas City R.R. v. Hadden*, 116 Tenn. 672, 94 S.W. 940 (1906).

[61]*Standing v. Morosco*, 43 Cal. App. 748, 184 P. 954 (1925). A memorandum sent from defendant to plaintiff while both parties were in New York included the following: "I will pay you one hundred and fifty ($150) dollars per week in Los Angeles for the length of your engagement there, under the terms of the usual theatrical contract." It was held that this did not constitute a sufficient memorandum because it contained no words fixing the term of service. In *Steward v. Blackwood Elec. Steel Corp.*, 100 W. Va. 331, 130 S.E. 447 (1925), a letter specified a salary for the first three months, an increase until the first of the following year, and a further increase after one year. The letter also provided that 20 shares of capital stock would be available for purchase by the employee over a period of two years. It was held that this was a sufficient writing under the statute of frauds. *Rua v. Bowyer Smokeless Coal Co.*, 84 W. Va. 47, 99 S.E. 213 (1919).

[62]*Southwell v. Parker Plow Co.*, 234 Mich. 292, 207 N.W. 872 (1926). The Supreme Court of Michigan followed what it termed the "Massachusetts rule" and held that the fixing of an annual salary imported an annual employment and standing alone was sufficient to support a finding that there was a hiring for that period.

An income tax statement is not a sufficient writing.[63] However, one case holds that if otherwise sufficient, the writing need not be signed.[64] Another case holds that sworn testimony in court by the employer is a substitute for any writing whatsoever.[65]

Detrimental Reliance and Past Performance as a Substitute for a Writing

Where it appears that the statute requires the contract to be in writing and there is none sufficient to satisfy the statute, the employee sometimes argues that detrimental reliance upon the promise estops the employer from raising the statute as a defense. The use of equitable estoppel to prevent the employer's use of a statute of frauds defense merits some comment. The doctrine of equitable estoppel and the common law applying the statute of frauds developed side by side, each for the ultimate purpose of preventing fraud and injustice.[66] It is anomalous that one doctrine is used to defeat the other. However, as long as the statute of frauds remains part of our law, the courts' problem is to define the field of operation of each.

Illinois has resolved the problem by requiring more than detrimental reliance on the oral promise as a basis for estoppel. In Illinois the conduct of the promising party who is asserting the statute-of-frauds defense must have amounted to a misrepresentation or concealment of material fact.[67] The moral wrong of refusing to be bound by an agreement because it does not comply with the statute does not of itself warrant application of the doctrine of promissory estoppel in Illinois.[68] Other jurisdictions permit the use of the doctrine of estoppel without engrafting the Illinois requirement that there has been a misrepresentation or concealment of a material fact. The experience of most jurisdictions is that the doctrine of estoppel will not eclipse the statute of frauds so long as the traditional elements of estoppel are strictly required. The essence of estoppel is detrimental reliance upon the conduct of the other party. In theory at least, this is substantially different from the disappointed expectations created

---

[63]*Marek v. Knab Co.*, 10 Wis.2d 390, 103 N.W.2d 31 (1960).

[64]*Grauer v. Valve & Primer Corp.*, 47 Ill. App.3d 152, 361 N.E.2d 863 (1977).

[65]*Adams-Riker, Inc. v. Nightingale*, 119 R.I. 862, 383 A.2d 1042 (1978). The case, however, is more representative of the rule that the statute does not apply where there is full performance on one side than of a rule that pleadings or sworn testimony in court is a substitute for the memorandum plainly required by the statute of frauds. Here an insurance agency sued one of its salesmen for commissions received by the salesman, and it was admitted that the salesman was bound to share his commissions with the agency.

[66]*Ozier v. Haines*, 411 Ill. 160, 103 N.E.2d 485 (1952); *Fireboard Prods. v. Townsend*, 202 F.2d 180 (9th Cir. 1953); *Monarco v. Lo Greco*, 35 Cal.2d 621, 220 P.2d 737 (1950).

[67]*Sinclair v. Sullivan Chevrolet Co.*, 31 Ill.2d 507, 202 N.E.2d 516 (1964).

[68]*Libby-Broadway Drive-Inn, Inc. v. McDonald's Sys.*, 72 Ill. App.3d 806, 811, 391 N.E.2d 1, 4 (1979).

by the promise and its abandonment.[69] Even if there is actual detrimental reliance, some cases present the further issue of whether the promise relied upon was sufficiently definite and certain to make reliance upon it reasonable.[70]

Where partial performance in reliance upon a promise does not have the ingredient of detrimental reliance or misrepresentation of material fact required to establish promissory or equitable estoppel to amount to a defense to the statute of frauds, the courts have devised another technique to permit at least some recovery in the face of the statute. Agreements that span several years are sometimes construed as encompassing two or more separate agreements, some of which are fully performed and some not. Those that are fully performed on one side then warrant enforcement of the corresponding promise.[71]

Oral Amendments to a Written Agreement and Automatic Renewals

If there is a written agreement sufficient to satisfy the statute before termination of employment, employers have sometimes argued that a salary increase in excess of the salary provided by the written agreement amounts to a new oral contract which is unenforceable under the statute and is a contract at will because it is not expressly subject to a term of employment. The cases that present these facts hold that the increase in salary is an oral amendment of the written contract and not an entirely new oral agreement. Therefore, the written agreement as orally amended complies with the statute of frauds.[72]

Where there is a valid agreement, whether written or oral, for one year of employment, the contract is presumed to continue in effect from year to year without any further agreement, written or oral, by the parties or any particular conduct to create a new agreement. The presumed renewal of such agreements on a year-to-year basis does not violate the statute of frauds.[73] If the original term of employment is more than one year, the statute of frauds does not foreclose a

---

[69]See *Fireboard Prods., Inc. v. Townsend*, 202 F.2d 180 (9th Cir. 1953) (quitting of job and relocation of family from Alabama to California on basis of oral promise were sufficient to estop company from asserting statute of frauds); *McLaughlin v. Ford Motor Co.*, 269 F.2d 120 (6th Cir. 1959) (quitting of job without relocation was not a detriment but only a necessary incident to placing employee in position to perform new assignment). *Pursell v. Wolverine-Pentronix, Inc.*, 91 Mich. App. 700, 283 N.W.2d 833 (1979) (severing of employment with former owner of factory and acceptance of position with new owner, with consequent loss of retirement benefits, was detrimental reliance). Accord: *Fireboard Prods., Inc. v. Townsend*, 202 F.2d 180 (9th Cir. 1953), and *Monarco v. Lo Greco*, 35 Cal.2d 621, 220 P.2d 737 (1950).

[70]*McMath v. Ford Motor Co.*, 77 Mich. App. 721, 259 N.W.2d 140 (1977) (oral promises concerning future economic security not sufficiently definite to justify reliance).

[71]*Mapes v. Kalva Corp.*, 68 Ill. App.3d 362, 386 N.E.2d 148 (1979) (employee held entitled to bonus attributable to calendar year, since performance for that year was complete). Accord: *White Lighting Co. v. Wolfson*, 68 Cal.2d 336, 438 P.2d 345, 66 Cal. Rptr. 697 (1968).

[72]See *Molostowsky v. Grauer*, 113 N.Y.S. 679 (App. Div. 1908), and *Evatt v. Campbell*, 234 S.C. 1, 106 S.E.2d 447 (1959).

[73]*Conrad v. Ellison-Harvey Co.*, 120 Va. 458, 91 S.E. 763 (1917). Accord: *McIntyre v. Smith-Bridgman & Co.*, 301 Mich. 629, 4 N.W.2d 36 (1942), citing *Sines v. Wayne County Superintendent of the Poor*, 58 Mich. 503, 25 N.W. 485 (1885).

presumption that employment continues under successive contracts for the original term. However, the statute has been read as making such a presumption rebuttable.[74]

Significance of the Statute in Employment Controversies

The statute will have little significance in employment litigation in the future. It appears that most jurisdictions construe the statute so that it rarely, if ever, operates on any employment contract. In the few jurisdictions that apply the statute to these contracts, the pitfalls can often be sidestepped by pleading and proving matters in avoidance of the statute which are inherent in any personal service contract and which make possible the end of employment before the lapse of twelve months.

Implied-In-Law Duty of Good Faith and Fair Dealing

The duty of good faith and fair dealing is implied as a matter of law in every contract, including employment contracts.[75] It is not something that must be proven with evidence. To determine what is embraced by the duty in any particular jurisdiction it will be necessary to compare the judiciary's application of the concept in insurance, uniform commercial code,[76] and franchise controversies as well as employment cases. No matter how ambitious and exhaustive the research, no final all-inclusive definition will ever be possible. It is evident from the most current authorities that the duty requires more than moral honesty. Where the boundary lies beyond honesty in fact is largely a matter of judicial discretion in each case. At a minimum, good faith and fair dealing also prohibits a party from using the contractual relationship or advantages derived from the relationship to extort a benefit not bargained for at the outset. Whether the courts

---

[74]*Borne Chem. Co. v. Dictrow*, 85 A.D.2d 646, 445 N.Y.S.2d 406 (1981).

[75]*Kravetz v. Merchants Distrib., Inc.*, 387 Mass. 457, 440 N.E.2d 1278 (1982); *Magnan v. Anaconda Indus., Inc.*, 37 Conn. Supp. 38, 429 A.2d 492 (1980); *Criscione v. Sears Roebuck & Co.*, 66 Ill. App.3d 664, 384 N.E.2d 91 (1978); *Stevenson v. ITT Harper*, 51 Ill. App.3d 568, 366 N.E.2d 561 (1977); *Foley v. U.S. Paving Co.*, 262 Cal.2d 499, 68 Cal. Rptr. 780 (1968); *Flying Tiger Line v. U.S. Air Coach*, 51 Cal.2d 199, 331 P.2d 37 (1958). See *Communale v. Traders & Gen. Ins. Co.*, 50 Cal.2d 654, 328 P.2d 198 (1958), a significant case concerning an insurance company's refusal to settle a claim. The implied duty of good faith and fair dealing was largely developed in cases of this type. Contra: *Perry v. Hartz Mountain Corp.*, 537 F. Supp. 1387 (S.D. Ind. 1982) (applying Indiana law); *Murphy v. American Home Prods. Corp.*, 58 N.Y.2d 293, 448 N.E.2d 86, 461 N.Y.S.2d 232 (1983).

[76]The code expressly defines good faith to mean "honesty in fact," U.C.C. §1–201 (19). Cf. U.C.C. §2–103 (1(b)), which expressly defines good faith in the case of a merchant as "honesty in fact and the observance of reasonable commercial standards of fair dealing in the trade." See also Burton, *Breech of Contract and the Common Law Duty to Perform in Good Faith*, 94 HARV. L. REV. 369 (1980); Stankiewicz, *Good Faith Obligations in the Uniform Commercial Code: Problems in Determining Its Meaning And Evaluating Its Effect*, 7 VAL. U.L. REV. 389 (1973); Powell, *Good Faith in Contracts*, 9 CURRENT LEGAL PROBLEMS 16 (1956); Madison, *The Employee's Emerging Right to Sue for Arbitrary or Unfair Discharge*, 6 EMPLOYEE REL. L.J. 422 (1980); CORBIN ON CONTRACTS pt. 1, §654D (1980 Supp.); Gellhorn, *Limitations on Contract Termination Rights—Franchise Cancellations*, 1967 DUKE L.J. 465 (1967); MacNeill, *Contracts: Adjustment of Long-term Economic Relations Under Classical, Neo-classical and Relational Contract Law*, 72 NW. U.L. REV. 854 (1978).

when faced with these questions are cut adrift on a sea of boundless discretion or whether at least the outer limits of the duty are identified is the subject of this discussion.

Dishonesty and Extortion as Bad Faith

The root meaning of the duty of good faith and fair dealing as a requirement to refrain from extortion is evident in *Monge v. Beebe Rubber Co.*[77] A short summary of the facts of that case will make the point. Olga Monge was an alien resident. She studied during the day to obtain the credentials necessary to become a licensed school teacher. She also cared for her minor children. To support herself and her family she worked the night shift in a factory until dismissed for refusing to yield to the sexual advances of a foreman. She sued for breach of the employment contract and a jury awarded modest damages. The employer appealed. The employer's attorney had the unenviable task of arguing that the employment-at-will doctrine required the court to close its eyes when the employer discharged this woman for an immoral reason having no connection with employment, namely, in retaliation for her refusal to be coerced into a meretricious relationship. The New Hampshire Supreme Court condemned this exploitative use of the employment relationship as a breach of the implied duty of good faith and fair dealing and affirmed judgment in favor of the employee. The employer's conduct in this case can fairly be described as extortionate.[78]

In *Fortune v. National Cash Register Co.*,[79] the plaintiff salesman was discharged by the employer to avoid paying the full commission earned on a $5 million sale. The Massachusetts Supreme Court held the discharge was a breach of the implied duty of good faith and fair dealing. The employment-at-will rule did not permit the employer to first obtain the fruits of the employee's services rendered in reliance upon the promise of a commission and then discharge the employee to deprive him of a part of that commission. This act by the employer was dishonest and therefore a breach of the duty of good faith.

The same result might have been reached in *Monge* by reading state or federal antidiscrimination statutes into the contract and finding an implied agreement against sexual discrimination. Likewise, in *Fortune* the salesman could have been held entitled to the

---

[77]114 N.H. 130, 316 A.2d 549 (1974).

[78]*Mason County Bd. of Educ. v. State Superintendent of Schools*, 295 S.E.2d 719 (1982) (a discharge motivated by malice is wrongful); but see *Brockmeyer v. Dun & Bradstreet*, 109 Wis.2d 44, 325 N.W.2d 70 (Ct. App. 1982).

[79]373 Mass. 96, 364 N.E.2d 1251 (1977). *Rees v. Bank Bldg. & Equip. Corp. of Am.*, 332 F.2d 548 (7th Cir. 1964), has facts and a conclusion close to *Fortune* but does not refer to the implied duty of good faith and fair dealing. Rather on the facts it finds an implied-in-fact agreement that was breached. See also *Ursic v. Bethlehem Mines*, 556 F. Supp. 571 (W.D. Pa. 1983), holding a discharge shortly before completion of 30 years of service and qualification for retirement pension was pretextual and a violation of Employment Retirement Income Security Act of 1974, 29 U.S.C.A. §1132 *et seq.*; *Maddaloni v. Western Mass. Bus Lines*, 422 N.E.2d 1379 (1981).

unpaid commission by holding that it was already earned and could not be forfeited.[80] The courts award relief in many ways against employers who invite trust and reliance and then unfairly take advantage of it. The stated legal grounds for relief may vary from one jurisdiction to another to conform more closely to governing precedent in the jurisdiction.[81] Some jurisdictions are reluctant, at least in employment cases, to afford a remedy when the only basis is employer dishonesty. For example, the *Monge* and *Fortune* use of the implied duty of good faith was rejected in *Moore v. Home Insurance Co.*[82] The plaintiff there claimed he was discharged shortly before his pension vested just so the employer could avoid paying the pension. The court applied Arizona law and was of the opinion that the implied duty of good faith did not apply.

There is authority dealing with insurers and the insured that expressly holds that the duty is a "two-way street." That is, both parties are bound.[83] In employment cases common sense compels the same conclusion, but research has disclosed no case expressly stating that result. Several cases hold that an employee's undisclosed self-dealing or conflicts of interest breach an implied duty of loyalty to the employer.[84] This holding appears to be the enforcement of a duty of honesty and fair dealing against the employee and in favor of the

---

[80]*Lucas v. Seagrave Corp.*, 277 F. Supp. 338 (D. Minn. 1967), presented the question whether a discharge of a large group of employees unjustly enriched the employer because the employees forfeited pension rights and the discharge was alleged to have been to accomplish that very purpose. The court held a *quantum meruit* recovery was a proper remedy if the facts alleged were proved. Cf. *Craig v. Bemis Co.*, 517 F.2d 677 (5th Cir. 1975) (*quantum meruit* recovery not permitted, since employer lacked dishonest motive). See also *Moore v. Home Ins. Co.*, 601 F.2d 1072 (9th Cir. 1979); *Maddaloni v. Western Mass. Bus Lines*, 386 Mass. 877, 438 N.E.2d 351 (1982); *Murphy v. American Home Prods. Corp.*, 58 N.Y.2d 293, 448 N.E.2d 86, 461 N.Y.S.2d 232 (1983).

[81]See, e.g., *O'Bier v. Safe Buy Real Estate Agency*, 256 Ark. 574, 509 S.W.2d 292 (1974), where it was held that it was a breach of the employment contract to induce a salesman to spend $30,000 of his own money to build up a territory and then fire him to benefit from the goodwill created by the salesman and his investment without paying a commission promised to the salesman. The implied duty of good faith and fair dealing was not mentioned.

[82]601 F.2d 1072 (9th Cir. 1979).

[83]*Commercial Union Assurance Cos. v. Safeway Stores, Inc.*, 26 Cal.3d 912, 918, 610 P.2d 1038, 1041, 164 Cal. Rptr. 709, 712, (1980). "[T]he insured status as such is not a license for the insured to engage in unconscionable acts which would subvert the legitimate rights and expectations of the * * * insurance carrier." *Id.* at 921, 610 P.2d at 1043, 164 Cal. Rptr. at 714. Accord: *Sargent v. Johnson*, 551 F.2d 221, 232 (8th Cir. 1977); *Kaiser Found. Hosps. v. North Star Reinsurance Corp.*, 90 Cal. App.3d 786, 792, 153 Cal. Rptr. 678, 682 (1979); *Liberty Mut. Ins. Co. v. Altfillisch Constr. Co.*, 70 Cal. App.3d 789, 139 Cal. Rptr. 91, 95 (1977). Numerous courts have held that the insured's breach of the duty of good faith excuses the insurer of its obligations under the contract. E.g., *Sargent v. Johnson*, 551 F.2d 221, 223 (8th Cir. 1977) (insured's "failure to deal with [the insurer] in good faith effectively severed the insured-insurer relationship") and *Kaiser Found. Hosps. v. North Star Reinsurance Corp.*, 90 Cal. App.3d 786, 792, 153 Cal. Rptr. 678, 682 (1979) (covenant of good faith and fair dealing applies to insured as well as insurers—it is "not a one-way street"). See also *Whitehead v. Van Leuven*, 347 F. Supp. 505, 508 (D. Idaho 1972) ("each of the parties" obligated to act in good faith) and *Silberg v. California Life Ins. Co.*, 11 Cal.3d 452, 460, 521 P.2d 1103, 1108, 113 Cal. Rptr. 711, 716 (1974) (covenant of good faith requires that "neither party will do anything to injure the right of the other to receive the benefits of the agreement").

[84]*Anthony Co. v. Johnson*, 20 Ill. App.2d 128, 155 N.E.2d 361 (1959) (employee who secretly dealt with employer's competitors was subject to enforcement by the employer of covenant not to compete); *Nogee v. Neisner Bros*, 351 Ill. App. 166, 114 N.E.2d 463 (1953) (termination before qualification for bonus was proper where the employee was about to compete directly with his employer); *Polyglycoat Corp. v. Holcomb*, 591 P.2d 449 (Utah 1979) (representing franchisee's product as that of franchisor is breach of implied duty of good faith).

employer. Such cases should stand as precedent for enforcement of good faith and fair dealing obligations in favor of the employee, and such precedent may be found in most jurisdictions. It should come as no shock that the courts are now stepping up to these issues and applying similar standards of loyalty and fair dealing to employers as well as employees. Breach of the duty is sometimes described as breach of an implied contract duty or a tort and sometimes as both.

In both *Monge* and *Fortune* the executive with the effective power to discharge was aware of the bad faith motive of the discharge. *Pstragowski v. Metropolitan Life Insurance Co.*[85] raises, but does not decide, the question of whether the employer corporation can be held liable for a bad faith discharge if the person who exercises the power to discharge is influenced by a subordinate who does not disclose his actual improper motive. Since the ultimate question is the bad faith of the employer corporation, it should be immaterial that the person with the power to discharge was in complete good faith. The corporation can act only through its agents. If one employee can cause the boss to discharge for a dishonest reason, the employer corporation should be held to have breached the implied duty of good faith and fair dealing. The ignorance of the executive with authority to discharge may be due to his own negligence or simply a bureaucratic lethargy interfering with communications.

What More Than Honesty Is Required by Good Faith and Fair Dealing?

The *Fortune* and *Monge* cases were read by some commentators as trumpeting the law's recognition of implied rights to job security.[86] The facts by themselves in those cases do not warrant such a sweeping conclusion. However, there is a growing body of authority that arbitrary discharge is a breach of the implied duty of good faith and fair dealing when it frustrates the employee's reasonable expectations to qualify for a pension or other form of deferred compensation or other benefits incident to longevity in the work place.

A discharge can result in a benefit to the employer even though the discharge was not, like *Fortune*, for the purpose of achieving that benefit. As workers advance in longevity, the rate at which they become entitled to deferred compensation and fringe benefits such as vacation and coverage in group health and life insurance plans accelerates. Even if at discharge the employer pays the present value of what is accrued to the date of discharge, the employee has foregone the opportunity to accrue benefits at a faster pace in the future and the employer has avoided higher labor costs in the future.[87] A discharge to intentionally accomplish this objective has been held to be

---

[85]553 F.2d 1 (1st Cir. 1977).
[86]Note, *supra* note 6.
[87]See *Hamilton v. Stockton Unified School Dist.*, 245 Cal. App.2d 944, 953, 54 Cal. Rptr. 463, 468–469 (1966), which comments on this characteristic of longevity in employment.

tortious.[88] Moreover, a worker's suitability for other employment or marketability as an employee may be limited or destroyed by continuation in the service of one employer for a number of years.[89] The question then narrows to whether the implied duty of good faith and fair dealing protects the employee from arbitrary discharge without proof that the employer intended to deprive the employee of particular benefits or deferred compensation for its own advantage. A few recent cases answer that question in the affirmative.

The plaintiff in *Zimmer v. Wells Management Corp.*[90] when hired received a stock option that would not vest until five years after employment commenced and then only if the holder were still employed. Eight months before it was to vest the plaintiff was fired because he was not a "swinger." It was held that the implied duty of good faith and fair dealing barred the employer from depriving the plaintiff of a valuable right for a trivial reason. Otherwise the opportunity to exercise the option would be illusory.

When the court characterizes the pension rights and other forms of deferred compensation as "mere expectancies" strictly subject to the conditions in the documents creating them, no relief is granted.[91] Deferred compensation is sometimes equated to the interest of a beneficiary under a will before the testator dies. The beneficiary cannot complain if he is disinherited. However, the difference between the beneficiary under a will and an employee is that the employer holds out deferred compensation and job security to obtain employee trust and reliance. Even a beneficiary under a will has an action in most jurisdictions against the deceased estate if the beneficiary confers some benefit upon the decedent in reliance on a promise to be included in the will.

Duty in Insurance Cases: Good Faith Performance of Reasonable Expectations

The concept of the implied duty of good faith and fair dealing has been extensively developed in actions between insurers and their

---

[88]*Savodnik v. Korvettes, Inc.*, 488 F. Supp. 822 (E.D.N.Y. 1980).

[89]*Maloney v. E.I. du Pont de Nemours & Co.*, 352 F.2d 936 (D.C. Cir. 1965), stressed the factor of employee longevity in holding an arbitrary dismissal to have been a breach of the employment contract.

[90]348 F. Supp. 540 (S.D.N.Y. 1972). *NLRB v. Knoxville Publishing Co.*, 124 F.2d 875 (6th Cir. 1942), held that failure to respond to plain, well-understood contractual obligations was bad faith. *Zimmer* goes beyond the definition of bad faith in *NLRB*. There was in *Zimmer* no right to the option except upon fulfillment of the condition (five years' continuous employment) and no "plain, well-understood" contract that until that condition was achieved Zimmer would be free from arbitrary discharge. See also *Sinnett v. Hie Food Prods., Inc.*, 185 Neb. 221, 174 N.W.2d 720 (1970) (employee may not be fired without good cause one day before bonus accrues). To the same effect, *Kollman v. McGreggor*, 240 Iowa 1331, 39 N.W.2d 302 (1949), and Annot., 28 A.L.R. 346 (1924). Other cases cite the employment-at-will rule as a rule of substantive law that bars any other implied-in-law covenant or implied-in-fact agreement. The following citations are typical: *Wright v. Standard Ultramarine & Color Co.*, 141 W. Va. 368, 90 S.E.2d 459 (1955) (retirement benefits forfeited); *Haag v. International Tel. & Tel. Corp.*, 342 F.2d 566 (7th Cir. 1965) (stock option rights forfeited); *Stevenson v. ITT Harper, Inc.*, 51 Ill. App.3d 568, 366 N.E.2d 561 (1977) (pension rights forfeited).

[91]*Finnell v. Cramet, Inc.*, 289 F.2d 409 (6th Cir. 1961) (based upon Illinois law).

insured. Many cases deal with the insurer's duty to settle a case that has a potential for a verdict against the insured in excess of the policy limits. Recent cases define and explain the duty in a manner consistent with the outcome in *Zimmer*. It has been defined as a duty "to cooperate and facilitate the performance of mutual promises."[92] Another opinion has held that the essence of the implied covenant of good faith in insurance policies is that neither party will do anything in which it injures the right of the other to receive the benefits of the agreement."[93]

The earliest insurance cases reasoned that the duty of good faith and fair dealing should be implied because the insurer had a fiduciary obligation toward the insured insofar as it exercised its right to defend claims covered by the policy. A fiduciary relationship, of course, is broad enough to include and does include the employment relation. One definition appears in *Mobil Oil Corp. v. Rubinfeld*:[94]

> "A fiduciary relationship is one founded on trust or confidence reposed by one person in the integrity and fidelity of another. The term is a very broad one. It is said that the relation exists and that relief is granted in all cases in which influence has been acquired and abused, in which confidence has been reposed and betrayed. The origin of the confidence and the source of the influence are immaterial. The rule embraces both technical fiduciary relations and those informal relations which exist whenever one man trusts in and relies upon another. Out of such a relation, the law raises the rule that neither party may exert influence or pressure upon the other, take selfish advantage of his trust or deal with the subject matter of the trust in such a way as to benefit himself or prejudice the other except in the exercise of the utmost good faith and with the full knowledge and consent of that other, business shrewdness and hard bargaining being totally prohibited as between persons standing in such a relation to each other. A fiduciary relation exists when confidence is reposed on one side and there is resulting superiority and influence on the other."

The duty of good faith and fair dealing as developed in insurance cases is implied in law in the sense that no evidence is necessary to establish the duty. But the duty is addressed to the reasonable expectations of the parties, and that may require evidence. In cases of an action by an insured against his insurer for bad faith refusal to settle a claim, the cases hold that the insurer defending an insured claim and faced with a probable verdict in excess of the policy limits is not entitled in good faith to refuse an offer to settle within policy limits. The reasonable expectations of the insured when the policy is purchased is that the insurer's right to defend claims covered by the policy will be reasonably exercised. When the insurer has, in effect, unreasonably gambled the insured's chance for a judgment in excess of the policy limits in order to have a chance for a verdict

---

[92]*Kansas City College v. Employer's Surplus Line Ins. Co.*, 581 F.2d 299, 303 (1st Cir. 1978), citing *Fortune*; *Gates v. Life of Mont. Ins. Co.*, 638 P.2d 1063 (Mont. 1982).
[93]*Commercial Union Assurance Cos. v. Safeway Stores, Inc.*, 26 Cal.3d 912, 918, 610 P.2d 1038, 1041, 164 Cal. Rptr. 709, 712 (1980).
[94]72 Misc.2d 392, 339 N.Y.S.2d 623 (Civ. Ct. 1972).

under the settlement offer or policy limits, the court holds that the duty of good faith has been breached. We will find that in the employment cases that expressly address this duty, there is the same attention to the reasonable expectations of the parties.

The Duty of Fairness Implied in Employment Contracts

Two recent cases squarely stand for the principle that the implied duty of good faith protects against arbitrary discharge where arbitrary discharge would make the prospect of qualifying for a pension plan or other benefits offered by the employer illusory. In *Cleary v. American Airlines*,[95] it was alleged that from 1958 to 1976, an 18-year period, plaintiff worked for the defendant employer as a payroll clerk, ramp agent, and, from 1961 forward, as an airport operations agent. It was alleged that the plaintiff was falsely charged with theft, leaving his work area without authorization, and threatening another employee with bodily harm in violation of the employer's regulations, and for these reasons was discharged. The complaint alleged further that the real reason for the discharge was the plaintiff's union-organizing activities. At the time of discharge plaintiff's salary was $22,000 per year. It was alleged that he had acquired, pursuant to the employment contract, certain retirement and pension benefits; the right to continue to earn such benefits to age 65; the right to borrow from, save in, and receive dividends from the credit union; the right to enjoy seniority status; and certain other unspecified rights. With respect to the implied-in-law duty of good faith and fair dealing, the court observed the following:[96]

> "Plaintiff herein has pleaded that the implied-in-law covenant of good faith and fair dealing was contained in his employment contract. The concept of good faith and fair dealing was first formulated by the California courts in insurance contracts. But it is clear that it has reference to *all* contracts. The doctrine was explained in *Comunale v. Traders & General Ins. Co.* (1958), 50 Cal.2d 654, 658, 328 P.2d 198, by the following observation: 'There is an implied covenant of good faith and fair dealing in *every* contract that neither party will do anything which will injure the right of the other to receive the benefits of the agreement.' [Emphasis added.]
> "The duty which arises from the covenant of good faith and fair dealing is unconditional and independent in nature; it is not controlled by events in the same manner as conditions precedent or subsequent. *(Gruenberg v. Aetna Ins. Co.* (1973) 9 Cal.3d 566, 578, 108 Cal. Rptr. 480, 510 P.2d 1032.) The only hint in California case law that, on occasion, it may be incumbent upon an employer to demonstate good faith in terminating an employee, was expressed in the early case of *Coats v. General Motors Corp.* (1934) 3 Cal. App.2d 340, 348, 39 P.2d 838, in these terms: 'It is equally well settled that the employer must act in good faith; and where there is evidence tending to show that the

---

[95]111 Cal. App.3d 443, 168 Cal. Rptr. 722 (1980).
[96]*Id.* at 453–456, 168 Cal. Rptr. at 728–730; *Gates v. Life of Mont. Ins. Co.*, 638 P.2d 1063 (Mont. 1982).

discharge was due to reasons other than dissatisfaction with the services the question is one for the jury.' (See also *Zimmer v. Wells Mgt. Corp.* (S.D.N.Y. 1972) 348 F. Supp. 540, utilizing the concept of good faith and fair dealing in an employment contract dispute.)

* * *

We have indicated herein the continuing trend toward recognition by the courts and the Legislature of certain implied contract rights to job security, necessary to ensure social stability in our society. As was concluded by a commentator in 26 *Stanford Law Review* at page 369 (see fn.3),[97] '[t]he existence of separate consideration, the common law of the job, and rights accruing through longevity are all factors for courts to consider in evaluating whether an implied contractual right to job security exists. The conflict between an employee's right to job security and an employer's right to fire for cause or with economic justification should be resolved by judicial balancing of the competing equities.'

"Two factors are of paramount importance in reaching our result that plaintiff has pleaded a viable cause of action. One is the longevity of service by plaintiff—18 years of apparently satisfactory performance. Termination of employment without legal cause after such a period of time offends the implied-in-law covenant of good faith and fair dealing contained in all contracts, including employment contracts. As a result of this covenant, a duty arose on the part of the employer, American Airlines, to do nothing which would deprive plaintiff, the employee, of the benefits of the employment bargain—benefits described in the complaint as having accrued during plaintiff's 18 years of employment

"The second factor of considerable significance is the expressed policy of the employer (probably in response to the demands of employees who were union members), set forth in Regulation 135-4. This policy involves the adoption of specific procedures for adjudicating employee disputes such as this one. While the contents of the regulation are not before us, its existence compels the conclusion that this employer had recognized its responsibility to engage in good faith and fair dealing rather than in arbitrary conduct with respect to all of its employees.

"In the case at bench, we hold that the longevity of the employee's service, together with the expressed policy of the employer, operate as a form of estoppel, precluding any discharge of such employee by the employer without good cause. We recognize, of course, that plaintiff has the burden of proving that he was terminated unjustly, and that the employer, American Airlines, will have its opportunity to demonstrate that it did in fact exercise good faith and fair dealing with respect to plaintiff. Should plaintiff sustain his burden of proof, he will have established a cause of action for wrongful discharge that sounds in both contract and in tort. He will then be entitled to an award of compensatory damages, and, in addition, punitive damages if his proof complies with the requirements for the latter type of damages. (See *Egan v. Mutual of Omaha Ins. Co.*, (1979) 24 Cal.3d 809, 157 Cal. Rptr. 482, 598 P.2d 452.)"

Pugh v. See's Candies, Inc.[98] followed and further developed the duty applied in *Cleary*. Pugh was an employee who worked his way up the corporate ladder from dishwasher to vice president in charge

---

[97]See Note, *supra* note 6, for analysis and criticism of the common law rule.
[98]116 Cal. App.3d 311, 171 Cal. Rptr. 917 (1981). See also *Cancellier v. Federated Dep't Stores*, 672 F.2d 1312 (9th Cir. 1982).

of production and was a member of the board of directors. After 32 years of employment, he was fired. The evidence presented to the jury was that when Pugh first went to work for See's, the then president of the company frequently told Pugh, "if you are loyal to [See's] and do a good job, your future is secure." The evidence also was that See's had a practice of not terminating administrative personnel except for good cause. During the entire period of his employment there had been no formal or written criticism of his work. He was never denied a raise or bonus. He received no notice or warning of any problem and had no idea that any disciplinary action was being contemplated before he was discharged. The court's opinion ranged over the development of the common law of employment in England and the rise of organized labor in the past several decades. It discussed cases concerning implied-in-fact promises for some form of continued employment or job security and then turned to the implied-in-law covenant of good faith and fair dealing:[99]

> [Quoting *Cleary v. American Airlines*, 111 Cal. App.3d 443, 168 Cal. Rptr. 722 (1980)] " 'In the case at bench, we hold that the longevity of the employee's service, together with the expressed policy of the employer, operate as a form of estoppel, precluding any discharge of such an employee by the employer without good cause.' (*Id.*, at pp. 455–456, 168 Cal. Rptr. 722.)
>
> "If '[t]ermination of employment without legal cause [after 18 years of service] offends the implied-in-law covenant of good faith and fair dealing contained in all contracts, including employment contracts,' as the court said in * * * *Cleary*, then *a fortiori* that covenant would provide protection to Pugh, whose employment is nearly twice that duration. Indeed, it seems difficult to defend termination of such a long-term employee arbitrarily, i.e., without some legitimate reason, as compatible with either good faith or fair dealing.
>
> "We need not go that far, however. In *Cleary* the court did not base its holding upon the covenant of good faith and fair dealing alone. Its decision rested also upon the employer's acceptance of responsibility for refraining from arbitrary conduct, as evidenced by its adoption of specific procedures for adjudicating employee grievances. While the court characterized the employer's conduct as constituting '[recognition of] its responsibility to engage in good faith and fair dealing' (111 Cal. App.3d at p. 455, 168 Cal. Rptr. 722), the result is equally explicable in traditional contract terms: the employer's conduct gave rise to an implied promise that it would not act arbitrarily in dealing with its employees.
>
> "Here, similarly, there were facts in evidence from which the jury could determine the existence of such an implied promise: the duration of appellant's employment, the commendations and promotions he received, the apparent lack of any direct criticism of his work, the assurances he was given, and the employer's acknowledged policies. While oblique language will not, standing alone, be sufficient to establish agreement (Drzewiecki v. H & R Block, Inc., *supra*, 24 Cal. App. 3d 695, 703, 101 Cal. Rptr. 169), it is appropriate to consider the totality of the parties' relationship: Agreement may be 'shown by the acts and conduct of the parties, interpreted in the light of the subject matter

---

[99]*Id.* at 327–329, 171 Cal. Rptr. at 926–927.

and the surrounding circumstances.' (*Marvin v. Marvin* (1976) 18 Cal.3d 660, 678, fn.16, 134 Cal. Rptr. 815, 557 P.2d 106; see Note, *Implied Contract Rights to Job Security* (1974) 26 STAN. L. REV. 335.)"

Both *Cleary* and *Pugh* explain their holding in terms of two factors. The first factor discusses the implied-in-law duty of good faith and fair dealing and the second factor considers the reasonable expectations of the parties. Both opinions address these factors as if they were separable and unrelated. We submit, however, that it is not possible to consider this implied-in-law duty without addressing the reasonable expectations of the parties, unless the law confers boundless discretion upon the court to remake the contract according to its own notions of fairness.

In effect, the two opinions both read the reasonable expectations of the parties into the contract. To the extent that the contract reserves the right of discharge to the employer, that right is construed in favor of the employee so as not to defeat his reasonable expectations. This is analogous to construing an ambiguity in a written agreement against the party who created it.

In short, the court finds bad faith or unfair dealing *because* the employer has violated the employee's reasonable expectation of job security.

What facts, one might inquire, give rise to enforceable reasonable expectations? In *Board of Regents v. Roth*[100] and *Perry v. Sindermann,*[101] the Supreme Court considered whether a public employee had a "property" right in the job sufficient to invoke the protections of due process of law.[102] Whether such an employee had a constitutional right to due process in connection with termination of employment, the Court said, turned on whether he had a reasonable expectation of job security. If the statutes, regulations, rules of the work place, or "common law of the shop" made an express or implied promise of job security, the Court ruled, the public employee was not terminable at will but only on a finding of good cause by a procedurally fair process.

The judicial recourse to reasonable expectation is premised on the rejection of an inflexible terminable-at-will doctrine. If employment were terminable at will because of the lack of a fixed term, independent consideration, or an authorized, express promise of permanent employment, then the employee ordinarily would have a reasonable expectation only of at-will employment.[103] Accordingly,

---

[100]408 U.S. 564 (1972).

[101]408 U.S. 593 (1972).

[102]The Fifth and Fourteenth Amendments prohibit government deprivation of "life, liberty, or property" without due process of law, so the relevant inquiry is whether the public employee's rights in the job are a protected "property interest." This turns on whether the applicable substantive law creates a contract or other right in the position.

[103]In the constitutional context, *Bishop v. Wood*, 426 U.S. 341 (1976), upholds a finding of no reasonable expectation of job security where the employee could not be terminated under the applicable regulation without good cause because the state common law held that employees are terminable at will. But see *Arnett v. Kennedy*, 416 U.S. 134 (1974) (federal employment was a property right where personnel manual provided for discharge for good cause only).

promises of discharge only for good cause, pension benefits, assurances of good prospects, and favorable job evaluations would be nothing more than indications of the employer's state of mind when the promises were made. They would mean nothing legally if discharge were permissible "for a good or bad reason or for no reason at all."

"Reasonable expectation" is an expression that connotes a judicial desire to examine the rights of employer and employee in the concrete setting of the actual relationship. The concept moves the employment relation out of the structured analytical framework which has grown up to rationalize the terminable-at-will rule, and into the customary search for a contractual "intent of the parties" found in their words, actions, and circumstances. It applies what has been called the objective theory of contracts to employment.

It also implies a view of the relationship more in sympathy with the employee. Rather than focus on the alleged business imperatives that require arbitrary employer discretion, the concept inquires into what the employee would naturally expect under all the circumstances. Common sense dictates that an employee would not accept a job and stay in it if he expected to suffer the economic and psychological prospect of termination without cause at any moment. Where employer statements were once held unenforceable because they were "words of expectation and not obligation,"[104] they now become evidence to support a claim that reasonable expectations have not been satisfied.

Before leaving *Cleary* and *Pugh*, a few other points deserve mention. *Cleary* reasons that the standard for discharge is "good cause." *Pugh* avoids the term "good cause" and instead speaks generally of a "legitimate reason" for discharge, something other than arbitrary discretion. The description of the standard for discharge is perhaps more carefully worded in *Pugh* because "good cause" is to arbitrators and labor lawyers shorthand for a number of procedural and substantive rights in the work place. Limiting the employer's right to discharge to good cause goes well beyond denying the employer the right to discharge arbitrarily. This is a subject that will be more fully addressed in Chapters 3 and 4.

Reasonable Expectations Read Into Employment Contracts Without Discussion of the Implied-In-Law Duty

Essentially the same employee protection was afforded in certain cases which found employee rights as a result of a breach of an implied-in-fact agreement as was afforded in cases that articulated their reasoning in terms of the implied duty of good faith and fair

---

[104]E.g., *Foster Wheeler Corp. v. Zell*, 250 Ala. 146, 33 So.2d 255 (1947) (statements in the nature of what the employer thought might reasonably be expected to occur and not of what the parties agreed would occur); *Heuvelman v. Triplett Elec. Instrument Co.*, 23 Ill. App.2d 231, 161 N.E.2d 875 (1959) (words expressing good faith and hopes for the future).

dealing. *Goodman v. Winn-Dixie Stores, Inc.*[105] serves as an example. An employee with nearly 15 years' satisfactory service was a participant in a retail chain's profit-sharing program. He had accumulated benefits in that program of about $6,000. When he took part in a lawful labor strike against the chain, he was permanently replaced, in accordance with an announced policy, and after refusing an invitation to return to work. The company informed him that, because of his voluntary termination of employment, he had forfeited all funds in his profit-sharing account. The court held that ordinarily an employee is not held to have resigned his employment by participating in a lawful strike and concluded that the express purpose of the profit-sharing program was to create an estate for employees who had continued for a long period of time. The employee should not have been denied his benefits and they were a measure of damages for breach of the employment contract.

In *Connor v. Phoenix Steel Corp.*,[106] an employee with 28 years' service who was 56 years old was discharged without prior warning, reprimand, or complaint about his performance. After discharge he was notified that he was ineligible to receive retirement benefits. At the time of his termination the employee was covered by a pension plan for employees with 15 years or more of continuous service. The company argued that the employee did not qualify for a pension because he had been discharged. The court observed that pension plans should, if possible, not be construed so as to permit the employer unilaterally to make illusory his promise to pay the benefits. Applying this general rule of construction, the court held that the employee's termination after 28 years of service without cause, complaint, or warning was equivalent to a layoff and not a discharge.

Reasonable Expectations of the Professional Employee and the Common Law of Fair Procedures

For several decades, a significant body of law has developed concerning membership of self-employed individuals in trade and professional associations and medical staffs of hospitals. The law governs exclusion from membership and termination of membership or curtailment of rights in associations where membership is a necessary precondition to the self-employed practice of certain businesses and professions. Although this subject is discussed in Chapter 10, it is mentioned here to alert the reader that the California Supreme Court bridged the common law of associations and common law of employment in *Ezekial v. Winkley.*[107] A professional employee at a hospital was held wrongfully discharged because the employer did not observe the same procedural safeguards that are required by law to protect

---

[105]240 So.2d 496 (Fla. Dist. Ct. App. 1970).
[106]249 A.2d 866 (Del. 1969). See also *Ursic v. Bethlehem Mines*, 556 F. Supp. 571 (W.D. Pa. 1983), and *Hovey v. Lutheran Medical Center*, 516 F. Supp. 554 (E.D.N.Y. 1981).
[107]20 Cal.3d 267, 572 P.2d 32, 142 Cal. Rptr. 418 (1977).

self-employed members of professional associations. The key factor referred to by the court was the plaintiff employee's expectation that the training he would receive as a surgical resident in the hospital would qualify him to practice surgery upon successful completion of the program. For that reason the hospital was not entitled to terminate his employment as a surgical resident without giving the plaintiff the benefit of "fair procedure" principles. Essentially this means fair notice of complaints against the employee and an opportunity to address such grievances on the merits.

Implied-In-Law Duty Does Not Go Beyond Reasonable Expectations

If the touchstone of this implied-in-law duty is a question of fact, namely, the reasonable expectations of the parties, then the duty should give way to a hard bargain openly and fairly made. Some support for this conclusion is given by examination of a controversy between franchisor and franchisee decided under the Uniform Commercial Code. In *Corenswet, Inc. v. Amana Refrigeration, Inc.*,[108] the question was whether the good faith obligation of U.C.C. Section 1-203 prevented the franchisor from acting under a termination clause in the written franchise agreement. The clause permitted termination by either party upon 10 days' notice, "at any time and for any cause."[109] Although the exercise of the franchisor's right of termination deprived the franchisee of a valuable business, the court held that the implied duty of good faith would not operate to modify or defeat the express agreement for termination. It did not appear that the franchisor was acting to appropriate to itself a benefit or advantage that the franchisee could reasonably expect to acquire in the face of the explicit termination provision. In other words, although the termination would injure the franchisee insofar as it could not recover a substantial investment and would never receive further benefits from the relationship, the termination provision was being invoked under circumstances contemplated by the parties when the contract was formed. Thus, the principle of freedom of contract protected a hard bargain arrived at freely and openly against a challenge in the form of the implied duty of good faith and fair dealing. If the contract had been formed under circumstances giving an unfair advantage to one party, theories of fraud, duress, mistake, and unconscionability might have been invoked to prevent enforcement.

There are difficulties in identifying the openly made hard bargain because of inequalities inherent in the employment relationship. The employer, by definition, is in a position of authority and control, and today usually enjoys a wide choice of applicants ready to accept

---

[108]594 F.2d 129, 134 (5th Cir. 1979).
[109]For similar cases see Gellhorn, *supra* note 76; and Hewitt, *Good Faith or Unconscionability—Franchise Remedies for Termination*, 29 Bus. Law. 227 (1973).

an offer of a job. The employee, on the other hand, rarely has more than a small number of offers to weigh; and if he aggressively bargains at the outset of the relationship or at any other point, he risks bargaining himself out of a job, since the employer will perceive his efforts as signifying something other than a subservient attitude. Further, as an employment relationship continues, the employee becomes dependent on the job and is vulnerable to a variety of petty on-the-job abuses if he displeases the boss, who very likely has others standing in line to take over if the employee is fired. As a rule, true equality of bargaining power obtains only in times of severe labor shortage, in situations involving collective employee bargaining, or in cases of specially situated employees.

Employers whose employees occupy positions of great discretion or who operate in a truly insecure economic climate are among those who should be permitted to rely on hard bargains. Their capacity to assume the risk of an unfruitful relationship and alternatives to the relationship are no greater than those of the employee. Since the essence of good faith and fair dealing is to prevent abuse of a superior position in the contract relationship, the duty ought not be interposed where the employer is not unjustly enriched, the circumstances of the relationship require broad discretion to terminate, and the situation has been understood by both parties in these terms.

Summary of the Implied Duty

No contract, no matter how detailed, can cover every conceivable eventuality that may arise in the course of performance. Insurance contracts, for example, do not describe the standard of judgment to be exercised by insurance carriers when refusing to settle an insured claim. The courts have been called upon to decide whether an insurer has honored its contractual duties during the course of performance. By taking a concept that originally embraced only honesty in fact and enlarging it to deny one party to a contract the right to frustrate the other party's reasonable expectations, an implied-in-law duty has been created, first for policing performance of insurance contracts and now of employment contracts.

If this duty has found application in the relatively well-settled field of insurance law where often insufferably complicated agreements are the rule, the field of employment law, with only a minority of workers covered by comprehensive written agreements, would appear ripe for frequent use of the doctrine. It is arguable that some form of the duty has already been applied by the courts in favor of employers insofar as a duty of employee loyalty has been read into contracts otherwise silent on the subject. Review of the breach of loyalty cases shows that they, like the implied-at-law duty of good faith, are largely influenced by the reasonable expectations of the parties.

Accepting the premise that the duty has a place in employment law, the question pertinent here is, "To what extent does the duty enhance job security?" If the discharge deprives the employee of a right to job security, pension, bonus, or other benefit he could reasonably expect to earn, the employer must be able to justify the discharge. At the least, this means the employer must satisfy a standard requiring a good faith business reason. In fact, a higher standard may be appropriate and it may be incumbent upon the employer to show good cause or even something more to justify the discharge. For instance, what is an appropriate reason for discharging a young worker many years from retirement may not be sufficient to justify a discharge of someone on the verge of accruing substantial pension rights and medical insurance benefits, or someone lured away from a secure job with another employer.

In the field of product liability, the law slowly developed from the principle of "let the buyer beware" to "let the manufacturer be careful." The common law over time adopted an approach that promoted customer safety by giving the consumer more power when a product case came to court. The same kind of development occurred between contracting parties with substantially unequal bargaining power in insurance and landlord–tenant controversies. Over the long haul, the common law does not turn a deaf ear to unfair conduct masquerading as business necessity. Employees, particularly those with substantial longevity in the work place, have a substantial interest in freedom from arbitrary discharge. We think this is an interest the courts will in the future more willingly protect.

3

The Employment Contract Formed

Reliance, Misinformation, and Temporizing Assurance

Refusal to Give Promised Employment

If employment-at-will permits the employer to discharge arbitrarily, does it permit the employer to refuse arbitrarily to honor a promise to hire? A host of cases can be found that stand for the proposition that arbitrary discharge is lawful "at any time." It might be fair to assume that "at any time" includes moments after the hiring. Case law, however, does not warrant the conclusion that because the employer of an "at will" employee may arbitrarily discharge, it may likewise arbitrarily refuse to honor a promise to hire. Examination of cases concerning an arbitrary refusal to honor a promise to hire or promote employees in jobs apparently covered by the at-will doctrine brings out two factors that often appear in wrongful discharge litigation: detrimental reliance on employer promises, and promises that amount to negligent or fraudulent misrepresentations. Only the exceptional refusal-to-hire case presents employee conduct as a ground for refusal to honor the promise of a job.[1]

It is evident that the promise of a job followed by a refusal to perform the promise presents a situation fraught with potential harm to the prospective employee. To remedy the harm and at the same time avoid dealing with the employment-at-will doctrine, two courts have cast the problem in terms of tort. In *Elizaga v. Kaiser Foundation Hospitals, Inc.*,[2] the hospital had established an employment and training program for surgeons. The hospital knew that the state board

---

[1]*Stoffel v. Metcalfe Constr. Co.*, 145 Neb. 450, 17 N.W.2d 3 (1945) (employee allegedly made disclosures to news media about his new job which concerned confidential national security matters).

[2]259 Or. 542, 487 P.2d 870 (1971). See also *Newton v. Johnson Organ & Piano Co.*, 180 Cal. 185, 180 P. 7 (1919), and *Lorson v. Falcon Coach, Inc.*, 214 Kan. 670, 522 P.2d 449 (1974).

of medical examiners did not intend to permit renewal of the program after June 30, 1969. In January 1969, a physician who was a citizen of the Philippines applied for the program. The hospital did not disclose to the applicant that the program might be shut down. In fact, the hospital admitted him as of July 1, 1969. He then moved his family from the Philippines to Portland, Oregon. When he arrived, the hospital notified him that he could not be hired because state authorities would not permit the hospital to renew the program. The physician then sued the hospital, contending that the offer of admission to the program for July 1, 1969, constituted a knowing misrepresentation because at the time he was accepted the hospital was aware that its authority to conduct the program was subject to cancellation by the governing authorities and this was not disclosed to plaintiff. The court held there was an actionable misrepresentation. The nondisclosure of material facts, it reasoned, can be a form of misrepresentation where the defendant has made representations that would be misleading without a full disclosure. In order to avoid misleading the physician, the defendant was under a duty to disclose the fact that the board of examiners might not permit renewal of the program for a term sufficient to allow the physician to complete the training or perhaps to even start the training. The court did not require an intent to mislead but rather based liability upon a reckless disregard of whether the physician would be misled. The court cited Prosser for the proposition that

> "A failure to perform a promise is not a basis for an action for fraud. Making a promise, however, with knowledge that it probably cannot be performed or with reckless disregard whether the promise can or cannot be performed can be the basis for an action of fraud."[3]

In *McAfee v. Rockford Coca-Cola Bottling Co.*,[4] an individual alleged he had had a discussion with certain employees of the prospective employer regarding the possibility of employment. He claimed he had been positively and without qualification promised a job and told he should report to work on a specific date. He inquired whether he was free to give notice of termination to his current employer and was told that he should. When he appeared for work he was told he was not needed. The Illinois court found the employer liable for negligent misrepresentations. Unlike *Elizaga*, however, the opinion does not identify any particular fact that was negligently or recklessly not disclosed. Perhaps this situation resembles what is known in the law of torts as *res ipsa loquitur*, the thing speaks for itself. In effect, the opinion puts the burden on the employer to explain how such representations could have been made in the absence of negligence— why it should not be liable for harm caused by its temporizing as-

---

[3]*Elizaga v. Kaiser Found. Hosps., Inc.*, 259 Ore. 542, 548, 487 P.2d 870, 874, citing W. Prosser, LAW OF TORTS (3d ed.) at 745.

[4]40 Ill. App.3d 521, 352 N.E.2d 50 (1976).

surances. This is an example of a movement in the law to protect persons in a disadvantaged bargaining position by requiring the disclosure of all material facts without regard to whether nondisclosure is the consequence of fraud, negligence, or innocent mistake.[5]

Grouse v. Group Health Plan, Inc.[6] is another example of the problem of the dishonored promise of a job. In reliance upon a promised job, an individual resigned his former position and turned down another attractive job offer. However, when he was ready to start, he learned that the employer had hired another person for the same position. In the lawsuit that followed, the employer argued that it had refused to honor its promise because it did not receive necessary favorable references. The Minnesota Supreme Court apparently believed the references question should have been resolved before the job was promised. It held that "it would be unjust" not to hold the employer to its promise because the plaintiff relied on the job offer.

Edgewater Beach Corp. v. Sugarman[7] found an implied duty to provide employment for a reasonable period of time. Plaintiff was to be employed to serve as a hotel manager. Before the promise of employment he was apparently unemployed. When he appeared to begin his employment, the hotel had no job for him. The court did consider the fact that after the promise of employment, plaintiff discontinued his efforts to find other employment. This is probably the least detrimental reliance one is likely to find in these situations.

In *Smith v. Pollack Co.*[8] an individual was hired as a bill collector. At the time he was hired he was told that he would have to furnish his own automobile for use in the work. Since he did not have an automobile, he borrowed money from friends to buy a car. When he got the car and tendered his service to the company, he was informed that another collector had been employed in his place. It was held he was entitled to recover the reliance damages claimed.

If an employee interviews in confidence for new employment, but before finding a new job is fired from the old job because the first employer learned about the confidential interviews, is there an enforceable claim against the prospective employer who could not keep a secret? A recent case held the employee had no claim for breach of confidence.[9] Nevertheless, this fairly common occurrence would appear to find a remedy for the employee in theories of negligence or breach of a confidential relationship.[10]

---

[5]See C. Fried, PROMISE AS CONTRACT (1981), for a discussion of this development. And see *Obde v. Schlemeyer,* 56 Wash.2d 449, 353 P.2d 672 (1960) (seller of house guilty of fraud for cosmetic changes to cover up termite damage).

[6]306 N.W.2d 114 (Minn. 1981); *Floyd v. Lamar Ferrell Chevrolet, Inc.,* 159 Ga. App. 756, 285 S.E.2d 218 (1981); *Eby v. York-Division, Borg-Warner,* 455 N.E.2d 623 (Ind. App. 1983).

[7]153 Fla. 555, 15 So.2d 260 (1943).

[8]9 La. App. 432, 121 So. 240 (1928).

[9]*Wadsworth v. Nalco Chem. Co.,* 523 F. Supp. 997 (N.D. Ala. 1981).

[10]Note, *Breach of Confidence,* 82 COLUM. L. REV. 1426 (1982).

Refusal to Give a Promised Promotion

A closely related fact pattern exists when the employee accepts employment in a subordinate position in reliance upon the promise of a better job and is fired before getting the better position. *McGrath v. Zenith Radio Corp.*[11] is an example. McGrath took a position and subsequently gave up a valuable stock option for no compensation in reliance upon a statement by a senior executive of a parent corporation that McGrath was the "heir apparent" to become president of the subsidiary upon the retirement of the current president. The court addressed the employer's argument that under the employment-at-will doctrine it had the right to discharge McGrath before or after he gave up the stock option:

"Defendants contend on appeal that even assuming arguendo that an agreement may have been entered into on that occasion, no actionable breach has been proven because the contract was only one for employment at will, and as such was terminable by either party at any time. For support defendants point to McGrath's own testimony that he asked for but was refused a three year written contract and to the absence of any other evidence as to the contemplated duration of plaintiff's prospective employment.

"The difficulty with this line of reasoning is that it misconstrues the nature of plaintiff's argument. McGrath does not assert merely that Zenith promised to continue his employment, but rather that Zenith promised to make him president of [the Zenith subsidiary] upon the retirement of [the current president] and to afford him career opportunities and benefits, including stock options at Zenith and participation in an executive bonus compensation group. In exchange for these promises according to plaintiff, he agreed to sell his stock and to waive the option he had to purchase shares in Basford. The alleged wrong lay in defendants' failure to either establish cause for not making him president or to make him president and then ease him out after a decent interval.

"We believe that the evidence produced at trial—including McGrath's testimony that [a Zenith officer] told McGrath that his becoming president was 'thoroughly acceptable to both Zenith and himself'; 'that as president * * * [McGrath] would be entitled to substantial stock options and * * * [to participate in] an executive * * * bonus program'; and 'that [McGrath] was the heir apparent'—formed a sufficient basis on which the jury could conclude that Zenith had promised to appoint plaintiff president of the new corporation and that a binding contract had been entered. While there was no representation that McGrath would be president for any specified tenure, the jury could find from the evidence a promise McGrath would be made president with a reasonable opportunity to give satisfactory performance. As the finder of fact, the jury was entitled to conclude that the agreement, although performed by McGrath by his selling his shares and executing the waiver, was breached by defendants when they terminated his employment."[12]

---

[11]651 F.2d 458 (7th Cir. 1981). See also *Bennett v. Eastern Rebuilders, Inc.*, 52 N.C. App. 579, 279 S.E.2d 46 (1981), where employer promised to demote rather than fire if employee took supervisory position and gave up security of a union job.
[12]*Id.* at 464-465.

Summary

The authorities described above, which give remedies premised upon breach of contract, fraud, negligent misrepresentation, or reliance, show that promissory obligation is only one basis of liability against persons who cause unnecessary harm to others by reneging on a promise to hire. Principles of tort are also available against persons who give vague and temporizing assurance that cause foreseeable harm. Justice often requires remedies for damages occasioned in circumstances in and around the contracting process. However, there are good reasons and a sound legal basis for premising liability upon the promise itself and looking to other considerations only to quantify the damages. There is a convention in our society that an individual is morally bound to keep his promise absent some good cause unknown at the time the promise is made. The promise of a job or the promise of a promotion in these cases is made to induce trust; in trusting, the prospective employee becomes vulnerable. Expectations have been created by the promisor. If the promise is not enforced, the promisor is given the benefit of the trust he has induced and the entire detriment falls upon the innocent party. Recognizing this, the law is now moving rapidly toward the enforcement of job promises made by the employer simply because it is wrong to make a promise on a matter of importance to another and to break it without good reason. We will see this development in many fairly recent cases described in this text.

Express Promise of Job Security

In the realm of employment controversies, an express promise if proven is only one factor to be weighed in concluding whether a civil obligation exists. In this section this factor is isolated to determine what issues develop once the employee claims the employer expressly promised job security.

Mere Expression of Goodwill and Optimism

The initial question is often whether there is in fact an express promise of job security or whether the employer's intent was merely a general expression of optimism and goodwill for the future. This is an issue that is sometimes addressed in terms of whether the promise is definite and certain enough to enforce. Employers and employees, like everyone else, sometimes speak in hyperbole to express their feelings of loyalty and friendship but without intent to invoke the heavy machinery of the law to enforce the literal meaning of these words.[13] For example, in *Brown v. Safeway Stores, Inc.*,[14] shortly after a merger, the company president addressed a meeting of district managers. One of the managers subsequently claimed that the president's statements at the meeting indicated that the company wanted and needed district managers to stay and that they would always be employed. This manager contended that these statements and others embodied in a pension plan constituted offers of lifetime employment or at least employment until age 65. The company answered that the president's statements were in the nature of a pep talk and could not reasonably be taken as offers of lifetime employment. The court held that contracts of life or permanent employment are extraordinary and unusual. An intention to make such a contract must be clear and unequivocal. Thus, standing alone, a casual remark made at a general meeting is too fragile a base on which to rest such a heavy obligation.

Similarly, the court refused to find an express promise where the employer merely inquired whether a nurse would be free to work all summer,[15] or where the alleged promise was in the form of an interoffice memorandum discussing additional training for the employee and which concluded, "If at the end of one week, things do not work out, we will see what other openings there are at night and transfer her."[16]

The Alaska Supreme Court and the Illinois Appellate Court both have ruled that a promise indicating the employee could remain employed until retirement alters an at-will employment relationship to one that requires just cause for termination.[17]

Authority to Make a Promise of Job Security

The more substantial the alleged promise of job security, the more likely the employer is to claim that his agent had no authority to make the promise. It has been held that even the president of a corporation has no real or apparent authority to bind the corporation

---

[13]*Bonnevier v. Dairy Coop. Ass'n,* 227 Ore. 123, 361 P.2d 262 (1961) (statement to disabled employee, who sold his house to employer upon promise of job, that "we will be glad to have you back to work when you are able" not enforceable because wages, job, and term of employment were not specified). Accord: *Croom v. Goldsboro Lumber Co.,* 182 N.C. 217, 108 S.E. 735 (1921); *Hedrick v. CCAT,* 7 Ohio App.3d 211, 454 N.E.2d 1343 (1982); *Grouse v. Group Health Plan, Inc.,* 306 N.W.2d 114 (Minn. 1981).

[14]190 F. Supp., 295 (E.D.N.Y. 1960). See also *Machen v. Budd Wheel Co.,* 294 Pa. 69, 143 A. 482 (1968).

[15]*Sproule v. Gulden,* 112 N.Y.S. 1076 (App. Div. 1908).

[16]*Zagar v. Field Enters. Educ. Corp.,* 58 Ill. App.3d 750, 374 N.E.2d 897 (1978). See also *Boleman v. Ols Congdon & Carpenter Co.,* 638 F.2d 2 (1st Cir. 1980), and *Bonnevier v. Dairy Coop. Ass'n,* 227 Ore. 123, 361 P.2d 262 (1961). In *Hobbs v. Gousha Co.,* 302 Ill. App. 508, 24 N.E.2d 240 (1940), a marginal notation alongside the part of an agreement that dealt specifically with rights of the parties in the event the employer terminated the employment was given no weight. The notation was "This paragraph is subject to further discussion." The court took into account the fact that it was the employer's attorney who had written the agreement and that the parties had worked harmoniously under the agreement for several years.

[17]*Eales v. Tanana Valley Medical-Surgical Group, Inc.,* Alaska Adv. Sh. 2686, 663 P.2d 958 (1983); *Martin v. Federal Life Ins. Co.,* 109 Ill. App.3d 596, 440 N.E.2d 998 (1982).

with a promise of lifetime employment.[18] However, the more substantial the detriment to the employee or other evidence of reliance, the more likely the court is to find apparent authority.[19] In *Fries v. Mine Workers*,[20] a union member claimed he had orally been promised retirement benefits by, among others, the union president, John L. Lewis. He also showed that he had relied substantially on the promise. The court found apparent authority of the union officers to make the promise claimed:

> "These men, along with Lewis, fill the highest and most powerful level offices within the union and were responsible for managing the union on a day-to-day basis. Even if no one of them acting alone could have bound the union, it was not unreasonable for plaintiff to believe that collectively they had sufficient authority to do so."[21]

Inconsistent Express Promises

Several cases present the problem of determining the intention of parties when there are two or more express promises which cannot both be taken literally. In *Carter v. Brodlee*,[22] the discharged plaintiff had entered into a contract which provided in part as follows:

> "This Agreement is made for two years from November 1st, 1925, but it is understood and agreed that we retain the right to terminate the Agreement and to discharge you at any time, should we feel called upon to do so for any reason."[23]

The question presented by this language was whether it was an agreement for two years or an agreement of employment-at-will or something else. In other words, what standard of discharge before the end of the two-year term should be read into the contract? All of the language could not be taken literally. The trial court held there was no job security of any kind and that the agreement was in effect one of employment-at-will. On appeal it was held that:

> "Such a construction would make the contract merely one at defendants' will though by its terms it was for two years. A construction will not be given a contract, if possible, that would place one of the parties at the mercy of the other (*Simon v. Etgen, et al.*, 213 N.Y. 589, 107 N.E. 1066). Under the clause in question, we are of the opinion

---

[18]*Brown v. Safeway Stores, Inc.*, 190 F. Supp. 295 (E.D.N.Y. 1960). See also *Bene v. La Grande Laundry Co.*, 22 Cal. App.2d 512, 71 P.2d 351 (1937); *Cox v. Baltimore & O.S.W. Ry.*, 180 Ind. 495, 103 N.E. 337 (1913); *Mannion v. Campbell Soup Co.*, 243 Cal. App.2d 317, 52 Cal. Rptr. 246 (1966) (personnel manager has no authority to promise employment until retirement.). Cf. *Stewart v. Blackwood Elec. Steel Corp.*, 100 W. Va. 331, 130 S.E. 447 (1925), and *Slabon v. St. Louis Car Co.*, 138 S.W.2d 673 (Mo. 1940) (company doctor has authority to promise "lifetime" employment).

[19]*Baltimore & Ohio R.R. v. Foar*, 84 F.2d 67 (7th Cir. 1936) (employee who agreed to work during violent strike could fairly assume those in charge had authority to offer lifetime employment).

[20]30 Ill. App.3d 575, 333 N.E.2d 600 (1975).

[21]*Id.* at 580, 333 N.E.2d at 604.

[22]245 A.D. 49, 280 N.Y.S. 368 (1935). See also *Burkhimer v. Gealy*, 39 N.C. App. 450, 250 S.E.2d 678 (1979) ("this agreement shall continue for the rest of my natural life or until terminated by mutual agreement").

[23]*Carter v. Brodlee*, 245 A.D. at 50, 280 N.Y.S. at 370.

that any discharge before the expiration date should have some 'reasonable' ground and that the reason must be attended with good faith."[24]

In effect, the court resolved the inconsistent language by inferring that the parties intended a standard for discharge which they did not articulate, i.e., a standard that discharge before the end of the term would be for a good business reason. Two inconsistent promises may sometimes be resolved by finding that one is unenforceable for some reason such as duress.[25]

Inconsistency Between Express and Implied Promises

Where the inconsistency in the alleged promise is between what is expressed in the language of the promise and what one party claims should be added to or read into the promise based upon a statute or corporate by-law, the cases show that the courts favor enforcement of the express promise. In *Seher v. Woodlawn School District,*[26] a teacher's contract stipulated a term for nine months. Four months into the contract the school board gave notice of dismissal and grounded their rights to terminate employment on a state statute which allowed the school board to dismiss a teacher at any time. It was held that the statute simply gave the board the power to dismiss with or without cause and that the employee would have no judicial remedies for reinstatement even if the dismissal was a breach of the employment contract. However, if there was no just cause for dismissal the employer would still be subject to liability for breach. Essentially the same result was reached where the employer claimed a corporate by-law gave the employer the right to terminate an employee at any time even though the written employment contract was for a definite period of one year.[27] The express language of an agreement has also been enforced over an inconsistent implied promise based upon the employer's published personnel policy.[28]

Express Language Defined in Court

Certain words and phrases in express promises for employment security have often been construed during the course of litigation and deserve mention. The term "permanent employment" has been construed to mean everything from indefinite employment termin-

---

[24]*Id.*

[25]*Goodwyn v. Sencore, Inc.,* 389 F. Supp. 824 (D.S.D. 1975).

[26]79 N.D. 818, 59 N.W.2d 805 (1953).

[27]*Cuppy v. Stollwerck Bros.,* 216 N.Y. 591, 111 N.E. 249 (1916).

[28]*George v. Wake County Opportunities, Inc.,* 26 N.C. App. 732, 217 S.E.2d 128 (1975) (existence of grievance procedure in written personnel policy did not create implied contract right to continued employment, where written contract of employment did not refer to grievance procedure); *Wills v. Gaff,* 136 Ind. App. 21, 191 N.E.2d 41 (1963) (personnel policy providing for renewal of yearly employment contracts after evaluation of work did not enlarge rights of employee hired for one-year period).

able at the will of either party to employment for one's working life.[29] Substantial detriment on the part of the employee or benefit to the employer in return for the promise shows the term was intended to be taken literally.[30] A sound definition of "permanent employment" comes from an old case, where the court reasoned "that plaintiff's employment * * * was to continue indefinitely and until one or the other of the parties wish *for some good reason* to sever the relation."[31]

Where "lifetime" employment was demanded as a prerequisite to concluding the sale of a business, it was held that the promise was enforceable.[32] Where the plaintiff released a substantial tort claim against the employer in return for a promise of employment for the balance of his life at a "living wage," it was held that the employer breached the contract by refusing the employee's request for higher salary.[33] An agreement to "guarantee" a certain annual salary has been held to be a promise of employment for one year.[34] A contract of employment for one year, with the provision "this contract shall be renewed during the strict performance of its provisions," was held to entitle the employee to a renewal for one year only.[35] Employment of the plaintiff "eternally" was held to be a contract for one year.[36] A job for one year and "each succeeding year * * * automatically" was held to be an engagement for one year.[37] A promise that "you will not be compelled to retire at 65 * * * [and f]rankly I hope you

[29]*Arie v. Intertherm, Inc.*, 648 S.W.2d 142 (Mo. Ct. App. 1983) ("permanent" means at will); *Borbely v. Nationwide Mut. Ins. Co.*, 547 F. Supp. 959 (D.N.J. 1981) (meaning depends upon all circumstances); *Martin v. Federal Life Ins. Co.*, 109 Ill. App.3d 596, 440 N.E.2d 998 (1982) ("permanent" means to regular age of retirement); *Jordan v. Mallard Exploration, Inc.*, 423 So.2d 896 (Ala. Civ. App. 1982) ("permanent" means not beyond existence of the business); *Roberts v. Wake Forest Univ.*, 55 N.C. App. 430, 286 S.E.2d 120 (1982) ("permanent" means at will); *Ohio Table Pad Co. v. Hogan*, 424 N.E.2d 144 (Ind. Ct. App. 1981) ("permanent" means dischargeable only for good cause if there is independent consideration); *Moody v. Bogue*, 310 N.W.2d 655 (Iowa Ct. App. 1981) ("permanent" means dischargeable only with good cause if promise is in exchange for independent consideration); *Alterman Foods, Inc. v. Ingram*, 158 Ga. App. 715, 282 S.E.2d 186 (1981) ("permanent" means at will); *Moorhouse v. Boeing Co.*, 501 F. Supp. 390 (E.D. Pa. 1980) ("permanent" means at will); *Green v. Medford Knitwear Mills, Inc.*, 408 F. Supp. 577 (E.D. Pa. 1976) ("permanent" employment means as long as satisfactory to employer); *Solomon v. Luria*, 45 Pa. D. & C.2d 291 (1967) ("permanent" means employment for one year); *Fireboard Prods. v. Townsend*, 202 F.2d 180 (9th Cir. 1953) ("permanent" employment means subject only to just cause discharge); *Roth v. Page's Pittsburgh Milk Co.*, 100 PITTSBURGH LEGAL J. 246 (No. 757, March 13, 1952) ("permanent" only means job is not temporary in nature); *Shuler v. Corl*, 39 Cal. App. 195, 178 P. 535 (1918) ("permanent" means month to month); *Saylor v. Marshall & Isley Bank*, 224 Wis. 511, 272 N.W. 369 (1937) ("permanent" means year to year); *McKelvy v. Choctaw Cotton Oil Co.*, 52 Okla. 81, 152 P. 414 (1915) ("permanent" employment is indefinite in term and thus terminable at will); *Pierson v. Kingman Milling Co.*, 92 Kan. 468, 139 P. 394 (1914) ("permanent" is not too indefinite to enforce); *Pennsylvania Co. v. Dolan*, 6 Ind. App. 109, 32 N.E. 802 (1812) ("steady and permanent" held to describe promise to furnish employment as long as employee was able, ready, and willing to perform services prescribed by company); *Siefert v. Arnold Bros.*, 138 Cal. App. 324, 39 P.2d 1059 (1934) ("steady" defined as satisfaction of employer); *Littell v. Evening Star Newspaper Co.*, 120 F.2d 36 (D.C. Cir. 1941) ("permanent" defined by circumstances).
[30]*Sullivan v. Detroit Ypsilanti & Ann Arbor Ry.*, 135 Mich. 661, 98 N.W. 756 (1904).
[31]*Lord v. Goldberg*, 81 Cal. 596, 601, 22 P. 1126, 1128 (1889).
[32]*Langendorf United Bakeries, Inc. v. Moore*, 327 F.2d 592 (9th Cir. 1964); *Slabon v. St. Louis Car Co.*, 138 S.W.2d 673 (Mo. 1940); *Page v. New Orleans Public Serv. Inc.*, 184 La. 617, 167 So. 99 (1936).
[33]*Fisher v. Roper Lumber Co.*, 183 N.C. 485, 111 S.E. 857 (1922).
[34]*Grauer v. Valve & Primer Corp.*, 47 Ill. App.3d 152, 361 N.E.2d 863 (1977).
[35]*McKinney v. Statesmen Publishing Co.*, 36 Ore. 509, 56 P. 651 (1899).
[36]*Horn v. Western Land Ass'n*, 22 Minn. 233 (1875).
[37]*Gressing v. Musical Instrument Sales Co.*, 222 N.Y. 215, 118 N.E. 627 (1918).

are around until at least you are 83" and signed by the president of the defendant company was held to be employment for life subject to termination only for good cause.[38]

An agreement that "this contract cannot be terminated or ended without the consent of both parties, and it is binding upon both parties" was held too indefinite and uncertain in duration to enforce.[39] Generally, inclusion in a written contract of specific events that justify a discharge does not imply that no other grounds may justify discharge.[40]

Summary

A close reading of the more recent cases shows a common thread. The courts enforced promises of job security more literally where all the circumstances of the case showed the employee could reasonably expect the job security promised. Evidence of misrepresentation on the part of the employer or detrimental reliance on the part of the employee was particularly persuasive. In the absence of these elements, the courts were less likely to take the alleged promise seriously but instead regarded it as a casual encounter between employer and employee with no legal significance.

The employer who wants to reduce the risk of wrongful discharge claims premised on breach of contract must make it clear to the employee that he may be discharged at will. At least one recent case holds that a statement made to that effect in a job application 12 years before the discharge occurred is sufficient.[41] However, many things may be said and done after the job application is completed that can fairly show employment will not be arbitrarily terminated. The employer who asks the court to ignore express promises of job security and look only at an old job application is probably asking too much.

Legitimate Expectations of Job Security Based Upon Personnel Policy

Personnel Policy Statements: Enforceable Contract Terms or Mere Gratuitous Statements of Intention?

The employer's personnel policy may be embodied in a formal personnel or supervisor's manual, a corporate bylaw, a personnel

---

[38]*Ward v. Consolidated Foods Corp.*, 480 S.W.2d 483 (Tex. Civ. App. 1972).

[39]*Mallory v. Jack*, 281 Mich. 156, 274 N.W. 746 (1937). See also *Hatch v. Sallinger*, 47 R.I. 395, 133 A. 621 (1926) (written agreement providing for rate of pay at $6,000 "per year" was hiring for one year considering the nature of the employment position and its responsibilities).

[40]*Corman Aircraft Corp. v. Weihmiller*, 78 F.2d 241 (7th Cir. 1935).

[41]*Novosel v. Sears, Roebuck & Co.*, 495 F. Supp. 344 (E.D. Mich. 1980) (employee with 12 years' service could have no reasonable expectation of job security because original job application made employment-at-will quite explicit).

department memorandum, or a statute governing termination procedures and tenure of public employees.[42] On the other hand, the policy may not be written anywhere. It may simply be a well-known industry practice or companywide policy; this is the so-called "common law of the shop."

The U.S. Supreme Court in *Perry v. Sindermann*[43] held that a public school teacher had a right of tenure because the college administration had raised his expectations in the college's "faculty guide." For many years the publication had provided:

> "Teacher Tenure: Odessa College has no tenure system. The administration of the college wishes the faculty member to feel that he has permanent tenure as long as his teaching services are satisfactory and as long as he displays a cooperative attitude toward his co-workers and his superiors and as long as he is happy in his work."[44]

The Court further held that a teacher's interest in the possibility of tenure is a property interest for due process purposes.

In whatever form a policy exists, the issue raised more frequently now is whether it is part of the employment contract. "Policy manual" or "employee rule book" cases have issues in common with cases concerning express promises of job security to an individual employee. Only one case, *Toussaint v. Blue Cross & Blue Shield*,[45] deals comprehensively with these issues. An examination of this case and a comparison with other cases that address the same issues show the potential of personnel policy as evidence of a contract for job security.

Charles Toussaint, employed by Blue Cross in a middle management position for five years, sued Blue Cross for wrongful discharge. A jury awarded him $72,835.52 in damages. An appellate court reversed, but the Michigan Supreme Court reinstated the judgment in favor of Toussaint.

The facts in the opinion that are of particular interest are the following:

> "Nowhere, either in the Manual or the Guidelines pamphlet, is there to be found any reference to Mr. Toussaint, by name or otherwise, to his specific duties, job description or the compensation to be paid him. The documents contain no reference to a contract of employment of any kind. Neither document is signed by the plaintiff or any representative of the defendant, nor is a place provided for such signatures.
> "Repeatedly throughout the manual notebook there appears the declaration that the document is a statement of company policy on the subjects addressed. Pages of the manual are regularly added and deleted by company officials unilaterally, under the supervision of the Blue Cross Personnel Department, without notice to any employee.
> "The record bears no evidence that during Mr. Toussaint's several pre-employment interviews any reference was made either to the Man-

---

[42]*Steinberg v. Chicago Medical School*, 69 Ill.2d 320, 371 N.E.2d 634 (1977) (catalogs, bulletins, circulars, and regulations of a university held to form contract between institution and student who makes application for admission).
[43]408 U.S. 593 (1972).
[44]*Id.* at 600.
[45]408 Mich. 579, 292 N.W.2d 880 (1980).

ual or Guidelines, or even to the subject of a written employment contract. Mr. Toussaint did not learn of the existence of the Manual and Guidelines until they were handed to him after he was hired on May 1, 1967. That is in keeping with the testimony of defendant's witnesses that the Manual is given to supervisory level employees as an aid in supervising persons in their charge and not as declarative of the contract terms of an employee's hire."[46]

Section VII of the manual provided in part:

> "III Policy—It is the policy of the company to treat employees leaving Blue Cross in a fair and consistent manner and to release employees for just cause only."[47]

The manual further defined grounds for discharge in terms of the employee's ability and willingness to perform and outlined detailed procedures for handling employee grievances and terminations.[48]

The gist of Toussaint's complaint was that the terms of his employment contract were largely embodied in the personnel manual. Those terms assured him of discharge only for good cause and that certain procedures for progressive discipline would be observed before a discharge. Thus, his complaint made out a claim for employment for an indefinite period of time, i.e., until he decided to quit or until there was good cause to discharge him.

A majority of the court viewed policy statements providing for some measure of job security as analogous to deferred compensation such as termination pay, death benefits, and profit-sharing benefits.[49] A promise of job security to induce employee trust and services, it reasoned, is not so different from a promise of deferred compensation that one should be enforceable and the other unenforceable.

The court held that a provision of an employment contract stating that an employee shall not be discharged except for cause is legally enforceable even though the contract is for an indefinite term. The provision may become part of the contract either by express oral agreement or by reason of an employee's legitimate expectation.[50] Employee reliance on the policy statement need not be shown.[51] (However, had he shown reliance, the dissent would have found for Toussaint on the basis of promissory estoppel.[52])

---

[46]*Id.* at 644, 292 N.W.2d at 906.

[47]*Id.* at 656, 292 N.W.2d at 911.

[48]*Id.* at 651-662, 292 N.W.2d at 909-915.

[49]The cases referred to by both the majority and the dissenting opinion in *Toussaint* (*id.* at 647 n.2, 292 N.W.2d at 907) are *Cain v. Allen Elec. & Equip. Co.,* 346 Mich. 568, 78 N.W.2d 296 (1956); *Psutka v. Michigan Alkali Co.,* 274 Mich. 318, 264 N.W. 385 (1936); *Gaydos v. White Motor Corp.,* 54 Mich. App. 143, 220 N.W.2d 697 (1974); *Clarke v. Brunswick Corp.,* 48 Mich. App. 667, 211 N.W.2d 101 (1973); and *Couch v. Administrative Comm. of the Difco Laboratories, Inc.,* 44 Mich. App. 44, 205 N.W.2d 24 (1972). See also *Hinkeldey v. Cities Serv. Oil Co.,* 470 S.W.2d 494 (Mo. 1971).

[50]*Toussaint, id.* at 598 n.2, 292 N.W.2d at 885. Several other cases have also held that the policy manual is part of an enforceable employment contract. E.g., *Gunsolley v. Bushby,* 19 Ore. App. 884, 529 P.2d 950 (1974) (hospital's written policy held to be part of the employee's employment contract).

[51]*Toussaint,* 408 Mich. at 613 n.25, 292 N.W.2d at 892. See also *Sullivan v. David City Bank,* 181 Neb. 395, 148 N.W.2d 844 (1967) (employment term described in articles of incorporation applied to employee, despite lack of reliance, acceptance, or knowledge).

[52]*Toussaint,* 408 Mich. at 649, 650, 292 N.W.2d at 908.

The objection to the employer's being bound to employ while the employee is not bound to be employed—mutuality of obligation — was disposed of in one sentence and a footnote. Mutuality of obligation was not regarded as a legal doctrine worthy of addressing. At best it was synonymous with consideration.[53]

The court's discussion of consideration ranged over several sub-issues. First, the majority held that no preemployment negotiation over job security need take place and parties' minds need not meet on the subject.[54] The dissent, however, regarded preemployment negotiation as a special circumstance —the equivalent of independent consideration—that would take the case out of the employment-at-will rule.[55]

The majority also held that it is not necessary that the employee know the "particulars" of the employer's policies and practices.[56] It may be inferred, however, that the employee must at least know in a general way that the policy is to deal fairly on the basis of performance. Of critical importance is the publication of the policy by the employer for the employee's benefit.[57]

That a promise may be accepted without knowledge of its substance may seem anomalous. However, there is some precedent in contract law. For example, when one apprehends a criminal suspect without knowing that an offer of a reward was made, many jurisdictions require the payment of the reward. [58] Moreover, the opinion does recognize continuing employment as constituting acceptance. Shortly after he was employed Toussaint was furnished with a copy of the manual. Certainly, if the policy is beneficial to the employee his acceptance is tacit; and several cases have resolved the acceptance issue this way.[59]

Under *Toussaint* the employer's power to change the policy unilaterally, and thus presumably change the contract, has no significance.[60] "[H]aving announced the policy," the employer may not treat it as illusory.[61] *Toussaint* thus places substantial limitations upon an employer's right to alter previously announced policies.

The most significant analysis in *Toussaint* identified what is exchanged between employer and employee that amounts to consideration. Instead of searching in vain for a reciprocal commitment

---

[53]*Id.* at 599, 292 N.W.2d at 885. See also *Piper v. Board of Trustees*, 99 Ill. App.3d 752, 426 N.E.2d 262 (1981) (policy manual is part of the employment contract; no discussion of mutuality), and *Carter v. Kaskaskia Community Agency*, 24 Ill. App.3d 1056, 322 N.E.2d 574 (1974) (mutuality found in requirement that employees give 30 days' notice before resigning).
[54]*Toussaint*, 408 Mich. at 613, 292 N.W.2d at 892.
[55]*Id.* at 641 n.4, 292 N.W.2d at 904.
[56]*Id.* at 613, 292 N.W.2d at 892.
[57]*Id.*
[58]See Fried, *supra* note 5, at 45.
[59]*Carter v. Kaskaskia Community Action Agency*, 24 Ill. App.3d 1056, 1059, 322 N.E.2d 574, 576 (1974) (continuing to work both assent to and consideration for employer's promise). Accord: *Scutt v. LaSalle County Bd.*, 97 Ill. App.3d 181, 423 N.E.2d 213 (1981); *Yartzoff v. Democrat–Herald Publishing Co.*, 281 Ore. 651, 576 P.2d 356 (1978). See *Wagner v. Sperry Univac*, 458 F. Supp. 505 (E.D. Pa. 1978), for an extensive discussion of the acceptance problem.
[60]*Toussaint*, 408 Mich. at 614, 292 N.W.2d at 892.
[61]*Id.* at 619, 292 N.W.2d at 895.

from the employee, the court found improved morale to be the benefit to the employer in exchange for its job security commitments:

"While an employer need not establish personnel policies or practices, where an employer chooses to establish such policies and practices and makes them known to its employees, the employment relationship is presumably enhanced. The employer secures an orderly, cooperative and loyal work force, and the employee the peace of mind associated with job security and the conviction that he will be treated fairly."[62]

The majority opinion does not explicitly overrule precedent that requires additional consideration or "special circumstances" in addition to services performed for enforcement of a promise of job security. Indeed, it describes the benefits accruing to the employer from a policy of providing job security as amounting to "special circumstances" under the prior authorities. The dissent found no special circumstances in the record of *Toussaint*.[63]

The employer, presumably for its own advantage, invited Toussaint and other employees to rely on a policy of observing an informal system of procedural and substantive due process in the work place. Having taken that initiative and received the benefit of the employees' trust, the employer must recognize its responsibility to treat employees as it had said it would. Several cases in the last decade have reached the same result.[64]

---

[62]*Id.* at 613, 292 N.W.2d at 892. See also *Dangott v. ASG Indus., Inc.*, 558 P.2d 379 (Okla. 1976) (consideration to employer from promulgation of administrative procedures for discharge was "stable and contented" work force; personnel policy is enforceable and no reliance need be shown); *Hepp v. Lockheed-California Co.*, 86 Cal. App.3d 714, 150 Cal. Rptr. 408 (1978); *Maloney v. E. I. du Pont de Nemours & Co.*, 352 F.2d 936 (D.C. Cir. 1965); *Schipani v. Ford Motor Co.*, 102 Mich. App. 606, 302 N.W.2d 307 (1981); *Marwill v. Baker*, 499 F. Supp. 560 (E.D. Mich. 1980).

[63]*Toussaint*, 408 Mich. at 641 n.4, 292 N.W.2d at 904.

[64]The courts apparently have taken employer personnel policies more seriously than some employers have. See *Greene v. Howard Univ.*, 412 F.2d 1128 (D.C. Cir. 1969) (policy of notice of nonretention of teachers gives rise to enforceable rights); *Carter v. Kaskaskia Community Action Agency*, 24 Ill. App.3d 1056, 322 N.E.2d 574 (1974) (where personnel manual required board hearing as condition of discharge, employer required to provide meaningful hearing, not merely pay lip service to policy). *Vallejo v. Jamestown College*, 244 N.W.2d 753 (N.D. 1976), reflects a novel application of a policy manual. The faculty handbook assured professors of academic freedom but gave no assurance that annual contracts would be renewed. A professor successfully argued that failure to renew was in retaliation for his exercise of academic freedom guaranteed by the handbook. Other cases approving an action premised upon the employer's personnel or policy manual include *Wolk v. Saks Fifth Avenue, Inc.*, 728 F.2d 221 (3d Cir. 1984); *Vinyard v. King*, 728 F.2d 428 (3d Cir. 1984); *Weiner v. McGraw-Hill, Inc.*, 57 N.Y.2d 458, 443 N.E.2d 441, 457 N.Y.S.2d 193 (1982); *Yartzoff v. Democrat-Herald Publishing Co.*, 281 Ore. 651, 576 P.2d 356 (1978); *Hepp v. Lockheed-California Co.*, 86 Cal. App.3d 714, 150 Cal. Rptr. 408 (1978); *Brooks v. Trans World Airlines*, 574 F. Supp. 805 (D. Colo. 1983); *Smith v. Kerrville Bus Co.*, 709 F.2d 914 (5th Cir. 1983); *Southwest Gas Corp. v. Ahmad*, 668 P.2d 261 (Nev. 1983); *Shah v. American Synthetic Rubber Corp.*, 655 S.W.2d 489 (Ky. 1983); *Arie v. Intertherm, Inc.*, 648 S.W.2d 142 (Mo. Ct. App. 1983); *Conley v. Board of Trustees*, 707 F.2d 175 (5th Cir. 1983); *Osterkamp v. Alkota Mfg., Inc.*, 332 N.W. 2d 275 (S.D. 1983); *Saunders v. Big Bros., Inc.*, 115 Misc.2d 845, 454 N.Y.S.2d 787 (Civ. Ct. 1982); *Hernandez v. Home Educ. Livelihood Program Inc.*, 98 N.M. 125, 645 P.2d 1381 (Ct. App. 1982); *Morris v. Chem-Lawn Corp.*, 541 F. Supp. 479 (E.D. Mich. 1982); *Sweet v. Stormont Vail Regional Medical Center*, 231 Kan. 604, 647 P.2d 1274 (1982); *Homby v. Genesco, Inc.*, 627 S.W.2d 373 (Tenn. Ct. App. 1981); *Simpson v. Western Graphics Corp.*, 53 Ore. App. 205, 631 P.2d 805 (1981); *Piper v. Board of Trustees*, 99 Ill. App.3d 752, 426 N.E.2d 262 (1981).

Cases refusing an action premised upon the policy manual include *White v. Chelsea Indus. Inc.*, 425 So.2d 1090 (Ala. 1983); *Reynolds Mfg. Co. v. Mendoza*, 644 S.W.2d 536 (Tex Civ. App.

It should be observed that the use of the policy manual to evidence terms of the employment contract is a two-way street. In fact, it was the employer in several early cases that relied successfully on the provisions of the manual to show it had fully honored its obligations.[65]

Can Personnel Policies Be Retroactively Changed?

After employment premised upon a promise of job security begins, what is the employer's power retroactively and unilaterally to diminish or downgrade job security? We know that defined compensation plans cannot be changed retroactively.[66] But there is little authority on the subject of job security that addresses the subject.[67]

Indiana ex rel. Anderson v. Brandy[68] concerned Indiana statutes that provided the terms for the employment contract between a school teacher and the school district. The 1927 Teacher's Tenure Act provided that a teacher who serves under contract for five or more successive years and enters into a contract for further service shall become a permanent teacher. This statute was amended in 1933 to eliminate the tenure provision. A teacher who had qualified for tenure under the original statute was then fired. The U.S. Supreme Court discussing the relationship between a teacher and a school district, noted that a teacher in the public schools is not a public officer but is employed under a contract between the teacher and the school corporation. The relationship remains contractual after the teacher has become a permanent teacher under the provisions of the Teacher's Tenure Act, the terms and conditions of the contract being governed primarily by the statute. The question was whether the alteration of the contract by amendment of the statute was a proper exercise of the police power. The Court held that it was not and that it did not otherwise disturb the contractual relationship based upon the 1927 statute before it was amended.

1982); *Cote v. Burroughs Wellcome*, 558 F. Supp. 883 (E.D. Pa. 1982); *Heideck v. Kent Gen. Hosp.*, 446 A.2d 1095 (Del. 1982); *Williams v. Delta Haven, Inc.*, 416 So.2d 637 (La. Ct. App. 1982); *Gates v. Life of Mont. Ins. Co.*, 638 P.2d 1063 (Mont. 1982); *Whittaker v. Care-More, Inc.*, 621 S.W.2d 395 (Tenn. Ct. App. 1981); *Muller v. Stromberg Carlson Corp.*, 427 So.2d 266 (Fla. Dist. Ct. App. 1983); *Pine River State Bank v. Mettille*, 333 N.W.2d 622 (Minn. 1983).

[65]*Jackson v. Minidoka Irrigation Dist.*, 98 Idaho 330, 563 P.2d 54 (1977) (employee not entitled to hearing because policy manual provided hearing only in certain circumstances not present); *Klekamp v. Blaw-Knox Co.*, 179 F. Supp. 328 (S.D. Cal. 1959); *Blackhurst v. E.I. du Pont de Nemours & Co.*, 294 F. Supp. 128 (S.D. W.Va. 1968); *Montgomery Ward & Co. v. Guignet*, 112 Ind. App. 661, 45 N.E.2d 337 (1942).

[66]*Roberts v. Mays Mills, Inc.*, 184 N.C. 406, 114 S.E. 530 (1922) (employer may not unilaterally withdraw offer of bonus); *Rochester Corp. v. Rochester*, 450 F.2d 118 (4th Cir. 1971) (employer may not retroactively change a pension plan).

[67]*Carter v. Kaskaskia Community Action Agency*, 24 Ill. App.3d 1056, 322 N.E.2d 574 (1974) (employer may not retroactively change quorum and other procedural requirements which relate to a hearing provided discharged employee); *Nichols v. National Tube Co.*, 122 F. Supp. 726 (N.D. Ohio 1954) (employer may not retroactively modify collective bargaining agreement by adopting mandatory retirement age of 65, where union agreement limited discharge to good cause). Accord: *Miller v. Dictaphone Corp.*, 334 F. Supp. 840 (D. Ore. 1971).

[68]303 U.S. 95 (1938).

Rensch v. General Drivers[69] concerned a union business representative who was elected to a three-year term commencing January 1, 1958. At a meeting in February 1958, the union's bylaws were amended to require all officers to retire at age 65. The representative turned 65 in June 1958 but continued working through December 1958, when his employment was terminated. A written request for reinstatement to his elected position was unconditionally rejected. The court held that the representative could not be deprived of his status as an elected officer by reason of the retroactive application of the bylaw. Dismissal or forced retirement pursuant to the bylaw constituted a breach of his employment contract.

In *People ex rel. Sterba v. Blaser*,[70] an employee understood that he had been hired by a state agency as a permanent employee. At no time prior to or during his service, he said, was he ever informed that he had been appointed or employed as an emergency "temporary or provisional" employee. Observing that all notations in the agency's records that the employee's position was temporary were made without notice to or knowledge of the plaintiff, the court stated:

> "This type of completely unilateral action should not be permitted to modify the conditions of plaintiff's employment and thus to affect his civil service status. It would indeed be an incredible state of affairs with alarming and indefensible connotations, if defendants here, *or any other employer*, could modify the status of an employee and the terms and conditions of his employment by merely making such entries as they saw fit upon official personnel records."[71] (Emphasis added.)

An employer who adopts and announces a less generous policy concerning job security might argue that the employees' continuation of employment after knowledge of the new policy is an acceptance. Such an argument should be rejected. In effect, the argument is that the employee has only two choices: quit or accede to the new terms. This argument is based upon the common law contract doctrine that silence plus additional circumstances may constitute acceptance of an offer as a matter of law.[72] The problem is that employees with seniority can argue persuasively that they have already earned the right to the originally promised job security. Where the employee specifically and repeatedly rejected the modification, no acceptance is understood even though he remains on the job.[73] If the modification does not benefit the employee, his acceptance is not tacit and cannot fairly be presumed from his silence.

Promulgation of the Policy

The *Toussaint* opinion conditioned incorporation of the personnel policy in the employment contract upon the employee's knowledge of

---

[69]268 Minn. 307, 129 N.W.2d 341 (1964).
[70]33 Ill. App.3d 1, 337 N.E.2d 410 (1975).
[71]*Id.* at 7, 337 N.E.2d at 415.
[72]CORBIN ON CONTRACTS, §75 at 121 (1952).
[73]*Bartinikas v. Clarklift of Chicago N., Inc.*, 508 F. Supp. 959 (N.D. Ill. 1981). Cf. *Anderson v. Seaton*, 14 Ill. App.2d 53, 143 N.E.2d 59 (1957).

at least its existence and purpose. The employee need not know the particulars of the policy. It is enough that he be aware of the general aspects of the policy by virtue of the environment of goodwill that it creates in the work place.[74]

Cederstrand v. Lutheran Brotherhood[75] focuses on the importance of some publication of the policy to employees who are subject to it. In the course of her work, the office manager and personnel director developed a personnel manual to be used by herself and other supervisors. One of the provisions in the booklet read, "A person is not dismissed without cause and it is customary to give a warning and an opportunity to make good before final dismissal." This provision, however, never appeared in the handbooks that were distributed to the employees. When she was later fired, the author of the manual sued for wrongful discharge, claiming that her employment contract included a provision that she could be dismissed only for cause by virtue of the personnel policy which she had drafted. The employer asserted the personnel manual was only a collection of the employee's own notes and not binding in any way upon the defendant-employer.

The court agreed with the employer primarily because the provision about just cause for discharge did not appear in the literature given to new employees. At least one other case requires some publication of the policy to employees before it will be regarded as part of the employment contract.[76]

Cases Rejecting Personnel Policy as Part of Contract

Personnel policy has been rejected as part of the employment contract where it was found that the policy on its face was nothing more than a general expression of goodwill or simply made general references to the employer's pension plan.[77] In *Sargent v. Illinois Institute of Technology*,[78] however, the heart of the court's refusal to incorporate the personnel policy in the employment contract was the absence of facts tending to show that the parties had bargained or negotiated over the terms.[79] Other cases rejecting personnel policy as part of the employment contract are often premised upon the employment-at-will doctrine.[80] In time, we believe, most courts will hold

---

[74]*Toussaint v. Blue Cross & Blue Shield*, 408 Mich. 579, 292 N.W.2d 880 (1980).

[75]263 Minn. 520, 117 N.W.2d 213 (1962).

[76]*Speciale v. Tektronix Inc.*, 38 Ore. App. 441, 590 P.2d 734 (1979).

[77]Some cases do not get into the employment-at-will rule because the policy statement is regarded as nothing but a general expression of goodwill. See, e.g., *Brookfield v. Drury College*, 139 Mo. App. 339, 123 S.W. 86 (1909), and *Schroeder v. Dayton-Hudson Corp.*, 448 F. Supp. 910 (E.D. Mich. 1977).

[78]78 Ill. App.3d 117, 397 N.E.2d 443 (1979). Cf. *Carter v. Kaskaskia Community Action Agency*, 24 Ill. App.3d 1056, 322 N.E.2d 574 (1974) (employee rule book is part of contract), and *Kepper v. School Directors*, 26 Ill. App.3d 372, 325 N.E.2d 91 (1975).

[79]*Sargent*, 78 Ill. App.3d at 121, 397 N.E.2d at 446.

[80]*Beidler v. W.R. Grace, Inc.*, 461 F. Supp. 1013 (E.D. Pa. 1978) (failure to adhere to company personnel policy is not grounds for action for wrongful discharge); *Johnson v. National Beef*

employers to the express promises in their personnel manuals.

Can an employer who states a generous personnel policy in an employee manual avoid responsibility for implied promises of job security by having employees acknowledge in writing that they are subject to dismissal at any time at the whim of the employer? In addition to contract law techniques for dealing with inconsistent documents, the hypothetical suggests an argument by the employees that the acknowledgment that employment is solely at the will of the employer is void because it is the product of economic coercion. Generally, the courts have not been receptive to such arguments unless the employee could show that the "coercion" was so aggravated it deprived him of his free will.[81] However, the substance of the economic coercion argument is no more fixed than any other legal doctrine. If the courts focus more on the unfairness of a withdrawal of benefits used to attract employees, or if the issue is framed in terms of whether the employer presents unreasonable choices, employees may have more success with this approach. In any event, the unfairness of an agreement and the inequality of bargaining power warrant a narrow construction of such agreements extracted from employees.[82]

Implied Promises and Reasonable Expectations

Even though an employer does not make an express promise of security, its behavior may imply such a promise. The factual question is then whether the employer could foresee that the employee would reasonably expect job security because of its words and actions. If so, the legal issue is whether those expectations can be enforced as the employer's implied-in-fact promise or read into the agreement by way of the implied duty of good faith and fair dealing. Questions of consideration, mutuality, the statute of frauds, and the employment-at-will doctrine are essentially the same whether the claim of job security is founded on general circumstances, an express personnel policy, or an express promise. Obviously, the employee's expectancy

---

Packing Co., 220 Kan. 52, 551 P.2d 779 (1976) (policy manual distributed to employees promising discharge only for just cause not enforceable in absence of commitment by employer or employee to fixed term of employment); *Shaw v. S.S. Kresge Co.*, 167 Ind. App. 1, 328 N.E.2d 775 (1975) (handbook providing for progressive discipline not a contract of employment in absence of commitment by employer and employee that employment should continue for fixed period of time); *Bernstein v. Pennsylvania State Univ.*, 80 YORK LEGAL RECORD 37 (Ct. Common Pleas, No. 4, June 23, 1966) (notice provision in faculty handbook not enforceable because university and faculty member did not agree on term of employment); *Chin v. American Tel. & Tel. Co.*, 96 Misc.2d 1070, 410 N.Y.S.2d 737 (Sup. Ct. 1978), *aff'd without opinion*, 70 A.D.2d 791, 416 N.Y.S.2d 160 (1979) ("Code of Conduct" was not part of employment contract because it did not define duties and responsibilities of particular position, length of employment, or terms of compensation, all of which are essential elements in employment agreement).

[81] *Alexander v. Standard Oil Co.*, 97 Ill App.3d 809, 423 N.E.2d 578 (1981); *Tidwell v. Critz*, 248 Ga. 201, 282 S.E.2d 104 (1981).

[82] *Bushman v. Pure Plant Food Int'l, Ltd.*, 330 N.W.2d 762 (S.D. 1983) (letter signed by employees acknowledging payment of promised bonus discretionary read as applicable only to year letter signed). Contra: *Whittaker v. Care-More, Inc.*, 621 S.W.2d 395 (Tenn. Ct. App. 1981) (refused to enforce generous policy in employee manual because signed employment application provided for at-will employment).

of job security must be founded upon something more than wishful thinking.[83]

The Hiring Letter

Art Miller responded to a newspaper ad and accepted a job as a trainee in Chicago. The personnel director sent him the following letter: "First, let me extend an official welcome to the Community family; we are certain you will have a rewarding and satisfying career ahead of you. For the record, I should like to confirm the employment arrangements with you. Your beginning salary will be $10,000 per year as a Store Management Trainee. Regarding moving expenses, we will pay one-half now and the balance after one year." Three months later, after moving from Toledo, Ohio, to Chicago, Miller was fired without cause. The court awarded judgment to Miller, finding in the moving expense language an intention to have the contract last for at least one year.[84]

A letter written by another employer to a prospective employee read as follows: "This letter will confirm my conversation with you. * * * Hodag Chemical Corporation * * * will employ you to perform such functions as assigned for two years minimum and at $15,400 per year. This employment begins today."[85] It was signed and accepted by both parties. The employee nevertheless was fired without cause a few months later. Plainly, the employer promised a term of employment. Just as plainly, the employee did not, by the language used, promise to stay in the job for any specific period of time. Yet, to enforce the promise against the employer, the court construed this letter to bind *both* the employer and the employee to a term of two years. Thus, the contract was characterized as having mutuality of obligation and was enforceable. This case and *Miller* arose in the same jurisdiction and were decided only a few months apart. Yet the second opinion turns upon a search for mutuality of obligation, which was ignored in the first opinion.[86]

Many of the cases discussed in this section raise a problem of consideration or mutuality of obligation. To hold the employer to an implied term of employment, the court may imply a term of employment binding on both employer and employee, neatly solving any problem of consideration or mutuality. And in fact, a mutual obligation to continue the relationship for a particular time may be what the parties had in mind. But unless the evidence shows such an intent, it is dangerous to infer one; to do so might subject an employee to an action for quitting without sufficient justification.

In reality, the employee's consideration is usually the surrender of another job and or simply the acceptance of the position offered.

[83]*Parker v. United Air Lines*, 32 Wash. App. 722, 649 P.2d 181 (1982).
[84]*Miller v. Community Discount*, 83 Ill. App.2d 439, 228 N.E.2d 113 (1967).
[85]*Hillman v. Hodag Chem. Corp.*, 96 Ill. App.2d 204, 206, 238 N.E.2d 145, 147 (1968).
[86]*Id.* at 208, 238 N.E.2d at 148.

Since the employee, unlike the employer, lacks discretion to alter working conditions, shifts, and job assignments, the common expectation of the parties is that the employee will give notice of termination—usually two weeks—so that the employer can adjust to the change without undue disruption. Accordingly, the suggestion that both parties agreed to a fixed term must be taken with a grain of salt, for such a finding is as often as not a fiction invoked to evade the consideration or mutuality issue.

Another letter offered a job in the following terms: "If you are willing to go to Miami and take charge of our service there we will pay you $165.00 per month with an extra living allowance of $30.00 per month for the winter, that is, up until May 1st." This offer when accepted by commencement of performance became a contract of employment until May.[87]

A prospective employee and an employer exchanged numerous letters and telegrams concerning a position as superintendent of construction for a railroad building project. In one telegram the employer said the work "will take about two years to complete." This was held to be a contract for two years of employment.[88] However, another court could not discern an implied agreement to hire for a term where the hiring letter provided: "It is scheduled that your assignment in Saudi Arabia will continue for a period of eighteen (18) months," and the employee went to Saudi Arabia in reliance upon the promise.[89]

A hiring letter is often the most concrete available evidence of the employment agreement. The large number of cases construing these documents as contracts and dissecting their language display no common theme, unless it is the careful examination of specific words, which often were written in a casual way. Excessive reliance on the hiring letter is seldom appropriate, for the letter is usually but a confirmation of an oral exchange. The cautious employer that chooses its words carefully should not be able to rely on the document to escape obligations orally undertaken, nor should a poor choice of words bind the employer to an obligation neither party intended. The letter ordinarily should be viewed as important evidence of the employment agreement, but not as the final word.

Nature of the Job

When an employee has to initiate a special operation, inaugurate a new office, or undertake some other job that is reasonably contemplated to last a particular length of time, it is implied that the period

---

[87]*Remington Typewriter Co. v. Hall*, 217 Ala. 128, 115 So. 74 (1928).

[88]*Costello v. Siems-Carey Co.*, 140 Minn. 208, 167 N.W. 551 (1918). Another case holding the hiring letter amounted to a contract or offer of a contract is *Ward v. Berry & Assocs., Inc.*, 614 S.W.2d 372 (Tenn. Ct. App. 1981).

[89]*Buian v. J.J. Jacobs & Co.*, 428 F.2d 531 (7th Cir. 1970). Other cases holding the letter did not create a contract are *Myers v. Coradian Corp.*, 92 A.D.2d 871, 459 N.Y.S.2d 829 (1983), *DuSesoi v. United Ref. Co.*, 540 F. Supp. 1260 (W.D. Pa. 1982), and *Roy Jorgensen Assocs., Inc. v. Deschenes*, 409 So.2d 1188 (Fla. Dist. Ct. App. 1982).

of employment will be at least sufficient to complete the assigned duty. For example, where an employment service had agreed to supply a number of laborers for the purpose of cleaning damaged cans of salmon, the court held that discharge without cause before completion of the job was a breach of the implied contract. Although the parties had not expressly agreed to a term of employment, it was clear that completion of the job was contemplated.[90] Likewise, where the purpose of employment was to build up a new insurance business, work requiring years of effort and labor, it was implied that no mere temporary arrangement would suffice.[91] Employment at the World Columbian Exposition implied a term coextensive with the duration of the exposition itself.[92] In agricultural employment, because work is often by the crop year, that year may be an implied term of employment.[93]

Tesstard v. Penn-Jersey Auto Stores, Inc.,[94] found an implied contract for a year because the plaintiff moved himself and his household from Memphis to Philadelphia to accept a new position which by its very nature was not temporary. Moreover, the salary was "by the year." In *Jones v. Pittsburgh Mercantile Co.*,[95] an individual's election to a corporate office by stockholders and directors together with the character of his position raised an issue for the jury whether he worked under an implied contract for a term of one year.

Common Law of the Shop

The common law of the shop is a neutral principle in the employment relationship. It is generally established by the policy of the company either expressly or impliedly. When there is no ascertainable company policy, the nature of the job or the customs and practices of the industry indicate what the parties reasonably expect in terms of job security and other conditions in the work place. Depending on the situation, the common law of the particular "shop" may imply either that an employee has job security or that he does not have it. The essential point for present purposes is that the common law of the job has recently been recognized as an element that helps define an employment contract.[96] One early case permitted a general sales manager to prove a one-year contract from the fact that employees previously employed in that position had been on one year contracts.[97]

---

[90]*Sarusal v. Seung*, 96 Wash. 295, 165 P. 116 (1917).
[91]*Woods v. Schumard & Co.*, 114 La. 451, 38 So. 416 (1905).
[92]*World Columbian Exposition v. Richards*, 57 Ill. App. 601 (1894).
[93]*Fletcher v. Crichton*, 183 La. 551, 164 So. 411 (1935); *Chenet v. Libby & Bloouin Ltd.*, 156 La. 503, 100 So. 697 (1924).
[94]154 F. Supp. 160 (E.D. Pa. 1956).
[95]295 Pa. 219, 145 A. 80 (1928).
[96]*Board of Regents v. Roth*, 408 U.S. 564 (1972); *Perry v. Sindermann,* 408 U.S. 593 (1972); *Steel Workers v. Warrior & Gulf Navigation Co.*, 363 U.S. 574 (1960).
[97]*Arkadelphia Lumber Co. v. Asman*, 85 Ark. 568, 107 S.W. 1171 (1907).

Salary Terms and the Ambience of the Work Place

Employment for a term has been inferred from the period the parties fix for the payment of salary;[98] just as often, the implication has been rejected. Another approach is that "a reasonable time" period of employment is implied when the employee "buys the job," but no time period is specified. For example, if a condition of hiring is assignment of patents, sale of business to the employer, or purchase of stock in the employer's business, the employee has in a sense bought the job and should not be subject to arbitrary discharge.[99]

An implied contract for a year was inferred in one case from the fact that the employee was promoted several times after a period of six years, was 58 years old, prepared yearly budgets for the employer that included her salary, scheduled her own work several months in advance, and expected to retire in two years. [100] This case appears to go too far. The implication of job security from the facts is plainly speculative.

Study of a number of cases either holding that facts pleaded or proved were inadequate to amount to an implied-in-fact agreement reveals no common thread; many, if not most of them could have been decided differently by another court.[101]

Longevity in the Job

Cleary v. American Airlines[102] enforced an implied contract for job security requiring just cause for discharge. The implied contract was based upon the employee's 17 years of service and the employer's general policy of fairness. This case was discussed in some detail in an earlier section dealing with the implied-in-law covenant of good faith and fair dealing (Chapter 2, pp. 68–69). *Pugh v. See's Candies, Inc.*, [103] also discussed earlier (pp. 69–71), presented a claim of wrongful discharge by a former senior executive of the employer who was abruptly dismissed after 32 years of employment. The court reviewed the earlier *Cleary* opinion with approval and found that the "totality

---

[98]*Mannion v. Campbell Soup Co.*, 243 Cal. App.2d 317, 52 Cal. Rptr. 246 (1966).

[99]See WILLISTON ON CONTRACTS §1940 (3d ed. 1978); RESTATEMENT OF THE LAW OF AGENCY §442 comment c (1958). See also *Brown v. National Elec. Works,* 168 Cal. 336, 143 P. 606 (1914) (employee paid $5,000 for stock in the employer's business).

[100]*Delzell v. Pope*, 200 Tenn. 641, 294 S.W.2d 690 (1956).

[101]In the following cases the court refused to find an implied contract from the general circumstances of the case: *Pearson v. Youngstown Sheet & Tube Co.*, 332 F.2d 439 (7th Cir. 1964); *Miller v. Missouri Pac. Transp. Co.*, 225 Ark. 475, 283 S.W.2d 158 (1955); *Littell v. Evening Star Newspaper Co.*, 120 F.2d 36 (D.C. Cir. 1941); *Heuvelman v. Triplett Elec. Instrument Co.*, 23 Ill. App.2d 231, 161 N.E.2d 875 (1959); *Degen v. Investors Diversified Serv., Inc.*, 260 Minn. 424, 110 N.W.2d 863 (1961); *Stevenson v. ITT Harper, Inc.*, 51 Ill. App.3d 568, 366 N.E.2d 561 (1977); *Rogers v. International Business Machs. Corp.*, 500 F. Supp. 867, (W.D. Pa. 1980). Contra: *Scholtes v. Signal Delivery Serv., Inc.*, 548 F. Supp. 487 (W.D. Ark. 1982) (good faith and fair dealing inferable from words and conduct); *Cancellier v. Federated Dep't Stores*, 672 F.2d 1312 (9th Cir. 1982); *Knowles v. Unity College*, 429 A.2d 220 (Me. 1981); *Viator v. City of New Iberia*, 428 So.2d 1329 (La. Ct. Ap. 1982).

[102]111 Cal. App.3d 443, 168 Cal. Rptr. 722 (1980).

[103]116 Cal. App.3d 311, 171 Cal. Rptr. 917 (1981).

of the parties' relationship" as pleaded in the complaint warranted a trial on the theory that the employee had an implied contract that insulated him from arbitrary discharge.

Foley v. Community Oil Co., Inc. [104] held that a jury could find an implied contract for some unspecified type of job security on the basis of the employee's 40 years of service and moving his family to accommodate the employer's interests.

McKinney v. National Dairy Council[105] is consistent with *Cleary* and *Pugh* and emphasizes longevity of service. *McKinney*, however, adds another factor for consideration. The employee charged that one motive for his discharge was his age. He argued that several different statutes prohibiting discrimination in employment based upon age must be read into the employment contract and that age discrimination contrary to such statutes would breach the implied duty of good faith and fair dealing. The court considered authorities on whether a civil remedy in contract could be implied from a statutory scheme to remedy age discrimination. It concluded that age discrimination legislation was embraced by the implied covenant of good faith and fair dealing in the contract. Accordingly, discharge because of age amounted to a breach of contract of employment.

Bussard v. College of St. Thomas, Inc.[106] found an implied promise of permanent employment in a situation where the plaintiff had never asked for permanent employment. In fact, the subject was never discussed. The implied promise was based upon the fact that all parties to the sale had to be aware that the plaintiff expected to continue indefinitely as editor-in-chief of the magazine. The opinion reviewed all the circumstances of the sale of the magazine publishing business from the former owner/ employer to the new owner. It concluded that express promises of job security were not necessary to prove the alleged promise of job security because job security was an obvious but unspoken premise of the entire transaction.

In *McNulty v. Borden, Inc.*,[107] the plaintiff alleged that during the course of his employment he rejected many offers of employment elsewhere. These rejections were made in reliance upon representations to him by his superiors that he would eventually be promoted to at least a position of district manager and possibly higher. The court felt that if these allegations were established at trial it would not be unreasonable for a trier of fact to conclude the promise was part of the contract.

The plaintiff in *Rowe v. Noren Pattern & Foundry Co.*,[108] quit another job upon accepting the defendant's offer of employment. The inducement for employment with the defendant was a somewhat higher salary and the opportunity after 45 days of employment to

---

[104]64 F.R.D. 561 (D.N.H. 1974).
[105]491 F. Supp. 1108 (D. Mass. 1980).
[106]294 Minn. 215, 200 N.W.2d 155 (1972).
[107]474 F. Supp. 1111 (E.D. Pa. 1979).
[108]91 Mich. App. 254, 283 N.W.2d 713 (1979).

become a union member and thereby obtain under the collective bargaining agreement the security of dismissal only for just cause. He was discharged before the 45 days elapsed. It was held that there was an implied agreement for dismissal only for just cause in the first 45-day period. The court was influenced by the fact that in the former position the employee had qualified for a favorable pension plan by long service and thereby suffered substantial detriment by giving up the former job.

Deferred Compensation

Pensions, bonuses, stock options, profit-sharing plans, insurance, commissions, and death benefits are recognized forms of deferred compensation. The question is whether and to what extent deferred compensation gives rise to reasonable expectations of job security. The problem is similar to that raised by long service. In some cases it may be the same problem in a different guise. Cases disclosed by our research address pension and bonus plans and consider whether the promise of such deferred compensation implies a right to remain on the job long enough to earn it.

An implied promise or reasonable expectation of job security, it is argued, is founded upon the employer's holding out an opportunity to earn a pension or bonus. Once the employee undertakes to fulfill the stated conditions, the promise of this compensation cannot arbitrarily be withdrawn nor can the employment itself be terminated arbitrarily. From the viewpoint of the employee, the offer of a pension or bonus upon the condition of fulfilling certain age and service standards is the offer of a unilateral contract, i.e., the offer of a promise for the employee's continued service to fulfill the condition. The employer, however, may view the holding out of a pension or bonus more in the nature of a promise to make a gift which may be withdrawn arbitrarily before the conditions are fulfilled.

Generally, an employer may not terminate pension and bonus plans either after the employee fulfills the express conditions or suspiciously close to the time for qualification. If there is a denial of promised benefits after qualification or vesting, the employer has breached the express terms of the contract. If the employment is terminated to avoid pension obligations, the employer is in breach of the implied covenant of good faith and fair dealing for frustrating the employee's reasonable expectation of earning the compensation. For example, where an employee who was discharged after 24 years of service brought suit to recover pension benefits which the employer refused to pay, the court, holding for the employee, said that the plan was an "integral part of the program" constituting a "continuing part consideration" and "a daily inducement to continuation of service and to exertion to satisfy."[109] The employee had been discharged for

---

[109]*Nilsson v. Cherokee Candy & Tobacco Co.*, 639 S.W.2d 226 (Mo. Ct. App. 1982) (promised bonus); *Titsch v. Reliance Group, Inc.*, 548 F. Supp. 983 (S.D.N.Y. 1982) (stock option exercisable only if employed; is not evidence of implied promise of job security); *Wilson v. Rudolph Wurlitzer Co.*, 48 Ohio App. 450, 454, 194 N.E. 441, 443 (1934).

trivial reasons; it was presumed that the employer was acting in bad faith.

In *Cantor v. Berkshire Life Insurance Co.,*[110] where the employee had produced the requisite business, served the necessary number of years, and attained the retirement age designated in the contract, rights had vested. Nevertheless, the employer attempted to destroy the employee's pension rights by exercising a termination clause in the employment contract. In holding for the employee, the court stated:

> "Even where an employer declares the plan is within the absolute discretion of the directors, the court will interpret the plan * * * so as to give effect to its general purpose in securing the loyalty and continued service of the employees, and the employer may not defeat the employee's reasonable expectations of receiving the promised reward.
> * * *
>
> * * *[W]hether a * * * plan is contributory or noncontributory and even though the employer has reserved the right to amend or terminate * * * once an employee * * * has complied with all the conditions entitling him to participate * * * his rights become vested and the employer cannot divest the employee of his rights thereunder."[111]

The more difficult case is the terminated employee whose rights have not vested and who is not terminated close to the time of vesting. Often, by the express terms of the bonus or pension, the employer retains the right for any reason to revoke the offer before vesting. The question is whether the courts will permit the reserved right of revocation to be enforced literally or only under circumstances that do not frustrate reasonable expectations created by the employer. It may be argued by the employer that an expectation of earning deferred compensation free of the threat of arbitrary discharge before vesting is not reasonable if the provisions of the plan clearly reserve that power to the employer. However, in any given controversy, the question is probably one for the jury if the express policy or known practice of the employer is not to exercise a right of discharge arbitrarily. Moreover, the employee's case is supported further if the employer has taken initiatives to foster or publicize the retirement or bonus plan as a morale-boosting incentive for attracting and keeping a loyal work force. It has been held that discharge only for good cause is implied if continued employment is induced by the offer of a bonus and discharge occurs before the bonus is fully earned.[112]

Thompson v. Burr[113] is another example of a court's unwillingness to permit an employer to lead the employee to a promised benefit but not let him receive it. The employer promised a bonus to all employees who were on the payroll on December 31 of each year. The

---

[110]*Cantor v. Berkshire Life Ins. Co.,* 171 Ohio St. 405, 171 N.E.2d 518 (1960).
[111]*Id.* at 410, 171 N.E.2d at 521. Cf. *Bos v. United States Rubber Co.,* 100 Cal. App.2d 565, 224 P.2d 386 (1950).
[112]*Roberts v. Mays Mills, Inc.,* 184 N.C. 406, 114 S.E. 530 (1922); *Frazer & Torbett, CPA's v. Kunkel,* 401 P.2d 476 (Okla. 1965).
[113]409 P.2d 157 (1971). See *Nilsson v. Cherokee Candy & Tobacco Co.,* 639 S.W.2d 226 (Mo. Ct. App. 1982); *McGraw v. Bill Hodges Truck Co.,* 629 P.2d 792 (Okla. Ct. App. 1981); *Lucian v. All States Trucking Co.,* 116 Cal. App.3d 972, 171 Cal. Rptr. 262 (1981).

bonus was payable in April of the following year, but nothing was said about a requirement of continued employment until April 1. One employee who quit between December 31 and April 1 was refused a bonus; the employee sued. While that suit was pending, the employer required the balance of his employees to sign a document which provided:

> "If an employee is on the payroll as of April 1st of any year, then he will be considered for a bonus based on his wages earned in the previous calendar year, but [the employer] is under no obligation to make payments unless we are actually employed on April 1st of any year."[114]

An employee who signed this document was discharged on March 12, allegedly for refusing to give testimony in the employer's behalf in an action brought by the employee who quit before April 1, and sued for his bonus. In spite of the statement signed by the plaintiff, it was held that the offer of the bonus became binding as a unilateral contract once the plaintiff stayed on the job for the entire calendar year and thereafter until the date of his discharge. The offer of a bonus could not be withdrawn nor could the bonus be arbitrarily withheld because the employee was discharged before April 1.

This approach is consistent with the theory of Professor Corbin:[115]

> "(1) Where an offer invites an offeree to accept by rendering a performance and does not invite a promissory acceptance, an option contract is created when the offeree begins the invited performance or tenders part of it.
>
> "(2) The offeror's duty of performance under any option contract so created is conditional on completion or tender of the invitee performance in accordance with the terms of the offer."

The *Thompson* case on its facts holds that an express right to withhold a bonus will not be enforced after the employee has fully performed his end of the bargain. Could the employee have been arbitrarily discharged before he fully performed the conditions of the bonus? Had he been discharged on New Year's Eve, a question of bad faith discharge to avoid liability for the bonus would be presented. This would be virtually the same as the issue faced by discharge between January 1 and April 1. An implied right of job security by virtue of an opportunity to earn deferred compensation requires recognition of an employee's right to avail himself of the offer. Such a right would be breached by an arbitrary discharge at any time after the employee begins to qualify. However, conditions of the bonus reasonably related to the incentive intended must be satisfied. For example, if the bonus is forfeitable in the event of an unexcused absence, it may not be recovered.[116]

---

[114]*Id.* at 158.
[115]CORBIN ON CONTRACTS §45 (Tent. Draft No. 1 (1964)).
[116]*Dove v. Rose Acre Farms, Inc.,* 434 N.E.2d 931 (Ind. Ct. App. 1982); *Moody v. Bogue,* 310 N.W.2d 655 (Iowa Ct. App. 1981); *Feola v. Valmont Indus., Inc.,* 208 Neb. 527, 304 N.W.2d 377 (1981); *Ward v. Berry & Assocs., Inc.,* 614 S.W.2d 372 (Tenn. Ct. App. 1981); *Gronlund v. Church & Dwight Co.,* 514 F. Supp., 1304 (S.D.N.Y. 1981).

One approach to finding an implied right to continue employment free of arbitrary discharge at least long enough to qualify for the pension or bonus or other promised deferred compensation is to give weight to two key factors. First, the employer seeks and receives a real benefit simply by offering these plans; they are "golden handcuffs" which discourage employees from quitting. Second, the employee views pension and bonus plans as deferred wages or salary that are in fact earned a little bit at a time, day by day, but paid out in a lump sum or over a term after retirement.

It is generally conceded by the courts that a pension plan is beneficial to the employer as well as to the employee;[117] and whenever the sense of the plan will allow, pension plans will be construed to create contractual rights. [118] Consideration is found in longevity of service not otherwise assured the employer,[119] his ability to attract better workers, the easier retirement and replacement of superannuated employees, and such intangible factors as better work attitudes and higher morale and productivity.[120]

Deferred compensation has also been recognized as "wages." In the *Inland Steel*[121] decision, the National Labor Relations Board determined and the court of appeals affirmed that an employer's refusal to bargain with a union over pension and retirement policies constituted an unfair labor practice under Sections 8(a)(5) and 9(a) of the National Labor Relations Act.[122] In its opinion, the Board reasoned that pension and retirement benefits were actually wages, stating:

> "With due regard for the aims and purposes of the Act and the evils which it sought to correct, we are convinced and find that the term 'wages' as used in Section 9(a) must be construed to include emoluments of value, like pension and insurance benefits, which may accrue to employees out of their employment relationship * * *.
> "* * * Realistically viewed, this type of wage enhancement or increase, no less than any other, becomes an integral part of the entire wage structure, and the character of the employee representative's interest in it, and the terms of its grant, is no different than in any other case where a change in the wage structure is effected."[123]

The view of pension benefits as a form of deferred wages has been increasingly recognized by the courts in recent years[124] and is

---

[117]See, e.g., *Cowles v. Morris & Co.*, 330 Ill. 11, 161 N.E. 150 (1928), and *Kroeger v. Stop & Shop Cos.*, 13 Mass. App. 310, 432 N.E.2d 566 (1982).

[118]See, e.g., *Magee v. San Francisco Bar Pilots Ass'n*, 88 Cal. App.2d 278, 198 P.2d 933 (1948).

[119]See, e.g., *Bos v. United States Rubber Co.*, 100 Cal. App.2d 565, 224 P.2d 386 (1950); *Hunter v. Sparling*, 87 Cal. App.2d 711, 197 P.2d 807 (1948); *Gearns v. Commercial Cable Co.*, 177 Misc. 1047, 32 N.Y.S.2d 856 (Mun. Ct. 1942), *aff'd*, 266 A.D. 315, 42 N.Y.S.2d 81 (1943), *aff'd*, 293 N.Y. 105, 56 N.E.2d 67 (1944) (dictum).

[120]See, e.g., *In re Schenectady Ry.*, 93 F. Supp. 67 (N.D.N.Y. 1950), and *Wilson v. Rudolph Wurlitzer Co.*, 48 Ohio App. 450, 194 N.E. 441 (1934).

[121]*Inland Steel Co. v. NLRB*, 77 NLRB 1, *enforced*, 170 F.2d 247 (7th Cir. 1948), *cert. denied*, 336 U.S. 960 (1949).

[122]29 U.S.C. §§168(a)(5), 159(a) (1964).

[123]*Inland Steel Co.*, 77 NLRB at 4-5.

[124]*Ball v. Victor Adding Mach. Co.*, 236 F.2d 170, 173 (5th Cir. 1956).

a realistic characterization of one of the factors common to employment in current times.

Under a deferred wages theory, benefits accrue to the employee from the moment the employee begins work. This leads to two possible conclusions. The first is that benefits may not be forfeited even upon dismissal for cause because they have been earned like wages and are the property of the employee no matter how long he works.

The second possible conclusion is that an employee dismissed arbitrarily has a claim for wrongful discharge. The measure of money damages would not necessarily be defined only by the deferred compensation constructively earned and what could reasonably have been earned but for the wrongful discharge. The measure would include everything that normally should enter into the estimation of damages due to wrongful discharge. Cases premising wrongful discharge upon breach of the implied duty of good faith and fair dealing and relying primarily upon longevity in the work place come closest to recognizing that implied rights of job security are undergirded by deferred compensation. It may be that the deferred wage theory will reinforce the equities the courts are recognizing in these cases.[125]

Presumed Renewal of Fixed Agreements for a Term

A contract of employment which provides for a definite term and expires is presumed to be renewed upon the same terms if the employee continues to render the same services.[126] This rule is said to be founded upon the general principle that a state of facts continuous in nature, once shown to exist, is presumed to continue until a change is shown.[127] To avoid the presumption of an automatic renewal of the contract for a year's term, a contrary intention must clearly be evidenced by some action taken by the employer.[128]

The presumption has been employed where the original term of the contract is longer than one year; however, the renewed term has been presumed to be only for an additional 12 months.[129] The original contract for one year need not be in writing if the jurisdiction does not bar enforcement of oral agreements for a year or more.[130] If the original agreement is not enforceable because of the statute of frauds

---

[125]Two cases have invoked the deferred wages theory to achieve an equitable result. In *Connor v. Phoenix Steel Corp.*, 249 A.2d 866 (Del. 1969), plaintiff's employment was terminated without cause. The court construed an ambiguity in the plan to allow recovery but articulated its holding in deferred wages terminology. In *Russell v. Princeton Laboratories, Inc.*, 50 N.J. 30, 231 A.2d 800 (1967), the plaintiff was forced to resign because his health was endangered by contact with substances with which he was required to work. The court, applying deferred wages theory, found him entitled to accumulated credits which had not yet vested.

[126]*Holton v. Hart Mill Co.*, 24 Wash.2d 493, 166 P.2d 186 (1946); *Moline Plow Co. v. Booth*, 17 Ill. App. 574 (1885); *Fish v. Marzluff*, 128 Ill. App. 549 (1906); *Henkel v. J.J. Henkel Co.*, 212 Cal. 288, 298 P. 28 (1931); *Harper v. Cedar Rapids Television Co.*, 244 N.W.2d 782 (Iowa 1976); *Hines v. Ward Baking Co.*, 155 F.2d 257 (7th Cir. 1946).

[127]*Mears v. O'Donoghue*, 58 Ill. App. 345 (1895).

[128]*Williams v. Schalk Chem. Co.*, 11 Cal. App.2d 396, 53 P.2d 1015 (1936).

[129]*Steranko v. Inforex, Inc.*, 5 Mass. App. 253, 362 N.E.2d 222 (1977).

[130]*McIntyre v. Smith-Bridgman & Co.*, 301 Mich. 629, 4 N.W.2d 36 (1942).

or some other defect, it is not presumed to have been renewed as an original agreement.[131] During the course of the original agreement or some presumed renewal of the original agreement, the salary and working conditions may be changed. These changes from the original contract do not disturb the force of the presumed renewal. The employment agreement is presumed to be renewed for additional terms, but upon working conditions such as salary and deferred compensation that applied at the time of the presumed renewal.[132]

---

[131]*Brown v. Oneida Knitting Mills, Inc.,* 226 Wis. 662, 277 N.W. 653 (1938).
[132]*Paxson v. Cass County Road Comm'n,* 325 Mich. 276, 38 N.W.2d 315 (1949).

4

The Employment Contract Terminated

The most vexing issues in the trial of an unjust discharge case are often without any significant legal precedent. These issues include the scope of jury review of an employer's discretion to discharge, whether the judge or jury decides what the standard of discharge is, and the measure of damages. The dearth of precedent in this area is typical of any rapidly moving legal frontier. Most of the appeals in employment discharge cases are occasioned by the trial judge's refusing the plaintiff an opportunity to present his case to the jury. The record on appeal often does not present the issues that are the subject of this chapter.

In prior chapters we examined issues peculiar to contract formation. In this chapter, after a brief discussion of preliminary issues, we will address questions raised by employment or contract termination where the contract expressly or impliedly requires good cause or some lesser standard for discharge.

Termination by Operation of Law

It has been held that a number of events terminate the relationship of employer and employee by operation of law. These include the death or other legal incapacity of the employer or employee, the bankruptcy of the employer, and even a state of war between the countries of the employer and the employee. Here we will focus upon only the death or physical incapacity of employer or employee.

The death of the employer or the employee ends the employment contract unless the employee is characterized as possessing a power coupled with an interest.[1] Consistent with the law's position on the death of the employee, early cases held that the death of a partner ends the partnership, which in turn ends the employment relation between a partnership and its employees;[2] in view of the Uniform Partnership Act and the corporate character of large partnerships, no one would now put any confidence in these early cases. The insanity of the employer does not terminate the relationship,[3] but the permanent disablement of the employee does.[4]

In *Williams v. Butler*[5] a bank sold a prospective employee stock in the bank at a bargain price in return for and to induce him to accept employment as vice president and treasurer. After nine months the employee became permanently disabled by insanity. The bank sued to recover the stock. The gist of the action was that because of the permanent disability of the employee, there was a failure of consideration for the stock. In effect, the bank claimed the bargain stock was payment in advance for the employee's services. The court held that the parties' mutual expectation of a long relationship was not equivalent to a contract for a term. Each party to the contract took the chance of events both knew were possible, such as death or sickness, that might intervene to end the contract. The employer lost the benefit of the bargain because it did not make a contract covering the possibility of the employee's disability.[6]

Resignation or Constructive Discharge

In many cases, before the issue of whether termination of employment was wrongful is reached, there is the question of whether the employee quit or was terminated. If he quit, the circumstances may nevertheless establish what is called a "constructive discharge." On the way to a decision, the judge or jury may also be required to determine the significance of a face-saving letter of resignation, forced retirement, or termination because of a physical disqualification under governing work rules.

It need hardly be said that there is no issue of whether the employee resigned or was discharged when the employer has given a written notice of discharge. One case so held where the employer

[1]*Ridges v. Williams*, 15 Tenn. App. 197 (1932); *Levy v. Wilmes*, 239 Ill. App. 229 (1926); *Casto v. Murray*, 47 Ore. 57, 81 P. 883 (1905); *Zinnell v. Bergdoll*, 19 Pa. Super. 508 (1902). And see RESTATEMENT OF AGENCY §§138–139 (1958).

[2]*Shumzte v. Sohon*, 12 F.2d 825 (D.C. Cir. 1926); *Deitrich v. Cashie & Chowan R.R. & Lumber Co.*, 127 N.C. 25, 37 S.E. 64 (1900).

[3]*Sands v. Potter* 165 Ill. 397, 46 N.E. 282 (1896).

[4]*Rollinger v. Dairyland Creamery Co.*, 66 S.D. 592, 287 N.W. 333 (1939); *American Nat'l Ins. Co. v. Jackson*, 12 Tenn. App. 305 (1930). Moreover, even if the employee later returns to work he is not entitled to pay for the period of his illness: *Shaw v. Ward*, 170 N.Y.S. 36 (Sup. Ct. 1918); *Wessl v. Haff*, 165 A.D. 705, 151 N.Y.S. 497 (1915).

[5]58 Ind. App. 47, 105 N.E. 387 (1914).

[6]See also *Rodgers v. Southern Newspaper, Inc.*, 214 Tenn. 335, 379 S.W.2d 787 (1963), (court enforced agreement that employee's wife could substitute her performance for his in event of his death).

claimed that the employee had quit and then asked for a notice of discharge, and that all it did was honor the request.[7] Words and actions that show a clear intent to dispense with the services of the employee amount to a termination.[8]

If there is a termination, the employer must make it evident to the employee that he has been terminated. If he does not, the employee who continues to perform is entitled to his salary.[9] Doubtless the same principle would apply to a commission salesman in the field even if the employer was unable to locate him to furnish notice of discharge. If there was an equivocal statement by the employer, the issue may be whether under all the circumstances it should have been understood as a discharge.[10]

There are cases of irresolute employees who offer to quit and then change their minds,[11] and indecisive employers who wait too long to accept an offered resignation.[12] If the employer promptly accepts an offer to quit, the termination is a "quit" even though the employee changes his mind. If the employer waits too long, the "acceptance" is a discharge.

The forced or face-saving employee resignation is a natural defense to a wrongful discharge case. The opinions on this point generally hold that such a resignation bars an action for wrongful discharge. One court held that a face-saving resignation, while not a true quit, nevertheless was not synonymous with a discharge.[13] Another held that an employee who resigns under protest or threat of termination "may not seek damages by reason of the termination of [his] services."[14] An employee who resigned when asked to do so was considered to have quit voluntarily,[15] and this was so even when a notice of termination preceded the request.[16] However, a resignation induced by a misrepresentation—that if the employee did not resign as general manager a bank would withdraw credit from the business—was held void.[17] The employee at least may make a jury question of duress or undue influence in the procurement of the resignation.[18]

The cases appear to attach an undue legal consequence to an

---

[7]*Signorelli v. Morice*, 174 So. 124 (La. Ct. App. 1937).

[8]*Salvatori Corp. v. Rubin*, 159 Ga. App. 369, 283 S.E.2d 326 (1981).

[9]*Mee v. Bowder Gold Mining Co.*, 47 Ore. 143, 81 P. 980 (1905).

[10]*Lewis v. Moorhead Bros. & Co.*, 201 Pa. 245, 50 A. 960 (1902) (permanent replacement of vacationing employee, after employee ignored suggestion that he resign, was constructive discharge); *Paine v. Hill*, 7 Wash. 437, 35 P. 136 (1893) (statements that employee's presence was "very disagreeable," that he was "not fit" for grocery business, and that he "had better go" evidenced constructive discharge).

[11]*Batts v. Review Bd.*, 179 Ind. App. 405, 385 N.E.2d 1174 (1979) (quit does not become discharge just because employer will not rehire when employee changes mind).

[12]*Akers v. Sedberry*, 39 Tenn. App. 633 (1955) (delayed acceptance of offer to quit, after employee had changed mind, was discharge); *Nesbit v. Giblin*, 96 Neb. 369, 148 N.W. 138 (1914) (acceptance of conditional resignation one month after tender was discharge).

[13]*Fredricks v. Georgia-Pacific Corp.*, 331 F. Supp. 422 (E.D. Pa. 1971).

[14]*Laiken v. American Bank & Trust Co.*, 34 A.D.2d 514, 308 N.Y.S.2d 111 (1970).

[15]*Blum Bros. Box Co. v. Wisconsin Labor Relations Bd.*, 229 Wis. 615, 282 N.W. 98 (1939).

[16]*Martin v. Gauld Co.*, 96 Ore. 635, 190 P. 717 (1920).

[17]*Hanaford v. Stevens & Co.*, 39 R.I. 182, 98 A. 209 (1916).

[18]*Piper v. Board of Trustees*, 99 Ill. App.3d 752, 426 N.E.2d 262 (1981).

empty formality or, at most, an attempt by the employee to minimize damage to his own reputation. A resignation to save face should not be given the same effect as a general release of claims. If that is what the employer wants, it should ask for one.

An employee's use of words like "suits me" does not signify agreement to be discharged.[19] However, an exchange of letters after the termination plainly showing that the former employee approved of his own discharge barred an action against the employer based on the discharge.[20]

Compulsory retirement is a forced termination.[21] Similarly, an indefinite layoff is a forced termination.[22] In both cases the employee is being given to understand that his services are no longer required, so there is a discharge.

Employee conduct inconsistent with an ability or intention to perform the agreed services is a constructive resignation. For example, a long failure to report to work[23] or taking a second full-time job[24] is a constructive resignation from the first job. It has been held that a knowing violation of a company rule is a constructive resignation.[25] Color blindness of a railroad engineer which disqualified him under company rules[26] was not called a constructive resignation, but was also not the same as a forced termination. Incarceration for a crime is a constructive resignation.[27] Of course, going on strike is protected conduct and does not amount to quitting.[28]

Constructive discharge cases have occurred in collective bargaining situations under the National Labor Relations Act.[29] The Fourth Circuit stated that constructive discharge occurs "[w]here an employer deliberately makes an employee's working conditions intolerable and thereby forces him to quit his job * * * ."[30] The Tenth Circuit found a constructive discharge from deliberate efforts by the employer to render the employee's working conditions intolerable.[31] The District of Columbia Circuit and the Eighth Circuit have also

---

[19]*Holton v. Hart Mill Co.*, 24 Wash. 2d 493, 166 P.2d 186 (1946).

[20]*NHA, Inc. v. Jones*, 500 S.W.2d 940 (Tex. Civ. App. 1973).

[21]*Nichols v. National Tube Co.*, 122 F. Supp. 726 (N.D. Ohio 1954).

[22]*Dunbar v. Orleans Metal Bed Co.*, 145 La. 779, 82 So. 889 (1919); *Schwarze v. Solo Cup Co.*, 445 N.E.2d 872, 112 Ill. App.3d 632 (1983).

[23]*American Nat'l Ins. Co. v. Jackson*, 12 Tenn. App. 305 (1930); *Becker v. Butler County Memorial Hosp.*, 249 Pa. Super. 321, 378 A.2d 316 (1977).

[24]*Caroll v. Reuben H. Donnelly Corp.*, 53 Pa. D. & C. 142 (1945).

[25]*Standard Oil Co. v. Review Bd.*, 119 Ind. App. 576, 88 N.E.2d 567 (1949) (woman married contrary to company rules).

[26]*Long v. Illinois Cent. R.R.*, 32 Ill. App.2d 103, 176 N.E.2d 812 (1961).

[27]*Powell v. Retirement Bd.*, 431 Pa. 396, 246 A.2d 110 (1968); *Pearson v. Equitable Life Assurance Soc'y of the United States*, 212 N.C. 731, 194 S.E. 661 (1938).

[28]*Goodman v. Winn-Dixie Stores, Inc.*, 240 So. 2d 496 (Fla. Dist. Ct. App. 1970).

[29]29 U.S.C. §151 *et seq.* (1976).

[30]*J.P. Stevens & Co. v. NLRB*, 461 F.2d 490, 494 (4th Cir. 1972).

[31]*Muller v. United States Steel Corp.*, 509 F.2d 923 (10th Cir.), *cert. denied*, 423 U.S. 825 (1975); *Vaughn v. Pool Offshore Co.*, 683 F.2d 922 (5th Cir. 1982); *Irving v. DuBuque Parking Co.*, 689 F.2d 170 (8th Cir. 1982); *Junior v. Texaco, Inc.*, 688 F.2d 377 (5th Cir. 1982); *Rimedio v. Revlon, Inc.*, 528 F. Supp. 1380 (S.D. Ohio 1982); *Walter v. KFGO Radio*, 518 F. Supp. 1309 (D.N.D. 1981).

followed the intolerable conditions rule.[32] These cases require a finding that the employer caused the resignation by deliberately making working conditions intolerable. The same controversy arising between the nonunion employee and his employer should be resolved by the same principles.

It is not a constructive discharge when an employee quits rather than follow a reasonable request. But an order to "do the work or quit" followed by a refusal to obey and resignation may be constructive discharge if the order was unreasonable.[33] An alleged five-year course of conduct between the general manager and the owner of a business was viewed as a failure to cooperate by the employee-general manager rather than a constructive discharge by the owner.[34]

Is there a constructive discharge where the employer refuses to pay the agreed salary? In two such cases the court found no constructive discharge.[35] These are close cases; on the same facts some courts have found constructive discharge.[36] It is unfair to put employees in the position of working for less than the agreed salary and suing for the small balance after the full term or, in the alternative, quitting and, under the approach of some cases, forfeiting the claim altogether. Under usual principles of contract, the employer's refusal to pay the agreed salary is a material breach of contract excusing further performance by the employee and entitling the employee to sue for damages.[37]

A clear case of constructive discharge was the action of the owner of a radio station who harassed his general manager and criticized, abused, and cursed employees who were under the general manager's supervision, causing many of them to leave. The constant turnover of personnel occurred at a time when because of war conditions it was difficult to obtain trained personnel. The owner failed to pay salaries and commissions and frequently violated the rules of regulatory agencies. These acts, coupled with numerous insults, were held to constitute constructive discharge of the general manager.[38]

A final case of interest here is that of the clothing designer working under a written contract of 21 months. Before 12 months had elapsed the employer refused to permit the employee to do the work for which he had been hired and instead ordered him to sit

---

[32]*Retail Store Employees, Local 880 v. NLRB*, 419 F.2d 329, 332 (D.C. Cir. 1969); *Thompson v. McDonnell Douglas Corp.*, 552 F.2d 220, 223 (8th Cir. 1977).

[33]*Burden v. Woodside Cotton Mills*, 104 S.C. 435, 89 S.E. 474 (1916); *Corrigan v. E.M.P. Producing Corp.*, 179 A.D. 810, 167 N.Y.S. 206 (1917).

[34]*Scotzin v. Brown*, 53 Dauphin County Rep. 129 (12th Dist. Pa. 1942).

[35]*Kottemann v. Gross*, 184 So. 380 (La. Ct. App. 1938); *Barnett v. Cohen*, 110 N.Y.S. 835 (Sup. Ct. 1908).

[36]*Fisher v. John L. Roper Lumber Co.*, 183 N.C. 485, 111 S.E. 857 (1922) (constructive discharge where plaintiff quit when employer refused to give "living wage"); *Farmers Coop. Ass'n v. Shaw*, 171 Okla. 358, 42 P.2d 887 (1935) (25 percent reduction in agreed salary was constructive discharge); *Harger v. Jenkins*, 17 Pa. Super. 615 (1901) (constructive discharge when employee quit rather than accept position inferior to one agreed to be given).

[37]*Kravetz v. Merchants Distribs., Inc.*, 387 Mass. 457, 440 N.E.2d 1278 (1982).

[38]*Carlson v. Ewing*, 219 La. 961, 54 So.2d 414 (1951). See also *Sullivan v. David City Bank*, 181 Neb. 395, 148 N.W.2d 844 (1967) (refusal to permit employee to perform duties is discharge).

unemployed in a dark room during work hours. The employee hired a lawyer, who accompanied him to the work place. The belligerent employer told them both to get out. It was held to be a jury question whether under all the facts the employee was discharged.[39]

Given an enforceable promise of job security and an involuntary termination, the stage is set for the second phase of the employer-employee controversy. Was the discharge unjust? This requires an examination of all the possible standards for discharge from employment and selection of that which is fairest under all the circumstances.

Standards of Employment Termination

Whether an employee has a legal remedy for discharge does not depend solely upon whether the governing standard for discharge was breached. An employee discharged for cause does not forfeit compensation already earned. In addition to wages or salary earned but unpaid at the time of termination, the employee may be entitled to deferred compensation such as vacation pay, pension, and bonuses. Earned sales commissions that would have been paid subsequent to the termination may still be recovered by the employee. What the employee is entitled to receive regardless of whether the termination accords with the governing standards of employer discretion is discussed under the heading of remedies in Chapter 11. Except for compensation already earned at the time of discharge, entitlement to damages depends upon whether the employer has breached the minimum standard governing employer discretion.

Employment-At-Will Caveat

Employment-at-will is sometimes misconceived as an absence of any standard governing employer discretion to discharge. This is not strictly true; given federal and state statutes barring discrimination and protecting the handicapped, and common law and statutes providing a remedy for discharge in derogation of public policy, the employer surely does not have unlimited discretion to discharge. But if common law and statutes have limited an employer's right to act arbitrarily or in bad faith, the employer still enjoys substantial freedom to discharge for any reason or no reason at all under the employment-at-will standard. The significance of the bare-minimum standard is simply that personnel decisions are less subject to challenge, and when challenged are more easily and simply defended.

---

[39]*Sigmon v. Goldstone*, 116 A.D. 490, 101 N.Y.S. 984 (1906). See also *Taylor v. Southern Univ.*, 554 F. Supp. 334 (E.D. La. 1983), and *Shawgo v. Spradlin*, 701 F.2d 470 (5th Cir. 1983).

Good Faith Business Reasons

Occasionally when courts require that employers not act arbitrarily or in bad faith,[40] they mean that the discharge must stem from a good faith belief that the termination will advance legitimate business interests. The business interests may embrace matters unrelated to the employee's performance. Likewise, actions could be prompted by the employer's opinion concerning the employee's ability or willingness to work well within the organization. All that the employer need do when an employment decision is challenged is come forward with evidence showing the decision was not arbitrary or in furtherance of a nonbusiness objective.

Satisfaction and Good Faith

The standard of performance to the employer's satisfaction holds the employer only to the requirement that a discharge be premised upon the employer's subjective but honest dissatisfaction with the employee's performance—even if a reasonable person would be satisfied with the same performance. This is a somewhat more stringent standard than one merely requiring a good faith business reason. The satisfaction standard is discussed in more detail below.

Just or Good Cause

The existence of just or good cause is the employer's defense for discharging an employee before the expiration of a fixed term of employment,[41] or without giving an agreed notice.[42] If the employer may discharge only for just cause, just cause must exist in fact.[43] The burden of proving just cause is on the employer.[44] In the case of a public employer, a requirement of just cause for discharge also includes a duty to afford the employee a hearing on whether just cause for discharge exists.[45] This standard is also covered more thoroughly below.

One case has held that a good faith belief that just cause exists was sufficient to justify a discharge.[46] The case appears to be without precedent and without any following in any other jurisdiction. In any event, this standard is somewhat stricter than the satisfaction standard because the employer's good faith belief must focus not only upon the employee's performance but upon assertions that if true would amount to just cause.

---

[40]*Siles v. Travenol Laboratories, Inc.*, 13 Mass. App. 354, 433 N.E.2d 103 (1982).
[41]*Bartlett v. Doctors Hosp.*, 422 So.2d 660 (La. Ct. App. 1982).
[42]*Chai Management, Inc. v. Leibowitz*, 50 Md. App. 504, 439 A.2d 34 (1982).
[43]*Chapin v. Klein*, 128 Ariz. 94, 623 P.2d 1250 (1981); *Alpern v. Hurwitz*, 644 F.2d 943 (2d Cir. 1981); *Advance Ross Elec. Corp. v. Green*, 624 S.W.2d 316 (Tex. Civ. App. 1981).
[44]*Staton v. Amax Coal Co.*, 122 Ill. App.3d 631, 461 N.E.2d 612 (1984).
[45]*Vinyard v. King*, 728 F.2d 428 (10th Cir. 1984).
[46]*Simpson v. Western Graphics*, 293 Ore. 96, 643 P.2d 1276 (1982).

Arbitration Standards for Just Discipline

It is common for arbitrators under collective bargaining agreements to resolve controversies concerning whether just or good cause for discharge exists. Although arbitrators and courts often use the same language, the just cause standard for discipline used by arbitrators is stricter than that used by the courts. For example, in addition to the existence of facts that amount to just cause, the arbitrator is concerned that the employee had fair notice that certain conduct warranted discipline and that the discipline is appropriate considering the employee's seniority and age and is not randomly or discriminatorily applied. In the first case in Illinois to define just cause for discharge from private employment, the court expressly adopted substantive and procedural arbitration standards for discharge.[47] More detail on arbitration standards is provided below.

Common Law of Fair Procedure

The common law of fair procedure has been applied in only a very limited way in employment controversies. More often it governs controversies between voluntary associations and their members. Examples of such associations are hospital medical staffs and professional and trade organizations. Generally, this common law permits the court to consider whether a member or prospective member was given an opportunity to question the merits of his being expelled or refused admission. This standard, which may find a larger sphere of operation in the future in employment law, is reviewed in detail in Chapter 10.

The Strict Good Faith Standard

The strictest standard for the exercise of employer discretion has been invoked when controlling shareholders of a closely held corporation force a fellow shareholder out of employment.[48] The shareholder of a closely held corporation typically does not invest for dividends, because taxes are lower if earnings are distributed in the form of salaries rather than dividends. And he does not invest for appreciation of his stock because there is no ready market for minority interests in closely held corporations. If he is deprived of his job, he is foreclosed from a fair chance to obtain the expected return on his investment. A rule foreclosing management from ever discharging an employee-shareholder would be subject to employee abuse. One court has held that the proper question is whether the controlling shareholders can demonstrate a legitimate business purpose for their

---

[47]*Staton v. Amax Coal Co.*, 122 Ill. App.3d 631, 461 N.E.2d 612 (1984).
[48]*Wilkes v. Springside Nursing Home, Inc.*, 370 Mass. 842, 353 N.E.2d 657 (1976), noted in 38 LA. L. REV. 214 (1977).

action. If so, the discharged employee can demonstrate that the same objective could have been achieved by an alternative course of action less harmful to the minority. The court "must weigh the legitimate business purpose, if any, against the practicability of a less harmful alternative."[49]

It is somewhat surprising that this standard is not incorporated into written employment agreements in situations where the employee has an opportunity to bargain for a substantial amount of job security. There are, however, cases in which agreed standards that closely resemble the strict good faith standard have been enforced. One example is a contract requiring notice of the reason for discharge and an opportunity to remedy the claimed deficient performance.[50]

The Arbitration Law of Unjust Discipline: Development of the "Just Cause" Concept*

Arbitrators have evolved standards for determining what constitutes just cause for discipline, developed procedures for determining the guilt or innocence of accused employees, exercised responsibility for reviewing the appropriateness of penalties, and provided effective remedies of reinstatement and back pay. For arbitrators, protection against unjust discipline has long ceased being "uncharted territory."

Collective agreements, with few exceptions, expressly prohibit unjust disciplinary action.[51] The contract language typically is terse, often simply prohibiting discipline "without cause," or "without just cause."[52] Even where such words are missing, arbitrators read them

---

*The text and notes under this heading are largely from Clyde W. Summers' article *Industrial Protection Against Unjust Dismissal: Time for a Statute*, 62 VA. L. REV. 481, 499–508 (1976). It is reproduced here with the permission of the publisher, the Virginia Law Review Association. This article was cited in *Staton v. Amax Coal Co.*, 122 Ill. App.3d 631, 461 N.E.2d 612 (1984), as authority for defining the essential characteristics for just cause in Illinois.

---

[49]*Id.* at 851, 852, 353 N.E.2d at 663. See also *Notzke v. Art Gallery, Inc.*, 84 Ill. App.3d 294, 405 N.E.2d 839 (1980) (remedy for discharge was dissolution of corporation). See generally, F. O'Neal, OPPRESSION OF MINORITY SHAREHOLDERS §3.06 (1975).
[50]*In re KDI Corp.*, 21 Bankr. 652 (S.D. Ohio 1982).
[51]See O. Phelps, DISCIPLINE AND DISCHARGE IN THE UNIONIZED FIRM 9–10 (1959). Such clauses were given a strong impetus by the National War Labor Board during World War II because the Board regularly ordered their inclusion in collective agreements in cases that came before it. See, e.g., *Brass Rail, Inc.*, 25 War Lab. Rep. 246 (1945); *Sunken Gardens Restaurant*, 20 War Lab. Rep. 101 (1944); *Cudahy Bros.*, 15 War Lab. Rep. 311 (1944); *Westinghouse Air Brake Co.*, 11 War Lab. Rep. 636 (1943); *Bethlehem Steel Co.*, 6 War Lab. Rep. 513 (1943); *Brown & Sharpe Mfg. Co.*, 4 War Lab. Rep. 20 (1942). Even when the parties had no agreement for arbitration or no just cause clause, the Board established a policy of referring disputes concerning discipline to arbitration for decision under a just cause standard. Discharges: Policy on Disciplinary Action, WLB Press Release B-2090 (May 17, 1945), *in* 24 War Lab. Rep. xxxix (1915). See *Goodyear Aircraft Corp.*, 26 War Lab. Rep. 143 (1945); *Nash-Kelvinator Corp.*, 19 War Lab. Rep. 24 (1944).
[52]2 BNA COLLECTIVE BARGAINING NEGOTIATIONS AND CONTRACTS 40:1 (April 10, 1975). General statements that employees may be discharged for "cause" or "just cause" appeared in 79 percent of agreements surveyed. Specific grounds for discharge named in collective agreements included unauthorized striking, violation of leave, violation of company rules, failure to obey safety rules, failure to meet work standards, intoxication, dishonesty, absenteeism, insubordination, and misconduct. *Id.* at 40:1–3.

into the contract as necessarily implied from seniority clauses or grievance and arbitration provisions.[53] As one arbitrator has stated, "It is part of the 'common law' of industrial relations—one of the tacit assumptions underlying all collective agreements—that an employer shall not exercise arbitrarily his power to discipline workers."[54]

On the bare words "just cause," arbitrators have built a comprehensive and relatively stable body of both substantive and procedural law.[55] Although what constitutes "just cause" inevitably depends on the industrial setting and the special circumstances, arbitrators have achieved substantial consensus about underlying principles and many detailed rules.[56] Thus, the National Academy of Arbitrators can discuss the principles to be applied in "long hair" and "dress code" cases,[57] and whether to allow the use of illegally obtained evidence or lie detector tests in arbitration proceedings.[58] Although arbitrators often cite no other decision in their opinions and never consider other cases as binding precedents, they usually are quite aware of the pattern of decisions by other arbitrators and are reluctant to deviate far from that pattern. Results in a discipline case may well depend on the length of the arbitrator's foot, but that leads to relatively small differences, for there are few peg-legs or abominable snowmen among arbitrators, and no one follows in their footsteps.

The extent to which arbitrators have produced an integrated and coherent body of law, rather than a mass of random individualized decisions, can best be demonstrated by briefly stating some of the general principles that have been developed by arbitrators and have gained acceptance among unions and employers. These principles

---

[53]Platt, *Arbitral Standards in Discipline Cases*, in THE LAW AND LABOR-MANAGEMENT RE-LATIONS 24–25 (1956).

[54]*Pilot Freight Carriers, Inc.*, 22 Lab. Arb. 761, 763 (Maggs, Arb., 1954).

[55]See F. Elkouri & E. Elkouri, HOW ARBITRATION WORKS (3d ed. 1973); M. Gollub, DISCHARGE FOR CAUSE (1948); D. Jones, ARBITRATION AND INDUSTRIAL DISCIPLINE (1961); J. Lazar, DUE PROCESS ON THE RAILROADS (1958); Phelps, *supra* note 51; P. Selznick, LAW, SOCIETY, AND IN-DUSTRIAL JUSTICE 161–178 (1969); M. Stone, LABOR MANAGEMENT CONTRACTS AT WORK Ch. 10 (1961); Bailer, *The Discipline Issue in Arbitration: Individual Differences and Shop Practices*, 15 LAB. L. J. 567 (1964); Holly, *The Arbitration of Discharge Cases: A Case Study*, and Ross, *The Arbitration of Discharge Cases: What Happens After Reinstatement*, both in National Academy of Arbitrators, CRITICAL ISSUES IN LABOR ARBITRATION 1, 2 (Proceedings of the 10th Annual Meeting, 1957); Myers, *Concepts of Industrial Discipline*, in National Academy of Arbitrators, MANAGEMENT RIGHTS AND THE ARBITRATION PROCESS 59–83 (Proceedings of the 9th Annual Meeting, 1956); Platt, *supra* note 53; Yagoda, *The Discipline Issue in Arbitration: Employer Rules*, 15 LAB. L.J. 571 (1964).

[56]On the face of it, "just cause" appears so vague as to give no guidance at all to the arbitrator. This is not true, however. Over the years, the "common law of arbitration" has defined this phrase in fairly understandable terms. *Lockheed Aircraft Corp.*, 27 Lab. Arb. 512, 514 (Warns, Arb., 1956). See Elkouri, *The Emerging Industrial Jurisprudence*, in COLLECTIVE BARGAINING AND THE LAW 245 (11th Annual Summer Institute of International & Comparative Law, University of Michigan Law School, 1959); Note, *Discharge in the "Law" of Arbitration*, 20 VAND. L. REV. 81 (1966).

[57]See Valtin, *Hair and Beards in Arbitration*; McDermott, *Drugs, Bombs and Bomb Scares, and Personal Attire*; Cohen, *Arbitrators and Changing Life Styles—Establishment or Impartial?*; all in National Academy of Arbitrators, LABOR ARBITRATION AT THE QUARTER-CENTURY MARK 235, 252, 272 (Proceedings of the 25th Annual Meeting, 1973).

[58]See Black, *Surveillance and the Labor Arbitration Process*, and Smith, Lipsitz, *Comments*, in National Academy of Arbitrators, ARBITRATION AND THE EXPANDING ROLE OF NEUTRALS 1, 15, 25 (Proceedings of the 23rd Annual Meeting, 1970).

also illustrate the fundamental character of this body of law and the sensitive protection it gives employees against arbitrary discipline. As Professor Phelps stated in his study of discipline cases, the arbitrator in these cases is "the 'Supreme Court' of industrial jurisprudence, the guarantor of due process of law to millions of employees."[59]

Management's Right to Manage

Requiring just cause for discipline does not take from management the right to manage the enterprise and direct the work force. Under most collective agreements management retains the right to prescribe plant rules specifying conduct that will warrant discipline. Management can prohibit smoking, limit employee conversations during working time, require the use of safety equipment, or insist on overtime work. Even where the collective agreement lists certain offenses or the parties negotiate plant rules, management may normally supplement the listed offenses or negotiated rules. Rules prescribed by management are subject to arbitral review, but they carry a presumptive validity and will be upheld so long as they are reasonably related to achieving efficient operation and maintaining order and are not manifestly unfair or do not unnecessarily burden employees' rights.

Management also is entitled to have its orders obeyed and may discipline employees for refusing to obey even improper orders. Arbitrators almost uniformly hold that an employee must obey first and then seek recourse through the grievance procedure, except where obeying would expose him to substantial risks to his health and safety.

Right of Employees to Know What Is Prohibited

Just cause, as articulated in the arbitration law of discipline, can include only conduct that the employee knows is subject to discipline. This does not mean that all offenses must be stated, either orally or in writing. An employee need not be told in advance that stealing the employer's property, sleeping on the job, attacking fellow employees, or engaging in a wildcat strike is prohibited. But he is not bound by plant rules that have not been brought to his attention, nor can he be punished for conduct he did not reasonably understand was prohibited. Management's right to prescribe rules is matched by its obligation to make those rules known to the employees.

Making the rules known to the employees is not enough, however, if the employees reasonably believe the rules will not be enforced. Where a no-smoking rule has regularly been ignored and no effort has been made to enforce it, an employee cannot be disciplined for smoking, even in front of a prominently posted "No Smoking"

---

[59]See Phelps, *supra* note 51, at 10.

sign. Employees who have openly been taking home scrap or supplies for personal use with the knowledge of management cannot be disciplined for stealing without warning. Management must first give clear warning that henceforth the rule will be enforced and violators punished.

Right of Employees to Equal Treatment

The evolved standard of fairness implicit in just cause requires that employees who have engaged in similar conduct be subject to similar discipline. An employee cannot be disciplined for wearing inappropriate clothing when other employees are not disciplined for similarly inappropriate dress. An employee disciplined for excessive absenteeism can defend on the grounds that other employees with similar records received lesser penalties. And wildcat strikers may not be selected at random for discharge. Even for indisputable offenses, such as dishonesty, refusing to obey orders, or loafing on the job, employees cannot be singled out and punished as an example to others.

Management need not catch all offenders, but it may not apply discipline mechanically to offenders it does catch. It must recognize differences in degrees of offenses and give weight to extenuating circumstances. But individualized treatment according to individual differences merely implements the basic principle that all employees must be judged by the same standard, rules must be uniformly enforced, and penalties must be equally applied.

It should be noted that these two basic principles—that an employee can be disciplined only for conduct he knows or reasonably understands is prohibited, and that discipline must be enforced evenhandedly—impose standards of fairness not required in the criminal law. People may be fined or sent to prison for conduct that they did not know was prohibited, and proof that others have committed the same offense and have not been prosecuted is no defense. Selective or random enforcement of the criminal law is, indeed, not only commonplace but often deliberate. This contrast between what has sometimes been called the common law of the work place and ordinary criminal law underscores the protection given employee job rights by arbitration under collective agreements and the fundamental character of the principles developed through arbitration.[60]

Principles of Procedural Fairness

Procedural provisions, when they appear in discipline clauses, relate almost entirely to notices to be given the employee or union.

---

[60]See Kadish, *The Criminal Law and Industrial Disciplines as Sanctioning Systems: Some Comparative Observations*, in National Academy of Arbitrators, LABOR ARBITRATION: PERSPECTIVES AND PROBLEMS 130 (Proceedings of the 17th Annual Meeting, 1964).

Principles of procedural fairness have been developed through arbitration without the aid of any contractual language, for few collective agreements even require a "fair hearing" in so many words. Certain basic procedural rights, however, have come to be commonly recognized. The offense with which the employee is charged must be specified, and this offense, not another one, must be proven. Disciplinary action must be taken promptly after the offense is discovered, and the penalty assessed cannot later be increased. The employee is not entitled to a hearing before discipline is imposed, unless the contract so provides, but in arbitration he obtains a full de novo hearing. He has a right to know all of the evidence against him, to confront and cross-examine witnesses, to present evidence, and to compel the employer to produce evidence and witnesses within the employer's control. He can refuse to answer questions in the absence of a union representative, refuse to testify against himself, and object to the admission of improperly obtained evidence.

Perhaps the most important procedural protection is that the burden of proof is on the employer to prove just cause rather than on the employee to prove that the employer has acted arbitrarily. Although arbitrators differ about whether the proof must be "beyond a reasonable doubt," "clear and convincing," or meet some other standard, there is a consensus that proof must be by more than a bare preponderance of the evidence. This is particularly true when the penalty is the "capital punishment" of discharge.

Principles of Corrective Discipline

Arbitrators not only determine the guilt or innocence of accused employees, but also review the appropriateness of the action taken against the guilty and exercise power to modify the sanction unless the contract explicitly provides otherwise. In reviewing sanctions, arbitrators have established the principle that discipline should be corrective and not punitive, that it should look toward saving and improving the future usefulness of the employee rather than wreaking vengeance or deterring others. The employee's past record becomes crucial, for it helps indicate whether he is incorrigible or is a potentially useful employee. Except for the most serious offenses, penalties must be progressive; reprimands and disciplinary layoffs must be used first to give the employee incentive and an opportunity to change his ways, and discharge may be used only as a last resort when corrective measures hold no promise of reform. When discharge is found inappropriate, arbitrators, with rare exceptions, order reinstatement, even though the employer strongly objects and reinstatement may create tension with supervisors and fellow employees.

These basic principles of the arbitration law of discipline, along with others, are firmly established and fully tested by experience. Their roots can be traced back to arbitration in the garment industry

in the 1920s;[61] they were articulated and elaborated by leading arbitrators in the 1940s;[62] and they were discussed as accepted principles in the arbitration literature of the 1950s. Arbitration of discipline
cases now consists largely of applying established principles to new
problems and special fact situations.[63]

These principles have demonstrated their acceptability and
workability, if by no other indicia than that the arbitrators who
articulate and apply them continue to be selected by the parties to
decide other discipline cases. More tellingly, parties negotiating new
agreements retain the language of "just cause" with a few or no
elaborations or limitations, prescribe few procedural rules, do not
alter the burden of proof, and seldom limit the arbitrator's power to
modify penalties.

It would be specious to claim that arbitrators in developing this
body of law have followed industry practice, particularly as it existed
prior to unionization. And it is probably an overstatement to say that
arbitrators have been guided by "modern concepts of enlightened
personnel administration,"[64] although arbitrators have sought to persuade management that these principles are in the long-term best
interests of their enterprises. It is probably more accurate to say that
the principles represent an accommodation of the needs of management and the legitimate claims of employees developed case by case
by arbitrators confronting the competing interests. They are drawn
from more general standards of justice and fair dealing, equal protection, and due process.[65]

Whatever the sources of this arbitration law, it has a force of its
own in shaping the attitudes and practices of the work place. Through
being articulated it establishes the standard of fairness and justice
against which disciplinary action is measured by management, by
the union, and by the individual employee. These principles have
become in a full sense part of the "law of the shop" defining the
nature of the employment relationship.

A fundamental assumption underlying these principles is that
an employee has a legally protected right to his job—a "property"
right protected through the processes of arbitration. The employee
owns the job and may not be deprived of it except on a showing of
just cause. The substantive and procedural rules are infused with

---

[61]See M. Sharp, DUE PROCESS OF LAW IN INDUSTRIAL GOVERNMENT (J. Commons ed. 1926).

[62]Gollub, *supra* note 55, presents a study of arbitration awards in discipline cases decided
by the New York State Board of Mediation between 1937–46. See H. Shulman & N. Chamberlain, CASES ON LABOR RELATIONS ch. 4 (1949).

[63]For the elaborate detail with which accepted rules have been developed, see Elkouri &
Elkouri, *supra* note 55, and Note, *supra* note 56.

[64]Ross, *supra* note 55, at 24. Professor Phelps point out that "[o]ut of more than a dozen
recent personnel texts and handbooks, published between 1949 and 1956, only four have so
much as a chapter on [discipline], and of these only two could be called adequate by any
standards of comparison with current industrial practice." Phelps, *supra* note 51, at 8–9.

[65]See Jones, *supra* note 55, at 18; Kadish, *supra* note 60; Tobriner, *An Appellate Judge's
View of the Labor Arbitration Process: Due Process and the Arbitration Process*, in National
Academy of Arbitrators, THE ARBITRATOR, THE NLRB, AND THE COURTS 37 (Proceedings of the
20th Annual Meeting, 1967).

principles of due process to protect the employee's interest. The burden rests not on the employee to prove that the employer has misused his authority, but on the employer to prove, at least beyond a preponderance of the evidence, that the employee should be deprived of his job rights. Arbitration law recognizes that an employee's job may be his most valuable asset, and the value of that asset increases with length of service. In a discharge case, where the job itself is at stake, the offense must be unusually serious or often repeated, and the proof must be particularly clear. Employees of long seniority who are plainly guilty of the most serious offenses may be ordered reinstated to avoid deprivation of their accumulated property right.

Common Law Standards for Just Cause

Statutes Requiring Just Cause for Discharge

Veterans and public service employees receive by statute a general protection against arbitrary discharge. Under the Veterans Reemployment Act,[66] veterans may not be discharged except for cause for one year after release from military duty and reemployment in jobs held before military service. Professor Summers, referring to the case law under this statute, noted that "cause has been broadly defined by the courts to be 'such cause as a fair-minded person may act upon.' "[67] Professor Summers cites the language of *Carter v. United States*[68] for a more specific description of "cause":

> "The 'cause' provision was inserted by Congress to provide the reemployed veteran with a protection of reasonableness similar to that enjoyed by a union member protected by provisions in a collective bargaining agreement limiting discharge to cause * * *. We think a discharge may be upheld as one for 'cause' only if it meets two criteria of reasonableness: one, that it is reasonable to discharge employees because of certain conduct, and the other, that the employee had fair notice, express or fairly implied, that such conduct would be ground for discharge."

The Civil Service Act (now the Merit Systems Protection Act), which protects the bulk of federal civil service employees, prohibits dismissal "except for such cause as will promote the efficiency of the service."[69] Apart from the Veterans Reemployment Act, no statute gives comparable protection to employees in the private sector.

---

[66]38 U.S.C. § 2021(a) (1976).
[67]Summers, *Individual Protection Against Unjust Dismissal: Time for a Statute*, 62 VA. L. REV. 481, 497 (1976) (citing *Keserich v. Carnegie-Illinois Steel Corp.*, 163 F.2d 889, 890 (7th Cir. 1947).
[68]407 F.2d 1238, 1244 (D.C. Cir. 1968); *Staton v. Amax Coal Co.*, 122 Ill. App.3d 631, 461 N.E.2d 612 (1984).
[69]5 U.S.C. § 7501(a) (1976).

What Is Just Cause?

The standard of good or just cause is addressed to employee misconduct; it does not embrace other good business reasons. For example, it may be good business to discharge employees to reduce expenses, but such business reasons are not equivalent to just cause.[70] The misconduct, in general, must have a necessary tendency to injure the employer's business and must have no reasonable excuse.[71] Actual damage to the employer is not necessary.[72] "Good cause" has been defined as a "failure of an employee to perform his duties in the scope of his employment in such manner as a person of ordinary prudence in the same employment would have performed under the same or similar circumstances."[73] Good cause includes inefficiency,[74] dishonesty,[75] failure to perform any regular duty,[76] and disability.[77] Refusal to accept a new position has been held not to be good cause.[78] Ordinarily, it is a jury question whether the employer has good cause in fact to terminate.[79]

A just cause discharge only warrants discharging the employee. The employee is still entitled to recover wages, salary, or commissions for services rendered.[80]

What Misconduct May Be Cited by Employer?

When a discharge for just cause is challenged by the employee, may the employer search the entire employment history to find grounds to justify the discharge? Early cases favor the view that the employer may justify a discharge upon any grounds whatsoever, whether or not known at the time of discharge.[81] More recent cases recognize that hindsight and resources for discovery during litigation sharpen the employer's ability to describe the employee's imperfections. Accordingly, these opinions define just cause as that cause that actuated discharge.[82] Individual acts of misconduct might be trivial or im-

---

[70]*Summers v. Colver*, 38 A.D. 553, 56 N.Y.S. 624 (1899).
[71]*Beckman v. Garrett*, 66 Ohio St. 136, 64 N.E. 62 (1902).
[72]*Bank of Am. Nat'l Trust & Sav. Ass'n v. Republic Prods., Inc.*, 44 Cal. App.2d 651, 112 P.2d 972 (1941).
[73]*Ingram v. Dallas County Water Control & Improvement Dist.*, 425 S.W.2d 366, 367 (Tex. Civ. App. 1968); *Mr. Eddie, Inc. v. Ginsberg*, 430 S.W.2d 5, 10 (Tex. Civ. App. 1968).
[74]*Lowenstein v. President & Fellows*, 319 F. Supp. 1096 (D. Mass. 1970).
[75]*Texas Employment Comm'n v. Ryan*, 481 S.W.2d 172 (Tex. Civ. App. 1972).
[76]*Clem v. Bowman Lumber Co.*, 83 N.M. 659, 495 P.2d 1106 (1972).
[77]*Fisher v. Church of St. Mary*, 497 P.2d 882 (Wyo. 1972).
[78]*Lanier v. Alenco*, 459 F.2d 689 (5th Cir. 1972).
[79]*Ward v. Consolidated Foods Corp.*, 480 S.W.2d 483, 486 (Tex. Civ. App. 1972).
[80]*Gillam v. Roadway Express, Inc.*, 1 Ohio App.2d 548, 206 N.E.2d 34 (1965).
[81]*Masonite Corp. v. Hand Shoe*, 208 Miss. 166, 44 So.2d 41 (1950) (not material that at time of discharge employer assigns ground not relied upon in later trial); *Haag v. Revell*, 28 Wash.2d 883, 184 P.2d 442 (1947); *Thomas v. Beaver Dam Mfg. Co.*, 157 Wis. 427, 147 N.W. 364 (1914) (employer not bound by grounds described in notice of discharge); *Loos v. George Walter Brewing Co.*, 145 Wis. 1, 129 N.W. 645 (1911); *Crescent Horseshoe & Iron Co. v. Eynon*, 95 Va. 151, 27 S.E. 935 (1897).
[82]*Cox v. Guy F. Atkinson Co.*, 468 F. Supp. 677 (N.D. Ind. 1979); *Corby v. 7100 Jeffery Ave. Bldg. Corp.*, 325 Ill. App. 442, 60 N.E.2d 236 (1945).

material but in the aggregate may amount to just cause for discharge.[83]

If the employment contract has an express or implied promise of graduated discipline or an opportunity to respond to charges of misconduct, it would seem fair to hold the employer to the actual grounds claimed at the time of discharge. Subsequently discovered misconduct that was serious in nature or concealed by the employee, however, may properly be cited to justify a discharge.

If alleged employee misconduct was known by the employer but not asserted as grounds for discharge until litigation, the employee may argue that the employer condoned the earlier misconduct. Condonation may mean waiver by the employer of the grounds for discharge forever. It may also mean that certain conduct of the employee will not be just cause for discharge unless the employee receives fair warning. It is the employer's knowledge, the lapse of time between the employer knowledge and the discharge, and the continued employment that creates this issue. In one case the employee, a store manager, had the store owner's wife arrested for shoplifting and called her "crazy." The employer took nine months to think this over and then discharged the manager for being rude to his wife. The former store manager sued for wrongful discharge. A jury found in favor of the store manager and against the employer. The appellate court held that under the circumstances both the issue of just cause and condonation were properly left to the jury.[84]

An employer's failure to discharge when cause exists undoubtedly gives the employee reason to believe that the same misconduct will not be used as an excuse for discharge at some arbitrary time in the future. If it were otherwise, one act of misconduct by an employee under a contract with some form of job security would, in effect, create an employment-at-will relationship. However, a delay in acting upon cause for discharge may not be viewed as condonation if it was the result of an investigation to determine the seriousness of the misconduct.[85]

The False Employment Application

This discussion is addressed exclusively to *intentional* falsification of an employment application. The materiality of a nondisclosure or misleading disclosure is central to the resolution of concrete cases. If a school bus driver fails to disclose a criminal record of child abuse, that is obviously more serious than a college graduate failing to

---

[83]*Smith v. Department of Human Resources, Greenwell Springs Hosp.*, 408 So.2d 411 (La. Ct. App. 1981).

[84]*Whittington v. Blank*, 18 Delaware County Rep. 208 (C.P. 1926). See also *Schaffer v. Park City Bowl, Inc.*, 345 Ill. App. 279, 102 N.E.2d 665 (1951); *Rafalo v. Edelstein*, 80 Misc. 153, 140 N.Y.S. 1076 (Sup. Ct. 1913); *Sharp v. McBride*, 120 La. 143, 45 So. 41 (1907); *Gordon v. Dickerson*, 100 W. Va. 490, 130 S.E. 650 (1925); *Hanaford v. Stevens & Co.*, 39 R.I. 182, 98 A. 209 (1916).

[85]*Austin's Rack, Inc. v. Austin*, 396 So.2d 1161 (Fla. Dist. Ct. App. 1981).

disclose his academic credentials for fear of being held overqualified for a blue collar job. The first kind of misrepresentation or omission can expose the employer to a continuing risk of harm.[86] The second kind of falsification enhances the applicant's opportunity to win the job without concealing a material risk from the employer.

Some cases disregard the materality of the misrepresentation and take a very mechanical approach to the problem. The falsifying employee is labeled "dishonest" and the employer is permitted to fire the "dishonest" employee on that ground alone.[87]

Failure to Satisfy Agreed Standards of Performance

Failing to perform according to agreed performance standards is just cause for discharge.[88] Ordinarily, employees are required to perform in a "reasonably skillful manner."[89] But performance to this standard is not a defense if the employee agrees to a higher standard.[90]

Conduct Reflecting Unfavorably Upon the Employer

It has been held that there is an implied condition in every employment contract that the employee will refrain from conduct that is likely to endanger his own reputation and injure his employer's interests.[91] The employer's business interests are the key consideration. Employee conduct that offends the employer's personal moral code is not just cause without a showing that the employer's business was or was likely to be harmed.[92] Likewise, misconduct in

---

[86]*Roundtree v. Board of Review*, 4 Ill. App.3d 695, 281 N.E.2d 360 (1972) (applicant for work as security guard did not disclose felony convictions); *Douglas v. Levingston Shipbuilding Co.*, 617 S.W.2d 718 (Tex. Civ. App. 1979).

[87]*Swanson v. American Mfg. Co.*, 511 S.W.2d 561 (Tex. 1974) (discharge for failure to disclose filing of workman's compensation claim, even though whether employee availed himself of statutory rights after injury in work place is not legitimate application question); *Hosking v. Hollaender Mfg. Co.*, 114 Ohio App. 70, 175 N.E.2d 201 (1961) (exaggeration of salary in prior employment to justify salary demand).

[88]*Tiedman v. American Pigment Corp.*, 253 F.2d 803 (4th Cir. 1958) (engineer unable to fulfill promise to produce synthetic oxides to industry standards); *Franklin v. Texas Int'l Petroleum Corp.*, 324 F. Supp. 808 (W.D. La. 1971) (manager unable to get along with company's bankers).

[89]*Rolfs v. Pooley Furniture Co.*, 176 Ill. App. 93 (1912).

[90]*Hatton v. Mountford*, 105 Va. 96, 52 S.E. 847 (1906) (failure, measured by student petition for discharge, to meet agreed standard of performance higher than would normally be required); *Gambrell v. Kansas City Chiefs Football Club*, 621 S.W.2d 382 (Mo. Ct. App. 1981).

[91]*Waymire v. Placer Joint Union High School Dist.*, 214 Cal. App.2d 372, 29 Cal. Rptr. 459 (1963) (male school bus driver fired for kissing sixteen-year-old female passenger); *Osborn v. Review Bd.*, 178 Ind. App. 22, 381 N.E.2d 495 (1978) (cocktail waitress returned after work as customer, became bibulous, and removed fire extinguisher from wall); *Turner v. Byers*, 562 S.W.2d 507 (Tex. Civ. App. 1978) (certified registered nurse anesthetist appeared on television and advocated nonpayment of taxes); *Associated Mills Producers v. Nelson*, 624 S.W.2d 920 (Tex. Civ. App. 1981); *Advance Ross Elec. Corp. v. Green*, 624 S.W.2d 316 (Tex. Civ. App. 1981).

[92]*Brownell v. Ehrich*, 43 A.D. 369, 60 N.Y.S. 112 (1899) (married man with another woman); *Campbell v. Fierlein*, 134 Ill. App. 207 (1907) (salesman who gambled).

a separate or different business or trust is not good cause for discharge.[93]

There is sometimes a clash between the public employee's view of his right to free expression and exercise of civil liberties and the employer's view of the boundaries of loyalty. The U.S. Supreme Court addressed this question in *Perry v. Sindermann*,[94] holding that refusal to renew a public school teacher's contract because of her exercise of the right of free speech was unlawful. However, a school janitor was held properly discharged for good cause for appearing before the school board and accusing its members of graft.[95] Filing a suit against one's employer and publicly charging it with incompetency also constituted just cause for discharge.[96]

Several cases present the issue of whether a public employee's First Amendment interest in speaking out against others in the employment relationship outweighs the employer's interest in ensuring harmony and loyalty among its employees. *Egger v. Phillips*[97] presents a compilation of representative cases.

Connick v. Myers[98] concerned a district attorney terminated for her refusal to accept a transfer to a different section of the criminal court and her distribution of a questionnaire, which was considered an act of insubordination. It was held the discharge did not breach her First Amendment right.

The interest of state police in maintaining high morale outweighed the employee's First Amendment claim in *Hughes v. Whitmer*.[99] The employee claimed that transfer within the state police was in retaliation for his allegations of wrongdoing by another member of the troup. Likewise, in *McBee v. Jim Hogg County*,[100] the Fifth Circuit upheld the termination of a dispatcher who made statements criticizing her employer. It was held there were no First Amendment protections because the nature of the employment required a close confidential working relationship.

In the following cases, the courts have found wrongful terminations premised upon violation of the First Amendment: In *Rookard v. Health and Hospital Corp.*,[101] a former nursing supervisor's complaints of wasteful and corrupt practices were constitutionally protected. In *Stern v. Shouldice*,[102] a professor's counseling of a student to seek legal advice about the student's suspension was a matter of public concern and protected under the First Amendment. In *McGee*

---

[93]*Gasbarra v. Park-Ohio, Inc.*, 382 F. Supp. 399 (N.D. Ill. 1974) (mishandling of funds as trustee of pension plan not good cause for discharge of company president).
[94]408 U.S. 593 (1972).
[95]*Board of Educ. v. Gossett*, 56 Okla. 95, 155 P. 856 (1916).
[96]*Osburn v. DeForce*, 122 Ore. 360, 257 P. 685 (1927).
[97]710 F.2d 292, 313 n.25 (7th Cir. 1983).
[98]461 U.S. 138 (1983).
[99]714 F.2d 1407 (8th Cir. 1983).
[100]703 F.2d 834 (5th Cir. 1983). See also *Gonzalez v. Benavides*, 712 F.2d 142 (5th Cir. 1983).
[101]710 F.2d 41 (2d Cir. 1983).
[102]706 F.2d 742 (6th Cir.), *cert. denied*, 464 U.S. ___ (1983).

v. South Pemiscot School District,[103] the termination of the school's track coach for writing a letter to the newspaper protesting the school board's decision to drop track was a violation of his constitutional rights. The First Amendment protected a probationary police employee union representative against discharge for publicly criticizing the city's decision not to give police officers an annual raise.[104]

If one's political beliefs reasonably present a threat to security in a sensitive defense-related business, discharge may be appropriate.[105] The employer's potential injury by the employee's political beliefs must either be obvious to the employee or have been brought to the employee's attention through some kind of notice.[106]

In *Carpenters v. Scott*,[107] the U.S. Supreme Court held that the anticonspiracy portion of the Civil Rights Act of 1871[108] did not apply to private conspiracies to deny First Amendment rights. In *Fiske v. Lockheed-Georgia Co.*,[109] the district court, applying *Scott*, found that Section 1985 (3) did not protect employees who were investigated and discharged in part because of their activity in support of the Socialists Workers' Party.

If the employer's public reputation may be injured, invoking the Fifth Amendment before a committee of Congress may warrant discharge from private employment.[110] A private employer with substantial government business may not have discretion to discharge for constitutionally protected conduct.[111] If, however, the constitutionally protected conduct amounts to insubordination, even the government may rely upon it as grounds to discharge a public employee.[112]

Intoxication

Drunkenness on the job is a well-recognized ground for discharge.[113] However, where the employee has given substantial con-

---

[103]712 F.2d 339 (8th Cir. 1983).

[104]*McKinley v. Eloy*, 705 F.2d 1110 (9th Cir. 1983). See also *Salerno v. O'Rourke*, 555 F. Supp. 750 (D.N.J. 1983) (rules instituted by county sheriff and members of county board limiting speech activities of deputy warden violated his First Amendment rights).

[105]*Lockheed Aircraft Corp. v. Superior Court*, 28 Cal.2d 481, 171 P.2d 21 (1946) (persons who believed in forcible overthrow of the United States were properly discharged by security-sensitive defense contractor).

[106]*Hale Hardware Co. v. Ragland*, 165 Ark. 258, 263 S.W. 962 (1924) (no reason for employee to believe bias in favor of strikers over nonstrikers employed by another business in same town would cause injury to employer).

[107]463 U.S. __ , 51 U.S.L.W. 5173 (July 5, 1983).

[108]42 U.S.C. §1985(3) (1976).

[109]568 F. Supp. 590 (N.D. Ga. 1983).

[110]*Electrical, Radio & Mach. Workers v. General Elec. Co.*, 127 F. Supp. 934 (D.C. Cir. 1954); *Twentieth Century-Fox Film Corp. v. Lardner*, 216 F.2d 844 (9th Cir. 1954) (screenwriters properly discharged for invoking Fifth Amendment before House Unamerican Activities Committee).

[111]*Holodnak v. Avco Corp.*, 514 F.2d 285 (2d Cir. 1975) (employee who accused employer of sabotaging collective bargaining grievance procedure was protected by First Amendment because of "governmental presence" at plant, 80 percent of employer's production being military hardware).

[112]*Chambliss v. Board of Fire & Police Comm'rs*, 20 Ill. App.3d 24, 312 N.E.2d 842 (1974).

[113]*Coleman v. Department of Labor*, 288 A.2d 285 (Del. 1972); *Monticello Cotton Mills, Inc., v. Powell*, 215 Ark. 492, 221 S.W.2d 33 (1949); *Mowbray v. Gould*, 83 A.D. 255, 82 N.Y.S. 162 (1903); *Van Vleet v. Hayes*, 56 Ark. 128, 19 S.W. 427 (1892).

sideration for his job security agreement, discharge may not be justified by even repeated instances of intoxication. In the case of chronic alcoholism, the employer's sympathetic assistance to achieve a cure may be required.[114]

Personality Problems and Disruptive Conduct

When an employee's belligerence undermines the possibility of an efficient relationship in the work place, someone has to go. That someone is the employee.[115] An employee may be discharged for belligerence toward his subordinates as well as a disrespectful attitude toward his superiors.[116] In some occupations, such as commercial airline pilot, a personality problem can easily present a question of public safety. In such circumstances any doubts should be resolved by the employer in favor of the public. Discharge, or at least a change of position, is warranted.[117]

An employee's belligerence or show of disrespect must, however, be real and substantial, not trivial. For example, where an employee's polite refusal of a gift of cuff links conveys a more significant message to the boss, it still does not amount to just cause for discharge.[118] Likewise, a subordinate's unhappiness with his salary does not warrant discharge.[119]

A Crime Against the Employer

A crime against the employer[120] or the employer's reasonable belief that the employee committed a crime against the employer[121] has been held sufficient to justify discharge. However, a crime that does not harm or threaten the employer does not amount to just cause for discharge.[122]

---

[114]*Kippen v. American Automatic Typewriter Co.*, 324 F.2d 742 (9th Cir. 1963) (franchisor not entitled to terminate franchisee for alcoholism without affording opportunity to correct problem).

[115]*Blue v. Chandler*, 5 So.2d 210 (La. Ct. App. 1941) (employee's belligerent attitude during disagreement with supervisor warranted discharge); *Farrakhan v. Sears, Roebuck & Co.*, 511 F. Supp. 893 (D. Neb. 1980).

[116]*Abendpost Co. v. Hertzel*, 67 Ill. App. 501 (1896); *Alexander v. Potts*, 151 Ill. App. 587 (1909).

[117]*Farris v. Alaska Airlines*, 113 F. Supp. 907 (W.D. Wash. 1953).

[118]*Frachtman v. Fox*, 156 N.Y.S. 313 (Sup. Ct. 1915).

[119]*Rench v. Hayes Equip. Mfg. Co.*, 134 Kan. 865, 8 P.2d 346 (1932).

[120]*Electrical, Radio & Mach. Workers, Local 453 v. Otis Elevator Co.*, 201 F. Supp. 213 (S.D.N.Y. 1962); *Taint v. Kroeger Co.*, 20 Ohio Misc. 29, 247 N.E.2d (1967) (irrelevant that employee caught stealing from employer was not stealing during working hours or from particular warehouse where he worked).

[121]*Lewis v. Magna Am. Corp.*, 472 F.2d 560 (6th Cir. 1972) (receiving stolen merchandise from fellow employee is just cause for discharge without evidence of guilty knowledge); *Food Fair Stores, Inc. v. Commonwealth*, 11 Pa. Commw. Ct. 535, 314 A.2d 528 (1974) (employee acquitted of crime after trial was nevertheless subject to discharge, since employer is entitled to expect higher standard of conduct).

[122]*Conway, Inc. v. Ross*, 627 P.2d 1029 (Alaska 1981).

Punctuality and Unauthorized Absences

An alarm clock that does not work or inadequate transportation is not a sufficient excuse for repeated tardiness after warnings.[123] If the absence is due to sickness, the employee must be away from the work place for a long duration compared to the entire period of service contemplated by the contract.[124] But a single day off for personal business without permission warrants discharge[125] unless the employee is a senior manager. High level supervisory personnel are less strictly accountable for their time.[126]

Insubordination

The largest number of discharges with just cause issues that appear in reported decisions concern insubordination. Generally, an intentional refusal to follow rules or instructions is just cause for discharge.[127] Whether insubordination is just cause for discharge turns upon several sub-issues. The first is whether the order or standing employer rule or regulation that was violated was reasonable. Blind obedience to an unreasonable demand is not the standard of employee conduct.[128] Emergencies enlarge the employee's responsibilities and govern the reasonableness of orders.[129] And the reasonableness of an order requires examination of the circumstances in which it was given.[130]

The problem is how reasonableness of employer orders is to be determined and who shall determine it. We are not aware of any opinions that explore this boundary line between reasonable and abusive exercise of management discretion. The issue is simply whether the rule was reasonably related to legitimate objectives of the employer.

Some cases support this conclusion. A railroad conductor was discharged for not reporting a near accident between a passenger train and work train. Such a report was required by a standing regulation. The reasonableness of the rule was indisputable. It was held that the reasonableness of the rule was not open to consideration by the jury.[131] In contrast, a court permitted the jury to consider whether

---

[123]*Ohio Ferro-Alloys Corp. v. Tichnor*, 83 Ohio L. Abstracts 254, 168 N.E.2d 334 (Common Pleas Ct., Muskingum County 1959); *Mandel Bros. v. Holguard*, 99 Ill. App. 75 (1901).
[124]*Gaynor v. Jonas*, 104 A.D. 35, 93 N.Y.S. 287 (1905).
[125]*Jerome v. Queen City Cycle Co.*, 163 N.Y. 351, 57 N.E. 485 (1900).
[126]*Moody v. Streissguth Clothing Co.*, 96 Wis. 202, 71 N.W. 99 (1897). But cf. *Farmer v. First Trust Co.*, 246 F. 671 (7th Cir. 1917) (senior manager's four-day absence was unreasonable in view of problems demanding his attention).
[127]*Circle Security Agency, Inc. v. Ross*, 107 Ill. App.3d 195, 437 N.E.2d 667 (1982); *Stokes v. Enmark Collaborative, Inc.*, 634 S.W.2d 571 (Mo. Ct. App. 1982); *Deason v. Mobil Oil Co.*, 407 So.2d 486 (La. Ct. App. 1981); *Central Alaska Broadcasting, Inc. v. Bracale*, 637 P.2d 711 (Alaska 1981).
[128]*Jones v. Review Bd.*, 399 N.E.2d 844 (Ind. Ct. App. 1980).
[129]*Keserich v. Carnegie-Illinois Steel Corp.*, 163 F.2d 889 (7th Cir. 1947).
[130]*S. Unterberger & Co. v. Wiley*, 170 Ark. 976, 281 S.W. 899 (1926); *Reynolds Mfg. Co. v. Mendoza*, 644 S.W.2d 536 (Tex. Civ. App. 1982).
[131]*Gregg v. Atlantic Coastline R.R.*, 143 F. Supp. 677 (E.D.S.C. 1956).

rules governing school teachers' social life were arbitrary.[132] However, the issue of reasonableness of rules and orders is one that courts have been reluctant to submit to juries.[133]

Insubordination is excused if the disobeyed order is inconsistent with the employment agreement—for example, an order inconsistent with managerial authority given when the employee was hired[134]— or implies a demotion from an agreed position.[135] A direction to substitute a different service than what was agreed to when the employee was hired may be a constructive wrongful discharge.[136] Likewise, if the employer orders the employee to do an illegal act, performance is excused.[137]

A simple misunderstanding may explain and excuse what appears to be misconduct.[138] Failure to complete a task may be explained by the fact that too much was expected in too short a time rather than disobedience.[139] The reasonableness of the employer's expectations is a question hardly different from the reasonableness of a rule or regulation and raises the question of how much second guessing by the jury is appropriate. The issues related to insubordination may be further complicated if the employee claims the discharge was actually motivated by a wrongful motive like retaliation for filing a worker's compensation claim.[140]

If compliance with the order would place the employee in physical jeopardy that was not understood at the time of employment, the order is unreasonable and obedience is excused.[141] If this issue is introduced, the trier of fact is dealing with the reasonableness of the employer's orders in a somewhat different form. The scope of inquiry by judge or jury into the reality of the jeopardy perceived by the employee may raise the policy questions discussed earlier.

Under some circumstances, the employer may provoke insubordination. For example, a disc jockey was fired for arriving for work 55 minutes late for his radio show. The employer, the night before,

---

[132]*Hall-Moody Inst. v. Copass*, 108 Tenn. 582, 69 S.W. 327 (1902). See also *Thornton v. Department of Human Resources Dev.*, 32 Cal. App.3d 180, 107 Cal. Rptr. 892 (1973) (pizza parlor owner's order to employee to shave beard, if motivated by belief that beard was unsanitary or detrimental to business, was reasonable). See *Indiana Civil Rights Comm'n v. Sutherland Lumber*, 394 N.E.2d 949 (Ind. Ct. App. 1979) for discussion of grooming requirements and their relationship to sexual discrimination. See also *Schumaker v. Heinemann*, 99 Wis. 251, 74 N.W. 785 (1898); *Trainer v. Trainer Spinning Co.*, 224 Pa. 45, 73 A. 8 (1909).

[133]*Corrigan v. G.M.P. Producing Corp.*, 179 A.D. 810, 167 N.Y.S. 206 (1917) (movie actor refused to come to set on time); *Moore v. Honeywell Information Sys.*, 558 F. Supp. 1229 (D. Hawaii 1983).

[134]*Mair v. Southern Minn. Broadcasting Co.*, 226 Minn. 137, 32 N.W.2d 177 (1948); *Spotswood Arms Corp. v. Este*, 147 Va. 1047, 133 S.E. 570 (1926).

[135]*Hayes v. Resource Control, Inc.*, 170 Conn. 102, 365 A.2d 399 (1976).

[136]*Loos v. George Walter Brewing Co.*, 145 Wis. 1, 129 N.W. 645 (1911).

[137]*Van Winkle v. Satterfield*, 58 Ark. 617, 25 S.W. 1113 (1894) (employee ordered to work on Sunday contrary to blue laws).

[138]*Embry v. Hargadine, McKittrick Dry Goods Co.*, 127 Mo. App. 383, 105 S.W. 777 (1907).

[139]*Goodwyn v. Sencore, Inc.*, 389 F. Supp. 824 (D.S.D. 1975).

[140]*Texas Steel Co. v. Douglas*, 533 S.W.2d 111 (Tex. Civ. App. 1976).

[141]*Spetz v. InterBorough Rapid Transit Co.*, 169 N.Y.S. 458 (Sup. Ct. 1918) (insufficient evidence of physical peril to justify railman's refusal to enter subway tunnel to dry out insulators without rubber boots). See also Note, *The Occupational Safety and Health Act of 1970: The Right to Refuse Work Under Hazardous Conditions*, 1979 WASH. U.L.Q. 571 (1979)

had requested his radio announcer to do an unscheduled broadcast until four o'clock in the morning to relieve another announcer who collapsed on the air while attempting to set a new record for sustained uninterrupted broadcasting.[142] Closely akin to this is the claim that the employer directly provoked the alleged insubordination by threatening the employee's contract rights. Thus, whatever is reasonably done by an employee in defense of contract rights or in the assertion of agreed employment rights is not insubordination.[143]

Disloyalty

It is taken for granted that employees have a duty of loyalty to their employer's interests. Thus, directing a potential customer to a competitor is good cause for discharge.[144] If an employee acquires a business interest adverse to his employer, the duty of loyalty is breached.[145] Although soliciting fellow employees to join in forming a new business would be grounds for discharge,[146] it is excusable if the employer has already indicated it is going out of business.[147] It has been held that an at-will employee may inform customers that he plans to quit and work for a competitor of his current employer.[148] Even if found to be disloyal, the employee is entitled to commissions earned before discharge.[149] Employee loyalty does not necessarily end after termination. At least this is the case with respect to confidential information obtained through employment.[150] A full discussion of employee conduct after employment terminates, however, is generally beyond the scope of this book.

Satisfaction

A "satisfaction contract" is a contract for a fixed term subject to the employer's satisfaction or for as long as the employer is satisfied with the employee. When an employee hired under such a contract

---

[142]*Krizan v. Storz Broadcasting Co.*, 145 So.2d 636 (La. Ct. App. 1962). Cf. *Blum Bros. Box Co. v. Wisconsin Labor Relations Bd.*, 229 Wis. 615, 282 N.W. 98 (1939) (employee was not excused for leaving work place without permission merely because others had done so without consequence), and *Woodson v. Unemployment Compensation Bd. of Review*, 461 Pa. 439, 366 A.2d 867 (1975).

[143]*Steranko v. Inforex, Inc.*, 5 Mass. App. Ct. 253, 362 N.E.2d 222 (1977) (vice president's continued assertion of contract rights after reduction in authority did not amount to insubordination). *Rudman v. Cowles Communications, Inc.*, 30 N.Y.2d 1, 280 N.E.2d 867, 330 N.Y.S.2d 33 (1972) (employer cannot punish employee for disobedience provoked by employer).

[144]*Katz v. Goodman*, 176 N.Y.S. 488 (Sup. Ct. 1919).

[145]*Weber v. Barnsdall*, 39 Okla. 212, 134 P. 842 (1913).

[146]*Brown v. Dupuy*, 4 F.2d 367 (7th Cir. 1924); *Puritas Laundry Co. v. Green*, 15 Cal. App. 654, 115 P. 660 (1911.)

[147]*Hawkins v. Crosby*, 71 Ohio App. 82, 130 N.E.2d 356 (1954). Cf. *Plastics Research & Dev. Corp. v. Norman*, 243 Ark. 780, 422 S.W.2d 121 (1967) (employee may solicit customers and fellow employees for planned new business while still employed), and *Hamilton Depositors Corp. v. Browne*, 199 Ark. 953, 136 S.W.2d 1031 (1940) (employee may organize but not operate business or solicit fellow employees while still with original employer).

[148]*Crane Co. v. Dahle*, 576 P.2d 870 (Utah 1978).

[149]*Barker v. Barker Artesian Well Co.*, 45 R.I. 297, 121 A. 117 (1923).

[150]*Bull v. Logetronics, Inc.*, 232 F. Supp. 115 (E.D. Va. 1971).

is discharged on the ground that the employer is dissatisfied, the question arises: to what standard should the employer be held in his determination that the employee was unsatisfactory? The courts are generally in agreement that the proper standard is simply that the employer be honestly and in fact dissatisfied with the employee[151] even if the dissatisfaction is unreasonable under the circumstances. The employer is the sole judge of whether the employee is satisfactory;[152] and as long as the employer is dissatisfied, the employee may be discharged even though there exist no real or substantial grounds for dissatisfaction.[153] The courts have tended to summarize the foregoing by stating that the standard to be applied is whether or not the employer acted in *good faith.*[154]

Whether an employer was in fact dissatisfied with the employee or merely used dissatisfaction as a pretext is a question of fact. But in keeping with the general rules set out above, the question presented to the trier of fact is limited. A jury or judge cannot supplant the employer's judgment. The question is not whether the employer should have been satisfied with the employee or whether a reasonable

---

[151]*Seitless v. Goldstein,* 164 N.Y.S. 682 (Sup. Ct. 1917); *Beck v. Only Skirt Co.,* 176 A.D. 867, 163, N.Y.S. 786 (1917); *Ginsberg v. Friedman,* 146 A.D. 779, 131 N.Y.S. 517 (1911); *Ray v. Georgetown Life Ins. Co.,* 94 Ill. App.3d 863, 419 N.E.2d 721 (1981); *Tiffany v. Pacific Sewer Pipe Co.,* 180 Cal. 700, 182 P. 428 (1919); *Paddock v. Bay Concrete Indus., Inc.,* 154 So.2d 313 (Fla. 1963); *Edwards v. Doherty,* 74 So.2d 686 (Fla. 1954); *Hazen v. Cobb,* 96 Fla. 151, 117 So. 853 (1928); *Sax v. Detroit, Grand Haven & Milwaukee Ry.,* 125 Mich. 252, 84 N.W. 314 (1900); *Koehler v. Buhl,* 94 Mich. 496, 54 N.W. 157 (1893); *Kramer v. Philadelphia Leather Goods Corp.,* 364 Pa. 531, 73 A.2d 385 (1950); *Corgan v. George F. Lee Coal Co.,* 218 Pa. 386, 67 A. 655 (1907); *Frary v. American Rubber Co.,* 52 Minn. 264, 53 N.W. 1156 (1893); *Atlanta Stoveworks v. Hamilton,* 83 Miss. 704, 35 So. 763 (1904); *Roxana Petroleum Co. v. Rice,* 109 Okla. 161, 235 P. 502 (1924); *Bailey v. Allied Properties, Inc.,* 262 Ore. 584, 500 P.2d 700 (1972); *Clem v. Bowman Lumber Co.,* 83 N.M. 659, 495 P.2d 1106 (1972); *Hortis v. Madison Golf Club, Inc.,* 92 A.D.2d 713, 461 N.Y.S.2d 116 (1983); *Lone Star Gas Co. v. Pippin,* 620 S.W.2d 922 (Tex. Civ. App. 1981); *Ray v. Georgetown Life Ins. Co.,* 94 Ill. App.3d 863, 419 N.E.2d 721 (1981).

[152]*Aquinto v. Clifford C. Fisher, Inc.,* 165 N.Y.S. 369 (Sup. Ct. 1917); *Mackay v. Arthur Hammerstein's Prods., Inc.,* 164 N.Y.S. 164 (1917); *Wynkoop Hallenbeck Crawford Co. v. Western Union Tel. Co.,* 268 N.Y. 108 (1935); *Brill v. Brenner,* 62 Misc.2d 102, 308 N.Y.S.2d 218 (Civ. Ct. 1970); *Fields v. Dinkins,* 156 Ill. App. 528 (1910); *Ray v. Georgetown Life Ins. Co.,* 94 Ill. App.3d 863, 419 N.E.2d 721 (1981); *Tiffany v. Pacific Sewer Pipe Co.,* 180 Cal. 700, 182 P. 428 (1919); *Hazen v. Cobb,* 96 Fla. 151, 117 So. 853 (1928); *Paddock v. Bay Concrete Indus., Inc.,* 154 So.2d 313 (Fla. 1963); *Edwards v. Doherty,* 74 So.2d 686 (Fla. 1954); *Sax v. Detroit, Grand Haven & Milwaukee Ry.,* 125 Mich. 252, 84 N.W. 314 (1900); *Corgan v. George F. Lee Coal Co.,* 218 Pa. 386, 67 A. 655 (1907); *Clem v. Bowman Lumber Co.,* 83 N.M. 659, 495 P.2d 1106 (1972).

[153]*Hazen v. Cobb,* 96 Fla. 151, 117 So. 853 (1928); *Paddock v. Bay Concrete Indus., Inc.,* 154 So. 2d 313 (Fla. 1963); *Edwards v. Doherty,* 74 So.2d 686 (Fla. 1954); *Kramer v. Philadelphia Leather Goods Corp.,* 364 Pa. 531, 73 A.2d 385 (1950); *Corgan v. George F. Lee Coal Co.,* 218 Pa. 386, 67 A. 655 (1907); *Frary v. American Rubber Co.,* 52 Minn. 264, 53 N.W. 1156 (1893); *Bailey v. Allied Properties, Inc.,* 262 Ore. 584, 500 P.2d 700 (1972); *Clem v. Bowman Lumber Co.,* 83 N.M. 659, 495 P.2d 1106 (1972).

[154]*Diamond v. Mendelsohn,* 156 A.D. 636, 141 N.Y.S. 775 (1913); *Bishop v. Bloomington Canning Co.,* 307 Ill. 179, 138 N.E. 597 (1923); *Bondi v. Jewels by Edwar, Ltd.,* 267 Cal. App.2d 672, 73 Cal. Rptr. 494 (1968); *Rife v. Mote,* 210 Ark. 629, 197 S.W.2d 277 (1946); *Hazen v. Cobb,* 96 Fla. 151, 117 So. 853 (1928); *Paddock v. Bay Concrete Indus., Inc.,* 154 So.2d 313 (Fla. 1963); *Edwards v. Doherty,* 74 So.2d 686 (Fla. 1954); *Kramer v. Philadelphia Leather Goods Corp.,* 364 Pa. 531, 73 A.2d 385 (1950); *Frary v. American Rubber Co.,* 52 Minn. 264, 53 N.W. 1156 (1893); *Roxana Petroleum Co. v. Rice,* 109 Okla. 165, 235 P. 502 (1925); *Bailey v. Allied Properties, Inc.,* 262 Ore. 584, 500 P.2d 700 (1972); *Clem v. Bowman Lumber Co.,* 83 N.M. 659, 495 P.2d 1106 (1972).

man would have been satisfied.[155] Rather, it is whether the alleged dissatisfaction is real and honest, and not feigned or pretended.[156] Indeed, where the only issue raised by the complaining employee is that the employer's dissatisfaction was unreasonable, the granting of motions to dismiss the complaint[157] or for a directed verdict[158] is appropriate. On the other hand, if the evidence tends to show that the employer had an ulterior motive for a discharge, the directing of a verdict at trial is improper.[159]

While the employer must show that he was dissatisfied with the employee and thus justified in discharging him, the burden of proof on the whole is on the employee, who must show that the claimed dissatisfaction is not genuine.[160] Stating this somewhat differently, the Illinois courts hold that "the employee makes out a cause of action if he proves that he was discharged before the expiration of the time provided for in the contract of employment, and either (1) that the employer was not dissatisfied with him, or (2) that the employer, whether dissatisfied or not, did not discharge him on account of dissatisfaction."[161] The second prong of this test is in accord with decisions holding that the employer's reasons for discharging the employee at the time of discharge are binding on him.[162] In other words, if the employee is, in fact, discharged for some reason other than dissatisfaction, the employer is in breach of the contract and cannot later be heard to say he had grounds to be dissatisfied. This issue is rarely directly discussed, though the language of the decisions generally indicate the courts are looking at the employer's grounds at the time of discharge. But there is at least one decision holding that regardless of the reason given at the time of the discharge, if in retrospect the employer had good grounds to have been dissatisfied with the em-

---

[155]*Beck v. Only Skirt Co.*, 176 A.D. 867, 163 N.Y.S. 786 (1917); *Kramer v. Wien*, 92 Misc. 159, 155 N.Y.S. 193 (App. Term. 1915); *Ginsberg v. Friedman*, 146 A.D. 779, 131 N.Y.S. 517 (1911); *Koehler v. Buhl*, 94 Mich. 496, 54 N.W. 157 (1893); *Corgan v. George F. Lee Coal Co.*, 218 Pa. 386, 67 A. 655 (1907); *Kramer v. Philadelphia Leather Goods Corp.*, 364 Pa. 531, 73 A.2d 385 (1950).

[156]*Beck v. Only Skirt Co.*, 176 A.D. 867, 163 N.Y.S. 786 (1917); *Ginsberg v. Friedman*, 146 A.D. 779, 131 N.Y.S. 517 (1911); *Kramer v. Wien*, 92 Misc. 159, 155 N.Y.S. 193 (App. Term. 1915); *Delano v. Columbia Mach. Works & Malleable Iron Co.*, 179 A.D. 153, 166 N.Y.S. 103 (1917); *Diamond v. Mendelsohn*, 156 A.D. 636, 141 N.Y.S. 775 (1913); *Rife v. Mote*, 210 Ark. 629, 197 S.W.2d 277 (1946); *Hazen v. Cobb*, 96 Fla. 151, 117 So. 853 (1928); *Paddock v. Bay Concrete Indus., Inc.*, 154 So.2d 313 (Fla. 1963); *Edwards v. Doherty*, 74 So.2d 686 (Fla. 1954); *Corgan v. George F. Lee Coal Co.*, 218 Pa. 386, 67 A. 655 (1907); *Kramer v. Philadelphia Leather Goods Corp.*, 364 Pa. 531, 73 A.2d 385 (1950); *Frary v. American Rubber Co.*, 52 Minn. 264, 53 N.W. 1156 (1893); *Atlanta Stoveworks v. Hamilton*, 83 Miss. 704, 35 So. 763 (1904); *Clem v. Bowman Lumber Co.*, 83 N.M. 659, 495 P.2d 1106 (1972); *Atkinson v. New Britain Mach. Co.*, 154 F.2d 895 (7th Cir. 1946).

[157]*Crawford v. Mail & Express Publishing Co.*, 163 N.Y. 404, 57 N.E. 616 (1900).

[158]*Daversa v. William H. Davidow's Sons Co.*, 89 Misc. 418, 151 N.Y.S. 872 (Sup. Ct. 1915).

[159]*Atkinson v. New Britain Mach. Co.*, 154 F.2d 895 (7th Cir. 1946) (refusal by employee to enter into lower-paying contract).

[160]*Delano v. Columbia Mach. Works & Malleable Iron Co.*, 179 A.D. 153, 166 N.Y.S. 103 (1917); *Rife v. Mote*, 210 Ark. 629, 197 S.W.2d 277 (1946); *Coker v. Wesco Materials Corp.*, 368 S.W.2d 883 (Tex. Civ. App. 1963).

[161]*Ray v. Georgetown Life Ins. Co.*, 94 Ill. App.3d 863, 419 N.E.2d 721 (1981).

[162]*Diamond v. Mendelsohn*, 156 A.D. 636, 141 N.Y.S. 775 (1913).

ployee, the contract was not breached by him when he discharged the employee.[163]

Frequently, the decisions will discuss the existence of two types of classes of "satisfaction contracts." The first concerns the personal taste, feeling, sensibility, fancy, or individual judgment of the party to be satisfied. The second involves mechanical utility or operative fitness to which an objective standard can be applied.[164] Contracts falling within the first class are interpreted by the courts as entitling the employer to discharge the employee at any time the employer is honestly and in good faith dissatisfied. That is, the courts apply the same subjective standard already discussed above. In the latter class of contracts, i.e., those involving mechanical utility or operative fitness, the decisions are conflicting; but the courts will frequently interpret the satisfaction clause as requiring the employer to have *reasonable* grounds for dissatisfaction—his subjective opinion being nondeterminative. Applying this standard, the jury can inquire whether the employer should have been dissatisfied or whether it was reasonable for him to be dissatisfied under the circumstances.

It is unfortunate that the courts have applied these classifications in employment contract situations, since upon close analyses their applicability is questionable and their use has tended only to create confusion in the decisions. The important factor is not necessarily the employee's finished product or the actual job he is performing. What is important is the employer-employee *relationship*. Is the employee trustworthy? Would the employer feel confident leaving him alone in the factory? Does the employee get along with the other employees? These questions and many more like them are the kinds of questions only the employer can answer. Such questions are present regardless of the operative fitness of the product. It is for this reason that the taste/fancy vs. operative fitness test is inappropriate in an employment context.

The courts that have, however, applied the taste/fancy vs. operative fitness test in an employment contract situation have generally held that the particular contract of employment in question falls within the taste/fancy category.[165] The logic of these decisions is strained, however, since they still appear to be concerned with the

---

[163]*Corgan v. George F. Lee Coal Co.*, 218 Pa. 386, 67 A. 655 (1907).

[164]*Duplex Safety Boiler Co. v. Garden*, 101 N.Y. 387, 4 N.E. 749 (1886); *Bishop v. Bloomington Canning Co.*, 307 Ill. 179, 138 N.E. 597 (1923); *Ray v. Georgetown Life Ins. Co.*, 94 Ill. App.3d 863, 419 N.E.2d 721 (1981); *Tiffany v. Pacific Sewer Pipe Co.*, 180 Cal. 700, 182 P. 428 (1919); *Jacobs v. Kraft Cheese Co.*, 310 Pa. 75, 164 A. 774 (1933); *Frary v. American Rubber Co.*, 52 Minn. 264, 53 N.W. 1156 (1893); *Hanaford v. Stevens & Co.*, 39 R.I. 182, 98 A. 209 (1916).

[165]*MacKay v. Arthur Hammerstein's Prods., Inc.*, 164 N.Y.S. 164 (Sup. Ct. 1917); *Brill v. Brenner*, 62 Misc.2d 102, 308 N.Y.S.2d 218 (Civ. Ct. 1970); *Rosen v. Druss*, 178 N.Y.S. 259 (App. Term. 1919); *Beiner v. Goetz*, 81 Misc. 244, 142 N.Y.S. 244 (1913); *Beck v. Only Skirt Co.*, 176 A.D. 867, 163 N.Y.S. 786 (1917); *Tiffany v. Pacific Sewer Pipe Co.*, 180 Cal. 700, 182 P. 428 (1919); *Bishop v. Bloomington Canning Co.*, 307 Ill. 179, 138 N.E. 597 (1923); *Ray v. Georgetown Life Ins. Co.*, 94 Ill. App.3d 863, 419 N.E.2d 721 (1981); *Frary v. American Rubber Co.*, 52 Minn. 264, 53 N.W. 1156 (1893).

employee's work product, which is often susceptible to an objective standard.

Statutory Defenses of Financial Institutions

The National Bank Act[166] and Federal Home Loan Bank Act[167] provide that bank officers serve at the pleasure of the bank's board of directors. Two cases have held that the statutes defeated the employee's assertion of a contract claim of employment security premised upon a personnel manual.[168] However, it has been held that a branch manager's employment was not governed by the National Bank Act because he was neither appointed nor dismissed by the bank's board of directors as required by the statute.[169]

---

[166] 12 U.S.C. §24 (1982).
[167] 12 U.S.C. §1432(a) (1982).
[168] *Inglis v. Feinerman*, 701 F.2d 97 (9th Cir. 1983), *cert. denied*, 464 U.S. ___ (1984); *Bollow v. Federal Reserve Bank*, 650 F.2d 1093 (9th Cir. 1981), *cert. denied*, 455 U.S. 948 (1982).
[169] *Wiskotoni v. Michigan Nat'l Bank-W.*, 716 F.2d 378 (6th Cir. 1983). See also *Mahoney v. Crocker Nat'l Bank*, 571 F. Supp. 287 (N.D. Cal. 1983).

II

Procedural Considerations and Alternate Remedies for Discharge

5

Preemption, Exhaustion, and *Res Judicata* Defenses

This chapter explores three procedural defenses that may be raised in employment cases. Some of the conditions that make these defenses available are peculiar to the field of employment; others frequently occur in employment controversies.

The first defense is preemption. A statutory scheme intended to provide comprehensive regulation of a situation arising in, or some aspect of, the employment relationship may bar an otherwise appropriate cause of action. The idea is that the legislature, having spelled out the appropriate rights and remedies, intended that they be all that are available; permitting other actions in this situation would undermine the legislative purpose. Federal labor laws and state workers' compensation laws are the most common sources of preemption.

The second defense is the requirement that a plaintiff exhaust other remedies before coming to court. Exhaustion problems are present where grievance arbitration under a collective bargaining agreement is available, where the controversy might be within the jurisdiction of an administrative agency, and where some alternative, nonjudicial remedy is available to the discharged employee. The exhaustion requirement may operate to bar an action because the court will simply enforce the decision reached in other proceedings.

The third defense is the collateral estoppel aspect of the *res judicata* doctrine. Other proceedings between employer and employee, such as unemployment compensation hearings, grievance arbitration, discrimination and unfair labor practice proceedings, and workers' compensation claims may establish facts that become binding in the employment case.

137

Preemption by Statutory Remedies

National Labor Relations Act Preemption

Federal labor law preemption was explained in *San Diego Building Trades Council v. Garmon.*[1] Reasoning that Congress entrusted labor law regulation to the National Labor Relations Board (NLRB) to ensure uniform application of the National Labor Relations Act (NLRA), the U.S. Supreme Court limited the power of a state to create rights affecting, or to adjudicate controversies arising from, labor disputes.

The rationale of preemption is that the NLRA is a carefully developed and delicately balanced regulatory scheme intended to prohibit certain conduct, protect certain conduct, and leave certain matters to the regulated economic power struggle between management and labor. Obviously, a state law designed to prohibit what the NLRA permits, or to protect what the NLRA prohibits, runs afoul of the Supremacy Clause and is invalid. For the NLRA merely to invalidate such openly unconstitutional measures, however, would not fulfill the federal statutory objective. The Court concluded in *Garmon* that the statute intended close questions to be resolved by the NLRB and thus if conduct was "arguably" protected or prohibited, state law could not be applied. In addition, since the NLRA also sought to allow freedom of action in certain areas under the "rules of the game," state regulation of conduct that was neither protected nor prohibited might impede NLRA policy and also would be preempted.[2]

The application of state law is not barred in all situations. The preemption doctrine does not apply to matters of "peripheral concern" to the implementation of national policy, or to cases in which the state's interest is "deeply rooted in local feeling and responsibility."[3]

Preemption by federal labor law is thus governed by a two-step inquiry: whether the state law affects national labor policy and, if so, whether the state interests are sufficiently compelling to make the impact on federal law tolerable.[4] The issue is one of ascertaining what is consistent with congressional intent, however, and this is the purpose of the test.[5]

The outer reach of preemption under the NLRA is generally controlled by the provisions of Sections 7 and 8 of the NLRA, which establish the rights of nonsupervisory private-sector employees to

---

[1]359 U.S. 236 (1959).
[2]*Id.* at 242–245; *Machinists v. Wisconsin Employment Relations Comm'n*, 427 U.S. 132 (1976). In a case of NLRA preemption, the "protected" and "prohibited" conduct generally refers to the rights created by Section 7 and the more specific unfair labor practices set out in Section 8 of the NLRA, 29 U.S.C. §§157, 158 (1976).
[3]*San Diego Bldg. Trades Council v. Garmon*, 359 U.S. 236, 243–244 (1959); *Street, Elec. Ry. & Motor Coach Employees v. Lockridge*, 403 U.S. 274, 289 (1971).
[4]*Farmer v. Carpenters*, 430 U.S. 290 (1977); *Linn v. Plant Guard Workers*, 383 U.S. 53 (1966).
[5]*Sears Roebuck & Co. v. Carpenters, San Diego County Dist. Council*, 436 U.S. 180 (1978); *Machinists v. Wisconsin Employment Relations Comm'n*, 427 U.S. 132 (1976).

organize and bargain collectively and define the legal restrictions imposed on management and labor.[6] Where a case arises out of the termination of employment, the first place to seek out federal policies that might be affected is these provisions of the NLRA or, in the case of common carriers, the Railway Labor Act.

There is room for argument that any termination of employment of any employee implicates federal labor policy. Any termination of a protected employee might *arguably* be motivated by an employer's desire to discourage, or might have the effect of discouraging, employee organization.[7] Any restraint on the power to fire unprotected supervisory employees might *arguably* diminish the absolute loyalty management may demand of such employees in labor matters.[8]

The Supreme Court has limited the *Garmon* doctrine and recognized countervailing state interests in a number of areas: maintenance of public safety and order,[9] restraint of violent public disorder,[10] obstruction of public highways,[11] and public access to the employer's place of business.[12] The Court has declined to block state court actions under state civil rights laws,[13] for defamation of character,[14] and for intentional infliction of emotional distress,[15] but it has barred certain state actions for interference with contract.[16]

Even a cursory examination of these decisions reveals that the outcome is not simply a function of the cause of action asserted.[17] Among the factors weighed in resolving the preemption issue are:

> (1) Whether there is a direct conflict between federal labor policy and the state law.[18]

---

[6]29 U.S.C. §§157, 158 (1976). For common carriers, similar provisions of the Railway Labor Act are applicable instead.

[7]Section 7 guarantees employees the right "to form, join, or assist labor organizations * * * and to engage in other concerted activities for the purpose of collective bargaining or other mutual aid or protection * * * ." 29 U.S.C. §157 (1976). However, in *Hentzel v. Singer Co.*, 138 Cal. App.3d 290, 188 Cal. Rptr. 159 (1982), the court found no arguable federal interest because the employee's discharge was allegedly for an individual grievance.

[8]The Taft-Hartley Act, which amended the NLRA, expressly excluded supervisory and confidential employees from protection against reprisals or discharge for union activity, 29 U.S.C. §§152(3), 152(11), 164(a) (1976), and the congressional intent was to provide the employer with absolute power over such employees—at least with respect to labor matters—to ensure their loyalty to management. See *Parker-Robb Chevrolet, Inc.*, 262 NLRB 402, 110 LRRM 1289 (1982).

[9]*Allen-Bradley Local 1111 v. Wisconsin Employment Relations Bd.*, 315 U.S. 740, 749 (1942).

[10]*Automobile Workers v. Russell*, 356 U.S. 634 (1958); *Construction Workers v. Laburnum Constr. Corp.*, 347 U.S. 656 (1954).

[11]*Youngdahl v. Rainfair, Inc.*, 355 U.S. 131 (1957).

[12]*Allen-Bradley Local 1111 v. Wisconsin Employment Relations Bd.*, 315 U.S. 740 (1942).

[13]*Colorado Anti-Discrimination Comm'n v. Continental Airlines*, 372 U.S. 714 (1963) (Railway Labor Act).

[14]*Linn v. Plant Guard Workers*, 383 U.S. 53 (1966).

[15]*Farmer v. Carpenters*, 430 U.S. 290 (1977). But see *Spielmann v. Anchor Motor Freight, Inc.*, 551 F. Supp. 817 (S.D.N.Y. 1982) (distinguishing *Farmer* where the outrageous conduct was the arguably prohibited conduct under the NLRA).

[16]*Operating Eng'rs Local 926 v. Jones*, 460 U.S. 669 (1983).

[17]*Street, Elec. Ry. & Motor Coach Employees v. Lockridge*, 403 U.S. 274, 292 (1971).

[18]In *Linn v. Plant Guard Workers*, 383 U.S. 53 (1966), the Court relied upon NLRB hostility to knowing falsehoods in organizing campaigns; concluding that state law and federal policy did not differ, the Court pronounced the matter one of "peripheral concern" to federal labor policy. In *Farmer v. Carpenters*, 430 U.S. 290, 303 n. 11 (1977), the Court noted that the NLRB had already found an unfair labor practice in the conduct complained of.

(2) Whether there is a substantial state interest of general application.[19]
(3) The similarity or difference between the focus or gist of the state law and federal labor law.[20]
(4) The possibility or difficulty of harmonizing state law with federal policy.[21]
(5) The sufficiency of federal labor law remedies to redress individual grievances fully.[22]

Analysis of the problem of preemption thus requires a specification of the particular federal policy or purpose affected, as well as consideration of the impact, if any, of the state law on that policy in the particular factual context of the case. If the state policy does not directly conflict with the federal policy, if it addressses general state concerns independent of the federal policy, and if it secures personal rights, preemption may not apply.

Defamation

Linn v. Plant Guard Workers[23] dictates partial preemption of a defamation action arising out of a labor dispute.[24] Reasoning that federal labor policy does not condone knowing falsehoods and finding "deeply rooted" local concerns, the Supreme Court created a qualified privilege to defame in a federal labor dispute. To maintain a state law action for defamation, the plaintiff must establish that the statements relied upon were knowingly false or were made in reckless disregard of their truth or falsity.[25]

Retaliatory Discharge

Preemption problems may be present in retaliatory discharge actions. Where a covered employee alleges discharge for union activity, the action is within the exclusive jurisdiction of the NLRB and will surely be preempted. Where other public policies are invoked, the conflict with federal labor policy may be less obvious. The presence of deeply rooted local concerns is likely to be found when state protection of public policy is the gist of the action. Still, the possibility

---

[19]Few state interests grounded in tort or statutory law appear to be "insubstantial"; it appears that laws of general application are most subject to question where conduct condoned by the NLRA is involved.

[20]If the state court could adjudicate the issues without considering the underlying Section 8 violation, this is a factor militating against preemption, *Linn v. Plant Guard Workers*, 383 U.S. 53, 59 (1966); *Farmer v. Carpenters*, 430 U.S. 290, 304 (1977).

[21]In *Linn v. Plant Guard Workers*, 383 U.S. 53, 65 (1966), the Court restricted the state defamation remedy by requiring that the statements relied upon be made knowingly or in reckless disregard of the truth, and authorized the use of a remitter to protect unions.

[22]*Farmer v. Carpenters*, 430 U.S. 290, 304 (1977); *Linn v. Plant Guard Workers*, 383 U.S. 53, 63 (1966). The factor may be a two-edged sword, however, if the court finds that federal labor policy requires a limited remedy.

[23]383 U.S. 53 (1966).

[24]The definition of "labor dispute" may be found at 29 U.S.C. §152(9) (1976), and is explained in this context in *Tosti v. Ayik*, 386 Mass. 721, 437 N.E.2d 1062 (1982).

[25]This standard is drawn from the First Amendment privilege to defame public officials established in *New York Times Co. v. Sullivan*, 376 U.S. 254 (1964).

of a conflict, in a given situation, between the state's policy and federal labor policy cannot be excluded.[26]

Interference With Contract

Preemption concerns may preclude most suits against a union for interference with contract. Union coercion or influence of employer discharge decisions may be "arguably protected or prohibited" by the Act, whether the employee is a rank-and-file worker protected by Section 7 of the statute or an unprotected "supervisor." *Iron Workers v. Perko*[27] found a suit for interference with contract to be barred because the NLRA prohibits a union from interfering with the right of employees to organize and collectively bargain, or to decline to do so,[28] and from causing an employer to discriminate on that basis.[29] As to supervisors, the Supreme Court found preemption based on the possibility of prohibited coercion of employees by discharge of a supervisor,[30] or on the prohibition of union coercion of an employer in the selection of its collective bargaining agents.[31]

In *Operating Engineers, Local 926 v. Jones*[32] an employee had sued the union for procuring his discharge because he had once worked for a non-union employer. The Supreme Court, aided by the employee's allegations in a charge he had filed with the NLRB's regional director,[33] concluded that since the union's action was arguably protected or prohibited, the action for interference with contract was preempted.[34] *Jones* demonstrates that *Perko* is still viable despite the erosion of the preemption doctrine in recent years. It decided, without expressly addressing the issue, that a union's procurement of discharge involved no "interest deeply rooted in local feeling and responsibility" that would defeat the preemption defense.

Jones left open the possibility that suits would not be preempted if the supervisory employee did not have collective bargaining responsibilities and if the greater risk of a coercive impact on rank-and-file employees that results from the unique structure of the construction industry was absent. Nevertheless, the Court took a broad view of the scope of preemption.

The initial finding by the regional director that the union had engaged in no unlawful conduct under the Act did not satisfy the

---

[26]*Peabody Galion v. Dollar*, 666 F.2d 1309 (10th Cir. 1981); *Vaughn v. Pacific N.W. Bell Tel. Co.*, 289 Ore. 73, 611 P.2d 281 (1980).
[27]373 U.S. 701 (1963).
[28]29 U.S.C. §158(b)(1)(A) (1976).
[29]29 U.S.C. §§158(b)(2), 158(a)(3) (1976).
[30]29 U.S.C. §158(a)(3) (1976).
[31]29 U.S.C. §158(b)(1)(B) (1976). Such a violation could occur only in an organized shop or in a shop likely to be organized.
[32]460 U.S. 669 (1983).
[33]The employee had claimed in the charge that his discharge violated §§8(b)(1)(A) and 8(b)(1)(B).
[34]The court noted that the issue did not arise under Georgia's right-to-work law, GA. CODE §34-6-24 (1982). Given the express authorization of such statutes in the NLRA, 29 U.S.C. §164 (b) (1976), actions within the scope of the congressional authorization would not be preempted.

preemption doctrine's concern with federal supremacy. The Court rejected the argument that, since a suit could be based on noncoercive union interference, the state law action should be allowed as outside the sphere of federal concern; the fact that the union's responsibility for the discharge had to be proved was sufficient to bar the claim of interference with contract.

The rationale of *Jones* and *Perko* does not necessarily mean that every action against a union for interference with employment is preempted. Actions under a state right-to-work statute, if within the scope of federal authorization,[35] will still be viable. Suits under the common law tort theories, however, will obviously be difficult to maintain, even on behalf of supervisors, whenever the employer and union are in a collective bargaining relationship or when the union is attempting to organize the employer's work place, even if the common law justification of action in pursuit of legitimate labor objectives[36] is absent.

Breach of Contract

Even a common law breach of contract action in an unorganized shop is subject to preemption. In *Morris v. Chem-Lawn Corp.*,[37] the court found preemption applied because the employee's rebuttal to the employer's claim of just cause for discharge consisted of proof that the real reason for his discharge was union activity.

Other Federal Statutory Actions

If more than one federal statute is involved, the preemption problem is more difficult to resolve. The court may be called on to harmonize policies of such statutes as the civil rights laws,[38] the antitrust laws,[39] the Fair Labor Standards Act,[40] and the Equal Employment Opportunity Act[41] with one another or with the NLRA.

Railway Labor Act Preemption

Preemption under the Railway Labor Act[42] (RLA) appears to be broader in scope than under the NLRA. In the absence of detailed

---

[35]29 U.S.C. §164(b) (1976).

[36]*Pugh v. See's Candies, Inc.*, 116 Cal. App.3d 311, 171 Cal. Rptr. 917 (1981).

[37]541 F. Supp. 479, 481 (E.D. Mich. 1982) (employment contract claim based promise that "if * * * I carried out my duties, I could expect to make Chem-Lawn my career").

[38]42 U.S.C. §1981 *et seq.* (1976). See, e.g., *Morris v. Chem-Lawn Corp.*, 541 F. Supp. 479 (E.D. Mich. 1982) (NLRA preemption applied), and *Iowa Beef Processors, Inc. v. Gorman*, 476 F. Supp. 1382 (N.D. Iowa 1979) (NLRA preemption applied).

[39]15 U.S.C. §1 *et seq.* (1982), See e.g., *Mackey v. National Football League*, 543 F.2nd 606, 615 (8th Cir. 1976)(no preemption). But see *Daley v. St. Agnes Hosp.*, 490 F. Supp. 1309, 1317–1318 (E.D. Pa. 1980) (alleged racially discriminatory blacklist could not be asserted under antitrust law because Title VII procedures must be followed).

[40]*Barrentine v. Arkansas-Best Freight Sys.*, 450 U.S. 728 (1981).

[41]42 U.S.C. §2000e(1) *et seq.* (1976). See e.g., *Alexander v. Gardner-Denver Co.*, 415 U.S. 36 (1974) (Title VII remedies independent of NLRA) and *Johnson v. Railway Express Agency, Inc.*, 421 U.S. 454 (1975) (older civil rights statute, 42 U.S.C. 1981, independent of Title VII).

[42]45 U.S.C. §151 *et seq.* (1976). The RLA covers railroad and air carrier employees.

authority from the U.S. Supreme Court, lower courts have found broader preemption because of the different structure of the RLA. The NLRA spells out "unfair labor practices" that are to be adjudicated in NLRB proceedings and leaves resolution of disputes over collective bargaining agreements to agreed-upon arbitration proceedings or court suits.[43] The RLA, by contrast, establishes a system of compulsory arbitration of employee grievances and collective bargaining disputes with the employer mandated by statute, rather than by agreement between the employer and bargaining representative.[44]

Breach of the Collective Bargaining Agreement

In NLRA cases the employee's claim that his discharge violated a collective bargaining agreement that provides for an exclusive arbitration remedy may be heard in court only if the union's handling of, or failure to pursue, the grievance is a breach of its duty of fair representation. In the absence of this factor, the employer may rely on the employee's failure to exhaust contractual remedies as a sufficient defense to the suit. The union's breach of its duty of fair representation creates an exception, because as a matter of policy and legislative intent the employer is not permitted to "hide behind" wrongful union conduct.[45]

Under the RLA the employee may also bring a court suit if the union's failure to process his grievance was a breach of the duty of fair representation, at least where the union and employer acted in concert. In the RLA case, however, the result is reached more as a matter of strict statutory construction. The statutory adjustment board has jurisdiction only over cases where the employee or union has a dispute with the employer—not where the employee has a dispute with the union or with the union and employer together.[46]

Other Employee Grievances

The RLA requires submission of disputes "growing out of grievances or out of the interpretation of application" of collective bargaining agreements to the appropriate adjustment board after

---

[43]29 U.S.C. §158 (1976) (unfair labor practices); 29 U.S.C. §185a (1976) (suits to enforce bargaining agreements).
[44]45 U.S.C. §153 (1976).
[45]*Vaca v. Sipes*, 386 U.S. 171 (1967). *Vaca* recognizes other exceptions where the employer repudiates arbitration and where the collective bargaining agreement does not make arbitration between employer and union the exclusive remedy. *Vaca* also holds that the availability of collective bargaining remedies does not operate to preempt state law tort claims as does the availability of statutory remedies under the provisions of §8 of the NLRA.
[46]*Glover v. St. Louis-San Francisco Ry.*, 393 U.S. 324 (1969); *Riddle v. Trans World Airlines*, 512 F. Supp. 75 (W.D. Mo. 1981); 45 U.S.C. §153 First (1976). *Glover* also relied upon the belief that the concerted employer-union activity made resort to a grievance process controlled by the defendants futile. There is no exception in RLA cases where the collective bargaining agreement does not provide for exclusivity of remedy, since arbitration before an adjustment board is mandated by the statute.

completion of any contractual grievance procedures.[47] Thus, the exclusive jurisdiction of the adjustment board is significantly different from that of the NLRB, which hears unfair labor practice charges. In many cases, NLRB policy may be largely unaffected by the availability of a state cause of action for employee termination. The RLA, by contrast, purports to cover all employee grievances.

In *Colorado Anti-Discrimination Commission v. Continental Air Lines*,[48] the Supreme Court allowed the application of state laws prohibiting racial discrimination in hiring to a carrier covered by the RLA. The Court reasoned that the RLA does not address the issue of discrimination in hiring. But in *Andrews v. Louisville & Nashville Railroad*,[49] the Court rejected the claim of a discharged employee that he could pursue a court action because he had accepted the severance of the employment relationship and sought damages for breach of contract. The decision was based on the necessity of reliance by the employee on the collective bargaining agreement. In *Andrews*, an employee who was not allowed to return to work after an auto accident claimed this was a "wrongful discharge." The decision, predating all but one of the retaliatory discharge cases that have been decided in the state courts, concluded that the claim was by definition contractually based:

> "[T]he very concept of 'wrongful discharge' implies some sort of statutory or contractual standard that modifies the traditional common law rule that a contract of employment is terminable by either party at will. Here it is conceded that the source of the petitioner's right not to be discharged, and therefore to treat an alleged discharge as a 'wrongful' one that entitles him to damages, is the collective bargaining agreement between the employer and the union."[50]

Thus *Andrews* provides little direct assistance in resolving preemption problems where the employee claims defamation, retaliatory discharge, fraud, or intentional infliction of mental distress. The Supreme Court's reliance on NLRB decisions in its opinion may indicate that such decisions will be followed in spirit; but because of the different remedial schemes the lower courts have been more willing to find preemption with RLA employers than with NLRA employers.[51]

In addition to the Supreme Court's denial of preemption for dis-

---

[47]45 U.S.C. §153 First (1976).

[48]372 U.S. 714 (1963). In light of the policy of federal antidiscrimination laws to encourage state resolution of such claims, the rationale of the case should not limit the result where other types of employment discrimination are involved. The Equal Employment Opportunity Act, 42 U.S.C. §2000e (1) *et seq.* (1972) had not yet been adopted when *Continental Air Lines* was decided.

[49]406 U.S. 320 (1972). Accord: *Bailey v. American Sugar Refinery*, 342 So.2nd 1268 (La. Ct. App. 1977) (similar argument rejected as to employee rights under NLRA collective bargaining agreement).

[50]406 U.S. at 324. Accord: *Waller v. Seaboard Coast Line R.R.*, 165 Ga. App. 490, 301 S.E.2d 654 (1983).

[51]Noting the differences between the NLRA and RLA, the court in *Jackson v. Consolidated Rail Corp.*, 717 F.2nd 1045 (7th Cir. 1983), ruled that only federal statutory claims and outrageous conduct unrelated to the collective bargaining relationship could escape RLA preemption.

crimination cases, federal statutory causes of action are generally found to be outside exclusive adjustment board jurisdiction. In *Railroad Trainmen v. Central of Georgia Railway*[52] a claim of discharge to coerce selection of a bargaining agent was held to be outside the adjustment board's exclusive jurisdiction; other cases have held that discharge for union activity in violation of the RLA is an independent statutory claim which is not preempted and may be pursued in court.[53] *Hendley v. Central of Georgia Railway*[54] held that a federal statutory claim arising out of a retaliatory discharge for providing information to another employee bringing a claim under the Federal Employer's Liability Act[55] was not preempted. Where the Interstate Commerce Commission has incorporated a negotiated labor protection agreement in an order approving a railroad merger, an employee's direct action to enforce the ICC order is not preempted.[56]

The RLA has been held to preempt state actions arising out of discipline or discharge asserting claims of defamation,[57] fraud,[58] false imprisonment,[59] and intentional infliction of mental distress.[60] The cases on retaliatory discharge are split.[61] These cases all attempt to follow the *Andrews* decision but reflect several different readings of that decision. Their divergent results could as easily apply to other state law causes of action.

Trombetta v. Detroit, Toledo & Ironton Railroad,[62] was a retaliatory discharge case alleging discharge for refusal to falsify pollution control reports to a state agency. The court held that RLA preemption applies only where the plaintiff is an employee covered by a collective bargaining agreement asserting a violation of the agreement. Since the employee was not covered by a bargaining agreement and relied on public policy rather than contract grounds, preemption did not apply.

---

[52]305 F.2d 605 (5th Cir. 1962).

[53]*Brady v. Trans World Airlines*, 401 F.2d 87 (3d Cir. 1968); *Machinists v. Eastern Airlines*, 320 F.2d 451 (5th Cir. 1963) (discipline and discharge cases only); *Conrad v. Delta Air Lines*, 494 F.2d 914 (7th Cir. 1974); *Burke v. Compania Mexicana De Aviacion*, 433 F.2d 1031 (9th Cir. 1970); *Kent v. Fugere*, 438 F. Supp. 560 (D. Conn. 1977); *Machinists v. Altair Airlines*, 481 F. Supp. 1359 (E.D. Pa. 1979); *Griffin v. Piedmont Aviation, Inc.*, 384 F. Supp. 1070 (N.D. Ga. 1974); *Lum v. China Airlines*, 413 F. Supp. 613 (D. Hawaii 1976).

[54]609 F.2d 1146 (5th Cir. 1980).

[55]45 U.S.C. §60 (1976) (criminal prohibition).

[56]*Nemitz v. Norfolk & W.R.R.*, 436 F.2d 841 (6th Cir. 1971), *aff'd on other grounds*, 404 U.S. 37 (1971).

[57]*Majors v. U.S. Air, Inc.*, 525 F. Supp. 853 (D.Md. 1981); *Carson v. Southern Ry.*, 494 F. Supp. 1104 (D.S.C. 1979); *Louisville & Nashville R.R. v. Marshall*, 586 S.W.2d 274 (Ky. App. 1979). But see *Franco v. Long Island R.R.*, 94 A.D.2d 756, 462 N.Y.S. 2d 697 (1983) (allowing suit against co-employees to stand after claim against employer dismissed).

[58]*Magnuson v. Burlington Inc.*, 576 F.2d 1367 (9th Cir. 1978).

[59]*Majors v. U.S. Air, Inc.*, 525 F. Supp. 853 (D.Md. 1981).

[60]*Choate v. Louisville & Nashville R.R.*, 715 F.2d 369 (7th Cir. 1983); *Beers v. Southern Pac. Transp. Co.*, 703 F.2d 425 (9th Cir. 1983); *Magnuson v. Burlington N., Inc.*, 576 F.2d 1367 (9th Cir. 1978).

[61]*Jackson v. Consolidated Rail Corp.*, 717 F.2d 1045 (7th Cir. 1983) (retaliatory discharge preempted). Contra: *Trombetta v. Detroit, Toledo & Ironton R.R.*, 81 Mich. App. 489, 265 N.W.2d 385 (1978) (retaliatory discharge not preempted); *Wiley v. Missouri Pac. R.R.*, 430 So.2d 1016 (La. App. 1982) (statutory retaliatory discharge not preempted).

[62]81 Mich. App. 489, 265 N.W.2d 385 (1978).

In *Magnuson v. Burlington Northern, Inc.*,[63] the court construed *Andrews* to apply to any action arising out of or seeking damages flowing from a discharge from employment. If the gravamen of the suit is a wrongful discharge, the court concluded that it was preempted.

Jackson v. Consolidated Rail Corp.[64] focused on the necessity of construing the collective bargaining agreement as the crucial question. In that case, since the employer's defense was that the discharge was pursuant to the terms of the agreement, the court concluded that the claim was preempted.[65]

Each of these approaches finds support in the *Andrews* opinion. The lower court RLA cases in this area, however, do little to follow the principle enunciated in the NLRA cases that state and federal interests must be balanced in an attempt to determine whether Congress intended to preclude state law remedies. Judge Posner's dissent in *Jackson*[66] suggested a more flexible approach, in which interpretation of the collective bargaining agreement would be done for the court by the adjustment board under RLA procedures, but the lawsuit would otherwise continue in court.[67]

Preemption by the Employee Retirement Income Security Act

The Employee Retirement Income Security Act (ERISA)[68] contains an express remedy for employees discharged for exercising rights under ERISA or testifying in ERISA proceedings, or to prevent them from obtaining rights under employee benefit plans.[69] Employees must exhaust their administrative remedies with the plan trustee before bringing suit under this statute.[70] Unlike the collective bargaining statutes, ERISA contains an express congressional declaration that it supersedes all state (but not federal) law that relates to employee benefit plans, unless the state law regulates insurance, banking, or securities.[71]

---

[63]576 F.2d 1367 (9th Cir. 1978). Accord: *Majors v. U.S. Air, Inc.*, 525 F. Supp. 853 (D. Md. 1981).

[64]717 F.2d 1045 (7th Cir. 1983).

[65]Accord: *De La Rosa Sanchez v. Eastern Airlines*, 574 F.2d 29 (1st. Cir. 1978); *Carson v. Southern Ry.*, 494 F. Supp. 1104 (D.S.C. 1979).

[66]*Jackson v. Consolidated Rail Corp.*, 717 F.2d 1045, 1057 (7th Cir. 1983) (dissenting opinion).

[67]This concept of "partial preemption" is a procedural variation on *Linn v. Plant Guard Workers*, 383 U.S. 53 (1966) (preemption used to create a qualified privilege in defamation cases to protect NLRA policy). *Bangor & Aroostook R.R. v. Locomotive Firemen*, 442 F.2d 812, 818 (1971), which permitted the lower court to refer a large volume of individual claims to the adjustment board for resolution, suggests that the coordinated approach between court and board that Judge Posner proposed could be followed in RLA cases. On the other hand, existing case law does suggest a clear line between judicial and adjustment board jurisdiction, *Hendley v. Central of Ga. Ry.*, 609 F.2d 1146, 1153 n.5 (5th Cir. 1980) (adjustment board resolution did not limit judicial remedy under statute); *Essary v. Chicago & N.W. Transp. Co.*, 618 F.2d 13 (7th Cir. 1980) (adjustment board resolution precluded claim for violation of duty of fair representation).

[68]29 U.S.C. §1001 *et seq.* (1975).

[69]29 U.S.C. §1140 (1975); *Dependahl v. Falstaff Brewing Co.*, 653 F.2d 1208 (8th Cir. 1981).

[70]*Kross v. Western Elec. Co.*, 701 F.2d 1238 (7th Cir. 1983).

[71]29 U.S.C. §1144 (1975).

In *Shaw v. Delta Air Lines*,[72] the U.S. Supreme Court held that state antidiscrimination laws that provide employee protection greater than federal equal opportunity laws are to that extent preempted by ERISA. Under *Shaw*, an employee discharged to save on insurance or pension costs might be precluded from proceeding on a claim of handicap discrimination or interference with contract where the underlying motive was to save on costs of employee benefits covered by ERISA. This was what happened, in fact, to the interference with contract claim in *Dependahl v. Falstaff Brewing Co.*[73]

Several cases have applied ERISA preemption to other state wrongful discharge claims. In *Gordon v. Matthew Bender & Co.*,[74] the court held that a state law claim that an employer acted in bad faith in discharging an employee 10 months before he fulfilled the 8-year vesting requirement of a pension plan was preempted. In *Witkowski v. St. Anne's Hospital*,[75] the court held that a retaliatory discharge action under state law based on the public policy embodied in ERISA was preempted. But in *Kelly v. IBM*[76] the court held that a claim for intentional infliction of mental distress was not preempted.

Preemption by State Workers' Compensation Exclusivity Provisions

At the heart of the workers' compensation scheme is the employee's statutory surrender of the right to sue the employer for industrial injury. Thus, state statutes creating the right to compensation contain strict "exclusivity" provisions that bar court suits for any bodily injury arising out of, and in the course of, the employment.[77] Language varies, but the statutes of different states tend toward uniformity.

Because of the Supremacy Clause, state workers' compensation laws cannot preempt actions based on federal law.[78] They are effective only to bar actions for bodily injury sustained on the job, but do so even if the employer is sued for fraud in concealing risks of injury[79] or for exposing the employee to a risk of injury in violation of the

---

[72] 463 U.S. 85 (1983).

[73] 653 F.2d 1208 (8th Cir. 1981).

[74] 562 F. Supp. 1286 (N.D. Ill. 1983). The court noted that *Moore v. Home Ins. Co.*, 601 F. 2d 1072 (9th Cir. 1979), and *Slavodnick v. Korvette's Inc.*, 488 F. Supp. 822 (E.D.N.Y. 1980), did not consider the preemption issue. See also *Johnson v. Trans World Airlines*, 149 Cal. App.3d 518, 196 Cal. Rptr. 896 (1983); *Shaw v. Delta Air Lines*, 463 U.S. 85 (1983); *Alessi v. Raybestos-Manhattan, Inc.*, 451 U.S. 504 (1981).

[75] 113 Ill. App.3d 745, 447 N.E.2d 1016 (1983). Accord: *Kelly v. IBM*, 573 F. Supp. 366 (E.D. Pa. 1983).

[76] 573 F. Supp. 366 (E.D. Pa. 1983).

[77] Note, *Exceptions to the Exclusive Remedy Requirements of Workers' Compensation Statutes*, 96 HARV. L. REV. 1641 (1983). See *Silkwood v. Kerr McGee Corp.*, 667 F.2d 908 (10th Cir. 1981).

[78] *Hutchings v. Erie City & County Library Bd.*, 516 F. Supp. 1265 (W.D. Pa. 1981).

[79] E.g., *Buttner v. American Bell Tel. Co.*, 41 Cal. App.2d 581, 107 P.2d 439 (1940). See 2A. A. Larsen, WORKMEN'S COMPENSATION LAW §68.32(a) at pp. 13–45 to 13–48.

employment contract.[80] Generally, however, actions for breach of contract[81] and retaliatory discharge[82] are not barred. Actions for non-physical injury based on torts such as invasion of privacy, fraud, and defamation are not barred because "these torts would not come within the basic coverage formula * * * when no workmen's compensation claim is possible."[83] If an otherwise viable action includes a claim for damages within the exclusivity bar, the usual course is to excise the preempted portion of the action.[84]

Termination: "In the Course of" Employment?

In *Hernandez v. Home Education Livelihood Program, Inc.*,[85] the employee claimed that discharge in an after-hours telephone call led to a mental breakdown, and the court held that the discharge was not "in the course of" employment because it was away from the work place. *Gates v. Trans Video Corp.*,[86] on the other hand, held that an altercation at the work place after the employment had been terminated, when the employee was dropping off keys and picking up personal items, was covered by the exclusivity statute. In *Jamison v. Storer Broadcasting Co.*,[87] the statute did not bar a claim that a discharge had triggered the employee's subsequent suicide, because the injury and the emotional impact took place after the employment was over.

Investigative Abuses

Insurance companies conducting investigations of claims for workers' compensation share the employer's protection under the exclusivity statute,[88] and are immune to suit for delay in payment where statutory penalties exist.[89] A purposefully deceitful investigation[90] or fraud practiced against the employee in the investigation,[91] however, is not protected.

---

[80]*O'Keefe v. Associated Grocers*, 120 N.H. 834, 424 A.2d 199 (1980) (union collective bargaining agreement); *Brinkman v. Buffalo Bills Football Club*, 433 F. Supp. 699 (W.D.N.Y. 1977) (standard player contract).

[81]*Milton v. County of Oakland*, 50 Mich. App. 279, 213 N.W.2d 250 (1973) (suit for additional compensation); *Hernandez v. Home Educ. Livelihood Program, Inc.*, 98 N.M. 125, 645 P.2d 1381 (1982).

[82]*Kelsay v. Motorola, Inc.*, 74 Ill.2d 172, 384 N.E.2d 353 (1978). See *Raden v. Azusa*, 97 Cal. App.3d 336, 158 Cal. Rptr. 689 (1979), and *Meyer v. Byron Jackson, Inc.*, 120 Cal. App.3d 59, 174 Cal. Rptr. 428 (1981).

[83]Larsen, *supra* note 79, §68.30 at pp. 13–40. See Annot., 46 A.L.R.3d 1279 (1972).

[84]E.g., *Stimson v. Michigan Bell Tel. Co.*, 77 Mich. App. 361, 258 N.W.2d 227 (1977); *Milton v. County of Oakland*, 50 Mich. App. 279, 213 N.W.2d 250 (1973). But see *Braman v. Walthall*, 215 Ark. 582, 225 S.W.2d 342 (1949).

[85]98 N.M. 125, 645 P.2d 1381 (Ct. App. 1982).

[86]93 Cal. App.3d 196, 155 Cal. Rptr. 486 (1979).

[87]511 F. Supp. 1286 (E.D. Mich. 1981).

[88]*Unruh v. Truck Ins. Exch.*, 7 Cal.3d 616, 498 P.2d 1063, 102 Cal. Rptr. 815 (1972).

[89]Larsen, *supra* note 79, §68.34(c) at pp. 13–70 to 13–76.

[90]*Unruh v. Truck Ins. Exch.*, 7 Cal.3d 616, 498 P.2d 1063, 102 Cal. Rptr. 815 (1972).

[91]Larsen, *supra* note 79, §68.32 at pp. 13–45 to 13–48.

Mental Distress Damages in Discrimination Cases

A number of Michigan decisions have debated the recoverability of mental or emotional distress damages in cases under that state's antidiscrimination law. In *Stimson v. Michigan Bell Telephone Co.*,[92] the court barred a claim for such damages since they could be recovered in a workers' compensation proceeding. However, in *Freeman v. Kelvinator, Inc.*,[93] the court resolved the issue as a matter of statutory construction, concluding:

> "[D]efendent would pit one great remedial statute against another and both against the plaintiffs. There is no indication whatever that the discrimination law was to have an exception for injuries arguably redressed by the [workers' compensation statute] nor is there any indication that the [workers' compensation statute] was impliedly expanded when the Civil Rights Act was passed.
> * * *
> "The discrimination injury is unique. Its source is deliberate or inadvertent disregard by the employer of the fundamental rights of his employees."[94]

The decisions since *Freeman* have followed it rather than *Stimson*,[95] and the same result has prevailed with respect to federal employees.[96]

Intentional Infliction of Mental Distress

The action for mental distress presents special problems because it is often accompanied by physical injury. In *Maggio v. St. Francis Medical Center, Inc.*,[97] the court found that the exclusivity statute did not apply because the action by its nature met the intentional tort exception.[98] In *Cohen v. Lion Products Co.*,[99] the court appeared to hold that an action for mental distress imposed even without a threat of physical harm was barred. The bar has been held applicable to cases where the emotional distress was accompanied by physical injury and disability,[100] but not where the physical injury was insignificant and the injury intentional.[101]

---

[92]77 Mich. App. 361, 258 N.W.2d 227 (1977). Accord: *Schroeder v. Dayton-Hudson Corp.*, 456 F. Supp. 652 (E.D. Mich. 1978).
[93]469 F. Supp. 999 (E.D. Mich. 1979).
[94]*Id.* at 1000.
[95]*Moll v. Parkside Livonia Credit Union*, 525 F. Supp. 786 (E.D. Mich. 1981); *Pacheco v. Clifton*, 109 Mich. App. 563, 311 N.W.2d 801 (1981).
[96]*Sullivan v. United States*, 428 F. Supp. 79 (E.D. Wis. 1977).
[97]391 So.2d 948 (La. Ct. App. 1980) (action based on discharge for reporting supervisor's alleged illegal actions to higherups). But see *Magliulo v. Superior Court*, 47 Cal. App.3d 760, 121 Cal. Rptr. 621 (1975) (citing limited statutory exception for willful physical act of aggression).
[98]The exception, which requires an intentional tort plus specific intent to inflict injury, is necessary to prevent the exclusivity statute from becoming a license to attack employees. See *Raden v. Azusa*, 97 Cal. App.3d 336, 158 Cal. Rptr. 689 (1979).
[99]177 F. Supp. 486 (D. Mass. 1959).
[100]*Ankeny v. Lockheed Missiles & Space Co.*, 88 Cal. App.3d 531, 151 Cal. Rptr. 828 (1979); *Raden v. Azusa*, 97 Cal. App.3d 336, 158 Cal. Rptr. 689 (1979); *Magliulo v. Superior Court*, 47 Cal. App.3d 760, 121 Cal. Rptr. 621 (1975).
[101]*McGee v. McNally*, 119 Cal. App.3d 891, 174 Cal. Rptr. 253 (1981); *Renteria v. County of Orange*, 82 Cal. App.3d 833, 147 Cal. Rptr. 447 (1978); *Ritter v. Allied Chem. Corp.*, 295 F. Supp. 1360 (D.S.C. 1968).

Exhaustion of Alternative Remedies

Collective Bargaining Grievance Procedures

Where there is an exclusive bargaining agent and a collective bargaining agreement is in effect between employees and employer, the individual employee's right to bring an action for breach of contract based on a discharge is severely restricted by the NLRA. Some recent cases suggest that a retaliatory discharge action may be unavailable as a matter of *state* law where a collective bargaining agreement is in effect. In each instance, the requirement that alternative remedies be exhausted is crucial.

Limitation by Other State and Federal Statutes

We cannot present here an all-inclusive catalog of common law actions that cannot be maintained because of the availability of other remedies under state or federal law. If the reason for a tort or contract claim is premised upon some form of age, sexual, racial, or religious bias, for instance, then limitation of the common law remedy may result from state human rights/fair employment practices acts or Title VII.[102]

Enforcement of Employee Contract Rights in the Organized Shop

Collective bargaining agreements as a rule prohibit discharge without just cause. The NLRA expressly provides for the enforcement in court of bargaining agreements[103] and permits employee suits for discharge in violation of the agreement.[104] However, most collective bargaining agreements also provide for resolution of grievances by conciliation and arbitration, and enforcement of the employee's right is usually in the hands of the bargaining representative.

Federal policy favors grievance arbitration as the primary means of resolving collective bargaining disputes.[105] This policy can be effectuated only if the means chosen by the parties to settle their dif-

---

[102]*Wolk v. Saks Fifth Avenue, Inc.*, 728 F.2d 221 (3d Cir. 1984); *Strauss v. A.L. Randall Co.*, 144 Cal. App.3d 514, 194 Cal. Rptr. 520 (1983); *Shaffer v. National Can Corp.*, 565 F. Supp. 909 (E.D. Pa. 1983).

[103]29 U.S.C. §185a (1976) (§301 of the Labor-Management Relations Act). The statute permits suits in state or federal court by employees and their employer or union. *Smith v. Evening News Ass'n*, 371 U.S. 195 (1962). Since the statute has been held to authorize development of a federal contract law, *Textile Workers v. Lincoln Mills*, 353 U.S. 448 (1957), a limited sort of preemption applies, invalidating state law where it is in conflict with federal policy. The usual preemption problem does not arise, however, since the NLRB has no jurisdiction over suits for violation of collective bargaining contracts; the contract action and federal claim are, in effect, merged.

[104]*Hines v. Anchor Motor Freight, Inc.*, 424 U.S. 554 (1976).

[105]"Final adjustment by a method agreed upon by the parties is declared to be the desirable method for settlement of grievance disputes arising over the application or interpretation of an existing collective bargaining agreement." *Aluminum Workers v. Chromalloy Am. Corp.*, 489 F. Supp. 536, 539, n.1 (N.D. Miss. 1980).

ferences under a collective bargaining agreement is given full play.[106] Accordingly, actions for breach of a bargaining agreement providing for arbitration may be brought only if the arbitration remedy has been exhausted.[107] The effect of this approach is to make arbitration the exclusive remedy in most cases; a court suit will be available only where the arbitration remedy has truly failed.

The burden on an individual employee is doubled by reason of the authority and discretion of the bargaining representative. In order to pursue a remedy for discharge without just cause, the employee must prove that his union violated its duty of fair representation in processing or refusing to process his grievance. To meet this standard, the employee must show arbitrary, discriminatory, or bad faith behavior and exhaust any available remedies within the union to correct the action.[108]

Thus, while the employee covered by a collective bargaining agreement cannot be discharged without just cause, that issue is usually resolved not in court but in an arbitration proceeding.[109] Only abuse of the arbitration process, or misfeasance by the union representative, will bring the controversy into court.

Impact of the Collective Bargaining Agreement on Other Civil Actions

The availability of grievance arbitration under a collective bargaining agreement may affect remedies other than the breach of contract suit. Employees seeking to enforce rights created by federal statute generally need not submit their claims to grievance arbitration.[110] Under the Equal Employment Opportunity Act an arbitration decision will be given great weight, but is not conclusive.[111]

The availability of arbitration under a collective bargaining agreement pursuant to the NLRA does not, as a matter of federal law, preclude a state law retaliatory discharge action.[112] If the em-

---

[106]*Steelworkers v. American Mfg. Co.*, 363 U.S. 564, 566 (1960).

[107]*Republic Steel Corp. v. Maddox*, 379 U.S. 650 (1965) (exhaustion required unless parties did not intend arbitration as exclusive remedy).

[108]*Vaca v. Sipes*, 386 U.S. 171 (1967). Where reversal of the union's position could not reinstate the grievance, however, exhaustion of internal union remedies is excused. *Clayton v. Automobile Workers*, 451 U.S. 679 (1981).

[109]There are no reported decisions on the applicability of permanent employment or good faith and fair dealing concepts to union employees. Since these concepts are for the most part subsumed in the just cause standards applied by arbitrators, there will rarely be any occasion to consider their applicability and effect in this context.

[110]*Barrentine v. Arkansas-Best Freight Sys.*, 450 U.S. 728 (1981); *Alexander v. Gardner-Denver Co.*, 415 U.S. 36 (1974). But see *United Technologies Corp.*, 268 NLRB No. 83, 115 LRRM 1049 (1984) (adopting a rule of deference to and preference for arbitration of disputes that raise issues of both breach of collective bargaining agreement and statutory unfair labor practices).

[111]See *Alexander v. Gardner-Denver Co.*, 415 U.S. 36 (1974); *Kremer v. Chemical Constr. Corp.*, 456 U.S. 461 (1982).

[112]*Peabody Galion v. Dollar*, 666 F.2d 1309 (10th Cir. 1981); *Vaughn v. Pacific N.W. Bell Tel. Co.*, 289 Ore. 73, 611 P.2d 281 (1980). However, fraud claims closely connected to the provisions of the collective bargaining agreement have been deemed to be within the exclusive jurisdiction of the arbitrator. *Johnson v. Johns-Manville Sales Corp.*, 409 So.2d 261 (La. 1982).

ployee has collective bargaining grievance arbitration available, however, *state* law may nevertheless deny an action for retaliatory discharge. Some courts have held that actions for retaliatory discharge are simply unavailable, out of deference to the NLRA structure of labor relations, or because only at-will employees need protection from discharge in violation of public policy.[113]

Other courts hold that resort to arbitration is required in a contract action, but not otherwise. These courts reason that the arbitration remedy is a creature of, and thus only applicable to, the employment contract. They argue that grievance procedures may be insensitive to public policy concerns, and that protection of union employees is necessary to vindicate the public interest.[114]

The issue is inextricably intertwined with the question of the appropriate scope of the action for retaliatory discharge itself. Limiting the action to unorganized at-will employees is simply one way to restrict the scope of the action.

Another way to approach the issue is suggested by cases decided under the Texas statute prohibiting reprisal for bringing workers' compensation proceedings. Those cases bind the employee who seeks a remedy by way of grievance arbitration to the result.[115] Where the employee's grievance is not pursued by the union,[116] or where he chooses to litigate in court instead of grieving,[117] he is free to bring suit. The result is, in essence, a binding election by the employee that precludes "two bites at the apple."[118]

Remedies Within the Employer Organization

It would be surprising to find that an action was barred, limited, or affected by a party's failure to change the adversary's mind. In the employment context, however, efforts to limit access to courts

---

[113]*Payne v. Pennzoil Corp.*, 672 P.2d 1322 (Ariz. 1983); *Embry v. Pacific Stationery & Printing Co.*, 62 Ore. App. 113, 659 P.2d 436 (1983) (retaliatory discharge claim not based on statutory right of action barred). See *Johnson v. Hydraulic Research & Mfg. Co.*, 70 Cal. App.3d 675, 139 Cal. Rptr. 136 (1977) (defamation claim held precluded by arbitration remedy).

[114]*Peabody Galion v. Dollar*, 666 F.2d 1309 (10th Cir. 1981); *Trombetta v. Detroit, Toledo & Ironton R.R.*, 81 Mich. App. 489, 265 N.W.2d 385 (1978); *Midgett v. Sackett-Chicago, Inc.*, 118 Ill. App.3d 7, 454 N.E.2d 1092 (1983) *aff'd* 117 LRRM 2807 (Ill. 1984); *Wyatt v. Jewel Cos.*, 108 Ill. App.3d 840, 439 N.E.2d 1053 (1982). See *Vaughn v. Pacific N.W. Bell Tel. Co.*, 40 Ore. App. 427, 595 P.2d 829 (1979), *aff'd*, 289 Ore. 73, 611 P.2d 281 (1980) (claim based on express statutory right of action for retaliatory discharge not subject to bar or exhaustion requirements). *Burkhart v. Mobil Oil Corp.*, 143 Vt. 123, 463 A.2d 226 (1983).

[115]*Thompson v. Monsanto Co.*, 559 S.W.2d 873 (Tex. Civ. App. 1977) (employee lost in arbitration); *Spainhouer v. Western Elec. Co.*, 592 S.W.2d 662 (Tex. Civ. App. 1979) (union pursued grievance through four steps but declined to arbitrate); *Hughes Tool Co. v. Richards*, 610 S.W.2d 232 (Tex. Civ. App. 1980) (union pursued grievance but declined to arbitrate).

[116]*Carnation Co. v. Borner*, 610 S.W.2d 450 (Tex. 1980).

[117]*Hughes Tool Co. v. Richards*, 610 S.W.2d 232 (Tex. Civ. App. 1980) ("employee must *choose*, before a final settlement of the grievance, whether he wishes to file suit * * * or proceed under the employment contract").

[118]In addition to the differences in procedure, the grievance arbitration remedy, which is usually reinstatement (with or without back pay), differs from the usual money damage remedy in a retaliatory discharge suit. But see *Brockmeyer v. Dun & Bradstreet*, 113 Wis.2d 561, 335 N.W.2d 834 (1983) (reinstatement and back pay adopted as remedy for retaliatory discharge action).

through internal, employer-operated grievance systems are to be expected, and cannot be disregarded.

The employer referred to by the recent cases creating employee rights is a large institution, not an individual. Its decisions concerning an employee are generally made at one or two levels in the hierarchy above the employee. Beyond the second level, there is often no personal involvement in a discharge decision, and perhaps not even an awareness of it.

Unionized employees customarily have the benefit of formal grievance proceedings through which discharge decisions may be reviewed. In an effort to provide nonunion employees a comparable corporate benefit—or to ward off union organization—many employers have adopted internal "due process" review procedures. As is noted elsewhere, courts have begun to enforce the substantive restrictions on discharge announced by an employer.

Other institutions that have internal review procedures have been deemed entitled to judicial deference. When a doctor is removed from a medical staff position, the court will require that the specified procedures of the hospital's medical staff bylaws be followed, but will not question the substantive result. Unions that discipline their members likewise must follow their own rules, but having done so will be upheld. Government agencies that fire career employees must provide due process, but are free to exercise independent judgment in reaching their conclusion.

It is logical that the large private employer that has set up a process for ensuring that its discharge decisions are fair would ask the court to support, not undermine, its grievance procedure. In the ordinary course of business, higher-level managers are frequently called upon to review decisions of their subordinates in other contexts. Assuming the process is fair, it should correct any erroneous or wrongful decision; the employee's discharge and damages could be viewed as the result of his failure to request, or to prevail in, an internal review.

However reasonable this position may seem, there is good reason to reject it as either a bar to suit or an exhaustion requirement. It is not possible to ensure that the decision-maker will not be influenced by those who participated in the initial action; there is, at least, a natural deference to the decision reached by the ordinary chain of command. The very announcement of the decision may destroy the employee's working relationships and make continued employment an unacceptable option. Such procedures have not been held enforceable by injunctive decree, so the employer may remain free to ignore them in sensitive or hard cases and litigate in court instead. The employer is in control of the process and may use that control to obtain strategic advantages in anticipated litigation (obtaining discovery, forcing admissions, framing issues). Finally, the employer becomes a judge in its own cause; it could not be expected, for instance, to award punitive damages against itself where appropriate.

In many discharge suits serious accusations of employer wrongdoing are made that would inevitably affect the grievance process profoundly. A court could not have confidence in the decision of a grievance panel of other employees that the employer had not, for example, suborned perjury, fixed prices, or condoned illicit overtures to subordinates. The employer's self-interest would be too strong.

In *Fortune v. National Cash Register Co.*,[119] the employee claimed he had been fired to prevent the vesting of his commission rights. After questioning whether the contractually mandated internal process was applicable, the court listed three reasons for excusing compliance with it: (1) it appeared likely that resort to the remedy would be futile; (2) the discharge was a breach excusing compliance; and (3) the employer could not be judge in its own cause.

In *Petermann v. Teamsters*,[120] the institutional procedure was that of a union. An individual had been fired from his job as an employee of the union and removed as a member because he refused to commit perjury. The court reasoned that the grievance procedure of the union governed membership questions and, because the employee did not pursue internal review, upheld the removal from membership. The procedure did not apply to the individual's employment, however, so the retaliatory discharge action was allowed to stand.

In *Jackson v. Minidoka Irrigation District*,[121] the discharged employee first sued to force the employer, a public entity, to provide a hearing. A court-ordered hearing failed to change the result. The Idaho Supreme Court accepted the facts found by the hearing in resolving the case. While the decision did not involve a private employer, it does imply that facts found in a procedurally fair hearing provided by employer policy, and which the employee chose to pursue, may not be relitigated.

The Maine Whistleblowers' Protection Act[122] requires an employee proceeding under that statute to make "a reasonable effort to maintain or restore his rights through any grievance procedure or similar process which may be available at his place of employment" before resorting to the courts. It is unclear whether an unfavorable result is binding on the employee, but the statute appears at least to require resort to grievance systems created and operated by the employer.

Exhaustion of Remedies: Administrative Procedures

The necessity of proceeding before an administrative agency with claims relating to discharge has posed three problems to date, all involving retaliatory discharge. The first problem involves suits that

---

[119]373 Mass. 96, 364 N.E.2d 1251 (1977).
[120]174 Cal. App.2d 184, 344 P.2d 25 (1959).
[121]98 Idaho 330, 563 P.2d 54 (1977). Contra: *Marion County School Bd. v. Clark*, 378 So.2d 831 (Fla. Dist. Ct. App. 1979) (school board hearing not entitled to *res judicata* effect).
[122]ME. REV. STAT. ANN. ch. 26, §834 (Supp. 1983).

cite antidiscrimination statutes providing express remedies as evidencing the public policy violated by the discharge. The second problem arises when the legislature creates an administrative remedy for some other type of claim that is within the scope of retaliatory discharge. The third problem is whether the availability of other legal devices to vindicate public policy will bar a retaliatory discharge suit.

The equal employment opportunity laws, state and federal, have been in place for about 20 years. Most statutes provide for conciliation or resolution of claims under these laws by a designated administrative agency. Recognition of equal employment opportunity as an actionable "public policy" would permit discriminatory discharge suits outside these procedures, circumventing both the conciliation process and the usual short limitations period for such claims. As a result, most courts have held that retaliatory discharge does not encompass claims for discharge contravening principles of equal employment opportunity.[123] Pennsylvania has gone a step beyond this by adopting an election-of-remedies approach under which a plaintiff who seeks relief under the state's discrimination law is barred from bringing any retaliatory discharge claim on the theory that retaliatory discharge may be invoked only where no other remedy is available.[124]

A number of states that have recognized retaliatory discharge have also adopted specific statutory prohibitions against discharge in retaliation for filing a workers' compensation claim. In *Lally v. Copygraphics*,[125] the New Jersey Supreme Court held that passage of the statute after recognition of the retaliatory discharge action did not affect or limit the common law tort action. The court explained that where the cause of action predated the statute, the legislature would have expressly preempted the private right of direct suit had it so intended. The statute was construed to create an alternative administrative remedy, and the employee was given a choice between a direct court action without exhaustion and the administrative remedy. In *Brown v. Transcon Lines*,[126] the Oregon Supreme Court held that an administrative remedy that was discretionary with the agency did not preclude, or limit, the common law right of action.

---

[123]*Bruffett v. Warner Communications, Inc.*, 692 F.2d 910 (3d Cir. 1982); *Strauss v. A.L. Randall Co.*, 144 Cal. App.3d 514, 194 Cal. Rptr. 520 (1983); *Kaufman v. Grant-Crawford Co-op Oil Co.*, 106 Wis.2d 771, 318 N.W.2d 26 (Ct. App. 1982); *Walsh v. Consolidated Freightways, Inc.*, 278 Ore. 347, 563 P.2d 1205 (1977); *Carrillo v. Illinois Bell Tel. Co.*, 538 F. Supp. 793 (N.D. Ill. 1983); *Manuel v. International Harvester Co.*, 502 F. Supp. 45 (N.D. Ill. 1980); *Howard v. Dorr Woolen Co.*, 120 N.H. 295, 414 A.2d 1273 (1980); *McCluney v. Jos. Schlitz Brewing Co.*, 489 F. Supp. 24 (E.D. Wis. 1980); *Wehr v. Burroughs Corp.*, 438 F. Supp. 1052 (E.D. Pa. 1977). See *Peterson v. Scott Constr. Co.*, 5 Ohio App.3d 203, 451 N.E.2d 1236 (1982), and *Dykstra v. Crestwood Bank*, 117 Ill. App.3d 821, 454 N.E.2d 51 (1983). Contra: *Placos v. Cosmair, Inc.*, 517 F. Supp. 1287 (S.D.N.Y. 1981); *Schipani v. Ford Motor Co.*, 102 Mich. App. 606, 302 N.W.2d 307 (1981); *McKinney v. National Dairy Council*, 491 F. Supp. 1108 (D. Mass. 1980).
[124]*Shaffer v. National Can Corp.*, 565 F. Supp. 909 (E.D. Pa. 1983).
[125]85 N.J. 668, 428 A.2d 1317 (1981). Accord: *Hentzel v. Singer Co.*, 138 Cal. App.3d 290, 188 Cal. Rptr. 159 (1982); *Meyer v. Byron Jackson, Inc.*, 120 Cal. App.3d 59, 174 Cal. Rptr. 428 (1981). Contra: *Portillo v. G.T. Price Prods., Inc.*, 131 Cal. App.3d 285, 182 Cal. Rptr. 291 (1982); *Cornejo v. Polycon Indus., Inc.*, 109 Wis.2d 649, 327 N.W.2d 183 (1982).
[126]284 Ore. 597, 588 P.2d 1087 (1978).

In *Schwartz v. Michigan Sugar Co.*,[127] however, the availability of an administrative procedure barred an action for discharge based on reporting of safety violations. At least one court has suggested that the action for retaliatory discharge is premised on the absence of any other remedy to redress a civil wrong.[128] It is plain enough, however, that the availability of a criminal prosecution of the employer does not preclude an action: "The imposition of a small criminal penalty for retaliatory discharge would do little to discourage retaliatory discharges, as there is a very real possibility that some employers would risk the threat of criminal sanctions in order to escape their responsibilities."[129] Similarly, other remedies that do not compensate the employee for the discharge do not preclude an action.[130]

Res Judicata in Employment Cases

In addition to the various causes of action that a discharged employee may choose to pursue in court, there are a substantial number of remedies outside the judicial system. Among these are the following:

(1) Unemployment compensation claims (typically before a state "employment security" department or commission).

(2) Workers' compensation proceedings (usually before the "industrial" commission).

(3) Collective bargaining grievance arbitration.

(4) Unfair labor practice proceedings (heard by state or federal labor relations boards).

(5) Employee compensation complaints (presented to state or federal labor departments).

(6) Race, sex, age, religion, national origin, handicap, or marital status discrimination proceedings (before municipal or state human rights or fair employment practices commissions or the federal Equal Employment Opportunity Commission or Office of Federal Contract Compliance Programs).

(7) Civil service, personnel, or tenure hearings (presided over by

---

[127]106 Mich. App. 471, 308 N.W.2d 459 (1981). Accord: *Ohlsen v. DST Indus., Inc.*, 111 Mich. App. 580, 314 N.W.2d 699 (1981); *Davis v. Boise Cascade Co.*, 288 N.W.2d 680 (Minn. 1979). See *McCarthy v. The Bark Peking*, 676 F.2d 42 (2d Cir. 1982) (failure to exhaust in suit claiming private right of action under federal law precluded any claim). Contra: *Hentzel v. Singer Co.*, 138 Cal. App.3d 290, 188 Cal. Rptr. 159 (1982) (adoption of Occupational Safety & Health Act after recognition of retaliatory discharge did not repeal cause of action or require compliance with statutory administrative remedy for retaliation).

[128]*Wehr v. Burroughs Corp.*, 438 F. Supp. 1052 (E.D. Pa. 1977).

[129]*Kelsay v. Motorola, Inc.*, 74 Ill.2d 172, 185, 384 N.E.2d 353, 359 (1978). Accord: *Petermann v. Teamsters*, 174 Cal. App.2d 184, 344 P.2d 25 (1959).

[130]*Frampton v. Central Ind. Gas Co.*, 260 Ind. 249, 297 N.E.2d 425 (1973). See *Meyer v. Byron Jackson, Inc.*, 120 Cal. App.3d 59, 174 Cal. Rptr. 428 (1981); *Raden v. Azusa*, 97 Cal. App.3d 336, 158 Cal. Rptr. 689 (1979); *Lally v. Copygraphics*, 173 N.J. Super. 162, 413 A.2d 960 (1980), *aff'd on other grounds*, 85 N.J. 668, 428 A.2d 1317 (1981); *Brown v. Transcon Lines*, 284 Ore. 597, 588 P.2d 1087 (1978).

federal, state, county, school, or municipal governing bodies or personnel boards).

When the discharged employee pursues one or more of these remedies, issues may be raised that advance, limit, or bar the employee's court case or one of the other options open to him. The possible effect of a resolution of the foregoing is governed by the doctrines of *res judicata*: merger and bar, and collateral estoppel.

The Principles of *Res Judicata* and Collateral Estoppel

The principles of merger and bar hold that a party may bring only one action on his claim. If the plaintiff prevails, the action merges with the judgment; if the plaintiff loses, all actions that were or could have been joined in the action are barred.[131] This general rule does not require a discharged employee to choose a single forum to the exclusion of all others, since the rules of merger and bar do not preclude subsequent actions if:

> "[T]he plaintiff was unable to rely on a certain theory of the case or seek a certain remedy or form of relief in the first action because of the limitations on the subject matter jurisdiction of the courts or restrictions on their authority to entertain multiple theories or demands for multiple remedies or forms of relief in a single action * * *."[132]

Thus, except where the judicial review is de novo and permits joinder of civil claims, merger and bar raise few issues peculiar to employment litigation.

While merger and bar principles are not ordinarily invoked by the presence of a prior administrative determination, collateral estoppel can easily come into play. The general rule is:

> "When an issue of fact or law is actually litigated and determined by a valid and final judgment, and the determination is essential to the judgment, the determination is conclusive in a subsequent action between the parties, whether on the same or a different claim."[133]

The range of issues that can result in collateral estoppel is limited only by the substantive rules of the administrative remedy and the particular facts in issue.

Unemployment Compensation Claims

The referee may deny an unemployment compensation claim if the employee left the job without good cause; this may amount to a determination that the employee breached the contract of employ-

---

[131]RESTATEMENT (SECOND) OF JUDGEMENTS §§17, 18, 19 (1983).

[132]*Id.* §26(c).

[133]*Id.* §27. One of the innovations of the Second Restatement is the inclusion of issues of law as well as issues of fact in the rule. Sections 28(2) and 28(3) significantly limit this new concept by permitting relitigation where the two actions are unrelated, where there is an intervening change in law, or where factors relating to the allocation of jurisdiction between tribunals call for relitigation.

ment and cannot himself sue for breach of contract. A denial may also be grounded on subsidiary findings that reject the basis for an employee claim of retaliatory discharge or tort claim. A finding in favor of the employee could resolve these same points against the employer.

Employees who are guilty of willful misconduct on the job may be disqualified from receiving benefits. A disqualification on this ground may resolve the issue of just cause for discharge in favor of the employer. While the absence of willful misconduct does not necessarily establish the absence of just cause, the finding of no willful misconduct may well resolve the facts in dispute to the point where there is no room for a finding of just cause.

Another ground for disqualification from unemployment compensation is the employee's failure to seek and accept work in a new position. Though the rulings are generally limited to short periods of time, they could be conclusive of mitigation of damage questions.

Workers' Compensation Proceedings

Workers' compensation proceedings adjudicate employee injury and disability claims. Issues affecting discharge cases or handicap discrimination claims, such as whether absences were excusable, the existence of physical handicaps, and ability to do the job, may be resolved in these proceedings.

Collective Bargaining Grievance Arbitration and
Civil Service Hearings

Arbitration of discharge grievances and civil service or tenure hearings will usually resolve the question of just cause for discharge and adjudicate the surrounding facts. The hearing will also resolve witness credibility questions, thereby precluding suits for defamation arising from false statements given in the hearing. If the collective bargaining agreement or civil service regulations prohibit discrimination of various types, actions for civil rights violations may be affected by a ruling that discrimination was present or absent. In reaching decisions on these questions, many of the facts and issues of the case may be resolved, thus affecting other discharge claims.

Unfair Labor Practice and Discrimination Proceedings

NLRB or state labor relations boards may consider whether an employee's discharge was for union activity or otherwise prohibited; state and federal discrimination proceedings determine whether the discharge resulted from discriminatory motives. Both types of cases generally involve the consideration of circumstantial evidence to weigh the likelihood of an illegitimate basis for the decision. In particular, the veracity of the employer's explanation for the discharge is invariably in issue. While an employer may have just cause for discharging an employee and still retaliate or discriminate (by discharging where lesser discipline would otherwise be applied), and may lack just cause to discharge and still not discriminate (by an honest error or judgment call), the resolution of a discrimination claim based on circumstantial evidence requires detailed factual findings that may affect other claims made by the employee.

Employee Compensation Complaints

State departments of labor frequently have power to adjudicate or enforce employee claims for unpaid wages or benefits. The U.S. Department of Labor enforces wage and hour laws, occupational safety and health laws, and the prohibitions on retaliation against whistleblowers. Actions involving these areas of regulation may resolve issues affecting discharge claims—for example, those relating to breach of contract, just cause for discharge, and constructive discharge.

With the proliferation of administrative agencies, the principles of *res judicata* have been extended to administrative decisions,[134] despite frequent holdings to the contrary in the past.[135] Not all jurisdictions accept this position,[136] and others limit it in special circumstances;[137] but the trend favors recognition of administrative decisions[138] if they are quasi-judicial in nature[139] and particularly where they are subject to judicial review.[140] The courts consider the absence of a jury trial, the limited scope of the inquiry, and the generally smaller amounts at stake in deciding whether to grant preclusive effect to administrative determinations, but these factors do not in themselves disqualify administrative rulings from having *res judicata* effect. Arbitration decisions also may have preclusive effect.[141] Arbitrators are not required to follow the law, and judicial review is strictly limited; these do not prevent points actually decided from working a collateral estoppel, since the parties have, by agreeing to arbitrate, stipulated to the fairness of this forum.[142]

Collateral estoppel operates against parties to the first proceed-

---

[134]*Salt Creek Freightways v. Wyoming Fair Employment Practices Comm'm*, 598 P.2d 435 (Wyo. 1979).

[135]*Corey v. Avco-Lycoming Div., Avco Corp.*, 163 Conn. 309, 307 A.2d 155 (1972).

[136]See, e.g., *Pratt v. Film Technicians*, 260 Cal. App.2d 545, 67 Cal. Rptr. 483 (1968).

[137]See, e.g., *Ferris v. Hawkins*, 135 Ariz. 329, 660 P.2d 1256 (1983).

[138]K. Davis, ADMINISTRATIVE LAW §21:2 (1983). See, e.g., *Corey v. Avco-Lycoming Div., Avco Corp.*, 163 Conn. 309, 307 A.2d 155 (1972); *Accountants v. City of Detroit*, 399 Mich. 449, 249 N.W.2d 121 (1976); *Bernstein v. Birch Wathen School*, 51 N.Y.2d 932, 415 N.E.2d 982, 434 N.Y.S.2d 994 (1980).

[139]*United States v. Utah Constr. & Mining Co.*, 384 U.S. 394 (1966); *Accountants v. City of Detroit*, 399 Mich. 449, 249 N.W.2d 121 (1976); *Walsh v. Pluess-Staufer (N. Am.), Inc.*, 67 Misc.2d 885, 325 N.Y.S.2d 19 (Sup. Ct. 1971). But see *Marion County School Bd. v. Clark*, 378 So.2d 831 (Fla. Dist. Ct. App. 1979) (findings at school board hearing not binding because board was adverse party to unemployment compensation proceedings).

[140]*Corey v. Avco-Lycoming Div., Avco Corp.*, 163 Conn. 309, 307 A.2d 155 (1972).

[141]E.g, *Freight Drivers, Local 208 v. Braswell Motor Freight Lines*, 422 F.2d 109 (9th Cir. 1970); *Bendix Corp. v. Radecki*, 158 Ind. App. 370, 302 N.E.2d 847 (1973); *Grubb v. Leroy L. Wade & Son*, 384 S.W.2d 528 (Mo. 1964).

[142]*Corey v. Avco-Lycoming Div., Avco Corp.*, 163 Conn. 309, 307 A.2d 155 (1972).

ing and those in privity with them. Where the staff of an agency is the moving party on behalf of the employee, who is the real party in interest, collateral estoppel still applies.[143] Similarly, where the union represents the employee in arbitration, the employee is bound to the issues determined.[144]

Limitations on Collateral Estoppel

Collateral estoppel, though available, may not be applied in a given case for a number of reasons. The major ones are lack of necessity to the judgment, absence of prior determination, absence of fair opportunity to contest, and legislative purpose problems.[145]

The finding must be essential to the judgment. In *Mississippi Employment Security Commission v. Philadelphia Municipal Separate School District*,[146] a teacher's contract was not renewed, and the school board cited various misconduct as the reason. Pursuant to statute, the school board held a hearing at which the administration's claim of just cause was sustained. This was held not to operate as collateral estoppel because the board was not required to find just cause, but merely some reason for discharge not prohibited by law.

The issue must in fact have been litigated and decided in the prior proceeding. In *Bernstein v. Birch Wathen School*,[147] a teacher left her job when she was demoted to assistant teacher. The unemployment compensation referee's finding that the teacher was ineligible because she left the job without good cause was given collateral estoppel effect in her subsequent breach of contract suit. While the teacher argued that her reassignment was a breach of contract entitling her to leave, the court noted that the contract and school handbook on this point were before the referee. Whether the principal had the right to reassign the teacher, the court held, had been conclusively decided when the referee determined that the teacher had left the job "without good cause."

The party to be estopped must have had a full and fair opportunity to contest the issue in the prior proceedings. In *Hunt v. OSR*

---

[143]*Newsday, Inc. v. Ross*, 80 A.D.2d 1, 437 N.Y.S.2d 376 (1981) (prior ruling against employee seeking unemployment benefits binding upon Industrial Commissioner). An issue might be raised as to the requisite "full and fair opportunity" to litigate a point where the agency prosecuted on behalf of the employee in the first action and a dispute over handling of the matter took place.

[144]*Corey v. Avco-Lycoming Div., Avco Corp.*, 163 Conn. 309, 307 A.2d 155 (1972). Where the union's handling of the arbitration rose to the level of a breach of the duty of fair representation, one might argue that the necessary "full and fair opportunity" to litigate was absent. However, the employee in such a case would be entitled to challenge the result by bringing an action against the union, and thus ought not be permitted to avoid the result.

[145]RESTATEMENT (SECOND) OF JUDGEMENTS §§27, 28(3), 28(5) (1983).

[146]437 So.2d 388 (Miss. 1983). See also *Goldsmith v. E.I. duPont de Nemours & Co.*, 32 FEP Cases 1879 (D. Del. 1983).

[147]71 A.D.2d 129, 421 N.Y.S.2d 574 (1979), *aff'd*, 51 N.Y.2d 932, 415 N.E.2d 982, 434 N.Y.S.2d 994 (1980). See also *Leftwich v. Harris-Stowe State College*, 540 F. Supp. 37 (E.D. Mo. 1982).

Chemical, Inc.,[148] collateral estoppel was denied because breach of contract issues had not been treated adequately by the parties before the referee. The court noted that the size of the unemployment compensation benefit was small in comparison to the lawsuit, and that complex contractual issues and circumstances surrounding them were not and could not have been litigated before the referee. Weighing the relative significance, formality, and time devoted to the two matters, the court found that the requisite full and fair opportunity to contest had not been provided in the administrative proceedings.

There may also be considerations of legislative policy that compel the denial of collateral estoppel. In *Ferris v. Hawkins*,[149] the court held that unemployment compensation decisions could not collaterally estop proceedings relating to a civil service board decision. Citing the social welfare purpose of unemployment compensation benefits, the court expressed doubt that the merits of employment disputes were intended by the legislature to be resolved in unemployment hearings. It noted that the effect of so holding would be to undermine the system by encouraging employers to contest the availability of benefits.

Effect of Collateral Estoppel

The usual reason for the assertion of collateral estoppel is to establish some fact that operates to bar the claim. Even when the requirements of collateral estoppel are met, the facts established or issues resolved do not necessarily prevent the plaintiff from prevailing, although they may greatly hamper the effort.

Unemployment Compensation Rulings

Where a referee had ruled that the plaintiff left work voluntarily without good cause, collateral estoppel did not bar the suit by the employee based on the breach of contract which led him to resign.[150] When the employer sought to bar a tort and breach of contract suit, the court held that the pretermination tort claims were unaffected, since the plaintiff's subsequent resignation did not establish that the pre-resignation wrongs had been waived.[151] A finding that an employee lacked good cause for leaving work voluntarily may defeat a claim that the employer's discrimination constituted constructive discharge, or even that the employer discriminated at all.[152] A deter-

---

[148]*Hunt v. OSR Chemicals, Inc.*, 85 A.D.2d 681, 445 N.Y.S.2d 499 (1981). See also *Rucker v. Higher Educ. Aids Bd.*, 669 F.2d 1179 (7th Cir. 1982); *Rawson v. Sears, Roebuck & Co.*, 554 F. Supp. 327 (D. Colo. 1983); *Lewis v. IBM*, 393 F. Supp. 305 (D. Ore. 1974).

[149]135 Ariz. 329, 660 P.2d 1256 (1983).

[150]*Schwarz v. Schnipper*, 87 A.D.2d 510, 447 N.Y.S.2d 488 (1982).

[151]But see *Bernstein v. Birch Wathen School*, 71 A.D.2d 129, 421 N.Y.S.2d 574 (1979), *aff'd*, 51 N.Y.2d 932, 415 N.E.2d 982, 434 N.Y.S.2d 994 (1980).

[152]*Salt Creek Freightways v. Wyoming Fair Employment Practices Comm'n*, 598 P.2d 435 (Wyo. 1979).

mination that an employee left work voluntarily does not establish the mental capacity of the employee to make a timely workers' compensation claim.[153]

A finding of willful employee misconduct, if enforceable, establishes just cause for the employee's discharge.[154] The converse is not true; that an employee was not guilty of willful misconduct still leaves room for a finding that he was discharged for just cause.[155]

Arbitration Rulings

An arbitration finding of just cause discharge is not dispositive of a federal[156] or state[157] discrimination claim. There is a split in authority if the collective bargaining agreement prohibits discrimination and a finding of discrimination is made in arbitration.[158] A finding of just cause is also conclusive with respect to any claim that the alleged reason for discharge was untrue,[159] which is effective to establish a defense of truth in a defamation case.[160]

---

[153]*Croon v. Breitfellers Sales, Inc.* 63 A.D.2d 1108, 406 N.Y.S.2d 390 (1978).

[154]*Newsday, Inc. v. Ross,* 80 A.D.2d 1, 437 N.Y.S.2d 376 (1981).

[155]*Silberman v. Penn Gen. Agencies, Inc.,* 63 A.D.2d 929, 406 N.Y.S.2d 93 (1978); *A.B. Mach. Works, Inc. v. Brissimitzakis,* 51 A.D.2d 915, 381 N.Y.S.2d 77 (1976).

[156]*Alexander v. Gardner-Denver Co.,* 415 U.S. 36 (1974).

[157]*State Div. of Human Rights v. Baker Hall, Inc.,* 80 A.D.2d 733, 437 N.Y.S.2d 160 (1981).

[158]Compare *Dewey v. Reynolds Metals Co.,* 429 F.2d 324 (6th Cir. 1980), *aff'd by an equally divided court,* 402 U.S. 689 (1971), with *Fekete v. United States Steel Corp.,* 424 F.2d 331 (3d Cir. 1970), and *Hutchings v. United States Indus., Inc.,* 428 F.2d 303 (5th Cir. 1970). The recent U.S. Supreme Court opinion in *Kremer v. Chemical Constr. Corp.,* 456 U.S. 461, 470 n.7 (1982), indicated that while in federal cases a state administrative proceeding reviewed by the state court is *res judicata,* arbitration proceedings are not entitled to *res judicata* effect but only to the statutory "great weight." In state cases, the decisions are divided. Compare *Corey v. Avco-Lycoming Div., Avco Corp.,* 163 Conn. 309, 307 A.2d 155 (1972); *Umberfield v. School Dist. 11,* 185 Colo. 165, 522 P.2d 730 (1974); and *Colorado Springs Coach Co. v. State of Colorado Civil Rights Comm.,* 35 Colo. App. 378, 536 P.2d 837 (1975), with *Hayworth v. Oakland,* 129 Cal. App.3d 723, 181 Cal. Rptr. 214 (1982).

[159]*Cooper v. Yellow Freight Sys.,* 589 S.W.2d 643 (Mo. App. 1979) (service letter statute case).

[160]*Conner v. Dart Transp. Serv.,* 65 Cal. App.3d 320, 135 Cal. Rptr. 259 (1976); *Bird v. Meadow Gold Prods. Corp.,* 60 Misc.2d 212, 302 N.Y.S.2d 701 (Sup. Ct. 1969); *Ashland Clothes, Inc. v. Cummings,* 35 Misc.2d 871, 231 N.Y.S.2d 509 (Sup. Ct. 1962).

6

Public Employee Job Security

The movement in employment law toward just cause and improper motive limitations on termination is manifest in public as well as private employment. The establishment of civil service and tenure systems providing job security to public employees dates back to the progressive era at the turn of the century. These systems protected public employees against politically motivated discharge by establishing a just cause standard. Public employees came to enjoy specific wrongful motive protection when the Supreme Court held that discharge could not be based solely on invocation by a public employee of the privilege against self-incrimination.[1]

In the private sector the courts are coming to recognize contract rights to job security based on "reasonable expectations." Similarly, the public employee enjoys protection under the Fourteenth Amendment against deprivation of property interests in the job without due process of law.[2] The private employee obtains a jury trial to determine whether job security expectations were reasonable and whether there is just cause for discharge. The public employee may obtain a judicial determination of whether job security expectations were reasonable, and the employer may be ordered to provide a due process hearing to resolve the just cause issue within the bounds of reason.

The private employee—with or without any job security—may be entitled to a remedy if the discharge was motivated by considerations violative of public policy. The public employee, even if subject to arbitrary and capricious termination, likewise has protection against discharge for reasons that are contrary to public policy. The "public

---

[1]*Slochower v. Board of Educ.*, 350 U.S. 551 (1956) (discharge of schoolteacher could not be based solely on employee's refusal to answer certain questions before McCarthy committee on claim of privilege against self-incrimination).

[2]Compare *Toussaint v. Blue Cross & Blue Shield*, 408 Mich. 579, 292 N.W.2d 880 (1980) (right to job security based on "reasonable expectation"), with *Board of Regents v. Roth*, 408 U.S. 564 (1972) (property right in job requiring due process before dismissal must be founded on "legitimate claim of entitlement" to job security).

policy" restraints on the government are spelled out in the Constitution and the Bill of Rights.

A private employee is protected by the law of defamation against impairment of his business reputation by the employer. A public employee has a constitutional "liberty" interest in his business reputation which is protected by constitutional due process standards. In place of a damage remedy, the public employee is entitled to a limited hearing to "clear his name" for the record but not necessarily restore him to his job.

There are, of course, sharp distinctions between the considerations that govern public and private employment. The government is not in business to earn a profit but lives off public funds; the government is responsible to a public electorate, not to the marketplace or profit-seeking shareholders; the business of government is to regulate, stimulate, subsidize, and educate, not to buy and sell; the government is restrained by a Constitution adopted to protect against tyranny and censorship, while the private business is restrained—by government.

These distinctions may explain such differences between the legal treatment of public and private employees as the more limited right of public employees to organize, collectively bargain, and strike; the greater willingness of the courts to reinstate public employees; and the greater judicial reluctance to interfere in the private employer's conduct of its business by recognizing employee rights. Yet, despite these distinctions and despite the different legal grounds on which the rights of private and public employees rest, the similarities between legal treatment of private and public employees are striking. The same issues are raised, the same concerns are voiced, and the same debate rages over judicial protection of employees against discharge. This chapter provides a broad outline of the federal constitutional case law governing discharged public employees, and focuses particular attention on the point where public employee rights present the most explosive conflict: politically motivated discharge.

The Fourteenth Amendment: Due Process Rights of Public Employees

This section will focus on the issue of whether a public employee has a constitutionally protected interest in his job. More specifically, it will examine when a public employee has a property or liberty interest in his job and what minimal procedural processes must be followed before involuntary termination.

Any inquiry into due process rights requires a twofold analysis: whether the employee was deprived of a protected interest in life, liberty, or property; and, if so, what process was due. When a "property" interest is claimed, the first question is answered by resort to state law;[3] while the second question is answered within a constitutional framework.[4] A state is free to decide what property interests are protected, but may not deny minimum procedural safeguards deemed constitutionally necessary to protect against arbitrary deprivation of the interest.

The Fourteenth Amendment recognizes three areas in which due process rights attach: life, liberty, and property.[5] A discharged public employee may, depending upon the circumstances, claim a denial of both liberty and property rights without due process. Deprivation of a liberty interest, analogous to a common law action for defamation, occurs when a public employee is discharged in such a manner that his reputation is stigmatized, thus inhibiting his chances of securing future employment. Deprivation of a property interest occurs when a public employee has demonstrated a vested property right in his job and is removed without having had the opportunity to present his case for a determination on the merits before the appropriate reviewing body.

It was not until 1972 that the Supreme Court expanded the concept of due process to incorporate minimal due process safeguards for public employees faced with termination. Since 1912, federal civil service employees had been protected from purely arbitrary discharge by the Lloyd-LaFollette Act,[6] which allowed removal only for such cause as will promote the efficiency of the service.[7] This protection, and the protections of similar state and local enactments, however, do not apply to non-civil service employees. Furthermore, even though the Lloyd LaFollette Act permitted dismissal only "for cause," it was not clear whether due process required a pre-termination or post-termination hearing.[8]

Board of Regents v. Roth[9] and its companion case, *Perry v. Sindermann*,[10] established the circumstances under which a public employee is entitled to a statement of reasons and a hearing before final termination. Roth was hired for one year as an untenured assistant professor at a Wisconsin university. The contract was not renewed upon its expiration. The university proferred no reason for the nonrenewal and no hearing was held. Roth filed suit alleging that his nonrenewal, in the absence of a hearing or a statement of the reasons for his dismissal, violated his constitutional due process rights. The

---

[3]"Property interests * * * are not created by the Constitution. Rather, they are created and their dimensions are defined by existing rules or understandings that stem from an independent source such as state law * * *." *Board of Regents v. Roth*, 408 U.S. 564, 577 (1972).

[4]"[T]he right to procedural due process * * * is conferred, not by legislative grace, but by constitutional guarantee." *Arnett v. Kennedy*, 416 U.S. 134, 167 (1974).

[5]The Fourteenth Amendment reads, in part, that no state shall "deprive any person of life, liberty, or property, without due process of law." U.S. CONST. amend. XIV, §1.

[6]5 U.S.C. §7501 (1970).

[7]§7501(a). More specific standards were enacted in 1978 as "merit systems principles." See *infra* note 119.

[8]See *The Supreme Court, 1973 Term*, 88 HARV. L. REV. 83 (1974), for a discussion of the procedural due process mandated by the Lloyd-LaFollette Act.

[9]408 U.S. 564 (1972).

[10]408 U.S. 593 (1972).

Court examined his Fourteenth Amendment claim in both a liberty and a property context.

Recognizing that liberty must be defined broadly, the Court acknowledged two circumstances in an employment situation which constitute denial or infringement of a liberty interest. The first such circumstance is employer statements that "seriously damage [an employee's] standing and associations in the community."[11] The second is a state's imposition of "a stigma or other disability that foreclosed his freedom to take advantage of other employment opportunities."[12] The Court found that Roth's dismissal had no stigmatizing effect.

The Court next focused on whether Roth had been denied a property interest, defined as a "security of interests that a person has already acquired in specific benefits."[13] The Court cited cases presenting a state-created property interest in public employment: a tenured college professor,[14] a staff member under contract,[15] and a teacher without the benefit of tenure of a contract but hired with a clearly implied promise of continual employment.[16] From these examples, the Court identified the thread common to all: "To have a property interest in a benefit, a person clearly must have more than an abstract need or desire for it. He must have more than a unilateral expectation of it. He must, instead, have a legitimate claim of entitlement to it."[17] Finding that Roth had no legitimate property interest in his employment, the Court did not reach the issue of due process.

Perry v. Sindermann,[18] decided the same day as *Roth*, defined one of the circumstances under which an implied promise of permanent employment could be found. Sindermann had worked for a state junior college for 10 years under a year-to-year contract. Like Roth, his contract was not renewed and he was not given a statement of the reasons or a hearing. Unlike the college in *Roth*, the college in *Sindermann* had a provision in its faculty guide[19] which the Court interpreted as a de facto tenure system. This provision, the Court found, created an implied contract. Reiterating that mere subjective expectancy did not create a property right, the Court held that the state had created a property right, thus triggering the due process procedures mandated by the Constitution.

In *Arnette v. Kennedy,*[20] the Court found that the Lloyd-La-Follette Act, which permitted dismissal only "for cause," created a property interest protected by the Fourteenth Amendment. The Court,

---

[11]408 U.S. 564, 573 (1972).

[12]*Id.*

[13]*Id.* at 576.

[14]*Slochower v. Board of Educ.*, 350 U.S. 551 (1956).

[15]*Wiman v. Updegraff,* 344 U.S. 183 (1952).

[16]*Connell v. Higgenbotham*, 403 U.S. 207 (1971).

[17]408 U.S. 564, 577 (1972).

[18]408 U.S. 593 (1972).

[19]The provision included the sentence, "[T]he Administration of the Colleges wishes the faculty member to feel that he has permanent tenure as long as his teaching services are satisfactory and as long as he displays a cooperative attitude toward his co-workers and his supervisors, and as long as he is happy in his work." *Id.* at 600.

[20]416 U.S. 134 (1974).

however, rejected the argument that due process required a pretermination hearing. The individual in question had a statutory right to a post-termination hearing, and this provided sufficient procedural protection.

Expansion of the Due Process Clause was arrested in *Bishop v. Wood*.[21] Bishop, classified as a permanent employee on the Marion, North Carolina, police force, was terminated. In accordance with a state statute and upon his request, he was notified as to the grounds for his dismissal but was not given a hearing. He brought a Section 1983[22] suit in federal court alleging denial of due process.

Bishop's claim, based upon both an implied and an express property right to employment, received short shrift from the Court. The Court found that he had been denied neither a property nor a liberty interest. In so finding, the Court limited the holding in *Sindermann* and enunciated a new element, publication, for a litigant claiming denial of a liberty interest.

Bishop's express property claim was derived from wording of the Personnel Ordinance of the City of Marion which provided that a permanent employee might be dismissed for failure to adequately perform his work, inefficiency, negligence, or unfitness to perform his duties—in other words, for cause. The Court, taking note of a state court decision holding that "an enforceable expectation of continued public employment * * * can exist only if the employer, by statute or contract, has actually granted some form of guarantee,"[23] concluded that Bishop was an employee at will. This determination precluded an inquiry into whether Bishop's permanent employee classification and length of service created an implied property interest. Additionally, by adopting the district court's findings,[24] the Court found that the limited procedural protections in the statute[25] justified the finding that no property right existed. In other words, because the state did not provide procedural due process protections, there was no property right which required constitutional procedural due process.

Bishop's claim of denial of a liberty interest also was dismissed. Noting that there had been no publication, the Court refused to find that Bishop's reputation had been impaired.[26]

Technically, it remains true that the rights of the employee in his job are defined by state law, while constitutional law determines whether the state law rights amount to a property right requiring due process. Practically, however, *Bishop* delivered control of both

---

[21]426 U.S. 341 (1976).

[22]42 U.S.C. §1983 (Civil Rights Act of 1871). The statute authorizes private suits for violations of constitutional rights by those acting under color of state law.

[23]*Id.* at 354. The quotation is from *Lance v. Still*, 279 N.C. 254, 182 S.E.2d 403 (1971), a case involving the interpretation of a statute governing teachers. Its application to the facts in *Bishop*, therefore, is questionable.

[24]377 F. Supp. 501 (W.D.N.C. 1973).

[25]It may be more accurate to say the lack of procedural protections in the statute, since notice and a hearing were not required before final termination.

[26]426 U.S. 341 (1976).

questions to state law. It opened the door for states to restrict an employee's reasonable expectation by establishing limitations upon procedural protections. It limited the circumstances under which an implied promise of permanent employment could be found. Finally, it curtailed liberty interests by requiring publication.

Policy Manuals as the Source of Property Rights in the Job

As discussed above, a public employee must show that he possesses a property or liberty interest in employment in order to trigger the due process protections afforded by the Fourteenth Amendment.[27] In *Vinyard v. King*,[28] the director of volunteer services of a public hospital was fired for alleged violation of a policy concerning confidentiality of personnel communications. She was given no hearing prior to discharge. At the time she was hired, there was no formal employees' policy manual. However, four years after commencement of employment, the employee was given a copy of the hospital's employee handbook. The handbook included a nonexclusive list of 23 specific causes for discharge. The court construed this list as a promise that employees would only be discharged for cause.

The court then turned to the law of Oklahoma to determine whether the handbook constituted a contract that created "a sufficient expectancy of continued employment to constitute a property interest, which must be afforded constitutionally guaranteed due process."[29] Under Oklahoma law, the employee's consideration for the employer's promise could consist merely in continuing to work and foregoing the option of quitting. This was sufficient to create a property interest in the job subject to constitutional protection. Moreover, as a public employee, the volunteer services director had a right to seek review of the hospital's policies and redress for discharge without cause, even though no right to a hearing was spelled out in the handbook. The court held that her termination without a hearing to determine if cause existed was a violation of Section 1983. The case was remanded to the district court to determine the amount of compensatory damages and possible reinstatement. The district court was also to consider her claim for punitive damages against the hospital's administrator for allegedly "knowingly, wilfully and wantonly" discharging her from her employment.[30] Since the plaintiff prevailed in the appellate court on her claim against the hospital, she was also entitled to reasonable attorney's fees as part of her costs.[31]

---

[27]*Board of Regents v. Roth*, 408 U.S. 564 (1972).

[28]728 F.2d 428 (10th Cir. 1984). See other cases in which federal courts examined state law to determine whether public employees had a property right in their employment that would require the public employer to comply with due process principles prior to termination. *Goetz v. Windsor Cent. School Dist.* 698 F.2d 606 (2d Cir. 1983); *Conley v. Board of Trustees*, 707 F.2d 175 (5th Cir. 1983); *Lyznicki v. Board of Education*, 707 F.2d 949 (7th Cir. 1983).

[29]728 F.2d at 432.

[30]*Id.* at 433.

[31]As provided by 42 U.S.C. §1988 (Supp. V 1981).

The critical element in this type of civil rights action is whether state law creates an enforceable claim of job security that the federal court will recognize as a property interest. Once a property interest is recognized, a pretermination hearing, even though not mentioned in any employment handbook or employer promise, is required as a matter of law. As the court held in *Vinyard*, the civil rights statute was violated whether or not the employee was discharged for cause. The failure to afford the employee a pretermination hearing violated her constitutional rights.

Political Patronage Dismissals Prior to *Elrod v. Burns*[32]

Political patronage[33] dismissals, in which government employees are discharged merely because their political beliefs or acts are not in accord with those of an elected official, are a form of retaliatory discharge. Recent Supreme Court decisions, not unlike those in the burgeoning area of wrongful discharge in the private sector, signal the curtailment of such unfettered employer discretion, in this case in the public sector.

The tradition of patronage appointments in American politics can be traced to the Administration of George Washington.[34] It is generally recognized that patronage in employment facilitated the democratizing of American politics by replacing "aristocrats" in the government with party loyalists. Patronage enabled immigrants to gain and hold political power. Thus, patronage is credited with broadening the base of political participation and increasing political discourse among the the citizenry.[35] According to the theory, patronage employees work for the good of the party, which, in turn, is responsible to the electorate. If the electorate becomes dissatisfied with the government official, he and his political appointees can be removed at the next election. Assurance against bureaucratic foot-dragging is thereby achieved.

Recognizing the inefficiency and injustice of the wholesale replacement of government employees because of party affiliation, Congress enacted the Pendleton Act[36] in 1883 which placed many federal jobs on a merit system. Hiring and firing of federal employees, as well as certain activities of federal employees, were proscribed by

---

[32]427 U.S. 347 (1976).

[33]Patronage is "the allocation of the discretionary favors of government in exchange for political support." M. Tolchin & S. Tolchin, To the Victor 323 (1972). Although patronage encompasses more than government jobs, for example, government contracts, this chapter is concerned with only patronage jobs.

[34]See *Farkas v. Thornburgh*, 493 F. Supp. 1168, 1169–1171 (E.D. Pa. 1980). For background on patronage, see D. Rosenbloom, Federal Service and the Constitution (1971).

[35]See generally Sorauf, *Patronage and Party*, 3 Midwest J. Pol. Sci. 115–116 (1959); *Elrod v. Burns*, 427 U.S. 347, 377-380 (Powell, J., dissenting). For a convincing and spirited defense of the patronage system in American politics, see *Loughney v. Hickey*, 635 F.2d 1063, 1065–1071 (3d Cir. 1980) (Aldisert, J., concurring).

[36]The Pendleton Act is presently codified at 5 U.S.C. §1101 *et seq.* (1976).

statute. Subsequently, states, counties, municipal governments, and other subdivisions of state government enacted similar statutes regulating state civil service jobs. Certain classes of public employees, however, are not within the protection of civil service statutes. It is these public employees, in the main, who face dismissal solely because of political party affiliation.[37]

Until recently, public employees dismissed because of party affiliation received little sympathy from the courts. Challenges to the practice of patronage dismissals were met with one of two responses: a patronage employee has no constitutionally protected right to his job,[38] or the acceptance of a patronage job constitutes a waiver of the right to challenge patronage dismissal.[39]

The notion that a person has no right to public employment was first credited to Oliver Wendell Holmes. In *McAuliffe v. Mayor of New Bedford*,[40] Justice Holmes opined, "[T] he petitioner may have a constitutional right to talk politics, but he has no constitutional right to be a policeman." [41] This right/privilege concept was ratified by the Supreme Court as late as 1951.[42]

Justice Holmes' right/privilege distinction failed to address the problem. The discharged patronage employee is not claiming a constitutional right to public employment; rather, he is challenging the basis for his dismissal: the exercise of a constitutional right to affiliate with the party of his choice. In *Perry v. Sindermann*,[43] the Supreme Court recognized the speciousness of the distinction. Holding that a public employee, even though he has no constitutional right to a government job and is therefore subject to dismissal for no reason at all, may not be discharged for exercising First Amendment rights, the Court explained:

> "For at least a quarter-century, this Court has made clear that even though a person has no 'right' to a valuable government benefit and even though the government may deny him the benefit for any number of reasons, there are some reasons upon which the government may not rely. It may not deny a benefit to a person on a basis that

---

[37]In 1975, nearly 15 million people were under the employ of federal, state, and local governments; half were not covered by civil service. U.S. Dep't of Commerce, Bureau of the Census, STATISTICAL ABSTRACT OF THE UNITED STATES 242, 272 (96th ed. 1975). Comment, *Political Patronage and the Fourth Circuit's Test of Dischargeability After Elrod v. Burns*, 15 WAKE FOREST L. REV. 655 n.7 (1979).

[38]See, e.g., *Alamar v. Dwyer*, 447 F.2d 482 (2d Cir. 1971), *cert. denied*, 404 U.S. 1020 (1972); *Indiana State Employees v. Negley*, 357 F. Supp. 38 (S.D. Ind. 1973); *Young v. Coder*, 346 F. Supp. 165 (M.D. Pa. 1972).

[39]*AFSCME v. Shapp*, 443 Pa. 527, 280 A.2d 375 (1971); *Nunnery v. Barber*, 503 F.2d 1349 (4th Cir. 1974), *cert. denied*, 420 U.S. 1005 (1975). This may be analogized to an equitable estoppel defense.

[40]155 Mass. 216, 29 N.E. 517 (1892).

[41]*Id.* at 220, 29 N.E. at 517.

[42]In *Baily v. Richardson*, 182 F.2d 46, 59 (D.C. Cir. 1950), *aff'd*, 341 U.S. 918 (1951), the Court noted:
  "The plain hard fact is that so far as the Constitution is concerned there is no prohibition against the dismissal of government employees because of their political beliefs, activities or affiliations. * * * The First Amendment guarantees free speech and assembly, but it does not guarantee government employ."

[43]408 U.S. 593 (1972). Plaintiff, a college professor, allegedly was discharged for publicly criticizing the board of regents.

infringes his constitutionally protected interests—especially, his interest in freedom of speech. For if the government could deny a benefit to a person because of his constitutionally protected speech or associations, his exercise of those freedoms would in effect be penalized and inhibited. * * * Such interference with constitutional rights is impermissible."[44]

This decision marked the final burial of the right-privilege distinction.

The waiver theory, the other basis for denying relief to public employees discharged for political reasons, was most colorfully expressed in *AFSCME v. Shapp*.[45] The implication of the waiver theory is that when one accepts a job premised on political loyalty he cannot later be heard to complain about dismissal because his political views do not accord with those of his newly elected superior. In the words of the *Shapp* court:

"State employees who obtain their positions * * * by politics or party patronage and complain of being fired solely on the grounds of political sponsorship or affiliation, have [no constitutionally protected right to their positions].
"Those who, figuratively speaking, live by the political sword must be prepared to die by the political sword."[46]

The waiver theory has a facile appeal, but it is premised on the assumption that the initial qualification is constitutional, a premise laid to rest in *Elrod v. Burns*.[47]

Elrod v. Burns: Defining the First Amendment Limitations on Political Patronage Dismissals

The Supreme Court squarely faced the constitutionality of political patronage dismissals in *Elrod v. Burns*.[48] Four Republican employees of the sheriff's office in Cook County, Illinois, sought to enjoin the newly elected Democratic sheriff from dismissing them.[49] The dismissal was based on the sole consideration that the four employees neither belonged to the Democratic party nor received sponsorship from Democratic party leaders. While the plurality opinion, written by Justice Brennan, found political patronage dismissals to be an unconstitutional violation of First and Fourteenth Amendment

---

[44]*Id.* at 597. Accord: *Keyishian v. Board of Regents*, 385 U.S. 589, 605 (1967), which rejected the argument that public employment "may be conditioned upon the surrender of constitutional rights which could not be abridged by direct government action."
[45]443 Pa. 527, 280 A.2d 375 (1971).
[46]*Id.* at 530, 280 A.2d at 378.
[47]427 U.S. 347, 359 n.13 (1976). See generally Comment, *Patronage Dismissals*, 41 U. Chi. L. Rev. 297, 311–315 (1974) for a discussion analogizing waiver in a criminal setting. Judge Stevens, now Justice Stevens, noted in *Illinois State Employees v. Lewis*, 473 F.2d 561, 573 (7th Cir. 1972), that the waiver defense would, at best, limit the relief, not completely foreclose it.
[48]427 U.S. 347 (1976).
[49]Three of the plaintiffs had already been dismissed. The fourth, although not yet discharged, feared imminent dismissal because he refused to alter his party allegiance.

rights, a concurring opinion found only dismissal of non-policy-making, nonconfidential employees unconstitutional. According to the "least common denominator" test,[50] it is only the latter that should be taken as the holding of the Court. But lower courts have been reluctant to enforce even this narrow holding.

After noting that the patronage system diminishes an individual's right to act in accordance with his beliefs and to associate with those whom he chooses,[51] the Court applied a "strict scrutiny" test in determining whether the state's interest outweighed the infringement to an individual's constitutional rights. [52] Three governmental interests were advanced: the need to ensure effective government and efficient public employees, the need for political loyalty among public employees to ensure implementation of policies, and the need to preserve the democratic process.[53] The Court criticized the validity of each of these interests.

Regarding the first governmental interest, the Court determined that dismissal for cause is a less intrusive method of ensuring effective government than across-the-board patronage dismissals. Moreover, the Court found wholesale patronage dismissals more disruptive of efficient government than the increased accountability presumably achieved by employee dependence upon patronage appointments.[54]

The second proffered justification, a corollary of the first governmental interest, was accepted by the Court in a modified form. The Court reasoned that implementation of a political party's platform policies, presumably sanctioned by the electorate, can be achieved by limiting patronage dismissals to individuals in a policy-making position.[55] Since non-policy-making individuals are not in a position

---

[50]"When a fragmented Court decides a case and no single rationale explaining the result enjoys the assent of five Justices 'the holding of the Court may be viewed as that position taken by those Members who concurred in the judgments on the narrowest grounds * * *.'" *Marks v. United States*, 430 U.S. 188, 193 (1977), quoting *Gregg v. Georgia*, 428 U.S. 153, 169 n.15 (1976). This has been referred to as the least common denominator test. *Branti v. Finkel*, 445 U.S. 507 (1980).

[51]The Court enunciated several examples of First Amendment restrictions imposed by the patronage system: By requiring support for the incumbent party, the average employee is left without time or money to pursue his own political beliefs. 427 U.S. 347, 356 (1976). Patronage favors the incumbent. *Id.* Imposing restrictions on political associations is contrary to basic constitutional freedom. *Id.* at 357, citing *Buckley v. Valeo*, 424 U.S. 1, 15 (1976) and *NAACP v. Button*, 371 U.S. 415, 430 (1958).

[52]"It is firmly established that a significant impairment of First Amendment rights must survive exacting scrutiny." *Id.* at 362, citing *Buckley v. Valeo*, 424 U.S. 1, 64–65 (1976) and *NAACP v. Alabama*, 357 U.S. 449, 460–461 (1958). "In short, if conditioning the retention of public employment on the employee's support of the in-party is to survive constitutional challenge, it must further some vital government end by a means that is least restrictive of freedom of belief and association in achieving that end, and the benefit gained must outweigh the loss of constitutionally protected rights." *Id.* at 363.

[53]*Id.* at 364–371.

[54]*Id.* at 366–367. The Court flatly rejected the notion that political persuasion imputes a disposition for ill-willed conduct which would motivate poor performance. *Id.* at 365, citing *Keyishian v. Board of Regents*, 385 U.S. 589, 606–608 (1967).

[55]"No clear line can be drawn between policymaking and nonpolicymaking positions. While nonpolicymaking individuals usually have limited responsibility, *that is not to say that one with a number of responsibilities is necessarily in a policy-making position.* The nature of the responsibilities is critical. Employee supervisors, for example, may have many responsibilities, but those responsibilities may have only limited and well-defined objectives. An employee with responsibilities that are not well defined or are of broad scope more likely functions in a policymaking position. In determining whether an employee occupies a policymaking position,

to thwart the goals of the party holding office, dismissal would not accomplish this end.[56]

The third governmental interest, that patronage dismissals are essential to the preservation of political parties and, a fortiori, to the democratic process itself, was found to be as much an impairment of, as a contributor to, the elective process. The entrenchment of one political party to the exclusion of others, the Court observed, retards the democratic process and in any event, patronage dismissals are neither the least restrictive method for, nor rationally related to, preserving the democratic process.[57]

Justice Stewart's concurring opinion qualified the plurality opinion: a non-policy-making, nonconfidential government employee cannot be discharged or threatened with discharge, upon the sole ground of his political beliefs, from a job that he is satisfactorily performing.[58] This is the narrower holding.

The Lower Courts' Interpretation of *Elrod*

Confusion, inconsistency, and reluctance to implement fully the holding of *Elrod* have characterized the lower courts' interpretation. Plaintiffs occupying identical positions have been deemed both protected and unprotected under the *Elrod* dischargeability test. Some courts, reasoning that whether an employee holds a policy-making position is a factual question, have refused to grant motions for summary judgment; other courts have held that it is a mixed question of law and fact, thereby making motions to dismiss inappropriate in some instances. The Fourth Circuit has extended only prospective relief to *Elrod* plaintiffs, explaining that the decision was not clearly foreshadowed and retrospective application would work an injustice to defendants.[59] The Fifth Circuit has interpreted the test as disjunctive: an employee need only be either confidential or a policy-maker, not both, in order to be constitutionally subject to discharge.[60] The Third Circuit, however, has regarded the test as conjunctive: the employee must be primarily in a policy-making position *and* in a

---

consideration should also be given to whether the employee acts as an adviser or formulates plans for the implementation of broad goals. * * * Since * * * it is the government's burden to demonstrate an overriding interest in order to validate an encroachment on protected interests, the burden of establishing this justification as to any particular respondent will rest on the petitioners on remand, *cases of doubt being resolved in favor of the particular respondent.*" (Emphasis added.)

Id. at 367–368. It is this distinction between policy-making and non-policy-making that has given the lower courts broad latitude in upholding patronage dismissals. See *infra* notes 85–93 and accompanying text.

[56]*Id.*

[57]*Id.* at 369–370.

[58]*Id.* at 375. The addition of the word "nonconfidential" to "non-policy-making" provided yet another means for the lower courts to emasculate the decision. It raised the question whether the test was conjunctive or disjunctive.

[59]*Ramey v. Harber*, 589 F.2d 753 (4th Cir. 1978).

[60]*Stegmaier v. Trammell*, 597 F.2d 1027 (5th Cir. 1979).

confidential relationship with the employer for his dismissal to pass muster under the Constitution.[61] Some jurisdictions have read *Elrod* to proscribe only actual dismissals of policy-making employees, while others have considered reassignment, demotion, and failure to rehire to be within the ambit of unacceptable patronage practices. In many cases, although the plaintiff has satisfied his burden of proof, an issue not addressed in *Elrod*, his action has been dismissed because the defendant demonstrated an independent, constitutional justification for the dismissal.

What Is a Policy-Maker?

The *Elrod* Court held that dismissal of non-policy-making, non-confidential public employees because of their political beliefs violated their constitutional rights.[62] Employees holding menial positions are clearly protected by the decision;[63] those holding positions with broad policy-making responsibilities are clearly without protection. It is cases involving employees who are not clearly in either group that have allowed lower courts to fashion their own tests.[64]

Before examining the criteria employed by the lower courts in determining what a policy-maker is, an important question must be addressed: Is the policy-making determination a question of fact, a question of law, or a mixed question of law and fact? The lower courts are split on this issue.

In *Rosenthal v. Rizzo*[65] there was conflicting testimony at the trial level regarding the plaintiff's status as a policy-maker. The trial court, apparently believing the issue to be a question of law, entered summary judgment for the defendant. The court of appeals reversed and remanded, noting that "[w]here there is evidence to support the employee's claim that he does not make policy, as there is here, he

---

[61]*Rosenthal v. Rizzo*, 555 F.2d 390 (3d Cir. 1977).

[62]427 U.S. 347 (1976).

[63]Employees with narrow responsibilities and those who perform narrow and well-defined tasks will seldom be considered policy-makers. *Elrod v. Burns*, 427 U.S. 347, 367–368 (1976).

[64]*Employee characterized as policy-making: Dipiro v. Taft*, 584 F.2d 1 (1st Cir. 1978), *cert. denied*, 440 U.S. 914 (1979) (fire chief); *Newcomb v. Brennan*, 558 F.2d 825 (7th Cir. 1977), *cert. denied*, 434 U.S 968 (1977) (deputy city attorney); *Alfaro de Quevedo v. De Jesus Schuck*, 556 F.2d 591 (1st Cir. 1977) (director of criminal justice office); *Mitchell v. King*, 537 F.2d 385 (10th Cir. 1976) (state museum regent); *Rivera Morales v. Benitez de Rexach*, 541 F.2d 882 (1st Cir. 1976) (assistant secretary of education); *Adams v. Walker*, 492 F.2d 1003 (7th Cir. 1972) (state liquor control commission chairman); *Indiana State Employees v. Negley*, 365 F. Supp. 225 (S.D. Ind. 1973), *aff'd*, 501 F.2d 1239, (7th Cir. 1974) (consultants in the federal projects division of a state government office); *Gould v. Walker*, 356 F. Supp. 421 (N.D. Ill. 1973) (assistant to the director of the governor's office of human resources); *McBride v. Griffin*, 62 A.D.2d 520, 405 N.Y.S.2d 353 (1978) (division director of drug abuse center); *Ause v. Regan*, 59 A.D.2d 317, 399 N.Y.S.2d 526 (1977) (county hospital supervisor); *Dyke v. Otlowski*, 154 N.J. Super. 377, 381 A.2d 413 (1977) (supervisor of senior citizen housing project).

Employee characterized as non-policy-making: Rivera Morales v. Benitez de Rexach, 541 F.2d 882 (1st Cir. 1976) (field coordinator for staff development project); *Vincent v. Maeras*, 447 F. Supp. 775 (S.D. Ill. 1978) (communications technician); *Boyce v. School Dist.*, 447 F. Supp. 357 (E.D. Pa. 1978) (school teacher); *Corbeil v. Canestari*, 57 A.D.2d 153, 393 N.Y.S.2d 796 (1977) (building inspector); *Pilarowski v. Brown*, 76 Mich. App. 666, 257 N.W.2d 211 (1977) (administrative assistant to county health department); *Dyke v. Otlowski*, 154 N.J. Super. 377, 381 A.2d 413 (1977) (senior housing inspector).

[65]555 F.2d 390 (3rd Cir. 1977).

is entitled to a full trial on the issue."[66] Thus, the appellate court found it to be a question of fact, as have other courts.[67]

The dissenting opinion in *Rosenthal* treated the issue as a question of law. Reasoning that there was agreement on the basic facts of the plaintiff's status, the dissent argued that whether the plaintiff was a policy-maker was a question of law.[68]

Perhaps the best approach is to treat the issue as a mixed question of law and fact. The court in *Tanner v. McCall* [69] noted that the resolution of the question "involves an evidentiary determination of the duties, responsibilities, terms and conditions of a particular job."[70]

The lower courts rely on many sources in determining whether a particular position is of policy-making stature. In general, if an employee's responsibilities are broad and undefined, he will more likely be deemed a policy-maker.[71] Broad discretion in the performance of duties is apparently the touchstone. Final decision-making authority, however, is not necessarily dispositive of the issue.[72]

When available, statutory job descriptions have been utilized. For example, in *Catterson v. Caso*[73] the court, in upholding the political dismissal of the county attorney, relied on local county statutes which outlined broad discretionary responsibilities for the office. Similarly, the court in *Newcomb v. Brennan*[74] took judicial notice of the

---

[66]*Id.* at 393 n.5.

[67]In *Elrod* the plurality stated that "justification is a matter of proof, or at least argument, directed at particular jobs." 427 U.S. 347 (1976). See, e.g., *McCollum v. Stahl*, 579 F.2d 869, 873 (4th Cir. 1978) ("The Court [in *Elrod*] emphasized that the determination of the quality of an employee's position is a matter of proof."); *Nekolny v. Painter*, 653 F.2d 1164, 1170 (7th Cir. 1981) ("[I]t [is] for the trier of fact to determine whether [the plaintiff is] a policymaker."); *Retail Clerks v. Leonard*, 450 F. Supp. 663, 667 (E.D. Pa. 1978) ("Since the nature of the status of plaintiffs is critical to the outcome of the case, we believe that a genuine issue of material fact exists [citation omitted] and therefore should not be resolved on a motion for summary judgment * * *."); *Brunton v. United States*, 518 F. Supp. 223 (S.D. Ohio 1981).

[68]555 F.2d 390, 395 (3d Cir. 1977). Accord: *Rivera Morales v. Benitez de Rexach*, 541 F.2d 882 (1st Cir. 1976); *Garretto v. Cooperman*, 510 F. Supp. 816 (S.D.N.Y. 1981); *Hollifield v. McMahan*, 438 F. Supp. 591 (E.D. Tenn. 1977); *Alfaro de Quevedo v. De Jesus Schuck*, 556 F.2d 591, 592 n.3 (1st Cir. 1977) ("[T]he question of who is and who is not a policymaker is ultimately a question of federal law.")

[69]441 F. Supp. 503 (M.D. Fla. 1977), *rev'd*, 625 F.2d 1183 (5th Cir. 1980).

[70]441 F. Supp. 503, 515 (M.D. Fla. 1977).

[71]In *Alfaro de Quevedo v. De Jesus Schuck*, 556 F.2d 591, 593 (1st Cir. 1977), the court found that the removal of an attorney holding the position of director of the office of criminal justice was constitutionally justified inasmuch as the "plaintiff's job gave her a broad discretion to carry out hazily defined purposes and to render advice to the secretary in an area that is far from non-controversial." The court noted that the relevant inquiry is whether the position itself is a policy-making one, not whether her superior placed trust and confidence in the person holding the position. *Id.* at 593 n.4. In *Nekolny v. Painter*, 653 F.2d 1164, 1170 (7th Cir. 1981), the test was stated as "whether the position held by the individual authorizes, either directly or indirectly, meaningful input into government decision making on issues where there is room for principled disagreement on goals or their implementation." It should be noted that *Nekolny* is a post-*Branti* decision: the test fashioned by the *Nekolny* court is, at best, an amalgam of the *Elrod-Branti* dischargeability test, and, at worst, a reversion to the *Elrod* test.

[72]*Indiana State Employees v. Negley*, 365 F. Supp. 225 (S.D. Ind. 1973), *aff'd*, 501 F.2d 1239 (7th Cir. 1974), cited in *Nekolny v. Painter*, 653 F.2d 1164, 1170 (7th Cir. 1981).

[73]472 F. Supp. 833, 837 (E.D.N.Y. 1979). The court also upheld the dismissal on the alternative ground that the employee was in a confidential position with his clients. *Id.* at 838. The alternative basis is questionable in light of *Branti v. Finkel*, 445 U.S. 507 (1980). See *infra* notes 113–118 and accompanying text.

[74]558 F.2d 825 (7th Cir. 1977), *cert. denied*, 430 U.S. 968 (1977). Accord: *Besig v. Friend*, 460 F. Supp. 134 (N.D. Cal. 1978); *McBride v. Griffin*, 62 A.D.2d 520, 405 N.Y.S.2d 353 (1978); *Ause v. Regan*, 59 A.D.2d 317, 399 N.Y.S.2d 526 (1977).

city charter and code of ordinances in determining that the deputy
city attorney occupied a policy-making position. The court in *Stegmaier v. Trammell*[75] intimated that if an employee's duties are specifically delineated rather than broadly defined by statute, he cannot
have the discretionary responsibilities inherent in policy-making positions.[76]

Statutes are not perforce controlling on the issue of policy-making positions. In *Committee to Protect First Amendment v. Bergland*,[77]
the court rejected an argument that Civil Service Commission regulations classifying a position as non-policy-making and nonconfidential was dispositive of the issue. Noting that the regulations were
written more than a decade before *Elrod*, the court concluded that
the basis for civil service classifications was different from the basis
underlying *Elrod*.[78]

Testimony and affidavits also provide a basis for determining
whether a position is a policy-making one. In *Alfaro de Quevedo v.
De Jesus Schuck*,[79] both the employee and a representative of the
employer were in agreement about the employee's duties. They included advising her superior on pending legislation, researching areas
affecting the department, counseling her superior before he addressed
the legislature, preparing annual reports of the work load anticipated
by the department and an annual budget for the department, briefing
and circulating current decisions in the area to other members of the
staff she supervised, and undertaking any additional research her
supervisor might assign her.[80] The court concluded that since the
plaintiff's duties were not "strictly cabined" she occupied a policy-
making position.[81]

The "Confidential" Employee

Policy-making employees may be discharged for their political
beliefs and associations. The lower courts are divided, however, on

[75]597 F.2d 1027 (5th Cir. 1979).
[76]*Id.* at 1037. This distinction provides little guidance. Few, if any, statutes are written
to encompass exact responsibilities.
    A similar argument was proffered by the plaintiffs in *Indiana State Employees v.
Negley*, 501 F.2d 1239, 1242 (7th Cir. 1974). The plaintiffs argued that they were so constrained
by statutes and regulations that they were mere administrative technicians, not policy-makers.
The court conceded that federal and state statutes restricted the plaintiffs' activities, but
concluded they were policy-makers nonetheless since their interpretation of the statutes provided the grounds for local policies. This same argument, advanced by a senior housing inspector, was accepted by the court in *Dyke v. Otlowski*, 154 N.J. Super. 377, 381 A.2d 413
(1977).
[77]626 F.2d 875 (D.C. Cir. 1979).
[78]*Id.* at 880. The court explained that it is not relevant what the civil service regulations
mean; the relevant inquiry is whether they are conclusive on the constitutional issue. *Id.* at
n.14.
[79]556 F.2d 591 (1st Cir. 1977).
[80]*Id.* at 593.
[81]Accord: *Loughney v. Hickey,* 480 F. Supp. 1352 (M.D. Pa. 1977), *remanded,* 635 F.2d 1063
(3d Cir. 1980) (the lower court's detailing of the duties of the plaintiffs, as established by
affidavit, covered six pages of the opinion); *Duff v. Sherlock,* 432 F. Supp. 423 (E.D. Pa. 1977);
Trippy v. Sams, 512 F. Supp. 5 (E.D. Tenn. 1980) (the court concluded that the plaintiff was
a policy-maker based on the affidavit, albeit self-serving, of the defendant); *Rosenberg v.
Redevelopment Auth.,* 428 F. Supp. 498 (E.D. Pa. 1977) (the court granted summary judgment
for the defendant based on nonconflicting affidavits of the plaintiff and defendant).

whether a confidential employee not in a policy-making position may be similarly discharged, or, stated differently, whether an employee must be both policy-making and confidential to be legally discharged for political reasons. If the employee need be only confidential, the number of protected employees under *Elrod* is, of course, drastically diminished.[82]

The court in *Rosenthal v. Rizzo*[83] determined that the term "confidential" is ancillary to the term "policy-maker" and therefore does not alter the basic logic of the dischargeability test:

> "It is true that Mr. Justice Stewart's concurrence in *Elrod* refers to a 'nonpolicy making, confidential government employee.' 427 U.S. at 375, 96 S.Ct. at 2690. In our view the additional adjective—nonconfidential—does not change the basic thrust [of] the plurality opinion, which is directed at policy *formulation* and representative government."[84]

Few courts have addressed this issue. The decision in *Rosenthal*, however, stands alone in finding the dischargeability test to be conjunctive.[85]

Other jurisdictions not only have found the test to be disjunctive, but have broadened the connotation of the word "confidential" to include employees in a confidential relation to non-policy-making positions. In *Stegmaier v. Trammell*,[86] the court found that a deputy circuit clerk did not occupy a policy-making position. The court upheld his discharge as constitutional, however, because he was in a confidential position to the circuit clerk, even though the circuit clerk was in a non-policy-making position.[87]

The question was phrased differently in *Loughney v. Hickey*.[88] The court narrowed the issue to "whether plaintiffs were municipal employees who were advisors to a policy maker and who constantly participated in and were privy to the discussions and information involved in the policy making process."[89] Answering in the affir-

---

[82]For example, a secretary, obviously in a non-policy-making job, may be discharged merely because he may have access to confidential material. The wording in the plurality opinion belies the constitutionality of such a dismissal. See *The Supreme Court, 1975 Term*, 90 HARV. L. REV. 186, 193–194 (1976) for a contrary view.

[83]555 F.2d 390 (3d Cir. 1977). See also *Livas v. Petka*, 711 F.2d 798 (7th Cir. 1983); *Gannon v. Daley*, 561 F. Supp. 1377 (N.D. Ill. 1983).

[84]*Id.* at 393 n.5.

[85]The court in *Finkel v. Branti*, 457 F. Supp. 1284 (S.D.N.Y. 1978), *aff'd*, 598 F.2d 609 (2d Cir. 1979), came to a similar conclusion. It is not cited in support of this proposition, however, since it is the case in which the Supreme Court later reformulated the criteria for constitutionally valid political patronage dismissals. 445 U.S. 507 (1980).

[86]597 F.2d 1027 (5th Cir. 1979).

[87]There were extenuating circumstances in this case which may explain the liberal interpretation of the *Elrod* dischargeability test. An Alabama statute empowered the deputy circuit clerk to conduct all the business which the clerk was authorized to conduct. Additionally, an Alabama statute provided that the clerk was civilly liable for failure to perform his duties. Since the clerk could be held liable for duties his deputy failed to perform, the court allowed that he must be able to select a deputy on whom he had absolute trust and confidence. *Id.* at 1040. While this rationale is commendable, it may not be within the confines of the *Elrod* holding. See also *McCollum v. Stahl*, 579 F.2d 869 (4th Cir. 1978).

[88]480 F. Supp. 1352 (M.D. Pa. 1979), *remanded*, 635 F.2d 1063 (3d Cir. 1980), in light of *Branti v. Finkel*, 445 U.S. 507 (1980).

[89]480 F. Supp. 1352, 1363 (M.D. Pa. 1979).

mative, the court held that the former superintendents of refuse and highways had the duty to discuss establishment and implementation of policy and were therefore part of the policy-making process.[90] Thus, in reaching its decision the court looked not to individual employees as confidential or policy-making, but to the entire process of policy-making.

Burden of Proof

Plaintiffs bringing political patronage dismissal actions under Section 1983 must show that the conduct engaged in by the defendant was under color of state law and that such conduct denied him privileges or rights guaranteed by the Constitution. If political association or belief is demonstrated to be the basis of the dismissal, the burden then shifts to the defendant to prove by a preponderance of the evidence that the plaintiff would have been discharged for other reasons in any case.

This shifting burden, enunciated in *Mt. Healthy City School District Board of Education v. Doyle*,[91] was elaborated in *Givhan v. Western Line Consolidated School District*.[92] The Supreme Court explained in *Givhan* that the initial burden is on the employee to show that his conduct is constitutionally protected. He must then establish that the conduct was a substantial or motivating factor in the employer's decision to discharge him. The burden then shifts to the employer to show by a preponderance of the evidence that it would have reached the same decision notwithstanding the protected conduct. The jury must find that the employee would not have been discharged "but for" the constitutionally immunized activity in order to find in his favor.

Lower courts have frequently found that even if party affiliation is a factor in the dismissal, the dismissal is not constitutionally tainted if independent justification existed. Thus, personnel and budgetary considerations,[93] reorganization of the department,[94] replacement with individuals better qualified than those dismissed,[95] and actions of dismissed employees shown to be disruptive and interfering with the efficient operation of the department[96] all have been held overriding

---

[90]*Id.* at 1364.

[91]429 U.S. 274 (1977). In *Mt. Healthy*, a nontenured school teacher was not rehired because of incidents ranging from making obscene gestures to students to publicly criticizing economic decisions of the school board. The letter notifying him of the board's decision not to rehire him acknowledged that the decision was based, in part, on his First Amendment activity. The Court held that even though the teacher's First Amendment activity was a substantial factor in the board's decision, there would be no constitutional violation if the board could show it would have reached the same decision in the absence of the protected conduct. *Id.* at 287.

[92]439 U.S. 410 (1979).

[93]*Branchick v. Commonwealth's Dep't of Labor & Indus.*, 496 Pa. 280, 436 A.2d 1182 (1981); *Rosaly v. Ignacio*, 593 F.2d 145 (1st Cir. 1979); *Wren v. Jones*, 635 F.2d 1277 (7th Cir. 1980).

[94]*Thompson v. Huecker*, 559 S.W.2d 488 (Ky. Ct. App. 1977).

[95]*Tanner v. McCall*, 625 F.2d 1183 (5th Cir. 1980); *Farkas v. Thornburgh*, 493 F. Supp. 1168 (E.D. Pa. 1980).

[96]*Serna v. Manzano*, 616 F.2d 1165 (10th Cir. 1980).

reasons for dismissal. Anticipation of morale problems within the department because an employee is running for the office held by his employer, however, is not sufficient independent justification.[97]

The Scope of *Elrod*: Failure to Rehire, Reassignment, and Demotion

The decision in *Elrod* dealt with the constitutional limitations of hiring and firing employees. It left unanswered the constitutionality of several related patronage practices: failure to rehire, demotion, failure to promote, and reassignment. Some lower courts have limited the holding to its facts while others have extended it to encompass all forms of patronage employment.[98].

Failure to rehire an employee was expressly found not to be the same as discharging an employee in *Reed v. Hamblen County*,[99] but failure to rehire or reappoint has also been found to be within the parameters of *Elrod*.[100] Failure to promote has been deemed to be within the proscription of *Elrod*,[101] as have demotion and reassignment.[102]

The interest sought to be protected in *Elrod*, freedom from impairment of First Amendment rights, is not accomplished if all forms of coercive activity are not included within the holding. The coercive effect of a demotion may be less in degree than outright dismissal, but it is the same in kind.[103]

Remedies

Both equitable and legal relief have been granted in patronage dismissal cases. Relief has been afforded against employers in both their individual and official capacities. Attorney's fees are also recoverable. Awards for pain and suffering, although not common, have been granted.

Reinstatement is the most favored form of equitable relief; it usually is accompanied by an award of back pay. In *Simmons v.*

---

[97]*Simmons v. Stanton*, 502 F. Supp. 932 (W.D. Miss. 1980).

[98]See Comment, *Political Patronage and the Fourth Circuit's Test of Dischargeability After* Elrod *v.* Burns, 15 WAKE FOREST L. REV. 655, 666–667 (1979).

[99]468 F. Supp. 2 (E.D. Tenn. 1978). Accord: *Ramey v. Harber*, 589 F.2d 753, 757 (4th Cir. 1978) ("the plurality opinion [in Elrod] expressly limited the Court's holding to patronage dismissals").

[100]*Rivera Morales v. Benitez de Rexach*, 541 F.2d 882 (1st Cir. 1976); *Brady v. Patterson*, 515 F. Supp. 695 (N.D.N.Y. 1981); *Bavoso v. Harding*, 507 F. Supp. 313 (S.D.N.Y. 1980).

[101]*DeLuca v. Sullivan*, 450 F. Supp. 736 (D. Mass. 1977); *Cullen v. New York State Civil Serv. Comm'n*, 435 F. Supp. 546 (E.D.N.Y. 1977).

[102]*Morris v. City of Kokomo*, 178 Ind. App. 56, 381 N.E.2d 510 (1978); *Delong v. United States*, 621 F.2d 618 (4th Cir. 1980).

[103]See *Morris v. City of Kokomo*, 178 Ind. App. 56, 381 N.E.2d 510, 518 (1978), and *DeLong v. United States*, 621 F.2d 618 (1980), for a discussion of why the *Elrod* decision should be read to procribe all forms of patronage employment.

Stanton[104] the court ordered reinstatement with seniority of an undersheriff, as well as damages, against the sheriff acting in his official capacity, for loss of pay and fringe benefits.[105] Similar relief has been granted by other courts.[106] The court in *McMullan v. Thornburgh*[107] ordered reinstatement even though the office had been filled subsequent to the improper dismissal. Though sympathizing with the incumbent officeholder, the court expressed the view that the wrongfully discharged employee had a superior legal claim to the position.

Attorney's fees,[108] against a defendant in his individual and official capacity and against a municipality,[109] have been awarded in patronage dismissal cases. The court in *Barrett v. Thomas*[110] awarded attorney's fees to a wrongfully discharged deputy sheriff. The award was against the sheriff and the county even though the county was not named as a defendant in the action.

Punitive damages as well as damages for pain and suffering and mental anguish have been recognized by a limited number of jurisdictions. The court in *Vega Matta v. Alvarez de Choudens*[111] found that an employee had suffered discomfort, anxiety, and economic hardship as a direct result of his termination. Accordingly, the court awarded him $20,000 in general damages, which included damages for mental anguish and emotional distress.[112]

Branti v. Finkel: An Unsuccessful Attempt to Clarify *Elrod v. Burns*

In *Branti v. Finkel*[113] the Court again grappled with the constitutionality of political patronage dismissals. In *Branti*, two republican assistant public defenders were threatened with dismissal by the recently appointed Democratic county public defender. Justice Ste-

---

[104]502 F. Supp. 932 (W.D. Miss. 1980).
[105]*Id.* at 938–939. The fringe benefits included hospital and life insurance and retirement benefits.
[106]See, e.g., *Francia v. White*, 594 F.2d 778 (10th Cir. 1979); *Vincent v. Maeras*, 447 F. Supp. 775 (S.D. Ill. 1978); *Miller v. Board of Educ.*, 450 F. Supp. 116 (S.D. W. Va. 1978); *Hollifield v. McMahan*, 438 F. Supp. 591 (E.D. Tenn. 1977) (legal damages granted but equitable relief based upon past work performance denied).
[107]508 F. Supp. 1044 (E.D. Pa. 1981).
[108]42 U.S.C. §1988 (1980) entitles prevailing plaintiffs in civil rights suits to recover attorney's fees. A party need not win a judgment in order to prevail. *Collins v. Thomas*, 649 F.2d 1203, 1205 (1981), citing *Maher v. Gagne*, 448 U.S. 122 (1980).
[109]If the acts of an official may fairly be said to represent official policy, then a county or municipality is considered to be a person for the purposes of a 42 U.S.C. §1983 action. *Monell v. New York City Dep't of Soc. Servs.*, 436 U.S. 658 (1978).
[110]649 F.2d 1193 (5th Cir. 1981).
[111]440 F. Supp. 251 (D.P.R. 1977), *aff'd*, 577 F.2d 722 (1st Cir. 1977).
[112]*See also Rivera Morales v. Benitez de Rexach*, 541 F.2d 882 (1st Cir. 1976); *Nekolny v. Painter*, 653 F.2d 1164 (7th Cir. 1981); *Carey v. Piphus*, 435 U.S. 247, 264 (1978) (mental and emotional distress resulting from denial of First Amendment rights compensable). But cf. *City of Newport v. Fact Concerts, Inc.*, 453 U.S. 247 (1981) (punitive damages not available against a municipality).
[113]445 U.S. 507 (1980).

vens,[114] writing for the majority, noted that unless the government can demonstrate an overriding vital interest, an employee's private beliefs cannot be the sole basis for depriving him of public employment.[115] The Court held that the critical inquiry hinged not on whether the employee was in a confidential or policy-making position, but on whether "party affiliation is an appropriate requirement for the effective performance of the public office."[116] The Court found no such justifiable requirement in the public defender's office.

Although the *Branti* test ostensibly places a higher burden on the hiring authority, it is less precise than the test proferred by the *Elrod* Court. No guidelines were suggested for making the determination. Consequently, courts considering the issue tend to cite *Branti* but rely on *Elrod* when rendering a decision,[117] or they altogether fail to distinguish the two tests.[118]

The *Branti* holding, on its face, is more restrictive than the *Elrod* dischargeability test. In its application in the short span since it was decided, however, it has proved to be more malleable than the *Elrod* test. Lower courts, themselves sensitive to political realities and pressures, continue to condone political patronage dismissals.

The Hatch Act: A Counterpoint to Impermissible Political Patronage Dismissals

A public employee's First Amendment rights, like those of a private citizen, are not unlimited. Federal employees fall within one of two categories: they are either civil service employees and thus enjoy the protection of a merit system,[119] or they are non-civil-service employees and are thus vulnerable to the vicissitudes of the political arena, subject to any constitutional limitations. Permissible political activities of civil service employees are defined by the Hatch Act.[120]

The *Elrod* Court addressed itself to the constitutionality of dismissing a non-civil-service employee merely because of his political beliefs and associations, not to the constitutionality of dismissing a civil service employee because of his political activities. The latter

---

[114]Justice Stevens did not participate in the *Elrod* decision. He did, however, author the opinion in *Illinois State Employees v. Lewis*, 473 F.2d 561 (7th Cir. 1972), an opinion extensively relied upon in *Elrod*.

[115]445 U.S. 507, 515–516 (1980).

[116]*Id.* at 518.

[117]See e.g., *Nekolny v. Painter*, 653 F.2d 1164 (7th Cir. 1981); *Barrett v. Thomas*, 649 F.2d 1193 (5th Cir. 1981).

[118]See e.g., *McMullan v. Thornburgh*, 508 F. Supp. 1044 (E.D. Pa. 1981).

[119]Until 1978, civil service employees were protected from arbitrary discharge by the Lloyd-LaFollette Act, 5 U.S.C. §7501 (1970), which permitted removal "only for such cause as will promote the efficiency of the service." In the 1978 Civil Service Reform Act, Congress adopted a more comprehensive set of "merit system principles" calling for "fair and equitable" treatment of affected federal employees; judgments about retention of employees based on "the adequacy of their performance"; and protection against "arbitrary action, personal favoritism, or coercion for partisan political purposes." 5 U.S.C. §2031 *et seq.* (1980).

[120]The Hatch Act is scattered throughout Titles 5 and 18 of the U.S. Code.

issue had been resolved in *CSC v. Letter Carriers*[121] three years earlier.

The Hatch Act seeks to achieve political neutrality among civil service employees. It prohibits a federal employee from using his authority or influence to interfere with or affect the result of an election and from taking an active role in political management or political campaigns.[122] An active role in political management or political campaigns is defined as those acts forbidden by civil service rules prior to June 19, 1940,[123] the date of enactment. The Act in effect incorporated by reference approximately 3,000 Civil Service Commission rulings rendered before 1940. Additionally, in 1970 the Civil Service Commission promulgated regulations outlining permissible and prohibited activities.[124] It does not cover federal em-

---

[121]413 U.S. 548 (1973).

[122]5 U.S.C. §7324 (1970) provides: "(a) An employee in an Executive agency or an individual employed by the government of the District of Columbia may not—

"(1) use his official authority or influence for the purpose of interfering with or affecting the result of an election; or

"(2) take an active part in political management or in political campaigns. For the purpose of this subsection, the phrase 'an active part in political management or in political campaigns' means those acts of political management or political campaigning which were prohibited on the part of employees in the competitive service before July 19, 1940, by determinations of the Civil Service Commission under the rules prescribed by the President.

"(b) An employee or individual to whom subsection (a) of this section applies retains the right to vote as he chooses and to express his opinion on political subjects and candidates.

"(c) Subsection (a) of this section does not apply to an individual employed by an educational or research institution, establishment, agency, or system which is supported in whole or in part by the District of Columbia or by a recognized religious, philanthropic, or cultural organization.

"(d) subsection (a)(2) of this section does not apply to—

"(1) an employee paid from the appropriation for the office of the President;

"(2) the head or the assistant head of an Executive department or military department;

"(3) an employee appointed by the President, by and with the advice and consent of the Senate, who determines policies to be pursued by the United States in its relations with foreign powers or in the nationwide administration of Federal laws;

"(4) the Commissioners of the District of Columbia; or

"(5) the Recorder of Deeds of the District of Columbia."

[123]5 U.S.C. §7324(a)(2).

[124]The pertinent regulations, appearing in 5 C.F.R. pt. 733 (1980), provide:

"PERMISSIBLE ACTIVITIES

"§733.121 Permissible activities.

"(a) All employees are free to engage in political activity to the widest extent consistent with the restrictions imposed by law and this subpart.

"(1) Register and vote in any election;

"(2) Express his opinion as an individual privately and publicly on political subjects and candidates;

"(3) Display a political picture, sticker, badge or button;

"(4) Participate in the nonpartisan activities of a civic, community, social, labor or professional organization, or of a similar organization;

"(5) Be a member of a political party or other political organization and participate in its activities to the extend consistent with law;

"(6) Attend a political convention, rally, fund-raising function, or other political gathering;

"(7) Sign a political petition as an individual;

"(8) Make a financial contribution to a political party or organization;

"(9) Take an active part, as an independent candidate, or in support of an independent candidate, in a partisan election covered by §733.124;

"(10) Take an active part, as a candidate or in support of a candidate, in a nonpartisan election;

"(11) Be politically active in connection with a question which is not specifically identified with a political party, such as a constitutional amendment, referendum, approval of a municipal ordinance or any other question or issue of a similar character;

ployees employed by an educational research institution,[125] an employee paid from the appropriations of the Office of the President, the head or assistant head of an executive or military department, an employee appointed by the President with the consent of the Senate who determines foreign or nationwide federal policies, the mayor of the District of Columbia, the members of the council of the District of Columbia, or the recorder of deeds in the District of Columbia.[126]

In *CSC v. Letter Carriers*,[127] individual federal employees and local Democratic and Republican political committees challenged the constitutionality of the Hatch Act. Specifically, they argued that the section of the Act that proscribes classified civil service employees from "taking an active part in political management or in political campaigns" was overbroad and infringed their First Amendment rights. The Court found otherwise.

After tracing the history of the Hatch Act and its predecessor, the Civil Service Act of 1883, the Court noted that federal service should depend upon meritorious performance and not political service.[128] The Court articulated four reasons why government efficiency, a compelling state interest, is promoted by the proscription of active politicking by civil service employees: First, fair and effective government, including the impartial execution of the laws, is more likely. Second, public confidence in representative government requires that civil service employees avoid even the appearance of impropriety. Third, the government is prevented from becoming a united political power block. And fourth, the temptation of public employees to act in accordance with their superior's political proclivities in order to gain favor instead of in the public interest is reduced.[129]

The *Letter Carriers* decision applied only to federal employees. Its companion case, *Broadrick v. Oklahoma*,[130] upheld a similar state statute proscribing political activities of state employees.[131]

"(12) Serve as an election judge or clerk, or in a similar position to perform nonpartisan duties as prescribed by State or local law; and

"(13) Otherwise participate fully in public affairs, except as prohibited by law, in a manner which does not materially compromise his efficiency or integrity as an employee or the neutrality, efficiency, or integrity of his agency.

"(b) Paragraph (a) of this section does not authorize an employee to engage in political activity in violation of law, while on duty, or while in a uniform that identifies him as an employee. The head of an agency may prohibit or limit the participation of an employee or class of employees of his agency in an activity permitted by paragraph (a) of this section, if participation in the activity would interfere with the efficient performance of official duties, or create a conflict or apparent conflict of interests.

"PROHIBITED ACTIVITIES

"§733.121 Use of official authority; prohibition.

"An employee may not use his official authority or influence for the purpose of interfering with or affecting the result of an election.

"§733.122 Political management and political campaigning; prohibitions.
        * * *"

[125]§7324(c).
[126]§7324(d).
[127]413 U.S. 548 (1973).
[128]*Id.* at 557.
[129]*Id.* at 565–566.
[130]413 U.S. 601 (1973).
[131]Each of the 50 states has a "little Hatch Act." See *id.* at 604 n.2 for a listing of individual state statutes.

At first blush it would seem that the rights of public employees are greater than those of their counterparts in the private sector, since public employees are afforded the additional protection of the Constitution. Closer examination, however, reveals that the protection is not significantly greater than that available to the private employee. As shown by the Hatch Act line of cases, public employees may have difficulty exercising their constitutional rights; lacking sufficient guidance from the Supreme Court, the lower courts still find reason to uphold patronage dismissals; and the application of the Due Process Clause to public employees is a very limited protection indeed.

7

Alternate Remedies for Improper Discharge

This chapter deals with eight types of legal actions which may grow out of the employment relationship or be created by the discharge itself. Defamation is treated separately in Chapter 9 because of its time-honored idiosyncracies and recently developed constitutional limitations. The newly developed tort of retaliatory discharge in derogation of public policy, a remarkable judicial innovation in employee protection, also is treated separately in Chapter 8.

The eight types of action discussed in the present chapter are the following:

Fraud. The action for fraud centers around the circumstances of the hiring, including misrepresented or undisclosed facts and false promises that induced the employee to accept the job.

Interference With Employment. Interference with the employment relationship, a frequently overlooked cause of action, may occur when a third party—sometimes even a fellow employee—persuades the employer to discharge an employee.

Emotional Distress. Where the treatment of the employee, usually including discharge, is particularly cruel and callous, an action to recover for emotional or mental distress may be brought, though the courts have been hesitant to recognize a right of action except in truly exceptional cases.

Negligent Performance. Negligent performance of the employment contract by the employer has so far addressed the employer's failure clearly to warn an employee that his conduct will lead to discharge if continued.

Assault and Battery. This action, involving employer liability for

185

the actions of supervisors, is sometimes a companion to a charge of sexual harassment.

Violation of the Right of Privacy. Employee privacy, a matter of special interest in this time of concern for individual rights, may be invaded by the employer's acquisition of personal information or by the disclosure of such information to third parties.

Violation of Antitrust Laws. The antitrust laws, intended to prevent unreasonable restraint of trade, may apply where employers combine to restrict employee mobility or may provide remedies to discharged employees in certain other situations.

Blacklisting and Adverse References. State statutes may protect terminated employees from being blacklisted or from certain employer practices with respect to references.

Tort remedies do not depend upon the existence of a contract; they represent socially imposed restraints on the employment relationship. Nevertheless, the common law has eschewed mechanical application of tort principles to employment cases, construing these principles with due recognition of the need to balance employer discretion and employee protection.

The treatment of these torts in this chapter is not comprehensive, but is focused on issues that arise in employment discharge cases. Other principles of recovery and defense must be examined by reference to general texts and the Restatements if the analysis of a case is to be complete.

Employment Fraud

The action in tort for deceit is applicable where an employee has been seriously misled concerning the employment, and the action typically begins with a discharge or refusal to hire. In a fraud case, the focus is generally on statements made to the employee at the time of hiring or when the employee was induced to stay on the job rather than accept an outside offer.[1]

As a general rule, the employee who is able to make out a claim of fraud may also have facts that prove a contract claim. Although ordinarily a contract theory requires a showing of an unfulfilled promise of some kind of employment security, the fraud theory requires more, i.e., proof of an intent to deceive and reasonable reliance by the

---

[1]In *Gardner v. Celanese Corp.*, 88 Ga. App. 642, 76 S.E.2d 817 (1953), however, the fraud consisted of telling the employee that he had been furloughed or laid off when in fact his employment had been terminated. Recovery was based on the employee's inability to find substitute work because prospective employers refused to hire him because he might go back to work for the defendant. *Silver v. Mohasco Corp.*, 94 A.D.2d 820, 462 N.Y.S.2d 917 (1983), found no fraud in the employer's failure to carry out its promise concerning references made at the time of termination.

employee.[2] At first blush, then, it would appear that fraud is at best a cumulative remedy, requiring a heavier burden of proof. But, it opens the door to a tort measure of damages and perhaps punitive damages.

If an employee seeks to make out a contract claim, several hurdles will be in the way. The terminable-at-will rule, for instance, may bar the contract claim; or a strict construction of the meaning of the words used may result in a finding that no bargain was reached. This does not necessarily bar the fraud claim. A promise which may at best be implied from specific statements of fact may not be actionable in contract; but if those statements were knowingly false when made, an action for fraud could arise. A court unwilling to enforce a claim based on a lifetime employment contract may be ready to provide damages in tort based on what the employee gave up on account of deceit.

The Existing Facts Rule

To make out a fraud, courts often recite a formula requiring proof of (1) a misrepresentation of material, existing fact (2) made with knowledge of falsity (or *scienter*) (3) with the intent to induce the plaintiff to rely (or "intent to defraud"); (4) reasonable reliance by the plaintiff; and (5) damages. This formula,[3] while it states the requirements of fraud generally, is not the sole test. Particular situations, including those most likely to involve employment, have special rules.

In the typical employment case, as described above, the strict requirements of the test would be met only on those rare occasions where the employer both falsified existing facts and made insincere promises. Even then, there would have to be a specific and positive assertion of fact by the employer for an action to be possible.

To increase protection for victims of deceit, courts have recognized two kinds of exceptions to the existing facts rule which have been relied on in employment cases. First, the courts have been willing to find fraud in representations of fact implied in promises, statements, and expressions of opinion or in concealment of related material facts. Second, the making of a promise with a present intent not to perform has been recognized as actionable in specified circumstances.

With these exceptions,[4] however, the existing facts rule governs; and opinions, predictions, projections, and statements of expectation

---

[2]See RESTATEMENT (SECOND) OF TORTS §525 (1977).

[3]W. Prosser, HANDBOOK ON THE LAW OF TORTS 685–686 (4th ed. 1971). See, e.g., *Hart v. McLucas*, 535 F.2d 516, 519 (9th Cir. 1976), and *United States v. Kiefer*, 228 F.2d 448 (D.C. Cir. 1955).

[4]Where there is no identifiable representation of fact, promise, or concealed fact, as was the case in *Senec v. L.M. Berry Co.*, 299 So.2d 433 (La. Ct. App. 1974), no action for fraud can lie. The Restatement position is that a misrepresentation may be of fact, opinion, intention or law, RESTATEMENT (SECOND) OF TORTS §525 (1977), but that nonfactual statements give rise to special problems of the reasonableness of reliance.

cannot form the basis for a fraud suit. An example of what is required may be found in *Espaillat v. Berlitz School of Languages*,[5] where the employee made a specific inquiry prior to hiring concerning whether noncitizen status would interfere with employment and was falsely told that citizenship was not a requirement of the job.[6] Among the misleading statements of the seller-employer in *Midwest Chevrolet Corp. v. Noah*[7] was a false supporting statement that another buyer had been provided with work.

Not suprisingly, many false prediction cases involve employees whose hopes of high compensation have been disappointed. Where statements of income are phrased as possibilities[8] or profits are simply "envisioned,"[9] an action for fraud is not available. In *Kelly Tire Service, Inc. v. Kelly Springfield Tire*,[10] the understanding of both parties that the projected income was no more than a projection was dispositive.

The courts are no more anxious to find a fraud in general employer expressions of good faith than they are to find a contract. Nor do "puffing" and overly optimistic statements of the outlook suffice to establish deceit. However, where the facts suggest that an employee has been misled in a serious way, and that the employer is responsible, the problem will be analyzed for implied misrepresentation or concealment, and for false promises. Where the exceptions do not apply, the existing fact rule will bar a suit.

Representations Implied in Hiring

Employment is always contracted for within a specific factual context. The surrounding circumstances may suggest that a promise was implied; the hiring negotiations, however short, will always be conducted in the context of certain mutually understood facts. Some of those are facts spelled out in writing or discussed openly; others

---

[5]217 A.2d 655 (D.D.C. 1966), *rev'd on other grounds*, 383 F.2d 220 (D.C. Cir. 1967).

[6]*Espaillat* shows that the distinction between fact and prediction is not always clear. The representation that alien status "would not interfere" with employment sounds like a future prediction, but is more correctly viewed as a statement that "citizenship is not a necessary qualification." In *Hartwig v. Bitter*, 29 Wis.2d 653, 139 N.W.2d 644 (1966), the court held that an expression of opinion as to future events that is incompatible with existing facts known to the speaker is fraud.

[7]173 Okla. 198, 48 P.2d 283 (1935). See also *Casale v. Dooner Laboratories, Inc.*, 503 F.2d 303 (4th Cir. 1973) (false statement concerning higher salary to accompany change in jobs and concerning nature of employer's business); *Hanson v. Ford Motor Co.*, 278 F.2d 586 (8th Cir. 1980) (false supporting statement of earnings of others); *Doody v. John Sexton & Co.*, 411 F.2d 1119 (1st Cir. 1969) (misrepresentations concerning "permanent" employment).

[8]*Peurify v. Congressional Motors, Inc.*, 254 Md. 501, 255 A.2d 332 (1969) (employee would "possibly" earn more than $45,000 in rest of year).

[9]*Lanzi v. Brooks*, 54 A.D.2d 1057, 388 N.Y.S.2d 946 (1976).

[10]338 F.2d 248 (8th Cir. 1964). See also *Jewell v. Shell Oil Co.*, 172 Wash. 603, 21 P.2d 243 (1933); *Lyxell v. Vautrin*, 604 F.2d 18 (5th Cir. 1979); *Shear v. National Rifle Ass'n of Am.*, 606 F.2d 1251 (D.C. Cir. 1979).

are so basic that no discussion is necessary,[11] or they are necessarily implied by the offer of a job itself.

A good example is the implied representation of continued availability of work. An employer who offers a fixed term contract offers employment that is necessarily temporary in nature. The employer who hires for an indefinite term may be free to terminate at will, but an indefinite term often, perhaps usually, implies that the job will continue to exist and be available in the foreseeable future. There is no representation that circumstances could not or will not change; but there is an implied representation that there are no presently existing facts that will cut the job off shortly after the employee comes to work.

In *Wildes v. Pens Unlimited Co.*[12] the court found fraud where shortly after the employee was hired for a specific sales representative position, his position was eliminated in a reorganization. The restructuring was known to have been contemplated at the time of hiring, and the termination took place three days after the employee, at the company's urging, relinquished another position elsewhere.

In *Andolson v. Berlitz School of Languages*[13] the school hired the employee knowing he was hesitant to leave his existing job, and shortly thereafter discharged him because of his alien status, of which it was aware at the time of hiring. The court found fraud in the luring away of this employee at the very time the employer was telling its customer, the U.S. Army, that it would try to employ only U.S. citizens and would get rid of all alien employees within the year.[14]

Another necessary implication of the offer of a job is that the employee is, at the time of hire, acceptable to the employer. In *McGrath v. Zenith Radio Corp.*,[15] the employee surrendered his stock and a stock option to the acquiring company based on an assurance that he would become president of the acquired company. The undisclosed collateral fact was that his superiors had met and decided that instead of promoting him, they would fire him. Discharge was plainly inconsistent with a promotion, and the promise of the promotion carried

---

[11]See RESTATEMENT (SECOND) OF TORTS §525 comment e (1977). Some basic "implied facts" are the following: The employee will be paid in U.S. dollars, not Hong Kong dollars; the employee will work on the employer's premises; customary workday hours will be applicable; pay increases will be considered or provided at some interval. Any of these or other points may be varied by agreement, but absent any discussion it is fair to assume that such basic points as those noted above are understood because they are customary.

[12]389 A.2d 837 (Me. 1978).

[13]196 A.2d 926 (D.C. 1964).

[14]A similar employee expression of concern was present in *Elizaga v. Kaiser Found. Hosp., Inc.*, 259 Ore. 542, 487 P.2d 870 (1971), where the employee specifically inquired whether, as a foreign medical student, he met the requirements for the preceptorship he was being offered. The hospital's response that he did was true, but its failure to disclose that the program that created the position was in jeopardy was found to be actionable misrepresentation.

In neither *Andolsun* nor *Elizaga* did the court hold that nondisclosure in the face of the expressed employee concern was the gist of the action, and perhaps both plaintiffs would have prevailed without the expression. The employer's knowledge of the employee's situation certainly was important in showing that an implied representation did exist.

[15]651 F.2d 458 (7th Cir. 1981).

with it an untrue representation that the employee was acceptable to the acquiring company.

Promise With Intent Not to Perform

In some cases the employer buttresses its promises of good fortune on the job with specific falsehoods; in others it withholds existing facts inconsistent with the offer of a job and allows the false and misleading implication of available work and employer satisfaction to stand. More usual, however, is the case of the employer who offers a specific job, or particular terms of a job, as a ruse to lure the employee into coming to work for it in some other job. No false facts are stated, nor is any existing fact inconsistent with hiring concealed. The deceit, however, is still present; to remedy that deceit the courts recognize a fraud action where a promise is made with a present intent not to perform.[16]

A promise without intent to perform requires that the employer, at the time the promise is made, have a present intent not to perform. The action for fraud does not lie simply because the promise, honestly made, is not fulfilled.[17] The violation of a promise is one of the requirements for this kind of action, but is not enough standing alone. When the employer makes the promise, it must be with a fraudulent intent, i.e., the intent to deceive the employee.[18]

Duty to Disclose Change of Intent

In *Yunkers v. Whitcraft*[19] the employee claimed fraud based on the employer's failure to disclose its change of intention. The promise in that case was to employ the plaintiff as director of a contemplated school, and the employee-plaintiff conceded that the promise was genuine when made. He argued that before he relied on the promise the employer had decided not to fulfill the promise, and that the employer was obligated to disclose its change of intent. The court found no liability because the evidence disclosed a deteriorating relationship, which the plaintiff must have recognized as such at the time he claimed to rely on the promise. On the other hand, in *McGrath*

---

[16]*Casale v. Dooner Laboratories, Inc.*, 503 F.2d 303 (4th Cir. 1973); *Sea-Land Serv., Inc. v. O'Neal*, 224 Va. 343, 297 S.E.2d 647 (1982); *Hamlen v. Fairchild Indus., Inc.*, 413 So.2d 800 (Fla. Dist. Ct. App. 1982). Justice Holmes once observed, in this context, that the state of a man's mind is as much a fact as the state of his digestion, and that a promise was no more than a representation of the promisor's state of mind. See also RESTATEMENT (SECOND) OF TORTS §530(1) (1977). The court in *Lanham v. Mr. B's Oil Co.*, 166 Ga. App. 372, 304 S.E.2d 738 (1983), contrary to the other cases cited in this section, held that false promises of employment terminable at will were not actionable.

[17]*Lanzi v. Brooks*, 54 A.D.2d 1057, 388 N.Y.S.2d 946 (1976); *Silver v. Mohasco Corp.*, 94 A.D.2d 820, 462 N.Y.S.2d 917 (1983) (refusal to provide references promised at time of termination).

[18]*Birmingham Broadcasting Co. v. Bell*, 259 Ala. 656, 68 So.2d 314 (1953); *Goodwin v. Dinkler St. Louis Management Corp.*, 419 S.W.2d 70 (Mo. 1967); *Hudson v.Venture Indus., Inc.*, 147 Ga. App. 31, 248 S.E.2d 9 (1978).

[19]57 N.M. 642, 261 P.2d 829 (1953).

v. Zenith Radio Corp.,[20] the decision not to fulfill the promise of employment was subject to serious doubt almost immediately after it was made and well prior to the acts of reliance by the employee. The court found that the failure to correct the mistaken impression was a continuing course of conduct amounting to fraud.[21]

Recovery for Unintentional Falsity in Job Promises

Jurisdictions that recognize negligent misrepresentation as a tort[22] may indirectly permit recovery for a promised job that is not provided. In *McAfee v. Rockford Coca-Cola Bottling Co.*,[23] the employer's agents promised a job which they had apparent, but not actual, authority to award to the plaintiff. Relying on an assurance that the job was his and on the new employer's telling him he should feel free to resign from his prior job, the employee quit his job. Two days later the employee was told he would not be hired.

The *McAfee* court recognized that an action for fraud could not be based on the misrepresentation of a future event.[24] However, it apparently allowed an action based on the direct statement to the plaintiff because authority to make the promise was impliedly represented, and the speaker had been negligent in ascertaining the extent of his authority and whether it was safe for the plaintiff to terminate his prior employment, even absent any intent to defraud. No element of *scienter* was required.[25] *McAfee* still requires, however, that the representation or promise be made in a situation where the employer's agent would know, in the absence of negligence, that the statement was untrue or the promise was unreliable. In most jurisdictions the *scienter* requirement for a fraud suit may be satisfied by a showing of reckless disregard for the truth or "conscious indifference" to the truth, a state of mind more serious than negligence.

Necessity of Proving a "Scheme or Device"

Proof that a promise was made without an intent to perform cannot generally be based solely on the fact that the promise was broken.[26] In *Doody v. John Sexton & Co.*,[27] the employer's admission that he had been "kidding" when specific promises about the job were made was enough to establish that there was no intent to perform at the time of the promise. Generally, however, circumstantial evi-

---

[20]651 F.2d 458 (7th Cir. 1981).
[21]*Id.* at 468.
[22]RESTATEMENT (SECOND) OF TORTS §552 (1977).
[23]40 Ill. App.3d 521, 352 N.E.2d 50 (1976).
[24]*Id.* at 523, 352 N.E.2d at 52.
[25]*Id.* at 527, 352 N.E.2d at 55.
[26]RESTATEMENT (SECOND) OF TORTS §530(1) comment d; *Bracewell v. Bryan*, 57 Ala. App. 494, 329 So.2d 552 (1976); *Lanzi v. Brooks*, 54 A.D.2d 1057, 388 N.Y.S.2d 946 (1976). Contra: *Boyd v. Bevilacqua*, 247 Cal. App.2d 272, 292, 55 Cal. Rptr. 610, 624 (1967). See *Sherman v. Mutual Benefit Life Ins. Co.*, 633 F.2d 782, 785 (9th Cir. 1980).
[27]411 F.2d 1119 (1st Cir. 1969).

dence must be relied upon to prove that the promise was not genuine when made.

In jurisdictions which require that the promise be shown to be part of a scheme of fraud, or to be a "device," fraudulent intent must be shown by more than just failure to perform.[28] Intent to defraud, after all, is a requirement of any intentional fraud action; the scheme or device requirement calls for the plaintiff to prove some larger design or ulterior purpose which was served by the promise.

Among the circumstances that have been held to establish the fraudulent intent are a scheme to eliminate the plaintiff as a competitor by false employment promises;[29] to obtain a sale of stock by the employee;[30] to make a sale to the employee;[31] and to obtain the benefit of the employee's reputation[32] or otherwise unavailable services.[33]

Reasonableness of Employee's Reliance

Actions for employment fraud have been founded on a variety of types of employee reliance. Investment of money[34] and purchases or sales of stock[35] or other property[36] are tangible forms of reliance recognized in the cases. An employee's giving up of other work[37] and giving a business the benefit of his reputation[38] are also recognized as actionable forms of reliance.

Employee reliance must be reasonable in the eyes of the law. Thus an employee who has good reason to doubt the sincerity of promises because of their equivocal nature or who knows of a lack of authority to make a promise cannot blindly rely.[39] The standard of caution imposed on the plaintiff in a fraud case, however, is not high; and so long as the plaintiff has acted with due regard for the protection of his own interests, he need not have anticipated or expected deception.[40]

Some cases suggest that an action cannot be based on a false

---

[28]*Wilhoute v. Fastenware, Inc.*, 354 F. Supp. 856, 858 (N.D. Ill. 1973).

[29]*Bondi v. Jewels by Elwar, Ltd.*, 267 Cal. App.2d 672, 73 Cal. Rptr. 494 (1968); *Page v. Pilot Life Ins. Co.*, 192 S.C. 59, 55 S.E.2d 454 (1939).

[30]*Powers v. American Traffic Signal Corp.*, 167 Minn. 327, 209 N.W. 16 (1926).

[31]*King Sales Co. v. McKey*, 104 Ga. App. 63, 121 S.E.2d 48 (1961) (employer refusal to rescind sale after repudiation of promise of employment); *Blasingame v. American Materials, Inc.*, 654 S.W.2d 659 (Tenn. 1983) (employer promised stock sale to induce employee to come to work).

[32]*Smyth v. Fleischmann*, 214 S.C. 263, 52 S.E.2d 199 (1949).

[33]*Lipsit v. Leonard*, 64 N.J. 276, 315 A.2d 25 (1974).

[34]*Hanson v. Ford Motor Co.*, 278 F.2d 586 (8th Cir. 1980); *Blasingame v. American Materials, Inc.*, 654 S.W.2d 659 (Tenn. 1983).

[35]*Powers v. American Traffic Signal Corp.*, 167 Minn. 327, 209 N.W. 16 (1926); *McGrath v. Zenith Radio Corp.*, 651 F.2d 458 (7th Cir. 1981).

[36]*Midwest Chevrolet Corp. v. Noah*, 173 Okla. 198, 48 P.2d 283 (1935).

[37]*Casale v. Dooner Laboratories, Inc.*, 503 F.2d 303 (4th Cir. 1973).

[38]*Smyth v. Fleischmann*, 214 S.C. 263, 52 S.E.2d 199 (1949).

[39]*Lanzi v. Brooks*, 54 A.D.2d 1057, 388 N.Y.S.2d 946 (1976).

[40]E.g., *McAfee v. Rockford Coca-Cola Bottling Co.*, 40 Ill. App.3d 521, 352 N.E.2d 50 (1976).

promise of lifetime employment unsupported by consideration.[41] This position may be based on the proposition that a misrepresentation of the law is not actionable. Other cases, however, permit recovery based on false promises of permanent employment,[42] or raise an estoppel to assert the legal right to terminate at will where the employer has promised not to invoke that right.[43] Since the premise underlying the claim that a promise was made with intent not to perform is that the defendant has falsely represented its intention, as distinguished from its legal rights, there is no apparent reason to require that the promise be legally enforceable.[44] In many cases, the inability to enforce the promise as a contract is the very circumstance which makes it possible for the promise to serve as a fraudulent device.

Related Fraud Remedies

In particular circumstances, an action for fraud might be based on SEC Rule 10(b)-5, which prohibits fraud in connection with the purchase or sale of securities.[45] The employment promise, statement or omission must be material to the transaction[46] and must be "in connection with" the sale.[47] In *McGrath v. Zenith Radio Corp.*,[48] the court found that a false promise of continued employment following acquisition of the employee's stock met the requirements for securities fraud.[49] While no reported cases address the issue, the Racketeering Influenced and Corrupt Organizations Act[50] could possibly,

---

[41]*Barrett v. Foresters*, 625 F.2d 73 (5th Cir. 1980) (Georgia law); *Sanis v. Duncan & Copeland, Inc.*, 153 Ga. App. 765, 266 S.E.2d 546 (1980); *Ely v. Stratoflex*, 132 Ga. App. 569, 208 S.E.2d 583 (1974). It should be pointed out that the terminable-at-will rule under Georgia law is based on an express statutory provision. GA. CODE §66–101 (1982).

[42]E.g., *Sherman v. Mutual Benefit Life Ins. Co.*, 633 F.2d 782, 785 (9th Cir. 1980) (California law); *Doody v. John Sexton & Co.*, 411 F.2d 1119 (1st Cir. 1969) (Massachusetts law).

[43]*Brawthen v. H&R. Block, Inc.*, 28 Cal. App.3d 139, 104 Cal. Rptr. 486 (1972), *appeal following remand*, 52 Cal. App.3d 139, 124 Cal. Rptr. 845 (1975).

[44]In *Morsinkhoff v. DeLuxe Laundry & Dry Cleaning Co.*, 344 S.W.2d 639 (Mo. App. 1961), however, the court denied a fraud remedy to an individual who left a prior position in reliance on a promise of a job on the premise that he accepted a position terminable at will and could be terminated lawfully on a moment's notice. But in *Grouse v. Group Health Plan, Inc.*, 306 N.W.2d 114 (Minn. 1981), the court relied on the doctrine of promissory estoppel to allow a remedy to an employee who resigned a prior position in reliance on a promise of employment for an indefinite term.

[45]Actions may be brought under Section 10(b) of the 1934 Securities Exchange Act, 15 U.S.C. §78j (1982), and SEC Rule 10(b)(5), 17 C.F.R. §240.10(b)(5) (1982); *Superintendent of Ins. v. Bankers Life & Casualty Co.*, 404 U.S. 6 (1971).

[46]*Robinson v. Cupples Container Co.*, 513 F.2d 1274 (9th Cir. 1975).

[47]*Ketchum v. Green*, 557 F.2d 1022 (3d Cir. 1977) (where sale of stock was mere incident of termination of employment resulting from struggle for corporate control, use of guile and deceit in power struggle was not "in connection with" sale of securities).

[48]651 F.2d 458 (7th Cir. 1981).

[49]While Rule 10(b)(5) is said to envision a lower standard of proof of fraud, the plaintiff must still prove a "security transaction" *Teamsters v. Daniel*, 439 U.S. 551 (1979); deception relating to the security transaction, *Santa Fe Indus., Inc. v. Green*, 430 U.S. 462 (1977); an intent to defraud, *Ernst & Ernst v. Hochfelder*, 425 U.S. 185 (1976); and that he was a "purchaser or seller" of a security, *Blue Chip Stamps v. Manor Drug Stores*, 421 U.S. 721 (1975).

[50]18 U.S.C. §§1961–1968 (1976) ("RICO").

in a proper case, create a federal treble damage remedy for multiple acts of employment fraud.[51]

Interference With the Employment Relationship

Though an employee may not have any legal right to continued employment as against the employer, tort law provides a substantial protection against third parties who procure the employee's discharge. As the law has been applied, a large portion of employee discharges without just cause are potentially within this protection.

The action for interference with contract[52] may remedy a discharge resulting from the improper exercise of influence by a third party, even, in some circumstances, another employee. The employment relationship is said to represent a valuable property interest of the employee,[53] and the employee has a manifest interest in the freedom of the employer to exercise its independent judgment without illegal interference or compulsion.[54]

Tortious interference requires a showing of (1) a contract relationship of the employee (2) known to the defendant; (3) an intentional procurement of the employee's discharge; (4) lack of justification; and (5) proximately caused damages. The critical element is invariably that of justification. Because of the various types of third parties and the many different reasons for interference that exist, the case law addresses a wide variety of situations.

Interference cases have been brought where a defendant who does business with the employer procures the employee's discharge;[55]

---

[51]RICO is a highly technical statute, but it has been broadly construed. See, e.g., *United States v. Turkette*, 452 U.S. 576 (1981); *Schact v. Brown*, 711 F.2d 1343 (7th Cir. 1983); *Bennett v. Berg*, 685 F.2d 1053 (8th Cir. 1982). Note, *Civil RICO: The Temptation and Impropriety of Judicial Restriction*, 95 HARV. L. REV. 1101 (1982).

The statute could apply to an employment fraud where multiple uses of the mails or telephone or telegraph wire transmissions took place in furtherance of a fraudulent scheme, constituting a "pattern of racketeering activity," as defined by 18 U.S.C. §1961 (1976). Any "person" who participated in the conduct of the affairs of an "enterprise" through that pattern would be exposed to treble damage liability by the literal terms of the statute. See 18 U.S.C. §§1962(c), 1964 (1976).

[52]The same general tort goes by several names: interference with contractual relations, inducing breach of contract, and the broader interference with prospective advantage. The prospective advantage tort reflects a situation in which no contract has been formed, and a prospective advantage is generally entitled to less legal protection against interference than a contract right. The general approach and basis for liability, however, are the same. See *Muller v. Stromberg Carlson Corp.*, 427 So.2d 266, 271 (Fla. Dist. Ct. App. 1983).

[53]*Byars v. Baptist Medical Centers, Inc.*, 361 So.2d 350 (Ala. 1978); *Tash v. Houston*, 74 Mich. App. 566, 254 N.W.2d 579 (1977); *Evans v. Swain*, 245 Ala. 641, 18 So.2d 400 (1944); *Blender v. Superior Court*, 55 Cal. App.2d 24, 130 P.2d 179 (1942).

[54]*American Surety Co. v. Schottenbauer*, 257 F.2d 6, 10 (8th Cir. 1958), citing *Truax v. Raich*, 239 U.S. 33, 38 (1915).

[55]E.g., *Smith v. Ford Motor Co.*, 289 N.C. 71, 221 S.E.2d 282 (1976) (manufacturer–dealership); *Pearse v. McDonald's Sys.*, 47 Ohio App.2d 20, 351 N.E.2d 788 (1975) (franchisor–franchisee); *Hopper v. Lennen & Mitchell*, 52 F. Supp. 319 (S.D. Cal. 1943) (radio sponsor–producer); *Sullivan v. Barrows*, 303 Mass. 197, 21 N.E.2d 275 (1939) (union–employer).

a number of such cases have involved insurance companies.[56] Creditors of the employee are also a source of interference with contract claims,[57] and some cases arise out of a former employer's interference with the employee's new job.[58] In a significant number of cases the interference is internal, with one employee, often a supervisor, charged with persuading the employer to discharge another employee.[59]

The overwhelming weight of authority holds that a terminable-at-will employment relationship is protected against unlawful interference by third parties.[60] While there are isolated decisions that hold to the contrary,[61] the rule is recognized by jurisdictions unwilling to extend even the most limited protection against wrongful discharge to employees at will when the employer is the defendant.[62]

Recognition of an action for interference with at-will employment is consistent with the growing trend toward permitting recovery for

---

[56]E.g., *Pino v. Protection Maritime Ins. Co.*, 454 F. Supp. 210 (D. Mass. 1978), *aff'd*, 599 F.2d 10 (1st Cir. 1979); *Green v. Lundquist Agency, Inc.*, 2 Mich. App. 488, 140 N.W.2d 575 (1966); *Zimmerman v. Gianelloni*, 206 S.W.2d 843 (Tex. Civ. App. 1947); *United States Fidelity & Guar. Co. v. Millonas*, 206 Ala. 147, 89 So. 732 (1921); *London Guar. Co. v. Horn*, 206 Ill. 493, 69 N.E. 526 (1904).

[57]E.g., *Doughty v. First Pa. Bank*, 463 F. Supp. 822 (E.D. Pa. 1978); *Messina v. Continental Purchasing Co.*, 272 N.Y. 175, 5 N.E.2d 62 (1937); *Southern Fin. Co. v. Foster*, 19 Ala. App. 109, 95 So. 338 (1923); *Doucette v. Salinger*, 228 Mass. 444, 117 N.E. 897 (1917).

[58]*Webster v. Holly Hill Lumber Co.*, 268 S.C. 416, 234 S.E.2d 232 (1977); *Stebbins & Roberts, Inc. v. Halsey*, 265 Ark. 903, 582 S.W.2d 266 (1979).

[59]E.g., *Ramsey v. Greenwald*, 91 Ill. App.3d 855, 414 N.E.2d 1266 (1980); *Ramsey v. Rudd*, 49 N.C. App. 670, 272 S.E.2d 162 (1980); *Straynar v. Jack W. Harris Co.*, 150 Ga. App. 509, 258 S.E.2d 248 (1979); *Harless v. First Nat'l Bank*, 289 S.E.2d 692 (W. Va. 1982); *Murtha v. Yonkers Child Care Ass'n*, 45 N.Y.2d 913, 383 N.E.2d 865, 411 N.Y.S.2d 219 (1978); *Ladd v. Roane Hosiery, Inc.*, 556 S.W.2d 758 (Tenn. 1977); *McGraw v. Hash*, 132 W. Va. 127, 51 S.E.2d 774 (1949); *Muller v. Stromberg Carlson Corp.*, 427 So.2d 266 (Fla. Dist. Ct. App. 1983); *Martin v. Federal Life Ins. Co.*, 109 Ill. App.3d 596, 440 N.E.2d 998 (1982); *Electrolux v. Lawson*, 684 P.2d 340 (Colo. App. 1982).

[60]RESTATEMENT (SECOND) OF TORTS §766, comment g (1977); *Cummings v. Walsh Constr. Co.*, 561 F. Supp. 872 (S.D. Ga. 1983); *Bachand v. Connecticut Gen. Life Ins. Co.*, 101 Wis. 2d 617, 305 N.W.2d 149 (Ct. App. 1981); *Hennessey v. NCAA*, 564 F.2d 1136 (5th Cir. 1977); *Ladd v. Roane Hosiery, Inc.*, 556 S.W.2d 758 (Tenn. 1977); *Tash v. Houston*, 74 Mich. App. 566, 254 N.W.2d 579 (1977); *American Surety Co. v. Schottenbauer*, 257 F.2d 6 (8th Cir. 1958); *Evans v. McKey*, 212 S.W. 680 (Tex. Civ. App. 1919); *Carter v. U.S. Coal & Coke Co.*, 84 W. Va. 624, 100 S.E. 405 (1919); *London Guar. Co. v. Horn*, 206 Ill. 493, 69 N.E. 526 (1904); *Ott v. Gandy*, 66 Ga. App. 684, 195 S.E.2d 180 (1942); *Southern Fin. Co. v. Foster*, 19 Ala. App. 109, 95 So. 338 (1923); *McCarter v. Baltimore Chamber of Commerce*, 126 Md. 131, 94 A. 541 (1915) (day-to-day contract); *Scott v. Prudential Outfitting Co.*, 92 Misc. 195, 155 N.Y.S. 497 (Sup. Ct. 1915); *Lopes v. Connolly*, 210 Mass. 487, 97 N.E. 80 (1912); *Ruddy v. Journeymen Plumbers*, 79 N.J.L. 467, 75 A. 742 (1911); *Chambers v. Probst*, 145 Ky. 381, 140 S.W. 572 (1911); *Tennessee Coal, Iron & Rail Co. v. Kelly*, 163 Ala. 348, 50 So. 1008 (1909); *Brennan v. Hatters*, 73 N.J.L. 729, 65 A. 165 (1906); *Holder v. Cannon Mfg. Co.*, 135 N.C. 392, 47 S.E. 481 (1904), *rev'd on rehearing*, 138 N.C. 308, 50 S.E. 681 (1906); *Donovan v. Berry*, 199 U.S. 612 (1905); *Monan v. Dunphy*, 177 Mass. 485, 59 N.E. 125 (1901); *Smith v. Ford Motor Co.*, 289 N.C. 71, 221 S.E.2d 282 (1976); *Kozlodsky v. Westminster Nat'l Bank*, 6 Cal. App.3d 593, 86 Cal. Rptr. 52 (1970); *Speegle v. Board of Fire Underwriters*, 29 Cal.2d 34, 172 P.2d 867 (1946); *Robbins v. Ogden Corp.*, 490 F. Supp. 801 (S.D.N.Y. 1980).

[61]E.g., *Lauter v. W. & J. Sloane, Inc.*, 417 F. Supp. 252 (S.D.N.Y. 1976); *Bradford v. Soret*, 64 N.Y.S.2d 876 (Sup. Ct. 1946). But see *Harris v. Home Indem. Co.*, 16 Misc.2d 702, 185 N.Y.S.2d 287 (Sup. Ct. 1959) (allowing no action but recognizing an action under *Rice v. Manley*, 66 N.Y. 82 (1876), where employer was willing to continue employment but was prevented by fraud from so doing); *Raycroft v. Tayntor*, 68 Vt. 219, 35 A. 53 (1896); *Chipley v. Atkinson*, 23 Fla. 206, 1 So. 934 (1887).

[62]Compare *Hinrichs v. Tranquilaire Hosp.*, 352 So.2d 1130 (Ala. 1977), and *Martin v. Tapley*, 360 So.2d 708 (Ala. 1978), with *Byars v. Baptist Medical Centers, Inc.*, 361 So.2d 350 (Ala. 1978) (recognizing a property right in employment) and *Georgia Power Co. v. Busbin*, 242 Ga. 612, 250 S.E.2d 442 (1978) (retaliatory discharge rejected but interference with contract claim sustained), *aff'g in part and rev'g in part* 145 Ga. App. 438, 244 S.E.2d 26, *appeal following remand*, 149 Ga. App. 274, 254 S.E.2d 146 (1979).

improper interference with prospective advantage;[63] indeed, at-will employment is a stronger candidate for protection than prospective advantage. At-will employment is, for most workers, the only available form of employment, and is of great practical value to the employee despite its limited legal protection. But tort liability has been applied in a way that does not impair the third party's legitimate rights; the protection provided by interference with contract is limited, and recovery generally depends on the legitimacy and reasonableness of the third party's motives and actions.

The Concept of Justification

Justification is at the heart of the action for interference with contract. The concept is analogous to the concept of privilege in defamation cases,[64] and yet in operation it calls for a broader scope of inquiry. Rarely, if ever, will interference take place without the presence of at least some factual basis for a justification claim. The interfering party will have acted for some reason, and that reason invariably involves a relationship with the employee or the employer which the third party is protecting or pursuing.

The defendant has in some cases been held to bear the burden of proving that the interference was justified.[65] Justification consists of showing that the defendant acted reasonably in pursuit of interests which are entitled, under the circumstances, to equal or greater protection than the plaintiff's employment relationship. In determining whether justification has been proved, the nature of the interference, the means employed by the defendant, the purpose or interest which motivated the interference, the relations of plaintiff and defendant with the employer, and the public or social importance of the conflicting interests of employee and defendant are considered.[66] Phrased in broad terms, the ultimate issue is whether the defendant's conduct was fair and reasonable under the circumstances.[67] Thus it is often an issue that must be left to the jury.[68]

Some cases speak of "malicious" interference with contract, and imply that malice must be proved as an element of tortious interference.[69] Malice in the sense of ill will, however, need not be proved to make out a case.[70] One court has observed that a defendant may

---

[63]See Annot., 6 A.L.R.4th 195 (1981).

[64]E.g., *American Pet Motels, Inc. v. Chicago Veterinary Medical Ass'n*, 106 Ill. App.3d 626, 435 N.E.2d 1297 (1982).

[65]E.g., *Pino v. Protection Maritime Ins. Co.*, 599 F.2d 10 (1st Cir. 1979).

[66]RESTATEMENT (SECOND) OF TORTS §767.

[67]*Basin Elec. Power Co-op.—Missouri Basin Power Project v. Howton*, 603 P.2d 402 (Wyo. 1979).

[68]*Id.*; *DeMarais v. Stricker*, 152 Ore. 362, 53 P.2d 715 (1936).

[69]E.g., *Ladd v. Roane Hosiery, Inc.*, 556 S.W.2d 758 (Tenn. 1977) (with "neither reason nor excuse" and out of a "spirit of vindictiveness and malice").

[70]*Pino v. Protection Maritime Ins. Co.*, 454 F. Supp. 210 (D. Mass. 1978), *aff'd*, 599 F.2d 10 (1st Cir. 1979); *Wyeman v. Deady*, 79 Conn. 414, 65 A. 129 (1906); *Holder v. Cannon Mfg. Co.*, 135 N.C. 392, 47 S.E. 481 (1904), *rev'd on rehearing*, 138 N.C. 308, 50 S.E. 681 (1905).

act out of a good motive and be guilty of tortious interference,[71] and another has pointed out that one may act out of ill will to bring about a discharge and still not be liable.[72] The intent element of the tort consists at most of intending the result: discharge of the employee.[73]

This is not to say that intent and motive are wholly irrelevant. Where the interfering party is performing a superior duty or is supported by a strong justification, malice will not render interference unlawful.[74] Outside the narrow confines of such absolute protection, however, the motive of the defendant may be relied upon to place the conduct outside the justification defense.[75]

Many justification cases turn on questions of whether the scope of the defendant's conduct exceeded the degree of interference required to protect the defendant's legitimate interest. A showing of conduct outside the scope of justifiable interference results in liability.

Abuse of justification is not a separate issue outside of the justification question. Rather, it is one method of overcoming a proferred justification. Just as certain justifications are important enough to shield even those who act out of ill will, certain forms of abuse are wrongful per se and strip the defendant of protection. Knowingly false statements,[76] independent tortious or predatory behavior,[77] and a purpose to coerce the employee in the exercise of his legitimate legal rights[78] are forms of abuse serious enough to overcome even a proper justification.

Cases that fall between these two extremes must be judged on their particular facts. In the absence of a compelling justification or a plain abuse, the defendant's conduct will be judged against a standard which considers the relative importance of the defendant's, the employee's, and the public interests along with the defendant's purposes and the reasonableness of his conduct in pursuit of his legitimate interests.

Justification: Strangers to the Employment Relationship

Control of the Market for Employees

It is sometimes said that third parties may lawfully cause the discharge of an employee of another in pursuit of a valid economic

---

[71]*Sullivan v. Barrows*, 303 Mass. 197, 21 N.E.2d 275 (1939).

[72]*DeMarais v. Stricker*, 152 Ore. 362, 53 P.2d 715 (1936).

[73]*Id.*

[74]*Woody v. Brush*, 178 A.D. 698, 165 N.Y.S. 867 (1917).

[75]*Id.*; *Hopper v. Lennen & Mitchell*, 52 F. Supp. 319, 327 (S.D. Cal. 1943).

[76]*Ramsey v. Greenwald*, 91 Ill. App.3d 855, 414 N.E.2d 1266 (1980); *Monan v. Dunphy*, 177 Mass. 485, 59 N.E. 125 (1901).

[77]*Murtha v. Yonkers Child Care Asss'n*, 45 N.Y.2d 913, 383 N.E.2d 865, 411 N.Y.S.2d 219 (1978) (predatory or tortious conduct); *Cavanagh v. Elliot*, 270 Ill. App. 21 (1934) (threats and intimidation).

[78]*Pino v. Protection Maritime Ins. Co.*, 454 F. Supp. 210 (D. Mass. 1978), *aff'd*, 599 F.2d 10 (1st Cir. 1979). See *Curnett v. Wolf*, 244 Iowa 683, 57 N.W.2d 915 (1953).

interest. Two decisions have found control over competition among
employers for the services of employees to be such an interest. In
Cesnik v. Chrysler Corp.,[79] the employer sold a division to the third
party, and to secure the transfer of the business agreed not to continue
the employment of managers like the plaintiff. The court held that
the acquiring corporation was justified by the pursuit of its economic
interest in insisting on the plaintiff's discharge. *Cesnik* is premised
on the right of the employer, as owner of a business, to sell the
business as a whole. The selling corporation has no ownership interest
in its employees, but the court found that the agreement to discharge
the division managers was an important means of assuring the buyer
that it would provide for the transfer of all the good will of the
division. So finding, the court held that the acquiring corporation
was not liable.[80]

In *Pearse v. McDonald's Systems*,[81] it was lawful for a franchisor
to enforce a provision of the franchise agreement it had with each of
its franchisees which prevented employees from leaving one franchise
and going to work for another. Pursuant to this provision, the franchisor required one franchise to discharge the plaintiff, who had previously worked for another franchise. The court held that the
franchisor's action had a valid relationship to its economic interest,
and the interference was held to be justified.

Every jurisdiction in the country has a body of law built around
attempts to enforce employee covenants not to compete, and most
states require that such covenants be narrowly drawn to protect employer property interests in trade secrets and, in some situations,
customer good will. In *Cesnik* and *Pearse* the courts have given effect
to such covenants, directly or indirectly, between *employers*. The
agreements were less restrictive of employee freedom than covenants
not to compete, since only the employers who joined them were affected; the restrictions were less deserving of judicial enforcement,
on the other hand, because they were "covenants" of which the employees could have been totally unaware. In *Cheek v. Prudential Insurance Co.*,[82] the Missouri court held that such employer agreements
were unlawful as against public policy.

Whether interference with contract or a covenant not to compete
is at issue, the legal standards for judging restraints on employee job
mobility should be roughly the same. If in *Pearse* the purpose of the
covenant was to protect individual franchise trade secrets from a
competitor, or perhaps if it was intended to prevent tortious inter-

---

[79]490 F. Supp. 859 (M.D. Tenn. 1980) (Tennessee and Kentucky law).

[80]Another way the court might have reached the same conclusion would have been to
inquire whether, upon selling the division, the selling corporation would have retained the
plaintiff in any case. *Cesnik* was not a case where, for example, the buyer threatened to abandon
the purchase if the seller agreed to continue the plaintiff's employment. A different case might
be presented were it shown that employer and employee preferred to continue the relationship,
but the buyer insisted on a discharge to coerce the employee to come to work for the buyer.

[81]47 Ohio App.2d 20, 351 N.E.2d 788 (1975).

[82]192 S.W. 387 (Mo. 1917).

ference by the second franchise in the form of a "corporate raid" on the first franchise's employees, then the employee's suit for interference should fail. If, on the other hand, the sole motive was to restrain competition for trained and skilled restaurant managers, this should hardly be found, as a matter of law, to be more weighty than the employee's interest in continued employment and a substantial market for his specialized skills. The public policies upon which the law governing the validity of covenants not to compete is based should be given due weight in interference-with-contract cases.

Insurer's Limited Privilege to Procure Discharge

Liability and workers' compensation insurers have, in common with the employers they insure, an interest in minimizing the risk of loss or injuries resulting from employee negligence or misconduct. In addition to concern over future claims by an accident-prone employee and *respondeat superior* liability for future unsafe behavior by the employee, insurers have concerns because courts are increasingly holding employers liable on "negligent hiring" claims brought by persons injured by employees who would otherwise not have had the opportunity to inflict injury.[83]

Because of this common interest with the employer, insurers have been held to be justified in efforts to procure the discharge of employees whose negligence has been found responsible for loss or injury, at least where this has been tied to future risks.[84] The protection of insurers is very limited; the courts have not protected insurer interference broadly because of the possible influence of improper motivation.

In *Pino v. Protection Maritime Insurance Co.*,[85] the insurer provided for a special "add-on premium charge" for any employee who had failed to settle an injury claim on a basis acceptable to the insurer. The effect of this program was an industrywide blacklist of any employee who did not compromise his legal rights for the insurer's benefit, and the interference that resulted was held to be unjustified. In other cases, courts have faced similar instances in which the insurer has retaliated against an employee for his refusal to settle by procuring his discharge.[86] They have uniformly found no justification in this circumstance.

---

[83]*Estate of Arrington v. Fields*, 528 S.W.2d 173 (Tex. Civ. App. 1979); *Hersh v. Kentfield Builders, Inc.*, 385 Mich. 410, 189 N.W.2d 286 (1971).

[84]*Green v. Lundquist Agency, Inc.*, 2 Mich. App. 488, 140 N.W.2d 575 (1966) (loss ratio based on fault accidents was important to decision to continue insurance). See *Pino v. Protection Maritime Ins. Co.*, 454 F. Supp. 210 (D. Mass. 1978), *aff'd*, 599 F.2d 10 (1st Cir. 1979) (legitimate loss-related reasons were not basis for insurer's interference). Cf. *Zimmerman v. Gianelloni*, 206 S.W.2d 843 (Tex. Civ. App. 1947) (employer's concurring judgment precluded liability).

[85]454 F. Supp. 210 (D. Mass. 1978), *aff'd*, 599 F.2d 10 (1st Cir. 1979).

[86]*Harris v. Trader's & Gen. Ins. Co.*, 82 S.W.2d 750 (Tex. Civ. App. 1935); *Hilton v. Sheridan Coal Co.*, 132 Kan. 525, 297 P. 413 (1931); *United States Fidelity & Guar. Co. v. Millonas*, 206 Ala. 147, 89 So. 732 (1921); *Johnson v. Aetna Life Ins. Co.*, 158 Wis. 56, 147 N.W. 32 (1914); *Gibson v. Fidelity & Casualty Co.*, 135 Ill. App. 290, *aff'd*, 232 Ill. 49, 83 N.E. 539 (1907); *London Guar. Co. v. Horn*, 206 Ill. 493, 69 N.E. 526 (1904).

The insurer who attempts to coerce settlement of an injury claim with a threat of discharge, or who causes the discharge of one who has refused to settle, plainly acts in its own economic interest. The interference is unjustified, however, because the effort is an abuse of another, separate right of the employee: the right to have his claim for compensation for an injury heard by a legal tribunal. The threat of retaliation is deemed to be predatory and unjustified.

Even absent this sort of sharp dealing, however, the insurer interferes with employment of a policyholder's workers somewhat at its peril. In *American Surety Co. v. Schottenbauer*,[87] the insurer threatened cancellation of its policy if a recently injured employee was not discharged. The court found that the company had exceeded the scope of justifiable conduct because of (1) the use of a threat; (2) the absence of a basis for the conclusion that the employee's injury was serious and created a substantial exposure; (3) the employer's satisfaction with the employee's physical recovery and work; and (4) the probable concern of the employer over the availability of substitute coverage.[88] Though the insurer may have acted out of perceived self-interest, the court concluded that it was not in fact protecting a substantial financial interest more weighty than the employee's interest in the job, and that it used questionable means to accomplish its purpose.

Interference by Creditors of the Employee

An employee's creditor with a just or unjust debt is in a strong position to compel payment if it holds the employee's livelihood in its hands. Given the traditional employer hostility to the garnishment of employee wages,[89] a creditor may well have this coercive power.

The creditor's privilege to interfere with employment has been narrowly construed. The creditor may serve a valid garnishment or wage assignment on the employer to collect its debt without liability, even if it knows the employee will be discharged when it does so.[90] There is little margin for error or other protection for a mistake by the creditor, however. In cases of mistaken identity the creditor has been held liable,[91] and attempts to shift the blame for the error to the employer have been unavailing.[92] Where the underlying obli-

---

[87]257 F.2d 6 (8th Cir. 1958).

[88]*Id.* at 12.

[89]In response to this industrial reality, Congress prohibited discharge of employees for garnishments on a single debt in the Consumer Credit Protection Act, 15 U.S.C. §674(a) (1982).

[90]*Messina v. Continental Purchasing Co.*, 272 N.Y. 175, 5 N.E.2d 62 (1937) (in the absence of fraud or overreaching); *Huchins v. Jones Piano Co.*, 209 Iowa 394, 228 N.W. 281 (1930); *Southern Fin. Co. v. Foster*, 19 Ala. App. 109, 95 So. 338 (1923) (if valid when served); *Haines v. M.S. Welker & Co.*, 182 Iowa 431, 165 N.W. 1027 (1918).

[91]*Lopes v. Connolly*, 210 Mass. 487, 97 N.E. 80 (1912).

[92]*Doucette v. Salinger*, 228 Mass. 444, 117 N.E. 897 (1917).

gation was invalid[93] or the papers were not valid when served,[94] creditors have been held liable for interference.

A direct and successful effort to procure discharge unless a debt is paid also is not justified.[95] In *Long v. Newby*[96] one hospital's bill collector made good on a threat to have the plaintiff discharged by a second hospital, and acted expressly in his capacity as bill collector to obtain the employer's cooperation in obtaining payment. In view of the employee's contest of her liability for the debt, the court upheld a verdict denying justification protection to the creditor.[97]

Interference by a creditor designed to compel payment of a claim is in plain pursuit of the creditor's economic interest, but that interest is subordinate to an employee's interest in his job for several reasons. First, the creditor shares no community of interest with the employer. Second, the creditor may be circumventing the legal process for determining whether the claim is just. Third, the creditor advances its economic interest only by its coercive power to force payment on threat of discharge; when the threat is carried out, the employee's ability to pay is diminished, not enhanced.

Interference by Former Employers

A former employer who interferes with the employee's subsequent employment relationship may be liable for such interference. In *Webster v. Holly Hill Lumber Co.*,[98] the former employer placed an unsolicited call to a later employer, supposedly to verify the employee's position there. The employee had a workers' compensation claim pending against the former employer based on a back injury, and without solicitation the former employer revealed this to the subsequent employer, who discharged the plaintiff for failure to disclose the back injury on his job application. Because the former employer had other means for confirming the employee's subsequent position, the court found an unjustified interference with contract.[99]

The former employer may not demand the employee's discharge by a subsequent employer where the employee has gone on strike against the former employer.[100] Nor may the former employer procure

---

[93]*Suarez v. McFall Bros.*, 87 S.W. 744 (Tex. Civ. App. 1905).

[94]*Southern Fin. Co. v. Foster*, 19 Ala. App. 109, 95 So. 338 (1923); *Kennedy v. Hub Mfg. Co.*, 221 Mass. 136, 108 N.E. 932 (1915); *Cotton v. Cooper*, 160 S.W. 597 (Tex. Civ. App. 1913).

[95]*McCarter v. Baltimore Chamber of Commerce*, 126 Md. 131, 94 A. 541 (1915).

[96]448 P.2d 719 (Alaska 1971). See also *Rhodes v. Industrial Fin. Corp.*, 64 Ga. App. 549, 13 S.E.2d 883 (1941), where the creditor fought with the employee at the work place, causing the employee's discharge for fighting.

[97]Cases involving the tort of intentional infliction of emotional distress often are marked by efforts to harass the debtor by calls and contacts at work and at late hours at home.

[98]268 S.C. 416, 234 S.E.2d 232 (1977).

[99]In a similar context it has been held that volunteering the existence of pending equal opportunity proceedings to a subsequent employer constitutes unlawful retaliation. *Rutherford v. American Bank of Commerce*, 565 F.2d 1162 (10th Cir. 1977).

[100]*Holder v. Cannon Mfg. Co.*, 135 N.C. 392, 47 S.E. 481, *rev'd on rehearing*, 138 N.C. 308, 50 S.E. 681 (1905). Today such a discharge might also be the subject of an unfair labor practice charge against the subsequent employer under Section 8(a)(1) of the NLRA, 29 U.S.C. §158(a)(1) (1976).

a discharge because of an unjust claim against the employee.[101] On the other hand, a former employer is privileged to refuse to respond to a reference request and to state that it would not take the employee back.[102]

Employers who give a subsequent employer notice of a covenant not to compete which the employee has signed also face exposure to interference claims. In *Stebbins & Roberts, Inc. v. Halsey*,[103] the former employer told a subsequent employer that the employee had signed a covenant not to compete and could not legally work for the latter. The former employer said privately that it would sue the employee and the subsequent employer and "make an example." The covenant not to compete did not protect any trade secrets and was of doubtful validity, and the court held that the former employer could be liable for interference with contract.

The *Stebbins & Roberts* case suggests that an employer who attempts to enforce a covenant not to compete against a subsequent employer is subject to liability if the covenant is invalid and its notice to the new employer results in discharge.[104] The decision also means that factual issues surrounding the validity of the covenant not to compete may be resolved by a jury, rather than the judge, in such instances.

Interference by Labor Organizations

Many cases arise out of union procurement of the discharge of a nonunion member or of a member who violates union rules.[105] Par-

---

[101]*Hill Grocery Co. v. Carroll*, 223 Ala. 376, 136 So. 789 (1931).

[102]*Creitz v. Bennett*, 273 Ill. App. 88 (1935). The privilege to respond in good faith to reference requests which exists in defamation law applies equally to interference with contract cases, but it is likewise lost if the former employer makes knowingly false accusations of wrongdoing. *Blender v. Superior Court*, 55 Cal. App.2d 24, 130 P.2d 179 (1942). Refusal to give a favorable reference is not actionable. *Brown v. Chem. Haulers, Inc.*, 402 So.2d 887 (1981). But under certain circumstances such a refusal may constitute an actionable violation of antireprisal or antidiscrimination statutes. *Pantchenko v. C.B. Dodge Co.*, 581 F.2d 1052 (2d Cir. 1978).

[103]265 Ark. 903, 582 S.W.2d 266 (1979).

[104]The holder of the covenant may not be able to make out an action against the subsequent employer unless notice has been given to the new employer. The employer would still be free to seek its remedy by injunction against the employee without risk of liability. The *Stebbins & Roberts* opinion, while acknowledging that the employer would be privileged to make a good faith statement of what it believed its legal rights were and that it would insist on its rights, held that it could not act out of an express purpose to obtain the employee's discharge. This fine distinction opens up almost any notice of an invalid covenant to question.

The outcome of most covenant not to compete cases is for practical purposes determined by a preliminary injunction hearing, so the right to a jury trial is of limited importance. This right will be important (1) where the new employer acquiesces in the covenant, and (2) where the trial court finds the facts for the employer at the preliminary stage. In such a case the employee will benefit from the availability of a jury trial.

Where the discharge occurs after a preliminary injunction which is later reversed, the employee may have an action on the bond, if one is set, or for "wrongful injunction."

[105]*Donovan v. Berry*, 199 U.S. 612 (1905); *Locomotive Firemen v. Hammett*, 273 Ala. 397, 140 So.2d 832 (1962); *Transportation Workers, Local 204 v. Richardson*, 245 Ala. 37, 15 So.2d 578 (1943); *Smetherton v. Laundry Workers*, 44 Cal. App.2d 131, 111 P.2d 948 (1941); *Patterson Glass Co. v. Thomas*, 41 Cal. App. 559, 183 P. 190 (1919); *Railway Conductors v. Jones*, 78 Colo. 80, 239 P. 882 (1925); *Conners v. Connolly*, 86 Conn. 641, 86 A. 600 (1913); *Wyeman v. Deady*, 79 Conn. 414, 65 A. 129 (1906); *Eschman v. Huebner*, 226 Ill. App. 537 (1922); *Sutton v. Workmeister*, 164 Ill. App. 105 (1911); *Kemp v. Street & Elec. Ry. Employees*, 255 Ill. 213,

ticularly where the cause of the dispute is the maintenance of a union shop, these cases may be outdated because of the provisions on that subject in the Taft-Hartley Act[106] and the preemption doctrine.[107] Today, the employee must demonstrate that the issue is not within the scope of exclusive NLRA jurisdiction, and the justification issue will depend on whether the union procured the discharge by legitimate means in pursuit of a legitimate labor objective.[108]

Interference by Parties Doing Business With the Employer

Those whom the employer serves, or who serve the employer, may have a legitimate right to insist on the discharge of an employee. The cases do not lay down a clear rule on this subject. It is unclear, for example, whether the individual customer "is always right" without regard to motive.[109] Where the defendant has an ongoing business relationship with the employer and the employee's position is related to that relationship, interference is justified if it has a reasonable basis[110] and, according to one older case, without reference to actual motive.[111]

---

99 N.E. 389 (1912), *rev'g* 153 Ill. App. 344 (1910); *Reeves v. Scott*, 324 Mass. 594, 87 N.E.2d 833 (1949); *Sullivan v. Burke*, 309 Mass. 493, 36 N.E.2d 371 (1941); *Hanson v. Innis*, 211 Mass. 301, 97 N.E. 756 (1912); *DeMinico v. Craig*, 207 Mass. 593, 94 N.E. 317 (1911); *Clarkson v. Liablan*, 202 Mo. App. 682, 216 S.W. 1029 (1919); *Carter v. Oster*, 134 Mo. App. 146, 112 S.W. 995 (1908); *Miller v. United States Rubber Co.*, 137 N.J. 682, 61 A.2d 241 (1948); *Malone v. Locomotive Firemen*, 94 N.J. 347, 160 A. 696 (1920); *Brennan v. Hatters*, 73 N.J.L. 729, 65 A. 165 (1906); *Barile v. Fisher*, 197 Misc. 493, 94 N.Y.S.2d 346 (Sup. Ct. 1949); *O'Brien v. Pappas*, 49 N.Y.S.2d 521 (1944); *Cusumano v. Schlessinger*, 90 Misc. 287; 152 N.Y.S. 1081 (Sup. Ct. 1915); *Wunch v. Shankland*, 59 A.D. 482, 69 N.Y.S. 349 (1901); *Tallman v. Gaillard*, 27 Misc. 114, 57 N.Y.S. 419 (Sup. Ct. 1899); *Smelter Workers v. Kyrk*, 199 Okla. 464, 187 P.2d 239 (1947); *Roddy v. Mine Workers*, 41 Okla. 621, 139 P. 126 (1914); *Savard v. Industrial Trades Union*, 76 R.I. 496, 72 A.2d 660 (1950); *Dukes v. Painters*, 191 Tenn. 495, 235 S.W.2d 7 (1950).

[106]29 U.S.C. §§158(b)(2), 158(a)(3) (1976). See also 29 U.S.C. §164(b), which authorizes state "right to work" statutes prohibiting compulsory union membership.

[107]*Operating Eng'rs, Local 926 v. Jones*, 460 U.S. 669 (1983). See discussion of preemption in Chapter 5. Where labor law permits a closed shop, for example, the union may enforce a collective bargaining provision to that effect without risk of liability, though concerted reprisals against a specific employee will probably be subject to civil suit. See *Barile v. Fisher*, 197 Misc. 493, 94 N.Y.S.2d 346 (Sup. Ct. 1949).

[108]*Pugh v. See's Candies, Inc.*, 116 Cal. App.3d 311, 171 Cal. Rptr. 917 (1981). If the employee is represented by the union, an NLRA duty of fair representation claim may be available. If the employee is not a union member or working in a bargaining unit, the union's quarrel with the employee is unlikely to serve as a justification. *Electrical Workers (IBEW) v. Briscoe*, 143 Ga. App. 417, 239 S.E.2d 38 (1977).

[109]Compare *Lancaster v. Hamburger*, 70 Ohio 156, 71 N.E. 289 (1904) (passenger may report misconduct even if motivated by ill will), and *MacKenzie v. Chrysler Corp.*, 607 F.2d 1162 (5th Cir. 1979) (complaint lodged with employer by defendant over employee's use of position to publicize dispute with defendant did not interfere with contract), with *Meadows v. South Carolina Medical Ass'n*, 266 S.C. 391, 223 S.E.2d 600 (1976) (members not privileged to procure dismissal of association employee). Most likely, in a case like *Lancaster*, a showing of knowing falsity and ulterior motive would alter the result, as would a legitimate good faith belief that there was cause to discharge in a case like *Meadows*.

[110]*Basin Elec. Power Co-op.—Missouri Basin Power Project v. Howton*, 603 P.2d 402 (Wyo. 1979) (defendant was project manager, employer a contractor on the project, and employee a construction worker).

[111]*O'Brien v. Western Union Tel. Co.*, 62 Wash. 598, 114 P. 441 (1911); *Pearse v. McDonald's Sys.*, 47 Ohio App.2d 20, 351 N.E.2d 788 (1975). In both cases, the defendant had a contract with the employer giving it the right to require discharge, which was at least a factor in the outcome. In *Heheman v. E.W. Scripps Co.*, 661 F.2d 1115 (6th Cir. 1981) it was held that the buyer of the entire business had no liability for discharge of the original employees.

In *Smith v. Ford Motor Co.*,[112] the manufacturer threatened to terminate a dealership if the dealership president was not fired. The alleged reason for the demand was the president's activities in connection with a dealer alliance—the small business equivalent of a union. The court found that the action was justified only if the manufacturer could show that it reasonably believed its legitimate business interests would be damaged or imperiled by the activity.[113] The court, however, recognized the right of a customer to refuse to deal with an employer because of dissatisfaction with services rendered by the employee, whether or not warranted. If there is a discharge as a result, the employee has no right of action against the customer because the discharge would be only an indirect consequence of the customer's exercise of its rights.[114]

Interference by Professional Regulating Bodies

Professional groups and others who regulate employee qualifications are also subject to interference liability. Two cases, *DeMarais v. Stricker*[115] and *Porter v. King County Medical Society*,[116] represent divergent approaches taken in the earlier cases. In *DeMarais* the employer's license was made contingent on discharge of the employee, and the court held that the case was one for the jury on that basis alone. In *Porter* the court held, as a matter of law, that a private medical society acted legitimately in barring local doctors from participating in a group clinic medical plan, similar to what is today called a health maintenance organization, thereby putting the business manager of the plan out of work.[117]

A more appropriate approach in this area is represented by *Byars v. Baptist Medical Centers, Inc.*,[118] where a hospital refused to permit the plaintiff, a nurse, to be placed on its registry of private care nurses. The court held that the justification issue turned on whether the refusal was because of the nurse's legal claim against the hospital or was based on a bona fide application to her of reasonable standards

---

[112]289 N.C. 71, 221 S.E.2d 282 (1976).

[113]Accord: *Hopper v. Lennen & Mitchell*, 52 F. Supp. 319 (S.D. Cal. 1943) (sponsor of program permitted to procure discharge of actress), *aff'd in part and rev'd in part*, 146 F.2d 364 (9th Cir. 1944). See *Blender v. Superior Court*, 55 Cal. App.2d 24, 130 P.2d 179 (1942) (defendant's action must have been in pursuit of legitimate business interests).

[114]Tortious or predatory conduct is an abuse of justification, and results in liability. *Taylor v. Pratt*, 135 Me. 282, 195 A. 205 (1937) (fraud or intimidation of employer creates liability).

[115]152 Ore. 362, 53 P.2d 715 (1936).

[116]186 Wash. 410, 58 P.2d 367 (1936).

[117]Such action by a medical society today would raise serious group boycott questions under the Sherman Antitrust Act, but in 1936 the professions were believed to stand outside the coverage of the act.

[118]361 So.2d 350 (Ala. 1978). In *Speegle v. Board of Fire Underwriters*, 29 Cal.2d 34, 172 P.2d 867 (1946), an association of insurance companies and agents compelled the discharge of one of the employees of a member agent for writing business for nonboard companies. The court held that this violated state antitrust laws and that an intent to stifle competition was no justification for interference with contract. But in *Hennessey v. NCAA*, 564 F.2d 1136 (5th Cir. 1977), an association's new rule limiting the number of assistant coaches, which led to plaintiff's discharge, was justified because it was a legitimate, well-intentioned regulatory action.

of fitness and competence to perform nursing duties. In cases like *DeMarais* and *Porter*, justification ought to depend upon a balancing of the legitimate objectives being pursued by the defendant, the impact of application of those standards to the employee's ability to find work elsewhere, and consideration of other, less legitimate reasons (retaliation, restriction of competition) which may lie behind the action.

In *Phillips v. Vandygriff*,[119] the employee attacked a practice of "de facto licensing" by a state banking official. A savings and loan association the employee had been connected with had had problems with misuse of funds, although the employee had not been implicated. The Savings and Loan Commissioner was familiar with the situation and, under an established custom in the business, conveyed what he knew about the situation to prospective employers of the employee. He also stated that, because of the employee's proximity to the derelictions, he could not recommend the employee. The court found that the situation was one that should be resolved by the jury.

Interference by Defendant in Employee Suit

A defendant in a civil action by the employee has no justification for procuring the discharge of the employee. In *Evans v. Swain*[120] the court held that where the employee's suit had no relationship to his employment, inducement of the discharge was actionable. In *Illinois Steel Co. v. Brenshall*,[121] the defendant, against whom the employee had a personal injury claim, had an arrangement by which it could and did procure the employee's discharge for refusal to release the claim. Such an agreement, the court held, is "unconscionable, unjust, tyrannical, unlawful, and subject to the severest condemnation," and the interference it permitted was actionable.

Justification: Interference by Other Employees

In most businesses the decision to discharge is deemed to be of such importance that it will be reviewed at more than one level of the organization, and in most businesses the "employer" is a corporate or other legal entity. Actions for interference with contract have been sustained where another employee, even the plaintiff's supervisor, procures the termination of the plaintiff's employment relationship with the corporate employer. Almost every discharge, then, is a potential source of an interference-with-contract claim. Given the obvious need of the employer to act through its agents and have the benefit of the judgments of its employees in making employment decisions, the courts have recognized a broad privilege or justification

---

[119]711 F.2d 1217 (5th Cir. 1983).
[120]245 Ala. 641, 18 So.2d 400 (1944).
[121]141 Ill. App. 36, 43 (1908).

for insiders to participate in discharge decisions without liability for interference with the employment relationship.

The corporate-insider justification is not available to one who is an insider but who acts in some other capacity to procure the discharge. In *Long v. Newby*,[122] the defendant hospital trustee was acting in his capacity as an agent of another business and not as a trustee when he procured the plaintiff's discharge; he was thus not entitled to the co-employee's privilege. Where the employee worked for a construction company and the owner's project manager, who directed the contractor's work, procured the employee's discharge, the court applied a general reasonableness justification test which gave far less discretion to the project manager than is customarily afforded to co-employees.[123]

Some courts have held that where one employee is given discretion to discharge, that employee is not subject to liability for interference with the employee's relationship with the company. The theory is that, so far as that decision is concerned, the final decision-maker *is* the employer for all practical purposes, and thus cannot be an interfering third party.[124] The rule does not apply where the decision is subject to the condition that it could be reversed by a higher authority[125] or where the defendant's authority is only to make recommendations to be acted on by others.[126] However, where the defendant's final authority is based on established practice of the employer and represents actual authority, the decision-maker is immune.[127]

Privilege to Report Truthfully on Wrongful Conduct on the Job

An employee has the right, and at least arguably the duty, to report wrongful conduct on the job by another employee; and an employee may be required by his job to make a discharge recommendation based on wrongful behavior. In neither of these situations

---

[122]488 P.2d 719 (Alaska 1971); *Eil v. Federal Reserve Bank*, 633 S.W.2d 432 (Mo. Ct. App. 1982).

[123]*Basin Elec. Power Co-op.—Missouri Basin Power Project v. Howton*, 603 P.2d 402 (Wyo. 1979).

[124]*West v. Troelstrup*, 367 So.2d 253 (Fla. Dist. Ct. App. 1979); *Ladd v. Roane Hosiery, Inc.*, 556 S.W.2d 758 (Tenn. 1977); *Georgia Power Co. v. Busbin*, 242 Ga. 612, 250 S.E.2d 442 (1978); *Straynar v. Jack W. Harris Co.*, 150 Ga. App. 509, 258 S.E.2d 248 (1979); *Wolcott v. Broughton*, 57 A.D.2d 1022, 395 N.Y.S.2d 705 (1977); see *Langley v. Russell*, 218 N.C. 216, 10 S.E.2d 721 (1940); *Kozlodsky v. Westminster Nat'l Bank*, 6 Cal. App.3d 593, 86 Cal. Rptr. 52 (1970); *May v. Santa Fe Trail Transp. Co.*, 189 Kan. 419, 370 P.2d 390 (1962); *Vuksta v. Bethlehem Steel Corp.*, 540 F. Supp. 1276, 1282 (E.D. Pa. 1982); *Cummings v. Walsh Constr. Co.*, 561 F. Supp. 872, 883 (S.D. Ga. 1983); *Wells v. Thomas*, 569 F. Supp. 426, 435 (E.D. Pa. 1983).

[125]*Schaeffer v. King*, 223 Ga. 468, 155 S.E.2d 815 (1967), *appeal following remand*, 123 Ga. App. 531, 181 S.E.2d 700 (1971); *American Standard, Inc. v. Jessee*, 150 Ga. App. 663, 258 S.E.2d 240 (1979).

[126]*Ramsey v. Greenwald*, 91 Ill. App.3d 855, 414 N.E.2d 1266 (1980).

[127]*Schaeffer v. King*, 123 Ga. App. 531, 181 S.E.2d 700 (1971), *prior appeal*, 223 Ga. 468, 155 S.E.2d 815 (1967).

is the employee liable for his actions.[128] The privilege to report protects statements made in the performance of duty with a reasonable belief in their truth.[129] The protection extends to reports of wrongdoing off the job that relate to the employee's fitness.[130]

If the report of wrongdoing is truthful and accurate, the fact that it is made out of ill will does not affect the privilege.[131] The hostility or other motive of the reporting employee is immaterial where the report is truthful or the recommendation is based on truth, and laxity in enforcing the rules against others does not make an otherwise appropriate recommendation of discharge unjustified.[132] The privilege to report does not protect false statements made out of an intent to injure the plaintiff, however, and such reports give rise to liability for interference with contract.[133]

An outsider may not be justified in threatening to terminate its at-will relationship with the employer to coerce the discharge of an employee solely out of a dislike for the employee.[134] An employee, by contrast, may report his hostility toward another employee and threaten to quit if the other employee remains.[135] Unlike the outsider, the employee is acting on a personal interest in his day-to-day working conditions when making the "either he goes or I go" ultimatum. Thus the honest statement of personal malice to induce a discharge is protected and deemed to be justified, but the knowingly false accusation of wrongdoing or recommendation based on known false information to accomplish the same goal is unjustified.

Improper Purpose or Means Test

As a general proposition, one employee is justified in procuring the discharge of another employee when he seeks to act in accordance with his duties and in the best interests of the employer.[136] In determining the question of justification outside the scope of the priv-

---

[128]E.g., *Ramsey v. Rudd*, 49 N.C. App. 670, 272 S.E.2d 162 (1980); *Petroni v. Board of Regents*, 115 Ariz. 562, 566 P.2d 1038 (App. 1977); *Fincke v. Phoenix Mut. Life Ins. Co.*, 448 F. Supp. 187 (W.D. Pa. 1978); *Menefee v. CBS, Inc.*, 458 Pa. 46, 329 A.2d 216 (1974); *Wells v. Thomas*, 569 F. Supp. 426 (E.D. Pa. 1983). In *Beckner v. Sears, Roebuck & Co.*, 4 Cal. App.2d 504, 84 Cal. Rptr. 315 (1970), the discharge was held to have been caused by the employee's inability to deny the claimed wrongdoing and not as a proximate result of the report itself. The result is better explained by the privilege to report, however, since the tort of interference generally recognizes liability where the defendant's conduct is the impetus for the discharge. See, e.g., *Webster v. Holly Hill Lumber Co.*, 268 S.C. 416, 234 S.E.2d 232 (1977) (discharge for falsification of employment application based on outsider's report).
[129]*Woody v. Brush*, 178 A.D. 698, 165 N.Y.S. 867 (1917).
[130]*Fisher v. J.C. Penney Co.*, 135 Ga. App. 913, 219 S.E.2d 626 (1975) (report that retail store employee had been arrested for shoplifting privileged).
[131]*Woody v. Brush*, 178 A.D. 698, 165 N.Y.S. 867 (1917). See *Ramsey v. Rudd*, 49 N.C. App. 670, 272 S.E.2d 162 (1980).
[132]*Feeley v. McAuliffe*, 335 Ill. App. 126, 80 N.E.2d 376 (1948).
[133]*Ramsey v. Greenwald*, 91 Ill. App.3d 855, 414 N.E.2d 1266 (1980); *Woody v. Brush*, 178 A.D. 698, 165 N.Y.S. 867 (1917); *Chambers v. Probst*, 145 Ky. 381, 140 S.W. 572 (1911).
[134]See *Smith v. Ford Motor Co.*, 289 N.C. 71, 221 S.E.2d 282 (1976).
[135]*Beame v. Weiman Co.*, 5 N.C. App. 279, 168 S.E.2d 233 (1969). Cf. *Kemp v. Street & Elec. Ry. Employees*, 255 Ill. 213, 99 N.E. 389 (1912), rev'g 153 Ill. App. 344 (1910).
[136]See e.g., *Wilkinson v. Trust Co. of Ga. Assocs.*, 128 Ga. App. 473, 197 S.E.2d 146 (1973), and *Bump v. Stewart, Wimer & Bump, P.C.*, 336 N.W.2d 731 (Iowa 1983).

ilege to report, the courts look to the actual purpose of the defendant and the means used.[137]

The defendant-employee acts in the corporation's best interest where the discharge is procured in response to corporate needs and the business climate[138] without an improper collateral purpose,[139] or based on a proper business reason.[140] An intent to injure the legitimate interests of shareholders or the shareholder interests of the employee is not in the best interests of the corporation,[140] but more than a general desire to control the corporation's affairs must be shown.[142] Where a personal advantage or purpose predominates[143] or vindictiveness and spite motivate the interference,[144] it is not justified.

Tortious or predatory conduct are the kinds of methods that will defeat the justification defense usually available to a co-employee.[145] The justification defense may also be lost by an employee who violates established corporate policy and procedure[146] or who acts outside the normal course of his duties.[147]

Employer Liability for Employee Interference

A suit for interference with contract must be brought against the individual who has committed the interference.[148] The employer whose employment relationship has been interfered with is not ren-

---

[137]*Worrick v. Flora*, 133 Ill. App.2d 755, 272 N.E.2d 708 (1971); *Kyriazi v. Western Elec. Co.*, 461 F. Supp. 894 (D.N.J. 1978). See *Harless v. First Nat'l Bank*, 289 S.E.2d 692 (W. Va. 1982). In *Wolcott v. Broughton*, 57 A.D.2d 1022, 395 N.Y.S.2d 705 (1977), the court rejected the "best interests" approach, holding that personal motive was irrelevant and that, within the agent's bounds of discretion, no action could lie no matter how malicious the discharge. Shortly thereafter, however, New York's highest court implied a more liberal test in *Murtha v. Yonkers Child Care Ass'n*, 45 N.Y.2d 913, 383 N.E.2d 865, 411 N.Y.S.2d 219 (1978), referring to the protection of an agent as limited to where he acted in good faith and engaged in no tortious or predatory conduct. Good faith is the essence of the "improper purpose or means" test. See *Gram v. Liberty Mut. Ins. Co.*, 81 Mass. Adv. Sh. 2287, 429 N.E.2d 21 (1981).

[138]*Stevenson v. ITT Harper*, 51 Ill. App.3d 568, 366 N.E.2d 561 (1977); *Heheman v. E.W. Scripps Co.*, 661 F.2d 1115 (6th Cir. 1981).

[139]*Balousek v. Milwaukee Cheese Co.*, 452 F. Supp. 920 (E.D. Wis. 1978).

[140]*Campbell v. Roseburg Lumber Co.*, 39 Ore. App. 671, 593 P.2d 1201, *aff'd on other grounds*, 288 Ore. 223, 603 P.2d 1179 (1979), *prior appeal sub nom. Campbell v. Ford Indus. Inc.*, 274 Ore. 243, 546 P.2d 141 (1976); *prior related case, Campbell v. Ford Indus. Inc.*, 266 Ore. 479, 513 P.2d 1153 (1973).

[141]*Campbell v. Ford Indus. Inc.*, 274 Ore. 243, 546 P.2d 141 (1976); *Godwin v. Westberry*, 231 Ga. 492, 202 S.E.2d 402 (1973).

[142]*Martin v. Federal Life Ins. Co.*, 109 Ill. App.3d 596, 440 N.E.2d 998 (1982).

[143]*Manuel v. International Harvester Co.*, 502 F. Supp. 45 (N.D. Ill. 1980). See *Petroni v. Board of Regents*, 115 Ariz. 562, 566 P.2d 1038 (App. 1977) ("individual advantage") and *Worrick v. Flora*, 133 Ill. App.2d 755, 272 N.E.2d 708 (1971). But cf. *Straynar v. Jack W. Harris Co.*, 150 Ga. App. 509, 258 S.E.2d 248 (1979) (no action proved where employee testified that demands for sexual favors were made in connection with creation of contract).

[144]*Ladd v. Roane Hosiery, Inc.*, 556 S.W.2d 758 (Tenn. 1977) (where no reason other than vindictiveness and malice is shown, supervisor may be liable for interference). See *Harless v. First Nat'l Bank*, 289 S.E.2d 692 (W. Va. 1982) (corporate officer personally liable for retaliatory discharge).

[145]*Ramsey v.Greenwald*, 91 Ill. App.3d 855, 414 N.E.2d 1266 (1980); *Murtha v. Yonkers Child Care Ass'n*, 45 N.Y.2d 913, 383 N.E.2d 865, 411 N.Y.S.2d 219 (1978).

[146]*Martin v. Federal Life Ins. Co.*, 109 Ill. App.3d 596, 440 N.E.2d 998 (1982).

[147]*Petroni v. Board of Regents*, 115 Ariz. 562, 566 P.2d 1038 (App. 1977).

[148]*Percival v. General Motors Corp.*, 539 F.2d 1126 (8th Cir. 1976).

dered liable for the resulting discharge.[149] Where the individual who is responsible for the interference is also an employee, a few cases have faced the question of whether the employer may be vicariously liable under the doctrine of *respondeat superior*. In *Ramsey v. Greenwald*,[150] the Illinois court found *respondeat superior* liability by the application of the usual principles of agency-tort liability, but most cases have barred such liability.[151] Where a group of employers subscribed to a custom of permitting a state official to screen and veto managerial employees, the court found that each might be liable for the official's interference with employment on a civil conspiracy theory.[152]

Proximate Cause and Damages in Interference Cases

In an action for interference with contract, the plaintiff must prove that the third party's actions caused the discharge to occur. The interference need not be so great as to deprive the employer of free will,[153] but must only be the efficient cause of the discharge.[154] It must be shown that the interference took place and that but for the interference the discharge would not have happened.[155] The employee is entitled to recover as damages the amount he would have earned but for the interference,[156] incidental and consequential dam-

---

[149]E.g., *Allison v. American Airlines*, 112 F. Supp. 37 (D. Okla. 1953); *West v. Troelstrup*, 367 S.2d 253 (Fla. Dist. Ct. App. 1979); *May v. Santa Fe Trail Transp. Co.*, 189 Kan. 419, 370 P.2d 390 (1962); *Gram v. Liberty Mut. Ins. Co.*, 81 Mass. Adv. Sh. 2287, 429 N.E.2d 21 (1981); *Walker v. General Motors Corp.*, 152 Ga. App. 526, 263 S.E.2d 266 (1979); *Sherman v. St. Barnabas Hosp.*, 535 F. Supp. 564 (S.D.N.Y. 1982).

[150]91 Ill. App.3d 855, 414 N.E.2d 1266 (1980). Cf. *Ex parte Young*, 209 U.S. 123, 159–168 (1908) (same treatment of analogous issue under Eleventh Amendment where state officer is sued for injunctive relief).

[151]*Georgia Power Co. v. Busbin*, 242 Ga. 612, 250 S.E.2d 442 (1978); *American Standard, Inc. v. Jessee*, 150 Ga. App. 663, 258 S.E.2d 240 (1979); *Walker v. General Motors Corp.*, 152 Ga. App. 526, 263 S.E.2d 266 (1979). Generally the agent's liability is said to depend on his being outside his privilege, which also places him outside the scope of employment for purposes of *respondeat superior*. *Houser v. Redmond*, 16 Wash. App. 743, 559 P.2d 482 (1977), *aff'd*, 91 Wash.2d 36, 586 P.2d 482 (1978); *Menefee v. CBS, Inc.*, 458 Pa. 46, 329 A.2d 216 (1974); *Wise v. Southern Pac. Co.*, 223 Cal. App.2d 50, 35 Cal. Rptr. 652 (1963).

[152]*Phillips v. Vandygriff*, 711 F.2d 1217, 1230 (5th Cir. 1983). The remaining cases are divided on the availability of civil conspiracy as a basis for employer liability. Compare *Wise v. Southern Pac. Co.*, 223 Cal. App.2d 50, 35 Cal. Rptr. 652 (1963), with *Jones v. Operating Eng'rs, Local 926*, 159 Ga. App. 693, 285 S.E.2d 30 (1981). See *May v. Santa Fe Trail Transp. Co.*, 189 Kan. 419, 370 P.2d 390 (1962).

[153]RESTATEMENT (SECOND) OF TORTS §766 comment h (1977) ("by persuasion or intimidation"). See *Cotton v. Cooper*, 160 S.W. 597 (Tex. Civ. App. 1913) (absence of threat and employer action based on established rule), and *Max v. Kahn*, 91 N.J. 170, 102 A. 737 (1917) (wrongful act did not break chain of causation).

[154]*Reardon v. Layton & Forsythe*, 190 Okla. 444, 124 P.2d 987 (1942).

[155]*Zimmerman v. Gianelloni*, 206 S.W.2d 843 (Tex. Civ. App. 1947); *Taylor v. Pratt*, 135 Me. 282, 195 A. 205 (1937). Compare *Joslin v. Chicago, Milwaukee, St. Paul & Pac. Ry.*, 319 Mo. 250, 3 S.W. 352 (1928) (no causation where employer's investigation could be expected), with *Webster v. Holly Hill Lumber Co.*, 268 S.C. 416, 234 S.E.2d 232 (1977) (causation found where interference triggered investigation by employer). Of course, an unintentional or incidental interference is not actionable. *Wadsworth v. Nalco Chem. Co.*, 523 F. Supp. 997 (N.D. Ala. 1981) (affirmative intentional steps required); RESTATEMENT (SECOND) OF TORTS §766 comment c (1977) (no liability for incidental or negligent interference).

[156]*Carmen v. Fox Film Corp.*, 269 F. 928 (D.C. Cir. 1919); *Kennedy v. Hub Mfg. Co.*, 221 Mass. 136, 108 N.E. 932 (1915); *Connell v. Stalker*, 20 Misc. 423, 45 N.Y.S. 1048 (City Ct.), *aff'd*, 21 Misc. 609, 48 N.Y.S. 77 (Sup. Ct. 1897).

ages,[157] damages for mental anguish,[158] and, in a proper case, punitive damages.[159]

Tortious Infliction of Mental Distress

Psychologists tell us that termination of employment ranks with divorce and death of a loved one as an emotional trauma. Discharge, even for neutral or good reasons, often produces feelings of rejection, self-doubt, festering resentment, humiliation, shame, and desperate fear of or worry over the future. Employees may lose professional respect, the camaraderie and moral support of co-workers, their sense of identity, and the dignity that goes with productive work. While the foregoing is not a universal or necessary result of discharge from employment, those who work regularly with recently fired employees will affirm that discharge customarily has an emotional impact. It is the knowledge of this impact that often makes discharge decisions painful for employers to make.

Recovery for mental suffering may be available as an element of damages where a discharge constitutes an intentional tort.[160] Likewise, an employee subjected to unusual on-the-job stress resulting in physical harm may have a workers' compensation remedy.[161] Tort law, traditionally reluctant to recognize mental suffering as a compensable injury in the absence of physical impact, has recently ameliorated the established restraints on recovery for wrongful conduct causing mental distress. The "tort of outrage" or "intentional infliction of emotional distress" provides that conduct otherwise not tortious can give rise to an action it if it sufficiently cruel and produces real and substantial emotional harm.

Courts have hesitated to apply the action to discharges from employment, presumably out of concern that so many firings may be candidates for inclusion. In doing so, the courts sometimes ignore or greatly understate the impact of employee discharge, but most often they deny recovery with the explanation that the conduct giving rise

---

[157]RESTATEMENT (SECOND) OF TORTS §774(A)(1)(b); *Sullivan v. Barrows*, 303 Mass. 197, 21 N.E.2d 275 (1939).

[158]RESTATEMENT (SECOND) OF TORTS §774(A)(1)(c); *United States Fidelity & Guar. Co. v. Millonas*, 206 Ala. 147, 89 So. 732 (1921); *Lopes v. Connolly*, 210 Mass. 136, 108 N.E. 932 (1915); *Carter v. Oster*, 134 Mo. App. 146, 112 S.W. 995 (1908); *Bachand v. Connecticut Gen. Life Ins. Co.*, 101 Wis.2d 617, 305 N.W.2d 149 (Ct. App. 1981).

[159]*Hill Grocery Co. v. Carroll*, 223 Ala. 376, 136 So. 789 (1931); *Hutton v. Sheridan Coal Co.*, 132 Kans. 525, 297 P. 413 (1931); *Illinois Steel Co. v. Brenshall*, 141 Ill. App. 36 (1908); *Gibson v. Fidelity & Casualty Co.*, 232 Ill. 49, 83 N.E. 539 (1907).

[160]For a discussion of the intentional tort grounds giving rise to recovery of emotional harm, see *Harless v. First Nat'l Bank*, 289 S.E.2d 692 (W. Va. 1982).

[161]The cases on heart attacks have long generated controversy before industrial commissions and the courts reviewing their decisions. E.g., *Lewter v. Abercrombie Enter., Inc.*, 240 N.C. 398, 82 S.E.2d 410 (1954); *Taylor v. Department of Labor & Indus.*, 69 Wash.2d 19, 416 P.2d 455 (1966). See also *Dwyer v. Ford Motor Co.*, 36 N.J. 487, 178 A.2d 161 (1962); *Coombe v. Penegar*, 348 Mich. 635, 83 N.W.2d 603 (1957); *Jackson v. Board of Indus.*, 12 A.D.2d 542, 206 N.Y.S.2d 737 (1960). Contra: *Mellen v. Industrial Comm'n*, 19 Utah 2d 373, 431 P.2d 798 (1967); *Bussone v. Sinclair Ref. Co.*, 210 Pa. Super. 442, 234 A.2d 195 (1967).

to the action, if shabby, is not sufficiently outrageous to justify liability. Nevertheless, in several well-defined circumstances, the courts have shown a willingness to permit recovery based on discharge from employment.

Summary of the "Tort of Outrage"

The *Restatement (Second) of Torts,* Section 46 (1965), has reflected and encouraged the development of the tort of outrage, and it is repeatedly relied upon in the case law. The Restatement identifies three elements of the tort:

> (1) extreme and outrageous conduct;
> (2) intentionally or recklessly caused;
> (3) resulting in severe emotional distress.

Each of these apparently simple elements in fact conceals a complicated analytical balancing process, with the end result being that only in the truly remarkable case will the elements be satisfied. At the same time it must be acknowledged that the issue of liability will generally turn on whether the facts "shock the conscience," and that at least until the case law is considerably more mature, analysis is subservient to intuition in determining the result.

Extreme and Outrageous. Conduct is extreme and outrageous when it goes beyond all possible bounds of decency and is utterly intolerable in a civilized society. Mere insults, indignities, and threats will not suffice.[162] This high threshold is lowered somewhat by two recognized aggravating circumstances: a relation giving the defendant authority over the plaintiff or power to affect his interests,[163] and knowledge by the defendant of a plaintiff's peculiar susceptibility to emotional distress.[164] On the other hand, a defendant is privileged to insist on his legal rights "in a permissible way," to act in self-defense, or to respond to extreme provocation.[165]

Intentional or Reckless Conduct. To be liable the defendant must act out of an intent to inflict severe emotional distress, or must at least know that such distress is substantially certain to result from the conduct in question.[166] Only where there is at least a threat of bodily injury can liability also be imposed for negligent infliction of emotional harm.[167]

Severe Emotional Distress. Hurt feelings as such do not justify

---

[162]RESTATEMENT (SECOND) OF TORTS §46 comment d (1977).
[163]*Id.* comment e. The comments and illustrations do not state whether the employer-employee relationship fits in this category; police, school officials, landlords, and creditors are the examples cited.
[164]*Id.* comment f.
[165]*Id.* comment g.
[166]*Id.* comment i.
[167]*Id.* §§312, 313, 436, 436A.

recovery; the mental distress must be so severe that no reasonable person could be expected to endure it, giving due consideration to both the intensity of distress and its duration. The severity of the defendant's conduct in itself can be important evidence of distress.[168]

Actions for emotional distress have been asserted for mistreatment on the job, for the particular circumstances of discharge, and for deprivation of employee benefits. Almost all of the cases turn on whether the conduct is outrageous and uncivilized, the first element of the tort. There has been little judicial appreciation of the psychological impact of discharge as such and a high threshold for proof of extreme and outrageous conduct has prevailed.

Analysis of mental distress cases is inherently difficult. The decisions inevitably build up a list of cruel actions where the plaintiff prevails, and minimize the severity of the claimed indignities where the decision is for the defendant. Classification of the varying factual circumstances is a necessary step to determining when conduct is likely to be actionable, but it cannot necessarily predict the result under the "totality of the circumstances" approach the courts use.

Independent Social Wrongs as Outrageous Conduct

Three identifiable forms of behavior toward employees are recognized as a basis for mental distress recovery because they violate generally accepted social standards of behavior. Such conduct may be tortious on independent grounds that might not allow recovery for emotional injury; or the action for mental distress may overlap another tort claim, just as defamation and interference with contract often overlap. The three repeated patterns of behavior are ridicule, harassment, or discharge based on race or sex; abuse of handicap; and discharge for conduct protected by public policy.

Racial and Sexual Harassment

For a long time—suprisingly so in the light of the relatively recent social upheavals over race of the 1950s and 1960s—courts have recognized racist behavior as outrageous.[169] The pattern in these cases generally consists primarily of racial slurs and a discharge or demotion.[170] Courts cite the employer's control of the work place as

---

[168]*Id.* §46 comment j.

[169]The earliest case was *Odom v. East Avenue Corp.*, 178 Misc. 363, 34 N.Y.S.2d 312 (1942) (refusal to serve hotel guests in dining room). Other race cases include *Guillery v. Godfrey*, 134 Cal. App.3d 628, 286 P.2d 474 (1955) (intimidation of business and customers for employment of black cook); *Browning v. Slenderella Sys.*, 54 Wash.2d 440, 341 P.2d 859 (1959) (refusal to serve customer because of race); *Ruiz v. Bertolotti*, 37 Misc.2d 1067, 236 N.Y.S.2d 854 (Sup. Ct. 1962) (housing discrimination); *Fisher v. Carrousel Motor Hotel, Inc.*, 424 S.W.2d 627 (Tex. 1967) (refusal to serve).

[170]*Alcorn v. Ambro Eng'rs, Inc.*, 2 Cal.3d 493, 468 P.2d 216, 86 Cal. Rptr. 88 (1970); *Contreras v. Crown Zellerbach Corp.*, 88 Wash.2d 735, 565 P.2d 1173 (1977); *Agarwal v. Johnson*, 25 Cal.3d 932, 603 P.2d 58, 160 Cal. Rptr. 141 (1979). Contra: *Lay v. Roux Laboratories, Inc.*, 379 So.2d 451 (Fla. Dist. Ct. App. 1980).

a ground for recognizing the action, and also speak of the particular sensitivity members of minority groups have to blatantly racist actions. In *Contreras v. Crown Zellerbach Corp.*,[171] the court specifically recognized that it was appropriate to apply contemporary social standards to the behavior in question. The racial harassment cases are testimony to the effect the recent revolution in race relations has had on standards of acceptable behavior.

The Equal Employment Opportunity Commission has defined sexual harassment to include "unwelcome sexual advances, requests for sexual favors, and other verbal or physical conduct of a sexual nature" which is treated by the employer as part of the job or which interferes with performance of the job.[172] The more blatant kinds of sexual harassment have traditionally been considered uncivilized or outrageous, though the milder forms have traditionally been accepted as "humorous." In today's climate, at least the former and perhaps also the latter will be recognized as the basis for a tort action for emotional distress.[173]

Rogers v. Loews L'Enfant Plaza Hotel[174] allowed an action for mental distress where insulting and demeaning remarks, as well as abusive language and physical advances, were directed at a woman employee. Similarly, *Robson v. Eva's Super Market, Inc.*[175] permitted an action where suggestive comments, leers, ridicule, and uninvited physical conduct were the basis for the suit. This is likely to be a fertile source of future litigation, since the remedies available under civil rights statutes may not allow recovery for mental distress, which is likely in many cases to represent the greater part of the actual injury.

Retaliatory Discharge Cases

A retaliatory discharge for reasons offensive to public policy would seem at first blush to be a perfect candidate for the operative test of the second Restatement. The tort of retaliatory discharge has been recognized in no small part because it produces the outraged reaction in the courts which is an element of the action for mental distress.[176]

---

[171]88 Wash.2d 735, 565 P.2d 1173 (1977).

[172]29 C.F.R. §1604.11(1) (1982). At least one state statute, adopted before the current women's rights movement, forbids employers to "permit any influence, practices or conditions calculated to injuriously affect the morals of female employees." ARK. STAT. ANN. §81-405 (1976). Sexual harassment was held to be a basis for a retaliatory discharge action in one early case in that area. *Monge v. Beebe Rubber Co.*, 114 N.H. 130, 316 A.2d 549 (1974).

[173]*Cummings v. Walsh Constr. Co.*, 561 F. Supp. 872 (S.D. Ga. 1983) (repeated demands for sexual favors, intimidating employee into sexual relations, and threats actionable); *Stewart v. Thomas*, 538 F. Supp. 891 (D.D.C. 1982) (periodic sexual advances, unconsented touching in sexual manner, and attempts to kiss actionable); *Rogers v. Loew's L'Enfant Plaza Hotel*, 526 F. Supp. 523 (D.D.C. 1981) (demeaning remarks and sexual advances actionable). But see *Wolk v. Saks Fifth Avenue, Inc.*, 31 FEP 859 (W.D. Pa. 1983) (two unconsented passionate kisses insufficient).

[174]526 F. Supp. 523, 529–531 (D.D.C. 1981).

[175]538 F. Supp. 857, 863–864 (N.D. Ohio 1982).

[176]RESTATEMENT (SECOND) OF TORTS §46 comment d (1977) ("[R]ecitation of the facts to an average member of the community would arouse his resentment against the actor, and lead him to exclaim, 'outrageous!'").

Nevertheless, the cases are divided. Where retaliatory discharge is not recognized, the action for mental distress has been an equally unsuccessful vehicle to recovery.[177] Where retaliatory discharge has been recognized as tortious, however, the public policy violation has been held to satisfy the first element of mental distress.[178]

Harassment of the Handicapped

Ridicule, abuse, or cruelty toward a handicapped employee literally adds insult to injury. The handicapped employee is particularly likely to be at the employer's mercy because of physical disadvantage and the emotional effect of the handicap. While courts have not generally been especially protective toward handicapped employees, there appears to be some sensitivity to the position such employees occupy.

The circumstances that have moved courts to permit recovery have arisen out of denial of benefits to the disabled.[179] In *Harris v. Jones*,[180] the employee brought suit for a supervisor's conduct in mimicking his stuttering speech pattern; but the court did not determine whether this was outrageous, denying recovery instead for failure to prove consequent emotional distress. A statement by a supervisor that the plaintiff's job was created for him because of his handicap was held insufficient as a matter of law in *Paris v. Division of State Compensation Insurance Fund*.[181]

Job-Related Harassment

The bulk of the employment mental distress cases have been brought by employees claiming varying degrees of harassment on the job. The courts, perhaps presuming that the employee-plaintiff has been subjected to justified disciplinary action and not wishing to chill employer disciplinary power, have been decidedly unsympathetic.[182]

---

[177]*Gellert v. Eastern Airlines*, 370 So.2d 802 (Fla. Dist. Ct. App. 1979); *Perdue v. J.C. Penney Co.*, 470 F. Supp. 1234 (S.D.N.Y. 1979) (applying Texas law).

[178]*Milton v. Illinois Bell Tel. Co.*, 101 Ill. App.3d 75, 427 N.E.2d 829 (1981), distinguishing *Palmateer v. International Harvester Co.*, 85 Ill. App.3d 50, 406 N.E.2d 595 (1980), *rev'd*, 85 Ill.2d 124, 421 N.E.2d 876 (1981) (premise that retaliatory discharge was not actionable overruled by state supreme court); *Harless v. First Nat'l Bank*, 289 S.E.2d 692 (W. Va. 1982) (recovery for mental distress allowed). See *Hudson v. Zenith Engraving Co.*, 273 S.C. 766, 259 S.E.2d 812 (1979) (no recovery where employee failed to show that discharge was in fact retaliatory).

[179]*Holmes v. Oxford Chems., Inc.*, 510 F. Supp. 915 (M.D. Ala. 1981); *Harrison v. Loyal Protective Life Ins. Co.*, 379 Mass. 212, 396 N.E.2d 987 (1979).

[180]281 Md. 560, 380 A.2d 611 (1977).

[181]517 P.2d 1353 (Colo. App. 1973).

[182]A good example of this view is *American Road Serv. Co. v. Inmon*, 394 So.2d 361 (Ala. 1980), in which the court reversed a finding of liability where the employee was the victim of harassment, false accusations, unwarranted investigation, and unjustified termination because the employer was held not to have intended mental distress. Discipline for misconduct away from the work place was not actionable in *Magruder v. Selling Areas Mktg., Inc.*, 439 F. Supp. 1155 (N.D. Ill. 1977), and in *Byrnes v. Orkin Exterminating Co.*, 562 F. Supp. 892 (E.D. La. 1983). But in *Armano v. Federal Reserve Bank*, 468 F. Supp. 674 (D. Mass. 1979), the court found outrageous conduct in the context of what the employee claimed was an attempt to force his resignation.

Involuntary job reassignment, in one instance[183] or repeatedly,[184] has been held insufficient to sustain an action for mental distress. Accusations that the employer has been uncooperative, annoying, or has actually obstructed the employee's performance of his job likewise do not shock the conscience.[185]

It is inherently difficult to separate the cases where the conduct characterized by the employee as on-the-job harassment is justifiable discipline and supervision from those where it is an attempt to induce the employee to resign.[186] While in the latter case the employer may specifically and deliberately intend mental suffering to result, the level of suffering and the type of conduct is not often viewed as outrageous.

The level of harassment can get beyond the judicial threshold, however. Knowingly false accusations of wrongful behavior if it is serious in nature, can be deemed outrageous.[187] Similarly, actions that have a continuing effect on the employee's professional career can be found outrageous.[188]

Discharge and Post-Termination Conduct as Outrage

Standing alone, termination of employment without cause is not outrageous conduct giving rise to an action for mental distress. For instance, in *Richey v. American Automobile Association*[189] discharge of an employee for absence due to hospitalization was not outrageous

---

[183]*Shewmaker v. Minchew*, 504 F. Supp. 156 (D.D.C. 1980), aff'd, 666 F.2d 616 (D.C. Cir. 1981); *Wenzer v. Consolidated Rail Corp.*, 464 F. Supp. 643 (E.D. Pa. 1979).

[184]*Ankeny v. Lockheed Missiles and Space Co.*, 88 Cal. App.2d 531, 151 Cal. Rptr. 828 (1979); *Wells v.Thomas*, 569 F. Supp. 426 (E.D. Pa. 1983).

[185]*Waldron v. Covington*, 415 A.2d 1070 (D.C. 1980); *Beidler v. W.R. Grace, Inc.*, 461 F. Supp. 1013 (E.D. Pa. 1978); *Magruder v. Selling Areas Mktg., Inc.*, 439 F. Supp. 1155 (N.D. Ill. 1977); *Cornblith v. First Maintenance Supply Co.*, 268 Cal. App.2d 564, 74 Cal. Rptr. 216 (1968); *Wells v. Thomas*, 569 F. Supp. 426 (E.D. Pa. 1983) (transfer, removal of secretary, poor performance rating, and no raise); *Pawelek v. Paramount Studios Corp.*, 571 F. Supp. 1082 (N.D. Ill. 1983) (telling Polish jokes); *Brynes v. Orkin Exterminating Co.*, 562 F. Supp. 892 (E.D. La. 1983) (cursing and embarrassing employee). In the following cases, circumstances were held sufficient: *Smith v. Montgomery Ward & Co.*, 567 F. Supp. 1331 (D. Colo. 1983) (failure to make timely payments under a benefit plan, withholding information, and intentionally disqualifying employee from certain benefits); *Cummings v. Walsh Constr. Co.*, 561 F. Supp. 872 (S.D. Ga. 1983) (repeated solicitation for sex with threats of discharge).

[186]The employee who resigns voluntarily is in a poor position to pursue a claim of any kind against the employer. More important, resignation spares the employer the distasteful and often painful task of telling the employee he is being let go.

[187]Compare *Perat v. Atkinson*, 213 Cal. App.2d 472, 28 Cal. Rptr. 898 (1963) (no liability for false accusation of failure to obey order), with *Armano v. Federal Reserve Bank*, 468 F. Supp. 674 (D. Mass. 1979) (rumors that plaintiff was suspected of theft as part of systematic harassment program).

[188]*Lagies v. Copley*, 110 Cal. App.2d 958, 168 Cal. Rptr. 368 (1980) (refusing to print reporter's stories, identifying confidential sources to destroy credibility, demotion, and preventing other employment).

[189]80 Mass. Adv. Sh. 1425, 406 N.E.2d 675 (1980). Accord: *Novosel v. Sears Roebuck & Co.*, 495 F. Supp. 344 (E.D. Mich. 1980) (termination for refusal to answer guard's inquiry concerning removal of property from employer's premises); *Lekich v. IBM Corp.*, 469 F. Supp. 485 (E.D. Pa. 1975) (termination for failure to report and pay for personal long-distance telephone calls); *Carrillo v. Illinois Bell Tel. Co.*, 538 F. Supp. 793 (N.D. Ill. 1982); *Cautilli v. GAF Corp.*, 531 F. Supp. 71 (E.D. Pa. 1982); *Elliott v. Employers Reinsurance Corp.*, 534 F. Supp. 690 (D. Kan. 1982); *Hobson v. Western Airlines*, 25 FEP Cases 1509 (W.D. Cal. 1980); *Brenimer v. Great W. Sugar Co.*, 567 F. Supp. 218 (D. Colo. 1983); *Crain v. Burroughs Corp.*, 560 F. Supp. 849 (C.D. Cal. 1983).

conduct. Recovery has been sought, with varying degrees of success, based on the manner of notification, the basis of the discharge, and accompanying efforts to extort money from the employee. There are also cases arising from arbitrary denial of employee benefits.

The notification cases reach contrary results. In *Agis v. Howard Johnson Co.*,[190] it was the communication to the employee of the purely arbitrary nature of the discharge that permitted an action. The employer, in hopes of eliminating an unknown thief from its staff, began firing one waitress a day in alphabetical order, starting with the plaintiff, which the court found to be outrageous. *Williams v. School District*,[191] held that notifying the employee of her termination while she was being treated by a physician and was under sedation was not outrageous.

In *Agarwal v. Johnson*,[192] false accusations concerning the employee's job performance causing discharge were one of many factors that added up to outrageous conduct accompanied by racial discrimination, bad references, moving of the employee's office, racial slurs, contradictory instructions, manipulation of working conditions, and frustration of the employee's effort to do his job. A false public announcement that an employee was dying of a rare disease was actionable in *Chuy v. Philadelphia Eagles Football Team*.[193] In *Dowling v. Blue Cross*,[194] the court denied an action based solely on discharge following erroneous accusations of immoral conduct, where it was alleged that a reasonable investigation would have proven that the conduct did not occur.

The courts have refused to find liability against those who bring about[195] or participate in[196] disciplinary proceedings against employees. The court in *Deaile v. General Telephone Co.*,[197] relied on a privilege analysis applicable to defamation cases to deny liability for necessary internal communication of admitted falsification of records.[198] The privilege analysis was relied on as a defense, though it actually was simply the determinative factor in characterizing the conduct as not outrageous.

The court permitted harsh investigatory techniques in *Food Fair*,

---

[190]371 Mass. 140, 355 N.E.2d 315 (1976).

[191]447 S.W.2d 256 (Mo. 1969).

[192]25 Cal.3d 932, 603 P.2d 58, 160 Cal. Rptr. 141 (1979). See also *Armano v. Federal Reserve Bank*, 468 F. Supp. 674 (D. Mass. 1979) (circulation of rumors that employee was suspected of theft and systematic harassment to induce resignation).

[193]595 F.2d 1265 (3d Cir. 1979).

[194]338 So.2d 88 (Fla. Dist. Ct. App. 1976).

[195]*Van Buskirk v. Bleiler*, 46 A.D.2d 707, 360 N.Y.S.2d 88 (1974) (malicious instigation of official action leading to discharge not actionable).

[196]*Agostini v. Strycula*, 231 Cal. App.2d 804, 42 Cal. Rptr. 314 (1965) (statements that employee's use of corporal punishment made him unsuited for duty not actionable).

[197]40 Cal. App.3d 841, 115 Cal. Rptr. 582 (1974).

[198]Two cases are based on the employer's public statements about the employee. In *Rosales v. City of Eloy*, 122 Ariz. 134, 593 P.2d 688 (App. 1979), a public statement of "charges" filed against the policeman-employee when only "accusations" had been filed was not outrageous. *Chuy v. Philadelphia Eagles Football Club*, 431 F. Supp. 254 (E.D. Pa. 1977), held that it was outrageous for the team physician to announce to the public, without any basis, that the player had a rare, terminal disease.

Inc. v. Anderson,[199] where the employer sought to determine the source of a cash shortage. The employee was required to submit to a polygraph examination and had an exchange with a security officer who said it was company policy to admit to theft and that anyone who had worked for the company as long as she must have removed some property. When the employee protested her innocence, she was told that the alternative to confession was termination. She confessed, and was terminated for theft. The court was not outraged.

Where the employer terminates an employee and also attempts to use its leverage to extort money from the employee or avoid liability to him, the courts have consistently permitted actions for emotional distress. In *MBM Co. v. Counce*,[200] the employee was terminated on accusations of theft and required to take a polygraph test before the employer would pay her final wages. She passed the test, but the employer still deducted "her share" of the missing money. This, the court held, could be found to be extreme and outrageous. The same result prevailed in *Beavers v. Johnson*,[201] where the employer threatened arrest and imprisonment if the employee did not pay money the employer claimed she had stolen, and in *Curnett v. Wolf*,[202] where the employer threatened to send and sent a bad reference to the new employer in an effort to force the employee to drop a breach of contract suit arising from his termination.

The cases on the employer's arbitrary termination of health and disability benefits are split. In *Steadman v. South Central Bell Telephone Co.*,[203] the court denied an action based on the employer's discontinuance of disability benefits during the employee's disability; but in other cases reduction of benefits[204] and threats of refusal to reemploy if benefits were claimed[205] were a sufficient basis for a mental distress action.

Other Necessary Elements of Mental Distress Cases

While the focus of a mental distress case is necessarily on the determination of whether the conduct in question rises to the level of "outrageous and uncivilized," and at times the nature of the conduct alone may be enough to satisfy the court that it was intentional and produced severe mental suffering, it nevertheless must be remembered that the action cannot be premised solely on the defendant's wrongful behavior. The plaintiff must show intent to inflict

---

[199]382 So.2d 150 (Fla. Dist. Ct. App. 1980). See also *Rosales v. City of Eloy*, 122 Ariz. 134, 593 P.2d 688 (App. 1979) (unsuccessful demand for search of employee's person not outrageous). But see *Agis v. Howard Johnson Co.*, 371 Mass. 140, 355 N.E.2d 315 (1976) (arbitrary alphabetical discharge program to locate thief gave rise to action for mental distress).
[200]268 Ark. 269, 596 S.W.2d 681 (1980). Accord: *Smith v. Montgomery Ward & Co.*, 567 F. Supp. 1331 (D. Colo. 1983).
[201]112 Ga. App. 677, 145 S.E.2d 776 (1976).
[202]244 Iowa 683, 57 N.W.2d 915 (1953).
[203]362 So.2d 1144 (La. Ct. App. 1978).
[204]*Holmes v. Oxford Chems., Inc.*, 510 F. Supp. 915 (M.D. Ala. 1981).
[205]*Harrison v. Loyal Protective Life Ins. Co.*, 379 Mass. 212, 396 N.E.2d 987 (1979).

emotional distress[206] and must show that the conduct did in fact cause severe emotional distress.[207]

Negligent Performance of the Employment Contract

In *Chamberlain v. Bissel, Inc.*,[208] an employee was terminated after 23 years of service. Three months before his termination, the employee received a routine performance appraisal involving both positive and negative comments. Although the supervisor who conducted the appraisal knew that the plaintiff was likely to be terminated in the near future, he failed to inform the employee of that fact. It was held that the employer was negligent in this respect and failed to exercise due care for the employee. Theoretically, this is a claim that can be characterized not only as a tort but also a breach of the implied duty to exercise due care which is implicit in any contract. The breach of that implied covenant is most frequently litigated in malpractice suits against physicians, lawyers, architects, engineers, and other professionals. The possibility of what effectively is a malpractice suit against employers opens many questions for consideration. Such a claim might be a blessing in disguise to the employer if it were coupled with other tort and contract claims made by the employee: The claim of negligence might well entitle the employer to at least a defense under its general liability insurance policy and perhaps also indemnity in the event of a loss.

Assault and Battery

Fortunately, physical aggression is an unusual occurrence in the relationship between employer and employee. Nevertheless, the possibility of such a claim must not be overlooked, particularly where the terminated employee alleges sexual harassment.[209] In general, the employer is liable for sexual assault and battery committed by its supervisory employees, particularly if they commit the offending acts while otherwise acting within the course and scope of their employment.[210]

---

[206]*American Road Serv. Co. v. Inmon*, 394 So.2d 361 (Ala. 1980).

[207]*Harris v. Jones*, 281 Md. 560, 380 A.2d 611 (1977) (particulars required); *Novosel v. Sears, Roebuck & Co.*, 495 F. Supp. 344 (E.D. Mich. 1980) (severe mental distress must result); *Wells v. Thomas*, 569 F. Supp. 426 (E.D. Pa. 1983) (possible increase in blood pressure insufficient to make out severe distress).

[208]547 F. Supp. 1067 (W.D. Mich. 1982); *Schipani v. Ford Motor Co.*, 102 Mich. App. 606, 302 N.W.2d 307 (1981). See *Bulkin v. Western Kraft E., Inc.*, 422 F. Supp. 437 (E.D. Pa. 1976) (negligent maintenance of personnel records).

[209]*Guyette v. Stauffer Chem. Co.*, 518 F. Supp. 521 (D.N.J. 1981).

[210]*Fitzgerald v. McCutcheon*, 270 Pa. Super. 102, 410 A.2d 1270 (1979); *International Distrib. Corp. v. American Dist. Tel. Co.*, 569 F.2d 136 (D.C. Cir. 1977).

Privacy vs. Disclosure: Balancing Employee and Employer Rights*

The conflict underlying the employee privacy problem is twofold: On the one hand, employers have an interest in obtaining and using personal information about their employees. They need such data for purposes ranging from administering benefit packages, to making employee selection decisions, to complying with government regulations. On the other hand, employees have an interest in preventing unwarranted intrusions into their private lives as well as in preventing discovery or use of information likely to create adverse consequences for them.

Employee privacy involves a number of related issues that can be organized into the following four categories: (1) employer acquisition of employee information, where both the types of data sought and the methods of obtaining it create potential privacy problems; (2) employer retention and internal use of personal information, where problems of accuracy and currency of the information, as well as its internal dissemination, arise; (3) employee access, where the issues are whether employees should see information retained about them and what types they should be allowed to see; and (4) employer disclosure to third parties, where the issues are what personal information employers should disclose and to whom. Third parties that pressure employers for data include government agencies, unions, prospective employers, and credit or consumer reporting agencies.

Federal Legislation

Privacy Act of 1974

There is at present no comprehensive federal regulation of private employees' privacy, but federal employees are protected by the Privacy Act of 1974. The Act requires federal government agencies to inform individuals (including federal employees) of the existence of record-keeping systems containing personal information about them. Agencies must permit individuals to examine, copy, correct, or amend that personal information. The Act also limits the type of data agencies may collect about an individual and prohibits, with certain exceptions, disclosure of personal information to outsiders without the written consent of the individual to whom the information pertains.

Privacy Protection Study Commission

The Privacy Act of 1974 also created the Privacy Protection Study Commission. The Commission's mandate was to investigate infor-

---

*This section on privacy is the contribution of D. Jan Duffy, J.D., Associate Professor at the California Polytechnic State University.

mation practices in private and regional government organizations, and to recommend to Congress the extent to which the principles and requirements of the Privacy Act should extend to them.[211]

In its 1977 report, the Commission concluded that the Privacy Act should not be extended to the private sector, but that employees should be given many new privacy protections. The Commission recommended that, for the most part, employers deal with privacy issues on a voluntary basis.

The Commission also concluded that certain employee privacy issues required immediate federal legislation. It recommended, among other things, that Congress (1) ban the use of polygraphs in the employment context; (2) ban "pretext interviews" in employment background investigations; (3) prohibit employers from seeking or using arrest records except as required by law; (4) require employers to exercise reasonable care in selecting investigative agencies; and (5) strengthen disclosure provisions of the Federal Fair Credit Reporting Act.

To date, Congress has not passed legislation to implement the Commission's recommendations.

Federal Fair Credit Reporting Act

Although the Federal Fair Credit Reporting Act essentially regulates the activities of consumer reporting agencies, it has some ramifications affecting employee privacy as well. "Consumer," within the meaning of the Act, includes employees and applicants; "user" of consumer agency services includes employers. Accordingly, any employer who procures a "consumer investigative report" (i.e., a report about an employee or applicant that is based on personal interviews) must (1) deliver or mail written notice to the employee or applicant that an investigative report possibly concerning his character, general reputation, personal characteristics, and mode of living will be made; and (2) at the employee's request, provide a complete disclosure of the nature and scope of the investigation.

If an employer denies employment or takes any other adverse action on the basis of information contained in a consumer investigative report, it must advise the employee of the adverse action and supply the name and address of the reporting agency.

State Legislation

State legislatures have been extremely active in the employee privacy area. As of 1983, nine states had enacted comprehensive

---

[211]PERSONAL PRIVACY IN AN INFORMATION SOCIETY: THE REPORT OF THE PRIVACY PROTECTION STUDY COMMISSION 496 (1977).

government privacy acts similar to the Federal Privacy Act of 1974.[212] Several others have imposed more limited restrictions on state agencies' personal information practices.[213]

Eleven states have enacted legislation requiring private employers to permit employees to examine their own personnel files.[214] Michigan's statute, which is the most detailed, incorporates many of the Privacy Protection Study Commission's recommendations. It provides that employees may, upon written request, examine and copy their personnel records at a reasonable time and place. The term "personnel records" appears to be rather broadly defined, although the Act specifically excludes from access certain reference letters, comparative evaluations, medical reports, and investigative or grievance files maintained separately. Employees may request that information in their personnel files be amended or corrected; if the request is denied, they may file dissenting statements that are to be kept in the file along with the disputed information. If an employer maintains investigative files, employees must be notified of their existence at the end of the investigation or after two years. Investigative files must be destroyed if no action is taken.

Michigan's statute also restricts the types of information that can be collected about an employee and imposes some limits on disclosure to third parties. To enforce its provisions, the statute authorizes injunctive relief, the award of actual damages and costs, and a $200 fine for willful and knowing violation. Other states' employee access statutes are somewhat less comprehensive. Several—for example, California, Oregon, and Pennsylvania—provide only rights of access and copying, although a few statutes incorporate provisions limiting disclosure to third parties or permitting employees to file dissents. For example, Connecticut's statute, like Michigan's, expressly limits disclosure to third parties. In addition, Connecticut, as well as North Carolina and Wisconsin, requires procedures for employees to challenge the accuracy of file information.

States have shown particular interest in regulating polygraphs and other truth verification devices; twenty-six states now impose some restrictions on their use. Two states—Massachusetts and New Jersey—and the District of Columbia absolutely prohibit polygraph

[212]See ARK. STAT. ANN. §16-804 (1979); CAL. CIV. CODE §1798, amended 1979 (Deering 1976); CONN. GEN. STAT. ANN. §4-190 (1969); IND. CODE §4-1-6 (1981); MASS. GEN. LAWS ANN. ch. 66A, amended 1976, 1977 (West 1969 & Supp. 1983); MINN. STAT. ANN. §15/162, amended 1979 (West 1977); OHIO REV. CODE ANN. §1347.01 (Page 1982); UTAH CODE ANN. §63-50-1 (1953); VA. CODE §2.1-377 (1950).
[213]See, e.g., N.Y. PUB. OFF. LAW §89, 1980 N.Y. Laws ch. 677 (Consol. Supp. 1983); COLO. REV. STAT. §24-72-204(3)(a) (1982).
[214]CAL. LAB. CODE §1198.5 (West Supp. 1983); CONN. GEN. STAT. ANN. §31-128a (West Supp. 1980); Act 83-1104, 1983 Ill. Leg. Serv. 7290 (West), to be codified at ILL. REV. STAT. ch. 48 §200 *et seq.*; ME. REV. STAT. ANN. tit. 26, §631, as amended 1979 (1974 & Supp. 1983-84); MICH. COMP. LAWS ANN. §423.501 (1978); N.H. REV. STAT. ANN. §275:56 (Supp. 1983). N.C. GEN. STAT. §126-22 (1981); ORE. REV. STAT. §652.750 (1981); PA. STAT. ANN. tit. 43, §1321 (Purdon 1964); WIS. STAT. ANN. §103.13, ch. 339 (West 1979). In Illinois, Pub. Act. No. 83-1104, 1983 Ill. Legis. Serv. 7290 (West) (to be codified at ILL. REV. STAT. ch. 48, §2001 *et seq.*).

use in employment.[215] Six states forbid employers to require, request, or suggest that an employee take a lie detector test.[216] Twelve states permit polygraph use only upon the employee's knowing and voluntary consent.[217] A few others impose more limited constraints, such as requiring that operators be licensed or prohibiting inquiries on certain subjects.[218] Malpractice liability may be asserted in some states against the polygraph examiner whose negligent examination results in discharge.[219]

Many states have enacted other miscellaneous statutes relating to employee privacy. Typical statutes restrict the use of arrest records in employment decisions; prohibit intentionally inaccurate employment references; require confidentiality of, or access to, medical records; and prohibit certain types of inquiries. In addition, sixteen states have enacted acts with provisions similar to those of the Federal Fair Credit Reporting Act.[220]

Judicial Protection: Tort and Constitutional Law

Employer Tort Liability

Defamation, which is an invasion of a person's interest in reputation and good name, is one traditional tort that bears on employee privacy.[221] Liability for this tort ordinarily arises when an employer communicates information to, e.g., a prospective employer or credit agency that is injurious to the reputation of an employee or former employee.

Since nothing prevents an individual from filing a lawsuit, employers have a healthy concern for potential defamation liability.

---

[215]D.C. CODE ANN. §36-803 (1981); MASS. GEN. LAWS ANN. ch. 149, §19B (West 1982); N.J. STAT. ANN. §2C:40A-1 (West 1982).

[216]ALASKA STAT. §23.10.037 (1982); DEL. CODE ANN. tit. 19, §704 (1979); ME. REV. STAT. ANN. ch. 32, §7166 (Supp. 1983-84); MINN. STAT. ANN. §181.75 (West Supp. 1984); N.Y. LAB. LAW §733 (Consol. 1983); WIS. STAT. ANN. §111.37 (West Supp. 1983-84).

[217]CAL. LAB. CODE §432.2 (West 1971); CONN. GEN. STAT. §31-51g (1979); HAWAII REV. STAT. §378.21 (1976); IDAHO CODE §44-903 (1977); MD. ANN. CODE art. 100, §95 (Supp. 1978); MICH. COMP. LAWS ANN. §338.1726 (1976); MONT. CODE ANN. §39-2-304 (1983); NEB. REV. STAT. §32 (1984); ORE. REV. STAT. §659.225 (1983); PA. CONS. STAT. ANN. ch. 18, §7321 (Purdon 1983); R.I. GEN. LAWS §28-6.1-1 (1979); WASH. REV. CODE ANN. §49.44.120 (Supp. 1983-84).

[218]ARIZ. REV. STAT. ANN. §32.2701 (1976) (operators must be licensed; must inform subjects that participation is voluntary; must inform subject of results; certain inquiries prohibited, e.g., those concerning religious, labor, and sexual activities and political affiliation); N.M. STAT. ANN. §67-31A-1 (1978) (operator must be licensed; certain inquiries prohibited unless subject gives written consent); ILL. REV. STAT. ch. 111, §2404 (1981) (operator must be licensed); VT. STAT. ANN. tit. 26, §2901 (Supp. 1983-84) (similar to Arizona's); VA. CODE §§40.1-51.4:3 and 54-729.916 (1981) (prohibits certain inquiries; subject must be provided copy of test).

[219]*Lawson v. Howmet Aluminum Corp.*, 449 N.E.2d 1172 (Ind. App. 1983).

[220]ARIZ. REV. STAT. ANN. §44-1693(A)(4) (1980); CAL. CIV. CODE §1785 (West 1982); CONN. GEN. STAT. ANN. §36-432(b) (West 1981); FLA. STAT. ANN. §559.72(3) and (6) (West 1972); KAN. STAT. ANN. §50-720 (1976); KY. REV. STAT. ANN. §431.350 (West 1967); ME. REV. STAT. ANN. tit. 10, §1311 (1980); MD. COMM. LAW CODE ANN. §14-201 (1982); MASS. GEN. LAWS ANN. ch. 93, §51 (West 1972); MONT. CODE ANN. §18-501 (1982); N.H. REV. STAT. ANN. §359B (1966); N.M. STAT. ANN. §50-18-1 (1978); N.Y. GEN. BUS. LAW §380 (Consol. 1980); OKLA. STAT. ANN. tit. 25 §81 (West 1955); TEX. REV. CIV. STAT. ANN. art. 9016(2) (Vernon 1967); VA. CODE §6.1-366(c) (1983).

[221]Prosser, *supra* note 3, §111 at 737.

Nevertheless, this tort actually affords employees little real protection against invasions of their privacy. The reason is that employers are protected by a qualified privilege; that is, employers generally are not held liable for injurious communications about an employee, even when the information given is false, so long as the communication is made in good faith in response to an inquiry by someone with a legitimate interest in the information (e.g., a prospective employer or a surety bonding company).[222] Accordingly, though disclosing personal information about an employee may violate his sense of privacy, it will not ordinarily constitute an actionable defamation. (The subject of defamation is treated in greater detail in Chapter 9.)

Another potential basis of employer tort liability is invasion of privacy. Courts have recognized four distinct forms of tortious invasions of privacy; the one most relevant to work place privacy is "public disclosure of true, embarrassing private facts about the plaintiff."[223] Much of the information contained in a personnel file—e.g., performance evaluations, test scores, salary history, and medical information—constitutes the "private facts" that, if disclosed, could form the basis of the tort. Nevertheless, this tort still falls short of providing significant protection of employees' privacy interests. One reason is that the tort requires public disclosure in the sense of "publicity" or communication to a large number of persons. Ordinarily, an employer does not communicate private facts about an employee to a sufficient number of persons to constitute public disclosure. The second reason is the employer's qualified privilege to communicate true information to those deemed by precedent to have legitimate interest in knowing it.

Some courts have recognized an additional basis of tort liability that relates to employee privacy. In *Quinones v. United States*,[224] an employee suffered adverse consequences when his employer, the federal government, released inaccurate information from his personnel file to a third party. Finding no precedent in existing state law, the Third Circuit held that Pennsylvania would allow the employee to maintain an action against his employer for negligence. The court reasoned that government regulations respecting maintenance of personnel records established a duty to maintain them accurately. Alternatively, the court concluded, one who gratuitously renders a service, such as providing employee references, assumes a duty to act carefully. Building on the Third Circuit's lead, a federal district court subsequently held in *Bulkin v. Western Kraft East, Inc.*[225] that Pennsylvania and New Jersey law would recognize an employee's action

---

[222]*Id.* §115 at 785-796.
[223]*Id.* §117 at 804-814. See also *Cort v. Bristol-Myers Co.*, 385 Mass. 300, 431 N.E.2d 908 (1982) (action for invasion of privacy premised upon employer's unsuccessful attempt to collect information dismissed).
[224]492 F.2d 1269 (3d Cir. 1974). Accord: *Moessmer v. United States*, 569 F. Supp. 782 (E.D. Mo. 1983). Contra: *Prouty v. National R.R. Passenger Corp.*, 572 F. Supp. 200 (D.D.C. 1983).
[225]422 F. Supp. 437 (E.D. Pa. 1976).

against his *private sector* employer for "negligent maintenance of employment records."

Phillips v. Smalley Maintenance Services, Inc.[226] concluded that a superior's coercive sexual demands are an invasion of privacy under Alabama law. The Alabama Supreme Court, answering questions certified by the Eleventh Circuit, rejected the argument that invasion of privacy requires a physical invasion of a private geographical place such as a home or hotel room. In the court's view, the plaintiff's psychological integrity had been violated—an intrusion upon seclusion form of invasion of privacy.

Constitutional Protection

Federal Guarantees. Federal courts have recognized a federal constitutional right to privacy arising from, variously, the First, Third, Fourth, Fifth, Ninth, and Fourteenth Amendments to the Constitution or from "penumbras" thereto.[227] It has not been established that such right of privacy extends to employment records. Nevertheless, in *Detroit Edison Co. v. NLRB*,[228] the Supreme Court held that an employer's refusal to disclose psychological tests, test scores, and other confidential material to the employees' union did not violate the National Labor Relations Act. The employees' so-called "privacy interest" was one factor the Court considered as weighing against disclosure. Moreover, in *E.I. du Pont de Nemours and Co. v. Finklea*[229] and *United States v. Westinghouse*,[230] two federal courts tacitly recognized the existence of employees' rights to privacy concerning medical records held by their employers. Although the courts held that the employers involved must surrender employee medical records to the National Institute for Occupational Safety and Health, each mentioned the employees' "privacy interest" as a factor to be considered.

In *Slevin v. City of New York*,[231] the court invalidated portions of New York City's law requiring public disclosure of the family finances of all city employees earning over $30,000 annually. Finding an intrusion upon firefighters' and police officers' interests in confidentiality and autonomy, the trial court concluded that the law violated their federal constitutional rights to privacy. Though it approved the filing of reports by all employees and the public disclosure of financial information by policy-making officials, the court held that the $30,000 salary standard was arbitrary since it included non-elected, non-policy-making employees and excluded certain sensi-

---

[226]711 F.2d 1524 (11th Cir. 1983). See also *Cummings v. Walsh Constr. Co.*, 561 F. Supp. 872 (S.D. Ga. 1983). Contra: *Kobeck v. Nabisco*, 166 Ga. App. 652, 305 S.E.2d 183 (1983).
[227]See, e.g., *Griswold v. Connecticut*, 381 U.S. 479 (1965); *Roe v. Wade*, 410 U.S. 113, *rehearing denied*, 410 U.S. 959 (1973).
[228]440 U.S. 301 (1979).
[229]442 F. Supp. 821 (S.D. W. Va. 1977).
[230]638 F.2d 570 (3d Cir. 1980).
[231]551 F. Supp. 917 (S.D.N.Y. 1982), *rev'd in pertinent part sub nom. Barry v. City of New York*, 712 F.2d 1554 (2d Cir. 1983).

tive policy-making positions. On appeal, the Second Circuit held that because the law required a finding by a Board of Ethics of a relationship of the financial information to the public employment or a possible conflict of interest before public disclosure could be made, no protected privacy interest was threatened.

In *Cole v. Dow Chemical Co.*,[232] employees charged that their employer had exposed them to a chemical that rendered them sterile and invaded their federal constitutional right to privacy by precluding them from making choices about procreation, contraception, and family relationships. The employees did not prevail because the court found there was no state action. Nevertheless, it concluded, without elaborating, that the employees' claims stated a violation of their Fourteenth Amendment right to privacy since the employer's action did interfere with (their) right to make decisions in the area of procreation and family matters."[233]

Police department attempts to regulate employees' off-duty conduct were the subject of *Shawgo v. Spradlin*.[234] The Fifth Circuit ruled that the First Amendment right to privacy of two disciplined police officers was not infringed by city regulations prohibiting off-duty employees from cohabitation outside marriage. In *Thorne v. City of El Segundo*,[235] the Ninth Circuit ruled that off-duty sexual activities of a police department clerk should not have been considered in deciding whether she could attend the police academy. The court held that her First Amendment guarantees of privacy and free association were bridged when she was forced, through a polygraph examination, to disclose information regarding personal sexual matters.

State Guarantees. State constitutions may prove even more protective of employee privacy interests. Ten states recognize the right of privacy in their constitutions.[236] Although some of those guarantees (e.g., those of Arizona, Florida, Hawaii, Louisiana, South Carolina, and Washington) appear to protect only against government intrusions, others seem to promise broader protection (e.g., Alaska, California, Illinois, and Montana).

In California, the developing case law may even extend state constitutional privacy protection to personnel records kept by private organizations. In *White v. Davis*,[237] a case involving police surveillance of a university class, the California Supreme Court held that the California constitutional guarantee of privacy was directed at four mischiefs:

---

[232]112 Mich. App. 198, 315 N.W.2d 565 (1982).
[233]*Id.* at 203, 315 N.W.2d at 568.
[234]701 F.2d 470 (5th Cir. 1983), *cert. denied*, 464 U.S.___ (1983). Compare, e.g., *Briggs v. North Muskegon Police Dep't*, 563 F. Supp. 585 (W.D. Mich. 1983), with *Baron v. Meloni*, 556 F. Supp. 796 (W.D.N.Y. 1983).
[235]726 F.2d 459 (9th Cir. 1983).
[236]ALASKA CONST. art. 1, §22; ARIZ. CONST. art. 2, §8; CAL. CONST. art. 1, §1; FLA. CONST. art. 1, §23; HAWAII CONST. art. 1, §5; ILL. CONST. art. 1, §§6, 12; LA. CONST. art. 1, §5; MONT. CONST. art. 11, §10; S.C. CONST. art. 4, §10; WASH. CONST. art. 1, §7.
[237]13 Cal.3d 757, 533 P.2d 222 (1975).

"1) 'government snooping' and the secret gathering of personal information; 2) the overbroad collection and retention of unnecessary personal information by government and *business interests* [emphasis added]; 3) the improper use of information properly obtained for a specific purpose, for example, the use of it for another purpose or the disclosure of it to some third party; and 4) the lack of a reasonable check on the accuracy of existing records."[238]

Subsequently, a California appeals court, in *Porten v. University of San Francisco*,[239] construed the state constitution's guarantee of privacy to protect not only against state action but against violation "by anyone." The court consequently held that a university student stated a constitution-based cause of action for invasion of privacy when he sued his university for unwarranted disclosure of his grades from a former school to a state scholarship commission. California's constitutional right of privacy recently surfaced again in two employment cases. In *Board of Trustees v. Superior Court*,[240] the court ruled that an employer need not turn over peer evaluations of a faculty member in response to his discovery request because, in part, such action would violate the constitutional privacy right of the persons who made those evaluations. The court in *Johnson v. Winter*[241] reached the same result with respect to confidential evaluations of an applicant for a deputy sheriff's position.

Recommendations for Employers

Given the potential for new regulation and the incentive to discover more mutually beneficial solutions, employers and employee representatives may themselves take the most significant steps toward fair information practices. Indeed, many employers and employee organizations have already acted. For those that have not yet done so, suggestions for developing and implementing fair information practices are set forth below.

One point should be clarified at the outset, however: In deciding whether to implement these recommendations, employers must balance employee privacy concerns against other, perhaps conflicting, practical concerns. Important as they are, employee privacy interests cannot and need not always outweigh the competing considerations of employer cost and effort, or the safety and welfare of other employees, customers, and the public.

General Practices

1. Identify applicable state and federal laws. Obviously, the starting point for any employee program must be compliance with existing legal requirements.

---

[238]*Id.* at 775, 533 P.2d at 234.
[239]64 Cal. App.3d 825, 134 Cal. Rptr. 839 (1976).
[240]127 Cal. App.3d 435, 179 Cal. Rptr. 585 (1982).
[241]119 Cal. App.3d 516, 174 Cal. Rptr. 160 (1981).

2. Review your information practices to determine what you are collecting; how you are maintaining it; what you actually need to collect and maintain; what safeguards you have to ensure accuracy and completeness of information; and what and to whom you are disclosing information. While this audit of existing practices may be costly and time-consuming, an effective new information practices program depends on an understanding and critical evaluation of current practices. Moreover, the findings of this audit will doubtless strengthen your resolve to implement new policies; employers are invariably surprised, even alarmed, by the inefficient and potentially dangerous practices they discover. Pay particular attention to records kept by persons outside the personnel office (e.g., front line supervisors), as many of the worst problems will be found there.

3. Establish formal policies relating to information handling. Express policies guide personnel charged with implementing them, assure consistent treatment of employees, and, if necessary, provide evidence of practice for defense purposes.

4. Inform employees of company information practices. A voluntary program, thoughtfully publicized and positively presented, will reap greater benefits in terms of employee morale and confidence in the employer's good will than will apparently grudging or ad hoc concessions. Incidentally, terming the policy an "information practices program" rather than a "privacy program" not only avoids the inference that the employer previously may have violated employees' rights, but also avoids raising unwarranted expectations (e.g., private offices and the like).

Acquisition of Personal Information

1. Limit information to what is relevant and necessary to the decision to be made. Not only does collecting irrelevant information potentially offend or demoralize employees, it adversely affects the quality of the decision for which it is obtained. Moreover, unnecessary information clutters up personnel files, decreasing their utility, and adds to information storage problems.

2. Collect information only from reliable sources. Avoid lie detector tests, pretext interviews, hearsay, and arrest records. None of these sources provide consistently reliable information, and unreliable information is at best useless to employers. At worst, it may expose them to tort, invasion of constitutional rights, or even discrimination law liability. Moreover, legislators have shown the greatest concern over use of these methods; abuses here are most likely to lead to further regulation.

3. If you rely on reports from consumer reporting agencies, choose such agencies carefully and periodically reevaluate your choice. Again, unreliable information is useless and potentially dangerous. Your selected agency should be not only competent but also ethical, since its actions may be attributed to you and will directly affect the quality of your decision-making.

4. If you rely on telephone interviews with prior employers, be wary of "off-the-record" information. Not only is such information suspect because it is often subjective, but it likely will prove impossible to rely on to explain resultant decisions, should there be an inquiry.

Maintenance and Internal Use of Personal Information

1. Establish policies concerning what, how long, and by whom employee personal information should be retained. Although this also is a time-consuming process, it is crucial for gaining control over information practices. Without specific guidance, even trained labor relations personnel, not to mention less well-indoctrinated supervisors, tend to follow the "more is more" principle regarding accumulating data. Irrelevant, redundant, outdated information adversely affects employer decision-making and increases storage problems.

2. Consider conducting a periodic audit of files kept and their typical contents; that is, require personal data record-keepers periodically to report the types of data they are collecting and retaining. This also requires a rather substantial effort; nevertheless, it is an effective method of encouraging record-keepers, particularly those outside the personnel office, to fulfill their responsibilities regarding information practices.

3. Periodically review files to remove inaccurate, outdated, or unnecessaray material. This step may be combined with Step 2. Eliminating such material greatly improves the quality of decision-making.

4. To the extent feasible in terms of cost and space, maintain the following separate personnel files for each employee:

(a) General file—routine personnel information unrelated to job performance (e.g., requests for payroll deductions, credit union or employees' club transactions);
(b) Job performance file—performance evaluations, letters of commendation, records of disciplinary actions, etc.
(c) Medical files—physicians' reports, insurance claims, etc.
(d) Criminal convictions—conviction records and, if such data are collected at all, arrest information; and
(e) Closed files—letters of reference, records of investigations, or other matters that you have determined should not be seen by employees.

There are several reasons for maintaining separate files. First, separating routine materials from job performance materials saves considerable time for decision-makers who typically wish to review only employee performance information. Second, segregating medical and criminal information ensures that such potentially irrelevant and prejudicial information is not inadvertently considered in making employment decisions. (It also provides proof of practice if an employee claims that such material *was* considered, where to do so would be illegal.) Finally, segregating sensitive data from routine information decreases the risk of inadvertently disclosing that material to outsiders.

5. Release employee personnel files only to those within your organization who have a "need to know." Consider establishing a routine sign-out procedure for sensitive material files. Restricting disclosure of personal information to those who have a need to know it minimizes intrusiveness and thereby improves employee morale and confidence in the organization. A sign-out procedure serves as a deterrent to unwarranted intrusions into sensitive areas.

Employee Access to Personnel Files

1. Permit employees to inspect and copy their own personnel files. A number of states already require this; others likely will do so soon. Allowing employees access to personnel files admittedly has some disadvantages: It may adversely affect the candor of supervisors or others who evaluate job performance; it may lead to disputes with employees who are dissatisfied with what they find; and it creates an additional burden for the personnel office, which must comply with access requests. However, the advantages of such a policy— which include the cost and time saved when employees police the accuracy and currency of their own files and the positive effect on employee morale—probably outweigh the disadvantages. In addition, drawbacks can be minimized by other efforts such as supervisor training.

2. Consider excluding from access information such as comparative evaluations, investigative materials, and medical data. You may also wish to exclude, or impose different policies for, inactive material that is difficult to retrieve. There is nothing wrong with refusing access to some types of information. Simply ascertain that there is a substantial, and explainable, reason for doing so.

3. Permit employees to request, in writing, amendments or corrections to their files. Permit employees whose request is refused to make a written explanation of their disagreement and include that explanation in the employee's file. Allowing employees to police their own files is the most effective and inexpensive way of assuring the accuracy and currency of the information in them. Permitting employees to file a dissent when the parties can't reach agreement ensures an end to the matter and enhances employee perceptions of employer fairness.

4. Maintain a log of employees' requests for access to their files.
This practice helps deter subsequent questions or complaints about
the accuracy of file information.

Disclosure to Third Parties

1. Strictly control release of information to outside parties; estab-
lish policies regarding what, to whom, and by whom information is
to be disclosed.

2. Ordinarily, only "directory information," such as position and
dates of employment, should be released without employees' consent,
a subpoena, or a judicial order. Restricting nonconsensual releases
to such information decreases the employers' potential for liability
and also decreases the administrative burden of complying with information requests.

3. The burden of providing consent may be placed on employees.
Refuse to release information other than directory information unless
the employee gives written consent on a form provided by the personnel
office. Such forms can list the types of information typically requested
by outsiders, with boxes employees can check if they consent to the
release of that information. Such forms should be dated and indicate
that the consent will expire after some period of time, usually not
more than thirty days.

4. Even with consent, release information only (1) in response to
a specific request, (2) from a properly identified individual, (3) who
has a legitimate right to know the information. These safeguards are
necessary to avoid potential tort liability.

5. Permit only certain designated and trained individuals to pro-
vide information to outsiders. Such a restriction helps monitor the
information released to third parties and provides the basis for defense, should it become necessary.

6. Keep a log of disclosures indicating what was disclosed and to
whom. This practice deters improper disclosures and provides a basis
for defense.

Antitrust Remedies

The antitrust laws are intended to protect the competitive, free-
market economy against unreasonable restraint of trade and monopoly power. They may also provide remedies to discharged employees in several situations. More than any other potential employee
cause of action, antitrust cases are an uncertain and expensive path
to relief from discharge or related injuries. The rapid rise and fall of
doctrine, the availability of some peculiar technical defenses, the

absence of other accepted defenses, the necessity for economic analyses, and the general absence of consistent and clearly defined rules all contribute to this fact. As today's pendulum swings against the antitrust complainant in a variety of doctrinal fields, tomorrow's decision may reshape today's law with unanticipated exceptions. Attorneys representing would-be employee antitrust plaintiffs must weigh the uncertainties and delays inherent in antitrust litigation before pleading a claim for the treble damages windfall the antitrust laws provide.

Section 1 of the Sherman Act[242] prohibits agreements, combinations, and conspiracies in restraint of trade. In recognition of common law precedent and logical necessity, the prohibition from its inception has been restricted to *unreasonable* restraints on trade.[243] Certain restraints have been held per se unlawful because of their necessarily pernicious effect on competition. These are price-fixing by competitors and related price restraints,[244] division of markets between competitors,[245] and group boycotts whose object is to exclude or punish competitors.[246] Other combinations or conspiracies that restrain trade are considered under the "Rule of Reason."[247] The Rule of Reason requires the court to examine all of the circumstances surrounding the restraint and weigh its overall impact on competition.

Section 2 of the Sherman Act[248] prohibits monopolizing by a single entity in a defined geographical and product market.[249] Monopolization requires willful acquisition or maintenance of monopoly power, as distinguished from superior business acumen, but it can even be inferred from market share.[250]

The Clayton Act specifically authorizes treble damage suits for violation of antitrust laws and allows recovery of attorneys' fees.[251] Certain other conduct, including mergers that create monopolies,[252] anticompetitive tying of the sale of one product to the purchase of another product,[253] and interlocking directorates in certain situations,[254] is also prohibited. The Federal Trade Commission Act[255] and Robinson-Patman Act[256] prohibit other specified commercial behavior.

The broad statutory standards of antitrust law and a substantial

[242]15 U.S.C. §1 (1982).
[243]*Standard Oil Co. v. United States*, 221 U.S. 1 (1911).
[244]E.g., *United States v. Socony-Vacuum Oil Co.*, 310 U.S. 150 (1940).
[245]E.g., *United States v. Topco Assoc., Inc.*, 405 U.S.. 596 (1972).
[246]E.g., *Klor's Inc. v. Broadway-Hale Stores, Inc.*, 359 U.S. 207 (1959).
[247]*Board of Trade v. United States*, 246 U.S. 231 (1918).
[248]15 U.S.C. §2 (1982).
[249]*United States v. E.I. du Pont de Nemours & Co.*, 351 U.S. 377 (1956).
[250]*United States v. Grinnell Corp.*, 384 U.S. 563 (1966).
[251]15 U.S.C. §15 (1982).
[252]*Id.* §18.
[253]*Id.* §14.
[254]*Id.* §19.
[255]*Id.* §41 *et seq.*
[256]*Id.* §§13(a), 13(b), 21(a).

volume of case law expounding it in a wide variety of factual settings have produced numerous tests and rules peculiar to the field. One doctrine particularly important for the employment case is the requirement that one who brings an antitrust action must have suffered an "antitrust injury."[257] An injured party is not barred from suit by prior coerced participation in the combination or conspiracy.[258] The determination under Section 1 of the Sherman Act of whether to apply a per se analysis or the Rule of Reason test is another troublesome area.[259]

Antitrust law has been applied to the employment setting in several kinds of cases. The most common cases have been those where employers have agreed among themselves whom they would or would not hire and, more recently, the cases in which employees have claimed they were discharged for refusal to participate in antitrust conspiracies. There are also cases, particularly in the field of athletics, where elaborate restraints on the market for employee services have been imposed, and other cases where employees, primarily in commission sales work, have challenged antitrust violations of the employer which adversely affect their financial rewards.

The Statutory Labor Antitrust Exemption

In the early part of this century, labor unions were held to be antitrust conspiracies.[260] Labor unions were seen as combinations of employees who sold their services to an employer or employers. When union members initiated strikes and boycotts to obtain recognition by unorganized employers, they were held to be engaged in a prohibited group boycott. According to this legal analysis, the typical union organizing campaign prior to enactment of the National Labor Relations Act (NLRA) was a violation of the Sherman Act.

The Sherman Act thus became a potent strikebreaking weapon for employers, creating a federal forum for labor disputes that favored the employer. The injunctive powers of the federal court and the contempt power that goes with it were at the employer's disposal. But Congress reacted to the proposition that union organization was a violation of federal law by enacting Section 6 of the Clayton Act,[261] which provides:

> "The labor of a human being is not a commodity or article of commerce. Nothing contained in the antitrust laws shall be construed to forbid the existence and operation of labor, agricultural, or horticul-

---

[257]*Brunswick Corp. v. Pueblo Bowl-O-Mat, Inc.*, 429 U.S. 477 (1977); *Illinois Brick Co. v. Illinois*, 431 U.S. 720 (1977).

[258]*Perma Life Mufflers, Inc. v. International Parts Corp.*, 392 U.S. 134 (1968).

[259]For a discussion of this and other related problems, see Baker, *Interconnected Problems of Doctrine and Economics in the Section One Labyrinth: Is Sylvania a Way Out?* 67 VA. L. REV. 1457 (1981).

[260]*Loewe v. Lawlor*, 208 U.S. 274, 304-305 (1908) (American Federation of Labor held to be antitrust conspiracy).

[261]15 U.S.C. §17 (1982).

tural organizations, instituted for the purpose of mutual help, and not having capital stock or conducted for profit, or to forbid or restrain individual members of such organizations from lawfully carrying out the legitimate objects thereof; nor shall such organization, or the members thereof, be held or construed to be illegal combinations or conspiracies in restraint of trade, under the antitrust laws."

On the surface, the broad conceptual language of this provision would also appear to bar most suits by employees under the antitrust laws. If the employee's suit is premised on an action by an employer or employers adversely affecting the market for his services, this provision appears to be an obstacle.

Despite the plain message to the courts, Sherman Act suits against unions continued. In *Duplex Printing Press Co. v. Deering*,[262] the Supreme Court held that

> "[T]here is nothing in the section to exempt [a union] or its members from accountability where it or they depart from its normal and legitimate objects, and engage in an actual combination or conspiracy in restraint of trade. And by no fair or permissible construction can it be taken as authorizing any activity otherwise unlawful, or enabling a normally lawful organization to become a cloak for an illegal combination or conspiracy in restraint of trade, as defined by the Antitrust Laws."[263]

This decision eventually led to the adoption of the even more explicit congressional commands of the Norris-LaGuardia Act[264] directing that the federal courts stay out of labor disputes. The Norris-La-Guardia Act expressly approves of labor unions and collective bargaining as a matter of federal policy[265] and was accepted by the courts as a reversal of *Deering*.[266]

The employer's first line of defense when charged with an antitrust violation by an employee has been to argue that since human labor is not within the scope of the antitrust laws, the employee cannot sue. The argument has been consistently rejected and, more frequently, ignored altogether. One decision directly addressing the issue at length is *Cordova v. Bache & Co.*[267]

The *Cordova* court relied on several points. First, the literal language of the statute says that "labor" of a human being is not "a commodity or article of commerce." Labor, as opposed to a contractual agreement to pay for work, is in the sole control of the employee or union itself. This argument is not persuasive, for in the same breath the court acknowledged that unions control labor, though labor is not by its nature controlled by anyone other than the employee. More to the point, *Cordova* pointed out that the context and history of the

---

[262]254 U.S. 443 (1921).
[263]*Id.* at 469.
[264]29 U.S.C. §101 *et seq.* (1976).
[265]*Id.* §102 (1976).
[266]*United States v. Hutcheson*, 312 U.S. 219, 235–237 (1941).
[267]321 F. Supp. 600 (S.D.N.Y. 1970).

statute show that its sole purpose was the protection of labor unions against antitrust liability:

> "It is readily apparent that Congress, in enacting §6, was concerned with the right of labor and similar organizations to continue engaging in [collective bargaining] activities, including the right to strike, not with the right of employers to band together for joint action in fixing the wages to be paid by each employer."[268]

The court concluded that, since the labor exemption sought to preserve the right of labor to organize but not that of capital,[269] the exemption must be read in this one-sided way. The language chosen by Congress, though couched in broad conceptual terms, was simply designed to make the exemption emphatic; the subsequent *Deering* decision shows that the congressional concern was well founded.

The Nonstatutory Labor Law Exemption

Even if employee conduct is not governed by the Clayton Act's exemption, the policies of federal labor law may preclude a treble damage suit by the employee. The Clayton Act provision is only a limitation on the scope of the antitrust laws. The administrative scheme of comprehensive labor regulation created by NRLA[270] may require that the employee seek a remedy only under that law and not under antitrust law. The problem is not one of determining whether labor law has "occupied the field" so as to exclude or preempt the applicability of antitrust law. Rather, the policies of the labor and antitrust laws must be weighed one against the other in the particular situation to determine whether both can be harmoniously applied and, if not, to select the proper rule to use. Both statutory schemes are intended to be all encompassing, and the contest is between the general conduct restrictions of antitrust law and the general subject matter regulation of labor law.

The courts have recognized a narrow exemption from antitrust law in favor of the employer based on the adoption of employment practices pursuant to a collective bargaining agreement. Where the challenged practice affects only the parties to the agreement and is adopted pursuant to arms-length negotiation on a mandatory subject of collective bargaining, an employee is precluded by the collective bargaining policy of the NLRA from challenging the practice as violative of antitrust law.[271] In this narrow area, employer combinations in restraint of trade and other conduct otherwise in violation of the antitrust laws are immune from employee attack.

The nonstatutory labor exemption to antitrust liability does not

---

[268]*Id.* at 606. "As an outstanding pioneer and fighter in the ranks of labor, [Samuel Gompers] would probably turn in his grave if he were credited with urging an exemption that would permit employers jointly and unilaterally to reduce wages of their employees." *Id.*

[269]*Id.* at 607.

[270]29 U.S.C. §151 *et seq.* (1976).

[271]*Mackey v. National Football League,* 543 F.2d 606 (8th Cir. 1976).

apply where the practice adopted by the employer is not in fact a collectively bargained provision of a labor agreement[272] or a joint agreement to wage rates or employment conditions formulated by a multi-employer collective bargaining group in anticipation of a labor agreement.[273] Not every practice vitally affecting the terms and conditions of employment is a mandatory subject of bargaining; the requirements of the exemption will not be met, for instance, in refusal-to-hire cases.[274] The disputed provision must be the subject of serious, bona fide bargaining[275] and cannot result from uncontested employer power in bargaining.[276] The exemption does not extend to anticompetitive conduct directed against third parties by a group of employers, even if the union concurs.[277] The union, unlike the employer, is entitled to the benefit of the broader statutory exemption of labor activities that may effect a restraint of trade.[278]

The National Labor Relations Board (NLRB) does not have exclusive jurisdiction over questions of the scope of this labor exemption to the antitrust laws[279] because it does not have special competence with respect to the antitrust laws. Since the question is one of harmonizing federal statutes with one another, rather than conflicts between state regulations and federal labor law, the federal courts are the appropriate forum.[280]

Standing Requirements for Suits Under the Antitrust Laws

Whether suit may be brought by a private plaintiff for alleged violation of the antitrust laws is a two-part inquiry. The judicial gloss on the simple language of Section 4 of the Clayton Act[281] is often a substantial barrier to an employee antitrust suit. The requirements are (1) injury to the plaintiff's business or property, (2) within the scope of protection provided by the antitrust laws.[282]

The requirement of injury to the plaintiff's "business or property" is specifically mentioned in the statute and generally presents little difficulty to the employee because of settled case law. The second

---

[272]*Kapp v. National Football League*, 390 F. Supp. 73 (N.D. Cal. 1974), *aff'd*, 586 F.2d 644 (9th Cir. 1975).

[273]*Cordova v. Bache & Co.*, 321 F. Supp. 600 (S.D.N.Y. 1970).

[274]*Mackey v. National Football League*, 543 F.2d 606, 615 (8th Cir. 1976).

[275]*McCourt v. California Sports, Inc.*, 600 F.2d 1193 (6th Cir. 1979).

[276]*Mackey v. National Football League*, 543 F.2d 606, 615–616 (8th Cir. 1976).

[277]*Meat Cutters v. Jewel Tea Co.*, 381 U.S. 676 (1965).

[278]15 U.S.C. §17 (1982). See Leslie, *Principles of Labor Antitrust*, 66 VA. L. REV. 1183 (1980).

[279]*Robertson v. National Basketball Ass'n*, 389 F. Supp. 867, 876–878 (S.D.N.Y. 1975).

[280]*Id.*

[281]15 U.S.C. §15(a) (1982): "[A]ny person who shall be injured in his business or property by reason of anything forbidden in the antitrust laws" is permitted to sue for and recover treble damages.

[282]The Supreme Court has restricted standing under the antitrust laws for two fundamental reasons. First, the drastic treble damage remedy could operate to impose such severe liability that its use must be deemed appropriate to the remedial scheme. Second, the expense, delay, and uncertainty of proper allocation of damages in suits involving derivative injuries have been found to justify limitations on recovery of damages remote from the immediate impact of the violation.

requirement is a judicial tool to restrict the breadth of antitrust liability exposure which looks in part to the factual inquiry of proximate causation, as well as focusing on the legislative purposes underlying the antitrust laws, imposing a sort of "protected class" requirement. No general analytical test has been enunciated that is particularly helpful in determining whether there is antitrust standing. Although the courts of appeal employ descriptive "target area" or "direct injury" tests, these labels are of limited value in predicting the result in a given case.

Employment: A "Business or Property"

The Supreme Court has twice ignored the issue of whether an employment injury is an "injury to business or property" in deciding cases in favor of employee-plaintiffs.[283] In both cases employers combined to boycott or blacklist the employee's services. Lower courts have often relied in part on these *sub silentio* decisions in concluding that employment is a "business or property."[284]

In one of the earlier of the lower court cases, *Roseland v. Phister Manufacturing Co.*,[285] the court defined "business" in terms of employment:

> "It signifies ordinarily that which habitually busies, or engages, time, attention or labor as a principal serious concern or interest. In a somewhat more truly economic, legal and industrial sense, it includes that which occupies the time, attention, and labor of men for the purpose of livelihood or profit—persistent human efforts which have for their end pecuniary reward. It denotes 'the employment or occupation in which a person is engaged to procure a living.'"[286]

The *Roseland* court distinguished prior holdings that stockholders, creditors, officers, and directors of a corporation did not have standing to seek recovery for injury to the business of a corporation. It found that the plaintiff, though not a competitor of his employer,[287] was to be treated as having, in his position as a commission salesman, a "business" for purposes of the Clayton Act.[288]

Subsequent cases addressing the issue have been to the same effect. In *Baughman v. Cooper-Jarrett, Inc.*,[289] which involved a truck driver, the court observed that "the little man is as much entitled to

---

[283]*Anderson v. Shipowners*, 272 U.S. 359 (1926); *Radovich v. National Football League*, 352 U.S. 445, 453 (1957) ("Petitioner's claim need only * * * meet the requirement that petitioner has thereby suffered injury" (responding to "technical objections to the pleading")).

[284]E.g., *Nichols v. Spencer Int'l Press, Inc.*, 371 F.2d 332 (7th Cir. 1967), and *Cesnick v. Chrysler Corp.*, 490 F. Supp. 859 (M.D. Tenn. 1980).

[285]125 F.2d 417 (7th Cir. 1942).

[286]*Id.* at 419.

[287]The case does not make clear whether the plaintiff was an employee or independent contractor; it speaks of his employment under an exclusive sales contract. *Nichols v. Spencer Int'l Press, Inc.*, 371 F.2d 332, 334 (7th Cir. 1967), concluded that Roseland was "apparently" an independent contractor.

[288]There is no independent discussion in *Roseland* of whether the injury was within the scope of antitrust protection.

[289]391 F. Supp. 671 (W.D. Pa. 1975).

be protected from violation of the antitrust laws as is the large business entity."[290] *Nichols v. Spencer International Press, Inc.*[291] observed:

> "Work as the employee of another is not, indeed, an independent business enterprise, and an opportunity to perform such work may not be property in the ordinary sense, but the interest invaded by a wrongful act resulting in loss of employment is so closely akin to the interest invaded by impairment of one's business as to be indistinguishable in this context."[292]

Mackey v. National Football League[293] supplied the most compelling rationale for finding employment generally to be a business or property under the Clayton Act when it noted that labor is one of the commodities essential to the operation of the business.[294] Those who sell the commodity are "in business" to that extent and thus should not be treated differently from other commodity suppliers.[295]

Employment and employment opportunities have satisfied the business or property requirements in several contexts. Cases attacking covenants not to compete and other postemployment restraints;[296] cases of employer refusals to hire or blacklists;[297] and cases where the employee claimed to be injured by employer antitrust violations through loss of compensation or termination of employment[298] have all reached this conclusion. In one case, the employee had standing based on her status as a new entrant into the product market.[299]

---

[290]*Id.* at 677.

[291]371 F.2d 332 (7th Cir. 1967).

[292]*Id.* at 334. The context was an alleged agreement between employers not to hire former employees of their competitors until six months after termination of their employment. The Tenth Circuit held in *Reibert v. Atlantic Richfield Co.*, 471 F.2d 727, 730 (10th Cir. 1973), that "to satisfy the business or property prerequisite, [plaintiff] must demonstrate that his job is a commercial venture or enterprise." In light of the burgeoning professional athlete antitrust litigation, and the cases cited and distinguished in *Reibert* itself, it appears the court combined the business or property requirement and the scope of antitrust protection requirement. See *Cesnick v. Chrysler Corp.*, 490 F. Supp. 859, 864 (M.D. Tenn. 1980) (implication that discharged managerial employees were injured in business or property is "inescapable").

[293]543 F.2d 606 (8th Cir. 1976).

[294]*Id.* at 617–619.

[295]The labor antitrust exemption to the Clayton Act was adopted to prevent the antitrust laws from treating labor as a commodity when the employer complained of employee combinations; to hold that labor is not a commodity for purposes of antitrust law when the employee complains of employer combinations would be anomalous. Once it is accepted that the labor exemption is not for the employer's benefit, reason dictates that the employee have a remedy under the antitrust laws against employer restraints on the market for employee services.

[296]*Bowen v. Wohl Shoe Co.*, 389 F. Supp. 572, 578–579 (S.D. Tex. 1975). See *Newburger, Loeb & Co. v. Gross*, 563 F.2d 1057, 1082 (2d Cir. 1977).

[297]*Quinonez v. NASD*, 540 F.2d 824, 829–830 (5th Cir. 1976); *Nichols v. Spencer Int'l Press, Inc.*, 371 F.2d 332, 334–335 (7th Cir. 1967); *Mackey v. National Football League*, 543 F.2d 606, 617–618 (8th Cir. 1976); *Baughmann v. Cooper-Jarrett, Inc.*, 391 F. Supp. 671, 677 (W.D. Pa. 1975); *Freeman v. Eastman-Whipstock, Inc.*, 390 F. Supp. 685, 688 (S.D. Tex. 1975); *Cesnick v. Chrysler Corp.*, 490 F. Supp. 859, 864 (M.D. Tenn. 1980). See also *Cheek v. Prudential Ins. Co.*, 192 S.W. 387 (Mo. 1917) (no-switching agreement violated antitrust laws or public policy).

[298]*Roseland v. Phister Mfg. Co.*, 125 F.2d 417, 419 (7th Cir. 1942); *Dailey v. Quality School Plan, Inc.*, 380 F.2d 484, 487 (5th Cir. 1967); *McNulty v. Borden, Inc.*, 474 F. Supp. 1111, 1116–1117 (E.D. Pa. 1979). See *Mans v. Sunray DX Oil Co.*, 352 F. Supp. 1095, 1099 (N.D. Okla. 1971) (assuming plaintiff's employment was property right).

[299]*Bowen v. Wohl Shoe Co.*, 389 F. Supp. 572 (S.D. Tex. 1975).

The Antitrust Injury Requirement

The employee antitrust cases disclose no consensus rule for determining whether the plaintiff has suffered a direct antitrust injury conferring standing. This is largely because the meaning of the test itself is disputed:

> "[S]ome courts * * * require that the plaintiff be a person against whom the conduct is directed. [Citation omitted.] This requirement is sometimes said to mean that the plaintiff's injury must be 'directly,' rather than 'remotely,' caused by the violation of which plaintiff complaints [citation omitted]. Other courts have adopted the somewhat different rule that a private party has standing when he is 'within the sector of the economy in which the violation threatens a breakdown' and is injured by the violation [citation omitted]. This requirement is sometimes described as meaning that the plaintiff must be within the 'target area' at which the illegal practices are directed."[300]

The antitrust injury standard, as the foregoing passage indicates, represents different concerns to different courts: specific intent to injure, or proximate cause, or statutory policy could be seen as the focus of the requirement.

Two recent Supreme Court decisions better demonstrate the meaning of "antitrust injury." In *Blue Cross v. McCready*,[301] an insured consumer alleged that she had had to pay personally for psychological services directly because a combination or conspiracy orchestrated by psychiatrists caused insurance coverage to be limited to mental health services provided by medical doctors. The Court held that because the consumer's having to pay for uninsured services was a direct result of the conspiracy in a factual sense and harmed her interests as a consumer, which were protected by the antitrust laws, it was an antitrust injury. In *Associated General Contractors v. California State Council of Carpenters*,[302] the union alleged that contractors in California, acting in concert, had manipulated their corporate structures and subcontracting practices to injure the union by weakening the business position of unionized contractors. The Court held that because the immediate victims of the alleged anticompetitive conduct were the unionized contractors and not the union, there was no antitrust injury. The "ripple effect" upon the union, although intended, was not a direct factual consequence of the alleged anticompetitive conduct, nor was it a necessary product of the anticompetitive aspect of the alleged conspiracy. These cases teach that an "antitrust injury," in today's legal climate, must be an economic loss imposed at the level in the distributive chain where the restraint has a direct, uninterrupted impact, and that it must result from the anticompetitive nature of the restraint.

---

[300]*Wilson v. Ringsby Truck Lines*, 320 F. Supp. 699, 701 (D. Colo. 1970).
[301]457 U.S. 465 (1982).
[302]459 U.S. 519 (1983).

Employment Market Restraints

A conspiracy to restrain trade may exist where two or more employers agree that a particular employee will not be hired or retained. The conspiracy may consist of open, well-developed controls on the hiring and retention of employees, as in the professional sports cases.[303] It may be a tacit "no-switching" arrangement between competitors intended to prevent unfair "raiding," or a secret pact to hold the line on pay increases. The conspiracy may be a covenant not to compete between employer and employee. It may also be a malicious blacklist.[304] For purposes of antitrust law, the surrounding circumstances are secondary to the economic consequences of the restraint; they are significant only to the extent they help demonstrate that, in the final analysis, the restraint of the market for employee services does or does not unreasonably restrain trade.

Standing Issues

In *Cesnick v. Chrysler Corp.*,[305] the employer sold a division to another company and, in order to encourage the employees to work for the acquiring business, agreed not to continue the employment of division personnel. Relying on the result in *Anderson v. Shipowners*[306] and the professional athlete cases, the court found the employees' jobs to be within the zone of protected antitrust interests. In *Quinonez v. NASD*[307] the employee alleged that the employers who had refused to hire him had combined to boycott him. He was held to have standing if he could show his intention and preparedness to work in the industry.

In re *Industrial Gas Antitrust Litigation*[308] held that the blacklisted employee lacked standing because he was boycotted in furtherance of an independent antitrust conspiracy directed at the employer's product market. On the same facts, the court in *Ostrofe v. H.S. Crocker Co.*[309] held that the employee had standing to sue for damages resulting from both antitrust conspiracies. *Industrial Gas* and *Ostrofe* are directed primarily toward the actionability of retaliatory discharge for refusal to participate in antitrust violations under Section 4 of the Clayton Act, and the *Industrial Gas* case does not discuss blacklisting at length. The court apparently concluded that the case differed from the other blacklist cases in that the em-

---

[303]The professional sports cases are collected in Annot., 18 A.L.R. FED. 489 (1974).
[304]See discussion of blacklisting *infra* pp. 246–247.
[305]490 F. Supp. 859 (M.D. Tenn. 1980). Accord: *Nichols v. Spencer Int'l Press, Inc.*, 371 F.2d 332, 335–336 (7th Cir. 1967) (no-switching agreement would affect both employee services market and product market), and, *Union Circulation Co. v. FTC*, 241 F.2d 652, 658 (2d Cir. 1957) (no-switching agreement may also inhibit new market entrants).
[306]272 U.S. 359 (1926).
[307]540 F.2d 824, 830 (5th Cir. 1976). Accord: *Freeman v. Eastman-Whipstock, Inc.*, 390 F. Supp. 685, 689–690 (S.D. Tex. 1975).
[308]681 F.2d 514 (7th Cir. 1982).
[309]670 F.2d 1378 (9th Cir. 1982).

ployee alleged that the ultimate employer motive behind the blacklist was to restrain trade in the product market. The court's assertion that the injury to the employee by reason of his blacklisting in the employment market (considered apart from any claim based on the impact of the conspiracy on the product market) "did not result from lack of competition in the labor market" appears to be mistaken, since a blacklist is by definition an agreement between employers not to compete for the employee's services.[310]

Necessity of a Conspiracy

An action under Section 1 of the Sherman Act requires an agreement, combination, or conspiracy; unilateral action to restrain trade does not violate the prohibition.[311] In *Thomsen v. Western Electric Co.*,[312] an employee who was unable to transfer between separate, but commonly managed, entities in the Bell System claimed that the system's no-switching rule violated the Sherman Act. Because the court found the rule to be a matter of internal management, it held that no conspiracy was present. Similarly, allegations of conspiracy between the employer and the committee administering its profit-sharing plan were found insufficient in *Graham v. Hodgins, Thompson, Ball & Associates, Inc.*[313] However, in *Bowen v. Wohl Shoe Co.*,[314] the conspiracy element was satisfied by the employer's attempt to enforce its own policy; the unwilling employee was the second party necessary to make the restraint actionable.

Proof of a conspiracy is necessarily circumstantial, but the two reported cases involving terminated employees who alleged blacklisting differ on the necessary amount of evidence. In *Daley v. St. Agnes Hospital*,[315] the court held that evidence of a single bad reference which prevented an individual's hiring was insufficient to prove a blacklist conspiracy; while in *Baughman v. Cooper-Jarrett, Inc.*,[316] evidence that the former employer had prevailed on two other

---

[310]*In re Industrial Gas Antitrust Litigation*, 681 F.2d 514, 517 (7th Cir. 1982). The court cited no authority for the distinction it made. It offered no explanation for relying on the employer's motive for blacklisting in holding that the employee suffered no antitrust injury from being excluded from the employment market. *Callahan v. Scott Paper Co.*, 541 F. Supp. 550, 561 (E.D. Pa. 1982), which agreed with *Industrial Gas* on the retaliatory discharge issue, distinguished *Ostrofe v. H.S. Crocker Co.*, 670 F.2d 1378 (9th Cir. 1982), because in *Callahan* the defendant "did not participate in any unlawful group boycott to prevent plaintiff from being employed in the paper products industry." Now that *Associated General Contractors v. California State Council of Carpenters*, 459 U.S. 519 (1983), has held that the immediate primary victim of an antitrust violation had standing, rather than the intended but remote ultimate victim, the reliance on the ultimate motive in *Industrial Gas* appears to be misplaced.

[311]*Freeman v. Eastman-Whipstock, Inc.*, 390 F. Supp. 685 (S.D. Tex. 1975) (independent decisions by two employers precluded finding of a blacklist conspiracy). For a discussion of the intracorporate conspiracy issue, see Areeda, *Intraenterprise Conspiracy in Decline*, 97 HARV. L. REV. 451 (1983). Not all antitrust violations require proof of a conspiracy; monopolization violations, under Section 2 of the Sherman Act, may be entirely unilateral.

[312]680 F.2d 1263 (9th Cir. 1982). See *Taketa v. Wisconsin Tel. Co.*, 394 F. Supp. 862 (E.D. Wis. 1975).

[313]319 F. Supp. 1335 (N.D. Okla. 1970).

[314]389 F. Supp. 572 (S.D. Tex. 1975).

[315]490 F. Supp. 1309 (E.D. Pa. 1980).

[316]391 F. Supp. 671 (W.D. Pa. 1975), *aff'd in part, rev'd in part*, 530 F.2d 529 (3d Cir. 1976).

employers not to hire the discharged employee was enough to prove a conspiracy.

Concerted Employer Restraints

Several cases deal with the issue of whether agreements between employers concerning employees may be actionable under Section 1 of the Sherman Act. In *Cesnick v. Chrysler Corp.*,[317] the employee lost his job when he refused to join the buyer of the corporate division he worked for. The discharge was a consequence of an agreement by the employer not to retain any of the division's managerial staff; and the court held that since the agreement was necessary to the sale of the division's good will, the restraint did not violate antitrust laws. In *Newburger, Loeb & Co. v. Gross*,[318] the court specifically determined that post employment restraints on employee job choice were to be analyzed under the Rule of Reason if they served a legitimate purpose. The protection of customer relations was held to be such a purpose, and the restraint accordingly was permissible.

In *Nichols v. Spencer International Press, Inc.*,[319] it was held that no-switching agreements between employers might be Sherman Act violations, but the court implied that the determining factor in evaluating such agreements was the impact of the restraint on the market for the employer's products. More recent cases, however, suggest that the Rule of Reason analysis must focus on the impact of the restraint on the employment market, since employees do not have standing to sue for anticompetitive behavior in the product market of which they are incidental victims.[320] Even so, the impact of the restraint on the product market may be relevant to show the history of and reason for the no-switching rule.

Cordova v. Bache & Co.[321] held that an agreement between securities dealers in the New York City area to limit employee commissions would be a *per se* price-fixing violation. In *Drayer v. Krasner*,[322] the court upheld a standard form of employment contract providing that disputes arising out of termination of employment would be arbitrated. The agreement was required by the rules of the New York Stock Exchange, and for that reason was alleged to be the product of an employer conspiracy. After determining that the Rule of Reason applied, the court upheld the arbitration provision because it was protected by regulatory provisions of the securities laws. *Kinzler v.*

---

[317] 490 F. Supp. 859 (M.D. Tenn. 1980).

[318] 563 F.2d 1057, 1081–1083 (2d Cir. 1977). Accord: *Smith v. Pro Football, Inc.*, 593 F.2d 1173 (D.C. Cir. 1978); *Quinonez v. NASD*, 540 F.2d 824 (5th Cir. 1976); *Kinzler v. NYSE*, 62 F.R.D. 196 (S.D.N.Y. 1974); *Kapp v. National Football League*, 390 F. Supp. 73 (N.D. Cal. 1974).

[319] 371 F.2d 332 (7th Cir. 1967); *Phillips v. Vandygriff*, 711 F.2d 1217 (5th Cir. 1983).

[320] *Reibert v. Atlantic-Richfield Co.*, 471 F.2d 727 (10th Cir. 1973). See *Mans v. Sunray DX Oil Co.*, 352 F. Supp. 1095 (N.D. Okla. 1971). Contra: *Wilson v. Ringsby Truck Lines*, 320 F. Supp. 699 (D. Colo. 1970).

[321] 321 F. Supp. 600 (S.D.N.Y. 1970).

[322] 572 F.2d 348 (2d Cir. 1978).

New York Stock Exchange[323] found that an emergency Stock Exchange order prohibiting the hiring of any employees of a failing brokerage house was open to challenge under the Rule of Reason. But in *NAACP v. New York City Clearing House Association*,[324] where employers allegedly combined to refuse to accept business from the city unless it withdrew an affirmative action requirement, employees were denied standing to attack the alleged conspiracy. *NAACP*, unlike the other cases, involved concerted employer resistance to government attempts to impose uniform conditions of employment, rather than agreements among employers to impose particular conditions.

Single Employer Violations

In *Bazal v. Beleford Trucking Co.*,[325] an employee was hired under a three-contract plan requiring him first to rent a truck, then to agree to drive exclusively for the employer, and finally to promise to furnish services on a 30-day renewable basis. He claimed that this plan was unlawful because it tied employment to rental of the truck. The court found that a contract of employment was analogous to recognized tying arrangements such as franchises, credit agreements, membership rights, and management service contracts. Since the employee had alleged the remaining elements of the offense—market power in the tying market and substantial business in the market for the tied product—the court held that the arrangement could be an unlawful tie.[326]

When a person accepts employment status, he takes on a common law duty of loyalty to the employer, which includes an implied covenant not to compete during the term of the employment. In *Farnell v. Albuquerque Publishing Co.*,[327] the court upheld the employer's right to terminate an employee for his insubordinate refusal to stop competing. In *Bowen v. Wohl Shoe Co.*,[328] on the other hand, the court upheld an employee's complaint alleging that her discharge for operating a specialty retail outlet 60 miles away from the employer's store violated the antitrust laws. The court found that depriving her of her salary, which subsidized the start-up of her store, could be a violation if it had a sufficient impact on competition in the market where the employee's store was located.

---

[323]62 F.R.D. 196 (S.D.N.Y. 1974).

[324]431 F.2d 405 (S.D.N.Y. 1977).

[325]442 F. Supp. 1089 (S.D. Fla. 1977).

[326]Statutes in a number of states prohibit employers from compelling employees to purchase from them or at designated stores: ARIZ. REV. STAT. ANN. §23–203 (1983); ARK. STAT. ANN. §81–307 (1976) (sales to employees at excessive prices); CONN. GEN. STAT. ANN. §31–48 (West 1972) (no overcharging of employees at company store); FLA. STAT. ANN. §448.03 (West 1981); ILL. REV. STAT. ch. 121-1/2 §205 (1981) (sales to employees out of ordinary line of business prohibited); IND. CODE ANN. §22–2–4–3 (West 1981) (sales to employees at high prices); NEV. REV. STAT. §613.140 (1980); N.M. STAT. ANN. §30–13–5 (1978); OHIO REV. CODE ANN. §4113.18 (Baldwin 1983); TENN. CODE ANN. §50–2–106 (1983); UTAH CONST. art. XVI, §3 (1971) (direction to legislature); W. VA. CODE §21–5–5 (1981).

[327]589 F.2d 497 (10th Cir. 1978).

[328]389 F. Supp. 572 (S.D. Tex. 1975).

Retaliatory Discharge

Is the retaliatory discharge of an employee who refuses to participate in an antitrust conspiracy a new per se violation of the antitrust laws? While case law in several jurisdictions recognizes such a discharge as giving rise to a common law cause of action,[329] an action under the antitrust laws would raise the stakes in such cases, permitting recovery of treble damages plus attorney's fees. The issue narrows to whether the plaintiff has suffered an antitrust injury.

Ostrofe v. H.S. Crocker Co.[330] illustrates the problem even though the case was vacated and remanded back to the Ninth Circuit for reconsideration. In *Ostrofe*, a sales manager was allegedly coerced to rig bids, fix prices, and allocate markets. For refusing to stop interfering with the scheme, he was threatened with reduced compensation, discharge, and blacklisting; and he resigned in the face of these threats. The manager claimed his resignation was a constructive discharge attributable to the underlying antitrust conspiracy. The conduct he refused to join was in fact an antitrust violation, he argued, and he was in effect discharged because of that refusal. Unlike a common law retaliatory discharge action, in which the discharge itself is actionable as a tort or breach of contract, under the Sherman Act the discharge would be seen as an injury flowing from the underlying antitrust conspiracy or violation. In a common law action, the discharge is the wrongful act; in a Sherman Act claim, the antitrust conspiracy is the wrongful act. Thus, the critical issue is whether an employee has antitrust standing, that is, whether discharge from employment in furtherance of an antitrust conspiracy is an injury "by reason of" the antitrust violation. The court of appeals in *Ostrofe* held that the discharge in question was.

Ostrofe relied in part on the enforcement benefits of the employee suit, noting that lack of employee cooperation could defeat the scheme's success before any harm resulted.[331] The court reasoned that the discharge was a unilateral act in furtherance of a conspiracy, which was actionable in other contexts,[332] and that the factual connection between the employee's injury and the violation was a close one.[333] Recognizing retaliatory discharge as a new basis for standing, the court found that the antitrust laws, by imposing criminal sanctions, showed a sufficient concern for individual conduct to justify redress for employees who obeyed the command of the federal criminal law.[334]

---

[329]*Tameny v. Atlantic Richfield Co.*, 27 Cal.3d 167, 610 P.2d 1330, 164 Cal. Rptr. 839 (1980); *Perry v. Hartz Mountain Co.*, 537 F. Supp. 1387 (S.D. Ind. 1982); *Shaw v. Russell Trucking Line*, 542 F. Supp. 776 (W.D. Pa. 1982); *McNulty v. Borden, Inc.*, 474 F. Supp. 1111 (E.D. Pa. 1979). See *Parnar v. Americana Hotels, Inc.*, 65 Hawaii 370, 652 P.2d 625 (1982). Contra: *Callahan v. Scott Paper Co.*, 541 F. Supp. 550 (E.D. Pa. 1982).

[330]670 F.2d 1378 (9th Cir. 1982), *vacated*, 460 U.S. 1007 (1983).

[331]670 F.2d at 1384. Accord: *Shaw v. Russell Trucking Line*, 542 F. Supp. 776 (W.D. Pa. 1982); *McNulty v. Borden, Inc.*, 474 F. Supp. 1111 (E.D. Pa. 1979), *modified*, 542 (F. Supp. 655, 661 (E.D. Pa. 1982).

[332]*Id.* at 1382.

[333]*Id.* at 1385.

[334]*Id.* at 1387–1388.

The decision was criticized in a strong dissent;[335] and it has since been rejected in a number of cases, most prominently in *In re Industrial Gas Antitrust Litigation*:[336]

> "We disagree with the majority analysis in [Ostrofe] for several reasons. First, we read *Brunswick [Corp. v. Pueblo Bowl-O-Mat*, 429 U.S. 477 (1977)] to hold that §4 [of the Clayton Act] protects only those persons injured as consumers or competitors in a defined market or a discrete area of the economy. Second, * * * we are convinced that in fashioning the antitrust laws, Congress was concerned with competition, not employee coercion or discharge.
> * * *

> "An appropriate balance is achieved by granting standing to those who, as consumers or competitors, suffer immediate injuries with respect to their business and property, while excluding persons whose injuries were more indirectly caused by the antitrust conduct. * * * Since [the plaintiff] is neither a consumer nor a competitor of Chemetron, his injury was indirectly caused by defendants' alleged price-fixing conspiracy and he does not have antitrust standing."[337]

Although the Supreme Court, in the light of its decision in *Associated General Contractors v. California State Council of Carpenters*,[338] vacated and remanded *Ostrofe*[339] for reconsideration by the court of appeals, and the Ninth Circuit has stated it is reconsidering the matter,[340] its implications for antitrust litigation are considerable. In the usual antitrust case, discovery of the violation is difficult and proof of a conspiracy is necessarily circumstantial.[341] If an employee fired for refusing to go along with the violation could bring a treble damage action, there necessarily would be a willing, firsthand witness to the unlawful conduct, and perhaps even to the conspiratorial meetings. The employee-plaintiff likely would bring suit over the discharge before competitors and the government filed actions, and proof of the violation would be a necessary element of his case. Not only would a verdict for the employee produce treble damages; it also would serve as a determination that the employer had violated the antitrust laws. That finding would be available to competitors and consumers bringing multimillion dollar class actions. The employee's antitrust case would become a high-stakes battle, perhaps involving stronger evidence than is usually available and a jury sympathetic to the terminated employee. While some of these risks for the employer are present in the common law cases, proof of an actual

---

[335]*Id.* at 1389.
[336]681 F.2d 514 (7th Cir. 1982). Accord: *Callahan v. Scott Paper Co.*, 541 F. Supp. 550 (E.D. Pa. 1982); *Broyer v. B.F. Goodrich*, 415 F. Supp. 193 (E.D. Pa. 1976); *McNulty v. Borden, Inc.*, 542 F. Supp. 655, 661 (E.D. Pa. 1982); *Perry v. Hartz Mountain Co.*, 537 F. Supp. 1387 (S.D. Ind. 1982).
[337]681 F.2d at 519, 520.
[338]See *supra* note 302 and accompanying text.
[339]460 U.S. 1007 (1983).
[340]*Chelson v. Oregonian Publishing Co.*, 715 F.2d 1368, 1371 n.2 (9th Cir. 1983).
[341]*Poller v. Columbia Broadcasting Sys.* 368 U.S. 464, 470–473 (1962).

violation may not be a necessary element;[342] and, if so, collateral estoppel would not apply.

Actions Based on Nonemployment Antitrust Violations

Employees can be adversely affected by antitrust violations of all kinds. When competition declines, there may be fewer jobs or less intense competition for talented employees as a result. By the same token, the inefficiencies resulting from antitrust violations may protect the jobs of people whose functions or performance do not contribute to economic efficiency. The fate of the employee is ultimately tied to the quality of the employer's management and to the employer's survival and fitness in the marketplace. Measuring the increment of benefit or injury to each employee that results from an antitrust violation is inherently speculative. Thus, in addition to the concerns raised in the discussion on retaliatory discharge, there are practical reasons for the general rule that an employee cannot sue for injury to his job caused by antitrust violations by, or affecting, the employer, apart from those in the employment market.[343]

There is a well-recognized exception, however, for employees on commission, or whose stake in some special phase of the employer's business is sufficiently outside the employment context to justify viewing the employee as an independent economic entity. Actions of this kind have been allowed to challenge mergers,[344] for relief from the impact of price-fixing and division of markets,[345] and for loss due to discriminatory pricing.[346]

State Statutory Remedies Relating to References

Chapter 8 discusses remedies based on state and federal statutes that provide protection against retaliatory discharge or set forth employee rights that could be the basis for retaliatory discharge actions. There are also statutes in a number of jurisdictions that provide postdischarge protection beyond the usual provisions for collection of unpaid wages and unemployment compensation.

---

[342]See, e.g., the Maine Whistleblowers' Protection Act, ME. REV. STAT. ANN. tit. 26, §832 (Supp. 1983).

[343]*Reibert v. Atlantic-Richfield Co.*, 471 F.2d 727 (10th Cir. 1973); *Mans v. Sunray DX Oil Co.*, 352 F. Supp. 1095 (N.D. Okla. 1971). Contra: *Wilson v. Ringsby Truck Lines*, 320 F. Supp. 699 (D. Colo. 1970). Employees also lack standing to sue for violations committed by third parties against the employer. *Curtis v. Campbell-Taggart, Inc.*, 687 F.2d 336 (10th Cir. 1982).

[344]*Dailey v. Quality School Plan, Inc.*, 380 F.2d 484 (5th Cir. 1967).

[345]*Roseland v. Phister Mfg. Co.*, 125 F.2d 417 (7th Cir. 1942).

[346]*Broyer v. B.F. Goodrich*, 415 F. Supp. 193 (E.D. Pa. 1976).

Blacklisting

A majority of the states have statutes prohibiting blacklisting,[347] which may otherwise be actionable in tort for interference with prospective economic advantage[348] or defamation,[349] or by an antitrust suit.[350] Blacklisting was originally associated with employer opposition to labor unions, and was a means of preventing possible union adherents from getting into the work place. Blacklisting to encourage or discourage union membership is a violation of the NLRA.[351] As a result, claims for blacklisting because of union membership or non-membership are within the exclusive jurisdiction of the NLRB and may not be brought in court,[352] unless the blacklist comes within the statutory "right to work" exception[353] permitting the states to restrict or prohibit agreements between unions and employers requiring union membership.[354]

During the 1950s, blacklisting took on a new meaning. It came to refer to

> "the practice prevalent in the entertainment industry of listing those entertainers who were accused of being Communists, or of having communist affiliations. Such listing invariably resulted in the cancellation of the engagements of one so listed and rendered him unemployable."[355]

In *Goins v. Sargent*,[356] the employer's threat to cease doing business with another employer if he hired the plaintiff was held to give rise to a statutory blacklisting action. *Andrews v. Stearns-Roger, Inc.*,[357]

---

[347]ALA. CODE §13A–11–123 (1975); ARIZ. CONST. art. 18, §9, ARIZ. REV. STAT. ANN. §23–1361 (1983); ARK. STAT. ANN. §81–211 (1976); CAL. LAB. CODE §§1050, 1051 (West 1971) (by misrepresentation); COLO. REV. STAT. §8–2–111 (1973); CONN. GEN. STAT. ANN. §31–51 (West 1972); FLA. STAT. ANN. §351.20 (West 1968) (railroads only); IND. CODE. ANN. §§22–2–5–3, 22–5–3–1 (West 1981); IOWA CODE ANN. §730.2 (West 1979); KANS. STAT. ANN. §44–117 (1981); LA. REV. STAT. ANN. §23:963 (West 1964) (no blacklist for failure to buy at designated store); ME. REV. STAT. ANN. tit. 17, §401 (1983); MINN. STAT. ANN. §§179.12(6), 179.60 (West 1966); MISS. CODE ANN. §77–9–725 (1972) (railroad and telephone companies' union membership); MONT. CODE ANN. §§39–2–802, 39–2–803 (1981); NEV. REV. STAT. §613.200, 613.210 (1981); N.M. STAT. ANN. §30–13–3 (1978); N.Y. LAB. LAWS §704.9 (Consol. 1983); N.C. GEN. STAT. §14–355 (1981); N.D. CONST. art. XII, §§17, 19; OHIO REV. CODE ANN. §1331.02 (Page 1979); OKLA. STAT. ANN. tit. 40, §172 (West 1954); ORE. REV. STAT. §659.230 (1981); R.I. GEN. LAWS §28–7–13(9) (1979); TENN. CODE ANN. §50–1–202 (1983) (union membership); TEX. REV. CIV. STAT. ANN. art. 5196(1) (Vernon 1971); UTAH CONST. art. XII, §19, art. XVI §4, UTAH CODE ANN. §§34–24–1, 34–24–2 (1971); VA. CODE §40.1–27 (1981); WASH. REV. CODE ANN. §49.44.010 (1962); WIS. STAT. §134.02 (1981).

[348]*Pino v. Protection Maritime Ins. Co.*, 454 F. Supp. 210 (D. Mass. 1978), aff'd, 599 F.2d 10 (1st Cir. 1979).

[349]*Faulk v. Aware, Inc.*, 19 A.D.2d 464, 244 N.Y.S.2d 259 (1963), aff'd, 14 N.Y.2d 899, 200 N.E.2d 778, 252 N.Y.S.2d 95 (1964).

[350]*Baughmann v. Cooper-Jarrett, Inc.*, 391 F. Supp. 671 (W.D. Pa. 1975), aff'd in part, rev'd in part, 530 F.2d 529 (3d Cir. 1976).

[351]29 U.S.C. §158(a)(3) (1976). See *Phelps Dodge Corp. v. NLRB*, 313 U.S. 177 (1941) (refusal to hire because of union membership).

[352]See discussion of preemption in Chapter 5.

[353]29 U.S.C. §164(b) (1976). See *Retail Clerks v. Schermerhorn*, 375 U.S. 96 (1963).

[354]In *Elsis v. Evans*, 185 Cal. App.2d 610, 8 Cal. Rptr. 565 (1960), the court held a claim for blacklisting of union members to be preempted. But in *Moore v. Plumbers Local 10*, 211 Va. 520, 179 S.E.2d 15 (1971), the court found the right-to-work exception applicable to an oral agreement between employer and union not to employ a nonunion member.

[355]*Faulk v. Aware, Inc.*, 19 A.D.2d 464, 244 N.Y.S.2d 259 (1963).

[356]196 N.C. 478, 146 S.E. 131 (1929).

[357]93 N.M. 527, 602 P.2d 624 (1979).

held that a request to other employers not to hire a former employee constituted blacklisting; and *Smithers v. Metro-Goldwyn-Mayer Studios, Inc.*[358] held that a threat by an employer to blacklist an employee if he did not make contractual concessions was a violation of the implied duty of good faith and fair dealing.

Although blacklisting is a rare phenomenon, the employer has reason for concern lest it be held to have blacklisted simply by giving an unfavorable reference. To alleviate this concern, the statutes generally provide that the employer may give a truthful response to reference requests without liability. While the gist of the action is affirmative efforts or threats by the former employer to prevent reemployment of the employee, doubtless false and defamatory statements could as easily serve the same purpose and could lead to liability for blacklisting in a proper case.

Service Letter Statutes

A discharged employee may be hurt in his search for new employment by the employer's refusal to respond in any way to reference requests by prospective employers. At common law, there is no duty to state, one way or the other, whether or when the employee was employed, what his position and pay were, and what the circumstances of his departure were. Such confirmation may be vital to the tendering of a job offer; but in this respect the employee is at the mercy of the former employer, who may fear liability for speaking freely, or simply prefer not to be bothered responding to reference requests.

In the early part of this century a practice existed in certain industries and regions whereby an employer would customarily issue a "service letter" to the employee upon termination.[359] Typically, the letter would state the dates of employment, pay, positions held, and reason for termination. Without such a letter, employment in certain industries was difficult to obtain.

Because of abuses of this practice resulting from unfriendly termination, legislatures in a number of states adopted "service letter" statutes that required employers to provide such a letter to a terminated employee on request.[360] These statutes have remained on the books for many years; Maine recently adopted a new statute on this model.[361] Attacks on the validity of service letter statutes have

---

[358]139 Cal. App.3d 643, 189 Cal. Rptr. 20 (1983).
[359]*Cheek v. Prudential Ins. Co.*, 259 U.S. 530 (1922); *Cleveland, Cincinnati, Chicago & St. Louis Ry. v. Jenkins*, 174 Ill. 398, 51 N.E. 811 (1898).
[360]CAL. LAB. CODE §1055 (West 1971) (public utility); IND. CODE ANN. §22–6–3–1 (West 1981); MO. ANN. STAT. §290.140 (Vernon 1965 & Supp. 1984); MONT. CODE ANN. §39–2–801 (1981); NEB. REV. STAT. §§48–209, 48–210, 48–211 (1981); NEV. REV. STAT. §613.240 (4) (1981); OKLA. STAT. ANN. tit. 40, §171 (West 1954) (public service corporations only); TEX. REV. CIV. STAT. ANN. art. 5196 (Vernon 1970). The Texas statute was held to violate that state's constitution in *St. Louis Southwestern Ry. v. Griffin*, 106 Tex. 477, 171 S.W. 703 (1914).
[361]ME. REV. STAT. ANN. tit. 26, §630 (Supp. 1983).

been largely unavailing.[362] Almost all of the litigation has been in Missouri.

Service letter statutes are not preempted by the NLRA.[363] If an employee demands a letter, the employer must provide a full statement on each of the matters set out in the statute[364] and is liable for damages if a false statement of the reason for discharge is given.[365] The service letter need not be exhaustive,[366] but a statement that the discharge was for "unsatisfactory work" is too general a statement of the reason for discharge.[367] A false statement of the reason for termination is not excused by an honest belief in its truthfulness.[368] To make out a claim for compensatory damages, the employee must show that he demanded a letter, that a letter satisfying the statute was not forthcoming, and that the absence or inadequacy of the service letter hindered his ability to obtain a specific position that was open.[369]

---

[362]*Cheek v. Prudential Life Ins. Co.*, 259 U.S. 530 (1922) (Missouri statute upheld); *Chicago, Rock Island, & Pac. R.R. v. Perry*, 259 U.S. 548 (1922) (Oklahoma statute upheld); *Rimmer v. Colt Indus. Operating Corp.*, 656 F.2d 323 (8th Cir. 1981) (Missouri statute upheld against void for vagueness attack). But see *Atchison Topeka & Santa Fe R.R. v. Brown*, 80 Kan. 312, 102 P. 459 (1909) (statute violated state freedom of speech provision), and *Wallace v. Georgia, Carolina & N. Ry.*, 94 Ga. 732, 22 S.E. 579 (1894) (state constitution violated by statute). See Annot., 24 A.L.R.4th 1115 (1983).

[363]*Collins v. Industrial Bearing Trans. Co.*, 575 S.W.2d 875 (Mo. App. 1978).

[364]*Labrier v. Anheuser Food, Inc.*, 621 S.W.2d 51 (Mo. 1981).

[365]*Rotermund v. Basic Materials Co.*, 558 S.W.2d 688 (Mo. App. 1977); *Comby v. Farmland Indus., Inc.*, 524 S.W.2d 132 (Mo. App. 1975); *Roberts v. Emerson Elec. Mfg. Co.*, 338 S.W.2d 62 (Mo. 1962); *Burens v. Wolfe Wear-U-Well Corp.*, 236 Mo. App. 892, 158 S.W.2d 175 (1942).

[366]See *Newton v. State Farm Mut. Auto Ins. Co.*, 700 F.2d 419 (8th Cir. 1983).

[367]*Stark v. American Bakeries Co.*, 647 S.W.2d 119 (Mo. 1983).

[368]*Newman v. Greater Kansas City Baptist & Community Hosp. Ass'n*, 604 S.W.2d 619 (Mo. App. 1980).

[369]*Herberholt v. dePaul Community Health Center*, 625 S.W.2d 617 (Mo. 1981), *appeal following remand*, 648 S.W.2d 160 (Mo. App. 1983).

8

Retaliatory Discharge and Public Policy

A newly developed rule of law is that an employee may not be discharged from employment for acting in furtherance of public policy or refusing to violate public policy. Discharge in violation of this rule gives rise to a civil action for compensatory and punitive damages.

Development of Retaliatory Discharge Action

Historical Development

The new cause of action, variously called "wrongful discharge," "abusive discharge," "retaliatory discharge," or "discharge in derogation of public policy," was first recognized in *Petermann v. Teamsters*,[1] a 1959 appellate court decision in California. The Teamsters Union, which at the time was being vigorously investigated for labor racketeering, employed an individual on an at-will basis. He was

---

[1]174 Cal. App.2d 184, 344 P.2d 25 (1959). Public policy was defined as "that principle of law which holds that no citizen can lawfully do that which has a tendency to be injurious to the public or against the public good * * *. [It consists of] the principles under which freedom of contract or private dealing is restricted by law for the good of the community. * * *[W]hatever contravenes good morals or any established interests of society is against public policy." *Id.* at 188, 344 P.2d at 27.

The *Petermann* decision was presaged by *Lockheed Aircraft Corp v. Superior Court*, 28 Cal.2d 481,486, 171 P.2d 21, 25 (1946), where employees discharged for political views relied upon a statute forbidding employer rules, regulations, and policies prohibiting employee political activity:

"The contract of employment must be held to have been made in light of, and to have incorporated, the provisions of existing law. [Citation omitted.] Hence, upon violation of this Section, an employee has a right of action for damages for breach of his employment contract."

Petermann, however, implied from the independent prohibition on perjury a limitation on the right to discharge, and was the first case to impose a limitation on that right without reference to a statute expressly protecting employee rights.

allegedly instructed by the union to perjure himself when he testified at a hearing before an investigative committee of the California legislature. He refused to do so and was fired, he alleged, for his refusal to commit perjury.

The California court held that these facts gave rise to an action for damages. The court emphasized the unlawful and reprehensible nature of the motivation, the impairment of legislative functions, and the fact that the employer could have been cited for contempt if it had sought to compel the employee to perjure himself in a court case. It reasoned that if such conduct was wrongful per se, it ought not go unremedied simply because the employee was otherwise subject to discharge at will. Allowing the action was in essence an extension of the court's contempt power. The court was not concerned that the discharge was arbitrary; the concern was that the employer's superior economic power was being used to force the employee into committing a crime, or to retaliate for the employee's refusal to commit a crime. The new rule was born.

Eight years later, Professor Blades' article "Employment at Will v. Individual Freedom: On Limiting the Abusive Exercise of Employer Power"[2] analyzed the potential for abuse inherent in the terminable-at-will rule. In a persuasive and thoughtful commentary examining the plight of nonunion workers, Blades called for recognition of a new tort that would limit the employer's power to discharge arbitrarily under the terminable-at-will rule.

In 1973, the Indiana Supreme Court relied on *Petermann* and an expansive interpretation of that state's workers' compensation statute to create a right of action for an employee discharged for filing a workers' compensation claim.[3] In 1974 the New Hampshire Supreme Court in *Monge v. Beebe Rubber Co.*[4] permitted an action where the discharge was a result of the sexual harassment of a married immigrant woman. The strongly worded opinion hinted that a general abrogation of the terminable-at-will rule itself was at hand and precipitated a flurry of articles in legal periodicals on the subject.

---

[2] 67 COLUM. L. REV. 1404 (1967). In the 15 years after it appeared, this seminal commentary was cited in almost every leading court decision on the subject. The article also contains numerous insights into particular problems that have arisen since retaliatory discharge was recognized. See also Blumberg, *Corporate Responsibility and the Employee's Duty of Loyalty and Obedience: A Preliminary Inquiry*, 24 OKLA. L. REV. 279 (1971); Note, *Implied Contract Rights for Job Security*, 26 STAN. L. REV. 335 (1974).

[3] *Frampton v. Central Ind. Gas Co.*, 260 Ind. 249, 297 N.E.2d 425 (1973). "When an employee is discharged solely for exercising a statutorily conferred right, an exception to the general rule must be recognized." *Id.* at 253, 297 N.E.2d at 428.

[4] 114 N.H. 130, 316 A.2d 549 (1974):
"In all employment contracts whether at will or for a definite term, the employer's interest in running his business as he sees fit must be balanced against the interest of the employee in maintaining his employment, and the public's interest in maintaining a proper balance between the two * * *. We hold that a termination by the employer of a contract of employment at will which is motivated by bad faith or malice or based on retaliation is not [in] the best interest of the economic system or the public good and constitutes a breach of the employment contract. * * * Such a rule affords the employee a certain stability of employment and does not interfere with the employer's normal exercise of his right to discharge, which is necessary to permit him to operate his business efficiently and profitably." *Id.* at 133, 316 A.2d at 551-552.

Doubtless the opinion's strong criticism of the abuse of employer power influenced courts in other jurisdictions to recognize retaliatory discharge as an exception to the terminable-at-will rule. Since *Monge*, most courts addressing the issue have recognized retaliatory discharge as a cause of action, though several states have specifically refused to join the trend.[5]

The principal feature of retaliatory discharge as a cause of action is that its wrongfulness is based on motivation. In the context of employment, however, basing liability for discharge or other discipline on wrongful motive is not a new idea. The wrongful motive approach appeared during the struggles of organized labor in the late nineteenth and early twentieth century. Oddly enough, motive-based torts were developed in favor of employers in the courts and in favor of employees in the legislatures.

Many of the early business tort cases arose out of what the common law courts perceived as excesses of organized labor. Intimidation of employees for their refusal to join the union and strikes and boycotts harmful to businesses that refused to bargain collectively were deemed actionable because of what the courts characterized as malicious purpose. These cases led to the development of business torts like interference with contract, which often look to the presence of "malice" and create defenses of "justification."

At the same time, state legislatures passed acts prohibiting yellow-dog contracts, in which employees were required to agree, as a condition of employment, not to join a labor organization. Statutes to this effect were initially struck down as an unconstitutional infringement on freedom of contract. The prohibition was expanded in the 1935 National Labor Relations Act, which forbade employer discrimination against employees for exercising their right to organize and bargain collectively. Similar prohibitions against wrongfully motivated discharge, including retaliatory discharge, were later adopted in favor of employees who reported violations of the Fair Labor Standards Act (minimum wage law) and the Equal Employment Opportunity Act. The tort of retaliatory discharge, which prohibits discharge prompted by certain wrongful motives, thus has its heritage in earlier

---

[5]The following 21 jurisdictions, in decisions by their highest appellate court or in uncontradicted lower appellate opinions, have recognized the action for retaliatory discharge by express language: California, Connecticut, Hawaii, Idaho, Illinois, Indiana, Kansas, Kentucky, Maryland, Massachusetts, Michigan, Montana, Nevada, New Hampshire, New Jersey, Oregon, Pennsylvania, Washington, West Virginia, and Wisconsin. New Mexico has recognized the action in a limited context. Two more jurisdictions have considered this question, found no cause of action in the case presented, but suggested that such an action might be recognized: Arkansas and Vermont.

Six jurisdictions have flatly rejected the action in decisions by their highest appellate courts: Alabama, District of Columbia, Florida, Georgia, Mississippi, and New York. Three other jurisdictions have reported appellate decisions rejecting the action: Louisiana, North Carolina, and Texas. Four jurisdictions have rejected claims for retaliatory discharge in specific cases and left the issue open, but by their language or because of the facts of the case appear unlikely to recognize the action: Arizona, Colorado, Iowa, and Nebraska. The 14 remaining jurisdictions have not considered the question since *Monge*.

statutory and common law precedents addressed to wrongful motives in the work place.

Reliance on public policy may also be viewed as an extension of the prohibition on enforcement of contracts that are contrary to public policy. The action for retaliatory discharge differs from this traditional doctrine in two important ways. First, the rule of contract law operates as a defense to an enforcement action; the action for retaliatory discharge uses public policy as a sword, not a shield. Second, the action for retaliatory discharge calls upon the court to transform a general public policy against, for instance, perjury, into a more specific and previously unstated public policy against discharge of an employee for refusing to commit perjury.

Legal commentators, almost uniformly, have applauded the development of the action for retaliatory discharge.[6] One might expect scholarly skepticism about a tort with such ill-defined contours and thin doctrinal basis. Doubtless the reason for the scholarly support lies in dissatisfaction with the logical inconsistencies and often harsh results of the terminable-at-will rule itself.

Reasons for Development of a Public Policy Exception to Employment-At-Will

Why, in the 1970s, did the courts generally begin to recognize a need for employee and public policy protection never before given serious consideration? Perhaps we are too much in the stream of this development to identify the reasons for its appearance at this particular time. One senses in many of the opinions the force of a "shock the conscience" test rather than careful legal analysis. Indeed, sharply contrasting results reached in similar cases in different courts show the presence of some degree of arbitrary adjudication. Different judges have different ideas of fairness and different philosophies about what kinds of discharge cases the courts should hear.

Central to the development of the cause of action is the growing recognition that the terminable-at-will rule, whether viewed as a rule of substantive law or a rule of construction, conflicts with the true expectations of the parties and exposes employees to abuse. Courts recognizing the action for retaliatory discharge have grown increasingly outspoken in challenging the premises of the at-will rule and acknowledging the injustice it engenders. Adopting retaliatory discharge as a cause of action is one way to mitigate the injustice and strike at one class of outrageous cases without taking the larger and more daring step of general abrogation of the terminable-at-will rule.

---

[6]E.g., Note, *Protecting At-Will Employees Against Wrongful Discharge: The Duty to Terminate Only in Good Faith*, 93 HARV. L. REV. 1816 (1980); Note, *A Common Law Action for the Abusively Discharged Employee*, 26 HASTINGS L.J. 1435 (1975); Note, *A Remedy for Malicious Discharge of the At-Will Employee: Monge v. Beebe Rubber Co.*, 7 CONN. L. REV. 758 (1974); Note, *Contracts-Employee: Discharge Motivated by Bad Faith, Malice or Retaliation Constituting a Breach of an Employment Contract Terminable at Will*, 43 FORDHAM L. REV. 300 (1974).

But the harshness of the terminable-at-will rule is not something new, as cases like *Comerford v. International Harvester Co.*[7] demonstrate.

Both opinions favoring and opinions rejecting recognition of the action for retaliatory discharge overstate the legal significance of the terminable-at-will rule in this context. That rule was created as, and remains, a rule of contract law, not tort law. The rule did not reflect a conscious determination that the absence of job security for employees was a socially beneficial state of affairs; this was, at most, a motivating opinion in the minds of nineteenth-century judges. The terminable-at-will rule comes into play in contract law to establish a presumed duration of the employment relationship when the parties have not expressly or impliedly agreed to a specific term or a term that ends upon the occurrence of a certain event. But a rule of contract law has no special place in the decision to recognize a tort for the abuse of a superior economic position in derogation of public policy. It is merely a circumstance which, like the absence of an enforceable contract between a store owner and business invitee in a negligence case, would preclude recovery in the absence of a tort remedy. Often in product and professional liability cases, the injured party has no contract remedy against the wrongdoer. That fact, however, has long since ceased to determine the scope or existence of a tort remedy. Judicial preoccupation with employment-at-will suggests the same sort of underlying bias as was reflected by the preoccupation with privity of contract prior to the development of modern product liability law.

In *Pierce v. Ortho Pharmaceutical Corp.*,[8] the court offered this view of industrial history to explain the development of retaliatory discharge:

> "[T]he common law developed in a laissez-faire climate that encouraged industrial growth and approved the right of an employer to control his own business, including the right to fire without cause an employee at will.* * * [In the twentieth century,] [b]usinesses have evolved from small and medium size firms to gigantic corporations in which ownership is separate from management. * * * The employer * * * has been replaced by a superior in the corporate hierarchy who is himself an employee."[9]

The historical assertion is dubious. The growth of giant corporations was well under way in the late nineteenth century when the terminable-at-will rule came into full flower. Laissez-faire thinking certainly contributed to the development of the terminable-at-will rule,

---

[7]235 Ala. 376, 178 So. 894 (1937). The employee alleged that the employer had discharged him because his wife refused to submit to romantic overtures of the employer's assistant sales manager. The court held that since the discharge was lawful, the fact that it was done from bad motives or with bad intent did not give the injured party a cause of action. See also *Odell v. Humble Oil Ref. Co.*, 201 F.2d 123, 127 (10th Cir. 1963) (discharge for truthful testimony).

[8]84 N.J. 58, 417 A.2d 505 (1980).

[9]*Id.* at 66, 417 A.2d at 509.

but the waning of that doctrine decades ago cannot explain the present trend toward recognition of retaliatory discharge.

In *Adler v. American Standard Corp.*,[10] the court noted that the majority of American workers do not have the job security of a collective bargaining agreement or civil service status, and that fired workers face an uncertain future. But in stating that this condition differs significantly from the state of affairs in the nineteenth century, the court is simply wrong. Indeed, oppression of employees was a fact of life during the "Gilded Age" when the terminable-at-will rule became firmly established, and in those days there was no unemployment compensation program to assist the fired employee in meeting continuing economic obligations, as there is today.

The Illinois Supreme Court correctly observed that the terminable-at-will rule was a "harsh outgrowth of the notion of reciprocal rights and obligations in the employment relationship."[11] But in its suggestion that specialized business operations have led to a relatively immobile work force, with workers unable to market their skills to other employers, the court relied on an unsupported description of industrial conditions. While the assertion may be true in certain sectors of the economy, turnover statistics in general tell a different story. In short, while the courts are correct in recognizing that the employer and unorganized employees are not on an equal footing, they cannot correctly attribute that fact to recent changes in the employment scene. The labor movement has been pointing to that same inequality for generations. Indeed, the leading treatise on employment at the turn of the century, recognizing that the terminable-at-will rule was firmly established, nevertheless criticized it as an "extreme" presumption that led in many instances to results contrary to those contemplated by the parties[12]

The rise of the retaliatory discharge cause of action is attribut-

---

[10]291 Md. 31, 432 A.2d 464 (1981).
[11]*Palmateer v. International Harvester Co.*, 85 Ill.2d 124, 128, 421 N.E.2d 876, 878 (1981).
[12]1 C.B. Labatt, COMMENTARIES ON THE LAW OF MASTER AND SERVANT §160, at 519-520 (2d ed., Lawyer's Cooperative, 1913):
"The preponderance of American authority in favor of the doctrine that an indefinite hiring is presumptively a hiring at will is so great that it is now scarcely open to criticism. But a commentator may perhaps be permitted to point out that, in many instances—more especially those in which the compensation is specified as being a certain sum per annum—it cannot be applied without entailing results different to those which may reasonably be supposed to have been within the contemplation of the parties. Having regard to the ordinary course of affairs in the business world, the higher the position to which the contract relates the more certainly may it be inferred that the employer and employed expect their relationship to continue for a considerable period. It seems questionable whether a doctrine resting on a presumption which ignores that expectation as an element indicative of intention can with propriety be treated as one of general application. Assuming that the social and economic conditions which prevail in the United States are such as to require the rejection of the English rule regarding the presumptive yearly duration of an indefinite hiring, it is by no means self-evident that those conditions, when viewed as a whole and with relation to the various descriptions of employment, afford a sufficient justification for going to the opposite extreme involved in the adoption of an unvarying presumption that such a hiring is not binding for any fixed period at all. It is at least fairly open to argument whether the more reasonable doctrine is not that which treats the duration of the engagement as an entirely open question of fact, unencumbered by any presumption whatever * * *."

able not so much to changes in the employment relationship or the economics of labor as it is to changes in the way Americans view themselves and a corresponding change in the judicial climate and perception of the employment relationship. A whole series of intangibles have contributed to the change: an emerging public rejection of authoritarian rules and of the surrender of basic liberties during working hours; the leading role the law played in bringing about the revolution in civil rights; the increased judicial sensitivity to individual rights brought about by the growth of individual constitutional rights; more open judicial selection procedures; increased awareness of the effects of discharge from employment brought about by press coverage of the problem; more judges who have been personally exposed to arbitrary conduct in the work place and the hardships of fired employees; and generally favorable experience with relatively abrupt judge-made policy changes in the law in areas such as product liability, equitable remedies, mental distress, right to privacy, and insurance law.

Private Rights of Action Under Antireprisal Statutes

Courts relied on public policy to limit exercise of the employer's power to discharge before the recognition of retaliatory discharge as a cause of action by finding private "rights of action" to be implied in statutes prohibiting discharge for specific forms of protected employee behavior. Where a statute prohibits discharge for specified reasons but does not declare a remedy, the courts must decide whether a private right of action may be implied on the prohibition. The action for retaliatory discharge goes a step further. The court infers not just the remedy of a private suit, but also the substantive prohibition against discharge for a "wrong reason"; the court thus creates both a prohibition on discharge and a remedy from a general public policy.

Courts that reject retaliatory discharge as a cause of action often do so out of deference to the legislature, arguing that any substantive prohibition of retaliation should be adopted by an elected body. Courts recognizing the action reply that the terminable-at-will rule is a judge-made rule, and that judge-made exceptions are just as appropriate as the rules they modify. In a larger sense, though, the action for retaliatory discharge often furthers legislative purposes by expanding the enforcement of legislative policy. As the court observed in *Harless v. First National Bank*,[13] to permit retaliation for the exercise of a statutory right or for compliance with statutory commands would be to withhold with one hand what the legislature has given with the other.

Where the action for retaliatory discharge is recognized, the necessity for considering implied private-right-of-action issues is re-

---

[13]246 S.E.2d 270 (W. Va. 1978).

moved. In *Perks v. Firestone Tire & Rubber Co.*,[14] the employee was discharged for refusing to submit to a polygraph examination, though the state's statute prohibited employers from making such tests a condition of employment. A private-right-of-action analysis would have considered whether the legislature intended a civil remedy and whether damages for the discharge were proper where the employee did not ultimately submit to the examination. These questions were swept aside in the retaliatory discharge analysis, with the court recognizing that as a practical matter the statute would be ineffective in the absence of a right to sue for discharge.

In *McKinney v. National Dairy Council*,[15] a federal district court, in recognizing a public policy action where the state had previously refused to allow a private right of action under the statute, explained the fundamental difference between the implied-right-of-action analysis and the retaliatory discharge analysis. The court noted that one of the basic premises that might reasonably have underlain the prior decision, that no claim could be established unless a civil remedy could be implied from the statute, was no longer true.

> "[I]n this resolution of a very close issue the public policy * * * manifested in the statute is a factor. But it is a factor in a way quite different from that urged and rejected in [the decision refusing to imply a private right of action.] Here, the force of the analogy to the statute moves in confluence with the greater flow of the principles and policies [prohibiting retaliatory discharge]."[16]

In jurisdictions that do not recognize the action for retaliatory discharge, private rights of action for statutorily prohibited reprisals provide a more limited form of employee protection. A private action under a statute may be appropriate where reprisal is specifically prohibited, or where the statute creates an employee right the assertion of which has led to discharge. In the former case the discharge itself is the wrongful act on which the suit is based; in the latter case it may be an injury flowing from the employer's violation of the statutory right.

Federal Statutes

Many federal statutes prohibit particular types of retaliatory discharge and provide for the enforcing agency to adjudicate or prosecute the action. Where the agency itself hears and adjudicates the question, the employee must proceed before the agency, but may be able to seek judicial review under the Administrative Review Act.[17]

If the statute is one that delegates to a government official or agency the sole authority to investigate violations and to enforce its

---

[14]611 F.2d 1363 (3d Cir. 1979).
[15]491 F. Supp. 1108 (D. Mass. 1980).
[16]*Id.* at 1122. The decision in *McKinney* was under Massachusetts law, which treats the public policy rule as a part of the doctrine of good faith and fair dealing.
[17]5 U.S.C. §701 (1982).

provisions by bringing suit against the employer, the decision of the enforcing officer or body not to bring suit often is not reviewable.[18] The employee in such cases may be left with no remedy because of bureaucratic indifference or a shortage of enforcement resources. In such cases the discharged employee will seek enforcement by a suit for damages. The federal court must then consider whether Congress intended private remedies to be available.

There is a particular concern in the federal cases that properly restricts implication of private rights of action. The U.S. Constitution creates a government of specific and limited powers, unlike the plenary powers of state government. While it may be proper to construe federal legislation broadly within its intended sphere to ensure that the objectives of Congress are accomplished, there is an ever-present danger that federal law will displace functions intended by Congress to remain within the scope of state law. Thus, especially where state concerns are affected by a federal law, the federal court will hesitate to provide private enforcement that may not have been intended by Congress and that would effectively displace any state law policy that strikes a balance less favorable to the plaintiff.[19]

The central focus of the question of a federal implied private right of action is on congressional intent. The general formula was set out in *Cort v. Ash*,[20] where the Supreme Court articulated a four-factor test for recognition or denial of an implied private right of action. If the plaintiff is a member of a class of persons especially to be benefited by the statute, the Court will examine evidence of specific legislative intent, which will be dispositive if it shows some congressional resolution of the question, even if only in the legislative history. It also will consider two more general indicators: whether there is an existing administrative scheme that a private right of action would disrupt, and whether matters of special state concern are involved. Where there is a protected class, no clear legislative intent, no disruption of administrative process, a special federal concern, and no other remedy, a right of action will generally be recognized.[21] Any substantial showing that Congress intended no private remedy will preclude an action, whether it be found in the legislative history or the context of the statute.[22]

Appendix A at the end of this volume lists federal statutes and regulations with provisions intended to protect employees against retaliatory discharge. These statutes and regulations are also noted in the appropriate sections in this chapter; complete references are

---

[18]*National Maritime Union v. NLRB*, 423 F.2d 625 (2d Cir. 1970) (NLRA); *Associated Builders & Contractors, Inc. v. Irving*, 610 F.2d 1221 (4th Cir. 1979) (NLRA); *Stewart v. EEOC*, 611 F.2d 679 (7th Cir. 1979) (EEOA); *Machinists v. Lubbers*, 681 F.2d 598 (9th Cir. 1982) (NLRA).

[19]See *Cannon v. University of Chicago*, 441 U.S. 677, 730 (1979) (Powell, J. dissenting).

[20]422 U.S. 66 (1975).

[21]*Cannon v. University of Chicago*, 441 U.S. 677 (1979).

[22]*Transamerica Mortgage Advisors, Inc. v. Lewis*, 444 U.S. 11 (1979); *Touche Ross & Co. v. Redington*, 442 U.S. 560 (1979).

provided in Appendix A. In jurisdictions recognizing the action for retaliatory discharge, they may be sufficient to establish a public policy that state law will enforce even though it would not be enforceable under a federal implied-right-of-action analysis.[23]

State Statutes

The *Restatement (Second) of Torts*, Section 874A6, calls for a civil remedy for violation of a statutory duty where the plaintiff is a member of the class of persons the statute is designed to protect and where the remedy is necessary to make the statute effective. This standard represents a general statement of the circumstances in which a suit for breach of statutory duty will be allowed, or of the grounds on which a right of action will be implied from a statute.

Unlike a federal court, the state court is free to make general law, and the presence of a statutory policy must be given substantial weight in that process. This is in part because it is the state's law that establishes the rights and obligations of the employment relationship in the first place. Experience with statutory enforcement through the doctrine of negligence per se is also a factor in resolving the private remedy issue.

Appendix A includes a summary of state statutes that suggest themselves as public policies for purposes of retaliatory discharge cases. Some are civil prohibitions with no stated remedy; others provide for an express employee right of action or administrative remedy, some with limitations periods as short as 30 days.[24] Still others specify criminal penalties. Some of the statutes only create employee rights that could be the subject of a retaliatory discharge suit or action for breach of statutory duty, while others expressly prohibit employer reprisal. The statutes that bar retaliation often extend to nondischarge cases by outlawing discrimination in the terms and conditions of employment on the basis of protected activity. Statutes not listed may have the effect of prohibiting discharge by expansive interpretation,[25] an unusual combination of circumstances,[26] or, in the case

---

[23]*Adler v. American Standard Corp.*, 538 F. Supp. 572 (D. Md. 1982).

[24]In *Hills v. Sleep Prod. Co.*, 41 Colo. App. 1, 584 P.2d 93 (1978), the court enforced a 30-day limitation period in a retaliatory discharge case, rejecting the employee's argument that compliance with the limitation provision was not necessary.

[25]In *Frampton v. Central Ind. Gas Co.*, 260 Ind. 249, 297 N.E.2d 425 (1973), for example, the statutory prohibition on any "device" to avoid liability for workers' compensation claims was applied to retaliatory discharge even though the employee received a workers' compensation settlement.

[26]For instance, Missouri's service letter statute, MO. ANN. STAT. § 290.140 (Vernon 1965 & Supp. 1984), requires the employer to provide a letter on request to a terminated employee stating, among other things, the true reason for discharge. Providing a false reason may give rise to liability, as in *Newman v. Greater Kansas City Baptist Community Hosp. Ass'n*, 604 S.W.2d 619 (Mo. Ct. App. 1980); since it is a rare employer who will concur when the employee claims the reason was an arbitrary or unlawful one, the statute may be employed to redress the wrongful discharge indirectly. Similarly, the failure of an employer to disclose documents on which discharge was based as required by a "personnel records" statute may, under the provisions of the new Illinois statute, Act. No. 83-1104, 1983 Ill. Legis. Serv. 7290 (West), to be codified at ILL. REV. STAT. ch. 48, §200 *et seq.*, be unavailable to the employer as evidence in the subsequent lawsuit over the discharge, thereby defeating the employer's otherwise sound defense and indirectly providing a remedy for the discharge.

of a broad, general statute, application to the employment setting.[27] State statutes, or the names of states having relevant statutes, are noted at appropriate points of the discussion of public policy protection in this chapter. Full references for each state's statutes may be found by consulting Appendix A. Other statutes applicable in a particular case may be located by searching for laws regulating the industry or field of activity involved in the employment relationship, and for statutes governing the employee conduct that led to the discharge—particularly those in the criminal code. The more the statute appears to be specifically directed toward the conduct in question, the more likely it is to represent a public policy.

Coverage and Scope of Retaliatory Discharge

Retaliation that takes the form of the "corporate capital punishment" of discharge is usually the only actionable form of retaliation. Moreover, the action for retaliatory discharge may not be available to all employees. There is growing debate over whether retaliatory discharge is a tort or contract action, or both.

In many cases it is the plight of the at-will worker, trapped between his desire to fulfill legal duties or assert legal rights and the employer's unrestrained power to discharge, that motivates the court to recognize a right of action.[28] But to justify the action, there must also be a need to protect public policy, and if that need is present it is difficult to see why the right of action should not be generally available. A person employed on a daily, weekly, or monthly basis is as a practical matter threatened by retaliatory discharge as much as an at-will employee. This is because the remedy provided by a suit for breach of contract usually will provide no more than a small award of severance pay—although organized employees, who are protected against discharge without just cause, have a more substantial remedy through grievance arbitration. There are decisions that restrict the cause of action to at-will employees,[29] and opinions that deny a cause of action to employees covered by collective bargaining agreements;[30] there are also cases to the contrary.[31] To date there is no consensus.

---

[27]Where the state has established an administrative remedy, however, exhaustion principles, discussed in Chapter 5, may preclude a retaliatory discharge action.

[28]E.g., *Palmateer v. International Harvester Co.*, 85 Ill.2d 124, 421 N.E.2d 876 (1981), characterizing the terminable-at-will rule as a harsh outgrowth of the notion of reciprocal rights and obligations in employment.

[29]*Pinsof v. Pinsof*, 107 Ill. App.3d 1031, 438 N.E.2d 525 (1982); *Harrison v. James*, 558 F. Supp. 438 (E.D. Pa. 1983); *Wehr v. Burroughs Corp.*, 438 F. Supp. 1052 (E.D. Pa. 1977).

[30]E.g., *Payne v. Pennzoil Corp.*, 672 P.2d 1322 (Ariz. 1983). This topic is explored at length in the discussion of exhaustion in Chapter 5.

[31]E.g., *Midgett v. Sackett-Chicago, Inc.*, 118 Ill. App.3d 7, 454 N.E.2d 1092 (1983) *aff'd* No. 59341, 59350 (Ill. 1984). See discussion of exhaustion in Chapter 5.

Government Workers

Public employees present yet another problem. They may have a greater duty to oppose and expose unlawful activity, since they are theoretically accountable to the general public. On the other hand, they also have constitutional protections not available to nongovernment employees. In the federal sphere, strict antireprisal protections administered by the Merit Systems Protection Board are written into the statutes.[32] Some courts have applied the public policy doctrine to protect public employees; and Montana has held that constitutional protections, including the due process rights of public employees with a "property interest" in the job, are public policy for purposes of the retaliatory discharge cause of action.[33] One New York court, recognizing that retaliatory discharge had been rejected as a cause of action for private employees, has allowed a public employee's suit for arbitrary discharge on constitutional substantive due process grounds.[34]

Retaliation Short of Discharge

The power of employer over employee is inherent in the employment relationship. There is a great deal that can be done to punish an employee short of discharge: close supervision, continual unjustified criticism and warnings, undesirable assignments, salary cuts or smaller raises, creation of peer antagonism, denial of promotions, and so on. Such discriminatory conditions may be imposed on a small or a large scale; they may be intended to drive the employee to quit.

The intrusive effect of permitting an action in the absence of a discharge is high, however. To attempt to distinguish between retaliatory actions affecting the employee and innocent or de minimus decisions involving something less drastic than termination of employment would open up a wide range of business decisions to litigation. While many of the employee protection statutes opt for more complete protection, the courts have allowed a common law action

---

[32]Merit Systems Protection Act, 5 U.S.C. §2301 (1982). The Board, which replaced the Civil Service Commission, protects many federal employees from employment decisions, including discharge, which are:
  "(1) based on political affiliation, race, color, religion, national origin, sex, marital status, age, handicapping condition, or in violation of rights of privacy and constitutional rights;
  "(2) based on personal favoritism, or which constitute coercion for partisan political purposes;
  "(3) reprisals for disclosure by the employee of information which the employee reasonably believes evidences:
    "(a) a violation of any law, rule or regulation, or
    "(b) mismanagement, a gross waste of funds, abuse of authority, or a substantial and specific danger to public health or safety."
5 U.S.C. §§2301(b)(2),(8),(9), 2302(b)(1),(2),(6),(8),(10) (1982).
[33]*Lovell v. Wolf*, 643 P.2d 569 (Mont. 1982); *Nye v. Department of Livestock*, 639 P.2d 498 (Mont. 1982); *Reiter v. Yellowstone Co.*, 627 P.2d 845 (Mont. 1981). See also *Hunter v. Port Auth.*, 277 Pa. Super. 4, 419 A.2d 631 (1980).
[34]*Bergamini v. Manhattan & Bronx Surface Transit Operating Auth.*, 94 A.D.2d 441, 463 N.Y.S.2d 777 (1983).

only for termination of employment.[35] However, the doctrine of constructive discharge is available where the termination of employment is forced on the employee.[36] *Hunter v. Port Authority*[37] allowed an action where the employee was promised employment but later was refused the job for a reason that violated public policy. In *Hurley v. Allied Chemical Corp.*,[38] however, the refusal to provide a promised job was held not actionable because no employment relationship had been formed.

Tort or Contract

Characterization of the action for retaliatory discharge as a contract or tort action may affect the availability of punitive damages, the applicable statute of limitations,[39] and the measure of damages. *Tameny v. Atlantic Richfield Co.*[40] concluded that retaliatory discharge was both a tort and a violation of an implied-in-law covenant of good faith in the employment contract. *Brockmeyer v. Dun & Bradstreet*[41] held that the action should be classified as a breach of contract, but in most cases involving the issue retaliatory discharge has been classified as a tort.[42]

Retaliatory Discharge Distinguished From Arbitrary Discharge

The action for retaliatory discharge does not protect the employee fired for a good reason or for no reason at all; nor does the action apply to all terminations for bad reasons. Only discharge that impairs a public policy gives rise to a cause of action; the absence of just cause for discharge or the presence of an unfair ulterior motive is insufficient.[43]

---

[35]*Bryce v. Johnson & Johnson, Inc.*, 115 Ill. App.3d 913, 450 N.E.2d 1235 (1983) (considerable friction between employer and employee over workers' compensation claim not actionable since employment terminated by subsequent disabling injury).

[36]*Id.* (suggesting that employment discrimination cases in this area are appropriate authorities); *Gates v. Life of Mont. Ins. Co.*, 638 P.2d 1063 (Mont. 1982), *appeal following remand,* 668 P.2d 213 (Mont. 1983).

[37]277 Pa. Super. 4, 419 A.2d 631 (1980).

[38]262 S.E.2d 757 (W. Va. 1980).

[39]*Henon v. Lever Bros.*, 114 Ill. App.3d 608, 449 N.E.2d 196 (1983); *Stanley v. Sewell Coal Co.*, 285 S.E.2d 679 (W. Va. 1981).

[40]27 Cal.3d 167, 610 P.2d 1330, 164 Cal. Rptr. 839 (1980).

[41]113 Wis.2d 561, 335 N.W.2d 834 (1983). See also *Monge v. Beebe Rubber Co.*, 114 N.H. 130, 316 A.2d 549 (1974); *Fortune v. National Cash Register Co.*, 373 Mass. 96, 364 N.E.2d 1251 (1977) (retaliatory discharge as in *Monge* an aspect of common law contract duty of good faith and fair dealing).

[42]*Scott v. Union Tank Car Co.*, 402 N.E.2d 992 (Ind. App. 1980); *Stanley v. Sewell Coal Co.*, 285 S.E.2d 679 (W. Va. 1981), *Harless v. First Nat'l Bank*, 246 S.E.2d 270 (W. Va. 1978). See *Vigil v. Arzola*, 22 N.M. Sт. B. Bull. 868 (1983).

[43]*Geary v. United States Steel Corp.*, 456 Pa. 171, 319 A.2d 174 (1974), indicated in dicta that a discharge motivated by malice, in the sense of a specific intent to cause harm for an ulterior purpose, would be actionable. The court hastened to add that it would not be enough simply to show that the employer knew of the probable harmful consequences of the discharge to the employee. By denying an action to the plaintiff in that case, the court demonstrated that the showing of malice would be exceedingly difficult to make out.

Illness

A discharge because of illness or an injury unrelated to the job does not give rise to an action for retaliatory discharge.[44] Such a discharge, if unaccompanied by absence or job performance problems, might raise problems of handicap discrimination. Discharge for pregnancy will generally violate federal equal employment opportunity law.[45] Discharge for on-the-job injury implicates the policy of protecting workers' compensation claimants. Public policy does not require the employer to retain sick employees generally, however.

Honesty

Discharge for honesty or refusal to lie, standing alone, is also insufficient. In *Adler v. American Standard Corp.*,[46] the court found no basis for a retaliatory discharge suit pleading general allegations of improper accounting, commercial "bribes," falsification of sales and income records, and personal use of corporate funds by other employees. The failure to find a specific criminal wrong in this alleged behavior was fatal to the claim, though the suit was later upheld because of specific illegalities alleged in an amended pleading.[47] Similarly, an employee's claim that he had been fired for complaining that the employer was not living up to its promise of good service to customers was insufficient in *Keneally v. Orgain*.[48] The appellate court in *Delaney v. Taco Time International, Inc.*[49] explained that honesty in business was so broad and general a concept that to recognize it as a public policy would involve the courts "with the more menial mendacities which lead to countless private quarrels in business, as they do in other spheres of life."[50] The Oregon Supreme Court, while not rejecting the principle, nevertheless reversed, finding that the public, societal duty of the employee to refrain from false and potentially defamatory statements concerning others was implicated by the employer's demand upon the employee to sign a statement accusing another employee of immoral behavior.[51] Honesty under oath[52] or in reports to the government[53] are also public policy concerns that can support an action.

---

[44]*Cuerton v. Abbott Laboratories*, 111 Ill. App.3d 261, 443 N.E.2d 1069 (1982); *Howard v. Dorr Woolen Co.*, 120 N.H. 295, 414 A.2d 1273 (1980); *Scarpace v. Sears, Roebuck & Co.*, 113 Wis.2d 608, 335 N.W.2d 844 (1983); *Hurley v. Allied Chem. Co.*, 262 S.E.2d 757 (W. Va. 1980). See also *Bruffett v. Warner Communications, Inc.*, 692 F.2d 910 (3d Cir. 1982) (refusal to complete hiring because of health questions raised by physical examination not bad faith.)
[45]42 U.S.C. §§2000e(k), 2000e-2(a)(1) (1976 & Supp. V 1981).
[46]291 Md. 31, 432 A.2d 464 (1981).
[47]538 F. Supp. 572 (D. Md. 1982).
[48]186 Mont. 1, 606 P.2d 127 (1979).
[49]65 Ore. App. 160, 670 P.2d 218 (1983), *rev'd*, 681 P.2d 114, 116 LRRM 2168 (Ore. 1984).
[50]670 P.2d at 222.
[51]*Delaney v. Taco Time Int'l, Inc.*, 681 P.2d 114, 116 LRRM 2168 (Ore. 1984).
[52]*Petermann v. Teamsters*, 174 Cal. App.2d 184, 344 P.2d 25 (1959) (perjury at legislative hearing).
[53]*Trombetta v. Detroit, Toledo & Ironton R.R.*, 81 Mich. App. 489, 265 N.W.2d 385 (1978) (pollution control reports to state). Cf. *Magnan v. Anaconda Indus., Inc.*, 37 Conn. Supp. 38, 429 A.2d 492 (Super. Ct. 1980) (report of theft conceded to raise public policy issue).

Employee Interests

An employer is not required by public policy to accommodate itself to an employee's personal interests absent a specific statutory mandate or strong public interest. An employee's interest in attending law school at night raised no public policy concern, despite the general public interest in encouraging education.[54] In *Becket v. Welton Becket & Associates*,[55] the employee served as executor of an estate holding stock in the employer, and was discharged for his refusal to drop a derivative suit against the employer. Finding that the decision to embark on the suit was not mandated by law, the court refused to allow a retaliatory discharge action. The opinion suggests that the employee should not have created the conflict of interest.

Pretextual Discharge

In equal employment opportunity cases, wrongful motivation for discharge is generally proven by showing that the reason offered by the employer was a pretext.[56] Pretext is also important as circumstantial proof of wrongful motive in retaliatory discharge cases. But it is not a violation of public policy simply to discharge without just cause and then give a baseless reason for the decision,[57] to discharge for violation of a rule though it was not possible to follow the rule,[58] or the employer ordered the employee to break the rule,[59] to discharge without reasonable inquiry into whether just cause existed,[60] to discharge for a trivial offense,[61] to discharge an employee so he can serve as a scapegoat,[62] to discharge an employee because he has embarrassing information about a superior,[63] to discharge on the basis of false accusations,[64] or to discharge on the basis of an erroneous belief of employee wrongdoing.[65]

The Meaning of "Public Policy"

The early cases speak in broad, general terms of public policy as a prohibition for the good of the community against "whatever con-

---

[54]*Scroghan v. Kraftco Corp.*, 551 S.W.2d 811 (Ky. App. 1977).
[55]39 Cal. App.3d 815, 114 Cal. Rptr. 531 (1974).
[56]*McDonnell Douglas Corp. v. Green*, 411 U.S. 792 (1973); *Aikens v. United States Postal Serv.*, 460 U.S. 711 (1983).
[57]*Holloway v. K-Mart Corp.*, 113 Wis.2d 143, 334 N.W.2d 570 (App. 1983).
[58]*Newton v. Brown & Root*, 280 Ark. 337, 658 S.W.2d 370 (1983).
[59]*Vandergrift v. American Brands Corp.*, 572 F. Supp. 496, 115 LRRM 2317 (D.N.H. 1983).
[60]*Gram v. Liberty Mut. Ins. Co.*, 384 Mass. 659, 429 N.E.2d 21 (1981); *Boresen v. Rohm & Haas, Inc.*, 526 F. Supp. 1230 (E.D. Pa. 1981).
[61]*Mead Johnson & Co. v. Oppenheimer*, 458 N.E.2d 668, 115 LRRM 3684 (Ind. App. 1984).
[62]*Siles v. Travenol Laboratories, Inc.*, 13 Mass. App. 354, 433 N.E.2d 103 (1982).
[63]*Hillenbrand v. Evansville*, 457 N.E.2d 236 (Ind. App. 1983).
[64]*Threlkeld v. Christoph*, 312 S.E.2d 14, 115 LRRM 3178 (S.C. Ct. App. 1984).
[65]*Zuniga v. Sears, Roebuck & Co.*, 671 P.2d 662, 115 LRRM 3189 (N.M. Ct. App. 1983).

travenes good morals or any established interests of society,"[66] against conduct "motivated by bad faith or malice or based on retaliation,"[67] or against action "for a socially undesirable motive" which "contravenes [values] high on the scale of American institutions and citizen obligations."[68] These pronouncements tell us only that the judicial conscience must be shocked, and that generally there must be some public concern beyond the private interests of the particular employee.

More recent cases have sought, with limited success, to infuse more specificity. The Wisconsin Supreme Court has said that public policy "must be evidenced by a constitutional or statutory provision,"[69] while the New Jersey Supreme Court will recognize legislation; administrative rules, regulations, and decisions; judicial decisions; or a professional code of ethics as creating public policy.[70] In *Palmateer v. International Harvester Co.*,[71] the court said that public policy

> "concerns what is right and just and what affects the citizens of the State collectively. It is to be found in the State's Constitution and statutes and, when they are silent, in its judicial decisions. * * * A matter must strike at the heart of a citizen's social rights, duties and responsibilities before the tort will be allowed."[72]

An attempt to discern the meaning of "public policy" in the context of retaliatory discharge must distinguish between the different situations to which the cause of action has been applied: where the claimed public policy is a duty or obligation of the employee; where it is a right of the employee; and where it is the opposition of the employee to unlawful conduct ("whistleblower" cases), or some similar situation also involving a less direct effect on public policy. Its meaning in a specific context must be constructed out of the results reached in decided cases arising out of similar facts.

Employee Duty as Public Policy

The most compelling kind of public policy is brought to bear where the employee refuses to commit an unlawful act. The terminable-at-will rule, in this situation, is used to coerce the employee to disobey the commands of law laid down by government. Allowing a cause of action reaffirms the fact that the citizen's first loyalty is

---

[66]*Petermann v. Teamsters*, 174 Cal. App.2d 184, 188, 344 P.2d 25, 27 (1959).
[67]*Monge v. Beebe Rubber Co.*, 114 N.H. 130, 133, 316 A.2d 549, 551 (1974).
[68]*Nees v. Hocks*, 272 Ore. 210, 218, 219, 536 P.2d 512, 515, 516 (1975).
[69]*Brockmeyer v. Dun & Bradstreet*, 113 Wis.2d 561, 573, 335 N.W.2d 834, 835 (1983). Accord: *Firestone Textile Co. Div., Firestone Tire & Rubber Co. v. Meadows*, 666 S.W.2d 730, 114 LRRM 3559 (Ky. 1983).
[70]*Pierce v. Ortho Pharmaceutical Corp.*, 84 N.J. 58, 417 A.2d 505 (1980). Accord: *Adler v. American Standard Corp.*, 291 Md. 31, 432 A.2d 464 (1981).
[71]85 Ill.2d 124, 421 N.E.2d 876 (1981).
[72]*Id.* at 130, 421 N.E.2d at 878-879 (1981).

owed not to any private party, but to the rule of law and legitimate regulations adopted by the elected government. In this area, the cases involving professional ethics raise a special concern, for licensed professionals are deemed to have a particular obligation to protect the public interest. A closely related problem arises in the case where discharge interferes with the machinery of government by punishing the performance of a civic obligation, whether or not it is a strict legal duty. In such a case, the employer's economic power under the terminable-at-will rule challenges the ability of the government to perform its basic constitutional functions. Thus, the first category of case includes situations where the employee refuses a direction to violate the prohibitions of the law or to neglect a professional or civic obligation.

Criminal Law and Tort Law as Public Policy

Where state law imposes a legal duty on the employee, and the employee is discharged for refusing to place his loyalty to the employer ahead of his obedience to the law, the case for recognizing the action for retaliatory discharge is strong. This is particularly so where the employee duty is imposed by the criminal law:

> "There is no public policy more basic, nothing more implicit in the concept of ordered liberty [citation omitted], than the enforcement of a State's criminal code. [Citation omitted.] There is no public policy more important or more fundamental than the one favoring the effective protection of the lives and property of citizens."[73]

If a jurisdiction recognizes the action for retaliatory discharge, it must necessarily allow a right of action where an employee is fired for refusing to commit a crime. An employer's insistence on employee participation in criminal conduct turns the employment relationship into a criminal conspiracy. Allowing the right of action is the court's affirmation that "the employer is not so absolute a sovereign of the job that there are not limits to his prerogative."[74] Thus, the general rule is that an action will be allowed where the employee is discharged for refusing to commit a criminal act.

In several states that define the terms of employment by statute, there is a specific provision to the effect that employees need not obey orders to commit unlawful, impossible, or unreasonably burdensome acts.[75] While the statutes are written in the context of defining an employee's contractual obligation and probably only reflect the com-

---

[73]*Id.* at 132, 421 N.E.2d at 879.

[74]*Tameny v. Atlantic Richfield Co.*, 27 Cal.3d 167, 178, 610 P.2d 1330, 1336, 164 Cal. Rptr. 839, 845 (1980) (discharge for refusal to violate antitrust laws actionable).

[75]The states are California, Montana, North Dakota, and South Dakota. References are given in the state-by-state listings in Appendix A at the subject name "Unlawful order." See also ME. REV. STAT. ANN. tit. 26, §833 (Supp. 1983–84) (whistleblower statute prohibiting discharge for refusal to commit unlawful act endangering the health or safety of any person, including employee), reproduced in Appendix B.

mon law, they imply legislative support for the general proposition that employees should not be punished for obeying the law.

None of the cases discusses the issue of the seriousness of the crime, for example, whether refusal to commit a petty offense such as a parking violation comes within the prohibition. In *Palmateer v. International Harvester Co.*,[76] however, the court intimated that the seriousness of the crime was not a proper basis for restricting the action. The question in *Palmateer* centered not upon committing a crime but upon reporting it, and the employer suggested that protection ought not apply to the reporting of minor offenses like petty larceny. In an analysis equally applicable to a case where the employee is told to commit a crime, the court responded that if the General Assembly made a minor or trivial offense criminal, its judgment was conclusive and that the law would be "feeble indeed" if it condoned retaliation in such circumstances.[77]

Tort law, although it overlaps criminal law in many ways, also protects social interests and imposes social duties. In *Delaney v. Taco Time International, Inc.*,[78] the court found a public policy to be implicated where the employee was discharged for refusal to sign a false statement that cast aspersions on the work habits and moral behavior of another employee. After citing provisions of the state's constitution concerning abuse of the right of free speech and the protection of reputations, the court found a public policy in the societal obligation not to defame others.

Discharge for Refusal to Disregard Health and Safety Prohibitions

Much of the government regulation of business concerns itself with protecting the health and safety of consumers and employees. Managerial and professional employees may be put into a difficult position where the employer wishes to circumvent these protections. In *Cloutier v. Great Atlantic & Pacific Tea Co.*,[79] a store manager was discharged when there was a theft of funds from his store on his day off. The manager had previously complained about the danger of taking the money to the bank in a dangerous neighborhood without police protection. Although other employees might have taken the money to the bank, the discharged manager had approved leaving the money in the store safe out of concern for the safety of those employees. The court concluded that the employee had been discharged for his compliance with a public policy of protecting employee safety, a policy expressed and embodied in the federal Occupational Safety and Health Act.

---

[76]85 Ill.2d 124, 421 N.E.2d 876 (1981).
[77]*Id.* at 133, 421 N.E.2d at 880.
[78]681 P.2d 114, 116 LRRM 2168 (Ore. 1984).
[79]121 N.H. 915, 436 A.2d 1140 (1981).

In *O'Sullivan v. Mallon*,[80] the employee, an X-ray technician, was discharged for refusing to perform a procedure that could be performed lawfully only by a physician or licensed nurse. The public has a foremost interest in compliance with proper medical procedures, the court held in allowing an action for retaliatory discharge.

The employee in *Sheets v. Teddy's Frosted Foods, Inc.*,[81] was a quality control director who was subject to criminal prosecution under the state's pure food and drug act if he approved products containing substandard raw materials. The court allowed him to bring a tort action when he was discharged for refusing to pass substandard products.

The state certainly has an interest in protecting employees charged with ensuring compliance with health and safety regulations. The Maine Whistleblowers' Protection Act[82] expressly provides that an employee has a cause of action for retaliatory discharge if he is fired for refusing to commit an unlawful act that endangers the health or safety of himself or others. A different problem is presented, however, when an employee insists on his own right to a safe work place, or "blows the whistle" on an unsafe product. These issues are addressed in the next two main sections (pp. 272–296). A personal legal responsibility on the part of the employee to comply with health and safety rules is what is central to the foregoing decisions.

Discharge for Refusal to Ignore or Violate Trade Regulation

The antitrust laws, which are criminal prohibitions, have served as a basis for retaliatory discharge actions. The employer in *Tameny v. Atlantic Richfield Co.*[83] allegedly coerced an employee to participate in a price-fixing conspiracy prohibited by the Sherman Act, and discharge of the employee for refusing to assist in the scheme gave rise to an action for wrongful discharge. Similarly, in *McNulty v. Borden, Inc.*,[84] the court held that refusal to participate in an allegedly illegal price-fixing scheme could not be the basis of a discharge. *Adler v. American Standard Corp.*,[85] held that general allega-

---

[80]160 N.J. Super. 416, 390 A.2d 149 (1978).

[81]179 Conn. 471, 427 A.2d 385 (1980).

[82]ME. REV. STAT. ANN. tit. 26, §833 (Supp. 1983–84), reproduced in Appendix B.

[83]27 Cal.3d 167, 610 P.2d 1330, 164 Cal. Rptr. 839 (1980). Accord: *Perry v. Hartz Mountain Corp.*, 537 F. Supp. 1387 (S.D. Ind. 1982); *Shaw v. Russell Trucking Line*, 542 F. Supp. 776 (W.D. Pa. 1982). See *Parnar v. Americana Hotels, Inc.*, 65 Hawaii 370, 652 P.2d 625 (1982) (employee discharged to further or conceal antitrust violations). Contra: *Callahan v. Scott Paper Co.*, 541 F. Supp. 550 (E.D. Pa. 1982).

[84]474 F. Supp. 1111 (E.D. Pa. 1979), *subsequent opinion*, 542 F. Supp. 655 (E.D. Pa. 1982).

[85]291 Md. 31, 432 A.2d 464 (1981). The case originated in federal court, and was certified to the Maryland Court of Appeals for resolution of questions of state law. The court held that Maryland recognized the action for retaliatory discharge, but that the employee's allegations were too general and conclusory to give rise to a cause of action. On remand to the federal court, however, the employee was able to plead a sufficient claim, *Adler v. American Standard Corp.*, 538 F. Supp. 572 (D. Md. 1982). But in *Martin v. Platt*, 179 Ind. App. 688, 386 N.E.2d 1026 (1979), and *Percival v. General Motors Corp.*, 400 F. Supp. 1322 (E.D. Mo. 1975), similar allegations concerning similar statutes were not sufficient to justify recognition of retaliatory discharge actions.

tions of commercial bribery and falsification of corporate records could not support a cause of action, but that alleged violation of specific federal trade regulations and tax laws raised public policy concerns. Misuse of government funds by a private employer raised a public policy question in *Vigil v. Arzola & Tierra Del Sol Housing Corp.*[86]

Professional Ethics as a Source for Public Policy

A special problem is created where an employee practicing a state-licensed occupation or profession is discharged for insistence on complying with the recognized ethical, legal, or professional standards of his calling. Unless the jurisdiction approves the use of economic compulsion to subvert the protection of the public provided by its program of licensing trades and professions, it must recognize a right of action.[87]

The problem exists with respect not only to medical, legal, and accounting professionals, but also to licensed electricians, insurance agents, real estate brokers, engineers, and a host of other trades, skills, businesses, and professions. Relatively few cases have faced the professional ethics issue, but those that have have demonstrated the importance of protecting the employee faced with a choice of breaching recognized professional standards or being discharged for insubordination.

In *Pierce v. Ortho Pharmaceutical Corp.*,[88] the court recognized that professional employees "owe a special duty to abide not only by federal and state law, but also by the recognized codes of ethics of their professions."[89] *Pierce* also acknowledged that this special duty may require an employee to decline to follow his employer's directions. However, the professional standard must be identifiable and explicit. In *Pierce*, the employee's judgment about a professional matter was simply at odds with that of her supervisor, who was also a physician. The employee's general invocation of professional obligations under such circumstances will not permit the overturning of employer discretion. The professional must point to a specific standard or ethical duty, not a broad statement of principle, to support a claim premised upon public policy.

In *Lampe v. Presbyterian Medical Center*,[90] a head nurse refused to comply with a directive to reduce the amount of overtime in her unit. She claimed that compliance with the order would be inconsis-

---

[86]22 N.M. ST. B. BULL. 868 (App. 1983). In *Gil v. Metal Serv. Corp.*, 412 So.2d 706 (La. App. 1982), the court denied a cause of action under unfair trade practice and consumer protection laws to an employee who was discharged for refusing to remove foreign identification marks from steel being delivered to buyers who had ordered domestic steel.

[87]For a general discussion of this topic see Note, *A Remedy for the Discharge of Professional Employees Who Refuse to Perform Unethical or Illegal Acts: A Proposal in Aid of Professional Ethics*, 28 VAND. L. REV. 805 (1975).

[88]84 N.J. 58, 417 A.2d 505 (1980).

[89]*Id.* at 71, 417 A.2d at 512. Contra: *Suchodolski v. Michigan Consol. Gas Co.*, 412 Mich. 692, 316 N.W.2d 710 (1982) (code of ethics of internal auditors not public policy).

[90]41 Colo. App. 465, 590 P.2d 513 (1978).

tent with the health and safety of persons under her care. The court held that the nurse's general reference to professional standards did not justify a conclusion that the discharge was in derogation of public policy. The nurse was discharged for her disagreement and insubordination regarding a managerial decision, not a decision concerning treatment that is particularly within the professional skill of a nurse. Hospital licensure statutes place control of managerial decisions affecting patient care, including staffing decisions, in the hands of the hospital governing board, not its employees. The nurse and the hospital simply differed upon a matter of managerial judgment that under hospital licensing laws was exclusively within the discretion of the hospital. It would have been a different case if the nurse had been ordered to inject the patient with a drug or to perform a nursing procedure in a manner inconsistent with a specific standard.[91]

Witt v. Forest Hospital, Inc.[92] protected a nurse who fulfilled her professional duty to report her employer's violation of the rights of mentally ill and disabled persons. A state statute cited in *Witt* specifically prohibited reprisals against employees who made such reports in good faith.

Professional obligations have been recognized outside the organized professions. In *Sheets v. Teddy's Frosted Foods, Inc.*,[93] the court extended protection to an inspector performing duties under a state pure food and drug act. *Geary v. United States Steel Corp.*[94] suggested that a retaliatory discharge action by an employee who complained about product safety might be recognized if it was the employee's duty to make judgments concerning product safety. In *Geary*, the complaining employee was a salesman. Although the complaint alleged that the salesman's opinion about the safety of a product had merit and was ultimately vindicated, the court relied partly on his lack of expertise in denying a cause of action.

Employee Civic Duties

Democracy requires citizen participation. Discharge to punish an employee's performance of a civic duty is a direct threat to self-government. The action for retaliatory discharge has been recognized as a protection for the employee who must choose between a civic obligation and the employer's wishes.

---

[91]*O'Sullivan v. Mallon*, 160 N.J. Super. 416, 390 A.2d 149 (1978) (technician improperly discharged for refusing to perform procedure in violation of law).

[92]115 Ill. App.3d 481, 450 N.E.2d 811 (1983). The court in *Maus v. National Living Centers, Inc.*, 633 S.W.2d 674 (Tex. Civ. App. 1982), recognized the legal duty of a nurse to report her employer's abuse and neglect of patients, but declined to recognize a cause of action because doing so would exceed its authority as an intermediate appellate court.

[93]179 Conn. 471, 427 A.2d 385 (1980). Accord: *Trombetta v. Detroit, Toledo & Ironton R.R.*, 81 Mich. App. 489, 265 N.W.2d 385 (1978) (employee refusal to falsify pollution control reports to state agency).

[94]456 Pa. 171, 319 A.2d 174 (1974).

Witnesses and Refusal to Commit Perjury

Petermann v. Teamsters[95] held that an employee may recover in an action for retaliatory discharge where the discharge was for refusal to commit perjury. In so concluding, the court cited the specific criminal prohibition and its tendency to interfere with the proper administration of justice. In *Petermann*, the testimony was before a legislative hearing. In *Reuther v. Fowler & Williams, Inc.*,[96] a jury service case, the court relied in part on the employer's direction to the employee to evade jury duty by falsely telling the court he had read about the case in the newspaper.

A number of state statutes protect the employment of witnesses who testify or who are about to testify in legal proceedings.[97] The protection of these statutes is not dependent on an employer request to commit perjury. The court in *Brockmeyer v. Dun & Bradstreet*[98] was unwilling to recognize such a public policy under the common law, refusing to find a cause of action where the employee was fired because he was about to testify truthfully. Anticipating this type of problem, the federal witness protection statutes[99] also generally provide protection to employees who are "about to testify" in specified proceedings.

Jury Service

Employees called upon to serve as grand and petit jurors are protected against discharge for such service. An express action is available to employees who serve on federal juries,[100] and most states

---

[95]*Petermann v. Teamsters*, 174 Cal. App.2d 184, 344 P.2d 25 (1959). Contra: *Ivy v. Army Times Publishing Co.*, 428 A.2d 831 (D.C. 1981) (holding retaliatory discharge not recognized in District of Columbia); *Phillips v. Goodyear Tire & Rubber Co.*, 651 F.2d 1051 (5th Cir. 1981) (holding retaliatory discharge not recognized in Georgia and Texas).

[96]255 Pa. Super 28, 386 A.2d 119 (1978).

[97]*General Witness Protection Statutes*: States having statutes are Arkansas, California, Connecticut, Hawaii, Illinois, Kentucky, Louisiana, Nevada, Oregon, and Vermont. See Appendix A at the subject name "Witnesses—general."

Occupational Safety Witness Protection Statutes: Alaska, Arizona, California, Connecticut, Hawaii, Indiana, Iowa, Kansas, Kentucky, Maine, Maryland, Michigan, Minnesota, Nevada, New Mexico, New York, North Carolina, Oregon, Rhode Island, South Carolina, Tennessee, Utah, Vermont, Virginia, Washington, Wisconsin, and Wyoming. See Appendix A at the subject name "Safety in the work place—complaint, testimony."

Labor and Wage Regulation Witness Protection Statutes: Alaska, California, Colorado, Idaho, Iowa, Kansas, Louisiana, Massachusetts, Minnesota, Nevada, New Jersey, New York, North Dakota, Ohio, Oregon, South Dakota, Utah, and Washington. See Appendix A at the subject name "Wage & hour—complaint, testimony."

[98]113 Wis.2d 561, 335 N.W.2d 834 (1983).

[99]*Labor Law Enforcement Testimony*: Coal Mine Health & Safety Act, Employee Retirement Income Security Act, Equal Employment Opportunity Act, Fair Labor Standards Act, Longshoremen's & Harbor Workers' Compensation Act, National Labor Relations Act, Occupational Safety & Health Act, Railroad Safety Authorization Act. See Appendix A for references.

Environmental Law Enforcement Testimony: Clean Air Act, Energy Reorganization Act (Nuclear Regulatory Commission), Hazardous Substance Release Act (Superfund), Safe Drinking Water Act, Solid Waste Disposal Act, Surface Mining Control & Reclamation Act, Toxic Substances Control Act, Water Pollution Prevention & Control Act. See Appendix A for references.

[100]28 U.S.C. §1875 (Supp. V 1981).

have statutes protecting the employment of jurors.[101] The leading common law case is *Nees v. Hocks*,[102] where the court cited the state constitutional provision for trial by jury, the criminal fine imposed for neglect of service, and the availability of contempt sanctions against employers who discharge for employee performance of jury service. The court concluded:

> "These actions by the people, the legislature and the courts clearly indicate that the jury system and jury duty are regarded as high on the scale of American institutions and citizen obligations. If an employer were permitted with impunity to discharge an employee for fulfilling her obligation of jury duty, the jury system would be adversely affected. The will of the community would be thwarted."[103]

Nees was followed in *Reuther v. Fowler & Williams, Inc.*,[104] which relied upon the state constitutional provision affording an accused a right to jury trial in finding the need to have citizens freely available for jury service.

The Electoral Process

The three cases to date on employee participation in elections were all based on special statutory prohibitions on employers, and two of them predate the development of retaliatory discharge as an independent tort. Many jurisdictions have statutes providing for time off to vote,[105] prohibiting employer coercion or influence of employee voting,[106] and protecting the right of employees to run for public office.[107]

Bell v. Faulkner[108] denied a private right of action under a statute punishing employer attempts to influence elections and voting. In

---

[101]Alabama, Arizona, Arkansas, California, Colorado, Connecticut, Florida, Hawaii, Idaho, Illinois, Indiana, Kentucky, Louisiana, Maine, Maryland, Massachusetts, Michigan, Minnesota, Mississippi, Nebraska, New Hampshire, New Jersey, New Mexico, New York, North Dakota, Ohio, Oklahoma, Oregon, Pennsylvania, Rhode Island, South Dakota, Tennessee, Utah, Vermont, Virginia, West Virginia, Wisconsin, and Wyoming. See Appendix A at the subject name "Jury service."

The Alabama Supreme Court rejected a suit arising out of alleged discharge for jury service under the 1975 version of that state's statute in *Bender Ship Repair, Inc. v. Stevens*, 379 So.2d 594 (Ala. 1980), but has recognized the availability of an action under the statute as amended, *Meredith v. C.E. Walther, Inc.*, 422 So.2d 761 (Ala. 1982).

[102]272 Ore. 210, 536 P.2d 512 (1975).

[103]*Id.* at 219, 536 P.2d at 516.

[104]255 Pa. Super. 28, 386 A.2d 119 (1978).

[105]Alaska, Arkansas, California, Colorado, Georgia, Hawaii, Illinois, Indiana, Iowa, Kansas, Kentucky, Maryland, Massachusetts, Minnesota, Missouri, Nebraska, Nevada, New Mexico, New York, Ohio, Oklahoma, South Dakota, Tennessee, Texas, Utah, West Virginia, Wisconsin, and Wyoming. See Appendix A at the subject name "Voting—time off."

[106]Alabama, Arizona, Arkansas, Colorado, Connecticut, Delaware, District of Columbia, Florida, Indiana, Iowa, Kentucky, Louisiana, Massachusetts, Minnesota, Mississippi, Missouri, Montana, Nebraska, Nevada, New Jersey, New Mexico, New York, Ohio, Rhode Island, Tennessee, Vermont, Wisconsin, and Wyoming. See Appendix A at the subject name "Voting—intimidation."

[107]California, Colorado, Connecticut, Louisiana, Mississippi, Missouri, Nebraska, and Nevada. See Appendix A at the subject name "Politics."

[108]75 S.W.2d 612 (Mo. App. 1934).

Kouff v. Bethlehem Alameda Shipyard, Inc.,[109] a statute prohibiting discharge of employees acting as election judges was applied and characterized as creating an exception to the terminable-at-will rule. More recently, *Davis v. Louisiana Computing Corp.*,[110] allowed an action for damages under a statute protecting employees who wish to participate in politics or become candidates for office.

The *Davis* case illustrates the problems an employer may face in such cases. Compliance with the statute in that case would have required the employer to risk the loss of substantial business, since its employee was apparently challenging an incumbent local government with which the employer did much of its business. How the balance between the duty of loyalty to the employer and the citizen's civic obligation and civil right to participate in electoral and political affairs will be struck in nonstatutory cases is unclear. The courts might follow *Davis* and protect the electoral process vigorously, or tilt in favor of the employer's right to preserve its business.

Military Service

Federal law requires that employees who leave their jobs to join the armed forces be provided reemployment with full seniority upon satisfactory completion of their duty.[111] It also protects the employment of reservists on active duty or in training exercises.[112] A number of state statutes require time off for training, create reemployment rights, and prohibit discrimination against members of the National Guard and, in some cases, reservists.[113] New Jersey prohibits discrimination on the basis of draft eligibility,[114] and Illinois prohibits discrimination on the basis of unfavorable discharge from the military service.[115]

Employee Legal Right as Public Policy

A second and entirely different situation exists when a legal right of the employee, usually involving some aspect of the employer–employee relationship, is the subject of a public policy. When the employee must choose between asserting the right and keeping his

---

[109]90 Cal. App.2d 322, 202 P.2d 1059 (1949). See also *Lockheed Aircraft Corp. v. Superior Court*, 28 Cal.2d 481, 171 P.2d 21 (1946).

[110]394 So.2d 678 (La. App. 1981).

[111]38 U.S.C. §§2021, 2024 (1976 & Supp. V 1981).

[112]38 U.S.C. §2024 (1976 & Supp. V 1981).

[113]States having such statutes are Arizona, Arkansas, California, Colorado, Connecticut, Delaware, Florida, Hawaii, Idaho, Illinois, Indiana, Kansas, Kentucky, Louisiana, Maine, Massachusetts, Michigan, Minnesota, Mississippi, Missouri, Montana, Nebraska, Nevada, New Hampshire, New Jersey, New Mexico, New York, North Carolina, North Dakota, Oklahoma, Oregon, Pennsylvania, Rhode Island, South Carolina, South Dakota, Tennessee, Texas, Vermont, Virginia, Washington, West Virginia, Wisconsin, and Wyoming. See Appendix A at the subject name "Military service."

[114]N.J. STAT. ANN. §§10:5-5(Q), 10:5-12 (West Supp. 1983–84).

[115]ILL. REV. STAT. ch. 68, §§1-103(Q), 2-102(A) (1981).

job, he will be restrained from asserting any right less valuable to him than the job itself. Thus, if employment can be terminated for the exercise of an employee right, the employer would be able to nullify most employee rights by the use of economic power.

If an employee discharged for exercising a legal right is allowed to pursue an action for retaliatory discharge, on the other hand, the court protects the right in the most meaningful way. Unless that protection is provided, the employee must risk his job to exercise the right. The public interest in these cases is simply the protection of employee rights. The earliest and most prominent cases in this area were brought by employees fired for seeking workers' compensation for on-the-job injuries. More recently, decisions involving numerous other employee rights have been rendered. Legislative activity in this field is as old as the National Labor Relations Act, but has spread in recent years into many new areas. New York, which has refused to recognize retaliatory discharge as a common law cause of action,[116] has adopted a statute providing a cause of action for employees discharged for the exercise of any right under that state's labor code.[117]

Employee's Political Beliefs and Free Expression

Public employees are protected by the First Amendment against reprisals for exercise of the right of free expression. *Novosel v. Nationwide Insurance Co.*[118] is the first common law decision finding a public policy in the private employee's First Amendment right to freedom of expression. The discharged employee had refused to participate in the employer's program intended to generate public support for the adoption of no-fault reform by the state legislature. In allowing a cause of action, the court relied upon the federal and state constitutions and upon judicial recognition of political expression as the "core" of the First Amendment. In finding that "the protection of an employee's freedom of political expression would appear to involve no less compelling a societal interest than the fulfillment of jury service,"[119] the court observed that employer economic power, left unregulated, could lead to corporate control of the political process. Rejecting an argument that the First Amendment protects individuals only against governmental action, the court found that the source of the threat to political freedom was irrelevant in view of the newly developed public policy doctrine.

Novosel suggests that the well-developed body of law protecting public employees from reprisal for the exercise of First Amendment rights applies equally to private employment. Given the special position freedom of speech occupies in American society and law, this

---

[116]*Murphy v. American Home Prods. Corp.*, 58 N.Y.2d 293, 448 N.E.2d 86, 461 N.Y.S.2d 232 (1983).
[117]N.Y.Lab. Law §§1, 215 (Consol. 1983).
[118]721 F.2d 894 (3rd Cir. 1983).
[119]*Id.* at 899.

is a distinct possibility. *Novosel* itself, however, addresses the narrower question of political speech, and other established limitations upon free speech would still apply in any event.[120] It could well be the first in a line of cases limiting the power private employers may exercise over employee freedom of expression.[121]

Several jurisdictions have statutes protecting the right of employees to hold political views and engage in political activity.[122] Other statutes protect employees who run for or hold elective office,[123] with some states providing leave of absence rights to employees who are elected to public office.[124]

Employee's Financial Situation

As the cases on interference with contract discussed in Chapter 7 show, garnishment of an employee's wages can cause an employer to discharge the employee. A similar reaction can result from the filing of bankruptcy proceedings. Under the Bankruptcy Code, a public employer cannot discharge an employee for seeking the protection of the bankruptcy laws.[125] While the prohibition is premised on case law establishing the obligation of state and local government not to interfere with federal bankruptcy rights, Congress left the door open to broader remedies:

> "The section is not exhaustive. * * * This section permits further development to prohibit actions by governmental or quasi-governmental organizations that perform licensing functions, such as a State bar association or a medical society, or by other organizations that can seriously affect a debtor's livelihood or fresh start, such as exclusion

---

[120]E.g, the court in *Harman v. LaCross Tribune*, 344 N.W.2d 536, 115 LRRM 3252 (Wis. Ct. App. 1984), denied an employee-lawyer's cause of action because his public attacks on a client of his law firm were properly proscribed by the Code of Professional Responsibility.

[121]*Redgrave v. Boston Symphony Orchestra, Inc.*, 557 F. Supp. 230 (D. Mass. 1983), refused to allow a cause of action where the orchestra allegedly cancelled a contract for narration of concerts because of the narrator's publicly stated political views. In *Redgrave*, however, the issue was limited to the availability of extracontractual damages; a breach of contract was assumed and the issue was the availability of tort damages. The court relied on the limited duration of the repudiated engagement to conclude that only contractual damages were available, and did not address the question of free speech as a public policy employee right.

The sole federal statute in this area, the Asbestos School Hazard Detection & Control Act, 20 U.S.C. §3608 (Supp. V 1980), protects employees of state and local educational agencies who bring asbestos problems in school buildings to public attention. The statute's protection is limited, however, to agencies funded or assisted by the Act. It is unusual among the federal statutes in that it protects publicizing rather than reporting to a government agency. The "opposition" to discrimination protection of federal and state antidiscrimination laws also protects public appeals if they are reasonable. See Note, *Protection From Employer Retaliation: A Suggested Analysis for Section 704(a)*, 65 VA. L. REV. 1155 (1979). It has also been held that the OSHA antiretaliation law, 29 U.S.C. §660(c) (1976), and interpretative regulations thereunder may protect communications with the media. *Donovan v. R.D. Anderson Constr. Co.*, 552 F. Supp. 249 (D. Kan. 1982).

[122]California, Colorado, District of Columbia, Louisiana, Minnesota, Mississippi, Missouri, and Nevada. See Appendix A at the subject name "Politics."

[123]California, Colorado, Connecticut, Louisiana, Mississippi, Missouri, Nebraska, and Nevada. See Appendix A at the subject name "Politics."

[124]Connecticut, Indiana, Maine, Minnesota, Nevada, Vermont, and West Virginia. See Appendix A at the subject name "Politics."

[125]11 U.S.C. §525 (1982); *In re Latchaw*, 24 Bankr. 457 (N.D. Ohio 1982). Hawaii has a statute applicable to private employees, HAWAII REV. STAT. §378-32(i) (Supp. 1982); and Kansas protects public employees under KAN. STAT. ANN. §75-4316 (1977).

from a union on the basis of [a bankruptcy] discharge of a debt to the union's credit union."[126]

To date no decisions have considered this language or the applicability of the statute to a private employer. *In re Terry*[127] spoke of an inherent power in the court to restrain discharge for filing bankruptcy proceedings, but other cases have refused to allow an action.[128] Where the outcome of a bankruptcy proceeding is a wage-earner plan, relief might be available under statutes prohibiting discharge for garnishment if the plan requires the employer to withhold wages.[129]

Federal law[130] and statutes in over half the states[131] prohibit discharge for garnishment. Some prohibitions apply only to a single debt and others to a limited number; still others are unlimited. Violation of the federal statute does not give rise to an implied private right of action,[132] but some of the state statutes expressly provide civil remedies.

Employee Privacy

Chapter 7 outlines the development of employee privacy rights in depth and notes the applicable statutes. Retaliatory discharge actions may be a vehicle for enforcement of statutory protections of employee privacy.[133] Several cases have provided common law protections. In *Monge v. Beebe Rubber Co.*[134] an action was allowed where the employee, a married woman, was discharged for her refusal to romance the boss. This is consistent with the legal recognition of the

---

[126]S. Rep. No. 989, 95th Cong., 2d Sess. 21, 81, reprinted in 1978 U.S. Code Cong. & Ad. News 5807, 5867.

[127]7 Bankr. L. Rep. 800 (E.D. Va. 1980).

[128]*McLellan v. Mississippi Power & Light Co.*, 545 F.2d 919 (5th Cir. 1977).

[129]*In re Jackson*, 424 F.2d 1220 (7th Cir. 1970), rejected an action on this basis, but the court relied upon the collective bargaining relationship to deny the action.

[130]Consumer Credit Protection Act, 15 U.S.C. §1674(a) (1982).

[131]California, Colorado, Connecticut, Delaware, District of Columbia, Georgia, Hawaii, Idaho, Illinois, Indiana, Iowa, Kansas, Kentucky, Louisiana, Maine, Michigan, Minnesota, Missouri, Montana, Nebraska, New Jersey, New York, North Dakota, Ohio, Oklahoma, Oregon, Utah, Vermont, Virginia, Washington, and Wisconsin. See Appendix A at the subject name "Garnishment."

[132]*Smith v. Cotton Bros. Baking Co.*, 609 F.2d 738 (5th Cir. 1980); *McCabe v. City of Eureka*, 664 F.2d 680 (8th Cir. 1981); *LeVick v. Skaggs Cos.*, 701 F.2d 777 (9th Cir. 1983), *overruling Stewart v. Traveler's Corp.*, 503 F.2d 108 (9th Cir. 1974); *Western v. Hodgson*, 359 F. Supp. 194 (W.D. La. 1973); *Simpson v. Sperry Rand Corp.*, 350 F. Supp. 1057 (W.D. La. 1972). Contra: *Nunn v. City of Paducah*, 367 F. Supp. 957 (W.D. Ky. 1973); *Maple v. Citizens Nat'l Bank & Trust Co.*, 437 F. Supp. 66 (W.D. Okla 1977).

[133]*Perks v. Firestone Tire and Rubber Co.*, 611 F.2d 1363 (3d Cir. 1979) (enforcing antipolygraph statute); *Polsky v. Radio Shack*, 666 F.2d 824 (3d Cir. 1981) (enforcing antipolygraph statute); *Molush v. Orkin Exterminating Co.*, 547 F. Supp. 54 (E.D. Pa. 1982) (enforcing antipolygraph statute). West Virginia recently held that requiring employees to submit to polygraph examinations violated public policy even before the legislature acted to prohibit such requirements, *Cordle v. General Hugh Mercer Corp.*, 116 LRRM 3447 (1984). Contra, *Larsen v. Motor Supply Co.*, 117 Ariz. 507, 573 P.2d 907 (App. 1977) (no retaliatory discharge action where state did not forbid use of voice-stress analyzer); see also *Smith v. American Cast Iron Pipe Co.*, 370 So.2d 283 (Ala. 1979).

[134]114 N.H. 130, 316 A.2d 549 (1974); see also *Phillips v. Smalley Maintenance Services, Inc.*, 711 F.2d 1524 (11th Cir. 1983) (invasion of privacy theory); but see *Wolk v. Saks Fifth Avenue*, 115 LRRM 3057 (W.D. Pa. 1983) (violation of public policy in sexual harassment discharge case not actionable under common law because sex discrimination remedies available).

institution of marriage and the right of privacy in personal decisions concerning sexual relations as fundamental individual rights.[135]

In *Cort v. Bristol-Myers Co.*[136] the court indicated that discharge for refusal to comply with a request for information that was an unreasonable, substantial, or serious interference with privacy would warrant liability.[137] In *Moore v. Honeywell Information Systems*,[138] however, the court found no public policy violation where an employee was discharged because her husband had formed a competing company and refused to give it up.

Bianco v. American Broadcasting Companies[139] held that the federal prohibitions on electronic eavesdropping could apply to employer electronic eavesdropping on employee conversations in which there was a reasonable expectation of privacy. Connecticut has a statute to this effect.[140] General state laws on wiretapping and surreptitious recording of conversations should also be consulted where electronic eavesdropping plays a part in discharge.

Employee Arrest or Criminal Record

In *Hunter v. Port Authority*,[141] the employee was a convicted criminal who had been pardoned, and the court found that public policy precluded his automatic disqualification from public employment. In Iowa, an employer is prohibited from discharging an employee for taking time off to attend classes for persons found guilty of driving while intoxicated.[142] A number of states prohibit employer reliance on arrest records in making employment decisions or employer inquiries into arrest records.[143] These statutes are premised in part on the fact that reliance on arrest records invariably leads to racial discrimination. In

---

[135]See *Griswold v. Connecticut*, 381 U.S. 479 (1965); *Eisenstadt v. Baird*, 405 U.S. 438 (1972).

[136]385 Mass. 300, 431 N.E.2d 908 (1982). The plaintiffs were sales representatives discharged for their refusal to answer questions relating to medical history and future plans, as well as self-evaluation of qualifications, job performance, and day-to-day activity at work. The employees objected that the questions could be used in a psychological evaluation program, but the court reversed a trial verdict in their favor.

[137]In *Geary v. United States Steel Corp.*, 456 Pa. 171, 184, 319 A.2d 174, 180 (1974), the court, in denying a cause of action in a whistleblower case, commented:

"It may be granted that there are areas of an employee's life in which his employer has no legitimate interest. An intrustion into one of these areas by virtue of the employer's power of discharge might plausibly give rise to a cause of action, particularly where some recognized facet of public policy is threatened."

[138]558 F. Supp. 1229 (D. Hawaii 1983). See also *Ward v. Frito-Lay, Inc.*, 95 Wis. 2d 372, 290 N.W.2d 536 (1980) (permitting discharge of unmarried cohabiting employees in plant prohibiting employment of relatives working on same shift). Oregon prohibits absolute antinepotism rules, ORE. REV. STAT. §659.340 (1981).

[139]470 F. Supp. 182, 185 (N.D. Ill. 1979).

[140]CONN. GEN. STAT. ANN. §31-48(b) (West 1972 & Supp. 1983–84). See also N.Y. LAB. LAW §704(1) (Consol. 1983) (eavesdropping on union activity).

[141]277 Pa. Super. 4, 419 A.2d 631 (1980). The decision relied upon a statute, PA. STAT. ANN. tit. 18, §9125 (1979), precluding reliance on irrelevant arrests and misdemeanor convictions, and on the established rule that a pardon extinguishes the crime.

[142]IOWA CODE ANN. §321.283 (West 1966 & Supp. 1983–84).

[143]California, Connecticut, Hawaii, Illinois, Michigan, New York, Oregon, Virginia, West Virginia, and Wisconsin. See Appendix A at the subject name "Arrest Record."

Salanger v. U.S. Air,[144] the employee, relying on New York's statute, brought an action following dismissal of criminal charges against her after her arrest for an alleged misappropriation of company funds. The court held that if her termination was motivated by the arrest, she would have a good action under the New York statute.

In *Cisco v. United Parcel Services, Inc.*,[145] a situation much like that of *Salanger*, a Pennsylvania court reached the opposite result:

> "U.P.S. was not examining a cold rap sheet of a job applicant. This case involves an arrest arising from [the employee's] performance of his extant duties * * * [and] gives rise to an inference that the reputation and business activity of U.P.S. were jeopardized by a mere arrest, even one which ultimately resulted in an acquittal. While the full panoply of rights incident to a criminal defendant were entitlements of [the employee] in his trial experience, including the right to be presumed innocent until proven guilty * * * they [cannot] be superimposed into an accused's remaining life experiences. Thus, marriages crumble even when one is adjudged guilty even without being considered innocent and jobs are lost when the employer, for a legitimate business reason, cannot risk even someone under suspicion of having committed theft * * * "

Religious and Moral Rights of Health Care Professionals

Congress has adopted statutory protection of the personal religious and moral standards of health care professionals with respect to sterilization, abortion, and research activity.[146] The statute prohibits discrimination in employment and in staff privileges against those who have performed or assisted in such operations or activity, and also forbids discrimination against those who have refused to participate. The statute is limited, however, to recipients of federal public health financial assistance. Most states also have statutes protecting health care professionals who refuse—and, in some instances, also those who are willing—to participate in abortions.[147] In many instances these statutes require the employee to serve a written statement of objection on the employer in advance.

Discrimination Laws

Federal[148] and state[149] civil rights statutes prohibit discrimination based on race, color, national origin or ancestry, religion or

---

[144]560 F. Supp. 202 (N.D.N.Y. 1983).

[145]116 LRRM 2514, 2517 (Pa. Super. 1984).

[146]42 U.S.C. §300a-7(b)(1) (Supp. V 1981).

[147]Arizona, Arkansas, California, Colorado, Delaware, Florida, Georgia, Idaho, Illinois, Indiana, Iowa, Kansas, Kentucky, Louisiana, Maine, Maryland, Massachusetts, Michigan, Minnesota, Missouri, Montana, Nebraska, New Jersey, New York, North Carolina, North Dakota, Ohio, Oklahoma, Oregon, Pennsylvania, Rhode Island, South Carolina, South Dakota, Tennessee, Texas, Utah, Virginia, Washington, Wisconsin, and Wyoming. See Appendix A at the subject name "Abortion."

[148]42 U.S.C. §2000e-2(a)(1) (1976 & Supp. V 1981) (Equal Employment Opportunity Act); 42 U.S.C. §1981 (1976) (1866–1871 Civil Rights Act). See Appendix A.

[149]With the exception of Alabama, Georgia, Louisiana, and Mississippi, all states have statutes addressing some or all of these issues. Complete references are given in Appendix A at the subject name "Discrimination." Also, Florida, Louisiana, North Carolina, and New Jersey have statutes addressing discrimination based on sickle cell trait or atypical blood trait (see Appendix A).

creed, and sex. Discrimination on the basis of age is also prohibited by federal law[150] and by statute in most states.[151]

Many jurisdictions prohibit discrimination based on handicap or disability,[152] pregnancy,[153] and marital status.[154] Some state statutes extend the protected attributes to include personal appearance,[155] sexual orientation, student status, and family responsibilities,[156] and receipt of public assistance.[157] These antidiscrimination statutes generally prohibit discharge for opposing unlawful discrimination, filing charges against the employer, testifying in proceedings, and participating in or assisting enforcement.[158] Equal Employment Opportunity Commission (EEOC) regulations[159] forbid sexual harassment,

---

[150]Age Discrimination in Employment Act, 29 U.S.C. §623(a)(1) (1982); Fair Labor Standards Act, 29 U.S.C. §215(a)(3) (1982). See Appendix A.

[151]Alaska, Arizona, California, Colorado, Connecticut, Delaware, District of Columbia, Florida, Georgia, Hawaii, Idaho, Illinois, Indiana, Iowa, Kentucky, Louisiana, Maine, Maryland, Massachusetts, Michigan, Minnesota, Montana, Nebraska, Nevada, New Hampshire, New Jersey, New Mexico, New York, North Carolina, North Dakota, Ohio, Oregon, Pennsylvania, Rhode Island, South Carolina, Tennessee, Texas, Utah, Vermont, Washington, West Virginia, and Wisconsin. See Appendix A at the subject name "Discrimination-age."

[152]29 U.S.C. §793 (1976 & Supp. V 1981) (Rehabilitation Act); 30 U.S.C. §938(a) (1976) (Black Lung Benefits Act). See Appendix A. States having statutes are Alaska, Arizona, California, Colorado, Connecticut, District of Columbia, Florida, Georgia, Hawaii, Illinois, Iowa, Kansas, Kentucky, Louisiana, Maine, Maryland, Massachusetts, Michigan, Minnesota, Missouri, Montana, Nebraska, Nevada, New Hampshire, New Jersey, New Mexico, New York, North Carolina, North Dakota, Ohio, Oklahoma, Oregon, Pennsylvania, Rhode Island, Tennessee, Texas, Utah, Vermont, Washington, West Virginia, and Wisconsin. See Appendix A at the subject name "Discrimination-handicap disability."

[153]42 U.S.C. §§2000e(k), 2000e-2(a)(1) (1976 & Supp. V 1981). See Appendix A. States having statutes are Alaska, California, Connecticut, District of Columbia, Hawaii, Maine, Maryland, Massachusetts, Michigan, Minnesota, Montana, North Dakota, Ohio, Oregon, South Carolina, Texas, and Wisconsin. See Appendix A at the subject name "Discrimination—pregnancy."

The state statutes generally define sex discrimination to include pregnancy discrimination; the federal law was a direct response to what Congress viewed as an overly restrictive view of sex discrimination in the courts which excluded pregnancy discrimination. State regulations may define sex discrimination to include pregnancy discrimination where the statute does not address the issue directly.

[154]Alaska, California, Connecticut, District of Columbia, Florida, Hawaii, Illinois, Maryland, Michigan, Minnesota, Montana, Nebraska, New Hampshire, New Jersey, New York, North Dakota, Oregon, Washington, and Wisconsin. See Appendix A at the subject name "Discrimination-marital status."

[155] District of Columbia, Michigan, and Wisconsin. See Appendix A at the subject name "Discrimination."

[156]District of Columbia, Oregon, and Wisconsin. See Appendix A at the subject name "Discrimination."

[157]Minnesota and North Dakota. See Appendix A at the subject name "Discrimination."

[158]42 U.S.C. §2000e-3(a) (1983) (Equal Employment Opportunity Act); 29 U.S.C. §215(a)(3) (1982) (Fair Labor Standards Act). See Appendix A. States having statutes are Alaska, Arizona, California, Connecticut, District of Columbia, Florida, Georgia, Hawaii, Illinois, Indiana, Iowa, Kansas, Kentucky, Louisiana, Maine, Maryland, Massachusetts, Michigan, Minnesota, Missouri, Montana, Nebraska, Nevada, New Hampshire, New Jersey, New Mexico, New York, North Dakota, Ohio, Oklahoma, Oregon, Pennsylvania, Rhode Island, South Carolina, South Dakota, Tennessee, Texas, Vermont, Washington, West Virginia, and Wisconsin. See Appendix A at the subject name "Discrimination—retaliation."

[159]29 C.F.R. §1604.11 (1982):

"(a) * * * Unwelcome sexual advances, requests for sexual favors, and other verbal or physical conduct of a sexual nature constitute sexual harassment when (1) submission to such conduct is made either explicitly or implicitly a term or condition of an individual's employment, (2) submission to or rejection of such conduct by an individual is used as the basis for employment decisions affecting such individual, and (3) such conduct has the purpose or effect of unreasonably interfering with an individual's work performance or creating an intimidating, hostile or offensive working environment.
* * *."

a form of sex discrimination that includes but is not limited to physical molesting and employer demands for sexual favors. Several states expressly forbid sexual harassment by statute,[160] while in other states enforcement agencies have adopted regulations patterned after those of the EEOC. The classic case of this type of civil wrong was presented and made the basis of common law retaliatory discharge relief in *Monge v. Beebe Rubber Co.*[161] Mississippi, which has refused to recognize an action for retaliatory discharge,[162] has a statutory prohibition, as yet never the subject of any reported decision, authorizing an employee suit for damages resulting from a corporate employer's interference with "social, civil or political rights."[163]

The discrimination laws protect the fundamental civil right of all individuals to employment free from invidious discrimination. They almost invariably provide express administrative remedies or civil rights of action, or both. These statutes have produced a body of law with its own peculiar conventions and doctrines. The most comprehensive treatment of this body of law may be found in Schlei and Grossman's *Employment Discrimination Law.*[164]

Employee Rights Under Labor Laws

The National Labor Relations Act (NLRA)[165] and the Railway Labor Act (RLA)[166] regulate the relationship between management and labor organizations. Both statutes provide for the protection of nonsupervisory employees against employer reprisal for employee

---

"(c) * * * [An employer] is responsible for its acts and those of its agents and supervisory employees with respect to sexual harassment regardless of whether the specific acts complained of were authorized or even forbidden by the employer and regardless of whether the employer knew or should have known of their occurrence. * * *

"(d) With respect to conduct between fellow employees, an employer is responsible for acts of sexual harassment in the workplace where the employer (or its agents or supervisory employees) knows or should have known of the conduct, unless it can show that it took immediate and appropriate corrective action.

"(e) An employer may also be responsible for the acts of non-employees, with respect to sexual harassment of employees in the workplace, where the employer (or its agents or supervisory employees) knows or should have known of the conduct and fails to take immediate and appropriate corrective action. * * *

"(g) Other related practices: Where employment opportunities or benefits are granted because of an individual's submission to the employer's sexual advances or requests for sexual favors, the employer may be held liable for unlawful sex discrimination against other persons who were qualified for but denied that employment opportunity or benefit."

[160]Arkansas, California, Connecticut, Michigan, North Dakota, and Wisconsin. See Appendix A at the subject name "Discrimination—sexual harassment." For the District of Columbia, see "Discrimination-family responsibilities."

[161]114 N.H. 130, 316 A.2d 549 (1974). See also *Phillips v. Smalley Maintenance Servs. Inc.*, 711 F.2d 1524 (11th Cir. 1983) (invasion of privacy action); *Wiley v. Georgia Power Co.*, 134 Ga. App. 187, 213 S.E.2d 550 (1975) (assault and battery action).

[162]*Kelly v. Mississippi Valley Gas Co.*, 397 So.2d 874 (Miss. 1981) (recognition of action for workers' compensation retaliatory discharge would violate legislative prerogative).

[163]MISS. CODE §79-1-9 (1972) (adopted pursuant to Mississippi Constitution, art. 7, §191).

[164]Washington, D.C.: BNA Books, 2d ed. 1983.

[165]29 U.S.C. §151 *et seq.* (1976). For a comprehensive treatment of the NLRA, see C. Morris ed., THE DEVELOPING LABOR LAW (Washington, D.C.: BNA Books, 2d ed. 1983).

[166]45 U.S.C. §151 *et seq.* (1976).

organizing or union activity.[167] Where the employee is outside the jurisdiction of these federal laws, statutes in most states likewise prohibit discharge for union activity and the conditioning of employment on not joining a union.[168] Actions for retaliatory discharge based on these state statutes have been allowed.[169] Federal[170] and state[171] statutes also forbid retaliation for reporting or testifying to violations of labor laws, including those regulating employee compensation and wage payment.

The "Right to Work"

The NLRA permits employers to agree to require new employees to join the union 30 days after being hired and thereafter to remain union members,[172] though in practice employees may meet this requirement by merely paying a service fee equal to union dues.[173] These are called "union security" provisions, and are a part of most collective bargaining agreements. Congress has, however, authorized state legislatures to limit or outlaw certain union security agreements.[174] Twenty-one state legislatures have done so, in statutes

---

[167]NLRA, 29 U.S.C. §158(a)(3); RLA, 45 U.S.C. §152. The involvement of a labor union or formal employee organization is not required; the employer is prohibited from discharging employees who are engaged in concerted efforts to protect their common interests related to the terms and conditions of employment. Complaints of discharge for union activity under the NLRA are brought before the National Labor Relations Board by its general counsel, except that where a discharge also allegedly violated a bargaining agreement, the issue will generally be heard and resolved by an arbitrator, subject to the Board's review. *United Technologies Corp.*, 268 NLRB No. 83, 115 LRRM 1049 (1984). Under the RLA the employee may bring a direct action in court for discharge in retaliation for union activity. *Adams v. Federal Express Corp.*, 547 F.2d 319 (6th Cir. 1976).

[168]Alabama, Alaska, Arizona, Arkansas, California, Colorado, Connecticut, Florida, Hawaii, Idaho, Illinois, Indiana, Iowa, Kansas, Kentucky, Louisiana, Maryland, Massachusetts, Michigan, Minnesota, Mississippi, Missouri, Nebraska, Nevada, New Hampshire, New Jersey, New Mexico, New York, North Carolina, Ohio, Oklahoma, Oregon, Pennsylvania, Rhode Island, South Carolina, South Dakota, Tennessee, Texas, Utah, Vermont, Virginia, Washington, West Virginia, Wisconsin and Wyoming. See Appendix A at the subject name "Labor union."

[169]*Glenn v. Clearman's Golden Cock Inn, Inc.*, 192 Cal. App. 2d 743, 13 Cal. Rptr. 769 (1961); *Wetherton v.Growers Farm Labor Ass'n*, 275 Cal. App. 2d 168, 79 Cal. Rptr. 543 (1969); *Montalvo v. Zamora*, 7 Cal. App. 3d 69, 86 Cal. Rptr. 401 (1970); see *Krystad v. Lau*, 65 Wash. 2d 827, 400 P.2d 72 (1965) (NLRB exercised discretion to decline jurisdiction); *Magnan v. Anaconda Ind., Inc.*, 37 Conn. Supp. 38, 429 A.2d 492 (Super. Ct. 1980) (refusal to sign false statement during labor disruption).

[170]§29 U.S.C. §215(a)(3) (1982) (Fair Labor Standards Act).

[171]See *supra* note 97, Labor and Wage Regulation Witness Protection Statutes.

[172]29 U.S.C. §158(a)(3) (1976).

[173]The statute prohibits the employer from discriminating against or discharging an employee denied membership for reasons other than failure to tender periodic dues and initiation fees. 29 U.S.C. §158(a)(3)(B) (1976). This has been construed to mean that the employee need only tender payment to the union and need not become bound by union rules, *Radio Officer's Union v. NLRB*, 347 U.S. 19, 41-42 (1954), or pay for costs not related to collective bargaining activities, *Machinists v. Street*, 367 U.S. 740 (1961).

[174]29 U.S.C. §164(b) (1976):
"Nothing in this subchapter shall be construed as authorizing the execution or application of agreements requiring membership in a labor organization as a condition of employment in any State or Territory in which such execution or application is prohibited by State or Territorial law."

commonly referred to as "right to work" laws.[175] These laws provide individuals who prefer not to join unions with a right to employment that is unavailable under the NLRA in most organized shops. Unions argue that in light of the NLRA limitation of maintenance of membership and union shop provisions to payment of dues or the equivalent, such laws only protect "free riders," who obtain the benefits of collective bargaining without paying the cost of the union's services.

Right-to-work laws usually provide for broad protection against discrimination toward nonunion workers. In *Retail Clerks v. Schermerhorn*,[176] however, the Supreme Court indicated that the statutory right-to-work exception to the preemption doctrine would be construed according to its statutory terms: "[S]tate power * * * begins only with actual negotiation and execution of [a bargaining agreement]."[177] In *Moore v. Plumbers, Local 10*,[178] the court held that this would permit the right-to-work statute to apply to oral agreements between employer and union to require union membership. At the same time, it appears that statutes prohibiting unilateral employer or union discrimination are preempted where NLRA jurisdiction exists.

Other Employee Statutory Rights

Several states prescribe the term of employment by statute, providing that in the absence of contrary evidence employment is presumed to be for a definite term equal to the period specified for wages or salary.[179] Twenty-eight states prohibit charges to employees for medical examinations,[180] and in Illinois employees cannot be required to open electronic funds transfer accounts.[181] Statutes also prohibit

---

[175]States with right-to-work laws are Alabama, Arizona, Arkansas, Colorado, Florida, Georgia, Iowa, Kansas, Louisiana, Mississippi, Nebraska, Nevada, North Carolina, North Dakota, South Carolina, South Dakota, Tennessee, Texas, Utah, Virginia, and Wyoming. See Appendix A at the subject name "Labor union—right to work (no union shop)."
    The New Hampshire statute, N.H. REV. STAT. ANN. §275:1 (1977), has been held to permit union security provisions permitted under the NLRA. *Tremblay v. Berlin Police Union*, 108 N.H. 416, 237 A.2d 668 (1968).
    [176]375 U.S. 96 (1963).
    [177]*Id.* at 105.
    [178]211 Va. 520, 179 S.E.2d 15 (1971).
    [179]GA. CODE §34-7-1 (1982); MONT. CODE ANN. §39-2-602 (1983); S.D. CODIFIED LAWS ANN. §§60-1-4, 60-2-7 (1978), 60-1-3 (1978 & Supp. 1983). The Georgia statute, unlike the other two, refers to the period of payment as distinguished from the period used for estimation of wages. Thus a salary of $12,000 per year would create not a year-to-year contract but a contract dependent upon the frequency of payment of wages. Moreover, under decisional law, after the first salary payment, absent an express agreement to the contrary, the contract becomes terminable at will. *Floyd v. Lamar Ferrell Chevrolet, Inc.*, 159 Ga. App. 756, 285 S.E.2d 218 (1981).
    [180]Arkansas, California, Colorado, Illinois, Louisiana, Maine, Massachusetts, Michigan, Minnesota, Montana, Nebraska, New Hampshire, New Jersey, New York, North Carolina, North Dakota, Ohio, Oklahoma, Oregon, Pennsylvania, Rhode Island, South Dakota, Tennessee, Utah, Vermont, Virginia, West Virginia, and Wisconsin. See Appendix A at the subject name "Medical examination—payment for."
    [181]ILL. REV. STAT. ch. 17, §1352(2) (1981).

employer fraud[182] and the extortion of money or gifts to provide a job.[183]

Other state statutes regulating the employment relation require a day off each week,[184] restrict sales to employees or coercion to buy from approved merchants,[185] and provide that employees may confront "spotters" who inform the employer of dishonesty.[186] In Alaska, the employer must provide employees with free return transportation to the place of hire.[187]

Employee Pension and Benefit Rights

The Employee Retirement Income Security Act (ERISA)[188] regulates pension programs of private employers. It prohibits discharge or discrimination for the exercise of rights under ERISA or related statutes and for providing information or testifying in proceedings under the Act, a standard federal employee protection provision. But it goes a step further, prohibiting discharge or discrimination "for the purpose of interfering with the attainment of any right to which such participant may become entitled."[189] An employee who can prove that he was discharged to prevent the vesting of pension or covered benefit rights or to minimize the employer's plan contributions may bring an action.[190] However, it has also been held of late that employees must exhaust their remedies by seeking reinstatement to the job through the trustees of the plan[191] and that this obligation cannot

---

[182]Alaska, Arizona, California, Colorado, Indiana, Massachusetts, Michigan, Minnesota, Montana, Nevada, New Hampshire, Oklahoma, Oregon, and Tennessee. See Appendix A at the subject name "Fraud."

[183]Alabama, Alaska, Arizona, Michigan, Nevada, New York, and Pennsylvania. See Appendix A at the subject name "Extortion of job applicants."

[184]Alabama, California, Connecticut, Georgia, Illinois, Kentucky, Louisiana, Maine, Maryland, Massachusetts, Michigan, Minnesota, Mississippi, Missouri, New Hampshire, New York, North Dakota, Oklahoma, Pennsylvania, Rhode Island, South Carolina, Virginia, West Virginia, and Wisconsin. See Appendix A at the subject name "Day of rest."

The "day of rest" statutes are the product of the biblical injunction to keep the sabbath, and many of them, but not all, expressly refer to Sunday or to the employee's sabbath. In *Caldor, Inc. v. Thornton*, 191 Conn. 336, 464 A.2d 785 (1983), the Connecticut Supreme Court held that state's statute unconstitutional as creating an establishment of religion, distinguishing *McGowan v. Maryland*, 366 U.S. 420 (1961). The U.S. Supreme Court avoided this issue in *Trans World Airlines v. Hardison*, 432 U.S. 63, 70 (1977), in the context of a religious discrimination case but has granted certiorari in *Caldor*.

The New Hampshire statute, which provides for "one day's rest in seven," and thus is valid under *McGowan* and *Calder*, was construed to prohibit the employer from holding a manager responsible for problems that took place on his day off in *Cloutier v. Great Atl. & Pac. Tea Co.*, 121 N.H. 915, 436 A.2d 1140 (1981).

[185]Arizona, Arkansas, Connecticut, Florida, Idaho, Illinois, Indiana, Louisiana, Nevada, New Jersey, New Mexico, New York, Ohio, Tennessee, and West Virginia. See Appendix A at the subject name "Sales to employees."

[186]California, Iowa and Nevada. See Appendix A at the subject name "Dishonesty—report to employer."

[187]ALASKA STAT. §§23.10.380, 23.10.385 (1981).

[188]29 U.S.C. §1001 *et seq.* (1976 & Supp. V 1981).

[189]29 U.S.C. §1140 (1976).

[190]*Titsch v. Reliance Group, Inc.*, 548 F. Supp. 983 (S.D.N.Y. 1982); *Ursic v. Bethlehem Mines*, 556 F. Supp. 571 (W.D. Pa. 1983); *Dependahl v. Falstaff Brewing Corp.*, 653 F.2d 1208 (8th Cir. 1981); *Bittner v. Sadoff & Rudoy Indus.*, 490 F. Supp. 534 (E.D. Wis. 1980); *Calhoun v. Falstaff Brewing Corp.*, 478 F. Supp. 357 (E.D. Mo. 1979).

[191]*Kross v. Western Elec. Co.*, 701 F.2d 1238 (7th Cir. 1983).

be bypassed by a retaliatory discharge suit under a state law.[192] Some state statutes also seek to protect employees against retaliation involving employee benefits, though these laws present preemption problems.[193]

Employee Right to a Safe Work Place

The federal Occupational Safety and Health Act (OSHA) requires employers to provide employees with a work environment free of recognized hazards causing or likely to cause death or serious physical harm to employees.[194] OSHA expressly prohibits retaliatory discharge of employees who accuse the employer of violating the statute or who testify in proceedings under it,[195] but no private right of action is available to enforce this prohibition.[196] Federal regulations authorize employees to refuse to perform work under unsafe conditions where the employee has no reasonable alternative.[197] Most states now have statutes requiring the employer to provide a safe work place,[198] many of which protect against retaliatory discharge.[199]

A number of states have recently adopted "toxic substances right to know" laws.[200] These statutes require employers to give notice to employees of the production or use of toxic substances in the work place, usually including labeling of specific items. Most require a full explanation of hazards upon employee request, special training in handling of such substances, detailed record keeping and reports to government, and protection of the jobs of employees who exercise their rights or testify in enforcement proceedings.

Job safety has been recognized as a protected employee right for

---

[192]*Witkowski v. St. Anne's Hosp., Inc.*, 113 Ill. App.3d 745, 447 N.E.2d 1016 (1983) (action preempted under ERISA provision for exclusive federal jurisdiction and requirement of exhaustion).

[193]Connecticut, Minnesota, and West Virginia have such statutes. See Appendix A at the subject name "Benefits."

[194]29 U.S.C. §§651 *et seq.* (1976).

[195]29 U.S.C. §660 (1976). See also 30 U.S.C. §815(c) (Supp. V 1981) (report of violation, accusation, or testimony concerning violation of Coal Mine Health and Safety Act); 45 U.S.C. §441(a) (Supp. V 1981) (accusation or testimony concerning violation of railroad safety laws); 46 U.S.C. §1506(a) (Supp. V 1981) (report of unsafe container or report of violation of Safe Containers For International Cargo Act to Labor Department).

[196]Claims for retaliatory discharge must be brought by the Secretary of Labor, and no private right of action exists under the statute. *Taylor v. Brighton Corp.*, 616 F.2d 256 (6th Cir. 1980).

[197]29 C.F.R. §1977.12(b)(2) (1983). The regulations were held valid in *Whirlpool Corp. v. Marshall*, 445 U.S. 1 (1980), as representing a "permissible gloss" on the statutory intent. Congress subsequently endorsed *Whirlpool Corp.* by enacting a similar provision relating to railroad safety, 45 U.S.C. §441(a) (Supp. V 1981). See H. REP. No. 1025, 96th Cong., 2d Sess. 1, 16, reprinted in 1980 U.S. CODE CONG. & AD. NEWS 3830, 3840-3841.

[198]Only Mississippi and North Dakota do not. See Appendix A at the subject name "Safety in the work place."

[199]Alaska, Arizona, California, Connecticut, Hawaii, Indiana, Iowa, Kansas, Kentucky, Maine, Maryland, Michigan, Minnesota, Nevada, New Mexico, New York, North Carolina, Oregon, Rhode Island, South Carolina, Tennessee, Utah, Vermont, Virginia, Washington, Wisconsin and Wyoming. See Appendix A at the subject name "Safety in the work place—complaint, testimony."

[200]Alaska, California, Connecticut, Hawaii, Illinois, Maine, Massachusetts, Michigan, Minnesota, Nevada, New Hampshire, New York, Rhode Island, West Virginia, and Wisconsin. See Appendix A at the subject name "Toxic substances—right to know."

purposes of retaliatory discharge in a surprisingly broad sense. In *Cloutier v. Great Atlantic & Pacific Tea Co.*,[201] the safety concern was the risk of robbery in a high-crime area, and the decision relied on the federal statute. In *Newton v. Brown & Root*[202] the court denied a right of action for employees discharged for failing to obey a safety rule requiring the use of lifelines although the employer had failed to equip the work area with lifelines. The decision rested, however, on the failure of the employees to give notice of or protest the unsafe condition.

The farthest-reaching case in this area is *Hentzel v. Singer Co.*,[203] where the unsafe condition was the employer's failure to provide no-smoking areas in the work place. The employee, a patent attorney, alleged he was discharged for protesting the employer's failure to provide a safe working environment; his special health problems, he asserted, required that he be protected from cigarette smoke by separation of smokers and nonsmokers in meetings. Noting the federal refusal to allow a private right of action to enforce OSHA, the court nevertheless permitted a retaliatory discharge suit. Because it cited and spoke to both the federal act and a state statute adopted to meet federal guidelines for state OSHA enforcement,[204] the decision is an appropriate authority for consideration in other states that have adopted such laws.

Retaliation for Seeking Workers' Compensation

Injury on the job is as old as employment, but in the late nineteenth and early twentieth centuries it produced substantial political controversy, presumably because the industrial revolution increased the risk of employee injury. The injured employee could bring suit against his employer for negligence in causing the injury, but the common law erected a new and often insurmountable impediment to recovery called the fellow-servant rule, which barred recovery if the injury was caused by another employee's negligence. The doctrine of assumption of risk likewise served to preclude many claims, with courts holding that the employee had voluntarily accepted the risk of injury inherent in the job. On the other hand, employers complained of juries, made up of sympathetic employees, which invariably resolved factual issues in the employee's favor and rendered generous damage awards against employers. The result was that many injured employees obtained no recovery, while a lucky few received substantial awards.

With the support of the labor movement, state legislatures adopted a compromise. Employees injured on the job would be absolutely entitled to compensation without regard to any of the legal bars to

---

[201]121 N.H. 915, 436 A.2d 1140 (1981).
[202]280 Ark. 337, 658 S.W.2d 370 (1983).
[203]138 Cal. App. 3d 290, 188 Cal. Rptr. 159 (1982).
[204]29 U.S.C. § 667.

recovery; no proof of employer negligence was required, and contributory negligence was no bar. If the employee was accidentally injured on the job, compensation was to be available through an administrative agency, often called the industrial commission. The recovery, however, was strictly limited, with modest fixed amounts to be paid for specific injuries and levels of disability. In return, the employee would be barred from bringing a suit to recover for personal injuries.

The possibility of a workers' compensation proceeding necessarily gives rise to an adversary relationship between employer and employee. While employers are generally required to carry workers' compensation insurance, the premiums depend on claims experience. Since an injury need not cause permanent disability to qualify for an award, the employer is often in a position to use its power of discharge as a weapon to discourage the filing or pursuit of a claim. The employer who resents paying the claim, who wishes to reduce future claims due to subsequent reinjury of the employee, or who hopes to inhibit other employees from making such claims, may punish the employee for filing a claim by firing him.

Discharge for the filing of a workers' compensation claim appears to be the single most frequent basis for a retaliatory discharge suit in the reported cases. The phenomenon is obviously widespread, and those jurisdictions that recognize retaliatory discharge as a cause of action invariably include workers' compensation claims among the employee acts that public policy protects.[205] The cause of action has added significance now that the National Labor Relations Board has reversed its prior stand and held that an employee fired for seeking workers' compensation will not have a remedy under the NLRA if he acts alone and on his own behalf.[206]

Recognition of Action

The recognition of an action based on discharge for the filing of workers' compensation proceedings was first sought in *Raley v. Darling Shop*,[207] and summarily rejected. On the basis of a criminal prohibition against retaliation, an action was brought six years later in Missouri, and again was rejected.[208]

In 1973 the Indiana Supreme Court recognized an action for a workers' compensation retaliatory discharge in *Frampton v. Central*

---

[205]The exception is New Mexico. Compare *Bottijliso v. Hutchinson Fruit Co..* 96 N.M. App. 189, 635 P.2d 992 (1981) (no action for workers' compensation retaliation), with *Vigil v. Arzola & Tierra Del Sol Housing Corp.*, 22 N.M. St. B. Bull. 868 (App. 1983) (recognizing action for retaliatory discharge generally but distinguishing *Bottijliso*).

[206]*Wabco Constr. & Mining Equip. Group*, 270 N.L.R.B. No. 126 (1984).

[207]216 S.C. 536, 59 S.E.2d 148 (1950).

[208]Christy v. Petrus, 365 Mo. 1187, 295 S.W.2d 122 (1956). Accord: *Narens v. Campbell Sixty-Six Express, Inc.*, 347 S.W.2d 204 (Mo. 1961). This position has been reversed by legislation, MO. ANN. STAT. §287.780 (Vernon 1973). See *Henderson v. St. Louis Housing Auth.*, 605 S.W.2d 800 (Mo. 1979).

Indiana Gas Co.[209] The court considered the absolute right of the employee to compensation and the practical impact of retaliatory discharge on the exercise of that right. It cited a statutory prohibition on "devices" operating to relieve the employer of such liability. Considering this prohibition a statement of public policy, the court concluded that a discharge in retaliation for an employee's availing himself of a statutory right is a "wrongful, unconscionable act" giving rise to a cause of action.

Workers' compensation retaliatory discharge was thereafter recognized as a "pure" public policy action in *Kelsay v. Motorola.*[210] Rejecting a contrary opinion on Illinois law by a federal appeals court,[211] *Kelsay* found a public policy without reliance on any express statutory prohibition. The court focused on the fact that permitting such firings would have the effect of relieving the employer of a responsibility imposed by statute. The action for retaliatory discharge for seeking workers' compensation has now been widely recognized both by decisional law[212] and by statute.[213] *Daniel v. Magma Copper Co.*[214] held that a provision of state law making it unlawful to require an employee to release the employer from liability for personal injury as a condition of employment does not give rise to a private right of

---

[209]260 Ind. 249, 297 N.E.2d 425 (1973). Contra: *Bay v. Western Pac. R.R.*, 595 F.2d 514 (9th Cir. 1979); *Greenwood v. Atchison, Topeka & Santa Fe Ry.*, 129 F. Supp. 165 (S.D. Cal. 1955).

[210]74 Ill.2d 172, 384 N.E.2d 353 (1978). See also *Leach v. Lauhoff Grain Co.*, 51 Ill. App.3d 1022, 366 N.E.2d 1145 (1977).

[211]*Loucks v. Star City Glass Co.*, 551 F.2d 745 (7th Cir. 1977).

[212]*Recognizing Action: Smith v. Atlas Off-Shore Boat Serv., Inc.*, 653 F.2d 1057 (5th Cir. 1981) (Jones Act and maritime law); *Piezo Technology v. Smith*, 413 So.2d 121 (Fla. Dist. Ct. App. 1982), *aff'd*, 427 So.2d 182 (1983) (implied private right of action under antiretaliation statute); *Good Samaritan Hosp. v. Bishop*, 413 So.2d 158 (Fla. Dist. Ct. App. 1982); *Kelsay v. Motorola, Inc.*, 74 Ill.2d 172, 384 N.E.2d 353 (1978); *Frampton v. Central Ind. Gas Co.*, 260 Ind. 249, 297 N.E.2d 425 (1973); *Murphy v. Topeka-Shawnee County Dep't of Labor Servs.*, 6 Kan. App.2d 488, 630 P.2d 186 (1981); *Firestone Tire & Rubber Co. v. Meadows*, 114 LRRM 3559 (Ky. 1983); *Sventko v. Kroger Co.*, 69 Mich. App. 644, 245 N.W.2d 151 (1976), *Hrab v. Hayes-Albion Corp.*, 103 Mich. App. 90, 302 N.W.2d 606 (1981); *Keneally v. Orgain*, 186 Mont. 1, 606 P.2d 127 (1979) (dictum); *Hansen v. Harrah's*, 115 LRRM 3024 (Nev. 1984); *Lally v. Copygraphics*, 85 N.J. 668, 428 A.2d 1317 (1981) (common law action independent of statutory action); *Brown v. Transcon Lines*, 284 Ore. 597, 588 P.2d 1087 (1978); *Shanholtz v. Monongahela Power Co.*, 270 S.E.2d 178 (W. Va. 1980) (dictum in case under antiretaliation statute).

Denying Action: Bay v. Western Pac. R.R., 595 F.2d 514 (9th Cir. 1979) (no private right of action for retaliatory discharge under FELA provision forbidding "device" to avoid liability similar to statute in *Frampton*); *Martin v. Tapley*, 360 So.2d 708 (Ala. 1978); see *Stephens v. Justiss-Mears Oil Co.*, 300 So.2d 510 (La. App. 1974) (distinguishing *Frampton*) (reversed by adoption of statute, LA. REV. STAT. ANN. §23:1361 (Supp. 1983), which provides for private right of action); *Kelly v. Mississippi Valley Gas Co.*, 397 So.2d 874 (Miss. 1981); *Bottijliso v. Hutchinson Fruit Co.*, 96 N.M. App. 189, 635 P.2d 992 (1981); *Dockery v. Lampart Table Co.*, 36 N.C. App. 293, 244 S.E.2d 272 (1978) (reversed by adoption of statute, N.C. GEN. STAT. §97.6.1 (1979), which provides for private right of action); *Raley v. Darling Shop, Inc.*, 216 S.C. 536, 59 S.E.2d 148 (1950).

[213]33 U.S.C. §948a (1978) (Longshoremen's & Harbor Workers' Compensation Act). States having statutes are Arkansas, California, District of Columbia, Florida, Hawaii, Illinois, Indiana, Louisiana, Maine, Maryland, Massachusetts, Michigan, Minnesota, Missouri, New Jersey, New York, North Carolina, Ohio, Oklahoma, Texas, Virginia, West Virginia, and Wisconsin. See Appendix A at the subject name "Workers' compensation."

[214]127 Ariz. 320, 620 P.2d 699 (App. 1980). Similarly, in *Britt v. Sherman Foundry*, 608 S.W.2d 338 (Tex. Civ. App. 1980), the employee had a common law cause of action against the employer for on-the-job injury, and no action for retaliatory discharge was allowed under the Texas statute.

action, but under the unusual circumstances of that case the injury to the employee was not within workers' compensation coverage.

The crux of the argument that public policy is not violated when an employee is discharged for pursuing workers' compensation remedies is that the policy of full compensation has been fulfilled for that employee or will be assured by the usual administrative remedies. This view ignores two related concerns: (1) the threat of discharge, whether explicit or implicit, will deter filing of a claim by employees unless the claim is substantial; and (2) if the claim is truly the reason for the discharge, the employer has improperly placed a very high price on the employee's exercise of a legal right the legislature intended to be freely exercised, thus diminishing its value.

Federal Employers Liability Act

In *Wiley v. Missouri Pacific Railroad*,[215] the discharged employee was a rail worker covered by the Federal Employers Liability Act (FELA).[216] The court construed Louisiana's statutory prohibition on workers' compensation retaliation to apply to an employee discharged for bringing an FELA claim. *Jackson v. Consolidated Rail Corp.*,[217] by contrast, concluded that there was no cause for action under federal or state law for discharge in retaliation for assertion of FELA rights. The absence of a statutory prohibition was conclusive of the federal law issue, and the availability of Railway Labor Act remedies for discharge rendered the action under state law unnecessary and therefore inappropriate.[218] In *Bay v. Western Pacific Railroad*[219] the court also held that no federal action for FELA retaliatory discharge was recognized, but in *Hendley v. Central of Georgia Railroad*[220] the court allowed private enforcement of a federal criminal prohibition[221] on retaliatory discharge of employees who provide information to FELA claimants.

Absence as an Independent Basis for Discharge

Employees injured seriously enough to render them temporarily disabled present the employer with an alternative basis for termination: absenteeism. The employee is typically entitled by statute to continuing compensation for temporary disability, and this implies

---

[215]430 So.2d 1016 (La. Ct. App. 1982).
[216]45 U.S.C. §51 *et seq.* (1976).
[217]717 F.2d 1045 (7th Cir. 1983).
[218]The court cited *Lamb v. Briggs Mfg. Div. of Celotex Corp.*, 700 F.2d 1092 (7th Cir. 1983), which held that organized employees had no right of action for retaliatory discharge because they were not at-will employees. The *Jackson* court also found that any action that existed would be preempted by the federal law under the Railway Labor Act. This issue is discussed in Chapter 5.
[219]595 F.2d 514 (9th Cir. 1979).
[220]609 F.2d 1146 (5th Cir. 1980).
[221]45 U.S.C. §60 (1976).

a right to be absent.[222] Unexcused absences of an employee who has been receiving compensation and leave, but which are not medically required, may be the basis of discharge.[223] Where the employee's injuries, rather than his absence, motivate the discharge, an action may be brought.[224] This is also the case where discharge for a long absenteeism problem comes only when the employee is absent because of a job-related injury.[225]

Other Prohibited Reasons for Discharge

In *A.J. Foyt Chevrolet, Inc. v. Jacobs,*[226] an action was allowed where the employee was discharged for refusing to fire his workers' compensation lawyer. Similar results prevail where the employer is motivated by a desire to keep insurance premium rates down.[227] In *Santex, Inc. v. Cunningham,*[228] the employer claimed the employee had shirked work, but the evidence also showed a pattern of employer conduct leading to discharge that began the day after a decision favoring the employee was rendered in the compensation proceedings. The employer had also openly displayed his anger and outrage at the decision. Dissatisfaction with the result in the proceedings was accepted as a wrongful motive.

The concurring opinion in *Sventko v. Kroger Co.*[229] suggested that discharge because the employer feared reinjury to the employee was permissible. Reinjury is a legitimate employer concern; moreover, the injury and other experience may lead the employer to conclude that the employee is "accident prone."[230] Since compensation is permitted even if the employee's negligence caused the accident leading to his injury, perhaps the injured negligent employee may be fired for violating company safety rules. On the other hand, since contributorily negligent employees are entitled to compensation, this

---

[222]*Clifford v. Cactus Drilling Corp.,* 109 Mich. App. 776, 312 N.W.2d 380 (1981); *LoDolce v. Regional Trans. Serv., Inc.,* 77 A.D.2d 697, 429 N.Y.S.2d 505 (1980). In *Murray Corp. v. Brooks,* 608 S.W.2d 897, 901-902 (Tex. Civ. App. 1980), the statutory case of retaliation was made out, in part, by evidence that the corporate policy of discharge after six months' absence was discretionary. *Rettinger v. American Can Co.,* 574 F. Supp. 306, 115 LRRM 3010 (M.D. Pa. 1983), recognized a possibility of employee recovery where the employee refused a call to return to work because his doctor forbade it and other employees with noncompensable medical problems were allowed to be absent on disability leave.

[223]*Mitchell v. St. Louis Co.,* 575 S.W.2d 813 (Mo. App. 1978); *Galante v. Sandoz, Inc.,* 470 A.2d 45, 115 LRRM 3370 (N.J. Super. 1983).

[224]*Arie v. Intertherm,* 648 S.W.2d 142 (Mo. App. 1983).

[225]*Griffin v. Eastman Kodak Co.,* 80 A.D.2d 689, 436 N.Y.S.2d 441 (1981). But see *Hansome v. Northwestern Cooperage Co.,* 115 LRRM 3027 (Mo. Ct. App. 1984) (rehiring of employee after filing of claim refuted claim that subsequent termination during probationary period for work-related absence was motivated by workers' compensation claim).

[226]578 S.W.2d 445 (Tex. Civ. App. 1979).

[227]*Murray Corp. v. Brooks,* 600 S.W.2d 897 (Tex. Civ. App. 1980) (workers' compensation coverage). See *Schrader v. Artco Bell Corp.,* 579 S.W.2d 534 (Tex. Civ. App. 1979) (health insurance coverage).

[228]618 S.W.2d 557 (Tex. Civ. App. 1981).

[229]69 Mich. App. 644, 245 N.W.2d 151 (1976).

[230]In *Murray Corp. v. Brooks,* 608 S.W.2d 897 (Tex. Civ. App. 1980), the employer offered an "accident prone" defense, but the court was not faced with the legal issue because there was no evidence to support the claim.

reason could be found so closely related to the compensation action as to be actionable. This issue is not resolved in the cases, but it can be expected to turn on the question of whether the employee would have been fired for violating the safety rule had he not been injured as a result.

Relation to Handicap Discrimination

An employee who is discharged after a serious injury may also have an action for handicap discrimination. The gravamen of this action is that an employee physically capable of doing the job is nevertheless terminated because of physical condition. The employer who offers a "fear of reinjury" defense may in effect be admitting to handicap discrimination.

A pattern of job injuries necessitating time off and compensation inevitably raises suspicion. The employer may believe that the injuries were not serious, or that the employee faked them. No doubt such things occur. Rather than be "taken" again, the employer may discharge the employee to save on insurance costs,[231] asserting that the employee's partial disability prevents him from doing the job or that he is accident prone and hence unfit.

In this situation, the employer may have greater difficulty defeating a handicap discrimination claim than a workers' compensation retaliatory discharge suit. The handicap discrimination laws are directed to employer prejudices about the capacity of partially disabled employees to do the job. The accident-prone argument will sound especially out of place. A claim of incapacity to do the job will be carefully scrutinized; such a claim may even be collaterally estopped by the outcome of the workers' compensation proceeding.[232]

Retaliation for Suing the Employer

In any employer–employee dispute, whether or not it arises out of the employment, the employer can exert considerable leverage to obtain a settlement on its own terms. Bringing legal proceedings may be a legal right of the employee, but it also creates tension in the employment relationship. To date, the decisions have held that public policy is not offended by the discharge of an employee who has sued the employer where no statutory employee right is invoked.[233] How-

---

[231]If the insurer makes the suggestion, it may be liable in tort for interference with contract, a topic discussed in Chapter 7.

[232]See the discussion on collateral estoppel in Chapter 5.

[233]*Daniel v. Magma Copper Co.*, 127 Ariz. 320, 620 P.2d 699 (App. 1980); *Buysse v. Paine, Weber, Jackson & Curtis, Inc.*, 623 F.2d 1244 (8th Cir. 1980); *Campbell v. Ford Indus., Inc.*, 274 Ore. 243, 546 P.2d 141 (1976), *prior appeal*, 266 Ore. 479, 513 P.2d 1153 (1973). See *Jones v. Keogh*, 137 Vt. 562, 409 A.2d 581 (1979) (discharge because of dispute over vacation pay and sick leave).

ever, a host of federal[234] and state[235] statutes confer on employees the right to institute specific administrative and legal proceedings against the employer free from retaliation.

Opposition to Unlawful Conduct: Whistleblowers

A third and considerably more troublesome situation exists where the duty that raises the public policy is one imposed on the employer or, conceivably, some third party. Most prominent in this category is the case of the "whistleblower," who acts as an internal policeman within the organization. Such an employee is a volunteer, not legally required to act; but to permit his punishment by discharge is to facilitate unlawful activity.

The employee who "blows the whistle" on management decisions or conduct may be perceived as disloyal or an officious intermeddler, and fired. In jurisdictions that recognize the action for retaliatory discharge, persons fired for whistleblowing may have a cause of action.[236]

Common Law Protection

The most emphatic case on whistleblowing is *Palmateer v. International Harvester Co.*,[237] which viewed whistleblowing as a civic duty and allowed an action by an employee who allegedly was fired for reporting a fellow employee to the police for stealing company property:

> "No specific constitutional or statutory provision requires a citizen to take an active part in the ferreting out and prosecution of crime, but public policy nevertheless favors citizen crime-fighters. 'Public policy favors the exposure of crime, and the cooperation of citizens possessing knowledge thereof is essential to effective implementation of that policy. Persons acting in good faith who have probable cause to believe crimes have been committed should not be deterred from reporting them * * *'
>
> * * *
>
> "* * *The magnitude of the crime is not the issue here. It was the General Assembly, the People's representatives, who decided that [petty

---

[234]*Labor*: Coal Mine Health & Safety Act, Employee Retirement Income Security Act, Equal Employment Opportunity Act, Fair Labor Standards Act, National Labor Relations Act, Occupational Safety & Health Act, Railroad Safety Authorization Act of 1978. See Appendix A.

Environmental: Clean Air Act, Energy Reorganization Act, Hazardous Substances Release Act, Safe Drinking Water Act, Surface Mining Control & Reclamation Act, Solid Waste Disposal Act, Toxic Substances Control Act, Water Pollution Prevention & Control Act. See Appendix A.

[235]Labor and wage regulation, see note 97 *supra*; equal employment opportunity, see note 158 *supra*; occupational safety and health, see note 199 *supra*; toxic substance right to know, see note 200 *supra*.

[236]For a discussion of this topic, see Comment, *Protecting the Private Sector At-Will Employee Who "Blows the Whistle": A Cause of Action Based Upon Determinants of Public Policy*, 1977 WIS. L. REV. 777.

[237]85 Ill. 2d 124, 421 N.E.2d 876 (1981).

larceny] was a problem that should be resolved by resort to the criminal justice system."[238]

The decision was criticized in a dissent, which expressed the view that the employer's interest in controlling its managers in an area that could injure its labor relations outweighed the public policy, and that the decision might also threaten the employer's internal plant security efforts.[239]

There is a division of authority on the recognition of a whistle-blower's cause of action. Appellate courts in some jurisdictions that have allowed a cause of action for retaliatory discharge, notably Indiana and Pennsylvania, have refused to extend protection to the whistleblower.[240] The rule for denial of an action was articulated in *Campbell v. Eli Lilly &Co.*:[241]

"[I]n order to fall within a recognized exception to the employment at will rule, a plaintiff must demonstrate that he was discharged in retaliation for either having exercised a statutorily conferred personal right or having fulfilled a statutorily imposed duty * * * "

Whistleblowers have sought and with limited success obtained judicial relief for opposing illegal conduct such as theft,[242] antitrust violations,[243] and violations of consumer credit laws.[244] Where health and safety considerations are at stake, they have had less success.[245]

Employees who uncover and blow the whistle on internal financial and business practices also have had surprisingly little support from the courts. In *Martin v. Platt*[246] the court found no cause of

---

[238]*Id.* at 133, 421 N.E.2d at 880.

[239]In *Goodroe v. Georgia Power Co.*, 148 Ga. App. 193, 251 S.E.2d 51 (1978), Georgia, which has refused to recognize the action for retaliatory discharge, denied a cause of action to an at-will employee allegedly discharged because he was about to uncover criminal behavior by another employee.

[240]*Martin v. Platt*, 179 Ind. App. 688, 386 N.E.2d 1026 (1979); *Campbell v. Eli Lilly & Co.*, 413 N.E.2d 1054 (Ind. App. 1980); *Geary v. United States Steel Corp.*, 456 Pa. 171, 319 A.2d 174 (1974); *O'Neill v. ARA Servs., Inc.*, 457 F. Supp. 182 (E.D. Pa. 1978).

[241]413 N.E.2d 1054, 1061 (Ind. App. 1980). See also *Campbell v. Dep't of Health & Human Servs.*, 682 F.2d 256 (D.C. Cir. 1982) (ruling on Freedom of Information Act request concerning Eli Lilly responses to FDA investigation of Campbell's allegations).

[242]*Palmateer v. International Harvester Co.*, 85 Ill.2d 124, 421 N.E.2d 876 (1981) (report to police of suspected theft of company property by fellow employee); *Petrick v. Monarch Printing Corp.*, 111 Ill. App.3d 502, 444 N.E.2d 588 (1982) (report to chief operating officer of possible embezzlement in situation allegedly involving chief operating officer himself.

[243]*McNulty v. Borden, Inc.*, 474 F. Supp. 1111 (E.D. Pa. 1979) (employee allegedly fired in furtherance of Robinson-Patman violations). See also *Parnar v. American Hotels, Inc.*, 65 Hawaii 370, 652 P.2d 625 (1982) (unwitting participant in price-sharing action who allegedly was discharged to further defense of criminal case).

[244]*Harless v. First Nat'l Bank*, 246 S.E.2d 270 (W. Va. 1978), *appeal following remand*, 289 S.E.2d 692 (1982).

[245]*Geary v. United States Steel Corp.*, 456 Pa. 171, 319 A.2d 174 (1974) (no action for employee who brought about withdrawal of allegedly unsafe tubular steel product); *Campbell v. Eli Lilly & Co.*, 413 N.E.2d 1054 (Ind. Ct. App. 1980) (no action for employee who reported to management on alleged unsafe drugs. Contra: *Sheets v. Teddy's Frosted Foods, Inc.*, 179 Conn. 471, 427 A.2d 385 (1980) (quality control inspector dismissed for insisting on compliance with pure food and labeling laws). *Witt v. Forest Hosp., Inc.*, 115 Ill. App.3d 481, 450 N.E.2d 811 (1983) (nurse who reported illegal threat to have patient committed).

[246]179 Ind. App. 688, 386 N.E.2d 1026 (1979). The court in *O'Neill v. ARA Servs., Inc.*, 457 F. Supp. 182 (E.D. Pa. 1978) reached the same result by construing the facts against an employee who claimed his discharge was in retaliation for heading an internal investigation which found evidence of organized crime infiltration, bribes, and loan sharking by corporate subsidiary. Contra: *Petrik v. Monarch Printing Co.*, 111 Ill. App.3d 502, 444 N.E.2d 588 (1982).

action in favor of employees who reported their supervisor for receiving kickbacks. *Adler v. American Standard Corp.*,[247] held that an employee who complained to management of commercial bribery he uncovered in an investigation had no cause of action for that reason (though specific federal securities and tax law violations were later held to raise public policy concerns).

Where the whistleblowing action is recognized, reports both to government[248] and to the employer[249] are protected. There is some reason to believe that an unwitting participant in improper conduct is permitted to bring an action,[250] but it is not clear whether an employee who has a change of heart after being a knowing participant in illegality will be protected.

Several unresolved issues remain to be decided in the whistleblower cases:

(1) Is blowing the whistle to the media protected?[251]
(2) Is the employee obligated to report to management before going to the government or to the public at large?
(3) Must the employee limit his whistleblowing effort to the least disruptive means of enforcing public policy?
(4) Is the employee protected if he blows the whistle on conduct that reasonably appears to be, but is not, illegal?[252]
(5) Must the employee's purpose be legitimate when he blows the whistle, or can he act out of self-serving motives and still be protected?

General Whistleblower Protection Laws

As a consequence of lobbying by organized labor or public interest groups, requests by government agencies, or simply a new legislative awareness that whistleblowers do get fired and have no sure legal

---

[247]291 Md. 31, 432 A.2d 464 (1981), *subsequent opinion*, 538 F.Supp. 572 (1982). Accord: *Percival v. General Motors Corp.*, 400 F. Supp. 1322 (E.D. Mo. 1975), *aff'd*, 539 F.2d 1126 (8th Cir. 1976) (employee who reported alleged SEC violations); *Suchodolski v. Michigan Consol. Gas Co.*, 412 Mich. 692, 316 N.W.2d 710 (1982) (internal auditor who reported alleged poor internal management, improper shifting of losses to rate payers, and low cost sales to employees). See also *Yaindl v. Ingersoll-Rand Co.*, 281 Pa. Super. 560, 422 A.2d 611 (1980) (no cause of action in favor of employees who reported machinery errors in investigation of failed equipment).

[248]E.g., *Palmateer v. International Harvester Co.*, 85 Ill.2d 124, 421 N.E.2d 876 (1981); *Witt v. Forest Hosp., Inc.*, 115 Ill. App.3d 481, 450 N.E.2d 811 (1983).

[249]E.g., *Harless v. First Nat'l Bank*, 246 S.E.2d 270 (W. Va. 1978); *Petrik v. Monarch Printing Co.*, 111 Ill. App.3d 502, 444 N.E.2d 588 (1982).

[250]See *Parnar v. Americana Hotels, Inc.*, 65 Hawaii 370, 652 P.2d 625 (1982) (unwitting participant in alleged antitrust violation).

[251]In *Donovan v. R.D. Anderson Constr. Co.*, 552 F. Supp. 249 (D. Kan. 1982), the court found a communication concerning safety on the job to a newspaper reporter to be protected by the federal OSHA retaliation statute, finding that the communication could lead to enforcement and thereby came within the remedial purposes of the statute and interpretative regulations.

[252]In *Hentzel v. Singer Co.*, 138 Cal. App.3d 290, 188 Cal. Rptr. 159 (1982), the court, citing Title VII retaliation cases as authority, construed an antireprisal statute to protect protests whether or not the employer was actually acting unlawfully, so long as they were made in good faith and with a reasonable basis.

remedy, Congress and state legislatures have enacted a number of statutes to protect whistleblowers in recent years. The three general whistleblowing statutes, enacted in Michigan, Connecticut, and Maine, are reproduced in Appendix B at the end of this volume. Two other states provide similar protection, but to public employees only.[253]

Michigan's Whistleblowers' Protection Act

In 1980, Michigan adopted the first statute prohibiting retaliatory discharge on a general basis.[254] It does not purport to codify the entire concept of retaliatory discharge, but it does cover whistleblowers regardless of the violation of law involved.

While the Michigan statute is the first one of general application, the law nevertheless operates in a narrow sphere, protecting only reports to public bodies of suspected violations of laws and assistance in any investigation. The protection does not necessarily go much beyond what the courts have done under common law. It does assure protection to employees who act on "reasonable suspicion," however; how the courts will interpret that language remains to be seen.

It would appear that if the underlying factual claims have any basis and if the conclusion of illegality in those claimed facts is reasonable, the employee's good faith in making the report may not be questioned. Does this mean that in such circumstances an employee who uses the report as a weapon in an ongoing battle with his superiors is protected? Ordinarily an employee who encounters suspected liability will go to superiors within the business to attempt to correct the situation. In common law actions, this conduct has been held to be both the basis for protection,[255] and independent wrongdoing justifying termination.[256] Since the Michigan statute speaks only to reports to public bodies, did the legislature intend to adopt the latter view or to leave the field open to common law adjudication? How will reports to the press be treated? The statute protects reports of suspected violations of state, federal, or local law. It expressly extends beyond the criminal law, but just how far beyond? Are parking or traffic violations included? Are common law torts and breaches of contract covered?

What the Michigan statute does do is cement in place a specific rule protecting reports to public bodies of suspected illegality, and create a civil action for reinstatement. It requires a clear and convincing showing of the protected conduct, and permits an award of attorney's fees. It also demonstrates a willingness on the part of legislative bodies to grapple with the retaliatory discharge issue and to seek an evenhanded resoluti)n of employer and employee interests.

---

[253]California and Illinois. See Appendix A at the subject name "Whistleblowing."
[254]MICH. STAT. ANN. §17.428(9) (Callaghan 1982).
[255]*Petrik v. Monarch Printing Co.*, 111 Ill. App.3d 502, 444 N.E.2d 588 (1982).
[256]*Geary v. United States Steel Corp.*, 456 Pa. 171, 319 A.2d 174 (1974).

Connecticut's Whistleblowers' Protection Act

Connecticut has adopted a statute patterned after Michigan's.[257] It differs in that reinstatement and attorney's fees are not a discretionary alternative remedy to damages; they are mandatory. It also calls for the employee to exhaust "all available administrative remedies." It is not clear whether grievance arbitration is to be construed as an administrative remedy.

Maine's Whistleblowers' Protection Act

Maine's statute[258] also follows the pattern of the Michigan law. The employee must give the employer an opportunity to correct the violation before reporting it. Maine also requires resort to grievance procedures in the work place, in language broad enough to include employer-operated, nonbargained systems. When the statute requires the employee to make a "reasonable effort to maintain or restore" employment through the grievance process, this may or may not imply that the outcome of that process is *res judicata* in a suit under the statute. The Maine law also prohibits discharge for refusal to follow an unlawful order, but only where the violation puts someone's health or safety at risk. It provides a mandatory civil penalty to be paid to the state and authorizes, but does not require, reinstatement.

Federal Whistleblower Statutes: Procedures

Regulations issued by the Secretary of Labor[259] govern the administrative enforcement of certain federal employee protection provisions contained in federal environmental protection statutes.[260] The procedure requires the filing of a complaint with a local office of the Department of Labor's Wage and Hour Division[261] within 30 days of the employer action.[262] The Labor Department must complete an investigation in 30 days and notify employer and employee of its findings.[263] Either side may demand a hearing by telegram within five days if an adverse determination is made.[264] Within a week after the demand, a hearing is to be scheduled on not less than five days'

---

[257]CONN. GEN. STAT. ANN. §31-51m (West Supp. 1983–84).

[258]ME. REV. STAT. ANN. tit. 26, §833 (Supp. 1983–84).

[259]29 C.F.R. §24.1 *et seq.* (1980).

[260]Clean Air Act, Energy Reorganization Act (Nuclear Regulatory Commission), Safe Drinking Water Act, Solid Waste Disposal Act, Toxic Substances Control Act, Water Pollution Control Act. See Appendix A.

[261]29 C.F.R. §24.3(d) (1980). Filing may also be made in Washington, D.C., with the Office of the Administrator of the Wage & Hour Division, Employment Standards Division, Department of Labor, Room S-3502, 200 Constitution Ave., N.W., Washington, D.C. 20210.

[262]29 C.F.R. §24.3(b) (1980). In *School Dist. v. Marshall*, 657 F.2d 16 (3d Cir. 1981), the court held that the 30-day limitation in federal employee protection statutes was tolled only if the delay in filing was brought about by the employer.

[263]29 C.F.R. §24.4(d)(1) (1980).

[264]*Id.* §§24.4(d)(2)(i), 24.4(d)(3)(i).

notice, at a point within 75 miles of the employee's residence, if possible.[265] An administrative law judge hears evidence and arguments[266] and issues a recommended decision, which is subject to review by the Secretary of Labor on the record.[267] Appeal from the Secretary of Labor's decision lies to the U.S. court of appeals,[268] and enforcement actions may be brought by the Secretary of Labor or the employee in U.S. district court.[269]

Specific Statutory Whistleblower Protections

The broadest specific whistleblower protection statutes are the antireprisal provisions of the Equal Employment Opportunity Act[270] and cognate state statutes,[271] which protect employees who "oppose" unlawful discrimination. Employees who provide information to investigations involving ERISA are also protected against retaliatory discharge.[272] A very limited federal statute, applicable to educational agencies receiving federal monies to detect and control asbestos in school buildings, protects agency employees who bring asbestos problems to public attention.[273]

Many of the federal environmental protection statutes protect employees who file (or are about to file) proceedings, who report (or are about to report) violations, and who assist or participate (or are about to assist or participate) in investigations under the statutes.[274] At least one state protects the employment of persons who report violations of environmental law.[275]

Employees who provide information to persons bringing FELA actions are protected against discipline and discharge.[276] Protection is available to employees who report violations of the Coal Mine Health and Safety Act,[277] and one state imposes a duty on miners to report unsafe conditions to their supervisors.[278] Similar protection applies to reports under the Safe Containers for International Cargo

---

[265]*Id.* §§24.5(a), 24.5(c).
[266]*Id.* §24.5(e).
[267]*Id.* §24.6.
[268]*Id.* §24.7.
[269]*Id.* §24.8.
[270]42 U.S.C. §2000e-3(a) (1981).
[271]See note 158, *supra.*
[272]29 U.S.C. §1140 (1976).
[273]Asbestos School Hazard Detection & Control Act, 20 U.S.C. §3608 (Supp. V 1981).
[274]Asbestos School Hazard Detection & Control Act, Clean Air Act, Energy Reorganization Act (Nuclear Regulatory Commission), Hazardous Substances Release Act (Superfund), Safe Drinking Water Act, Solid Waste Disposal Act, Surface Mining Control & Reclamation Act, Toxic Substances Control Act, Water Pollution Prevention & Control Act. See Appendix A.
[275]LA. REV. STAT. ANN. §30:1074.1 (West Supp. 1984).
[276]45 U.S.C. §60 (1976): *Hendley v. Central of Ga. Ry.*, 609 F.2d 1146 (5th Cir. 1980); *Stark v. Burlington N., Inc.*, 538 F. Supp. 1061 (D. Colo. 1982). Ironically, employees who *bring* FELA proceedings have no federal law protection. *Bay v. Western Pac. R.R.*, 595 F.2d 514 (9th Cir. 1979). State law, however, may provide a remedy. *Wiley v. Missouri Pac. R.R.*, 430 So.2d 1016 (La. App. 1982).
[277]30 U.S.C. §815(c) (Supp. V 1981).
[278]IND. CODE ANN. §22-10-11-9 (Burns Supp. 1983). Under the analysis of *Frampton v. Central Ind. Gas Co.*, 260 Ind. 249, 297 N.E.2d 425 (1973), an action for retaliatory discharge is probably available to employees fired for complying with this statute.

Act,[279] for reporting violations of some state OSHA statutes,[280] and in at least two states to employees who report patient abuse.[281]

Discharge in Furtherance of Public Policy Violation or for Causing Employer to Comply With Public Policy

The employee who is discharged to further a violation of public policy, or in retaliation for causing employer compliance with public policy, is in a situation somewhat similar to that of the whistleblower, in that he has not exercised protected rights or refused a demand to break the law. Like the whistleblower cases, such cases involve a more attenuated relationship between the discharge and the public policy.

In *Cloutier v. Great Atlantic & Pacific Tea Co.*[282] the employee was a store manager who, with the employer's acquiescence, violated a company policy by storing money in the supermarket's safe instead of sending employees to deposit it in a bank located in a dangerous neighborhood. The manager was discharged when the supermarket safe was robbed, and the court held that the discharge was actionable because it punished the manager for acting in compliance with the public policy of assuring employee safety.

Parnar v. Americana Hotel, Inc.[283] involved an employee who unknowingly participated in conduct violative of the antitrust laws by sharing information with competitors at the employer's direction. When the government took action, the employee was interviewed by company lawyers and became upset upon learning that she might have acted illegally. After being discharged, she moved away from the state and thus became unavailable as a witness. The court found that her discharge, if motivated by a desire to further an antitrust violation, was actionable.

"Retaliation" and the Necessity of an Impact on Public Policy

A discharge is retaliatory only if there is some relationship between the discharge and a public policy. Once a recognized public policy has been identified, the court must decide what relationship between the public policy and the discharge makes the termination actionable. To date the courts appear not to have recognized the complexity of this inquiry and its importance to the resolution of

---

[279]46 U.S.C. §1506(a) (Supp. V 1981).
[280]See note 199, *supra*.
[281]CAL. PENAL CODE §11161.8 (West Supp. 1984); ILL. REV. STAT. ch. 91½, §734 (1983).
[282]121 N.H. 915, 436 A.2d 1140 (1981). See also *Sheets v. Teddy's Frosted Foods, Inc.*, 179 Conn. 471, 427 A.2d 385 (1980).
[283]65 Hawaii 370, 652 P.2d 625 (1982).

retaliatory discharge cases. There are a number of possible relationships: the discharge is part of an unlawful or criminal act; the employer's motivation for discharge is based on hostility to the public policy; the discharge is punishment for conduct protected by public policy; the discharge is a consequence of protected conduct; or the discharge may be perceived by other employees as a punishment for protected conduct and operate to deter such conduct by others.

Cloutier v. Great Atlantic & Pacific Tea Co.[284] adopted

> "a two-part test which plaintiffs must meet to establish a wrongful discharge cause of action. First, a plaintiff must show that the defendant was motivated by bad faith, malice, or retaliation in terminating the plaintiff's employment. * * * Second, the plaintiff must demonstrate that he was discharged because he performed an act that public policy would encourage, or refused to do something that public policy would condemn."[285]

The cases bear out the *Cloutier* court's view that one must consider both whether the discharge was causally related to employee behavior that was in compliance with or protected by public policy, and whether the totality of the circumstances surrounding the employer's decision was of a character that justifies a cause of action. It is necessary to consider (a) whether the employee conduct was within the protection of the applicable public policy, (b) whether the employer had a motive for discharge that contravened the public policy and, if so, whether the motive caused the discharge, and (c) whether the discharge was justifiable for some independent reason. Failure to distinguish between these different factors can lead the court to confuse the factual issue of employer motivation with legal issues like the protected nature of the conduct or the presence of legal justification.

Conduct Must Be Protected by Public Policy

An employee's conduct must be closely related to a public policy to justify protection against retaliation. The point at which protection should attach depends largely on one's perspective: Does the court examine the case from the employee's point of view or the employer's?[286] The difference can be crucial, as the decided cases demonstrate. For the employee, the issue is: Would I have been discharged if the issue presenting public policy concerns had not come up? For the employer, the issue is: Was there a direct confrontation between public policy and employer policy? Cases like *Petermann v. Teamsters*,[287] where the employer allegedly ordered the employee to break

---

[284]121 N.H. 915, 436 A.2d 1140 (1981).

[285]*Id.* at 921, 922, 436 A.2d at 1143, 1144.

[286]For a treatment of the question of judicial perspective in the employment discrimination field, see Freeman, *Antidiscrimination Law: A Critical Review*, in THE POLITICS OF LAW, D. Kairys ed. (1982).

[287]174 Cal. App.2d 184, 344 P.2d 25 (1959).

the law, threatened to fire the employee if he did not comply, and carried out the threat when the employee obeyed the law, do not present the issue, because any conceivable standard is met.

The second generation of cases shows the distinction between the employer and employee perspectives. In *Brockmeyer v. Dun & Bradstreet*,[288] the court found no public policy issue in a case one step removed from *Petermann*. The employee was called as a pretrial witness in a suit against the employer, and prior to giving testimony was asked by the employer and counsel what he would say. He gave his version of the facts, unfavorable to the employer's case, and added that he would tell the truth under oath. The employer settled the case on an unfavorable basis, and immediately thereafter discharged the employee. The court held that no public policy was violated by the discharge. In *Donovan v. Stafford Construction Co.*,[289] the court construed the employee protection provisions of the Coal Mine Health and Safety Act to protect an employee against such retaliation. The "right to testify freely in mine safety proceedings," the court held, "encompasses the giving of statements to MSHA personnel conducting preliminary investigations." The court went on to extend protection where the employee refused a company request to provide investigators with a particular statement, explaining that the statement was not true. The court conceded that denying protection against retaliation to the employee might fit the literal language of the statute, but it declined to adopt "such a hypertechnical and purpose-defeating interpretation."

From the employee's perspective, in each case, his discharge would not have taken place had he not insisted that he would testify truthfully. From the employer's perspective, in each case, there was no demand that the employee commit perjury and no opportunity for him to do so. The *Brockmeyer* court chose the employer's side, refusing to recognize employee affirmations of intent to comply with public policy as protected conduct in the absence of an employer order to commit perjury; while the *Stafford Construction Co.* court broadened the scope of protection by seeing the issue more from the employee's perspective.

In *Geary v. United States Steel Corp.*,[290] the employee claimed to be protected by the public policy favoring product safety, reflected in the case law creating strict liability for unreasonably dangerous products. The claim was rejected, in part, because the court found that the employee was not exposed to personal liability in tort. But in *Delaney v. Taco Time International, Inc.*,[291] the court held that refusal to sign a false statement that was only *potentially* defamatory raised a public policy issue. In the one instance, the court appeared willing to find for the employee only if he would be personally liable for the

---

[288]109 Wis.2d 44, 325 N.W.2d 70 (App. 1982).
[289]732 F.2d 954 (D.C. Cir. 1984).
[290]456 Pa. 171, 319 A.2d 174 (1974).
[291]681 P.2d 114, 116 LRRM 2168 (Ore. 1984).

tortious conduct, while the second case suggests that a good faith concern that the conduct the employer demanded was tortious was sufficient. The issue is open: to be protected, must the employee be correct in his claim that the conduct asked of him is legally condemned?[292]

Some courts hold that an employee who is only *preparing* to file for workers' compensation is not protected against retaliatory discharge.[293] This approach insulates prompt retaliation, and has been rejected in other cases.[294] While a discharge prior to the actual filing of the claim may be motivated by unrelated concerns, it is more appropriate to determine whether that was the case[295] than to bar recovery simply on the basis of the date papers are filed.

Darnell v. Impact Industries, Inc.[296] is an example of a hard case in this area. When hired, the employee denied having received workers' compensation benefits in the past; a reference check showed that she had previously filed for benefits. Though she explained that she had dropped the claim and had received no benefits, she nevertheless was discharged. The court held that the case was one for the jury, implicitly deciding that the filing of a claim against a prior employer may be protected conduct. In *Setzer v. Columbia Basin Irrigation District*,[297] the employee alleged that his discharge was for garnishment. At the time of his rehiring the employee had incorrectly told the employer that his previous family and creditor problems had been cleared up. The employer learned shortly thereafter that this was not true. The court held that a discharge, in the absence of any actual or threatened garnishment, was not actionable. In each of the two cases the employer had reason to question the employee's honesty; but in one case the presence of a related employer concern with the public policy was acknowledged and made a basis for suit, while in the other it was disregarded entirely.

When the court in *Cloutier v. Great Atlantic & Pacific Tea Co.*[298] suggested that the determination of what public policy is should be left to the jury, perhaps it had in mind the issue of what the scope of protection surrounding a recognized public policy should be. Whether the matter is decided by judge or jury, both the degree of interference with the public policy in the specific factual context and the possible chilling effect of the discharge on other employees should be weighed

---

[292]The antiretaliation provisions of the federal Equal Employment Opportunity Act (Title VII), 42 U.S.C. §2000e-3(a) (1976) permit employees to take protected legal steps and engage in limited opposition based on a reasonable, good faith belief that the practice in question is prohibited.

[293]*Bryant v. Dayton Casket Co.*, 69 Ohio St. 357, 433 N.E.2d 142 (1982); *Genheimer v. Clark Grave Vault Co.*, 70 Ohio App.2d 65, 434 N.E.2d 744 (1980).

[294]*Hrab v. Hayes-Albion Corp.*, 103 Mich. App. 90, 302 N.W.2d 606 (1981); *Texas Steel Co. v. Douglas*, 533 S.W.2d 111 (Tex. Civ. App. 1976).

[295]*Armstrong v. Freeman United Coal Mining Co.*, 112 Ill. App.3d 1020, 446 N.E.2d 296 (1983); *Cunningham v. Addressograph-Multigraph Corp.*, 87 Ill. App.3d 396, 409 N.E.2d 89 (1980).

[296]119 Ill. App.3d 763, 457 N.E.2d 125 (1983) *aff'd*, No. 59525 (Ill. 1984).

[297]19 Wash. App. 502, 576 P.2d 82 (1978).

[298]121 N.H. 915, 436 A.2d 1140 (1981).

carefully against the employer's interest in control of the work place in determining whether the conduct is protected. Where the employer was in fact motivated to discharge by hostility to the public policy, the employee's conduct that should probably be protected.

The Wrongful Motive Issue

In *Geary v. United States Steel Corp.*,[299] the court was unwilling to acknowledge obvious factual inferences relating to the motive for discharge. The employee had persisted in objecting to an unsafe product, and succeeded in having it taken off the market. He was then discharged by his superiors, who had originally directed him to drop the issue. The court's opinion rested on a finding that the employer discharged Geary out of its "legitimate interest in preserving its normal operational procedures." This conclusion, in turn, rested on a supremely ironic observation:

> "We see no basis for inferring that Geary's discharge was a spiteful retaliatory gesture designed to punish him for noticing and calling attention to the asserted defect in the company's product. * * * In scrutinizing the complaint we are not required to put aside our common sense or attribute to parties a perversity which the facts alleged do not warrant."[300]

The court simply presumed that no retaliatory motive existed; it resolved an obvious factual issue raised by the pleadings. It is hardly contrary to common sense to suggest that Geary's superiors might have been embarrassed over the disclosure of the safety problem, lost prestige as a result of the success of his campaign, and been resentful of his successful challenge to their authority. When they found themselves in a position to do so, perhaps they acted as people sometimes do—they avenged their corporate defeat.

The court apparently wanted proof to be as compelling and uncontroverted as the pleadings in *Petermann*; it would not allow the trier of fact to examine the issue of motive if it was necessary to rely on circumstantial or inferential evidence as proof of motive. This is an unrealistic approach that could eliminate the protection promised by the action for retaliatory discharge. The discharge in *Petermann*, for example, would have been no less wrongful if the employer had ascertained indirectly that the employee would tell the truth when called to testify and had then invented a pretext for termination and fired the employee before the hearing took place. Proving the case might have been more difficult, but the employee still would have been fired because he would not commit perjury.

In *Hentzel v. Singer Co.*,[301] the employer argued that the issue was whether it had broken the law by not acceding to the protests of an employee who asserted his right to a safe work place. The court

---

[299] 456 Pa. 171, 319 A.2d 174 (1974).
[300] *Id.* at 183 n.15, 319 A.2d at 180 n.15.
[301] 138 Cal. App.3d 290, 188 Cal. Rptr. 159 (1982).

rejected this formulation, identifying the issue as being whether the employer had violated express statutory objectives or had undermined public policy by firing the employee. Similarly, while the dissent in *Palmateer v. International Harvester Co.*[302] argued that the employer might have had legitimate interests to protect and thus should not have been liable, the majority responded that the only issue was whether the discharge was in contravention of a clearly mandated public policy, and that this was a factual question.

Many motives may lie behind a retaliatory discharge. Human emotions such as anger, frustration, embarrassment, fear, revenge, greed, jealousy, and lust may trigger the discharge, and examples of each can be found in the cases. But just as often there is a rational motive, alone or in conjunction with an emotional response. The employer's purpose may be to facilitate the wrongdoing[303] or to cover up past wrongdoing.[304] The employer may be carrying out a threat to discharge used in an attempt to coerce employee obedience,[305] or it may be providing an object lesson to like-minded employees.[306] The purpose of the discharge may be to eliminate an irritant,[307] to shift blame,[308] to satisfy a third party,[309] or simply to save money.[310] The employer may act out of prejudice[311] or even an honest belief that it is punishing wrongdoing.[312]

Whether the employer acts from blind emotion or calm deliberation, its motive must be deemed wrongful if the discharge is in some way a response to actual or anticipated protected employee behavior.

Standards for Evaluating Claims of Wrongful Motive

There are no perfect employees; to err is human. There are no perfectly stable businesses; no one is indispensable. Accordingly, there will frequently be some reason other than retaliation in violation of public policy that could explain a discharge. Determination of whether and to what extent retaliation played a role in the discharge often must be resolved by resort to circumstantial evidence.

Precedent that may be helpful in evaluating claims of wrongful motive may be found in several sources: decisions considering discharge for union activity in violation of the NLRA,[313] opinions in-

---

[302] 85 Ill.2d 124, 421 N.E.2d 876 (1981).
[303] E.g., *Sheets v. Teddy's Frosted Foods, Inc.*, 179 Conn. 471, 427 A.2d 385 (1980).
[304] E.g., *Petrik v. Monarch Printing Corp.*, 111 Ill. App.3d 502, 444 N.E.2d 588 (1982).
[305] E.g., *Fortune v. National Cash Register, Inc.*, 373 Mass. 96, 364 N.E.2d 1251 (1977); *Monge v. Beebe Rubber Co.*, 114 N.H. 130, 316 A.2d 549 (1974).
[306] E.g., *Kelsay v. Motorola, Inc.*, 74 Ill.2d 172, 384 N.E.2d 353 (1978).
[307] E.g., *Pierce v. Ortho Pharmaceutical Corp.*, 84 N.J. 58, 417 A.2d 505 (1980).
[308] E.g., *Cloutier v. Great Atl. & Pac. Tea Co.*, 121 N.H. 915, 436 A.2d 1140 (1981).
[309] E.g., *Davis v. Louisiana Computing Corp.*, 394 So.2d 678 (La. App. 1981).
[310] E.g., *Dependahl v. Falstaff Brewing Co.*, 653 F.2d 1208 (8th Cir. 1981).
[311] E.g., *Flowers v. Crouch-Walker*, 552 F.2d 1277 (7th Cir. 1977).
[312] E.g., *Perks v. Firestone Tire & Rubber Co.*, 611 F.2d 1363 (3d Cir. 1979).
[313] 29 U.S.C. §158(a)(3) (1976). See *Wright Line, A Division of Wright Line, Inc.*, 251 NLRB 1083 (1980).

volving discrimination or retaliation in violation of equal employment opportunity laws,[314] cases brought under various state and federal employee protection statutes, and decisions based on discharge of public employees for the exercise of constitutional rights.[315]

The special concerns of each of these areas must be considered when reading the decisions. Cases under the NLRA reflect a strong protective policy, since the retaliation prohibition is the linchpin of the entire collective bargaining system. If union activists are easily gotten rid of, employee organization is doomed.

The equal opportunity cases focus on somewhat different issues. Title VII and the other statutes attempt no general regulation of the employment relationship. Instead, they seek to ensure equality of treatment, and arise out of claimed personal prejudice rather than a spirit of retribution. Naturally enough, the Title VII cases are concerned with whether treatment varies according to protected status. This different emphasis is a function of both the statutory objective of equal treatment and the nature of discrimination, which is more the result of a passive bias, presumption, or attitude concerning classes of people than it is a response to specific behavior.

The public policy cases, like the equal opportunity cases, seek to avoid intruding on employer discretion over the work force. The type of public policy involved in the particular situation may play a part in determining the likelihood that a wrongful motive is at work, just as the nature of the policy will help determine the motives the court will consider wrongful.

Proof of Wrongful Motive

Proof of wrongful motive must begin with a showing of the employer's awareness of the protected conduct. Any direct evidence of motive, the timing of and the circumstances surrounding the discharge, and the stated reasons for the discharge must also be examined. While the question is often a factual issue, the court may find the proof of a wrongful motive insufficient as a matter of law.[316]

Direct evidence may consist of employer admissions, threats, harassment, criticism, anger, chagrin, or protestations plainly directed at the protected behavior or toward the public policy in question. An order by the employer to violate public policy, or its failure to cooperate with the employee's efforts to vindicate public policy, is also direct evidence of retaliatory motivation.

The timing and circumstances surrounding the discharge may suggest a wrongful motive. The proximity in time of the protected

---

[314]42 U.S.C. §2000e-2(a)(1) (1976). See *McDonnell Douglas Corp. v. Green*, 411 U.S. 792 (1973); *Aikens v. United States Postal Serv.*, 460 U.S. 711 (1983).

[315]See *Mt. Healthy City Bd. of Educ. v. Doyle*, 429 U.S. 274 (1977).

[316]E.g., *Hansome v. Northwestern Cooperage Co.*, 115 LRRM 3027 (Mo. Ct. App. 1984) (rehiring of employee after workers' compensation claim rebutted possibility that subsequent discharge during probationary period for work-related absenteeism was wrongfully motivated).

conduct to the discharge is important evidence, and whether the asserted reason for discharge is recent or stale likewise is important. Other evidence may include proof of a "setup" or provocation by the employer; close supervision or surveillance following the protected behavior; changes in the employee's status, pay, or working conditions before discharge, and the timing of those changes; how the employer learned of the grounds for discharge and reached its decision; and the employer's handling of the termination (notice, termination benefits) and its impact on the employee.

Stated reasons for discharge can be based on the behavior of the employee or the independent business needs of the employer. They may be related to or independent of the protected conduct. Where the reason for discharge is related to the protected conduct, difficult questions of the scope of protection and the reasonableness of the employee's behavior come into play.

The specificity of the reasons for discharge is a critical concern: a general reason unsupported by specific facts or particular events does little to rebut an alleged wrongful motive; an outright false reason may actually support the employee's claim by destroying employer credibility; but a serious wrongful act by the employee or the culmination of a pattern of employee disobedience or failure to perform will refute a claim of wrongful motive. Inconsistency with past practice in similar situations or deviation from published standards detracts from the inference of a legitimate motive. By the same token, a history of treating similar problems the same way, or publication of a policy of discharge for the conduct in question, tends to rebut a claim of wrongful motive. The triviality or seriousness of the reason, especially in the absence of a past practice or published policy, is another important consideration.

Mixed Motives

In a substantial number of cases, after credibility judgments are made and the facts established, it will be clear that the employer's decision was partly wrongful and partly justifiable. This presents the mixed-motive problem.

There are actually two types of mixed-motive cases. One is the case where the employer has an independent persuasive reason for discharge and a possible wrongful motive as well. The second type of case is presented when the employee's protected conduct and a legitimate reason for discharge are inextricably intertwined with one another. An example of the latter type of case is *Perks v. Firestone Tire & Rubber Co.*[317] The employer suspected the employee of wrongdoing, and in violation of a statutory policy asked the employee to take a polygraph examination. When he refused, he was discharged. Evidence was developed after the discharge which added weight to

---

[317]611 F.2d 1363 (3d Cir. 1979).

the employer's conclusion that the employee had been guilty of improprieties. Arguing that it had merely drawn an adverse inference from the employee's refusal to take the lie detector test, and had discharged for wrongdoing, the employer moved for summary judgment. The employee could as easily have moved for summary judgment, arguing that it was his exercise of the right not to undergo a polygraph examination that resulted in his discharge. The court held that the issue was one of fact, that is, whether suspicion of wrongdoing or the exercise of a statutory right was the real reason for discharge.

The mixed-motive problem is more one of evidentiary evaluation by the trier of fact than a question of the legal standard to be applied. Given a minimum of evidence suggesting both a legitimate motive and a wrongful one, the issue will invariably be one for the trier of fact. There is no persuasive reason to vary from the traditional "but for" test of causation. Other tests such as "sole cause" or "contributing factor" require abstract speculation about the employer's state of mind. If the court has concerns about the reliability of circumstantial evidence of wrongful motive, those concerns should be faced directly and consideration given to adjusting the standard of proof to require "clear and compelling evidence." The "but for" test presents a simple question—whether the employer would have discharged the employee in the absence of the protected behavior. If so, the employee has not been injured as a consequence of complying with public policy; he would have been fired anyway. If not, the employee has not been injured as a consequence of complying with public policy; he would have been fired anyway. The test can be adapted to a situation where the legitimate and wrongful motives are closely related; it is simply a matter of isolating and identifying the wrongful and legitimate components of the motivation.

Rebutting a Claim of Retaliatory Discharge

Two grounds appear in the cases for rebutting a charge of retaliatory discharge. These may be viewed simply as types of employee conduct outside the scope of public policy protection or as creating mixed-motive problems; but the courts might treat them as legal defenses that defeat the claim. They are (a) excessive employee activity after substantial employer compliance with the public policy; and (b) compelling just cause for discharge in the manner of and purpose for assertion of the public policy.

Employer Compliance With Public Policy

In *Pierce v. Ortho Pharmaceutical Corp.*,[318] the employee objected to the testing of a drug on humans, believing it to be unsafe. The court recognized an issue of public policy—professional ethics—in

---

[318]84 N.J. 58, 417 A.2d 505 (1980).

this case, but held that because the employer's view was supported by a contrary competent professional position on the issue, no cause of action was established. What changed the dispute from a public policy retaliatory discharge into a permissible discharge over the exercise of judgment was the employer's prompt and careful attention to the public policy issue.

An employee who asserts public policy concerns should not be ignored. If the employer studies the issue objectively, takes steps to comply with public policy, and explains its actions to the employee, it may discharge an employee who persists in refusing to cooperate and does not follow directions. Once there is substantial compliance with public policy, the dispute becomes a matter of business judgment, and the employee must subordinate his personal views about what is right to the employer's right to run the business. Of course, this does not excuse discharge where the employer promptly complies with public policy and the employee's protests then cease.

Employee Not Deserving of Protection

An employee who pursues public policy may be a less than ideal representative of the public interest. While in most cases just cause for discharge is inconsistent with a retaliatory discharge claim, decisions in cases brought under the NLRA[319] and Equal Employment Opportunity Act[320] show that this is not necessarily the case. The employer who does not discharge for known misconduct until after the employee has engaged in protected conduct will have difficulty persuading the trier of fact that the employee deserved discharge, but the chain of events may unfold in a way that makes it impossible to separate the just cause for discharge from the protected behavior.

In *Liberty Mutual v. NLRB*,[321] the court of appeals reversed an NLRB finding that an insurance salesman who had attempted to organize his fellow salesmen was discharged for protected activity. Though couched in the language of factual inquiry, the decision pro-

---

[319]*Edward G. Budd Mfg. Co. v. NLRB*, 138 F.2d 86, (3d Cir. 1943) (agent for company union discharged after he joined efforts of legitimate labor organization to unionize the plant): "The case of Walter Weigand is extraordinary. If ever a workman deserved summary discharge, it was he. * * * Weigand's immediate superiors demanded again and again that he be discharged, but each time higher officials intervened on Weigand's behalf * * *. In return for not working at the job for which he was hired, [the employer] gave him full pay and on five separate occasions raised his wages. * * * The [employer] contends that Weigand was discharged because of accumulated grievances. But about the time of the discharge it was suspected by some of the representatives that Weigand had joined the complaining CIO union. One of the representatives taxed him with this fact * * *. We think that he was discharged because his work on behalf of the CIO had become known to the plant manager. That ended his sinecure at the Budd plant. * * * [H]e was discharged because of his activities on behalf of the union."
[320]*McDonnell Douglas Corp. v. Green*, 411 U.S. 792, 804 (1973) ("Title VII does not * * * permit [the employer] to use [the employee's] conduct as a pretext for * * * discrimination"); *McDonald v. Santa Fe Trail Transp. Co.*, 427 U.S. 273, 284 (1976) ("It may be that theft of property entrusted to an employer for carriage is a more compelling basis for discharge than obstruction of an employer's traffic arteries, but this does not diminish the illogic in retaining guilty employees of one color while discharging those of another color").
[321]592 F.2d 595 (1st Cir. 1979).

vides an excellent example of the situation in which a court might deem an employee whose firing was motivated by purposes inimical to public policy to be unprotected.

> "[T]he Company was probably motivated by two reasons to discharge Agacinski: his organizational activity and his personal rebellion against the Company. It is difficult to determine where one ends and the other begins. The bright line demarcation which both the Board and Company insist upon is simply not present.
> * * *
> "While the Act clearly insulates organizing activity from retribution by the employer, it does not authorize carte blanche action by an employee in pursuit of the lawful end of union organization.
> * * *
> "[W]hen he threatened to be disruptive, declared war on management, missed appointments, and refused to meet with his superior as requested, he cast off the protective mantle of the Act and exposed himself to the disciplinary rigors of his employer. * * * Agacinski's behavior * * * may be fairly characterized as constituting a partial strike, or 'a strike on the installment plan'.
> * * *
> [Aldrich, J., Concurring]
> "* * * [A]s a matter of business judgment there can be only one course open to management when an employee perists in giving it the finger."[322]

Employees who come into court as representatives of the public interest will rarely be flawless, but the court can insist on employee good faith. It can expect the employee to have genuine concern about the public policy in issue. It can reject claims of employees who would use public policy solely as a weapon in a personal power struggle with the employer. It can ask that the employee have a sound basis for his position, and it can require that the employee's steps within and outside the employer organization not be calculated unnecessarily to aggravate the harm and embarrassment to the employer inherent in the situation.

---

[322]*Id.* at 604–606.

9

Defamation in the Work Place

Americans have a tradition that one can speak and write as he pleases without fear of prior restraint or being called to account. The tradition resembles reality only when the subject of the speech concerns the public arena, for example, politics, the selection of government officials, or the basic concepts of freedom, democracy, and equality. It is stood on its head in the private sphere, which embraces most employment activity. The vast majority of Americans who deal only in the private sphere lack such complete freedom of speech in their daily lives. The law of defamation with its collection of quirky distinctions and time-honored anachronisms gives virtually unlimited discretion to judges to declare months and years after a statement was uttered that it will or will not be the basis for money damages even when no damages can be established.

Statements that are legally defamatory and may be proved to be so in future lawsuits are uttered in the work place every day. They may be found in business correspondence concerning requests for references and in records of performance evaluations. They may be recorded at or recalled from informal meetings where there is comment upon why someone was let go or whether someone who voluntarily quit will be missed.

The most important ingredient in any business is its human resources. A free flow of information concerning these resources is essential. The common law of defamation, accordingly, is not a benign factor, given our litigious society. Even if qualified privilege ultimately comes to the rescue of the defendant, defense is expensive and nonproductive.

It is possible that if the superstructure of the common law of defamation were left to itself, it would sooner or later collapse under the weight of meaningless distinctions that frustrate and punish efficient and fruitful communication. However, there is an emerging recognition that the First Amendment to the U.S. Constitution should be and perhaps is as applicable to the private sphere as to the public sphere. If private speech within the work place ultimately receives constitutional protection, most of the discussion in this chapter will happily be rendered moot. However, for the time being, defamation law in the work place deserves attention, and that is the first subject to which we turn. The developing constitutional protections of private speech are discussed later in the chapter.

Summary of the Elements of Defamation

Commentators have long decried the lack of clear thinking and consistent adjudication in defamation law.[1] Generally, however, there is agreement that a statement is actionable as defamation if four elements are present. First, there must be a communication inpugning the reputation of another. Second, the communication must be received by a third party—there must be "publication." Third, the defendant must be unable to prove the utterance was true or substantially true or show that he was "privileged" to make the statement. Fourth, the communication must proximately cause damages that can be proved, unless the nature of the communication allows the court to presume that it must have caused damages.

The Defamatory Statement

Generally in the area of employment, a statement is defamatory if it imputes to another the commission of a crime or disparages the other's fitness to perform the duties of his office, employment, trade, or profession.[2] *Bobenhauser v. Cassat Avenue Mobile Homes, Inc.*[3] provides an example of an obviously defamatory statement and also an example of the importance of keeping personal opinions of the

---

[1]F. Pollock, LAW OF TORTS (13th ed. 1929); Veeder, *History and Theory of the Law of Defamation*, 4 COLUM. L. REV. 33 (1904); Courtney, *Absurdities of the Law of Slander and Libel*, 36 A.L.R. 552 (1902).

[2]At common law, the traditional distinction between a written or printed defamation (libel) and a spoken defamation (slander) had a direct impact upon pleading a cause of action. A printed statement classed as libel carried a presumption of special damages in favor of the one defamed and was actionable per se. A statement classed as slander, no matter how insulting it was, in general carried no such presumption of damages and was actionable only upon a plea of special damages. Certain slanders, however, were considered damaging in and of themselves and were actionable per se. These were statements that fit into certain defined categories, two of which are important for our purposes: (1) imputations that one had committed a crime, and (2) imputations that one was unfit to perform duties of his office, employment, trade, or profession.

In *Crinkley v. Dow Jones & Co.*, 67 Ill. App.3d 869, 385 N.E.2d 714 (1978) *appeal following remand*, 119 Ill. App.3d 147, 456 N.E.2d 138 (1983), the court held that an action for disparagement of services of an employee was distinguishable from an action for defamation of character. The opinion does not exclude the possibility that in a proper case an employee might be able to state a cause of action under trade disparagement common law or under statutory deceptive trade practices provisions, if the words cited suggested incompetence (disparaging services) rather than lack of integrity (defamation of character).

[3]344 So.2d 279 (Fla. Dist. Ct. App. 1977).

employer confidential. A discharged sales manager was characterized in communications to prospective employers as a "thief and a crook" who "stole [the former employer] blind." When the sales manager then attempted to obtain financing to become self-employed, he was turned down for credit as a result of a report to the prospective lender stating that "prior to purchasing this business, Mr. Bobenhauser was employed with Cassat Avenue Mobile Homes as a general manager, but his employer states he was discharged due to his stealing from the company." The court held that such spoken words falsely imputing a criminal offense to another are actionable.[4]

Statements implying that a former employee was guilty of a crime or untrustworthy in his performance are likewise defamatory. An example of such a statement is provided by *Rogozinski v. Air Stream by Angell*,[5] where a discharged employee applied for unemployment compensation. The former employer informed the compensation board that the employee "had to be continually watched and reminded with respect to collection of monies, ordering of parts and supplies, and treatment of customers."[6]

To be defamatory, communications injuring one in his profession, trade, office, or employment must be made with reference to some quality or attribute important to that employment. Analysis of allegedly defamatory material focuses not on reflections about an individual's general character, but on statements relating explicitly to the capacity of the person for effective performance in his calling. In general, such statements may either describe specific events or occurrences in the course of employment, or address general ability to perform. In both cases, the defamatory character of the statement is determined from the words and from the particular business, trade, or profession of the person who is the subject of the statement. In *Jamison v. Rebenson*,[7] two women members of a union whose membership included many women signed affidavits against a union organizer. One affidavit stated, "I surmised that his intentions were not honorable when he made improper advances and his chosen route

---

[4]Other examples are found in *McCorkle v. Jefferson*, 252 Ark. 204, 478 S.W.2d 47 (1971) ("You have stole $10 from his register"); *Cook v. East Shore Newspapers, Inc.*, 327 Ill. App. 559, 64 N.E.2d 751 (1945) ("We have enough now to start an investigation by the State's Attorney. You know, that's a criminal offense, bribing a public official to keep your job"); *Cook v. Safeway Stores*, 266 Ore. 77, 511 P.2d 375 (1973) (store manager told three employees that plaintiff had been fired for stealing from company); *Axelrod v. Califano*, 357 So.2d 1048 (Fla. Dist. Ct. App. 1978) (employer told third persons that former skin-diving instructor had stolen large sums of money from YMCA and forged checks).
[5]152 N.J. Super. 133, 377 A.2d 807 (1977).
[6]For other examples of statements found to contain implications of criminality, see the following cases: For the crime of theft, *Farnum v. Colbert*, 293 A.2d 279 (D.C. 1972); *Washington Annapolis Hotel Co. v. Riddle*, 171 F.2d 732 (D.C. Cir. 1947); *Gasbarra v. Park-Ohio, Inc.*, 382 F. Supp. 399 (N.D. Ill. 1974), *aff'd*, 529 F.2d 529 (7th Cir. 1976); *Boston Mut. Life Ins. Co. v. Varone*, 303 F.2d 155 (1st Cir. 1962). For the crime of embezzlement, *Stephenson v. Marshall*, 104 F. Supp. 26 (D. Alaska 1952); *Stewart v. Nationwide Check Corp.*, 279 N.C. 278, 182 S.E.2d 410 (1971); *Zeinfeld v. Hayes Freight Lines*, 41 Ill.2d 345, 243 N.E.2d 217 (1969); *De Ronde v. Gaytime Shops, Inc.*, 239 F.2d 735 (2d Cir. 1957). For the crime of bribery, *Flannery v. Allyn*, 47 Ill. App.2d 308, 198 N.E.2d 563 (1964). For the crime of reckless use of a weapon, *Prahl v. Brosamle*, 98 Wis.2d 130, 295 N.W.2d 768 (1980).
[7]21 Ill. App.2d 364, 158 N.E.2d 82 (1959).

commenced to lead to isolated territory. After I threatened to vacate his automobile, he then agreed to control his impulse." The other affidavit stated that he "made ungentlemanly and improper advances to me and I was forced to flee next door." The statements were repeated orally to the executive board of the union by the two women. It was held that because there were many women in the union and many prospective members of the union were women, the statements reflected on the organizer's fitness to perform his duties and therefore were defamatory.

Similarly, in *Presnell v. Tell*[8] the principal of a school accused a teacher of bringing liquor onto the school premises and giving it to painters. The court found that these accusations imputed reprehensible conduct to the teacher, tended to prejudice her standing among her fellow workers, stained her character as an employee of the public school system, and damaged her chances of serving in other public capacities in the future. Perhaps the rationale underlying this opinion is that such accusations as the principal's in this case destroy a teacher's ability to serve as a role model for students. If a carpenter or bricklayer were accused of giving spirits to other tradesmen, the statement would doubtless not be defamatory.[9]

An example of a more generalized disparagement of performance is *McGuire v. Jankiewicz*.[10] An insurance adjuster, after being informed by the insured that she had obtained a lawyer to represent her, stated, "You could not have chosen a worse attorney." The statement, according to the court, had the effect of characterizing the lawyer as the least competent of all licensed practicing attorneys. Thus, the words imputed a lack of ability in the legal profession even though they did not allege specific unprofessional acts.[11]

---

[8]298 N.C. 715, 260 S.E.2d 611 (1979).

[9]For other examples of specific event disparagement, see *Glynn v. City of Kissimmee*, 383 So.2d 774 (Fla. Dist. Ct. App. 1980) (employee accused by supervisor of being drunk on job); *White v. Postal Workers*, 579 S.W.2d 671 (Mo. Ct. App. 1979) (president of union wrote letter regarding male nurse accused in letter of attempting "to probe female visitors in debauchery"); *Book v. Severino*, 51 A.D.2d 911, 380 N.Y.S.2d 692 (1976) (employees told in letter by former owner of business that $16,000 supposed to have been distributed to employees had been kept by new owner); *Savage v. Seed*, 81 Ill. App.3d 744, 401 N.E.2d 984 (1980) (commodity trader accused of misrepresenting expertise and of giving advice to buy futures while secretly selling for own accounts).

[10]8 Ill. App.3d 319, 290 N.E.2d 675 (1972).

[11]Other cases presenting examples of general statements found to be defamation per se include *Atkinson v. Equitable Life Assurance Soc'y of the United States*, 519 F.2d 1112 (5th Cir. 1975) (successor of plaintiff stated to plaintiff's former client "[H]e was selling for his own gain and not yours * * * he ain't looking out for you"); *Welch v. Chicago Tribune Co.*, 34 Ill. App.3d 1046, 340 N.E.2d 539 (1976) ("John Welch's services have been terminated as of this date because of alcoholism, inefficiency, lack of punctuality and unreliability"); *Reynolds v. Arentz*, 119 F. Supp. 82 (D. Nev. 1954) (nurse accused by representative of private corporation of activities detrimental to county, causing widespread dissatisfaction with nurse); *Rogozinski v. Air Stream by Angell*, 152 N.J.Super. 133, 377 A.2d 807 (1977) (unemployment commission told by former employer that "drastic reduction in the sales in the store from the time she took the job indicated a lack of capability on her part to adequately accomplish the tasks at hand"); *Barlow v. International Harvester*, 95 Idaho 881, 522 P.2d 1102 (1974) (potential financer of plaintiff's business told by employee that business had "absolutely no records and no semblance of records" and that "there was no accounting—there was no management. It just was not operating as a business entity"); *Stuempges v. Parke, Davis & Co*, 297 N.W.2d 252 (Minn. 1980) (employment agency told by former employer that employee was poor salesman, was not industrious, and had been fired because he sold on friendship, would not get products

Some statements that neither imputed the commission of a crime nor depreciated the employee's ability or competence have nonetheless been held defamatory. In *Drennen v. Westinghouse Electric Corp.*,[12] the employer's representative read a communication to 300 employees which stated that an employee bundled company property together and put it in his truck without a pass. Although the court could not clearly discern in the statement the imputation of a crime or inability to perform a profession or calling, it found that the statement accused the employee of conduct incompatible with the proper exercise of his employment and was therefore defamatory. Thus, as with obscenity, judges may not know how to define defamation but they know it when they see it.

If an explanation of the circumstances attending a statement is required to show that it was defamatory, it must also be shown that the statement was understood in a defamatory sense. For example, in *M.F. Peterson Dental Supply Co. v. Wadley*[13] a salesman was discharged after 20 years of service. The employer then sent the following letter to the salesman's former customers:

> "Over the years Mr. Cullom Wadley has contributed a great deal to this firm. He has made many friends in the dental profession, with our laboratory customers, and in our firm.
>
> "Therefore, it is with a great deal of regret that we have reached the conclusion that, for the best interests of both our customers and our firm, we must release him from our employ. Believe me this action has not been taken without a great deal of thought and investigation, for we do not take lightly our responsibilities to not only you, but also to our employees.
>
> "Mr. T.E. (Tom) Warwick will take over most of the territory formerly covered by Mr. Wadley. I am sure you will find him reliable, dependable and easy to do business with."[14]

In reaching its decision that a cause of action for defamation had been pleaded, the court stated:

> "The complaint averred that the language of the letter was intended to mean that Wadley 'was unfit to further represent the company, or to any longer enjoy a relationship of trust with his dentist customers, and further, by innuendo indicated that he was guilty of some unprecedented and unpardonable public or personal misconduct or activity * * * that he would be replaced by someone that was "reliable, dependable and easy to do business with," further imputing that

---

out, was hard to motivate, and could not sell); *Soley v. Ampudia*, 183 F.2d 277 (5th Cir. 1950) (worker called "'informer,' 'stooge,' 'stool pigeon,' and 'traitor' to the union" by union officer); *Anderson v. Kammeier*, 262 N.W.2d 366 (Minn. 1978) (customer of plaintiff told by former employer that plaintiff "should not be trusted" and "would stab anyone in the back if given a chance"); *Chambers v. National Battery Co.*, 34 F. Supp. 834 (W.D. Mo. 1940) ("Chambers is * * * an undesirable employee; is inefficient, careless and indifferent, and lacks ability").

[12]328 So.2d 52 (Fla. Dist. Ct. App. 1976). See also *Williams v. Rutherford Freight Lines*, 10 N.C. App. 384, 179 S.E.2d 319 (1971), in which a company manager accused two union agents of being "nothing but a bunch of goddamned s.o.b. gangsters." It was held the statement accused the union agents of a crime because a gangster is a member of a gang of criminals. However, the court believed that the statement did not impeach the agents' occupational ability because the statement did not attack a quality important to the pursuit of their occupation.

[13]401 F.2d 167 (10th Cir. 1968).

[14]*Id.* at 169.

(Wadley) wasn't reliable, dependable and easy to do business with.' It was further averred that the letter was so understood by the recipients * * *. As we read the letter in the context in which it was written, we readily agree * * * that it is susceptible of the defamatory imputations set forth in the complaint. A claim upon which relief can be granted is thus stated."[15]

Foul, abusive, or vituperative language is usually held nondefamatory unless it attacks, at least as innuendo, someone's ability to perform his trade, profession, or employment or otherwise imputes a crime. In *Skolnick v. Nudelman,*[16] an attorney called another attorney a "regular nut," a "screwball," and a "meshuggener." The court held the words nonactionable, stating that while they might have been abusive, they amounted to no more than name calling. At most, the terms were simply epithets describing a peculiar or eccentric person.[17]

Expressions of worry or concern have also been found nondefamatory, as in *Ornatek v. Nevada State Bank.*[18] The vice president of a bank telephoned a borrower's employer, another bank, to state that he was "concerned about a $4,700 note" owed by the borrower. The court found that this statement was not defamatory, since it did not impugn the integrity of the borrower. Additionally, the words complained of were held not to be capable of a defamatory meaning absent a showing of extrinsic fact that would make them defamatory.[19]

Words requiring artificial or unreasonable construction to reveal an alleged defamatory meaning are nonactionable. In a Ninth Circuit case, *Pond v. General Electric Co.,*[20] an employee resigned from his job of 17 years and was given a service letter as he departed. The letter contained very favorable comments on his ability and personality. Each of four potential new employers read the letter and then wrote the former employer, who responded:

> "This is in reply to your letter * * * in which you request information concerning [Pond].
>
> "The official in International General Electric to whom Mr. Pond reported passed away several years ago, and I am unable to give you first hand information concerning him. His personnel record with the Company indicates that he had approximately 17 years of service in the International General Electric family. His initial engagement was with General Electric, S.A., Argentina. During the early 40's he came to the United States of his own violition, seeking opportunity for en-

---

[15]*Id.* at 169, 170.
[16]95 Ill. App.2d 293, 237 N.E.2d 804 (1968).
[17]Other cases illustrating nonactionable though objectionable language include *Wainman v. Bowler,* 176 Mont. 91, 576 P.2d 268 (1978) ("bully boy"); *McGuire v. Jankiewicz,* 8 Ill. App.3d 319, 290 N.E.2d 675 (1972) ("Your lawyer is an asshole"); *Bucher v. Roberts,* 198 Colo. 1, 595 P.2d 239 (1979) ("You did not need two fucking gabardine resources. You are presently jacking yourself off with Metro slacks, and another fucking resource, Buccaneer slacks, called today").
[18]93 Nev. 17, 558 P.2d 1145 (1977).
[19]Similarly, in *Haynes v. Alverno Heights Hosp.,* 515 P.2d 568 (Okla. 1973), defendant's letter to plaintiff's employer stating, "We realize that you cannot act as a collection agency for us, but your cooperation in urging your employee to pay this bill will sincerely be appreciated," was held nonactionable.
[20]256 F.2d 824 (9th Cir.), *cert. denied,* 358 U.S. 818 (1938).

gagement here while in the process of securing naturalization as a U.S. citizen. He was hired by International General Electric after his arrival in the U.S., and was assigned to our Air Conditioning and Refrigeration Department. Our records further indicate that he submitted his res- ignation on August 9, 1950, which was accepted by mutual agreement.

"Insofar as I can determine from his records, we would not be prepared to consider him for re-engagement."[21]

The employee claimed this letter created, in the mind of his prospective employers, the impression that the service letter might not be authentic, that the company files contained information un- favorable to the former employee, and that General Electric could not give him a favorable recommendation. The Ninth Circuit disa- greed, stating that the extrinsic circumstances pleaded did not make the letter reasonably susceptible to a defamatory interpretation and that there was nothing obviously defamatory in the letter. The gist of the complaint, the court noted, was that the General Electric rep- resentative had refused to speak, not that he had spoken falsely. That silence or a perfunctory response might cause prospective employers to draw unfavorable inferences was not sufficient to make the letter at issue actionable. The court grounded these findings on its belief that an employer does not have a duty to recommend a former em- ployee. Thus, absent a falsehood in the letter, no cause of action could be stated.

Publication

"Publication" is the term of art used to describe communication of defamatory matter to at least one person other than the subject of the communication. Publication is required to make the matter ac- tionable as defamation: Without such communication, one's reputa- tion cannot be harmed;[22] further, the third person who hears or receives the communication must understand the language to be defama- tory.[23]

To be publication, communication must be either intentional or negligent and not accidental. In *Harbridge v. Greyhound Lines*,[24] defamatory remarks made over the telephone by an employer to an employee were overheard by the employee's wife, who was eaves-

---

[21]256 F.2d at 826.

[22]Thus, the mere *threat* of defamatory publication, no matter how imminent, is not itself actionable as defamation. *Pinkney v. District of Columbia*, 439 F. Supp. 519 (D.C. 1977) (entry made in plaintiff's personnel record known only by plaintiff); *Pressley v. Continental Can Co.*, 39 N.C. App. 467, 250 S.E.2d 676 (1979) (report kept in plaintiff's file not read by anyone). Similarly, a publication procured or invited by a plaintiff is usually held unactionable. See, e.g., *Pressley*, 39 N.C. App. at 467, 250 S.E.2d at 678 (allegedly defamatory report read at meeting held at plaintiff's request). But see *Ramacciotti v. Zinn*, 550 S.W.2d 217 (Mo. 1977) (general rule will not insulate defendant from liability simply because plaintiff discussed libelous matter with others). For a discussion of the defense of consent, see *infra* notes 87-92 and accompanying text.

[23]*Bergman v. Oshman's Sporting Goods, Inc.*, 594 S.W.2d 814 (Tex. Civ. App. 1980).

[24]294 F. Supp. 1059 (E.D. Pa. 1969).

dropping by pressing her ear close to the telephone. The court found against the employee for lack of publication. The employer's statements clearly were not intentionally communicated to the wife, nor were they negligently communicated since the employer had no reason to suspect the wife was listening. The court termed this "accidental" publication and held that an act not intended to communicate defamatory matters to a third person and not creating an unreasonable risk of such communication is not a publication.

Communications within corporations are sometimes held nonactionable for lack of publication. For example, where an allegedly defamatory letter was dictated by a company president to his secretary, it was found nonactionable because both the president and the secretary were acting as instruments of a single corporate entity in the performance of a single corporate act. If the complaint had named the president individually as a defendant as well as the corporate entity, perhaps the result would have been different.[25]

A repetition of defamatory language is another publication and thus creates another cause of action separate and distinct from the cause of action which arose upon the original publication.[26] Thus, in the case of an oral defamatory utterance (slander), each utterance gives rise to a separate cause of action. In the case of written defamatory statements (libel), the majority of courts have developed a "single publication rule" providing that where a single impression or printing is used, only one publication exists regardless of the number of copies sold or the number of people exposed to the libel.[27]

A cause of action for defamation exists at the time of the original publication. Thus, statutes of limitation run from this date even if the person defamed was not initially aware of the publication.[28] However, at least one court has suggested creating an exception for private libels to allow the statute of limitations to run only from the time the defamed person first learns or should have learned of the publication.[29]

---

[25]See also *Mims v. Metropolitan Life Ins. Co.*, 200 F.2d 800 (5th Cir.), *cert. denied*, 345 U.S. 940 (1952).

[26]*Nance v. Flaugh*, 221 Ark. 352, 253 S.W.2d 207 (1952); *Lubore v. Pittsburgh Courier Publishing Co.*, 101 F. Supp. 234 (D.D.C. 1951), *aff'd*, 100 F.2d 255 (D.C. Cir. 1952).

[27]*Rinaldi v. Viking Penguin, Inc.*, 101 Misc.2d 928, 422 N.Y.S.2d 552 (Sup. Ct. 1979); *Applewhite v. Memphis State Univ.*, 495 S.W.2d 190 (Tenn. 1973). This rule reflects an adaptation to the contemporary publishing world, where large numbers of copies of books, newspapers, and magazines are circulated.

[28]*Applewhite v. Memphis State Univ.*, 495 S.W.2d 190 (Tenn. 1973); *Wild v. Rarig*, 302 Minn. 419, 234 N.W.2d 775 (1975).

[29]*Wild v. Rarig*, 302 Minn. 419, 234 N.W.2d 775 (1975). The court reasoned that where a defamed person is unaware of a defamation because of limited publication, he may nevertheless be seriously damaged. Thus, private libels such as intraoffice memoranda, intracompany correspondence, and private letters would be treated differently from widespread public libels. See also *Applewhite v. Memphis State Univ.*, 495 S.W.2d 190 (Tenn. 1973) (most reasonable date to mark beginning of statute is first time publication is distributed in county where action is brought).

The Defense of Privilege

The defense of privilege to a defamation claim assumes that the statement is defamatory, was published, and either caused damage or was of such character that damage is assumed. The law classifies privileges generally as either absolute or qualified.

Absolute Privilege

Absolute privilege is a bar to a defamation action even though the words were knowingly false and uttered with malice. Traditionally, communications so protected are (a) statements made during legislative proceedings by legislators, (b) statements published in the course of judicial or quasi-judicial proceedings by lawyers and judges, (c) statements published by lawyers in the course of their professional duties, and (d) statements concerning acts of executive officers or public officials.[30] By custom or court rule, confidential relationships such as attorney–client, physician–patient, priest–penitent, husband–wife, and parent–child are clothed with absolute privilege. Moreover, some states have special statutory privileges that protect persons acting in the course of hospital quality control proceedings[31] and statements by insurance companies explaining why insurance is not to be renewed or is terminated.[32]

Proceedings to discipline or terminate the employment of civil service and other public employees sometimes involve quasi-judicial proceedings. It has been held that defamatory statements made in the course of such proceedings enjoy absolute immunity.[33]

In determining whether the words complained of are pertinent and material to the proceedings and therefore privileged, courts are often very liberal.[34] It has been held that an employer's affidavit detailing his rationale for discharging an employee was clearly relevant to an arbitration proceeding and was thus clothed with an absolute privilege.[35] Further, it has been held that a communication may be privileged even if it merely initiates judicial or quasi-judicial proceedings.[36]

---

[30]There appear to have been no cases involving an employment setting for defamations in a legislative proceeding. Generally, this is a broad category protecting legislators and those who testify before their committees from defamation suits. Immunity applies to all federal, state, and, in some jurisdictions, municipal legislatures. See Yanwich, *The Immunity of Congressional Speech—Its Origin, Meaning and Scope*, 99 U. PA. L. REV. 960 (1951), and Field, *The Constitutional Privilege of Legislators*, 9 MINN. L. REV. 442 (1975).

[31]*E.g.*, ILL. REV. STAT. ch. 110, §8-2102 (1981).

[32]*E.g.*, ILL. ANN. STAT. ch. 73, §755.1 (Smith-Hurd 1965).

[33]See *Hanzimanolis v. City of New York*, 88 Misc.2d 681, 388 N.Y.S.2d 826 (Sup. Ct. 1976), in which a deputy police commissioner issued an allegedly defamatory memorandum of findings after a lawfully authorized formal departmental investigation of a police officer. It was held that the memorandum, having been made pursuant to quasi-judicial proceedings, was absolutely privileged.

[34]*Mock v. Chicago, Rock Island & Pac. R.R.*, 454 F.2d 131 (8th Cir. 1972).

[35]*Nizinski v. Currington*, 517 P.2d 754 (Alaska 1974).

[36]However, the intent to do so must be clear. *Cushman v. Day*, 43 Ore. App. 123, 602 P.2d 327 (1979) (communication to police chief of intent to file criminal charge was not on its face request that charge be filed). But see *Toker v. Pollack*, 44 N.Y.2d 211, 376 N.E.2d 163, 405 N.Y.S.2d 1 (1978) (absolute immunity does not attach to information to district attorney concerning alleged commission of crime).

Absolute immunity also extends to official acts of an executive officer of government. It is usually argued that this immunity is essential to an effective functioning of government by freeing such officers from the fear of lawsuits. Traditionally, however, a privilege extended only to superior officers in the executive departments and branches of the federal government and only to the communications required or authorized in the performance of their duties.[37] *Barr v. Matteo*[38] expanded the scope of this privilege. In that case, the director of a federal agency issued a defamatory press release announcing personnel action planned against certain employees. The U.S. Supreme Court first stated that the duties and not the title of an office must guide the application of the rule, because activities can fall within the realm of protection even though they are exercised by officers of a lower rank. The Court then held the director's office within the privilege. Second, the Court extended traditional protection to include publication made within the "outer perimeter" of an officer's duties, and it considered a defamatory press release within those bounds.[39]

Other courts have extended the *Barr* holding. Statements of elected board of education employees at open meetings,[40] a press release by a city manager detailing reasons why an employee was fired,[41] and a job performance evaluation written by an associate director of a university division,[42] have all been held to be absolutely privileged communications.

At least one court has even protected private sector employees. In *Becker v. Philco Corp.*,[43] a defense contractor executed a security agreement with the U.S. Department of Defense to safeguard classified information. Certain employees lost their jobs with the contractor when their security clearances were suspended on the basis of a report by the contractor noting suspicions that the employees were compromising classified information. Because, in the court's view, the contractor was a link in the government's overall system for protecting classified information, it was performing a governmental function and its report was absolutely privileged.[44]

---

[37]W. Prosser, HANDBOOK OF THE LAW OF TORTS 782-783 nn. 34-50 (4th ed. 1971).

[38]360 U.S. 564 (1959).

[39] See *Bush v. Lucas*, 598 F.2d 958 (5th Cir. 1979) (director's statement to press concerning employee); *Rowe v. Pierce*, 467 F. Supp. 14 (E.D. Tenn. 1979) (National Guard supervisor's letter to employee); *Ammons v. Bodish*, 308 F. Supp. 1149 (S.D. Ohio 1970) (postmaster's statements to press concerning employee); *LeBurkein v. Notti*, 365 F.2d 143 (7th Cir. 1966) (official notification of personnel action by regional director of Housing & Home Financing Agency); *Snurf v. DiCara*, 42 A.D.2d 791, 346 N.Y.S.2d 546 (1973) (Veterans Administration doctor's report concerning employee).

[40]*Brubaker v. Board of Educ.*, 502 F.2d 973 (7th Cir. 1974). See also *McAulay v. Maloff*, 82 Misc.2d 447, 369 N.Y.S.2d 946 (Civ. Ct. 1975) (evaluation report from school principal to superintendent only qualifiedly privileged).

[41]*Densmore v. City of Boca Raton*, 368 So.2d 945 (Fla. Dist. Ct. App. 1979).

[42]*Cripe v. Board of Regents*, 358 So.2d 244 (Fla. Dist. Ct. App. 1978).

[43]234 F. Supp. 10 (E.D. Va. 1964), *aff'd*, 372 F.2d 771 (4th Cir.), *cert. denied*, 389 U.S. 979 (1967).

[44]For another extension of governmental duties giving rise to absolute protection, see *Shipp v. Waller*, 391 F. Supp. 283 (D.C. Cir. 1975) (filing by General Services Administration employees of affidavits in connection with investigation of fellow employee held within outer perimeter of duties).

Courts differ on the question of whether an employer's communications to the labor departments of governments are absolutely privileged. Some decisions hold all information to and from such departments immune from suit on the basis of the traditional privilege.[45] Others recognize that such a broad privilege could lead to abuse. In *Sanders v. Stewart*,[46] the Indiana Employment Security Division sent a form to an employer requesting reasons for a former employee's discharge. The employer's allegedly defamatory response led to denial of unemployment compensation. The trial court dismissed the complaint on the basis of absolute privilege. On appeal, however, the court stated that if such forms were absolutely privileged, employers could report anything, whether true or not, with any kind of intent, including malice, and be immune from libel action. Thus, the report was protected only by a qualified privilege.[47] (Qualified privilege is discussed in the next section.)

Where an absolute privilege is recognized, the boundaries are governed by the subject of the statement made, the circumstances in which it was made, and the duties of the person who uttered it. In *Clark v. McGee*,[48] a town supervisor publicly accused the town clerk of illegally raising her own salary. As the town supervisor was concerned with the expenditure of public funds, the subject of his comments was clearly related to his duties. The court held, however, that statements made about a public servant in a news interview were not part of the supervisor's public responsibilities and thus were not entitled to absolute protection.[49]

Express and Implied Consent To Be Defamed

In some cases it has been held that the plaintiff instigated the defamatory communication and thereby consented to it. The consent led to the defamation, and it constituted a complete defense to the

---

[45]*Land v. Delta Airlines*, 147 Ga. App. 738, 250 S.E.2d 188 (1978) (report to Employment Security Agency of Georgia Department of Labor); *Taylor v. St. Joseph Hosp. Inc.*, 136 Ga. App. 831, 222 S.E.2d 67 (1975) (report to Georgia Department of Labor). At least one court has found absolute protection based on a quasi-judicial theory. See *Krenek v. Abel & Abel Air Conditioning*, 594 S.W.2d 821 (Tex. Civ. App. 1980) (statements by employer to state employment commission having quasi-judicial powers in determination of plaintiff's eligibility for unemployment compensation).

[46]157 Ind. App. 74, 298 N.E.2d 509 (1973).

[47]See *Rogozinski v. Air Stream by Angell*, 152 N.J. Super. 133, 377 A.2d 807 (1977) (employer cannot claim whatever privilege might have been asserted by unemployment compensation commission). See also *Wardlow v. City of Miami*, 372 So.2d 976 (Fla. Dist. Ct. App. 1979), in which an individual was denied employment when a deputy commander of internal security for the Miami police department told a police captain of criminal acts allegedly committed by the applicant. It was held that absolute privilege was not warranted and that the privilege was qualified. See also *Hoesl v. United States*, 451 F. Supp. 1170 (N.D. Cal. 1978) (U.S. Navy psychiatrist has qualified privilege) and *Martinez v. Cardwell*, 25 Ariz. App. 253, 542 P.2d 1133 (1975) (superintendent of Arizona State Prison has qualified privilege).

[48]49 N.Y.2d 613, 404 N.E.2d 1283, 427 N.Y.S.2d 740 (1980).

[49]See Also *Butler v. Wayne County Sheriff's Dep't*, 75 Mich. App. 202, 255 N.W.2d 7 (1977) (forwarding by county police of defamatory information about plaintiff to state police and plaintiff's prospective employer served no governmental purpose), and *Colaizzi v. Walker*, 542 F.2d 969 (7th Cir. 1976) (repeating by director of office of special investigations of charges in news conference went beyond protected interofficial communications).

defamation charge. The consent defense often arises in cases concerning union membership, where it is held that employees consent to all communications contemplated by the collective bargaining agreement.[50] Consent has also been found where nonunion employees request an explanation of employer action. In *Christensen v. Marvin*,[51] a nontenured teacher requested a written statement from the school board as to why her contract was not renewed. Even though the teacher was unaware of the exact language that would be used to answer her request, the court held that she had reason to know it would be defamatory. Thus, statements by the board were absolutely privileged.[52] An absurd extension of the consent defense is found in *Gengler v. Phelps*,[53] in which a nurse affirmatively answered a hospital job application question asking whether prior employers could be contacted. Subsequently, she sued one of her prior employers because of its response to the hospital's inquiry. The court, observing that the nurse knew from the application that hospital personnel would contact her former employer, held that when an employee consents to an inquiry concerning prior work, a former employer's response to the inquiry is absolutely privileged. It may be noted, however, that there is nothing in the opinion to indicate that the nurse consented to defamatory, untrue statements, but merely to the truth.[54]

Qualified Privilege

Generally, an employer is afforded what the courts describe as a "qualified" privilege to defame. The basic elements of qualified privilege are set out in *Judge v. Rockford Memorial Hospital*[55] where the court stated:

> "[W]here circumstances exist, or are reasonably believed by defendant to exist, from which he has an interest or duty or in good faith believes he has an interest or duty to make a certain communication to another person having a corresponding interest or duty, and the defendant is so situated that he believes, in the discharge of his interest or duty or in the interests of society, that he should make the communication,

---

[50]Such communications are usually written or spoken statements of cause for dismissal or discipline, as provided by the agreement. See, e.g., *Brockman v. Detroit Diesel Allison Div. of Gen. Motors Corp.*, 174 Ind. App. 240, 366 N.E.2d 1201 (1977); *Joftes v. Kaufman*, 324 F. Supp. 660 (D.D.C. 1971); *Louisville & Nashville R.R. v. Marshall*, 586 S.W.2d 274 (Ky. App. 1979); *Turner v. Gateway Trans. Co.*, 569 S.W.2d 358 (Mo. 1978). But see *Ezekiel v. Jones Motor Co.*, 374 Mass. 382, 372 N.E.2d 1281 (1978) (voluntary compliance with union grievance procedure does not give rise to consent). Further, at least one court applied the privilege where plaintiff's union requested a statement of cause even though such a statement was not contemplated by the collective bargaining agreement. *Peterson v. Mountain States Tel. & Tel. Co.*, 349 F.2d 934 (9th Cir. 1965).
[51]273 Ore. 97, 539 P.2d 1082 (1975).
[52]Accord: *Westbrook v. Mack*, 575 S.W.2d 921 (Mo. 1978) (hearing requested by police sergeant to consider his suspension).
[53]92 N.M. 465, 589 P.2d 1056 (1979).
[54]This rationale was recognized in *Rogozinski v. Air Stream by Angell*, 152 N.J. Super. 133, 377 A.2d 807 (1977) (mere application for unemployment benefits consents only to furnishing of reasons for separation).
[55]17 Ill. App.2d 365, 150 N.E.2d 202 (1958).

and if he makes the communication in good faith, under those circumstances, believing the communication to be true, even though it may not be true, then the communication is qualified, or conditionally privileged, even though the defendant's duty may not necessarily be a legal one, but moral or social and imperfect in character. [Citation omitted.] * * * The essential elements are: good faith by the defendant, an interest or duty to be upheld, a statement limited in its scope to the purpose, a proper occasion, and publication in a proper manner and to proper parties only."[56]

If any one element of the qualified privilege is missing, the privilege is lost. Despite its conditional status, this privilege, like all privileges, admits that the statements are defamatory but asserts, nevertheless, a right to defame under the circumstances. Courts clearly favor qualified protection for communications concerning an employer's business operations and have found protection in many circumstances.[57]

The qualified privilege encompasses communications heard or seen only within the employer's organization.[58] Public policy and sound business principles demand that employers be able to discuss freely charges of employee misconduct with their own employees.[59] For example, in *Porterfield v. Burger King Corp.*,[60] when a restaurant was burglarized under circumstances indicating that the burglar had a key, an assistant district manager listed a former manager on a company-required crime report under the heading "personnel involved." The form was mailed to the parent company, where it was read by two employees. When the named party brought suit, the court found the document protected under qualified privilege because it was required by the parent company, prepared on the day of the theft, and read only by the proper employees.[61]

Communications from managerial to nonmanagerial employees fall less easily into the qualified privilege classification. In *Gordon*

[56]*Id.* at 376-377, 150 N.E.2d at 207.
[57]*Matviuw v. Johnson*, 70 Ill. App.3d 481, 388 N.E.2d 795 (1979); *Matviuw v. Johnson*, 111 Ill. App.3d 629, 444 N.E.2d 606 (1982).
[58]A plaintiff's knowledge of in-house publication usually occurs in one of three ways: Plaintiff is present when publication occurs, he is notified after it has occurred, or he infers it when confronted with disciplinary action.
[59]*Benson v. Hall*, 339 So.2d 570 (Miss. 1976); *Gray v. Allison Div., Gen. Motors Corp.*, 52 Ohio App.2d 348, 370 N.E.2d 747 (1977).
[60]540 F.2d 398 (8th Cir. 1976).
[61]Accord: *White v. Postal Workers*, 579 S.W.2d 671 (Mo. 1979) (letter from union division head to postmaster of union); *Burns v. Smith Corona Marchant, Inc.*, 36 A.D.2d 400, 320 N.Y.S.2d 869 (1971) (statements by manager to regional managers in office meeting); *McAulay v. Maloff*, 82 Misc.2d 447, 369 N.Y.S.2d 946 (Civ. Ct. 1975) (report from school principal to superintendent); *Weenig v. Wood*, 169 Ind. App. 413, 349 N.E.2d 235 (1976) (chief operating officer's statement to board of directors); *Green v. Kinsella*, 36 A.D.2d 617, 319 N.Y.S.2d 780 (1971) (board of education employee's letter to administrators); *Campbell v. Willmark Serv. Sys.*, 123 F.2d 204 (3d Cir. 1941) (supervisor's report sent by store manager to home office); *Hamilton v. U.S. Pipe & Foundry Co.*, 213 F.2d 861 (5th Cir. 1954) (letter from plant manager to vice president of corporation); *Swanson v. Speidel Corp.*, 110 R.I. 335, 293 A.2d 307 (1972) (written termination notice from manager to personnel department); *Glynn v. City of Kissimmee*, 383 So.2d 774 (Fla. Dist. Ct. App. 1980) (supervisor's accusation of plaintiff's drinking communicated to plant manager); *Baldwin v. Shell Oil Co.*, 71 A.D.2d 907, 419 N.Y.S.2d 752 (1979) (district sales manager's statement to plaintiff in presence of district manager).

v. Allstate Insurance Co.,[62] an insurance agent's superiors told his fellow agents that he had been fired for "kiting" remittances to the company. The communication was found qualifiedly privileged because both parties had a mutual interest in the agent's job performance and the reasons for his termination.[63] On the other hand, in *Drennen v. Westinghouse Electric Corp.*[64] a supervisor's statement of reasons for an employee's suspension that was read to 300 other employees was found unprotected by the qualified privilege. The court stated that while the corporation was serving its interest of restoring morale, no corresponding interest accrued to the fellow employees. They were not supervisors, personnel department representatives, or company officials but were simply other employees doing essentially the same work.[65]

Communications from security personnel to managerial employees generally are qualifiedly privileged. In *McBride v. Sears Roebuck & Co.*,[66] a security guard accused an employee of stealing merchandise, and the employee was fired as a result. The court stated that communications during investigations of employee misconduct are made upon a proper occasion and for a proper purpose because of the employer's interest in protecting itself and the public from harmful employees.[67] Other in-house communications routinely found conditionally privileged are employee evaluation reports[68] and written notices of discharge.[69]

A conditional privilege is found also whenever a prior employer

---

[62]71 A.D.2d 907, 419 N.Y.S.2d 173 (1979).

[63]Accord: *Welch v. Chicago Tribune Co.*, 34 Ill. App.3d 1046, 340 N.E.2d 539 (1976) (posting of memorandum stating reasons for plaintiff's dismissal); *Stephenson v. Marshall*, 104 F. Supp. 26 (D. Alaska 1952) (reasons for dismissal of vice president communicated to 75-100 employees of lower rank); *Bergman v. Oshman's Sporting Goods, Inc.*, 594 S.W.2d 814 (Tex. Civ. App. 1980) (employee asked by manager whether plaintiff stole money from store).

[64]328 So.2d 52 (Fla. Dist. Ct. App. 1976).

[65] Accord: *Presnell v. Tell*, 298 N.C. 715, 260 S.E.2d 611 (1979) (school principal's statement to plaintiff's fellow teachers concerning plaintiff's discharge). At least one court found little difficulty in finding privileged a communication flowing in the opposite direction: *Andrews v. Mohawk Rubber Co.*, 474 F. Supp. 1276 (E.D. Ark. 1979) (production employees' disclosure to management that plaintiff had admitted union organizers through back gate).

[66]306 Minn. 93, 235 N.W.2d 371 (1975).

[67]See *Pierson v. Robert Griffin Investigations*, 92 Nev. 605, 555 P.2d 843 (1976) (background investigation of employee prepared by private investigation firm qualifiedly privileged); *Rezey v. Golub Corp.*, 73 A.D.2d 772, 423 N.Y.S.2d 535 (1979) (security director's statements to manager); *Merkel v. Carter Carburetor Corp.*, 175 F.2d 323 (5th Cir. 1949) (FBI agents' statements to employer accusing plaintiffs of sabotaging government work); *May Dep't Stores Co. v. Devercelli*, 314 A.2d 767 (D.C. 1973) (store detective's accusation of theft); *Ross v. Duke*, 116 Ariz. 298, 569 P.2d 240 (Ariz Ct. App. 1977) (private accounting firm's audit of financial secretary's activities requested by vice president). See also *Rogeau v. Firestone Tire & Rubber Co.*, 274 So.2d 454 (La. Ct. App. 1973); *Cangalosi v. Schwegmann Bros. Giant Supermarkets*, 379 So.2d 836 (La. Ct. App. 1980); *Washington Annapolis Hotel Co. v. Riddle*, 171 F.2d 732 (D.C. Cir. 1947); *Hall v. Hercules, Inc.*, 494 F.2d 420 (10th Cir. 1974); *Smith v. District of Columbia*, 399 A.2d 213 (D.C. 1979); *Lee v. Canon Mills Co.*, 107 F.2d 109 (4th Cir. 1939).

[68]*Land v. Delta Airlines*, 147 Ga. App. 738, 250 S.E.2d 188 (1978); *Benson v. Hall*, 339 So.2d 570 (Miss. 1976); *Kamberos v. Schuster*, 132 Ill. App.2d 392, 270 N.E.2d 182 (1971); *Greenya v. George Washington Univ.*, 512 F.2d 556 (D.C. Cir. 1975).

[69]*Silveira v. Aircraft Casting Co.*, 291 So.2d 19 (Fla. Dist. Ct. App. 1974); *Sowell v. IML Freight, Inc.*, 30 Utah 2d 446, 519 P.2d 884 (1974). But see *Welch v. Chicago Tribune Co.*, 34 Ill. App.3d 1046, 340 N.E.2d 539 (1976). Other examples include *British Am. & E. Co. v. Wirth Ltd.*, 592 F.2d 75 (2d Cir. 1979) (communication by ex-owner with financial interest to parent corporation about deficiencies of successor), and *Ashe v. Hatfield*, 13 Ill. App.3d 214, 300 N.E.2d 545 (1973) (interoffice memorandum).

honestly evaluates a former employee at a prospective employer's request. Even if ultimately proved inaccurate, such evaluations are privileged if made in good faith.[70] Without such protection, it is felt that the necessary free exchange of opinion between employers would be severely hindered.[71]

The privilege is also applied to communications from prior employers to current employers[72] and private agencies hired to investigate a prospective employee's background.[73] Further, even communications from past or present employers to an entrepreneur's customers have been protected.[74]

Certainly, not every defamatory publication by an employer is qualifiedly privileged. When a communication is published to those lacking a corresponding interest, courts have little difficulty denying

---

[70]*Konowitz v. Archway School, Inc.*, 65 A.D.2d 752, 409 N.Y.S.2d 757 (1978). See also *Cash v. Empire Gas Corp.*, 547 S.W.2d 830 (Mo. 1977) (employees acting in good faith may and should communicate all relevant information regardless of belief in its truth). While other elements of qualified privilege must be present, good faith seems particularly stressed in this area.

[71]*Alford v. Georgia-Pacific Corp.*, 331 So.2d 558 (La. Ct. App. 1976); *Calero v. Del Chem. Corp.*, 68 Wis.2d 487, 228 N.W.2d 737 (1975). In *Zuschek v. Whitmoyer Laboratories, Inc.*, 430 F. Supp. 1163 (E.D. Pa. 1977), *aff'd*, 571 F.2d 573 (3d Cir. 1978), a prospective employer sent a "confidential management personnel record" to an applicant's prior employer. On the reverse side of the form, the former employer wrote: "Dr. Zuschek is an intelligent and hardworking individual with thriving ambition and good orientations. However, as a manager, he is very dictatorial, quite devious and often demoralizing. With close supervision, he can be very effective, but left alone, very destructive." It was held that the communication enjoyed the qualified privilege. See also *Wynn v. Cole*, 91 Mich. App. 517, 284 N.W.2d 144 (1979) (prior employer's statement to prospective employer that "Vickie did not really apply herself to the best of her ability * * * eager to get on the bandwagon if trouble existed"); *Hoover v. Perilous Publications, Inc.*, 461 F. Supp. 1206 (E.D. Pa. 1978) (statement from prior to prospective employer that worker "had mental problems"); *Edwards v. James Stewart & Co.*, 160 F.2d 935 (D.C. Cir. 1947) (letter from prior to prospective employer stating, "Although this office gave him a letter * * * stating that he was released from our employ at his own request and without prejudice, his services in Trinidad were not satisfactory"); *Swanson v. Speidel Corp.*, 110 R.I. 335, 293 A.2d 307 (1972) (disclosure to prospective employers of termination notice stating that plaintiff was chronic absentee, indifferent, irresponsible, and needed constant supervision); *Alford v. Georgia-Pacific Corp.*, 331 So.2d 558 (La. Ct. App. 1976) (statements from prior to prospective employer that plaintiff was qualified electrical engineer but could not work in field and could not supervise people); *Calero v. Del Chem. Corp.*, 68 Wis.2d 487, 228 N.W.2d 737 (1975) (disclosure that employee was dismissed for starting competing company, appropriating confidential corporate records about suppliers and formulations, and attempting to hire away key personnel).

[72]*Gross v. Abernathy*, 47 Mich. App. 703, 209 N.W.2d 813 (1973); *Walsh v. Consolidated Freightways, Inc.*, 278 Ore. 347, 563 P.2d 1205 (1977).

[73]*Bloomfield v. Retail Credit Co.*, 14 Ill. App.3d 158, 302 N.E.2d 88 (1973); *Stuempges v. Parke, Davis & Co.*, 297 N.W.2d 252 (Minn. 1980); *Hold-A-Way Drugs v. Braden*, 582 S.W.2d 646 (Ky. 1979); *Cash v. Empire Gas Corp.*, 547 S.W.2d 830 (Mo. 1977); *DeSapio v. Kohlmeyer*, 52 A.D.2d 780, 383 N.Y.S.2d 16 (1976). Other examples include *Rios v. Smithtown Gen. Hosp.*, 65 A.D.2d 808, 410 N.Y.S.2d 366 (1978) (statements concerning employee by customer of current employer); *Russell v. Variety Artists*, 53 Hawaii 456, 497 P.2d 40 (1972) (union agent's letter to plaintiff's booking agent concerning nightclub performer's discharge); *Interstate Transit Lines v. Crane*, 100 F.2d 857 (10th Cir. 1939) (prior employer's statements to bonding company). Further, at least one court has found information *volunteered* by a former employer to be qualifiedly privileged: *Gengler v. Phelps*, 92 N.M. 465, 585 P.2d 1056 (1979).

[74]In *Hahn v. Kotten*, 43 Ohio St.2d 237, 331 N.E.2d 713 (1975), a district manager was discharged by an insurance company after he admitted withholding funds from the company. When he formed a new company, his old customers began transferring their insurance to him. Agents of his former employer were instructed to show his customers a written listing of the circumstances under which an agent must be terminated for cause. The copy bore the words "upon termination of this contract for cause because of district manager's embezzlement, fraud, willful violation of any provision of the contract or willful violation of any insurance law or regulation." The court held the statements privileged by finding a common interest between the insured and the insurer.

privileged status. In *Brown v. First National Bank*,[75] a bank gave information implying an individual's involvement in a bank theft to a local newspaper. The court stated that while a shortage of money at the bank may have been of public interest, the communication was not made to a person empowered to act. Instead, it was made to the general public and was therefore not privileged.

Abuse of Qualified Privilege: Malice

When a defendant demonstrates the essential elements of a qualified privilege—an interest or duty to be upheld, the statement limited in its scope to serving that interest, a proper occasion for publication, and publication in a proper manner to serve the defendant's business interest in good faith—the burden of proof shifts to the plaintiff to show that the privilege was abused or its boundaries exceeded. The boundaries of the qualified privilege have been traced in the preceding subsection; we turn now to how plaintiffs show abuse of the defendant's claimed qualified privilege to defame.

It is often said in the cases that the plaintiff must show malice to overcome the qualified privilege. For this purpose, the common law usage of the term "malice" focuses entirely upon the motive of the defendant at the time the defamatory statement was uttered. The motive that amounts to malice is an intent to injure the plaintiff. Malice is commonly defined or explained in terms of ill will, spite, envy, or revenge.[76] The common law's preoccupation with motive stems from the early history of defamation in the law. Originally, actions for defamation were outside the jurisdiction of courts of law and could be brought only in the ecclesiastical courts. The ecclesiastical courts had jurisdiction because defamation was considered a sin, the root of which was a hurtful utterance intentionally made.

The common law concept of malice, which the plaintiff must show in the defendant to overcome the defense of qualified privilege, should be distinguished at this point from the modern concept of actual malice, which a plaintiff must show to overcome a defendant's privilege to defame that stems from the First Amendment of the U.S. Constitution, a subject addressed in detail in the next section. While common law malice, as stated above, requires showing that the defendant intended to injure the subject of the defamatory statement, actual malice requires showing that at the time the defamatory statement was made, the defendant knew the statement was untrue or

---

[75]193 N.W.2d 547 (Iowa 1972). See also *Weenig v. Wood*, 169 Ind. App. 413, 349 N.E.2d 235 (1976); *Melton v. Bow*, 241 Ga. 629, 247 S.E.2d 100 (1978); *Stephenson v. Marshall*, 104 F. Supp. 26 (D. Alaska 1952); *Smith v. Anheuser Busch Brewing Co.*, 346 So.2d 125 (Fla. Dist. Ct. App. 1977).

[76]See *Stuempges v. Parke, Davis & Co.*, 297 N.W.2d 252 (Minn. 1980); *Weenig v. Wood*, 169 Ind. App. 413, 349 N.E.2d 235 (1976); *Bloomfield v. Retail Credit Co.*, 14 Ill. App.3d 158, 302 N.E.2d 88 (1973); *Pierce v. Northwestern Mut. Life Ins. Co.*, 444 F. Supp. 1098 (D.S.C. 1978); *Baldwin v. Shell Oil Co.*, 71 A.D.2d 907, 419 N.Y.S.2d 752 (1979); *Martinez v. Cardwell*, 25 Ariz. App. 253, 542 P.2d 1133 (1975); *Boston Mut. Life Ins. Co. v. Varone*, 303 F.2d 155 (1st Cir. 1962).

acted in reckless disregard of whether it was true. The distinction has been blurred in some jurisdictions, however, where the original common law concept of malice has been enlarged to embrace reckless or negligent conduct constituting a wanton disregard of the rights of others.[77] The expanded definition of common law malice certainly includes the definition of actual malice in the constitutional cases. To many jury members, one definition of malice may seem about the same as another; the significance of the differences lies primarily in whether the judge can be persuaded that the plaintiff has offered sufficient proof of malice to warrant presenting the case to the jury.

If cases are examined to identify the facts that tended to establish common law malice, the boundaries of the concept can be appreciated. In *Stuempges v. Parke, Davis & Co.*,[78] a salesman resigned because of friction with his district manager. An employment agency was told by the manager that the salesman could not sell, was not industrious, and was hard to motivate. The court found the statements conditionally privileged, but also noted the importance of protecting job seekers from malicious undercutting by former employers. State of mind was thus the significant issue; if the statement was made with ill-will and for an improper motive, the privilege would be deemed abused. Noting the district manager's threat to "blackball" the salesman from the industry, the court refused to overturn the jury's determination that malice had been shown.[79]

Konowitz v. Archway School, Inc.[80] concerned a teacher who was told that her termination was due to budget problems. A school official, responding to a request for a reference, wrote a letter to a local teacher registry stating, "Miss Konowitz was let go because she was not effective with the difficult children." The school's motion for summary judgment was denied, and the denial was upheld on appeal, the court noting that abuse of privilege could be shown by evidence of ill-will, culpable recklessness, or gross negligence constituting a wanton disregard of the rights of others. Because the teacher had alleged that the school official had never personally observed her work, and because of the discrepancy between the allegedly libelous statement and the reason given for discharge, the court found sufficient basis to raise a triable question of fact on the issue of motive.[81]

From these two cases, it can been seen that ill-will sufficient to

---

[77]See *Konowitz v. Archway School, Inc.*, 65 A.D.2d 752, 409 N.Y.S.2d 757 (1978); *Interstate Transit Lines v. Crane*, 100 F.2d 857 (10th Cir. 1939); *De Ronde v. Gaytimes Shops, Inc.*, 239 F.2d 735 (2d Cir. 1957).

[78]297 N.W.2d 252 (Minn. 1980).

[79]Other cases using ill will to defeat a privilege include *Bloomfield v. Retail Credit Co.*, 14 Ill. App.3d 158, 302 N.E.2d 88 (1973); *Weenig v. Wood*, 169 Ind. App. 413, 349 N.E.2d 235 (1976); *Gray v. Allison Div. of Gen. Motors Corp.*, 52 Ohio App.2d 348, 370 N.E.2d 747 (Ohio 1977).

[80]65 A.D.2d 752, 409 N.Y.S.2d 757 (1978). Accord: *Andrews v. Mohawk Rubber Co.*, 474 F. Supp. 1276 (E.D. Ark. 1979) (ill will or reckless disregard of the rights of another will defeat a qualified privilege).

[81]Other cases using the culpable recklessness or gross negligence standard to defeat a privilege include *Interstate Transit Lines v. Crane*, 100 F.2d 857 (10th Cir. 1939), and *De Ronde v. Gaytimes Shops, Inc.*, 239 F.2d 735 (2d Cir. 1957).

324 Employment Termination

create an issue of fact for the jury on whether the qualified privilege has been abused may be inferred from only a few facts or a small amount of testimony, all of which may be from the mouth of the plaintiff. Qualified privilege hangs by a slender thread.

However, in *Martinez v. Cardwell*,[82] a prison guard was accused by his superior of using marijuana. The guard presented no evidence of actual ill will but argued that his superior's failure to investigate before making the charge raised an inference of malice. The court did not agree, saying, "The mere fact that Cardwell made no independent investigation of the appellant's activities is insufficient to raise a genuine issue as to his motives."[83]

Boston Mutual Life Insurance Co. v. Varone[84] demonstrates that malice or ill will must actuate the defendant to make the utterance. It is not sufficient that there has been no love lost between the plaintiff and the defendant. A discharged insurance agent claimed that a letter written by his employer to the state insurance commissioner was defamatory. The court held that there was no abuse of privilege because the letter was responsive to a requirement of the department of insurance. This was true even if the employer was pleased to see the agent in difficulty, as long as this "incidental gratification of personal feelings" did not motivate the letter.[85]

First Amendment Protection of Private Speech in the Work Place

New York Times Co. v. Sullivan,[86] was the first case to introduce the modern concept of actual malice into the law. A police commissioner brought a libel action concerning an advertisement in the *New York Times* protesting treatment of southern blacks and civil rights demonstrators. Believing that free speech, including sharp attacks on governmental officials, should not be inhibited by fear of a defamation action, the U.S. Supreme Court held that the plaintiff could not recover unless he showed actual malice, that is, showed either that the newspaper knew the statement about the plaintiff was false when it was published, or that the newspaper published the advertisement in reckless disregard of its truth. In subsequent cases, the Supreme Court has made it clear that reckless disregard of truth is not merely negligence or gross negligence. Rather, the plaintiff must show that the individual defendant "in fact entertained serious doubts as to the truth of the statement."[87] A district court wryly summed up the redefinition of old terms:

---

[82]25 Ariz. App. 253, 542 P.2d 1133 (1975).
[83]25 Ariz. App. at 257, 542 P.2d at 1137.
[84]303 F.2d 155 (1st Cir. 1962).
[85]303 F.2d at 159. *Pierce v. Northwestern Mut. Life Ins. Co.*, 444 F. Supp. 1098 (D.S.C. 1978), citing *Boston Mut. Life Ins. Co. v. Varone*, 303 F.2d 155 (1st Cir. 1962), with approval.
[86]376 U.S. 254 (1964).
[87]*St. Amanti v. Thompson*, 390 U.S. 727, 731 (1968).

"Although these definitions distort common English, they must be taken at face value. In the context of a libel suit 'actual malice' simply does not mean ill-will or spite. Rather, 'malice' must be taken to mean fraudulent, knowing, publication of a falsehood, or reckless disregard of falsity. And we also note that reckless does not mean grossly negligent, its common use, but rather intentional disregard. When the Supreme Court uses a word, it means what the Court wants it to mean. 'Actual malice' is now a term of art having nothing to do with actual malice."[88]

Left unresolved was whether and to what extent media defendants are protected by the actual malice standard when they print defamatory statements about private individuals. *Gertz v. Welch, Inc.*[89] addressed this issue. A magazine publisher stated that a private lawyer was a Communist who had engineered perjured testimony in a wrongful-death action. In the trial court, the jury returned a verdict in favor of the lawyer, but judgment was entered notwithstanding the verdict largely on the ground that there had been no showing of actual malice. On appeal, the Supreme Court was faced with the question of whether to expand the *New York Times* standard to embrace private individuals. The Court refused to do that, but applied two new restrictions upon traditional libel law as it pertains to private individuals claiming defamation by the media. The Court held that the state may not impose liability for defamation without a showing of fault, at least negligence; and that where the actual-malice standard is not satisfied, the state may permit recovery only for "actual injury" and not for presumed or punitive damages. Left unanswered in *Gertz* is the question whether these standards are to be applied in an action by a private plaintiff against a nonmedia defendant. A growing number of state courts answer the question in the affirmative.

In *Jacron Sales Co. v. Sindorf*,[90] a salesman stated in a resignation letter that he regarded inventory in his possession as part payment of commissions due him. Accordingly, he refused to return it. Shortly thereafter, the company told the salesman's new employer that when the salesman resigned there were "quite a few cash sales and quite a bit of merchandise that were unaccounted for." In the defamation suit that arose over this statement, the salesman prevailed. This decision was reversed on appeal, and an appeal from that decision was taken. The second appeal was heard to determine the applicability of *Gertz* to the case.

In reaching its decision to apply *Gertz* to purely private actions, the Maryland Court of Appeals reasoned that the state's interest in protecting private persons from defamation must be balanced against the threat of self-censorship by defendants regardless of their status. It found no persuasive basis for distinguishing media and nonmedia

[88]*Reliance Ins. Co. v. Barron's*, 442 F. Supp. 1341, 1349-1350 (S.D.N.Y. 1977).
[89]418 U.S. 323 (1974).
[90]*Jacron Sales Co. v. Sindorf*, 276 Md. 580, 350 A.2d 688 (1976).

defendants, because issues of public interest may be discussed equally in either context. Undoubtedly, one reason for this belief was concern that common law strict liability would accord less favorable treatment to nonmedia defendants, who are less likely to cause substantial harm to a person than are media defendants. Also, the court noted that the need for consistency and simplicity in the law demanded such across-the-board application of *Gertz.*

Applying *Gertz* to a defamation claim by a private plaintiff against a nonmedia defendant means there can be no punitive or presumed damages without a showing of actual malice and that there can be no liability whatsoever without some fault—negligence in determining the truth, at the least. The second aspect of *Gertz* adds no new requirements in defamation actions where the defendant claims a qualified privilege and there is no issue of the defendant's exceeding the boundaries of the privilege. In that event, the only question is whether the plaintiff can show an abuse of the privilege by proving common law malice, that is, an intent to injure.

Nevertheless, if state courts engraft the standards of *Gertz* upon defamation actions between private individuals, would they go further and apply the *New York Times v. Sullivan* actual-malice standard of liability when a private individual makes a defamation claim against a nonmedia defendant? At least one court, the Illinois Supreme Court, has done so: In *Colson v. Steig,*[91] a college professor claimed he had been slandered by his department head in a committee meeting to determine whether the professor should receive tenure. The Illinois Supreme Court held that the credentialing of a college professor was a matter of public interest that warranted the same protection of free speech and freedom of the press as *New York Times v. Sullivan.* Since the plaintiff could not prove by clear and convincing evidence that the defendant had made the allegedly defamatory remarks with actual knowledge that they were false or with reckless disregard of their truth or falsity, no action would lie.[92]

Arguably, the *Colson* decision can be viewed as applying the actual-malice constitutional standard to all cases of defamation regardless of who the parties are. However, the Illinois Supreme Court did not specifically address this issue, and at least one Illinois appellate court has refused an invitation to interpret *Colson* this way.[93] A district court, applying Illinois law, held that actual malice was

---

[91]89 Ill.2d 205, 433 N.E.2d 246 (1982).

[92]In *Rosenbloom v. Metro Media,* 403 U.S. 29 (1971), the Supreme Court refused to apply the *New York Times v. Sullivan* test to a private individual suing a nonmedia defendant. Of course, that decision does not foreclose any state supreme court from itself applying that standard on state constitutional grounds or by distinguishing *Rosenbloom* on the facts.

[93]*American Pet Motels, Inc. v. Chicago Veterinary Medical Ass'n,* 106 Ill. App.3d 626, 435 N.E.2d 1297 (1982). This case is of interest for another reason. It applies the constitutional defamation standard of actual malice to a claim of tortious interference with prospective business advantage. *Id.* at 633-634, 436 N.E.2d at 1303. This extension of the privilege was necessary, the court reasoned, because the particular words that were the subject of the complaint could as well have been framed in one common law action as another. If speech were to be protected, the standard must apply to both common law actions. See also *Brown & Williamson Tobacco Corp. v. Jacobson,* 713 F.2d 262 (7th Cir. 1983).

required to overcome a claim of qualified privilege in a defamation action between a private individual and a nonmedia defendant.[94] At least one court, however, has refused to extend the actual-malice standard to defamation claims that arise in employment controversies.[95]

The Defense of Truth and Substantial Truth

At common law, the falsity of a defamatory publication was presumed unless the defendant affirmatively pleaded and proved its truth. If successful, the defendant was said to have erected an absolute, unqualified defense to a defamation action. Although this is still the approach in some jurisdictions, the defense of truth is an area being affected by the emergent constitutional analysis. A jurisdiction that requires proof of fault as a precondition to liability or to punitive or presumed damages is in effect requiring the plaintiff to show at least the defendant's negligent disregard of truth; and this, in turn, requires the plaintiff to show that the defamatory statement is untrue. Thus, where the new constitutional standards apply, there is a reallocation of the burden of proving whether the defamatory statement is true or untrue.

Where truth is an issue and the defendant has the burden, is it enough for the defendant to show that the alleged defamatory statement is substantially, though not literally, true? Or, on the other hand, if the plaintiff has the burden of proving the statement untrue, is it enough for the plaintiff to prove that the statement is literally untrue even if it is substantially truthful? It has been held that literal truth need not be shown. It is enough that the "gist" or "sting" of the statement be shown to be true to serve as a complete defense.[96] For example, where the defendant stated that the plaintiff had wrongfully withheld money "as far back as September," it was held that the substance of the statement was true since it was shown that money was wrongfully withheld as far back as October.[97]

Damages

In general, three types of compensable damages are recognized as flowing from a defamation: general, special, and punitive. General damages are peculiar to defamation actions. In order to permit a plaintiff to recover for injury to his reputation, courts have created the concept of presumed, or general, damages. General damages need not be proved. They are allowable whenever the immediate result of

---

[94]*International Adm'rs, Inc. v. Life Ins. Co. of N. Am.*, 564 F. Supp. 1247 (N.D. Ill. 1983).
[95]*Calero v. Del Chem. Corp.*, 68 Wis.2d 487, 228 N.W.2d 737 (1975).
[96]*International Adm'rs, Inc. v. Life Ins. Co. of N. Am.*, 564 F. Supp. 1247 (N.D. Ill. 1983).
[97]*Id.*

a defamation is to impair the plaintiff's reputation even though no provable pecuniary loss can be demonstrated.[98] The amount of such damages is entirely within the province of the trier of fact. In determining that amount, the trier of fact considers the character of the publication, the probable effect of the language used, the area of dissemination of the defamation, and the duration of the statement's circulation.[99]

As noted earlier, in *Gertz* the Supreme Court, pursuant to its concerns over freedom of the press, struck down the concept of strict liability and, to an extent, its sibling, presumed damages.[100] Specifically, *Gertz* requires an award of presumed damages to be premised upon a finding of actual malice as set out in *New York Times v. Sullivan*, that is, actual knowledge of falsity or reckless disregard for truth or falsity.[101]

Special damages are never presumed and must be proved by specific evidence as to time, cause, and amount.[102] Special harm must arise by the time a cause of action is filed.[103] Further, the evidence must show that the defamation was the proximate cause of the harm or at least was a substantial factor in bringing it about.[104]

Most special damage awards arise from evidence concerning a plaintiff's inability to secure employment as a result of the defamation. The particularity with which a plaintiff must show evidence of financial loss, however, is usually left to the discretion of the court. For this reason, results are often inconsistent. As previously noted, proof of special damages may also be an element of proof required in certain cases.

---

[98]*Riss v. Anderson*, 304 F.2d 188 (8th cir. 1962); *Cook v. Safeway Stores*, 266 Ore. 77, 511 P.2d 375 (1973); *Barlow v. International Harvester Co.*, 95 Idaho 881, 522 P.2d 1102 (1974); *Bloomfield v. Retail Credit Co.*, 14 Ill. App.3d 158, 302 N.E.2d 88 (1973); *Cook v. East Shore Newspapers, Inc.*, 327 Ill. App. 559, 64 N.E.2d 751 (1945); *Corbin v. Madison*, 12 Wash. App. 318, 529 P.2d 1145 (1974); *Weenig v. Wood*, 169 Ind. App. 413, 349 N.E.2d 235 (1976); *Bobenhauser v. Cassat Ave. Mobile Homes, Inc.*, 344 So.2d 279 (Fla. Dist. Ct. App. 1977); *Stuempges v. Parke, Davis & Co.*, 297 N.W.2d 252 (Minn. 1980).

[99]Courts usually consider mental suffering and anguish and injured feelings arising from the defamation in fixing the amount of general damages. In *Van Norman v. Peoria Journal Star*, 31 Ill. App.2d 314, 175 N.E.2d 805 (1961), 35,000 copies of a newspaper article characterizing a city councilman as "a man who came to city hall in a drunken condition carrying a gun" were circulated. Because of the wide publication and the councilman's prominence in the community, general damages of $5,000 were awarded. Similarly, in *Cook v. East Shore Newspaper, Inc.*, 327 Ill. App. 559, 64 N.E.2d 751 (1945), front-page articles accusing a judge of taking payoffs from employees gave rise to a $20,000 general award. See also *Calero v. Del Chem. Corp.*, 68 Wis.2d 487, 228 N.W.2d 737 (1975) ($3,000 award); *Stuempges v. Parke, Davis & Co.*, 297 N.W.2d 252 (Minn. 1980) ($10,000 award); *Corbin v. Madison*, 12 Wash. App. 318, 529 P.2d 1145 (1974). In *Eulo v. Deval Aerodynamics, Inc.*, 47 F.R.D. 35 (E.D. Pa. 1968), *rev'd in part*, 430 F.2d 325 (3rd Cir. 1970), a corporation sent a letter to a shareholder stating that because of huge losses its president had resigned. Although the former company president prevailed in a defamation action, the jury awarded him only six cents. In upholding the award, the appellate court noted that it was unable to hold that the jury's assessment that the president had suffered only a "technical" libel was unreasonable.

[100]*Gertz v. Welch*, 418 U.S. 323 (1974).

[101]*Id.*

[102]*M.F. Peterson Dental Supply Co. v. Wadley*, 401 F.2d 167 (10th Cir. 1968); *Barry College v. Hull*, 353 So.2d 575 (Fla. Dist. Ct. App. 1977).

[103]*Williams v. Rutherford Freight Lines*, 10 N.C. App. 384, 179 S.E.2d 319 (1971).

[104]Thus, mere allegations that plaintiff suffered special damages to personal reputation were insufficient to impose damages in *Haynes v. Alverno Heights Hosp.*, 515 P.2d 568 (Okla. 1973).

Punitive damages, like general damages, can be recovered only if actual malice as defined in *New York Times v. Sullivan* can be proved.[105] This is a topic covered in more detail in Chapter 11.

It is one of the anomalies of employment law that the more serious the reason for discharge of an employee, the greater the danger to the employer of a defamation lawsuit. If, for example, a clerk is discharged from a grocery store or a nurse is discharged from a hospital for lack of punctuality, it is likely that each will get another job even if prospective employers know the reason for the discharge. They might well believe that the employee had learned a lesson or that the tardiness was a consequence of family problems that were now under control. However, if the clerk is discharged for stealing from the cash register or the nurse is discharged for suspicion of murder, it is unlikely that either will be rehired in a similar position if prospective employers are fully informed of the reason for the discharge. It is the very difficulty of obtaining substitute employment that may motivate an action for defamation. The employee may have little to lose from further publicizing the reason for the discharge and a great deal to gain by vindicating his name, avenging all real and imagined wrong, and possibly recovering a lot of money.

Yet complete silence on the employer's part is not realistic. If a crime has been committed, there is a civic duty to disclose it to the proper authorities. Whether or not damage has been suffered by or claims have been made against the employer, insurance coverage may require notice of the possibility of a claim. If the employee was terminated for innocent conduct, silence in the face of legitimate requests for references conveys an unfair message to prospective employers. No hard and fast governing rules for all situations can be laid down with confidence. Senior managers must exercise judgment in threading their way through this bramble patch of the law.

---

[105]*Gertz v. Welch*, 418 U.S. 323 (1974)

III

Status Analysis

10

Beyond Property and Contract: Fair Procedure in Denial of Group Membership and Its Applications to Employment

Historically, individuals seeking relief from arbitrary exclusion or expulsion from private voluntary associations have shared the frustrations of employees seeking to protect their job security. Courts have traditionally refused to interfere with the actions of voluntary associations out of respect for group autonomy and an unwillingness to substitute the judge's or jury's judgment for the association's in the group's private affairs.[1] Accordingly, if an individual was unable to characterize his grievance as a deprivation of tangible property or breach of contract, he was denied judicial relief, regardless of the severity of injury resulting from lack of group membership or employment.[2] In the past two decades, however, the courts have begun to fashion a doctrine of fair procedure applicable to situations in which the economic power wielded by an association is such that denial of or expulsion from membership threatens the individual's power to earn a living. Nonmembers as well as members have thus

---

[1]Note, *Exclusion From Private Associations*, 74 YALE L.J. 1313 (1965); Affeldt & Seney, *Group Sanctions and Personal Rights—Professions, Occupations and Labor Law* (pt. 1), 11 ST. LOUIS U.L.J. 382, 384–385 (1967); Chafee, *The Internal Affairs of Associations Not for Profit*, 43 HARV. L. REV. 993, 1020–1029 (1930); *Developments in the Law—Judicial Control of Actions of Private Associations*, 76 HARV. L. REV. 983, 990–994 (1963); Pasley, *Exclusion and Expulsion From Non-Profit Organizations—The Civil Rights Aspect*, 14 CLEV.–MAR. L. REV. 203 (1965); Annot., 20 A.L.R.2d 344 (1951); Annot., 20 A.L.R.2d 531 (1951); *Blende v. Maricopa County Medical Soc'y*, 96 Ariz. 240, 244, 245, 393 P.2d 926, 929, 930 (1964); *Kronen v. Pacific Coast Soc'y of Orthodontists*, 237 Cal. App.2d 289, 301, 302, 46 Cal. Rptr. 808, 816, 817 (1965); *Schooler v. Tarrant County Medical Soc'y*, 457 S.W.2d 644 (Tex. Civ. App. 1970).

[2]Chafee, *supra* note 1, at 998, 1001; Affeldt & Seney, *Group Sanctions and Personal Rights—Professions, Occupations and Labor Law* (pt. 2), 12 ST. LOUIS U.L.J. 177, 177–181 (1967–68).

been enabled to seek judicial review of their claims of unfair treatment.

The primary purpose of this chapter is to acquaint the reader with this developing area of the common law. It has obvious importance for the self-employed and those employed by others who must belong to medical staffs, boards of realtors, jockey associations, or other voluntary associations as a condition of practicing their profession or business. Near the end of the chapter we shall discuss the few cases, primarily from California, in which attempts have been made to apply the common law of fair procedure, initiated in association and hospital staff admissions cases, to the traditional employment relationship. First, however, we will survey the spectrum of issues that arise in these cases.

Common Law Issues in a Voluntary Association's Membership Decisions—The Medical Staff Controversy

Controversies between hospitals and self-employed physicians who wish to become members of hospital medical staffs or who challenge disciplinary action, exclusion, or expulsion from medical staffs present the whole array of issues that voluntary associations of all kinds may encounter in their decisions respecting membership. The following outline relies heavily upon hospital medical staff cases because these cases constitute the largest part of this body of law.

The Question of Judicial Review

The threshold question is whether a court will take cognizance of the controversy. When a court considers whether there should be judicial review, it is really deciding whether an association may arbitrarily, irrationally, or discriminatorily exclude applicants or discipline or expel members. A refusal of judicial review is not unlike a recognition of employment-at-will in the familiar employer-employee discharge case. In both cases, courts refuse to intervene no matter how arbitrary the conduct of the association or employer is alleged to be.

Constitutionally, actions by public hospitals are state action. Consequently, their medical staff decisions with respect to credentials are subject to judicial review under the standards of the Fourteenth Amendment of the U.S. Constitution.[3] Private hospital decisions concerning staff appointments and discipline are not subject to uniform common law standards of judicial review. Some authorities hold that no judicial review of private hospital credential decisions is permit-

---

[3]*Foster v. Mobile County Hosp. Bd.*, 398 F.2d 227 (5th Cir. 1968).

ted.[4] One case, however, refers to private hospitals as "quasi-public" if they are so invested with state action by virtue of extensive government regulation and funding that their decisions must meet the tests of the Fourteenth Amendment.[5] The Seventh Circuit has held, however, that staff decisions in private hospitals are subject to judicial review under standards of constitutional due process only if the state actively and directly supports the challenged conduct.[6]

Many jurisdictions permit judicial review of a private voluntary association's membership decisions that affect members' ability to earn a living. The rejection by a professional association of an applicant for membership has been held subject to judicial review if membership is an economic necessity.[7] One court has held that termination of membership privileges by a grocers' association was "tinged with public stature and purpose" and could be reviewed for a fair hearing before an impartial tribunal if "an important economic interest" was at stake.[8] In Florida, a statute places public and private hospitals on the same footing with respect to membership standards.[9]

Procedural Due Process and Minimum Standards for Fair Procedure

After the court decides that there will be judicial review, the question becomes: judicial review of what and judicial review by what standards? When the disappointed member of the association or applicant for membership attacks the association's procedures, the issue is whether the procedures conform to the standards of the Fourteenth Amendment if state action is involved, or conform to the prerequisites of fair procedure when significant economic interests of the member or applicant are in the balance. A basic tenet of procedural due process is that a party is entitled to an opportunity to be heard "at a meaningful time and in a meaningful manner."[10] There is, however, no set inflexible judicial procedure for guaranteeing due process.[11]

Buttrey v. United States,[12] while not a credentials controversy of

---

[4]*Tigua v. General Hosp., Inc. v. Feuerberg*, 645 S.W.2d 575 (Tex. Civ. App. 1982); *Kahn v. Suburban Community Hosp.*, 45 Ohio St.2d 39, 44, 45, 340 N.E.2d 398, 402 (1976) ("The great weight of authority in the United States is that * * * the action of hospital trustees in refusing to appoint a physician to its medical or surgical staff or declining to renew an appointment that has expired or changing the requirements for staff privileges, is not subject to judicial review").

[5]*Peterson v. Tucson Gen. Hosp.*, 114 Ariz. 66, 559 P.2d 186 (Ct. App. 1976).

[6]*Cannon v. University of Chicago*, 559 F.2d 1063 (7th Cir. 1976); *Doe v. Berlin Memorial Hosp.*, 479 F.2d 756 (7th Cir. 1973). Accord: *Mauer v. Highland Park Hosp. Found.*, 90 Ill. App.2d 409, 232 N.E.2d 776 (1967); *Hoffman v. Garden City Hosp.-Osteopathic*, 115 Mich. App. 773, 321 N.W.2d 810 (1982); *Settler v. Hopedale Medical Found.*, 80 Ill. App.3d 850, 400 N.E.2d 577 (1980); *Knapp v. Palos Community Hosp.*, ___ Ill. App.3d___, 465 N.E.2d 554 (1984).

[7]*Treister v. American Academy of Orthopaedic Surgeons*, 78 Ill. App.3d 746, 396 N.E.2d 1225 (1979).

[8]*Van Daele v. Vinci*, 51 Ill.2d 389, 282 N.E.2d 728 (1972).

[9]*Carida v. Holy Cross Hosp., Inc.*, 427 So.2d 803 (Fla. Dist. Ct. App. 1983).

[10]*Armstrong v. Manzo*, 380 U.S. 543, 552 (1965).

[11]"[D]ue process is flexible and calls for such procedural protections as the particular procedure demands." *Morrisey v. Brewer*, 408 U.S. 471, 481 (1972).

[12]690 F.2d 1170 (5th Cir. 1982); 690 F.2d 1186 (5th Cir. 1982).

a voluntary association, presents the constitutional analysis for determining what process is due, and also demonstrates the flexibility of due process. In *Buttrey*, a private real estate developer challenged a decision by the U.S. Army Corps of Engineers denying the developer permits for the rechanneling of a stream for flood control and real estate development purposes. The Corps of Engineers gave the developer a "paper hearing"—basically an exchange of correspondence, with one informal and off-the-record meeting between the Corps commander and the developer. The court stated:

> "The starting point for any inquiry into how much 'process' is 'due' must be the Supreme Court's opinion in *Mathews v. Eldridge*, 424 U.S. 319, 96 S.Ct. 893, 47 L.Ed.2d 18 (1976). Implicitly adopting the three-part analysis developed by Judge Friendly the previous year, Friendly, *'Some Kind of Hearing,'* 123 U. PA. L.REV. 1267, 1278 (1975), the court set out the three most important considerations that a court should balance:
>
> > 'First, the private interest that will be affected by the official action; second, the risk of an erroneous deprivation of such interest through the procedures used, and the probable value, if any, of additional or substitute procedural safeguards; and finally, the Government's interest, including the function involved and the fiscal and administrative burdens that the additional or substitute procedural requirement would entail.'
>
> * * *
>
> "The procedures adopted by the Corps of Engineers in reviewing Buttrey's Section 404 permit application afforded him considerable protection. The Corps in effect gives applicants a 'paper hearing.' After public notice of the pending application has been given, the Corps usually receives numerous comments from other federal agencies and the interested public. As the comments arrive, they are (and were in this case) immediately forwarded to the applicant.* * *
> * * *
> "Even if this case did depend upon conflicting scientific testimony, as Buttrey claims it does, the right of cross-examination provided by full trial-type procedures would probably serve little purpose. Many courts and commentators have concluded that cross-examination of scientific witnesses in a case of this sort is often, if not always, an exercise in futility. See, *See, e.g., Eldridge, supra*, 424 U.S. at 343-44, 96 S.Ct. at 907 (noting probable worthlessness of opportunity to cross-examine expert physician specialists); *Basciano v. Herkimer*, 605 F.2d 605, 610-11 (2d Cir. 1978) ('[T]he value of cross-examination to discredit a professional medical opinion at best is limited'), *cert. denied*, 442 U.S. 929, 99 S.Ct. 2858, 61 L.Ed.2d 296 (1979); 3 K. Davis, *supra*, § 15:10 at 184 (2d ed. 1980) (recommending that cross-examination be 'rarely allowed' in cases involving mixtures of legislative fact and judgment); Ames & McCracken, *supra*, at 35 ('Cross-examination * * * will be most cumbersome when the issues are complex * * * '); Friendly, *supra*, at 1285 ('in many such [recondite scientific or economic] cases the main effect of cross-examination is delay.'); Korn, *Law, Fact and Science in the Courts*, 66 COLUM. L. REV. 1080, 1086–87 (1966) (the value of cross-examination 'is often negligible where the dispute turns on matters of expert judgment rather than veracity'), *but cf.* Boyer, *Alternatives to Administrative Trial-type Hearings for Resolving Complex Scientific, Economic, and Social Issues*, 71 MICH. L. REV. 111, 127–28, (1972)

(noting controversial nature of cross-examination of expert witnesses)."[13]

Hospital medical staff controversies that address standards for due process have evolved some practical applications of the general principles outlined in *Buttrey*. However, when considering due process within a voluntary organization, there is a difference between committees that exercise an investigative function and those that perform an adjudicative function. Only in the case of the latter are due process or fair procedure standards required.[14] An opportunity to present and cross-examine witnesses must be afforded, but the challenger is not entitled to challenge the competence of the persons acting on behalf of the association and cross-examine persons not presenting evidence.[15] One is entitled to an impartial hearing, but bias is not shown by the fact that the persons making up the review panel participated in other panels considering other charges of incompetence.[16] Although a staff member is entitled to an unbiased hearing, the mere fact that officers of the hospital saw it as their duty to oppose the staff member's renewal of membership or privileges is not enough to prove that proceedings within the hospital were unfair or biased.[17]

Whether the review of membership decisions of voluntary associations is premised upon rights originating in tort, property, con-

---

[13]*Id.* at 1177–1183.

[14]*Koelling v. Board of Trustees*, 259 Iowa 1185, 146 N.W.2d 284 (1966).

[15]*Woodbury v. McKinnon*, 447 F.2d 839, 844 (5th Cir. 1971). This is the single best opinion outlining the analysis of issues in hospital medical staff cases. The court stated:

"It is the plaintiff's position that inasmuch as his surgical judgment was being considered by members of the medical staff who practiced in the hospital, they must submit themselves to the test of their own surgical judgment. In effect, he would try the judges. We do not believe that this is a constitutional necessity. *United States v. Morgan*, 313 U.S. 409, 422, 61 S.Ct. 999, 85 L.Ed. 1429 (1941).

"The hearing was an informal discussion by the medical staff of the cases specified in the charges against the plaintiff. There were no witnesses presented at the hearing. Nor did any of the doctors testify in any sense of the word. The members of the medical staff, including plaintiff, were free to make comments or ask questions concerning each particular case as reflected in the hospital records. Under these circumstances, there was no one to cross-examine. The plaintiff's attorney, although present, was not permitted to question the other doctors present. However, the plaintiff was allowed to ask questions and exercised that privilege freely. Since the attorney and the plaintiff could confer at will, we will see no due process violation in the refusal to permit the attorney to ask questions. Dr. Woodbury was in a familiar setting, with familiar people, discussing a familiar subject. His expertise and acquaintance with the facts of each case thoroughly qualified him to be effective in discussion with his fellow doctors.

"We have held that cross-examination need not be a part of every hearing in order to satisfy due process. *Dixon v. Alabama State Board of Education*, 294 F.2d 150 (5th Cir. 1951). Whether it is required depends upon the circumstances. Because of the nature of the charges (professional competence) and the nature of the hearing (informal discussion of medical records with no witnesses) cross-examination was not required in this case." See also H. Robert, ROBERT'S RULES OF ORDER §75 Trial of Members of Societies (rev. ed. 1979). And see the statement that

"[a] notorious pickpocket could not even be arrested, much less convicted by a civil court, simply on the ground of being commonly known as a pickpocket; while such evidence could convict and expel him from any ordinary society.

"The moral conviction of the truth of the charge is all that is necessary in an ecclesiastical or other deliberative body to find the accused guilty of the charges." See also *Knapp v. Palos Community Hosp.*, ___ Ill. App.3d___, 465 N.E.2d 554 (1984).

[16]*Yarnell v. Sisters of St. Francis Health Servs.*, 446 N.E.2d 359 (Ind. App. 1983).

[17]*Id.*

tract law, or otherwise is unclear. *Virgin v. American College of Surgeons*,[18] which concerned the expulsion of a member from a professional society concluded:

> "Whether the 'interest of substance' which accrues to a member of a professional association is called a 'property right,' 'contract right' or merely the 'member's relation to the association,' there is a growing awareness that wrongful expulsion from a voluntary professional association has such a serious effect on the ability of the professional man to successfully pursue his livelihood that it is a judicially protectable interest [citation omitted]."[19]

If the interest to be protected is merely the member's economic interest in his relationship to the voluntary association, judicial review, if appropriate, is invoked by the common law writ of certiorari rather than an action at law or in equity for tortious conduct or breach of contract.[20] The nature of the action, however, can influence the choice of governing substantive law and the extent to which the court scrutinizes the conduct of the voluntary association. Under the common law writ of certiorari, there may be no right to a jury trial. The trial court simply reviews the record of the association's decision to determine whether it proceeded according to appropriate due process or fair procedure standards and whether there is anything in the record that fairly tends to sustain the action of the association.[21] Although the procedure confines the trial judge to the record of proceedings during the decision process, the record consists of both documentation and testimony concerning what occurred. The Illinois Medical Studies Act[22] specifically permits physicians to obtain discovery of the membership decisions of hospital medical staffs for purposes of judicial review.

The medical staff member who is disciplined must be given written notice of the complaint against him. However, a letter notice and an opportunity to be heard are sufficient procedures.[23] If the disciplined member or disappointed applicant is not misled or prejudiced

---

[18]42 Ill. App.2d 352, 192 N.E.2d 414 (1963).

[19]*Id.* at 369, 192 N.E.2d at 422.

[20]*Ladenheim v. Union County Hosp. Dist.*, 76 Ill. App.3d 90, 394 N.E.2d 770 (1979).

[21]*Odell v. Village of Hoffman Estates*, 110 Ill. App.3d 974, 443 N.E.2d 247 (1982).

[22]ILL. REV. STAT. ch. 110, §8-2101 *et seq.* (1983).

[23]*Bryant v. City of Lakeland*, 158 Fla. 151, 28 So.2d 106 (1947) (public hospital); *Van Daele v. Vinci*, 51 Ill.2d 389, 282 N.E.2d 728 (1972); *Landenheim v. Union County Hosp.*, 76 Ill. App.3d 90, 394 N.E.2d 770 (1979); *Mufson v. Pennsylvania Dep't of Pub. Welfare*, 72 Pa. Commw. 404, 456 A.2d 736 (1983). The physician's knowledge of his own patients' charts is a factor to consider in determining whether a physician received proper notice and adequate time to prepare. See *Klinge v. Lutheran Charities Ass'n*, 523 F.2d 56 (8th Cir. 1975); *Kaplan v. Carney*, 404 F. Supp. 161 (E.D. Mo. 1975); *Woodbury v. McKinnon*, 447 F. 2d 839 (5th Cir. 1971). The adequacy of a notice is a function of its language and the knowledge of the subject matter that the recipient of the notice has:

"The charges in administrative proceedings need not be drawn with the same precision required of pleadings in judicial action. *Kelly v. Police Board of Chicago* (1st Dist. 1975) 25 Ill. App.3d 559, 323 N.E.2d 624. They need only be sufficiently clear and specific to

by the original notice, no violation of due process has occurred.[24] Extensive and formal trial procedures need not be followed. Due process in private hospitals requires that the hospital must follow its own bylaws.[25] It also means that the decision-maker must be impartial.[26] The burden of proof and the burden of going forward may be placed upon the person challenging the credential decision. The complaining applicant for membership or disciplined member has been held to have a right to counsel during the course of the pro-

---

allow preparation of a defense. *Kelly v. Police Board of Chicago; Carro v. The Board of Education, City of Chicago,* (1st Dist. 1977) 46 Ill. App.3d 33, 4 Ill. Dec. 600, 360 N.E.2d 536. The test of the adequacy of notice is whether the party receiving the notice should have anticipated the possible effects of the hearing on the basis of the notice. *Hyon Waste Management Services v. City of Chicago,* (1st Dist. 1977), 53 Ill. App.3d 1013, 11 Ill. Dec. 725, 369 N.E.2d 179, *Department of Revenue v. Jamb Discount,* (2d Dist. 1973), 13 Ill. App.3d 430, 301 N.E.2d 23."

Baker v. Illinois Racing Bd., 101 Ill. App.3d 580, 584, 427 N.E.2d 959, 962 (1981). In *Kaplan v. Carney,* 404 F. Supp. 161, 164 (E.D. Mo. 1975), addressing the plaintiff's claim that a letter did not provide adequate notice under principles of procedural due process, the court stated:

"The record establishes that plaintiff was given adequate notice on June 16, 1972, and an opportunity to be heard at the June 26, 1972 meeting with the Executive Committee. That only ten out of twenty-four charts were discussed at that meeting does not change this court's conclusion that due process was complied with. Plaintiff had been given the charts involved earlier that day. The charts were his own and '[p]resumably, he had some existing recollection of the particular cases that would be considered by the hearing panel' [quoting *Klinge v. Lutheran Charities Ass'n,* 523 F.2d 56, 60 (8th Cir. 1975)]."

See also *Woodbury v. McKinnon,* 447 F.2d 839 (5th Cir. 1971); *Storrs v. Lutheran Hosp. Home Soc'y of Am., Inc.,* 609 P.2d 24 (Alaska 1980); *Duffield v. Charleston Area Medical Center, Inc.,* 503 F.2d 512 (4th Cir. 1974).

[24]In *Anton v. San Antonio Community Hosp.,* 19 Cal.3d 802, 828, 567 P.2d 1162, 1177, 140 Cal. Rptr. 442, 457 (1977), a physician filed suit to compel a hospital to reappoint him to the medical staff and reinstate his staff privileges. One of the issues raised on appeal was whether a particular hospital bylaw, which placed on the physician both the burden of proof and the burden of going forward with the evidence, was inconsistent with the minimum requirements of a fair and impartial hearing. The California Supreme Court relied upon its decision in *Pinsker v. Pacific Coast Soc'y,* 12 Cal.3d 541, 555–556, 526 P.2d 253, 263, 116 Cal. Rptr. 245, 255 (1974), in which it stated:

"The common law requirement of a fair procedure does not compel formal proceedings with all of the embellishments of a court trial * * * nor adherence to a single mode of process. It may be satisfied by any one of a variety of procedures which afford a fair opportunity for an [affected party] to present his position. As such, this court should not attempt to fix a rigid procedure that must invariably be observed. Instead, the associations themselves should retain the initial and primary responsibility for devising a method which provides an [affected party] adequate notice of the 'charges' against him and a reasonable opportunity to respond. In drafting such procedure * * * the organization should consider the nature of the tendered issue and should fashion its procedure to insure a *fair* opportunity for [an affected party] to present his position. Although the association retains discretion in formalizing such procedures, the courts remain available to afford relief in the event of the abuse of such discretion."

The court concluded that the adoption and application of this bylaw did not amount to an abuse of discretion and therefore upheld its use against the physician.

Hosptials are entitled to adopt reasonable rules for the conduct of their internal management. See, e.g., *Fahey v. Holy Name Hosp.,* 32 Ill. App.3d 537, 336 N.E.2d 309 (1975); *Sosa v. Board of Managers,* 437 F.2d 173 (5th Cir. 1971); *Kaplan v. Carney,* 404 F. Supp. 161 (E.D. Mo. 1975).

[25]*Nagib v. St. Therese Hosp., Inc.,* 41 Ill. App.3d 970, 355 N.E.2d 211 (1976); *Spencer v. Community Hosp.,* 87 Ill. App.3d 214, 408 N.E.2d 981 (1980); *Settler v. Hopedale Medical Found.,* 80 Ill. App.3d 850, 400 N.E.2d 577 (1980); *Jain v. Northwest Community Hosp.,* 67 Ill. App.3d 420, 385 N.E.2d 108 (1978); *Knapp v. Palos Community Hosp.,* __ Ill. App.3d __, 465 N.E.2d 554 (1984); *Scappatura v. Baptist Hosp.,* 120 Ariz. 204, 584 P.2d 1195 (1978); *Schulman v. Washington Hosp. Center,* 222 F. Supp. 59 (D.D.C. 1963).

[26]*Van Daele v. Vinci,* 51 Ill.2d 389, 282 N.E.2d 728 (1972); *Ladenheim v. Union County Hosp.,* 76 Ill. App.3d 90, 95, 394 N.E.2d 770, 774 (1979) ("The only bias and familiarity which disqualifies a member of a tribunal is that which derives from an extra-judicial source and which results in an opinion on the merits based on something other than that which was learned by participating in the case").

ceedings, but procedural errors that are neither prejudicial nor determinative of the issues do not violate due process.[27] And a procedural error at one point in the proceedings may be cured by a proceeding at a later stage.[28]

Substantive Due Process—Whether the Governing Rule or Regulation Is Reasonably Related to the Association's Purpose

Generally, a hospital's discretion in the setting of rules and regulations is limited only by the requirement that standards for medical staff privileges be reasonably related to furthering the goal of providing high-quality patient care and that the power of the hospital not be exercised in an unreasonably arbitrary and capricious manner.[29] Broad subjective standards are permitted.[30] A Fifth Circuit opinion describes the common sense deference courts show when rules and regulations are the product of the expertise of a hospital board or medical staff:

> "It is the Board, not the court, which is charged with the responsibility of providing a competent staff of doctors. The Board has chosen to rely on the advice of its Medical Staff in executing this responsibility. Human lives are at stake, and the governing Board must be given discretion in its selection so that it can have confidence in the competence and moral commitment of its staff. The evaluation of professional proficiency of doctors is best left to the specialized expertise of their peers, subject only to limited judicial surveillance. The court is charged with the narrow responsibility of assuring that the qualifications imposed by the Board are reasonably related to the operation of the Hospital and fairly administered."[31]

---

[27]*Silver v. Queen's Hosp.*, 63 Hawaii 430, 629 P.2d 1116 (1981).

[28]*Even v. Longmont United Hosp. Ass'n*, 629 P.2d 1100 (Colo. Ct. App. 1981); *Brickman v. Board of Directors*, 372 So.2d 701 (La. Ct. App. 1979) (de minimis violations of bylaws insufficient to warrant reversal of hospital action). See also *Ritter v. Board of Comm'rs*, 96 Wash.2d 503, 637 P.2d 940 (1981) (postsuspension hearing cured defects in previous meeting).

[29]*Sarasota County Pub. Hosp. Bd. v. El Shahawy*, 408 So.2d 644 (Fla. Dist. Ct. App. 1982).

[30]*Huffaker v. Bailey*, 273 Ore. 273, 540 P.2d 1398 (1975). See also *Spencer v. Community Hosp.*, 87 Ill. App.3d 214, 408 N.E.2d 981 (1980) (physician charged in part with "failure to cooperate with the utilization review committee and/or failure to complete records to justify continued hospitalization; and improper or excessive prescription of narcotics; improper or excessive prescription of steroids or antibiotics; improper medical treatment of patients * * *"); *Anton v. San Antonio Community Hosp.*, 19 Cal.3d 802, 567 P.2d 1162, 140 Cal. Rptr. 442 (1977) (physician charged in part with "over utilization of hospital facilities and services, as evidenced by the following records: [citation to chart numbers of 10 hospital records]"); *Kaplan v. Carney*, 404 F. Supp. 161 (E.D. Mo. 1975) (physician charged with exaggerated diagnoses, inappropriate treatment, and errors of medical judgment; precise standards of competency are not required or even possible).

[31]*Sosa v. Board of Managers*, 437 F.2d 173, 177 (5th Cir. 1971). Accord: *Miller v. Eisenhower Medical Center*, 27 Cal.3d 614, 614 P.2d 258, 166 Cal. Rptr. 826, (1980). In *Campbell v. St. Mary's Hosp.*, 312 Minn. 379, 389, 252 N.W.2d 581, 587 (1977), the court stated:

> "Our ignorance of such multisyllable terms found in the present records as 'parathyroidectomy' and 'aneurysmectomy' is no less than that shared by the general public. Simply stated, courts are ill-equipped to pass judgment on the specialized expertise required of a physician, particularly when such a decision is likely to have a direct impact on human life."

Grounds for Challenging Association Decisions

If substantive rules further the objectives of the association and procedures are fair and were followed, to what extent can the outcome be challenged? When a disciplined member of a voluntary association or a disappointed applicant for membership claims the decision against him was wrong on its merits, the standard for review under well-settled administrative law principles is whether the decision is supported by substantial evidence.[32] Substantial evidence has been defined as the amount and quality of evidence that would warrant a reasonable man's reaching a conclusion.[33] The issue is not whether the voluntary association arrived at the proper conclusion on the basis of conflicting evidence, but whether it acted arbitrarily and without regard to the facts.[34] A hospital decision is supported by substantial evidence even if it considers matters that do not relate to current or existing cause for terminating a staff member. The hospital can consider past conduct and an entire pattern of conduct, elements of which would not have been sufficient in and of themselves to warrant drastic discipline or termination from the staff.[35] Refusal of staff membership privileges based upon the physician's inadequate preparation of patient records may alone be sufficient to warrant discipline.[36] It is up to the hospital board to resolve inconsistent testimony.[37] It is irrelevant that the sample of patient charts examined by peer review committees is not a recognized statistical sample if the sample is regarded as valid by the staff or the hospital board.[38] The hospital board need not follow the recommendation of the medical staff. Indeed, there may be substantial evidence to support the board's action even when medical staff recommendations are inconsistent.[39] Where a hospital credentials committee took no action

---

[32]See K. Davis, ADMINISTRATIVE LAW TREATISE §15.1 (2d ed. 1980); *Unterthiner v. Desert Hosp. Dist.*, 33 Cal.3d 285, 656 P.2d 554, 188 Cal. Rptr. 590 (1983).

[33]*Silver v. Queens Hosp.*, 63 Hawaii 430, 629 P.2d 1116 (1981); *Anderson v. Board of Trustees*, 10 Mich. App. 348, 159 N.W.2d 347 (1968) (well-documented disruptive behavior by a physician).

[34]*Laje v. R.E. Thomasen Gen. Hosp.*, 564 F.2d 1159 (5th Cir. 1978).

[35]*Peterson v. Tucson Gen. Hosp.*, 114 Ariz. 66, 559 P.2d 186 (1976); *Miller v. Indiana Hosp.*, 277 Pa. Super. 370, 419 A.2d 1191, 1194 (1980), in which the court stated:
"Merely reappointing appellant annually to the staff did not indicate an intention on the part of the hospital to ignore the cumulative effect of appellant's prior misconduct. Appellant has not alleged nor proven any reliance upon the assumption that the actions of the hospital constituted a waiver. It was therefore proper for the hospital committee to consider prior misconduct which might not have been so egregious in any one year as to warrant denial of reappointment, but the cumulative effect of which called for Appellant's dismissal from the staff."
Contra: *Wyatt v. Tahoe Forest Hosp. Dist.*, 174 Cal. App.2d 709, 345 P.2d 93 (1959) (hospital must consider only current cause for termination).

[36]*Peterson v. Tucson Gen. Hosp.*, 114 Ariz. 66, 559 P.2d 186 (Ct. App. 1976).

[37]*Laje v. R.E. Thomasen Gen. Hosp.*, 564 F.2d 1159 (5th Cir. 1978).

[38]*Id.*

[39]*Yarnell v. Sisters of St. Francis Health Servs., Inc.*, 446 N.E.2d 359 (Ind. App. 1983). In *Ritter v. Board of Comm'rs*, 96 Wash.2d 503, 515–516, 637 P.2d 940, 947–948 (1981), the court stated:
"Administrative action is not arbitrary or capricious if there are grounds for two or more reasonable opinions and the agency reached its decision honestly and with due consideration of the relevant circumstances. Such action is not arbitrary or capricious merely because an appellate court believes it would have reached a different decision on the same

because at least one of its members did not want to get involved and the medical staff passed a resolution reappointing the plaintiffs to the staff, the board members still had an independent and nondelegable duty to refuse appointment to a physician they believed unqualified. Affirming the board's discretion, an appellate court stated that board members were not entitled to look the other way when they believed the medical staff was wrong; moreover, the board members were individually liable for damages to a patient injured by an incompetent staff member known to be incompetent at the time his privileges were renewed.[40] The substantial evidence test itself presents the risk that confidential patient information will be disclosed in the course of judicial review of hospital credential decisions. Thus, judicial review of hospital matters may be more circumspect than that of questions involving other voluntary organizations.[41]

Remedies

If a court finds a substantial violation of the rights of the individual, what remedy is appropriate? The remedy of money damages is open to an individual found to be wrongfully injured by a voluntary association's membership or disciplinary proceedings. Chapter 11 discusses damages and specific injuries that may warrant recovery of

---

facts. *See, e.g., Barrie v. Kitsap County*, 93 Wash.2d 843, 850, 613 P.2d 1148 (1980). Our scope of review should be specially unobtrusive in this context given the gravity of interests at stake, the inherent difficulty of precisely defining fitness to be a member of a hospital staff, and the judiciary's limited capacity to question competently a hospital administration's discretion in such matters. *See Sosa v. Board of Managers of Val Verde Memorial Hospital*, 437 F.2d 173, 176–177 (5th Cir. 1971); *Shulman v. Washington Hosp. Center*, 222 F. Supp. 59 (D.D.C. 1963); *Khan v. Suburban Community Hosp.*, 45 Ohio St.2d 39, 44, 340 N.E.2d 398 (1976). '[S]o long as [initial] staff selections are administered with fairness, geared by rationale compatible with hospital responsibility, and unencumbered with irrelevant considerations, a court should not interfere'. *Sosa* at 177. There is no reason why judicial review should not be similarly limited when staff privileges are withdrawn." See also *Suckle v. Madison Gen. Hosp.*, 362 F. Supp. 1196, 1209 (W.D. Wis. 1973).

[40]*Branch v. Hempsted County Hosp.*, 539 F. Supp. 908 (W.D. Ark. 1982).

[41]Only by wholesale disclosure of confidential information can judicial review of medical staff decisions in public and private hospitals embrace more than the questions of whether established procedures were followed, the procedures were fair, and the decision-makers were without bias. Further inquiry to decide whether the correct decision was reached concerning physician competence, alleged overuse of drug therapy or other therapeutic procedures, improper maintenance of patient records, or other such matters requires examination of the original patient records that were the basis for the hospital's decision. That information is also subject to the statutory physician–patient privilege. Such privilege may permit disclosure of confidential material for purposes of medical research and hospital decisions on credentials, but apparently no statute creating the privilege opens the material for use by physicians to vindicate their private interests and challenge decisions on credentials. The privilege is that of the patient, not of the physician; only the patient may waive it. See, e.g., ILL. REV. STAT. ch. 110, §8-802, which prohibits the release of patient charts without patient permission, and *Parkson v. Central DuPage Hosp.*, 105 Ill. App.3d 850; 435 N.E.2d 140 (1982), which holds that hospitals may assert the physician–patient privilege on behalf of patients. But see *United States v. Nixon*, 418 U.S. 683 (1974), which indicates that in some circumstances courts may have inherent power to set privileges aside. It is likely that courts will hold that hospitals have a duty to assert all available privileges for such documents in their custody. Even if the physician–patient privilege could or should be brushed aside to protect physicians' private interests in staff membership, judicial encroachment upon the hospital's decision-making process raises the question of judicial competence in matters of life and death if the court is unguided by expert testimony. Moreover, licensing and regulation by a state indicates that the legislature believes the sensitive credentials process is not only a matter of overarching public importance, but one best left to the hospitals themselves.

money in wrongful discharge cases. These are applicable here. The heart of the remedy problem, however, is whether and to what extent the voluntary organization may be ordered to reinstate a member or admit a new member.

Entitlement to an equitable remedy requires the plaintiff to satisfy several prerequisites for equitable relief. One requirement is that the prevailing party must show he has no adequate remedy at law because he will suffer irreparable harm if the requested relief is not granted.[42] This means the plaintiff must show that money alone is not enough. One is said to have suffered irreparable harm "when it is of such nature that the injured party cannot be adequately compensated therefor in (money) damages, or when damages which result therefrom cannot be measured by any certain pecuniary standard."[43] Court decisions have specifically addressed the question of whether threatened loss of income, inconvenience, and possible damage to reputation established irreparable injury and have rejected the argument. For example, in *Rutledge v. St. Vincent Memorial Hospital*,[44] a physician who had been a member of the medical staff of a private hospital for 11 years filed suit against the hospital and members of its governing board after being informed that the credentials committee had voted not to renew his privileges for the upcoming year. As a basis for his request that the trial court enjoin the defendants from denying him use of hospital facilities, the physician alleged he had built up a substantial medical practice, that the failure to reappoint him would cause him great damage, and that the denial of his medical staff privileges would cause irreparable harm. The trial court denied injunctive relief and the physician appealed. The appellate court affirmed, and specifically held as follows:

> "In his amended complaint, plaintiff alleges that the defendant hospital is the only hospital in Taylorville, that by reason of the denial of the use of the defendant hospital's facilities, his practice is curtailed and he will suffer irreparable damage unless the injunction is issued. Unquestionably, the loss of those privileges has caused inconvenience, and probably, loss of income, but we cannot hold that this fact, of itself, would require the trial court to enjoin the defendants from refusing to reappoint plaintiff to the staff of the defendant hospital. The bylaws provide that 'final responsibility' for such action rests with the Governing Board, and the issuance of a temporary injunction, would, in fact, determine for the Governing Board the manner in which that responsibility is to be discharged."[45]

---

[42]*Midwest Micromedia, Inc. v. Machotka*, 76 Ill. App.3d 698, 395 N.E.2d 188 (1979); *Shorr Paper Prods., Inc. v. Frary*, 74 Ill. App.3d 498, 292 N.E.2d 1148 (1979); *National Bank v. River Forest State Bank*, 3 Ill. App.3d 209, 278 N.E.2d 501 (1971).

[43]*Washingtonian Home v. City of Chicago*, 281 Ill. 110, 119, 117 N.E. 737, 741 (1917).

[44]67 Ill. App.2d 156, 214 N.E.2d 131 (1966). See *Jain v. Northwest Community Hosp.*, 67 Ill. App.3d 420, 385 N.E.2d 108 (1978), and *Fahey v. Holy Name Hosp.*, 32 Ill. App.3d 537, 336 N.E.2d 309 (1975). See also *Kurle v. Evangelical Hosp. Ass'n*, 89 Ill. App.3d 45, 411 N.E.2d 326 (1980) (where injunctive relief granting reinstatement of nurse to hospital was reversed on appeal for several reasons including finding that monetary damages provided adequate remedy at law).

[45]*Rutledge v. St. Vincent Memorial Hosp.*, 67 Ill. App.2d 156, 161, 214 N.E.2d 131, 134 (1966).

Courts have also denied injunctive relief where the only injury claimed was loss of income or damage to reputation. In *Early v. Bristol Memorial Hospital, Inc.*,[46] a physician filed an antitrust suit against a hospital after it suspended his medical staff privileges and requested a temporary restraining order enjoining the hospital from carrying out the suspension. In denying the plaintiff's request for injunctive relief, the court stated:

> "This Court will not grant injunctive relief where the party seeking the same appears to have an adequate remedy at law. *O'Shea v. Littleton* (1974), 414 U.S. 488, 499, 94 S.Ct. 669, 677, 38 L.Ed.2d 674, 685 [9,10]; *Roseboro v. Fayetteville City Board of Education*, D.C. Tenn. (1977), 491 F. Supp. 110 112[4], affirmed C.A. 6th (1980), 617 F.2d 603 * * *. If the defendants have in fact violated the Sherman Act, as is claimed by Dr. Early, then he is entitled to recover '* * * three-fold the damages sustained by them, and the cost of suit, including a reasonable attorney's fee. * * *' 15 U.S.C. §15. Although Dr. Early contends that his loss economically would be difficult to prove, nevertheless, he had demanded damages aggregating $250,000, which presumably would be trebled. This would appear to constitute an adequate remedy at law."[47]

It is often assumed that reinstatement will avoid future damage or undo reputation damage already done. That assumption may not be warranted, and *Dos Santos v. Columbus-Cuneo-Cabrini Medical Center*[48] is one of only a few cases that address the point. The Seventh Circuit Court of Appeals considered whether the district court had abused its discretion in granting injunctive relief to an anesthesiologist who was no longer permitted to provide anesthesia services at the hospital. The hospital had entered into an exclusive contract with an anesthesia group which had employed the plaintiff. When the anesthesiologist was terminated from employment, the hospital advised her that it could no longer allow her to provide anesthesia services although she could remain a member of the medical staff.

The Court of Appeals reversed the district court's grant of injunctive relief, holding that temporary loss of income does not establish irreparable harm because it can be remedied by an award of monetary damages. With respect to the claimed damage to reputation, the court stated:

> "Plaintiff sought and obtained a preliminary injunction invalidating the exclusive contract, which was the sole basis on which she was denied access to Columbus Hospital. But this injunction cannot redress the claimed injury to her professional standing because the exclusive contract is not the source of that injury. Plaintiff has suffered an injury to reputation not because of the operation of the exclusive contract (such arrangments are, as noted, prevalent among hospitals in the Chicago area) but rather because of the decision by the plaintiff's employer, Associates, to terminate her employment summarily. The relief awarded by the district court is simply incapable of erasing the fact that plaintiff was fired by her employer and it cannot remove the stigma

---

[46]508 F. Supp. 35 (E.D. Tenn. 1980).
[47]*Id*. at 37; *Kreutzer v. Clark*, 271 Ark. 243, 607 S.W.2d 670 (1980).
[48]684 F.2d 1346 (7th Cir. 1982).

and damage to reputation that often accompanies such a termination of employment. Thus, even if plaintiff's injury to reputation is both real and irreparable, it does not support the preliminary injunction that was granted."[49]

If the equitable remedy requires the association not to strike the name of a member from the membership list, that alone may permit the member to enjoy all the benefits of membership. For example, if a member of a professional nursing organization were eligible by virtue of membership to seek specialized nursing positions, an injunction prohibiting the cancellation of membership would maintain the status quo. Such an injunction is referred to as prohibitory or passive. An injunction that orders the defendant to do something affirmative is a mandatory injunction. A mandatory injunction carries a greater burden of proof.[50]

The reinstatement of a physician to a position on a medical staff is mandatory in character. The impact of reinstatement on the hospital is felt on a daily and even an hourly basis. The hospital must make available to the staff the full use of and access to all departments, admit patients when and as ordered by the staff, and provide nursing, laboratory, radiology, cardiology, surgical, and X-ray services and a host of other related health care and accounting services. The hospital becomes the unwilling servant of the staff physician during the course of the injunction.

If the injunction not only is mandatory but is to be awarded before there is a final trial on the merits, the standards of proof require a showing of great necessity and emergency.[51] The plaintiff's right that requires the protection of an equitable remedy must be clearly ascertainable from the evidence; and there must be a showing of probable ultimate success on the merits.[52]

Finally, entitlement to equitable relief requires a balancing of the equities. The court must conclude that its injunction will benefit the plaintiff more than it will harm the defendant. In a medical staff dispute, there may be no significant hospital interest at stake if the challenging physician was disciplined for nonpayment of dues or infrequent attendance at staff meetings. However, if discipline was the result of a staff decision critical of the plaintiff's competency, rein-

---

[49]*Id.* at 1350.

[50]In *Whitaker v. Pierce*, 44 Ill. App.3d 148, 152, 358 N.E.2d 61, 64 (1976), the plaintiff sought reinstatement after having been removed from his position as an organist-choir director at a church. The court held:

"Finally, we observe that the injunction here is mandatory in character because, in asking that defendants be restrained from terminating him and from hiring another in his place, plaintiff in effect asks the court to direct his reemployment and the discharge of his already employed successor. See *Liberty National Bank v. Newberry* (1955), 6 Ill. App.2d 252, 127 N.E.2d 269."

[51]*Grillo v. Sidney Wanzer & Sons*, 26 Ill. App.3d 1007, 1012, 326 N.E.2d 180, 184 (1975).

[52]*Grillo, id.* at 1013, 326 N.E.2d at 185, provides as follows:

"All that is necessary is that the petitioning party raise a fair question as to the existence of the right claimed, lead the court to believe that he will probably be entitled to the relief prayed for if the proof should sustain his allegation and make it appear advisable that the positions of the parties should stay as they are until the court has had an opportunity to consider the case on the merits."

statement can carry substantial risk of harm to patients and to the power and authority of the hospital to determine its own quality control standards.[53]

To obtain a full understanding of this subject and its possible application to employment law controversies, we will turn to a more detailed examination of the history and development of this law and its current status in several jurisdictions.

The Traditional Approach

As noted above, only in the past two decades have courts begun to develop a doctrine of fair procedure applicable to cases where individuals challenge the membership decisions of voluntary associations. Prior to this, it was generally held that a nonmember had no right to judicially compelled membership in an association.[54] Members who had been expelled obtained judicial relief against arbitrary action only if they could frame their dispute as a denial of a property right or a breach of contract. A property interest was found in the right to use the association's physical property,[55] in a member's right to a pro rata share of the association's assets in the event of dissolution,[56] and, occasionally, in any pecuniary interest whether or not related to the association's property.[57] Property was also found in the member's interest in the corporate franchise of a medical society,[58]

---

[53]In *Early v. Bristol Memorial Hosp., Inc.*, 508 F. Supp. 35, 37–38 (E.D. Tenn. 1980), the court succinctly set forth the interest of the public in a medical staff privilege dispute:

"The competency of Dr. Early as a physician and the propriety of permitting his practice of his chosen profession at the defendant hospital are in dispute. Those issues, in turn, implicate the health and welfare of those patients whom he might attend at the hospital. If this court were to order the defendants to reinstate Dr. Early to staff privileges pending the final resolution of this action, and should it develop at or after trial on the merits that the defendants had acted properly in removing him from the hospital, then immeasuarble harm could be suffered by hospital patients in that interval. The public has a strong interest in seeing that only competent physicians receive staff-privileges at hospitals and that qualified medical experts, and not judges, made the determination of whether a particular physician should enjoy such privileges. Absent the most compelling reason, the court will not attempt to substitute its judgment for that of the defendants prior to a full hearing of this action on its merits."

On the basis of these considerations, the court in *Early* denied the plaintiff's request for reinstatement. See also *Dayan v. Wood River Township Hosp.*, 18 Ill. App.2d 63, 152 N.E.2d 205 (1958); *Woodbury v. McKinnon*, 447 F.2d 839 (5th Cir. 1971); *Dos Santos v. Columbus-Cuneo-Cabrini Medical Center*, 684 F.2d 1346 (7th Cir. 1982).

[54]*Elizabeth Hosp., Inc. v. Richardson*, 167 F. Supp. 155 (W.D. Ark. 1958), *aff'd*, 269 F.2d 167 (8th Cir.), *cert. denied*, 361 U.S. 884 (1959); *State ex rel. Hartigan v. Monongalia County Medical Soc'y*, 97 W. Va. 273, 124 S.E. 826 (1924); *Harris v. Thomas*, 217 S.W. 1068 (Tex. Civ. App. 1920); *Trautwein v. Harbourt*, 40 N.J. Super. 247, 123 A.2d 30, *cert. denied*, 22 N.J. 220, 125 A.2d 233 (1956); Annot., 89 A.L.R.2d 964 (1963); Note, *supra* note 1.

[55]*Davis v. Scher*, 356 Mich. 291, 97 N.W.2d 137 (1959) (minority prevented from using synagogue); *Heaton v. Hull*, 51 A.D. 126, 64 N.Y.S. 279 (1900) (use of sorority's local chapter house).

[56]*Stein v. Marks*, 44 Misc. 140, 89 N.Y.S. 921 (Sup. Ct. 1904); *Evans v. Philadelphia Club*, 50 Pa. 107, 119 (1865).

[57]*Barr v. Essex Trades Council*, 53 N.J. Eq. 101, 30 A. 881 (Ch. 1894) (right to practice profession); *Joseph v. Passaic Hosp. Ass'n*, 38 N.J. Super. 284, 118 A.2d 696 (1955) (right to earn a livelihood).

[58]*State ex rel. Waring v. Georgia Medical Soc'y*, 38 Ga. 608, 626 (1869).

the opportunity to become trustee of a church,[59] and the possibility of being elected to a salaried office in the group.[60]

Other courts, emphasizing the consensual basis of the member's relation to the group, treated the group's rules as terms of a contract, which became the sole source of legally cognizable rights enforceable in the courts according to ordinary contract doctrine.[61] While a member might have benefited from the group's own rules if they provided for fair procedures, it was clear that a nonmember would not, since it was held that nonmembers had no standing in the courts to seek enforcement of the association's own bylaws.[62]

Members achieved some success in fitting their disputes within traditional tort theories. Where, for example, an expulsion ceremony involved physical torture[63] or physical force was used to implement a group decision,[64] courts characterized the conduct as battery. Others focused on the impact a group decision had on an individual's reputation and permitted suits premised on defamation.[65] Also, where a group decision affected the economic interests of an individual, the tort was considered interference with an advantagous economic relation.[66]

Because of a member's ability to draw on contract, property, and tort theories, courts generally intervened to guard against arbitrary expulsions.[67] It was well established that an accused member had rights to reasonable notice and an opportunity to be heard prior to expulsion.[68]

Problems With the Traditional Approach

Some of the problems and injustices that resulted from the traditional judicial approach were identified in Professor Chafee's classic article, "The Internal Affairs of Associations Not for Profit," published in 1930. Chafee noted that, while courts paid lip service to the principle that a member would be protected from an improper ex-

---

[59]*Halcombe v. Leavitt*, 124 N.Y.S. 980 (Sup. Ct. 1910).
[60]*Williams v. District Executive Bd., Mine Workers*, 1 Pa. D. & C. 31 (1921).
[61]*Developments in the Law—Judicial Control of Actions of Private Associations, supra* note 1, at 1001; *O'Brien v. Matual*, 14 Ill. App.2d 173, 144 N.E.2d 446 (1957) (union actions scrutinized for compliance with union regulations); *Nagib v. St. Therese Hosp.*, 41 Ill. App.3d 970, 355 N.E.2d 211 (1976) (removal of hospital staff privileges scrutinized for compliance with regulations).
[62]*Treister v. American Academy of Orthopaedic Surgeons*, 78 Ill. App.3d 746, 396 N.E.2d 1225, 1232 (1979). See also *Knapp v. Palos Community Hosp.*, __Ill. App.3d__, 465 N.E.2d 554 (1984). But see Op. Ill. Att'y Gen. (April 4, 1984) (Illinois Hospital Licensing Requirements Rule 3-1.1 interpreted to require public and private hospitals to afford "due process and a fair hearing" to applicants to medical staff). And see *Developments in the Law—Judicial Control of Actions of Private Associations, supra* note 1, at 1001.
[63]*State v. Williams*, 75 N.C. 134 (1876).
[64]*Innes v. Wylie*, 174 Eng. Rep. 800 (1844).
[65]*Developments in the Law—Judicial Control of Actions of Private Associations, supra* note 1, at 1005.
[66]*Id.*; *Schlesinger v. Quinto*, 201 A.D. 487, 194 N.Y.S. 401 (Sup. Ct. 1922).
[67]Annot., 20 A.L.R.2d 531 (1951); *Falcone*, 34 N.J. at 590, 170 A.2d at 796.
[68]*Swital v. Real Estate Comm'r*, 116 Cal. App.2d 677, 679, 254 P.2d 587, 588 (1953); *Berberian v. Lancaster Osteopathic Hosp. Ass'n*, 395 Pa. 257, 149 A.2d 456 (1959); *Developments in the Law—Judicial Control of Actions of Private Associations, supra* note 1, at 1028.

pulsion or other wrongful act of an association only if he had a property interest, any such interest was largely a fiction, a guise for protecting personal interests, e.g., social reputation.[69] Moreover, property analysis created absurd results. For example, many clubs were proprietary, i.e., the property was owned not by the club or its members but by a group of proprietors who permitted members to make use of it. Expulsion from a proprietary club was often just as destructive of the reputation of a member as expulsion from a club whose premises were owned by the members; yet courts denied relief for wrongful expulsions in proprietary clubs while granting relief in the case of the member-owned clubs. Chafee pointed out that the injuries in both types of clubs were often the same, and that relief should not turn on an analysis of property interests.[70]

The contract approach was also criticized by Chafee as artificial. If an association was unincorporated and could not be treated as an entity, then each member had a contract with every other member, which complicated matters and distracted courts from the real issues. Also, if a wrongful expulsion were a breach of contract, then the members who voted for expulsion would be liable at law for damages. Yet this did not happen since the few actions at law brought for expulsion were against the entity and not its members. Finally, principles frequently cited by the courts as a basis for relief from wrongful acts of associations were inconsistent with contract law. For example, if an association's constitution and bylaws formed a contract by which the member was bound, the fact that some of the clauses were "contrary to natural justice" should not prevent them from being operative. Nevertheless, courts often disregarded such clauses.[71]

Additionally, the courts usually held that an expulsion from an association might not be malicious, even if the group had followed its own rules. But there was in fact no basis in the so-called contract or bylaws of the association for such a "bad faith" rule with respect to expulsion.[72] Chafee concluded:

> "In short, the member's 'contract,' like his 'property interest,' is often a legal fiction which prevents the courts from considering attentively the genuine reasons for and against relief.
> "The members' relation to the association is the true subject matter of protection in most cases where relief is given against wrongful expulsions. The wrong is a tort, not a breach of contract, and the tort consists in the destruction of the relation rather than in a deprivation of the remote and conjectural right to receive property."[73]

Other commentators have noted that the property and contract approaches are also ineffective in remedying injuries to nonmembers, as nonmembers clearly have no property right in an organization

---

[69]Chafee, *supra* note 1, at 999.
[70]*Id.* at 1000.
[71]*Id.* at 1003–1007.
[72]*Id.* at 1006.
[73]*Id.* at 1007.

they do not belong to, or, ordinarily, a contractual relationship with it.[74] Yet exclusion from a group may be just as harmful as expulsion. For example, denial of membership in a certifying organization will often seriously impair a professional person's ability to find employment and, perhaps, to practice the profession at all.[75]

The Decision in *Falcone*

The inability of contract and property law to protect individuals from associations wielding monopoly power was first recognized judicially in *Falcone v. Middlesex County Medical Society.*[76] In that case, an osteopathic physician sued to compel the medical society to admit him to full membership. It was alleged that membership in the society was an absolute prerequisite to hospital staff privileges in the physician's area of practice. The physician had successfully passed the New Jersey medical boards and had been originally admitted to the society as an associate member. During this time he was serving on two hospital medical staffs. However, he was not recommended for active membership in the society when it was discovered that he had received his medical degree from a foreign university. After his associate membership expired, he was removed from the society's membership roles. The two hospitals subsequently terminated his staff membership and precluded him from admitting and treating patients.

The trial court noted the general rule that the court may not compel membership in a voluntary medical association but observed that earlier cases had granted writs of mandamus to compel admission under a contract theory, i.e., the association's bylaws or constitution might be enforceable in equity when the organization acted contrary to those laws. Generally, however, plaintiffs were required to show a property right as a condition precedent to judicial intervention. Noting Chafee's criticism of the contract and property right theory, the trial court suggested that the nature of the organization and the injuries incurred from expulsion or exclusion should be the proper focus:

> "This court is of the opinion that where an organization is in fact involuntary and/or is of such a nature that the court should intervene to protect the public, and where an exclusion results in a substantial injury to a plaintiff, the court will grant relief, providing that such exclusion was contrary to the organization's own laws, was without procedural safeguards, or the application of a particular law or laws of an organization was contrary to public policy. It follows that each case must stand on its own facts."[77]

---

[74]Note, *supra* note 1, at 1314–1315.
[75]Wallace, *Occupational Licensing and Certification: Remedies for Denial,* 14 Wm. & Mary L. Rev. 46, 110–111 (1972).
[76]62 N.J. Super. 184, 162 A.2d 324 (1960), *aff'd,* 34 N.J. 582, 170 A.2d 791 (1961).
[77]62 N.J. Super. at 197, 162 A.2d at 331.

The trial court pointed out that many organizations are essentially involuntary and cited antitrust actions that had been brought against them. The court concluded that the society was virtually a monopoly and accordingly had certain public responsibilities. These responsibilities it could not escape by claiming to be a private, voluntary organization. It was, rather, "an involuntary organization, clothed with such public responsibilities that its actions are subject to judicial scrutiny."[78]

The court stressed that the plaintiff did not complain that the society had denied him procedural safeguards. He had pursued an appeal to the judicial counsel of the state medical society and the judicial counsel of the American Medical Association. Unsuccessful, he then sought judicially compelled membership. The court ordered his admittance, noting that if the society continued to hold monopolistic control on the practice of medicine it had no alternative but to admit all doctors duly licensed by New Jersey who met reasonable requirements.

The Supreme Court of New Jersey affirmed the trial court, approving its abandonment of property and contract principles in favor of focusing on the nature of the group's power and the injuries resulting from abuse of that power.[79] The earlier case of *Trautwein v. Harbourt*,[80] which held that allegations of malicious exclusion from a fraternal order did not state a cause of action, was distinguished.

> "We are here in nowise concerned with a social or fraternal organization such as the Order of the Eastern Star. We are here concerned with and therefore deal solely with an organization, membership in which may here, in the language of *Trautwein*, be viewed as 'an economic necessity'; in dealing with such an organization, the court must be particularly alert to the need for truly protecting the public welfare *and advancing the interests of justice by reasonably safeguarding the individual's opportunity for earning a livelihood while not impairing the proper standards and objectives of the organization*" [emphasis added].[81]

Significantly, the court justified judicial intrusion by the need to protect an "individual's opportunity for earning a livelihood," as well as to protect the public interest in fair delivery of medical services. Moreover, it did not view protecting the right to earn a living as limited by contract or property law.

While the *Falcone* court's departure from traditional contract and property analysis was at first criticized,[82] later commentators viewed the decision as necessary in view of the increasing power of groups over individuals.[83] For example, Tobriner and Grodin cited

[78]*Id.* at 200, 162 A.2d at 332.
[79]34 N.J. 582, 170 A.2d 791 (1961).
[80]40 N.J. Super. 247, 123 A.2d 30 (1956).
[81]34 N.J. at 591–592, 170 A.2d at 796–797.
[82]*Expulsion and Exclusion From Hospital Practice and Organized Medical Societies*, 15 RUTGERS L. REV. 327 (1961); 75 HARV. L. REV. 1186 (1962); Wallace, *supra* note 75, at 118.
[83]Tobriner & Grodin, *The Individual and the Public Service Enterprise in the New Industrial State*, 55 CALIF. L. REV. 1247, 1258–1260 (1967); Affeldt & Seney, *supra* note 1, at 399–403; Affeldt & Seney, *supra* note 2, at 179.

Falcone in support of their thesis that courts are responding to the new "organized society" by reformulating common law principles to impose duties and obligations on the basis of status or relationship.[84] They noted that much of the early common law was based on concepts of "public" or "common" vocations that focused on the nature of relationships. The advent of the mercantile economy and a liberal laissez-faire philosophy, however, brought about the demise of status concepts. Doctrines such as negligence and, in particular, contract served to free businesses and individuals from static hierarchies. Through consent, it permitted individuals to make law for themselves.[85] On the other hand, increased organization and specialization now make it necessary to revive the status approach:

> "Contract doctrine, for example, at one time the instrument of transition from status to individualism, may today, if rigidly applied produce a quite different result. Thus, an individual today does not bargain meaningfully over a union or professional society's constitution and by-laws, an automobile manufacturer's warranty, or an insurance policy. He accepts these as given; they are part of his economic environment. If they are contracts at all, they are 'contracts of adhesion,' imposed on a take-it-or-leave-it basis by the party possessing superior 'bargaining' strength.
> * * *
> "We believe that our legal system is reviving status concepts—not from nostalgia for a bygone society, but to meet the challenges of today—and that one important aspect of that trend lies in the application to certain relationships of principles originating in the 'public service' doctrine * * *. In short, certain institutions and enterprises are viewed as quasi-public in nature: the important products or services which these enterprises provide, their express or implied representations to the public concerning their products or services, their superior bargaining power, legislative recognition of their public aspect or a combination of these factors, lead courts to impose on these enterprises obligations to the public and the individuals with whom they deal, reflecting the role which they have assumed, apart from and in some cases despite the existence of a contract. Such obligations flow from status rather than consensual relationships between the parties."[86]

The "public service" approach is but one aspect of the larger field of status concepts. It is not in itself so much a rule of law as it is a tool of understanding, a metaphor, a way of explaining what courts are doing in a variety of situations.[87] Tobriner and Grodin discussed how some courts, despite a traditional "hands-off" attitude, applied status concepts to admission to labor unions and professional societies (discussing *Falcone*), and to protection of organization members from arbitrary actions of the group.[88] They also cite bailor–bailee, landlord–tenant, and manufacturer–customer relationships, and banks, hospitals, and insurance companies as situations and settings where

---

[84]*Tobriner & Grodin, supra* note 83.
[85]*Id.* at 1250–1251.
[86]*Id.* at 1252–1253.
[87]*Id.* at 1254.
[88]*Id.* at 1256–1263.

traditional theories have been discarded in favor of a status approach.[89] Interestingly enough, Tobriner and Grodin did not discuss cases involving the application of status concepts to the employer–employee relationship.

While Affeldt and Seney[90] did address the employer–employee relationship in connection with some union cases, these commentators also viewed the question of the right to earn a living as primarily a battle between the employee and an association:

> "Today the new property takes the form of status or citizenship within the group. The most important right for the majority of men is the right to earn a livelihood, and it is this right over which private groups have a stranglehold. This right to prospective advantage is a basic right which is indispensable to the realization of the more human values. The average man places much more value on his union card, his license, and his franchise than on his home, his TV set, or his car. Citizenship within these private societies involves much more than the right to a paycheck; it involves his past, present, and future life. For instance, a union card provides a member with a bill of rights in the form of the grievance procedure, citizenship in the form of pension and insurance rights, and a host of other advantages much more important to him that state citizenship. Short of prison, group disenfranchisement is the most severe kind of punishment the modern world can inflict upon the individual. The doctor who loses his American Medical Association membership, the pastor who loses his pastorate, and the lawyer who loses his license are outcasts who also lose access to the more human values.
>
> "The time has come to protect group citizenship in quasi-public groups in the same manner in which we protected the old property. We should surround it with the strongest constitutional safeguards, once reserved for personality; for 'status is so clearly linked to personality that distruction [sic] of one may well destroy the other.' "[91]

Affeldt and Seney reviewed university student relationships, professional associations and hospital staff admissions (citing *Falcone*),[92] trade associations, and labor unions. They advocated greater judicial supervision of such groups to protect the right to earn a living. Yet they too failed to address the nonunion employer-employee situation, which is still the dominant relationship in the work force.[93]

Recently, Glendon and Lev[94] have observed that the structure

---

[89]*Id.* at 1267–1282.

[90]*Affeldt & Seney, supra* notes 1 & 2.

[91]*Affeldt & Seney, supra* note 1, at 387, 388.

[92]*Id.* at 409–410.

[93]Note, *Patronage, Arbitrary Discharge and Public Policy: Redefining the Balance of Interests in Employment*, 14 J. MAR. L. REV. 785, 795, 796 (1981):

> "One standard feature of nearly every collective bargaining agreement is the prohibition of arbitrary dismissal, whereby no employee covered by the agreement may be discharged except for cause. Like the cause requirement in the civil service legislation, this statutory provision has been judicially interpreted to convey to the employee a constructive property right protectible under the due process clauses of the fifth and fourteenth amendments. *The weakness in current statutory protection, however, is that it extends to only about one-third of the working population. Sixty-seven percent of the United States work force, nearly 57 million employees, have no protectible interest in their major source of income.*" (Emphasis supplied, footnotes omitted.)

[94]Glendon & Lev, *Changes in the Bonding of the Employment Relationship: An Essay on the New Property*, 20 B.C.L. REV. 457, 475–477 (1979).

of society has developed in such a fashion that continued employment in a particular job is one of the most important rights to protect from arbitrary action:

"An individual's decision to change or leave a job is more complex than her decision to take a job. Nevertheless, there is nothing particularly new about many of the factors that constrain an employee from shifting from one employer to another, or from one type of work to another. Inertia and the fear of unknown ills have always weighed against any prospective advantage of a job change. Job satisfaction, while extremely significant, usually yields to the employee's perception of his economic condition. This is an overriding consideration unless the employee's income is already well above a level which he deems appropriate to his needs, desires, and expectations. What is new and what merits discussion here, is the increasing significance in recent years of pensions, and the benefits accruing from an accumulation of seniority among the ties that bind an employee to his present job.

"Pensions, in the private sector at least, are largely a post-World War II phenomenon. However, by 1973, according to one estimate, over half of the labor force was covered by pension plans, and enrollment was growing at a faster rate than the labor force. Significantly, until vesting occurs in private, nonambulatory pension plans, an employee can accumulate credits toward vesting only by staying with his present employer. Thus, at some point in the early years of employment, an employee begins to sense that he has made an investment which will be lost if he leaves before vesting occurs. By this time (ten years under ERISA) he may also be reluctant to forfeit the seniority, experience, and the other benefits of extended employment he has gained with his employer. The point at which an employee senses that he has accumulated sufficient pension or seniority credits to warrant staying where he is in order to avoid the forfeiture to be suffered by leaving varies with the particular employee, his family situation, his age, his health, and the perceptions he has of himself and his current job. In short, once it becomes distasteful for an employee to give up an accumulation of service credits toward vesting, he will tend to remain where he is. Just as the employee nearing the year in which his pension will vest is apt to remain with his employer, the vested employee feels the tug of the increase in retirement amount anticipated with each year's employment service. In both cases, each year is a strand which strengthens the cable binding the employee to his particular employer. The anticipated benefits of an increased pension, added to the difficulties older employees experience in securing new employment, are formidable deterrents to a change in jobs."[95] (Footnotes omitted.)

While recognizing the importance of protected job security, scholarly commentators still ignore status concepts in favor of justifying relief on contract, tort (defamation, libel, unjust interference), or property principles.[96] On the other hand, a recent article has in essence adopted the status approach by suggesting that the "at will"

---

[95]*Id.* at 475–477 (1979).

[96]E.g., Note, *Recognizing the Employee's Interests in Continued Employment—The California Cause of Action For Unjust Dismissal*, 12 PAC. L.J. 69 (1980); note, *Protecting At Will Employees Against Wrongful Discharge: The Duty to Terminate Only in Good Faith*, 93 HARV. L. REV. 1816 (1980); Glendon & Lev, *supra* note 94.

rule be replaced with a balancing of employer and employee interests.[97]

Subsequent to *Falcone's* rejection of property and contract analysis, an Illinois court explicitly recognized that the presence or absence of traditional contract or property rights was insignificant when
determining whether a duty of fair procedure would be imposed in
expulsion cases:

> "Whether the 'interest of substance' which accrues to a member of a
> professional association is called a 'property right,' 'contract right,' or
> merely the 'member's relation to the association,' there is a growing
> awareness that wrongful expulsion from a voluntary association has
> such a serious effect on the ability of a professional man to successfully
> pursue his livelihood and that it is a judicially protectable interest.
> [Citations omitted.]
>
> "Courts annul expulsions from voluntary associations when they
> are (1) not in accordance with the constitution and by-laws of the as-
> sociation, (2) influenced by bias, prejudice or lacking in good faith, or
> (3) contrary to rudimentary due process or natural justice."[98]

The demise of the contract and property requirements in situations where an individual's right to earn a living is threatened has
not only allowed courts to deal with expulsion cases in a more flexible
and realistic fashion, it has permitted the nonmember to seek judicial
review of exclusions as well. In *Blende v. Maricopa County Medical
Society*, the Arizona Supreme Court adopted *Falcone* and additionally
noted that no real distinction existed between expulsion and exclusion from associations where nonmembership seriously impaired a
person's ability to pursue his occupation.[99] Most of the cases applying
a fair procedure duty in such a context appear to agree with that
observation since they no longer distinguish between expulsion and
exclusion, presumably because they are not bound to a contract or
property analysis.

When membership is viewed as an "economic necessity," the
courts will intervene to balance the individual's opportunity for earning a livelihood against the goals, standards, and objectives of the
organization.[100] The rationale for such intervention was first expressed in *Falcone*. Where an association has a virtual monopoly, it
is under a fiduciary duty not to exercise its power in an arbitrary or
unreasonable manner. Such a duty was likened to that imposed early
in the common law against innkeepers and carriers who were required to serve all comers on reasonable terms because of their monopolies in defined geographical areas.[101] The *Falcone* court also noted
that the county medical society was not a private voluntary membership association with which the public had no concern. Its engagement in activities vitally affecting the health and welfare of the

---

[97]Note, *supra* note 93, at 788–789, 798.
[98]*Virgin v. American College of Surgeons*, 42 Ill. App.2d 352, 192 N.E.2d 414, 422 (1963).
[99]*Blende v. Maricopa County Medical Soc'y*, 96 Ariz. 240, 243 n.1, 393 P.2d 926, 928 (1964).
[100]*Falcone*, 34 N.J. at 592, 170 A.2d at 796–797.
[101]*Id.* at 594, 170 A.2d at 798.

people tinged it with a public interest. The society could no longer be treated as a private, voluntary organization not subject to judicial review.[102]

Many cases that follow *Falcone* focus on either the monopoly-fiduciary duty rationale or the public interest justification, depending on their facts. However, the standards for invoking judicial review are in reality not nearly as stringent as the case language would indicate. Something closer to importance or convenience is enough to warrant judicial review. The resulting judicial review and its concept of fair procedure, a mix of substantive and procedural due process applied to private entities, will be examined on a state-by-state basis.

Physician/Medical Staff Privilege: Problems and Related Controversies

New Jersey

Shortly after *Falcone*, the New Jersey courts expanded its holding to apply to private hospitals and their medical staffs. In *Greisman v. Newcomb Hospital*,[103] an osteopath sued for admission to the courtesy medical staff of the hospital. The osteopath complained of a hospital bylaw requiring that all staff members be graduates of a medical school approved by the AMA or a full or associate member of the county medical society. The New Jersey trial court noted the general rule that an exclusion of a physician from practicing in a private hospital rests in the discretion of the managing hospital authorities. The osteopath argued, however, that the reasoning of *Falcone* was not confined to medical societies or other membership groups but applied equally to private hospitals and their medical staffs, especially when there is a public interest in a hospital's operations. The trial court agreed, holding that the hospital's receipt of public funds transformed its status to that of a public charity, and that since it was the only general hospital open to the public within the metropolitan area and consequently functioned as a monopoly, it had certain public responsibilities. The bylaw requiring membership in the county medical society was clearly unreasonable and offensive to public policy. The court applied the *Falcone* reasoning, i.e., that if the state had licensed the physician to practice, no bylaw of the medical society *or the hospital* would be reasonable if it effectively excluded that physician from practicing in the state. The court ordered the hospital to consider the osteopath's application without using those bylaws as part of the consideration.

The New Jersey Supreme Court affirmed the trial court's rul-

---

[102]*Id.* at 596–597, 170 A.2d at 799.
[103]76 N.J. Super. 149, 183 A.2d 878 (1962).

ing.[104] The court observed that, although the managing officials of the hospital had discretionary powers in the selection of the medical staff, those powers were reviewable for policy reasons comparable to those expressed in *Falcone*. The managing officials had a fiduciary duty to the public to exercise their powers reasonably and for the public good. The court noted there was a public interest in seeing that patients who chose the osteopath as a physician could be treated by that physician at their local hospital.

Schneir v. Englewood Hospital Association,[105] followed the *Greisman* case, noting that the *Falcone* decision, which struck down an arbitrary membership requirement of a nonprofit organization, applied to private hospitals and that an applicant for staff membership was entitled to have his application evaluated on its merits. The court observed, however, that *Greisman* merely invalidated an illegal bylaw and did not discuss the medical's staff discretion to consider an individual applicant pursuant to valid bylaws. In *Schneir*, the court found that the hospital had given full consideration to an individual's application through its regular procedure. The application was not rejected but deferred. Since it appeared that the applicant was not discriminated against because he was an osteopath, the court sustained the decision to defer the application and suggested that the applicant wait a reasonable period of time to let the hospital observe his character and professional standing during the deferral period. Thus, *Greisman* was viewed as a case addressing the substance or reasonableness of a bylaw; *Schneir* addressed the fairness of the procedure that applied the bylaws.

Sussman v. Overlook Hospital Association[106] was an action by physicians to compel a private hospital to set up fair procedures involving a court hearing on their rejected applications for medical staff membership. The court commented that the physicians were professionally competent but there was some evidence to indicate they had been rejected because of personality problems. One physician, who had difficulty in personal relationships, argued that the hospital's failure to investigate and allow him a hearing was arbitrary and discriminatory. Although the physicians had memberships in other hospitals and the defendant hospital did not possess a monopoly, the court ordered the hospital to provide such a hearing. The fact that membership on a hospital staff is a privilege and not a right was not viewed by the court as a reason for withholding review. It observed that there were many types of privileges and rights and that labels alone should not determine whether actions regarding them are subject to judicial review. A physician does not have a right to hospital affiliation, but *Greisman* held that a medical staff by-law could not be respected if it imposed arbitrary conditions on member-

---

[104]*Greisman v. Newcomb Hosp.*, 40 N.J. 389, 192 A.2d 817 (1963).
[105]91 N.J. Super. 527, 221 A.2d 530 (1966).
[106]92 N.J. Super. 163, 222 A.2d 530 (1966).

ship.[107] It was *not* necessary for the hospital to operate as a monopoly before judicial review would be granted. A significant impact on the physician's livelihood would suffice:

> "It is true that in this case there is no element of monopoly power in economic deprivation of a right to earn a living as was present in *Falcone* [citations omitted], and to a more limited extent in *Greisman*. Doctor Sussman admitted that he has a large income and will continue to have one although denied appointment to Overlook's Medical Staff. Also, his membership on the staffs of Muhlenberg and Perth Amboy General shows that his livelihood is not affected. The same is true of Dr. Scialabba. However, it is not necessary to find monopoly or deprivation of all economic opportunity before there is a case for judicial review. *Greisman* indicates that since the function of the private organization in question is public, judicial review is available to hold said organization to conduct becoming a fiduciary."[108]

The court also held that following its internal bylaws and not exercising bad faith were insufficient in themselves to constitute a proper exercise of the hospital's ficuciary duty. A substantial inquiry into the fitness of plaintiffs to serve on the medical staff also was necessary. Fairness dictated that Dr. Sussman be afforded an opportunity to be heard and to present proof that might indicate that the disfavor he incurred with the hospital administrators had been occasioned by his frank and perhaps tactless criticisms of certain hospital practices and of deficiencies in nursing personnel. In summary, reasonable bylaws and fair procedures were required.

While the *Sussman* case held that one of the bases for the *Falcone* decision's case for judicial review, i.e., monopoly power, was not necessary, *Davis v. Morristown Memorial Hospital*[109] held that the other rationale, public policy, was also not necessary to justify judicial review. In this case plaintiffs were obstetricians who were refused admission to the hospital staff because the hospital in consideration of its limited number of beds already had a sufficiently large number of patients served by obstetricians and gynecologists. The court appeared to recognize that the hospital did not have a monopoly over the obstetricians' right to practice their profession, since it was noted they had access to other hospitals. Nevertheless, the court believed judicial review was warranted because the hospital's decision affected the obstetricians' professional status. Significantly, in addition to noting the absence of a monopoly, the court specifically indicated that no issue of public policy was involved; but it concluded:

> "Even though no matter of public policy is here involved, I conclude from the holding in *Greisman* that this court has the duty to exercise 'broad judicial authority to ensure that exclusionary policies are lawful and are not applied arbitrarily or discriminatorily.'"[110]

---

[107]*Id.* at 175, 222 A.2d at 536.
[108]*Id.* at 176, 222 A.2d at 537.
[109]106 N.J. Super. 33 n.31, 254 A.2d 125 (1969).
[110]*Id.* at 42, 254 A.2d at 130.

The holding in this case was broader than in *Falcone* since it essentially abandoned *Falcone*'s two reasons for court participation in favor of ensuring fair procedures whenever an individual's professional status is affected. Despite the *Davis* court's decision to review judicially the actions of the hospital, the hospital's refusal to admit the obstetricians on the basis of the limited number of available beds was upheld. The court indicated, however, that if more beds became available and physicians were not admitted, the hospital would steer into a collision course with the court.

While the latter cases have effectively expanded judicial review of the procedures of private entities, one New Jersey court has limited the fiduciary duty outlined in *Greisman* to hospitals only. In *Grodjest v. Jersey City Medical Center*,[111] board-certified oral surgeons sought reinstatement to the hospital's emergency room rotation and expunging of a censure by the executive committee of the hospital until a hearing could be held. Additionally, they sued to use the facilities of a dental school predicated on its connections with the hospital and a fiduciary duty of the dental school. The surgeons sought reinstatement to the emergency room rotation on the ground that their exclusion from this service adversely affected them professionally by limiting their exposure to trauma cases, denying them an opportunity for continuing professional education and excluding them from an academic atmosphere. The courts specifically noted that the surgeons did not contend they had suffered any economic loss by reason of their nonparticipation in the rotation schedule. The record also failed to contain any evidence that it was economically beneficial for an attending oral surgeon to participate in the rotation schedule. Despite this, the court did not refuse judicial review of the hospital's decision to exclude them from the rotation schedule. It observed that the surgeons did not have an absolute right to use the emergency room facility but that they could not be excluded without a cause or reason. However, finding that the exclusion in this case was not arbitrary, the court denied the surgeon's applications for reinstatement.

With regard to the censure by the hospital's executive committee, the court held that this had unquestionably damaged the surgeons' reputations and their professional standing. Thus, the failure of the executive committee to notify the surgeons that they were being considered for reprimand, and to give them a hearing, constituted a denial of their procedural due process rights. The court expunged the censure and remanded the case for a hearing consistent with due process.

Grodjest demonstrates again that the courts have gone beyond requiring a public interest or a monopoly and will review arbitrary decisions made by private entities when such decisions affect an individual's professional reputation. On the other hand, *Grodjest* limited such review to hospitals. The court refused to consider the surgeons'

---

[111]135 N.J. Super. 393, 343 A.2d 489 (1975).

claims against the dental school that were based on an asserted fiduciary duty because the primary responsibility of the school was dental education and not medical treatment. Therefore, the unique responsibility delegated to the dental school militated against the imposition of fiduciary duties commonly associated with general hospitals.

The case of *Guererro v. Burlington City Memorial Hospital*[112] involved doctors who sought admission to the medical staff of the hospital for the purpose of practicing general surgery at the hospital's satellite facility. Staff privileges were denied on the ground that the satellite hospital's general surgery staff should not be enlarged, given its limited bed capacity. The trial court entered judgment for the doctors, the appellate court affirmed, but the New Jersey Supreme Court reversed, indicating that under *Greisman* judicial review is restricted to situations in which the hospital's actions constitute an unreasonable exercise of discretion, a condition found not to be present in this case. The court was careful to point out, however, that the holding should not be construed as suggesting that hospitals may routinely deny staff privileges to doctors moving into the area. Any denial of such privileges, the purpose of which was to exclude newcomers in order to maintain the status quo of the staff, would not be judicially tolerated. Implicit in *Falcone*, the court said, was the belief that the power to exclude must be reasonably and lawfully exercised in furtherance of the interest of both the public and the medical profession. A denial predicated upon policies fostering only the well-being of those staff members who were already admitted would clearly violate the spirit of *Falcone*. The *Guererro* decision is interesting since it finds that the well-being of the staff members alone is insufficient to justify an exclusion of a new physician from the private hospital's medical staff. The welfare of the applicant, as well as of the members, must be considered.

One of the most recent cases dealing with the application of fair procedure in the hospital staff context is *Garrow v. Elizabeth General Hospital*, a 1979 case.[113] The New Jersey Supreme Court stated that a nonprofit private hospital serving the public in general is a quasi-public institution whose obligation to serve the public creates a fiduciary relationship. *Falcone* was cited for support of judicial review when an individual's professional reputation was at stake. The court did, however, state that the plaintiff must exhaust all internal remedies prior to seeking court relief. Fundamental fairness dictated that the hospital apprise the physician of the specific charges and give him an opportunity to be heard, including the right to present witnesses to contradict or explain the charges. The hospital might also have to afford the physician the right to have counsel at the hearing. Additionally, relevant material and documents upon which the board

---

[112]70 N.J. 344, 360 A.2d 334 (1976).
[113]79 N.J. 549, 401 A.2d 533 (1979).

of trustees relied in arriving at a conclusion should be made available to enable the physician to prepare for the hearing. In *Garrow*, the court did not require a trial-type hearing but did require a record-making hearing—a difference that will be examined in more detail later in this chapter.

The *Falcone* rule was not applied to a policemen's benevolent association to require judicial review of decisions excluding applicants. In this case, there was no proof that membership was "in any way necessary to either employment or advancement in police work."[114] However, participation in the benefit plans of the fraternal organization was in the nature of an insurance agreement and as such constituted a property interest sufficient to require that notice and a hearing be afforded prior to expulsion of members. In another case involving a policemen's benevolent association, the court, citing *Falcone*, held that mandamus would lie for irregular removal of an individual even if the association were a private corporation.[115]

The *Falcone* and *Greisman* cases were also cited in support of a medical technologist's lawsuit to compel the American Society of Clinical Pathologists to renew her certification and to reinstate her name on its registry of medical technologists. In *Higgins v. American Society of Clinical Pathologists*,[116] the medical technologist argued that the society's standards of conduct, which required her to work at all times under the supervision of a pathologist, were against public policy. The trial court refused judicial review on the ground that the technologist continued to be actively employed in her profession and that her certification indicated no more than that she was a medical technologist approved by the society. In supervising the training of such technologists and later certifying them, the society was not exercising a monopolistic control over the practice of medical technology in the state. Certification had not been shown to be an economic necessity or a sine qua non for employment or advancement. The alleged injuries of failure to receive bulletins from the society and loss of voting rights were insufficient to invoke review. The court entered a summary judgment in favor of the society.

This case was later reversed by the New Jersey Supreme Court.[117] The court agreed that the society did not exercise monopolistic control and that the technologist suffered no present economic loss from lack of the certification. The trial court was incorrect, however, in concluding that in the absence of an economic necessity of membership for employment or advancement there was no basis for judicial intervention. The technologist's cause of action extended beyond *Falcone* and *Greisman*. She alleged that her primary injury related to her professional identity, reputation, and status. The court noted that

---

[114]*Schwankert v. New Jersey State Patrolman's Benevolent Ass'n*, 77 N.J. Super. 224, 230, 185 A.2d 877, 881 (1962).
[115]*Calabrese v. Policemen's Benevolent Ass'n*, 157 N.J. Super. 139, 384 A.2d 579 (1978).
[116]94 N.J. Super. 243, 227 A.2d 712 (1966).
[117]51 N.J. 191, 238 A.2d 665 (1968).

in an expulsion case, as opposed to an exclusion situation, the plaintiff would not be required to show economic necessity. Here the plaintiff sought reinstatement of her preexisting membership rather than, as in *Falcone* and *Greisman*, membership in an organization that had refused to admit her initially. It was noted that while the general rule is that courts will not compel admission of an individual into a voluntary association, they have been willing to intervene and compel the reinstatement of a member who has been wrongfully expelled. The law accords important rights and status to members of voluntary organizations not extended to mere aspirants to membership.[118] Significantly, the court commented that the legal basis for according judicial review for exclusions, that is, property or contract rights, had been under severe criticism and added:

> "*The loss of status* resulting from the destruction of one's relationship to a professional organization often times may be more harmful than a loss of property or contractual rights and properly may be the subject of judicial protection.
> * * *
> "This State's highest court has recognized that personal rights, as distinguished from property or contractual rights, are a proper subject for judicial protection."
> * * *
> "It is beyond doubt that plaintiff's standing in her profession has been impaired by a loss of this distinction. We conclude that the plaintiff's stake in her professional status is substantial enough to warrant at least limited judicial examination of the reason for her expulsion."[119]

The court did note that its review as to the reasons for expulsion would be limited. Private associations must have considerable latitude in rule-making in order to accomplish their objectives, and their private laws are generally binding on those who wish to remain members. However, the court would strike down laws in conflict with public policy when an expulsion is involved. The summary judgment in favor of the society was reversed on the ground that the rule that denied the technologist her certification violated public policy.

The *Falcone* rule has also been applied to real estate associations operating multiple listing services. In *Grillo v. Board of Realtors*,[120] a broker sued the board seeking fair consideration of his application for membership. He did not demand a judgment compelling admission but rather asserted that the board's restrictions upon membership constituted a harmful and unlawful combination in restraint of trade. *Falcone* was cited as support for giving a private citizen who alleges his business has been damaged by a combination of competitors a common law cause of action. The court held that the monopolistic effects of restraint of trade had historically been regarded as a matter of public concern rather than a mere private wrong to be remedied

---

[118]*Id.* at 199, 238 A.2d at 669.
[119]*Id.* at 201–202, 238 A.2d at 670.
[120]91 N.J. Super. 202, 219 A.2d 635 (1966).

by a private suit. The board was permitted to continue to operate as long as it did not enforce its illegal rules and regulations.

More significant is *Oates v. Eastern Bergen Co. Multiple Listing Service, Inc.*,[121] where a real estate broker brought an action to compel the multiple listing service to admit him as a member. The court held that operation of the multiple listing service from which plaintiff was excluded was illegal per se since it deprived the broker of access to listings of hundreds of properties. The case was decided on the basis of the New Jersey antitrust statute as well as applicable common law principles. *Falcone* was cited for the proposition that the court could intervene to protect an individual's opportunity for earning a livelihood without impairing the proper standards and objectives of the organization. The trial court concluded that the association's rules were illegal and that the broker was to be admitted as a member of the corporation.

The above cases, in addition to two dealing with an automobile club[122] and a local union,[123] demonstrate that the courts will protect the right to earn a living in many different contexts. The traditional unwillingness of courts to review the affairs of private associations has given way to a policy of review when this right is at issue.

Despite the fact that the arbitrary discharge of an employee may impinge on his ability to earn a living, there have been no New Jersey cases in such controversies drawing on the preceding opinions.

New York

The first case in New York that referred to *Falcone* was *Salter v. New York State Psychological Association*.[124] A practicing psychologist of many years' standing sued to obtain a court order requiring the association to admit him to membership. The psychologist asserted that he was a qualified and successful practitioner certified by the state of New York since 1959 and that the association was the most important organization of psychologists in the state, acting as spokesman for the profession. The association argued that it was not a public or governmental body but a private corporation governed by its own bylaws. One of these bylaws required graduate work in psychology for admission, and the psychologist had not done any such graduate work. The principal issue in the lawsuit was whether the association occupied such a monopolistic position or was so nearly an arm of the state itself that equal protection and due process constitutional requirements would make it unlawful for the association to reject qualified and certified applicants. The court noted that there was no showing in the record that the association was in effect an arm of the state or that it had monopoly power over the profession

---

[121]113 N.J. Super. 371, 273 A.2d 795 (1971).
[122]*Valle v. North Jersey Automobile Club*, 125 N.J. Super. 302, 310 A.2d 518 (1973).
[123]*Moore v. Iron Workers, Local 483*, 66 N.J. 527, 334 A.2d 1 (1975).
[124]14 N.Y.2d 100, 198 N.E.2d 250, 248 N.Y.S.2d 867 (1964).

or that its refusal to accept the applicant was arbitrary or unreasonable. The court commented that the applicant had gained state certification without examination or study under a "grandfather clause" which excused certain requirements for individuals who had been practicing at least 12 years prior to a new state law mandating graduate work prior to certification. Since the association's demands of its members were no more rigorous than those of the state itself, the association's bylaws could hardly be held to be arbitrary or unreasonable as a matter of law.

The court concluded that the petitioner had not made a showing that the association was an arm of the state. Allegations of cooperation, leadership, advice, and reliance between agencies of the state and the association did not demonstrate sufficient state action to apply constitutional principles. As an alternative, however, petitioner had argued that fair procedure should be applied in light of the *Falcone* decision, since the association was a monopoly in plaintiff's field of practice. The court distinguished the *Falcone* decision on the basis that decisions on exclusion from membership would be reviewed only when economic necessity was demonstrated. Enhancement or damage to professional reputation was not sufficient:

> "The last of petitioner's relied-on 'facts' is that the association has 'monopoly power over the profession', but even petitioner sees that 'monopoly' as operating only to restrict the professional activities and diminish the reputation of nonmembers. As to downgrading of petitioner's reputation, exclusion from any selective group of high-standard professionals leaves the rejected ones without desired kudos and prestige—but no court has ever taken it upon itself to review such selections. As to nonmembership in respondent association restricting petitioner's professional activities, there is just no proof at all.
> "The courts, it seems, interfere in such matters only when there is a showing of 'economic necessity' for membership. Typical of such interventions is the *Falcone* case."[125]

While *Salter* recognized the *Falcone* rule, it was not applied until the case of *Kurk v. Medical Society*.[126] *Kurk* was a mandamus proceeding to compel the county medical society to admit a physician who had been rejected because he was an osteopath and did not have a medical degree from a school of medicine approved by the society. The trial court distinguished between membership in a professional society upon which one's livelihood may well depend and membership in a social club or fraternal organization. Public policy is involved when a medical society, which in many ways is an arm of the state, denies membership for reasons based not on an individiual's lack of moral integrity or lack of attainment in the profession but on an arbitrary classification of osteopaths. Membership in a medical society was necessary, the court reasoned, for the osteopath's economic survival. The court commented that the facts in *Falcone* were similar

---

[125]*Id.* at 107, 198 N.E.2d at 253, 248 N.Y.S.2d at 872.
[126]46 Misc.2d 790, 260 N.Y.S.2d 520 (Sup. Ct. 1965).

since the osteopath had alleged a denial of hospital staff privileges because of his lack of membership in the society.

The trial court granted the osteopath's petition for mandamus, but the appellate court reversed because the osteopath apparently had received a medical license by mistake. The appellate court held that since the society was a group of individuals with medical degrees, its members had every right to maintain it as such unless they were party to a monopoly. The complaint did not allege a monopoly. The osteopath did allege he had been denied hospital staff privileges at a nearby hospital, but the record indicated there were numerous other hospitals in the county which did not require graduation from medical school as a prerequisite to staff membership. The allegation of economic hardship was merely conclusory.

In *Jacobson v. New York Racing Association*,[127] a licensed owner of thoroughbred horses sued the nonprofit racing association, seeking stall space at tracks owned by the association. In 1970, the owner's license had been suspended by the New York State Racing Commission for 45 days. After the license was restored, he was still denied stall space, which virtually barred him from thoroughbred racing in New York. The court discussed the common law rule that proprietors of private enterprises such as places of amusement and resorts had no obligation to serve all individuals without discrimination and were privileged to provide services to whomever they pleased. It held, however, that the common law rule did not shield the racing association from liability since it had a virtual monopoly over thoroughbred racing in New York. Exclusion from its tracks was tantamount to keeping the owner from plying his trade and effectively infringing on the state's power to license horse racing. The *Falcone* and hospital staff admission cases were cited as providing a justification for judicial review, but the court emphasized that the plaintiff would have a heavy burden in proving that denial of the stall space was not a reasonable discretionary business judgment, and instead was actuated by motives other than those relating to the best interests of racing. The appellate court remanded the case for trial. Again, *Jacobson* demonstrates the reluctance on the part of New York courts to interfere with decisions of private associations concerning credentials for membership. Even though the right to review was acknowledged and the association possessed a monopoly, the court was quick to emphasize that the association's decision would be upheld if it were in the best interests of racing generally.

Fritz v. Huntington Hospital,[128] also illustrates that the New York courts are not as willing to protect professional reputation through judicial review of private entities. In this case, two physicians brought an action to compel their appointment to a hospital medical staff. The appellate court held that the hospital's refusal to grant staff

---

[127]33 N.Y.2d 144, 305 N.E.2d 765, 350 N.Y.S.2d 639 (1973).
[128]48 A.D.2d 684, 367 N.Y.S.2d 847 (1975).

privileges to the physicians, who were graduates of an osteopathy college, was not a subject for judicial review. The physicians, it pointed out, had been practicing their profession for over a decade, treated an average of over 170 patients per week, and enjoyed staff privileges at another hospital. Under all the circumstances, the court held that economic necessity, as distinguished from economic and professional convenience and improvement, was not shown nor was it demonstrated that the hospital's decision was arbitrary.

While the *Falcone* decision has been acknowledged in New York and used as a justificiation for judicial review of some membership decisions, it appears that New York courts are adhering to a very conservative course when embarking on such review. To date there have been no cases in which an association, even if reviewed, was required to admit anyone to membership or change its bylaws or internal rules.[129]

Illinois

Van Daele v. Vinci[130] was the first case in Illinois to recognize and apply the *Falcone* rationale. The organization involved was a private, voluntary, incorporated association of independent retail grocers. The association's purpose was to secure lower prices through large-volume purchases of various grocery items; these items would then be sold to its members at a slightly higher price. Members of the association sued to enjoin its directors from taking disciplinary action against them. The association held a special meeting where it gave notice to the members that the board of directors was considering censuring, suspending, or expelling them, since they were disrupting the association's activities. The notice advised the members that each could be assisted by legal counsel during the proceedings. The members contended, however, that they would not receive a fair hearing since many members of the board were defendants in a lawsuit they had filed, and also were involved in events which had given rise to the planned disciplinary action. Although the board followed the procedure outlined in its bylaws for disciplinary hearings, the court believed the potential bias of the various board members might have deprived plaintiffs of a fair hearing and, consequently, denied them due process. The resolution expelling them from the association was held invalid and the association was enjoined from enforcing the resolution.

The *Van Daele* court justified judicial review on two grounds. First, the court cited *Falcone* as support for invoking judicial review when an important economic interest of an individual has been af-

---

[129]Cf. *Fried v. Straussman*, 82 Misc.2d 121, 369 N.Y.S.2d 591 (Sup. Ct. 1975), where the trial court issued an injunction to compel physician's admission to a nursing home facility because the facility was immersed in state action. The *Falcone* and *Salter* cases were referred to but an injunction did not issue pursuant to those decisions.

[130]51 Ill.2d 389, 282 N.E.2d 728 (1972), *cert. denied*, 409 U.S. 1007 (1972).

fected by an improper administrative proceeding. Second, it relied on the traditional principle that members subjected to disciplinary actions should be accorded a fair hearing. The court stated that a private organization, particularly if tinged with a public interest or purpose, may not expel or discipline a member if such action would adversely affect substantial property, contract, or other economic rights, except as a result of fair proceedings which may be provided for in the organization's bylaws, carried forward in an atmosphere of good faith and fair play. Moreover, the organization's purpose was more than social, and its endeavor to benefit from various state and federal laws subjected its actions to judicial review.

There is no discussion in *Van Daele* concerning any total inability to pursue the occupation of retail grocer without membership in the association. The Illinois court appeared to view "economic necessity" as any "important economic interest."

In *Jain v. Northwest Community Hospital*,[131] a physician sought an injunction on compelling his admission to the hospital staff. The physician alleged that the hospital was dedicated to the vital public purpose of serving the sick and injured and that it derived funds directly and indirectly from public sources, including the state of Illinois. He also alleged that the hospital's wrongful exclusion had caused him irreparable damage in that he had been unable to use the hospital's emergency room and had been substantially inhibited from expanding and developing his medical practice in certain residential areas.

A state appellate court affirmed the trial court's dismissal of the action. The fact that the hospital received federal and state funds, enjoyed tax exemptions, and was licensed by the state, the court held, did not transform its private hospital staff appointments into state action for purposes of due process protections. The court did note another possible basis for reviewing the decision—the power of courts to regulate private businesses impressed with a public interest to ensure that their discretionary powers are exercised reasonably and for the public good, and in accord with minimal common law requisites of fair procedure. Citing *Greisman* and noting its derivation from *Falcone*, the court listed a number of citations from other jurisdictions which had adopted the *Greisman* rationale. But the court believed it could not overturn its decision in *Mauer v. Highland Park Hospital Foundation*,[132] in which it had considered and rejected the policy grounds on which *Greisman* was based and had held that a private hospital had the absolute right to refuse to appoint a physician to its medical staff and that such a refusal was not subject to

---

[131]67 Ill. App.3d 420, 385 N.E.2d 108 (1978). See also *Knapp v. Palos Community Hosp.*, __Ill. App.3d__, 465 N.E.2d 554 (1984). But see Op. Ill. Att'y Gen. (April 4, 1984) (Illinois Hospital Licensing Requirements Rule 3-1.1 interpreted to require public and private hospitals to afford "due process and a fair hearing" to applicants to medical staff).

[132]90 Ill. App.2d 409, 232 N.E.2d 776 (1967).

judicial review. The court also distinguished the *Van Daele* case on the ground that it involved an expulsion rather than an exclusion:

"[W]e cannot agree that the decision in *Van Daele* relating to expulsions from associations, necessarily abrogated the rule of the *Mauer* case, relating to initial applications to private hospitals. The principle that voluntary associations which affect important economic interests must conduct expulsion proceedings according to their by-laws had already been established in decisions of our appellate courts. See *Virgin v. American College of Surgeons* First Dis. 1963, 42 Ill. App. 352, 192 N.E.2d 414 (surgeons' association) [additional citations omitted]. Indeed, this has long been the majority common law rule existing side-by-side with the general rule of non-review of private hospital staff appointments. [Citations omitted.] Similarly, as we have noted, the rule in Illinois has been that although private hospitals' staff decisions are not generally reviewable, reductions of privileges or dismissals must be in accord with the hospital by-laws. The court in *Van Daele* simply extended the rule to cover expulsions conducted by biased tribunals, though in accord with by-law procedures. We cannot agree that in so doing the court intended to overturn the rule of the *Mauer* case so as to require private hospitals to conduct a hearing on every application for staff membership they receive. Neither do we believe that by citing *Falcone*, the court necessarily adopted all subsequent judicial extensions of that case."[133]

One of the reasons for the *Jain* court's refusal to apply *Van Daele* was that *Van Daele* dealt with a voluntary business association rather than with a hospital medical staff. *Treister v. American Academy of Orthopaedic Surgeons*[134] suggests, nevertheless, that the Illinois courts take a restrictive view of judicial review even in the context of voluntary associations. In this case Dr. Treister brought an action challenging the academy's denial of his membership application and seeking the chance to confront his accusers and an opportunity to be heard. The court expressed approval of the *Falcone* decision but granted the Academy's motion to dismiss because the complaint demonstrated that lack of membership had not precluded Dr. Treister from successfully practicing orthopedic surgery:

"[W]e hold that our courts can review the application procedures of a private association when membership in the organization is an economic necessity. We approve of the opinions in *Falcone* and *Blende* which hold that a medical society cannot arbitrarily deny membership to an applicant when the society controls access to local hospital facilities and thus can deprive the applicant of his ability to practice medicine. We find, however, that the plaintiff has not alleged that membership in the American Academy of Orthopaedic Surgeons is an economic necessity. Membership is not a requisite to hospital staff privileges as evidenced by the fact that plaintiff is a member of the attending staff

---

[133]*Jain v. Northwest Community Hosp.*, 67 Ill. App.3d at 427, 385 N.E.2d at 114. See also *Spencer v. Community Hosp.*, 87 Ill. App.3d 214, 408 N.E.2d 981 (1980); Horan & Grasso, *Judicial Review and Due Process in Health Care Privilege Cases*, in REPRESENTING HEALTH CARE INSTITUTIONS—ILLINOIS INSTITUTE FOR CONTINUING LEGAL EDUCATION HANDBOOK 18–1 (1980).

[134]78 Ill. App.3d 746, 396 N.E.2d 1225 (1979).

at seven Chicago Hospitals. In addition, the plaintiff was board-certified and licensed by the State without academy membership."[135]

Dr. Treister argued that the *Van Daele* case controlled his fact situation, asserting that Illinois courts recognized no distinction between expulsion and exclusion with respect to a private association. The appellate court disagreed, pointing to the *Mauer* and *Jain* hospital staff decisions as examples of such distinctions. The *Treister* decision, in contrast to the New Jersey cases, adopted a very strict economic necessity test for exclusions from associations and more closely resembles the New York approach. The fact that membership in the association might have been a practical necessity for gaining maximum professional recognition in orthopedic surgery was not sufficient to permit judicial review of the Academy's decision not to admit Dr. Treister.

It appears that the standards for judicial review of membership decisions are more strict and limiting for hospital medical staff than for other voluntary professional associations. *Knapp v. Palos Community Hospital*[136] holds that the hospital will only be held to a standard of substantial compliance with its bylaws when refusing to renew the privileges of members and that members may not premise claims of procedural and substantive rights upon custom and usage at the hospital. The *Van Daele* case suggests that decisions disqualifying former members of other kinds of professional organizations will be reviewed more broadly to ensure that fair procedures are applied. Differences in standards of judicial review between medical staffs and other associations are also found in cases concerning admission of applicants to membership. The *Treister* decision adopted a strict economic necessity test for exclusion from professional societies. The *Mauer* and *Jain* decisions hold that even an allegation of strict economic necessity will not be sufficient to warrant judicial review when admission to a hospital staff is sought. The substantially limited judicial review of decisions of hospital medical staffs stems from the court's sensitivity to the unique expertise of hospitals in these matters of public health and safety.

Arizona

The *Falcone* decision was adopted by the Arizona Supreme Court in *Blende v. Maricopa County Medical Society.*[137] This case involved a mandamus proceeding by a licensed physician against the county medical society and its board to obtain review of the denial of his application for permanent membership after automatic expiration of his probationary membership. The trial court dismissed the action

---

[135]*Id.* at 755, 396 N.E.2d at 1231, 1232.
[136]___ Ill. App.3d___, 465 N.E.2d 554 (1984). See also *Maimon v. Sisters of the Third Order of St. Francis*, 120 Ill. App.3d 1090, 458 N.E.2d 1317 (1983).
[137]96 Ariz. 240, 393 P.2d 926 (1964).

on the ground that a voluntary association may "arbitrarily" determine its membership. The Arizona Supreme Court reversed, indicating that it agreed with the reasoning of the *Falcone* decision. The court commented that there are legitimate interests such as freedom of association that make it desirable for private associations to determine their own membership. But when a medical society controls doctors' access to hospital facilities, the society's exercise of such quasi-governmental power is the legitimate object of judicial concern. The court examined the society's articles and bylaws and concluded that there was no formal relation between membership in the society and maintenance of staff privileges in local hospitals. Finally, the society had complied with the procedural requirements of its articles and bylaws in considering the physician's application for membership, and therefore his allegations of procedural irregularity and bad faith were without merit. However, the court stated there still might exist the question of a definite, although informal, relation between membership in the society and maintenance of staff privileges in local hospitals. If the physician could show such a relation, his membership application might not be denied arbitrarily but only on a showing of just cause established by the society under proceedings embodying the elements of due process.

When determining just cause, the court must consider whether the grounds for exclusion were supported by substantial evidence and were reasonably related to legitimate purposes of the society. This involves essentially a balancing of individual, group, and public interests: the right of the individual to practice his profession without undue restrictions, the right of the public to have unrestricted choice of a physician, and the justification for the society's action.[138] The court cautioned that in making such an inquiry, the judiciary must guard against unduly interfering with a society's autonomy by substituting its judgment for that of the society in an area where the competence of the court does not equal that of the association. For example, the court questioned whether the *Falcone* decision might have gone too far in determining that the plaintiff's medical training was sufficient for admission into the society. Commenting that such de novo reviews appeared unwise, court proposed a very limited type of judicial review:

> "Therefore, the scope of the judicial review of the Society's action should be narrow. If the Society has refused membership on the basis of factual findings supported by substantial evidence and reasoned through the application of a reasonable standard—one which comports with the legitimate goals of the Society and the rights of the individual and the public—then judicial inquiry should end. Broad judicial review would unduly interfere with the autonomy of the Society and its competence to determine its membership affairs."[139]

---

[138]*Id.* at 245, 393 P.2d at 930.
[139]*Id.*

After this case was remanded, the trial court ordered the society to admit the physician to membership. This order was upheld on appeal by the supreme court, despite the fact that the society had taken no action to influence hospital requirement of society membership. The trial court found with sufficient evidence that there was a requirement of membership in the society in order to attain staff privileges. It did not matter that the society was not affirmatively involved in bringing about this influence on the hospitals.[140]

It is difficult to determine from the *Blende* series of cases whether or not Arizona has adopted the strict economic necessity test. There were indications in these opinions that the complaining physician had attained staff privileges at some hospitals even though he was not a member of the county medical society. Nevertheless, the supreme court ordered that the decision to deny his application for membership be judicially reviewed to ensure that he received due process. The next case to deal with judicial review of voluntary associations intimated that the Arizona courts might not have adopted the strict economic necessity test and instead would invoke broader review such as that advocated in the *Greisman* case. In *Quimby v. School District No. 21*,[141] an individual challenged the eligibility requirements of an athletic association. The association argued that it was a voluntary, nonprofit association and courts should not interfere with its affairs. The court held that judicial review could occur when compelling reasons of public interest were involved, and the medical association cases were cited in support of that proposition. But it is difficult to determine from the *Quimby* case if judicial review was premised on the rationale in the medical cases, because while the court recognized the athletic association as a nongovernmental agency, it suggested there was a connection with the government since the rules adopted by the association directly affected participation in tax-supported programs of an educational institution. The court reviewed the association's eligibility rules and found that such rules had a reasonable relation to the association's legitimate purposes and denied plaintiff relief.

Similarly ambiguous was *Peterson v. Tucson General Hospital, Inc.*,[142] where an osteopathic physician sued the hospital for wrongful denial of his reapplication to staff membership. The court acknowledged the general rule that exclusion of a physician from staff privileges in a private hospital ordinarily rests within the discretion of the managing authorities and is not subject to judicial review. This rule does not apply, however, when there is a contention that a hospital has failed to meet certain procedural requirements set forth in its constitution, bylaws, or rules and regulations. Citing *Greisman* and *Falcone*, among other cases, the court noted a growing trend

---

[140]104 Ariz. 12, 448 P.2d 68 (1968).
[141]10 Ariz. App. 69, 455 P.2d 1019 (1969).
[142]114 Ariz. 66, 559 P.2d 186 (Ct. App. 1976).

toward reviewing decisions of quasi-public hospitals. Since the hospital was the only osteopathic institution in Tucson and therefore a virtual monopoly, the court held that judicial review was proper, but limited:

> "If the hospital has refused staff privileges on the basis of factual findings supported by substantial evidence and reached its decision by the application of a reasonable standard, i.e., one that comports with the legitimate goals of the hospitals and the rights of the individual and public, then judicial inquiry should end."[143]

The Arizona appellate court determined that the evidence showed that the doctor had failed to maintain proper medical records as required by the hospital and therefore the hospital's refusal to admit him was proper. Whether judicial review was premised on the hospital's monopoly or its public policy connections is unclear.

Pima County Medical Society v. Felland[144] did cite the *Blende* cases as espousing a strict economic necessity test and refused to liberalize that requirement. In that case, a physician requested that the county medical society act on her membership application. The trial court found that membership in the society was a prerequisite for membership in the state and national organizations and was also required for serving on certain state medical groups such as the board of examiners. Holding that the physician had met the society's reqirements and that the society had held her application for too long without taking action, the trial court ordered the application to be considered. The appellate court reversed, however, stating:

> The only issue which might suggest the exercise of a quasi-governmental function justifying judicial intervention, was the fact that at one time appellee was denied malpractice insurance because she was not a member of the Society, such insurance being a prerequisite to practice at Tucson Medical Center, one of Tucson's private hospitals. However, at the time of trial appellee had secured malpractice insurance."[145]

The appellate court directed the trial court to dismiss the physician's complaint, apparently because she had not demonstrated a strict economic necessity for membership in the society. This 1977 decision suggests that Arizona has adhered to a stricter test of judicial review than New Jersey and appears to agree with Illinois and New York on the question of such review. Significantly, in no instance have these Arizona decisions ordered the defendants to admit plaintiffs; nor have the courts struck down an association's rules and by-laws, even though they have been willing to embark on some judicial review.

As in Illinois, in Arizona courts provide greater judicial protection to individuals who have been expelled from an association than

---

[143]*Id.* at 71, 559 P.2d at 191.
[144]115 Ariz. 811, 565 P.2d 188 (Ct. App. 1977).
[145]*Id.* at 312, 565 P.2d at 189.

to those who have been excluded. For example, in *Holmes v. Home-mako Hospital*,[146] a duly licensed physician challenged a hospital's suspension of his staff privileges because he was not going to renew his professional liability insurance. The court of appeals reversed the trial court's holding that the physician was afforded procedural due process and his suspension was not arbitrary or capricious. In reversing that finding, the court of appeals noted:

> "We are well aware of the fact that the right to follow any lawful vocation or profession is constitutionally protected. *City of Tucson v. Steward*, 45 Ariz. 36, 40 P.2d 72 (1935); *Meyer v. State of Nebraska*, 262 U.S. 390, 43 S.Ct. 625, 67 L.Ed. 1042 (1923)."[147]

Apparently, such constitutional protections extend to expulsion cases only, as the foregoing Arizona decisions denied relief in admission cases absent a showing a strict economic necessity.

California

California has been at the forefront of according broad judicial review to the actions of private voluntary associations. Indeed, one of the cases relied on by *Falcone, James v. Marinship Corp.*,[148] was decided by the California Supreme Court in 1944. In that case the court sustained an order which restrained interference with the employment of the plaintiff where the union had a closed shop agreement with his employer but declined to admit the plaintiff to union membership for racial reasons. The *Falcone* case quoted the following portion of the California Supreme Court's opinion in *James*:

> "Where a union has, as in this case, attained a monopoly of the supply of labor by means of closed shop agreements and other forms of collective labor action, such a union occupies a quasi-public position similar to that of a public service business and it has certain corresponding obligations. It may no longer claim the same freedom from legal restraint enjoyed by golf clubs or fraternal associations. Its asserted right to choose its own members does not merely relate to social relations; it affects the fundamental right to work for a living."[149]

In 1962, the Supreme Court of California reiterated this position in *Willis v. Santa Ana Community Hospital Association*.[150] This case involved an action by an osteopathic physician against a hospital association for damages for an alleged conspiracy to deny him access to hospital facilities and deprive him of his ability to practice. The court held that while there was no state antitrust liability in the case, there was an established principle at common law that an action may be brought when the pursuit of a lawful business, calling, trade, or occupation is intentionally interfered with either by unlawful means

---

[146]117 Ariz. 403, 573 P.2d 477 (Ct. App. 1978).
[147]*Id.* at 405, 573 P.2d at 479.
[148]25 Cal.2d 721, 155 P.2d 329 (1944).
[149]*Falcone*, 34 N.J. at 593–594, 170 A.2d at 797–798.
[150]58 Cal.2d 806, 376 P.2d 568, 26 Cal. Rptr. 640 (1962).

or by means otherwise lawful when there is a lack of sufficient justification.[151] The court held that a cause of action is stated under such principle when it is alleged that a physician of the highest qualifications is denied access to necessary hospital facilities as a result of a conspiracy designed to restrain competition and deprive him of his practice in order to benefit competing members of the conspiracy.[152]

In *Kronen v. Pacific Coast Society of Orthodontists*,[153] the trial court specifically found that the society had not conspired to inhibit a complaining orthodontist's professional practice. In addition, the court found that the dentist was not qualified in all respects for admission into the association, had not complied with its bylaws requiring proper sponsors, and had refused to avail himself of the remedies available from the association. It concluded that the orthodontist had no enforceable right to membership and that the society had no legal obligation to show cause why his application for active membership was not or should not be granted. On review, the appellate court observed that as a general rule, membership in a voluntary association is a privilege which may be granted or withheld by the association at its pleasure. The courts will not interfere to compel admission to membership, no matter how arbitrary or unjust the rejection of the candidate may be. The appellate court did note the distinction between explusion and refusal to admit, indicating that limited review is available when a member is expelled from an association. The purpose of such review is to determine whether the association acted within its powers and in good faith, according to its laws and the law of the land. In *Kronen*, the orthodontist had argued that he should be subject to the expulsion standard of review because he had been a temporary associate member of the association. The court rejected this; it did not believe the orthodontist had a contractual right to become an active member simply because he had been an associate member. The court did conclude, however, that it was proper to review his exclusion from the association, because without membership he could not announce his specialty, could not serve welfare patients, and would be unable successfully to limit his practice to orthodontics. However, review of the facts indicated that the orthodontist received no improper arbitrary treatment, since he had failed to comply with several of the admission requirements.

Pinsker v. Pacific Coast Society of Orthodontists[154] departs from the requirement of a strict economic necessity allegation prior to review of an admission case. Dr. Pinsker's application for membership to the society's Southern Component, which would have qualified him for membership in the society and in the American Academy of Orthodontists, was denied. When he asked the reasons for his denial,

---

[151]*Id.* at 810, 376 P.2d at 570, 26 Cal Rptr. at 642.
[152]*Id.*
[153]237 Cal. App.2d 289, 46 Cal. Rptr. 808 (1965).
[154]1 Cal.3d 160, 460 P.2d 495, 81 Cal. Rptr. 623 (1969) (*Pinsker I*).

he was told that it was because he was sharing patients with a non-member. Dr. Pinsker segregated his patients from this nonmember, reapplied, and was again denied admission. The trial court applied the *Falcone* decision but rejected Dr. Pinsker's case because it found on the evidence that there was no "economic or other necessity" to justify judicial intervention. The California Supreme Court reversed, holding that Dr. Pinsker's allegations that membership would be *economically advantageous* and that he had suffered financial loss by reason of his rejection were sufficient to invoke judicial review:

> "In cases involving exclusion from membership in trade and professional organizations, the emphasis has been upon the economic necessity as opposed to the mere social utility, of membership.
>
> * * *
>
> "Because of the unique position in the field of orthodontics occupied by defendant AAO and its constituent organizations, membership, therein, *although not economically necessary in the strict sense of the word* (as was the case in *Falcone*), would appear to be a *practical necessity for a dentist who wishes not only to make a good living as an orthodontist but also to realize maximum potential achievement and recognition in such specialty* [emphasis added]. Defendant associations hold themselves out to the public and the dental profession generally as the sole organizations recognized by the ADA, which is itself a virtual monopoly to determine standards, both ethical and educational for the practice and certification of orthodontics. Thus, a public interest is shown and the associations must be viewed as having a fiduciary responsibility with respect to the acceptance or rejection of membership applications. (See Tobriner and Grodin, *The Individual and The Public Service Enterprise in the New Industrial State* (1967) 55 CAL. L. REV. 1247.) Under the circumstances, an applicant for membership has judicially enforceable right to have his application considered in a manner comporting with the fundamentals of due process, including the showing of a cause for rejection."[155]

The court added that the society had the right to show that its rejection was in fact reasonable and remanded the case for trial.

Five years later the case returned to the California Supreme Court.[156] On remand, the society had claimed that Dr. Pinsker violated its ethical rules by sharing patients with an unqualified person, while Dr. Pinsker replied that he had not disobeyed the rules and that his rejection was invalid because of unfair procedures. The trial court upheld the society's construction of its rule and its claim that Dr. Pinsker had violated it, and held that Dr. Pinsker had no right to respond to the charges against him. The California Supreme Court again reversed:

> "As our past cases recognize, an organization's decision to exclude or expel an individual may be 'arbitrary' either because the reason for the exclusion or explusion is itself irrational or because, in applying a given rule in a particular case, the society has proceeded in an unfair manner. Although the fair procedure required in this setting clearly

---

[155]*Id.* at 165–166, 460 P.2d at 498–499.
[156]12 Cal.3d 541, 526 P.2d 253, 116 Cal. Rptr. 245 (1974) (*Pinsker II*).

need not include the formal embellishments of a court trial, an affected individual must at least be provided with some meaningful opportunity to respond to the 'charges' against him."[157]

The court held that Dr. Pinsker had the right to fair procedures as well as reasonable admission standards. This right was traced through the *Falcone* case to the California union cases such as *James v. Marinship Corp.* While many of the previous cases had dealt with expulsion situations, rather than exclusions, the court believed that the same judicial standard should be applied to an association with monopoly power which sufficiently affected significant economic and professional concerns to clothe it with a "public interest." The court specifically stated that, even though such a showing may not be an "economic necessity," the applicant would still have a right to obtain judicial review.

The court pointed out, however, that the common law requirement of fair procedure does not compel formal proceedings with all the embellishments of a court trial. Referring to the ruling of the Arizona Supreme Court in *Blende v. Maricopa Medical Society*,[158] the court noted that the judiciary must guard against interfering unduly with a society's autonomy by substituting its judgment for that of the society in an area where the competence of the court does not equal that of the society. Applying this standard to the facts in *Pinsker*, the court held that the application to Dr. Pinsker of the rule that members could not associate in practice with nonmembers was not arbitrary. However, the court stated that Dr. Pinsker was entitled to a fair hearing as to whether he had actually associated with a nonmember once he was warned against doing so. If the society properly concluded during such a hearing that Pinsker had in fact continued sharing patients with nonmembers, the court said, such a practice would provide a nonarbitrary ground for rejecting his application. Since Dr. Pinsker had not yet received such a hearing, his rejection from the society was set aside and the society was ordered to reconsider his application pursuant to fair procedure.

The *Pinsker* standard was applied to a real estate association in *Marin County Board of Realtors v. Palsson.*[159] A broker was denied membership in the association and, consequently, access to its multiple listing service, on the ground that he was not a full-time broker. He brought suit under the antitrust laws. The California Supreme Court held that the association was not immune from judicial review. While noting that it has never been the law in California that a voluntary association can be forced to open its membership rolls to all who apply, the court stated that when membership in an association is a "practical economic necessity," judicial review is available to examine the reasons for exclusion. The *Pinsker* and *Falcone* cases

---

[157]*Id.* at 545, 526 P.2d at 256, 116 Cal. Rptr. at 248.
[158]96 Ariz. 240, 393 P.2d 926 (1964).
[159]16 Cal. 3d 920, 549 P.2d 833, 130 Cal. Rptr. 1 (1976).

were cited in support of this proposition. The court was quick to point out that the *Pinsker* decision had not been decided under the antitrust laws and that the scope of review under the antitrust act would be broader in order to focus on possible anticompetitive effects of the association's bylaws.

The *Pinsker* rule was also applied to support a cause of action by a horse trainer and stable agent against a racetrack for excluding him from the stable area of the track. In *Greenberg v. Hollywood Turf Club*,[160] a California appellate court rejected the club's argument that it was immune from judicial review under the common law rule that places of amusement, such as racetracks, have no common law duty to provide access to all individuals. The court held that stable areas constituted a natural place for future employment negotiations since that is where prospective employers of the horse trainer would be found. Moreover, the court took judicial notice of the fact that by virtue of the licensing powers of the California horse racing board, racing associations have a quasi-monopoly in that the number of tracks in operation is limited. Such a monopoly imposed upon the club certain obligations which other landowners may not be subject to. It is interesting that the court found a "monopoly" in this case simply because the racetrack was regulated by the state, which limited the number of tracks as part of the regulation plan. Such reasoning could obviously be applied in a number of different contexts to support judicial review of a private entity's actions.

While the *Pinsker* decision appears to announce the broadest basis for judicial review of voluntary associations, the California courts have limited its holding in some situations. For example, in *Blatt v. University of Southern California*,[161] a law student sought to compel his admission to membership in the Order of the Coif, a national honorary legal society. The trial court dismissed the complaint with prejudice, and the reviewing court affirmed on the ground that membership in the Order "does not affect [the student's] basic right to earn a living."[162] The student had alleged that election to the Order elevates the law student in the eyes of the legal profession and public at large and greatly enhances his employment possibilities and economic position after graduation. He alleged that nonelection would adversely affect his professional and economic interests to a degree sufficient to bring him within the *Pinsker* line of cases, at least to create a question of fact, and therefore he should be permitted to offer evidence in support of his allegations. The court characterized the student's position as one advocating compulsory admission to membership in a voluntary organization in *any* situation where membership might enhance or affect one's professional or economic interests. The *Pinsker* cases, the court stated, do not support such a

---

[160]7 Cal. App.3d 968, 86 Cal. Rptr. (1970).
[161]5 Cal. App.3d 935, 85 Cal. Rptr. 601 (1970).
[162]85 Cal. Rptr. at 606.

contention since they are expressly limited to situations affecting the right to work in a chosen occupation or specialized field. The court noted and rejected the broad implications of deciding in favor of the plaintiff:

> "To adopt plaintiff's contention would subject to judicial review the membership selection activity and policies of *every* voluntary organization, because it is difficult to conceive of any organization that does not in some respect involve or affect a professional or economic interest of its members. It would also subject to judicial review procedures used in selecting persons for advanced and honorary degrees, and for selection of members for such honorary societies as Phi Beta Kappa, each of which presumably have some resultant professional or economic benefit.
>
>   * * *
>
> "Membership in the Order does not give a member the right to practice the profession of law. It does not signify qualification for any specialized field of practice. It has no direct bearing on the number or type of clients that the attorney-member might have or on the income he will make in his professional practice. It does not affect his basic right to earn a living. We hold that in the absence of allegations of sufficient facts of arbitrary or discriminatory action, membership in the Order is an honor best determined by those in the academic field without judicial interference. Plaintiff's allegations of arbitrary or discriminatory action on the part of the election committee are insufficient to state a cause of action. No justifiable issue has been presented."[163]

The California courts have also refused to extend the *Pinsker* rule for the benefit of certain bar associations suing other such associations alleging that the defendant's bylaws prohibiting the plaintiff from being represented at state bar meetings were arbitrary. It was noted that it was not a matter of practical necessity for the plaintiff organization's survival to be represented by delegates at an advisory conference.[164]

A corporation alleging that it had been economically harmed by the enforcement of a medical association's bylaws also was denied relief despite the *Pinsker* decision. The court observed that the medical association was formed to protect and advance the interests of both its member doctors and the public. A special relationship existed between the association and its members concerning the conduct of a member within the association's ambit. That special relationship justified the association's interference in the conduct of its members, and those who suffered adverse economic effects from such interference had no standing to complain.[165] A California court also refused to apply the *Pinsker* decision to strike down association rules limiting an optometrist's right to advertise.[166]

Even if the *Pinsker* case is found to be applicable to an associ-

---

[163]*Id.* at 605–606.
[164]*Criminal Courts Bar Ass'n v. State Bar*, 22 Cal. App.3d 681, 99 Cal. Rptr. 661 (1972).
[165]*Cal-Medicon v. Los Angeles County Medical Ass'n*, 20 Cal. App.3d 148, 97 Cal. Rptr. 530 (1971).
[166]*Jacobs v. State Bd. of Optometry*, 81 Cal. App.3d 1022, 147 Cal. Rptr. 225 (1978).

ation, there has been some willingness to implement procedural protections so as to minimize the intrusion on an association's internal affairs. For example, in *Bunzel v. American Academy of Orthopaedic Surgeons*,[167] an orthopedic surgeon brought an action against the academy for damages and for an order admitting him to membership. During the course of litigation the surgeon sought discovery of the academy's membership deliberations regarding his candidacy. The academy objected to this on the ground that evaluations of the applicants were privileged under the First Amendment and disclosure would inhibit its members from participating in the selection of future applicants for fear of harassment or legal actions by those rejected. While such membership deliberations might be relevant to the surgeon's cause of action, the trial court required the surgeon to show, prior to obtaining discovery of the members' evaluations of the applicants, that the academy was a *"Pinsker"* type of organization, i.e., that membership therein was a "practical economic necessity." Subsequently, the trial court entered summary judgment in favor of the academy, holding that the overwhelming weight of evidence indicated that the academy was not a *"Pinsker"* type of organization. On appeal, the decision was reversed on the ground that the issue of whether the academy was a *"Pinsker"* type of organization was for the trier of fact. The case was remanded for trial on that issue. While the academy did not ultimately prevail on its motion for summary judgment, this case illustrates how a lawsuit may be structured to minimize intrusion into an association's internal affairs. Only if the plaintiff were able to prove that membership in the academy was a "practical economic necessity" would he be permitted to invoke judicial review of the academy's confidential membership deliberations. Such procedural steps may go a long way toward balancing and protecting interests of both the plaintiff and the defendant in cases where courts have judicially refrained from reviewing. It should be kept in mind, however, that his case dealt with an exclusion, not an expulsion. In an expulsion case, it is unlikely that plaintiffs would be required first to prove "practical economic necessity," since expelled members have traditionally been accorded judicial review and fair procedure.[168]

Like the courts in other states surveyed in this chapter, the California courts have applied rules developed in the association cases to hospital staff admission disputes. In *Ascherman v. San Francisco Medical Society*,[169] a physician denied staff privileges by three hospitals compared his right to judicial review to the law of fraternal societies, labor unions, mutual benefit societies, and trade associations. He argued that he was entitled at least to minimum due process protections against arbitrary action by any of the hospitals. The hos-

[167]107 Cal. App.3d 165, 165 Cal. Rptr. 433 (1980).
[168]*California Dental Ass'n v. American Dental Ass'n*, 80 Cal. App.3d 653, 145 Cal. Rptr. 772 (1978), *aff'd*, 23 Cal.3d 346, 590 P.2d 401, 152 Cal. Rptr. 546 (1979).
[169]39 Cal. App.3d 623, 114 Cal. Rptr. 681 (1974).

pitals conceded that they were required to comply with their bylaws but asserted that there was no requirement that a bylaw provide a right to a hearing before a licensed physician could be deprived of or denied staff privileges. They argued that cases dealing with membership in professional societies involved associations monopolizing the practice of a particular profession, whereas they constituted only a small fraction of the many hospitals in the San Francisco Bay area and therefore did not have monopolistic control over the physician's right to practice his profession. The court ruled that this argument construed the type of economic advantage the courts will protect too narrowly. The physician alleged with supporting evidence that he had suffered economic loss by reason of his exclusion. This was sufficient to warrant judicial review.

A similar result was reached in *Ascherman v. St. Francis Memorial Hospital*,[170] where a physician petitioned for a writ of mandamus to compel a private hospital to consider his application for staff privileges. The lower court had entered judgment denying the petition but the court of appeals reversed, holding that a bylaw permitting rejection of an application not accompanied by letters of recommendation from hospital staff members was not rational and violated minimum common law standards of fair procedure. The *Pinsker* case was cited for the proposition that the physician had a judicially enforceable right to have his application considered in a manner comporting with fundamental due process. *Pinsker* was based on the fiduciary responsibilities arising out of public service functions performed by associations and hospitals. The mere existence of other hospitals to which the physician might apply was not a sufficient safety valve to prevent deprivation of substantial economic advantages.

The "common law duty of fair procedure" subsequently has been imposed on private hospitals in many cases.[171] It appears from these decisions that the showing of a monopoly enjoyed by the defendant may no longer be critical to securing judicial review of arbitrary actions by private entities. Instead, the California courts appear to permit judicial review when an individual's right to earn a living or pursue his profession is affected. One court has cautioned, however, that although the *Pinsker* and *Ascherman* cases stand for the proposition that a showing of strict economic necessity may no longer be required, judicial intervention in staff exclusion cases, in contrast to expulsion cases, is generally limited to situations involving *substantial* economic ramifications.[172]

---

[170]45 Cal. App.3d 507, 119 Cal. Rptr. 507 (1975).
[171]*Westlake Community Hosp. v. Superior Court*, 17 Cal.3d 465, 551 P.2d 410, 131 Cal. Rptr. 90 (1976); *Anton v. San Antonio Community Hosp.*, 19 Cal.3d 802, 815, 567 P.2d 1162, 1168, 140 Cal. Rptr. 442, 448 (1977); *Hackethal v. Loma Linda Community Hosp.*, 91 Cal. App.3d 59, 153 Cal. Rptr. 783 (1979); *Miller v. Eisenhower Medical Center*, 27 Cal.3d 614, 614 P.2d 258, 166 Cal. Rptr. 826 (1980); *Applebaum v. Board of Directors*, 104 Cal. App.3d 648, 163 Cal. Rptr. 831 (1980).
[172]*Lewin v. St. Joseph Hosp.*, 82 Cal. App.3d 368, 393, 146 Cal. Rptr. 892, 908 (1978).

Not only has the *Pinsker* holding been expanded to control hospital staff admission cases, it has also been relied on to increase an individual's rights against various quasi-governmental entities. For example, the Califonia Supreme Court has held that prejudgment attachment without prior notice or hearing upon the filing of such an action violated due process. The Supreme Court required the lower court to afford the plaintiff a hearing prior to the attachment, noting that the California courts of law preserved the individual's right to notice and a meaningful hearing in instances in which a significant deprivation is threatened by a private entity or a governmental body.[173] Another court has applied the *Pinsker* common law rule of fair procedure to the Board of Behavioral Science Examiners, a state accrediting association.[174] One of the more significant decisions in this area is *Bixby v. Pierno*,[175] in which minority shareholders alleged that the state corporation commissioner's approval of a recapitalization plan substantially injured them. The *Pinsker* and *Falcone* cases were cited in support of the California Supreme Court's holding that where vested, fundamental rights, such as the right to practice one's trade or profession, are affected, administrative agency decisions will be reviewed by the courts de novo:

> "In a case involving the agency's initial determination whether an individual qualifies to enter a profession or trade, the courts uphold the agency decision unless it lacks substantial evidentiary support [citations omitted] or infringes upon the applicant's statutory or constitutional rights. Once the agency has initially exercised its expertise and determined that an individual fulfills the requirements to practice his profession, the agency's subsequent revocation of the license calls for an independent judgment review of the facts underlying any such administrative decision. Although we recognize that the California rule yields no fixed formula and guarantees no predictably exact ruling in each case, it performs a precious function in the protection of the rights of the individual. Too often the independent thinker or crusader is subjected to the retaliation of the professional or trade group; the centripetal pressure to conformity will often destroy the advocate of reform. The unpopular protestant may well provoke an aroused zeal of scrutiny by the licensing body that finds trivial grounds for license revocation. Restricted to the narrow ground of review of the evidence and denied the power of an independent analysis, the court might well be unable to save the unpopular professional or practitioner. Before his license is revoked, such an individual, who walks in the shadow of the governmental monoliths, deserves the protection of a full and independent hearing."[176]

---

[173]*Randone v. Appellate Dep't of Superior Court*, 5 Cal.3d 536, 550, 488 P.2d 13, 21, 96 Cal. Rptr. 709, 717 (1971).

[174]*Packer v. Board of Behavioral Science Examiners*, 52 Cal. App.3d 190, 125 Cal. Rptr. 96 (1975).

[175]4 Cal.3d 130, 481 P.2d 242, 93 Cal. Rptr. 234 (1971).

[176]*Id.* at 146–147, 481 P.2d at 253–254, 93 Cal. Rptr. at 245–246.

Other Jurisdictions

In *Hawkins v. Kinsie*,[177] the Colorado Court of Appeals confronted the question of whether a court may intervene in the decisions of a private hospital with regard to staff admissions and commented that the case was one of first impression in Colorado. Observing that the hospital in the case was a private institution, the reviewing court held that there was no basis for imposition of constitutional due process standards and that dismissal of the plaintiff's claim premised on violations of procedural due process requirements was proper. However, the trial court's action in dismissing the claim that the hospital's decision was unreasonable, arbitrary, and capricious was premature. The court of appeals noted that the majority rule was that private hospitals have unfettered discretion in choosing whether to appoint a physician to its medical staff. The New Jersey *Greisman* case was cited as the minority rule, i.e., courts should grant relief where the action of the private hospital has been demonstrated to be unreasonable, arbitrary, and capricious. The latter rule was adopted by the Colorado Court of Appeals. Accordingly, the case was remanded for trial on the issue of whether the private hospital's decision was arbitrary.

While Florida has not had occasion to rule directly on the application of fair procedure requirements to private entities, one recent case has suggested that the *Falcone* and *Pinsker* decisions might be applied to accord judicial review to the actions of an association if an applicant is denied membership in contravention of due process rights.[178]

Two Massachusetts cases that address the *Falcone* decision are difficult to harmonize. In 1971 the Massachusetts Supreme Judicial Court in *Godfrey v. Massachusetts Medical Service*[179] denied declaratory relief to several podiatrists seeking to participate as a matter of right in a Blue Shield medical service plan. One of the issues in the case was whether the nonprofit medical service plan, as embodied in a Massachusetts state statute, discriminated unconstitutionally and arbitrarily between physicians and podiatrists. The court held that the statute was not unconstitutional, since differences in educational levels afforded a rational basis for making a distinction between the two professions. Relying heavily on *Falcone*, the podiatrists also contended that the medical service was a quasi-public corporation and that its discretionary power to exclude podiatrists was being exercised in an arbitrary and unreasonable manner. Distinguishing *Falcone*, the court held that exclusion from the Blue Shield program did not affect the right of the podiatrists to practice their profession. The court commented that in any event much of the force of the

---

[177]540 P.2d 345 (Colo. Ct. App. 1975).
[178]*Feldman v. Houle*, 400 So.2d 180, 181 (Fla. Dist. Ct. App. 1981) (per curiam).
[179]359 Mass. 610, 270 N.E.2d 804 (1971).

Falcone case had been weakened by the case of *Hayman v. Galveston*,[180] where a regulation by a municipal hospital board excluding osteopathic physicians from its staff was held not to violate the Constitution.

Despite the court's comment that *Falcone*'s force had been weakened, however, the *Falcone* decision was apparently applied in a Massachusetts federal district court several years later. In *Marlboro Corp. v. Association of Independent Colleges*,[181] the district court cited *Falcone* in support of its ability to review the private association, a business school accrediting agency recognized by the U.S. Commisioner of Education. The association was "quasi-public" and was required to follow fair procedures reasonably related to its legitimate purposes.

A Michigan federal district court in *Dietz v. American Dental Association*[182] adopted the *Falcone* rule in favor of a dentist who had been denied diplomate status by the dental association. The dentist alleged he was a licensed practioner and a member of the American Dental Association and that he had met all the qualifications for diplomate status in endodontics. He alleged that diplomate status permitted a dentist to announce that he is a specialist without exclusively limiting his practice to endodontics, command higher fees, attend special classes, teach, and more freely locate, all privileges which a nondiplomate might not enjoy. The association's board was the sole authority for certifying dentists as diplomates, and the board, the dentist alleged, remained under the control of the association. The association and its board argued that the dentist's certification was outside the court's competence. The U.S. Court of Appeals for the Sixth Circuit had previously ruled that the case involved no state action. Hence, the trial court noted, the dentist's recourse was to state law. Although noting the general rule that courts are reluctant to interfere with the internal workings of private associations, the trial court, citing *Falcone*, stated that if justice and equity required, the courts would review the decision of a private association. The court appeared to make no distinction between an exclusion and an expulsion and did not invoke the "economic necessity" test that some courts have required in an exclusion. Instead, it relied on the monopoly power of the association and whether membership would significantly affect an individual's professional practice:

> "Where a professional association has monopoly power and membership in the association significantly affects the member's practice of his profession, courts will hold the association has a fiduciary duty to be substantively rational and procedurally fair. The association must exercise its powers according to its by-laws and constitution; it cannot decide *to exclude or expell* a member or deny rights of membership for arbitrary, capricious or discriminatory reasons."[183] (Emphasis added.)

---

[180] 273 U.S. 414 (1927).
[181] 416 F. Supp. 958 (D. Mass. 1976).
[182] 479 F. Supp. 554 (E.D. Mich. 1979).
[183] *Id.* at 557.

The court denied the association's motion for summary judgment on the ground that material issues of fact existed concerning the length of required oral examinations and whether they were so meager in content that it would be arbitrary and capricious to deny diplomate status to the dentist on the basis of his failure to pass those tests.

Ohio adopted the *Falcone* and *Greisman* holdings in *Davidson v. Youngstown Hospital Association*.[184] This involved a proceeding by a licensed podiatrist for a mandatory order compelling a private hospital to grant him hospital staff privileges. The Ohio appellate court agreed that any rule or regulation of a professional society that has the effect of depriving an individual of an opportunity to earn a livelihood in a profession in which he is duly licensed by the state is subject to judicial scrutiny. The court did indicate that if exclusion from the staff of a private hospital was based on sound and reasonable exercise of discretionary judgment, it would not intervene. However, if the exclusion stemmed from unreasonable, arbitrary, capricious, or discriminatory considerations, the court would grant equitable relief. In *Davidson*, the court found that the bylaw resulting in the podiatrist's exclusion was not arbitrary.

In *Straube v. Emanuel Lutheran Charity Board*,[185] the Oregon Supreme Court recognized the principles set forth in the *Pinsker* cases but did not directly rule on whether a duty of fair procedure existed. Faced with a situation in which a radiologist brought suit against a hospital for wrongful suspension of his staff privileges, the court stated:

> "The term 'common-law due process' is unfortunate because of the tendency to confuse it with fourteenth Amendment due process; 'fair procedure' is a better term. In those states which recognize it, it is a rule having both substantive and procedural aspects which controls the actions of some private entities."[186]

The court did not decide whether a *Pinsker* type of duty applied to the case, since, assuming the duty existed, there was sufficient procedural fairness:

> "Fair procedure in a common-law sense is not constitutional due process. When plaintiff joined defendant's medical staff, he signified 'his agreement to abide by these [the hospital's] by-laws and regulations' and they provided for immediate suspension if required by 'the best interest of patient care in the hospital.' "[187]

It appears that most of the courts applying the common-law concept of fair procedure tacitly agree with the Oregon's court view that common law fair procedure is something less than constitutional due process. Both the California cases and the leading Arizona case, *Blende*,

---

[184] 19 Ohio App.2d 246, 250 N.E.2d 892 (1969).
[185] 287 Ore. 375, 600 P.2d 381 (1979).
[186] *Id*. at 379, 600 P.2d at 384.
[187] *Id*. at 382, 600 P.2d at 385–386.

repeatedly stressed that while judicial review may now be available, it is limited and defendants are not required to provide full-blown adversary proceedings, such as those found in the courts, for hearings relating to expulsion or exclusions. While Pennsylvania has not explicitly adopted the *Falcone* rationale, its courts have expressed a willingness to review the membership decisions of voluntary associations when such decisions affect individuals economically.[188] In one case, a Pennsylvania court ruled that a board of realtors must accept all brokers who fulfill the state-mandated minimum requirements for licensing on the assumption that membership and access to the listing service is essential for all brokers.[189]

Texas courts will afford judicial review for unfair expulsions from private associations,[190] but the application of *Falcone* to an exclusion situation was rejected by one appellate court in *Schooler v. Tarrant County Medical Society*.[191] In *Schooler*, a licensed physician petitioned for a writ of mandamus compelling a voluntary medical society to admit him to membership. A Texas appellate court held that the writ was properly denied where the physician failed to establish that membership in the society was a prerequisite to staff privileges at various hospitals. The physician had been a provisional member prior to applying for membership. The society indicated that during the physician's provisional membership, there were numerous complaints about his ethics and alleged overcharging. The general rule, which Texas follows, is that courts cannot compel admission of an individual into a voluntary association since membership is a privilege and not a right. This is true even if a person's application is arbitrarily refused. Additionally, the constitution and bylaws of such as association confer no legal rights on nonmembers. The court specifically noted that the *Falcone* and *Blende* cases were contrary to Texas law. While most jurisdictions do afford some type of due process hearing for expulsion situations, since contract or property rights may be involved, certain states, like Texas, continue to observe the rule that nonmembers have no right to judicially compelled admission to a private voluntary association. Among such states are Alabama,[192] Arkansas[193] and Indiana.[194]

---

[188]*Collins v. Mainline Bd. of Realtors*, 452 Pa. 342, 304 A.2d 493 (1973) (admission to multiple listing service compelled); School Dist. v. Pennsylvania Interscholastic Athletic Ass'n, 453 Pa. 495, 309 A.2d 353 (1973).

[189]*Collins v. Mainline Bd. of Realtors*, 452 Pa. 342, 304 A.2d 493 (1973).

[190]*Hatley v. American Quarter Horse Ass'n*, 552 F.2d 646, 655–656 (5th Cir. 1977).

[191]457 S.W.2d 644 (Tex. Civ. App. 1970).

[192]*Medical Soc'y v. Walker*, 245 Ala. 135, 16 So.2d 321 (1944); *Walker v. Medical Soc'y*, 247 Ala. 169, 22 So.2d 715 (1945).

[193]*Ware v. Benedikt*, 225 Ark. 185, 280 S.W.2d 234 (1955); *Elizabeth Hospital, Inc. v. Richardson*, 167 F. Supp. 155 (W.D. Ark. 1958), aff'd, 269 F.2d 167 (8th Cir.), cert. denied, 361 U.S. 884 (1959).

[194]*Hamilton County Hosp. v. Andrews*, 227 Ind. 217, 84 N.E.2d 469, cert. denied, 338 U.S. 831 (1949); *STP Corp. v. United States Auto Club, Inc.*, 286 F. Supp. 146 (S.D. Ind. 1968) (judicial review appropriate only if club's powers exercised in unlawful, arbitrary, or malicious fashion *and in such manner as to affect plaintiff's property rights*).

Summary

Even though there are still some states that adhere to the traditional property and contract right approach, the foregoing survey leaves no doubt that there has been widespread abandonment of the traditional approach and that the *Falcone* and *Pinsker* decisions have been largely responsible for this trend. The underlying rationale of these landmark cases, i.e., the need to protect an individual's right to earn a living, has been applied in a variety of situations, including hospital staff admissions, administrative licensing agencies, and attachment proceedings. It is logical that some attorneys have seized on the principles announced in *Falcone* and *Pinsker* and argued that they warrant judicial review of employment decisions. Such efforts, however, have been primarily limited to the California courts and have not always been successful.

Fair Procedure and the Employment Relationship

Bogacki v. Board of Supervisors[195] involved a petition for writ of mandamus to compel a county board of supervisors to set aside an individual's allegedly wrongful dismissal from county employment. The California Supreme Court held that the dismissal of the petitioner did not violate due process, even though neither ground assigned by the director in the letter of termination was supported by concrete evidence. The county had not adopted the civil service system of employment; under the terms of its ordinances and resolutions governing county employment, employees served at the pleasure of their department heads, subject to certain limited appeal rights. The plaintiff had alleged that he was discharged because of his work with a particular association, and that the dismissal accordingly violated his right of free speech and assembly. The court ruled, however, that it had not been proved that this was the reason for his dismissal. The law in California, it stated, is that a public employee serving at the pleasure of the appointing authority is by the terms of his employment subject to removal without judicially cognizable good cause. The power of the department head to remove from his particular department an employee deemed unsuitable by him was absolute within the terms of applicable county law.

Justice Tobriner, who participated in both *Pinsker* decisions, dissented on the ground that case law relating to labor unions and professional associations, in situations in which the private action has a significant impact on an individual's livelihood, was ignored by the majority. Justice Tobriner traced the history of these cases back to *James v. Marinship Corp.*, where it was held that a labor organization maintaining a closed shop, and effectively controlling

---

[195]5 Cal.3d 771, 489 P.2d 537, 97 Cal. Rptr. 657 (1971).

the availability of specific employment for an individual, could not "arbitrarily" exclude applicants for membership. Judicial review would be accorded when the fundamental right to work for a living was affected by the union's decision. Tobriner pointed out that the principles reflected in the union cases had been applied to trade and professional associations. Such cases held that whenever membership in an association would have significant economic and professional bearing on an applicant's livelihood, "an applicant for membership has a judicially enforceable right to have his application considered in a manner comporting with the fundamentals of due process, including the showing of cause for rejection"[196] (quoting *Pinsker*). Justice Tobriner did caution, however, that such judicial review should be limited:

> "Although I agree that we must recognize a 'broad discretion' residing in employing agencies or supervisory personnel, it does not follow that we must similarly acknowledge this discretion to be 'absolute' or 'unfettered' or that it may be abused at will without any opportunity for review. * * * Nevertheless, when the government does discharge an employee 'arbitrarily,' thereby abusing this broad discretion, I believe the courts must be open to afford relief. 'Where discretion is conferred upon an administrative officer to render a decision, this decision must be honestly rendered, and if it is arbitrary or capricious, or rendered in bad faith, then the courts have the power to review the decision and set it aside.' (*Crocker v. United States* (1955) 127 F. Supp. 568, 573, 130 CT. CL. 567)."[197]

In addition to citing the *Pinsker* cases as support for review of the board's actions, Justice Tobriner referred to the U.S. Supreme Court decision in *Sniadach v. Family Finance Corp.*,[198] where it was determined that a Wisconsin prejudgment wage garnishment provision was unconstitutional because it authorized the withholding of the debtor's wages without affording the debtor the due process protections of notice and a meaningful hearing. In decisions following *Sniadach*, minimal due process requirements applicable to governmental actions were extended to termination of welfare benefits and the suspension of an automobile driver's license. Justice Tobriner found a comparison of the instant case with the Court's analysis in *Sniadach* revealing. In *Sniadach*, the Court emphasized the great hardships that would frequently befall a wage earner and his family as a result of the withholding of a significant portion of his earnings. The Court concluded that where the taking of one's property was so obvious, failure to provide a hearing violated the fundamental principles of due process. In the instant case, Tobriner pointed out, petitioner had been deprived not merely of a portion of his wages but of his entire livelihood.

Most important, Justice Tobriner's dissent provides a justifica-

---

[196]*Id.* at 801, 489 P.2d at 558, 97 Cal. Rptr. at 678.
[197]*Id.* at 802–803, 489 P.2d at 559–560, 97 Cal. Rptr. at 679–680.
[198]395 U.S. 337 (1969).

tion for applying the rules found in the voluntary association and certification cases to the employment situation through the following analysis:

> "The due process analysis in *Bell* decisively points out the incongruity of a decision denying the applicability of procedural due process in the instant case. In *Bell* the suspension of a driver's license was recognized as *affecting* an interest of sufficient importance to bring the procedural due process safeguards into play, precisely because such licenses 'may become essential in the pursuit of a livelihood.' (91 S.Ct. at p. 1589) In the instant case we deal not with an incidental interest, the denial of which may detrimentally affect one's livelihood, but with the question of the actual termination of the 'livelihood' itself. Given *Bell* the instant matter must surely be the paradigmatic *a fortiori* case.
>
> "The majority cannot avoid the force of these recent decisions by falling back on the claim that public employment is merely a 'privilege' which may be withdrawn summarily."[199]

The majority did not state why it failed to apply the body of case law cited by Justice Tobriner to the employment situation. It is quite possible that the presence of the ordinance specifically declaring that an employee served at the pleasure of the appointing authority removed the situation from the common law principles set forth in the *Pinsker* decisions. In other words, statute or contract law precluded the application of the common law of fair procedure.

Justice Tobriner also dissented in *Barthuli v. Board of Trustees*.[200] In this case a former school superintendent sought a writ of mandamus to compel reinstatement to his job. The California Supreme Court held that in the absence of a deprivation of a constitutional right, reinstatement was not available. Also, the court held that the former superintendent had no property right in continued employment and was not entitled to due process prior to his termination. The majority spent some time defining the nature of the property right and determined that the petitioner in his position as an administrator was not a permanent employee since the legislature had not given him a property right. Justice Tobriner dissented from that portion of the opinion denying the former superintendent a right to be heard by the board of trustees, the body that possessed the ultimate discretionary authority over his employment. Such a right, Tobriner argued, was justified by the *Pinsker* series of cases.

In *Centeno v. Roseville Community Hospital*,[201] a Califonia appellate court refused to apply the common law of fair procedure or due process to an exclusive contract situation. A radiologist had been involved in a partnership which had an exclusive radiology services contract with the hospital. The radiologist became embroiled in a controversy with his partners which culminated in his withdrawal from the partnership. The hospital then refused to allow him to use

[199]*Bogacki v. Board of Supervisors*, 5 Cal.3d at 805–806, 489 P.2d at 561–562, 97 Cal. Rptr. at 681–682.
[200]19 Cal.3d 717, 566 P.2d 261, 139 Cal. Rptr. 627 (1977).
[201]107 Cal. App.3d 62, 167 Cal. Rptr. 183 (1979).

its radiology facilities, claiming it had an exclusive contract with the remaining partners. The radiologist sued the hospital, alleging that one of the parties to the contract had maliciously, unlawfully, and wrongfully deprived him of his right to practice his profession; that he would suffer irreparable damage unless injunctive and declaratory relief were granted; and that the hospital intentionally and maliciously had interfered with his present and prospective economic and professional benefits by refusing to allow him complete radiological clinical privileges. The radiologist cited the *Pinsker* case in support of his contention that the hospital was required to hold a hearing before he was excluded from use of the radiology department. In the court's view the *Pinsker* case was not applicable. If municipalities can grant exclusive contracts without violating the due process clause, the court reasoned, a private hospital should be able to grant an exclusive contract such as the one involved in this case. The court commented that it could not give serious consideration to the demand that the award of a public contract must be preceded by an evidentiary hearing as to afford all potentially interested persons an opportunity to contest the award.

In *Heath v. Redbud Hospital District*,[202] the U.S. Court of Appeals for the Ninth Circuit refused to apply the common law duty of fair procedure to the employment relationship. A former hospital administrator had brought a civil rights action arising out of her termination from that position. The reviewing court affirmed the summary judgment entered in favor of the hospital. A California statute, it noted, specifically stated that officers hold their positions at the pleasure of the hospital boards. The former administrator asserted that she had a constitutionally protected "property" interest in continued employment with the hospital, but the court held the state statute controlling in determining what a property interest was. The former administrator sought to invoke the "California common law right of fair procedure," citing *Pinsker* among other decisions, but the court rejected this effort:

> "Two factors militate against reliance on *Ezekial* to support the conclusion that plaintiff had a legitimate expectation of continued employment. First, there is absent in this case the licensing or certification factor, denial of which made pursuit of an individual's chosen trade or profession impossible in *Marinship, Pinsker* and *Ezekial*. Second, is the fact that '[n]o case has yet applied the *Marinship* doctrine directly to a relationship dependent on employment.' *Ezekial*, 142 Cal.Rptr. at 423, 572 P.2d at 37."[203]

Despite the broad ramifications of applying the *Pinsker* and *Falcone* decisions to all types of employment situations, some court decisions have provided a bridge between the association cases and employment situations. The majority and dissenting opinions of the

---

[202]620 F.2d 207 (9th Cir. 1980).
[203]*Id.* at 210–211.

California Supreme Court in *Ezekial v. Winkley* are a case in point.[204] In *Ezekial*, a former resident who had been terminated brought an action against a private hospital, claiming the existence of enforceable contracts of employment. The California Supreme Court held that the fair procedure principles developed in *Pinsker* applied to the case:

> "The underlying rationale of the *Marinship-Pinsker* line of cases is that certain private entities possess substantial power either to thwart an individual's pursuit of a lawful trade or profession, or to control the terms and conditions under which it is practiced. [Citations omitted.] Thus in *Marinship, Directors Guild* and *Thorman*, all *supra*, a labor union's arbitrary policies of exclusion have important effects on the employment opportunities of persons already qualified and employed in a craft or trade. In *Kronen* and in the *Ascherman* and *Pinsker* cases, all *supra*, private organizations, by controlling access to vital professional privileges and certifications, had a similar practical ability to foreclose from practice one who had already obtained a professional license. We had said that the right to practice a lawful trade or profession is sufficiently 'fundamental' to require substantial protection against arbitrary administrative interference, either by government [citations omitted] or by a private entity [citations omitted]."[205]

The court acknowledged that no prior cases had applied the common law doctrine of fair procedure to dismissals from a private hospital residency. Because residency was a part of the regulatory plan of hospitals, however, and because the hospital sought to expel the former resident from a program to which he had already been admitted, he would be entitled to fair procedure protection prior to the dismissal from the residency program.

The hospital had claimed there was a critical distinction in status between the medical resident and the independent practicing professionals involved in the *Pinsker* series of cases. Common law rights of fair procedure, it argued, apply neither to an employer-employee relationship nor to the training opportunity by which a physician seeks to qualify as a medical specialist. The hospital urged that, unlike an independent physician with hospital staff privileges, the resident was merely an employee whose connection with the hospital was terminable at will in the absence of a contrary agreement, and whose only remedy would be money damages for any contractual breach.

The court acknowledged that no case had yet applied the common law of fair procedure directly to a relationship dependent on employment alone. Nor had the rule against arbitrary *explusion* from a private association been invoked in the employment context. A careful reading of the decision shows that the court decided to apply the fair procedure doctrine, not because petitioner was an employee, but rather because of his professional status. Referring to the hos-

---

[204]20 Cal.3d 267, 572 P.2d 32, 142 Cal. Rptr. 418 (1977).
[205]*Id.* at 272, 572 P.2d at 35, 142 Cal. Rptr. at 421.

pital's argument that fair procedure should not apply in an employee context, the court stated:

> "These common law principles were, of course, never intended to invoke legal sanctions, beyond those found either on contract or statute, on behalf of every employee threatened with discharge by a private employer. Rather, *Marinship* and successive cases have emphasized that the membership privileges, or the professional recognition, which certain private institutions may arbitrarily grant, deny, or withdraw are practical prerequisites to *any* effective employment in a chosen field.
>
> "In the instant case we look beyond plaintiff's immediate status as an employee of Kaiser and examine an entirely distinct interest which also inheres in his residency, namely, his expectation of achieving necessary certification as a surgeon. We conclude that defendants may not defeat application of *Marinship-Pinsker* principles on the basis alone that plaintiff, as a resident, is also necessarily an employee of the hospital."[206]

This excerpt suggests that the court was exercising caution in its application of the common law of fair procedure to a situation that can be viewed as an employer-employee relation. The court pointed out that this was not the only factor present. Additionally, the former resident alleged that failure to complete his residency would affect his ability to practice his specialty. Hence, the justification for applying fair procedure appears to rest, as in the previous cases, on ensuring that an individual is not blocked from practicing his chosen profession by a private entity's arbitrary actions. Nevertheless, Justice Mosk dissented on the ground that the fair procedure concept had been extended too broadly:

> "I fear my learned colleagues in the majority are extending the amorphous common law right to 'fair procedure' far beyond any previous contemplation. In so doing they create a cumbersome burden on employer-employee contractual relations, substitute judicial rather than professional determination of professional qualifications and potentially affect the ability of medical institutions to provide the type of care they desire for their own patients."[207]

Justice Mosk insisted that the common law right of fair procedure extends only to circumstances where the association or private entity has obtained a monopoly over the supply of labor or an individual's ability to practice a certain calling. He justified the application of the common law doctrine as similar to the equivalent of a common law action for restraint of trade. In *Ezekial*, however, Justice Mosk found no monopoly of access to a profession or a conspiracy by petitioner's competitors. To the contrary, the former resident conceded that the hospital's residency program was unlike those of most private hospitals. He had not been denied the right to practice medicine, nor had he been barred by competitors from access to the patients and facilities of the community. Rather, he had been thwarted in his

---

[206]*Id.* at 275–276, 572 P.2d at 37–38, 142 Cal. Rptr. at 423–424.
[207]*Id.* at 280, 572 P.2d at 40, 142 Cal. Rptr. at 426.

expectation of completing his residency in surgery at a particular hospital.

In Justice Mosk's view, the former resident was attempting to bootstrap an alleged breach of an employment contract into an equitable proceeding by adding claims of irreparable injury. For the majority to permit this was going too far:

> "Undoubtedly, there are untoward detrimental effects after every employment dismissal. But I doubt that the majority realize, in attempting to ameliorate that result by approving plaintiff's theory, they are establishing precedent for requiring employers to provide a 'fair hearing' to every employee who alleges a subjective expectation of continued employment and injury for having that expectancy toward it. The burden on the normal employer-employee contractual relationship will become intolerable.
> * * *
> "A staff physician treats *his* patients at the hospital. He has full authority to prescribe the patient's treatment, he is subject to no supervision during the course of treatment, and he generally bears full responsibility for negligence. The situation of the medical resident is entirely different. He treats his *employer's* patients by assignment of his employer, subject to supervision by the hospital's chief of surgery, and because of the employer-employee relationship, the hospital is liable for his negligence under accepted principles of *respondeat superior*."[208]

The additional element of *respondeat superior*, as mentioned by Justice Mosk, is one of the outstanding differences between the employer-employee relationship and that of a professional and a medical association or hospital staff. The argument could be made that the employer's various liability for acts of his employees necessitates granting the employer complete discretion in terminating his relationship with an employee where employee competence is the issue. Perhaps this was a substantial influential factor in the Ninth Circuit Court of Appeals decision in *Heath v. Redbud Hospital District*,[209] where the court refused to apply *Ezekial* to a situation involving purely an employment relationship without a licensing or certification factor precluding a professional from practicing his calling.

While the *Heath* case strongly suggested that the common law of fair procedure would not be applied to an employment relation absent a certification or licensing factor, the California Supreme Court, in a 1979 decision, held fair procedure principles applicable to an employment situation which did not involve a profession. In *Gay Law Students Association v. Pacific Telephone & Telegraph Co.*,[210] an association advocating equal rights for homosexuals sought declaratory, injunctive, and monetary relief against a public utility on the ground that it engaged in discriminatory employment practices, and against the Fair Employment Practice Commission on the ground

---

[208]*Id.* at 281–283, 572 P.2d at 41–42, 142 Cal. Rptr. at 427–428.
[209]620 F.2d 207 (9th Cir. 1980).
[210]24 Cal.3d 458, 595 P.2d 592, 156 Cal. Rptr. 14 (1979).

that it improperly refused to take any action to remedy the alleged employment discrimination. The California Supreme Court focused on the *Marinship* decision and quoted portions of the opinion holding that when a union occupies a quasi-public position similar to that of public service businesses, it has certain corresponding obligations and can no longer claim the freedom from legal restraint enjoyed by golf clubs or fraternal associations. This is because the union's asserted right to choose its own members does not relate to social relations but affects the fundamental right to work for a living. The court commented that the *Marinship* doctrine does not apply only to unions but has been extended to any "public service enterprise," including professional and business associations and private and public hospitals. These entities, tinged with a public interest, are bound under common law principles to refrain from arbitrary exclusion of individuals from employment opportunities. Since a utility is tinged with a public interest, the *Marinship* and *Pinsker* series of cases are applicable.

The telephone company argued that as a utility it was free to hire or fire employees as it saw fit. The court rejected this argument, noting that the utility enjoyed a state-protected monopoly and could not be compared to the ordinary private employer. It should be observed that in *Marinship* the court held the union had no right arbitrarily to deny certain persons membership because it had monopoly power over jobs in the shipyard. In *Gay Law Students*, the court reasoned that the telephone company had no power arbitrarily to deny employment because, as a publicly regulated utility, it had a monopoly in the delivery of telephone services. The relationship in *Gay Law Students* between monopoly power and jobs is substantially less direct than in *Marinship*, but the same bar to arbitrary conduct is applied.

The final comment made by the court suggests that even *private* employers might be subject to the common law of fair procedure:

> "Indeed, the *Marinship* decision itself establishes that employers are not automatically exempt from these common law principles, for, as noted above, the injunction upheld in *Marinship* specifically prohibited the employer as well as the union from discrimination against black workers."[211]

In 1981 the California Supreme Court, in *Graham v. Sissor-Tail, Inc.*,[212] again applied the common law requirement of fair procedure to an employee dispute not involving licensing or certification. In *Graham*, a nonunion member promoter of concerts brought suit against a musician for breach of a contract, one provision of which provided for arbitration. The court held, that if a party resisting arbitration can show that the rules under which the arbitration is to proceed will operate to deprive him of the common law right of fair procedure,

---

[211]*Id.* at 485, 595 P.2d at 608, 156 Cal. Rptr. at 30.
[212]28 Cal.3d 807, 623 P.2d 165, 171 Cal. Rptr. 604 (1981) (en banc).

the agreement to arbitrate will not be enforced. *Pinsker* was cited as the basis for imposition of the common law right of fair procedure. This case, as well as *Ezekial*, illustrates the court's willingness to import the *Falcone* and *Pinsker* principles to situations not involving associations and licensing or certification. All of these cases, however, have involved factors in addition to the employment relation. The *Gay Law Students* case, for example, involved an employer-employee situation, but the defendant was a public utility. A case has yet to surface that involves a purely private employer-employee relationship and the application of the common law of fair procedure. Apparently the *Gay Law Students* opinion, where the California Supreme Court indicated that private employers would not necessarily be exempt from the common law of fair procedure, is as far as any case has gone.

The only other situation that has touched on the application of fair procedure to employment termination is *Dimond v. Samaritan Health Service.*[213] A discharged supervisor in the clinical pathology department of a private hospital requested a hearing pursuant to the rules and regulations of the hospital relating to termination of employment. At the hearing, she was not permitted to have legal counsel, and no provision was made for the compulsory attendance of witnesses. The Arizona appellate court ruled that even assuming they constituted a contract, the hospital's rules and regulations did not provide for representation by legal counsel and compulsory witnesses. Since the discharged supervisor had no contractual right to procedures, any right to a lawyer and compulsory witness attendance must rest on a constitutional basis such as denial of due process, which in turn would require that the hospital's conduct be regarded as state action. This, however, was a private hospital and in no sense any agent of the state.

There are parallels that can be drawn between the evolution of the law governing judicial review of the membership decisions of voluntary associations and the law governing termination of employment. In dealing with employment controversies, courts are now at the point where they were several decades ago in dealing with membership decisions of voluntary associations: They are in the early stages of seriously questioning whether employers (associations) may act arbitrarily, irrationally, or discriminatorily if the decision has a substantial impact on the livelihood of the employee (member). Perhaps in time the courts will borrow from the voluntary association cases, discard attempts to shoehorn employment rights and remedies into tort and contract theories, and declare that there are inherent

---

[213]27 Ariz. App. 682, 558 P.2d 710 (1976). See also *King v. Regents of Univ. of Cal.*, 138 Cal. App.3d 812, 189 Cal. Rptr. 189 (1982), and *Marmion v. Mercy Hosp. & Medical Center*, 145 Cal. App.3d 72, 193 Cal. Rptr. 225 (1983).

in the status of employer and employee certain reciprocal rights and duties—such as fair procedure by the employer in termination and loyalty by the employee during the course of employment.

The law of voluntary associations, however, affects relatively few professionals, whereas much of the populace would be affected by changes in the law governing employee termination. This doubtless explains much of the inertia in the development of fair procedure as a right in employment law; for certainly there is a sense evinced by the courts that changes in employment law, if they should come, are best taken in small steps to minimize unfair or unexpected burdens on employers.

Another explanation for a slower development of standards of fair procedure in employment law is that judges, themselves professionals, tend to relate to the interests of employers and professional people more than they do to the concerns of discharged employees. Whether or not this explanation is true, the law's long history of benign indifference to unjust discharge contrasts sharply with the sympathetic attention of judges to the claims of expelled and excluded members of professional associations.

IV

Remedies

11

Money Damages and Reinstatement

Introduction to Remedies

Few cases have analyzed in any depth the principles used to determine what remedy is appropriate for wrongful discharge. Many employment cases reach the reviewing court on the basic question of whether the discharged employee has made his case against the former employer. Relatively few cases, on the other hand, develop the subject of remedies. Although our focus here is on cases dealing with discharge from employment, the lawyer seriously researching this topic will find helpful analogies in cases dealing with civil rights, franchise termination, and business interruption occasioned by antitrust action, intentional tort, or casualties.

Our discussion of remedies is generally divided between remedies at law and remedies in equity, and concludes with a brief discussion of whether confidential evaluations are subject to disclosure in litigation. In the framework of an employment controversy, the difference between law and equity is usually expressed in whether the employee is entitled to court-awarded money damages or court-ordered reinstatement. An orthodox prerequisite for equitable relief, or reinstatement, is that relief at law, i.e., money damages, must be inadequate to compensate for the actual or threatened injury. Accordingly, we shall first address the system of money damages that has developed in employment controversies.

Money Damages

Court-awarded damages measured by (1) the plaintiff's reasonable expectations, (2) the plaintiff's reliance upon the promises or

397

conduct of the defendant, or (3) the benefits conferred by the plaintiff upon the defendant. The first measure, the plaintiff's reasonable expectations, is referred to in the cases and texts as a measure that attempts to quantify the benefit of the bargain that the plaintiff was unfairly denied by the defendant. For example, a wrongfully discharged employee who had been promised permanent employment would roughly measure the benefits of the unfulfilled promise by the stream of income that he would have received had he not been fired, less what he expected to receive in other employment.[1]

The second measure, reliance, is generally intended to put the plaintiff in the same place he would have been in had he never encountered the defendant.[2] An example is the damage suffered by an employee who, in reliance upon a promise of employment, moves himself and his family across the country and upon presenting himself for work is told the job has been filled. If the promised employment was for no certain term, a measure of damages based upon the expected duration of employment would be highly speculative. Reliance damages at least permit the recovery of travel expenses and the value of lost opportunities.

In a very few cases, the employee's best measure of damages for wrongful discharge is the third measure, i.e., the benefit the employee conferred upon the employer by agreeing to be employed. If the promise of a job is an integral part of a sale of a business, patent, plan, copyright, or special advantage to the employer, it may be easier and more certain, and amount to a more generous measure of damages, for the employee to measure damages by the value to the employer of what was given up in return for the promise of the job.

If the facts in a particular case permit more than one measure of damages, the plaintiff may select the one that will yield the largest recovery or which is easiest to prove. Indeed, the plaintiff can attempt to prove more than one measure of damages so long as there is no danger of recovering more than once for the same injury. In many employment situations, the reliance measure may be congruent with the expectation or benefit measure. For example, if in reliance upon a promise of permanent employment an employee forgoes an attractive alternative position, damages for wrongful discharge from the permanent employment position measured by either expectation or reliance will be nearly the same.

In employment cases, the measure of money damages is a func-

---

[1]This same subject is described in textbooks as a problem of direct and consequential damages and lost profits. *Hadley v. Baxendale*, 9 Ex. 341, 156 Eng. Rep. 145 (1854), laid down what is referred to as the "rule of *Hadley v. Baxendale*" that in a contract case the defendant is liable only for the risks he explicitly or tacitly agreed to assume. This standard has generally been rejected in favor of a measure of damages governed by what the defendant had "reason to know" at the time of the agreement. See Dunn, RECOVERY OF DAMAGES FOR LOST PROFITS, ch. 2 (2d ed. 1981). See Appendix C.

[2]*Pepsi-Cola Gen. Bottlers, Inc. v. Woods*, 440 N.E.2d 696 (Ind. Ct. App. 1982) (only out-of-pocket damages permitted for refusal to honor promise of at-will employment); *Langenderfer v. Midrex Corp.*, 660 F.2d 523 (4th Cir. 1981) (reliance warranting equitable estoppel against employer entitles employee to promised bonus and cost of living increases).

tion of the theory of liability, i.e., whether contract, tort, status, or statutory. Where there is an express or implied promise of job security, the employee's measure of damages will be enhanced by arguing a contract theory in addition to any other theory of liability permitted by the facts. Under contract theory the plaintiff can obtain the benefit of the bargain or expectation damages. Tort theory ordinarily permits only actual or reliance damages. However, tort theories and tort measures of actual damages are ordinarily more tolerant of the problem of uncertainty in ascertaining the amount of damages so long as the fact of damages is certain.

The cases described in this section are premised entirely upon tort and contract theories. Research has not disclosed a money damage case where liability was founded upon a status theory. When such a case arises, presumably the court will borrow a measure by analogy from the tort and contract cases. Likewise, where liability stems from a statutory duty, if the statute itself does not describe the measure, the court will examine the alternatives suggested by the common law.

Elements of Money Damages

This section is organized according to the particular losses for which the employee will seek money damages. Agreed compensation, whether salary, wages, or commissions, is the usual ingredient. Other common injuries for which employees seek recompense are damage to reputation; mental anguish; expenses incident to relocation; and lost pension, insurance, stock options, and other fringe benefits. In particularly egregious circumstances, punitive damages may also be available.

Agreed Compensation Earned at the Time of Discharge

Even where a discharge is proper, the employer has no right to refuse to pay the employee for services rendered up to the time of discharge.[3] Any other result would amount to a forfeiture. Even if the employee's services resulted in damages to the employer, the employer is not permitted the self-help remedy of withholding the employee's compensation. Employees paid in whole or in part by commission are entitled to commissions earned before termination or that would have been paid if they had not been fired.[4] Many jurisdictions bar that course of action by statute and sometimes pro-

---

[3]*NHA, Inc. v. Jones*, 500 S.W.2d 940 (Tex. Civ. App. 1973); *Hildebrand v. American Fine Art Co.*, 109 Wis.171, 85 N.W. 268 (1901).

[4]*Perry v. Al George, Inc.*, 428 So.2d 1309 (La. Ct. App. 1983) (recovery allowed on *quantum meruit* theory even though commission not immediately payable and salesman, if still employed, would be required to provide further services); *Hudman v. Century 21 Cent., Realtors*, 411 So.2d 569 (La. Ct. App. 1982) (commissions recoverable on sales procured but unclosed at time of discharge); *Gelfand v. Horizon Corp.*, 675 F.2d 1108 (10th Cir. 1982) (agreed upon commission recoverable even though executive did not make sale); *Vector Eng'g and Mfg. Corp.*

vide for recovery against the employer of multiples of the amount of the salary wrongfully withheld as well as attorney's fees. If the jurisdiction provides such a statutory remedy, the employee has the alternative of pursuing his claim in a state administrative forum rather than in court. The alternative in large municipalities will often prove cheaper and faster and perhaps provide a more sympathetic forum for the employee than a lawsuit would. State labor boards may issue orders for payment, interest, and sometimes attorney's fees, which may be enforced through a court action if necessary.[5]

One substantial form of compensation that may be forfeited upon discharge, however, is the pension. Few cases address this subject. Where compensation is in the form of commissions, nice questions of fact are sometimes raised as to whether at the time of termination the commission claimed had actually been earned even if the paper work was not complete.[6]

Agreed Compensation Where Discharge Is Conditioned Upon Notice

If an employment contract provides that the employer must give notice of termination, either of two situations may arise. In the first, the employer gives the correct notice and either permits the employee to remain at least through the notice period or pays the stipulated compensation through the notice period after removing the employee from the work place. Where the employee is permitted to remain on the job, his potential for finding substitute employment is usually somewhat enhanced. When he is terminated immediately, he loses one of the benefits of the notice period even though he receives the same compensation.

In the second situation, where the contract notice is not given or is defective—for example, less notice than is required by the contract is given—the question arises whether and to what extent the defective notice influences the measure of damages. When the theory of damages is premised only upon contract liability, the courts generally measure damages for wrongful discharge by the period of the notice that should have been given less mitigation (see below, p. 407) and any other appropriate setoffs or deductions.[7] This result is ra-

---

v. Pequet, 431 N.E.2d 503 (Ind. Ct. App. 1982); *Barrows v. Maco, Inc.*, 94 Ill. App.3d 959, 419 N.E.2d 634 (1981); *Basic Four Corp. v. Parker*, 158 Ga. App. 117, 279 S.E.2d 241 (1981) (recovery of commission defeated by written waiver given by employee in course of resignation). *Contra: Mackie v. LaSalle Indus., Inc.*, 92 A.D.2d 821, 460 N.Y.S.2d 313 (1983); *Diaz v. Indian Head, Inc.*, 686 F.2d 556 (9th Cir. 1982) (executive who did not solicit sales and whose job did not require persuasion could not be procuring cause of sales); *Reyna v. Gonzalez*, 630 S.W.2d 439 (Tex. Civ. App. 1982).

[5] See, e.g., Illinois Wage Payment And Collection Act, ILL. REV. STAT. ch. 48, §39m-1 *et seq.* (1983).

[6] *Technical Representatives, Inc. v. Richardson-Merrell, Inc.*, 107 Ill. App.3d 830, 438 N.E.2d 599 (1982) (under procuring cause rule, employee may be entitled to sales made after termination of employment).

[7] *Hold v. Seversky Electron Adam Corp.*, 452 F.2d 31 (2d Cir. 1971); *Raynor v. Burroughs Corp.*, 294 F. Supp. 238 (E.D. Va. 1968); *Protective Workers, Local 2 v. Ford Motor Co.*, 223 F.2d 49 (7th Cir. 1955).

tionalized on the ground that the employee could not reasonably have expected more compensation at the time of severance than for the period of the notice. Moreover, the courts observe that the employee's contract measure of damages should not be enhanced simply because the employer breached the agreement.

There are two general exceptions to the rule that measures damages by the period of the notice that should have been given. The first is that if the employee suffers damages as a consequence of the employer's failure to give proper notice, then those damages, in addition to the agreed compensation for the notice period, will be part of the measure of damages. The second exception comes into play where the contract of employment gives the noticed party the right during the stipulated notice period to perform certain acts or bring into existence certain conditions which will nullify or negate the employer's right to terminate.[8]

Agreed Compensation for a Specified Duration of Employment

In the case of a fixed term contract where the employee is wrongfully terminated after payment up to the time of termination, the measure of damages is simply the salary that would have been paid for the balance of the term less mitigation and other proper deductions.[9] If by the time of the trial the contract term that measures damages has not yet expired, estimated future salary, wages, or commissions must be discounted to present value.[10] In addition, the employer is entitled to offer evidence concerning the probability that the employee will obtain future employment that would then serve as a deduction under a mitigation theory. The uncertainty of life and the possibility that the employee may become physically or mentally handicapped before the expiration of the term of employment may justify further deduction on the theory that the employee might never have been able to complete the fixed term of the employment and thus should not recover damages measured by the full term.[11] But a person violating his contract ought not to be permitted to escape liability entirely for the reason that the amount of damages that he has caused is uncertain. Losses sustained and gains prevented are proper elements of damages even if they are prospective and to some extent uncertain and problematical.[12]

---

[8]See Annot. 99 A.L.R.2d 272 (1965).

[9]*Seher v. Woodlawn School Dist.*, 79 N.D. 818, 59 N.W.2d 805 (1953); *Tollesson v. Green Bay Packers, Inc.*, 256 Wis. 318, 41 N.W.2d 201 (1950); *District of Columbia v. Jones*, 442 A.2d 512 (D.C. 1982); *Vieira v. Roberts' Hawaii Tours, Inc.*, 2 Hawaii App.23, 630 P.2d 120 (1981); *Chapin v. Klein*, 128 Ariz. 94, 623 P.2d 1250 (1981); *Fogelman v. Peruvian Assoc.*, 127 Ariz. 504, 622 P.2d 63 (Ct. App. 1980).

[10]*Sheshunoff & Co. v. Scholl*, 564 S.W.2d 697 (Tex. 1978).

[11]*Fulton v. Tennessee Walking Horse Breeders*, 63 Tenn. App. 569, 476 S.W.2d 644 (1971).

[12]*Chapin v. Klein*, 128 Ariz. 94, 623 P.2d 1250 (1981); *Goodwyn v. Sencore, Inc.*, 389 F. Supp. 824 (D.S.D. 1975); *Jeffers v. Stanley*, 486 S.W.2d 737 (Tenn. 1972); *Krause v. Bell Potato Chip Co.*, 149 Ore. 388, 39 P.2d 363 (1935); *Olson v. Naymark*, 177 Minn. 383, 225 N.W. 275 (1929); *Smith v. Pallay*,130 Ore. 282, 279 P. 279 (1929); *Helfferich v. Sherman*, 28 S.D. 627, 134 N.W. 815 (1912).

*Agreed Compensation After Discharge From Lifetime
Employment or Employment Conditioned Upon Discharge
Only for Good Cause*

When an employment contract provides for dismissal only for good cause or describes employment or tenure as "permanent" or "for life" and those terms are construed to mean literally for life or as long as the employee is able to perform the services required, the problem is very much like measuring damages in the fixed term contract that extends beyond the date of the trial. It is simply a matter of the uncertainty introduced when damages are prospective. The difficulty of estimating such damages, however, is no greater than exists in many other cases involving reputation in defamation cases or ongoing personal injuries in product liability, automobile accident, or medical malpractice cases, where a present value must be assigned to estimated future damages that result from a known injury.[13] One factor that the courts usually address is the employee's actuarially estimated life expectancy.[14] Another approach is arbitrarily to determine a reasonable employment expectancy subsequent to the date of the trial in the absence of wrongful termination.[15] This approach recognizes that employment can end by an event less drastic than death. For example, the employer might become bankrupt or the employee might give good cause for discharge at some point in the future.

In measuring what an employee could have earned had there been no wrongful discharge, it seems fair to distinguish probable working life expectancy from life expectancy. However, attempting to factor in a possible employer bankruptcy or future employee misconduct moves the question into the realm of pure speculation. It also permits the wrongdoer an unfair advantage just because of the breach. If the same logic were followed in awarding damages for the repair of a fender crumpled in an intersection collision, the plaintiff would be denied full recovery for the fender because it might have been damaged in some other way sooner or later. Once it is known that the employer caused damage reasonably contemplated by the contract, i.e., denial of the job security that was promised, uncertainties in the estimation of prospective damages should be resolved against the party who committed the breach and not against the innocent employee.

*Agreed Compensation and Reliance Damage in the Absence
of a Fixed or Determinable Term of Employment*

If employment security is not premised upon a fixed term or lifetime duration of employment or an agreed condition for discharge

---

[13]*Molitor v. Chicago Title & Trust Co.*, 325 Ill. App. 124, 59 N.E.2d 695 (1945).
[14]*Nichols v. National Tube Co.*, 122 F. Supp. 726 (N.D. Ohio 1954); *Royster Guano Co. v. Hall*, 68 F.2d 533 (4th Cir. 1934).
[15]*Rabago-Alvarez v. Dart Indus., Inc.*, 55 Cal. App.3d 91, 127 Cal. Rptr. 222 (1976).

such as just cause, or some demonstrable employment policy fostering job security expectations, the expectation approach to measuring money damages has a serious shortcoming, namely, it is difficult for the employee to claim that he reasonably expected to be employed for a given period of time. Nevertheless, disappointed employees who were essentially "at will" have sometimes recovered expectation damages. Typically this has occurred where the employee gave up one good job to take another job, sometimes moving himself and his family a great distance to accept the new position.[16] Where an employer refuses to honor a promise of employment with no fixed or reasonably determinable duration, however, reliance damages are more commonly awarded. Such damages include traveling expenses, the cost of seeking other employment, special expenses such as the purchase of an automobile to qualify for the employment, or the value of a business or profession that was given up in reliance on the promised employment.[17]

If there is no promise of a fixed or determinable period of employment, a tort theory of damages may have more potential for recovery by the employee. The jury can first focus upon the period that has elapsed between the date of discharge and the date of the trial. If the employee is still healthy and the employer is still in business, the assumption can be indulged that, but for the tortious wrongful discharge, the employee would still be employed. Prospective damages subsequent to the date of the trial may be substantially more difficult to prove.[18] Thus, the length of time it takes a case on the court's docket to be called for trial may be significant to fixing the amount of damages.

Reputation and Mental Anguish

The mental suffering that is ordinarily a companion to discharge from employment, whether the discharge is wrongful or not, is generally not compensable in tort or contract actions. The justification for denying damages on a contract theory is simply that damages

---

[16]*Hackett v. Food Maker, Inc.*, 69 Mich. App. 591, 245 N.W.2d 140 (1976); *Magnolia Miss Dress Co. v. Zorn*, 204 Miss. 1, 36 So.2d 795 (1948).

[17]*Lorson v. Falcon Coach, Inc.*, 214 Kan. 670, 522 P.2d 449 (1974); *Smith v. Pollack Co.*, 9 La. App. 432, 121 So. 240 (1928); *McLean v. News Publishers Co.*, 21 N.D. 89, 129 N.W. 93 (1910).

[18]*Petermann v. Teamsters*, 214 Cal. App.2d 155, 129 Cal. Rptr. 399 (1963) (*Petermann II*). The court in an earlier case of the same name held that the plaintiff's discharge for refusing to commit perjury stated a cause of action; $32,000 was awarded as a loss of earnings up to the time of trial, and $18,000 was awarded as prospective earnings after the trial. The court observed that, taking plaintiff's age into consideration, $18,000 was less than his predictable earnings to the age of retirement. But see *McGrath v. Zenith Radio Corp.*, 651 F.2d 458 (7th Cir. 1981), where the court reduced a $1 million compensatory damage award premised largely upon lost earnings subsequent to trial to $300,000, which was the amount of lost earnings that were proved for the period between discharge and the time of trial, five years. The court believed that plaintiff had not adequately proved the prospect of loss of earnings, and held that specific proof of the probability of continued life, employability, and favorable professional experience was required. However, the lost earnings from discharge to the trial date did include substantial sums based upon promotion and pay increases received by similarly situated employees.

were not reasonably contemplated as a risk the employer was undertaking at the time the employment contract was entered into by both parties. The contingency is sometimes described as "too remote" for damage measurement.[19] Generally, to recover for mental suffering in tort, either the defendant must have intended to cause the suffering, or it must be a consequence of a physical impact. Neither of these two circumstances is likely to occur in the employment setting, though there are some authorities on the subject.[20]

In a time when the livelihood of most people is in the hands of others, one's employment reputation is a singularly valuable asset. A person who leaves his employment usually must have an explanation if he wishes to prevent the inference that he was discharged or that his leaving was due to his attitude, misconduct, or inability to perform. If an employee was in fact discharged, the problem of detriment to his reputation arises whether the discharge was proper or wrongful. Where the discharge was wrongful, a demonstrable injury to his reputation is a proper element for measuring damages where the economic impact can be quantified with concrete evidence.[21] The impact of discharge upon the opportunity to obtain substitute employment has been the subject of scholarly study.[22]

Cost of Locating Substitute Employment

The employee's expenses in attempting to locate substitute employment may be included as additional elements of damages. The cases that describe mitigation often state that the cost of mitigating or attempting to mitigate may be included as damages.[23]

Pensions, Insurance, Fringe Benefits, Taxes, and Inflation

In addition to whatever compensation is included, the measure of damages in both tort and contract includes the value of unused

[19]*Gunsolley v. Bushby*, 19 Ore. App. 884, 529 P.2d 950 (1974); *Flagler Museum v. Lee*, 268 So.2d 434 (Fla. Dist. Ct. App. 1972).

[20]*Sea-Land Serv., Inc. v. O'Neal*, 224 Va. 343, 297 S.E.2d 647 (1982); *Cancellier v. Federated Dep't Stores*, 672 F.2d 1312 (9th Cir. 1982).

[21]*Skagway City School Bd. v. Davis*, 543 P.2d 218 (Alaska 1975); *Sea-Land Serv., Inc. v. O'Neal*, 224 Va. 224 Va. 343, 297 S.E.2d 647 (1982); *Gram v. Liberty Mut. Ins. Co.*, 429 N.E.2d 21 (Mass. 1981); *Greater Fort Worth and Tarrant County Community Action Agency v. Mims*, 627 S.W.2d 149 (Tex. 1982); *Santex, Inc. v. Cunningham*, 618 S.W.2d 557 (Tex. Civ. App. 1981); *Budge v. Post*, 643 F.2d 372 (5th Cir. 1981) (future earnings must be discounted to present value); *Traighten v. Miller Bros. Indus., Inc.*, 80 A.D.2d 802, 437 N.Y.S.2d 101 (1981) (salary plus commissions proved reasonable probabilities); *O'Leary v. Sterling Extruder Corp.*, 533 F. Supp. 1205 (E.D. Wis. 1982).

[22]See, e.g., Parnes and King, *Middle-Aged Job-Losers*, prepared under a contract with the Employment and Training Administration, U.S. Department of Labor, by the Center for Human Resource Research, College of Administrative Science, Ohio State University; Block and Stieber, *Discharged Workers and the Labor Market: An Analysis of Employer Attitudes and Experience and Arbitration Decisions*, prepared under a contract with the Employment and Training Administration, U.S. Department of Labor, by the School of Labor and Industrial Relations, Michigan State University.

[23]*Vallejo v. Jamestown College*, 244 N.W.2d 753 (N.D. 1976); *Beggs v. Dougherty Overseas, Inc.*, 287 F.2d 80 (2d Cir. 1961). This case also held that the employees were entitled to recover the value of the loss of tax benefits they would have had if they still had been employed.

sick leave,[24] vacation pay,[25] and other fringe benefits.[26] Pension rights lost as a consequence of the discharge[27] and promised bonuses are part of damages.[28] This result is reasonable since pensions are fairly viewed a form of deferred compensation. For example, the replacement costs of medical and life insurance that the employee enjoyed as a member of a group plan when employed is a fair element of damages. The measure is the cost of comparable insurance to the employee, not what the employer was required to pay for such insurance when the plaintiff was a member of a group policy.[29] Moreover, in the event the employee in the period between discharge and the time of trial could have availed himself of medical insurance benefits or his beneficiaries could have collected life insurance benefits, the measure of damages may fairly include such benefits.[30] If the discharge foreclosed the employee from qualifying for a promised stock option that would have accrued before the time of trial, that may also be an element of damages under tort or contract theories.[31] If the stock option would accrue or mature subsequent to the date of trial, the uncertainty of qualification is at least no worse than the problem common to awarding compensation or other prospective damage subsequent to the trial.

At least under a contract theory, the employee is not entitled to recover estimated profits he would have earned had he invested his salary. This is too speculative and not contemplated as damages by the employer at the time of the commencement of the employment contract.[32]

Recovery of damages from an employer may have more adverse tax consequences than the receipt of a stream of payments as wages or salary. However, it has been held that excess tax liability "is not a loss within the meaning of the term as used in the law of damages."[33] This conclusion is without merit. Increased tax liability is a factor that can and should be considered.[34] The inflationary impact must also be taken into account when calculating the present cash value of lost future income. This is a technical subject largely within the expertise of economists.[35]

---

[24]*Logue v. City of Carthage*, 612 S.W.2d 148 (Mo. Ct. App. 1981).
[25]*State ex rel. Roberts v. Public Fin. Co.*, 59 Ore. App. 234, 651 P.2d 728 (1982); *Hamby Co. v. Palmer*, 631 S.W.2d 589 (Tex. Civ. App. 1982); *Suastez v. Plastic Dress-Up Co.*, 31 Cal. 3d 744, 183 Cal. Rptr. 846, 647 P.2d 122 (1982).
[26]*Schwarze v. Solo Cup Co.*, 112 Ill. App.3d 632, 445 N.E.2d 872 (1983).
[27]*Sulyok v. Penzintezeti Cozpont Budapest*, 304 N.Y. 704, 107 N.E.2d 604 (1952).
[28]*Bushman v. Pure Plant Food Int'l Ltd.*, 330 N.W.2d 762 (S.D. 1983).
[29]*Wise v. Southern Pac. Co.*,1 Cal. 3d 600, 463 P.2d 426, 83 Cal. Rptr. 202 (1970).
[30]*McAleer v. McNally Pittsburgh Mfg. Corp.*, 239 F.2d 273 (3d Cir. 1964).
[31]*Ebling v. Masco Corp.*, 79 Mich. App. 531, 261 N.W.2d 74 (1978).
[32]*Bartinikas v. Clarklift of Chicago N., Inc.*, 508 F. Supp. 959 (N.D. Ill. 1981).
[33]*McLaughlin v. Union-Leader Corp.*, 100 N.H. 367, 372, 127 A.2d 269, 273 (1956).
[34]*Oltersdorf v. Chesapeake & Ohio R.R.*, 83 Ill. App. 3d 457, 404 N.E.2d 320 (1980) (error to refuse evidence of impact of taxation on plaintiff's lost future earnings and in refusing to instruct jury award of damages not subject to taxation).
[35]Lebrenz, *The Inflationary Impact Upon the Economic Loss From Impaired Earning Capacity*, 69 ILL. BAR. J. 372 (1981). See Appendix C.

Punitive Damages

Punitive damages are a sum of money in excess of whatever the court awards to a plaintiff to compensate for his injury, however the compensation is measured. Punitive damages are supposed to serve as a warning and an example to deter others from similar misconduct. The measurement is a jury question if the parties have submitted the case to a jury.

Punitive damages are ordinarily not awarded for a breach of contract unless the defendant's conduct also amounts to an independent tort that justifies punitive damages.[36] *Kelsay v. Motorola, Inc.*[37] described a standard for punitive damages that has been repeated in almost the same words in many other jurisdictions: "It has long been established * * * that punitive damages may be awarded when torts are committed with fraud, actual malice, deliberate violence or oppression or when the defendant acts willfully or with gross negligence as to indicate wanton disregard of the rights of others."[38] In *Kelsay*, the plaintiff's action for wrongful discharge was permitted where the plaintiff alleged that the discharge was in retaliation for filing a workers' compensation claim. The court observed that the retaliatory discharge "mocks the public policy of this state."[39] The largest reported punitive damage award in an employment case was $1 million, awarded in addition to $1 million awarded for actual damages (the latter reduced on appeal to $300,000), in *McGrath v. Zenith Radio Corp.*,[40] in which a fraud theory warranted punitive damages. It was alleged that the employer had promised to make the employee president of a subsidiary corporation to induce him to give up valuable stock options knowing that it expected to discharge him within 100 days.

Liquidated Damages

Occasionally, when an employee is in the enviable position of being able to negotiate a written contract with a prospective employer, he will include a provision that stipulates the amount of money he is to recover in the event he is discharged with or without cause prior to the expiration of the term of the agreement. Such a provision is known in the law of contracts as a "liquidated damage

---

[36]*Kamiar Corp. v. Haley*, 224 Va. 699, 299 S.E.2d 514 (1983) (punitive damages not permitted for discharge "actuated by malicious motives" where only theory of liability is contract).
[37]74 Ill.2d 172, 384 N.E.2d 353 (1978).
[38]*Id.* at 186, 384 N.E.2d at 359.
[39]*Id.* at 187, 384 N.E.2d at 359. See also *Scheps v. Giles*, 222 S.W. 348 (Tex. Civ. App. 1920); *Peterson v. Culver Educ. Found.*, 402 N.E.2d 448 (1980); *Cox v. Guy F. Atkinson Co.*, 468 F. Supp. 677 (N.D. Ind. 1979); *Fincke v. Phoenix Mut. Life Ins. Co.*, 448 F. Supp. 187 (W.D. Pa. 1978); *Sinclair Ref. Co. v. McCullom*, 107 Ind. App. 356, 24 N.E.2d 784 (1940).
[40]651 F.2d 458 (7th Cir. 1981). See also *Cancellier v. Federated Dep't Stores*, 672 F.2d 1312 (9th Cir. 1982) (long-service employee arbitrarily terminated contrary to personnel policy); *Davis v. Tyee Indus., Inc.*, 58 Ore. App. 292, 648 P.2d 388 (1982) (award of punitive damages for withholding commissions due); *Schwarze v. Solo Cup Co.*, 112 Ill. App.3d 632, 445 N.E.2d 872 (1983); *Carnation Co. v. Borner*, 610 S.W.2d 450 (Tex. 1980).

provision." In a real sense, notice provisions serve substantially the same purpose, at least where the discharge is not for good cause. Liquidated damage provisions in contracts are governed by the same standards that apply to contracts generally; if negotiated in good faith and not oppressive, they will be enforced.[41]

Mitigation of Damages

Generally, the employee's damages must be diminished by the amount of compensation received from employment of a like nature subsequent to wrongful discharge. Damages are to be reduced not only by what was actually received, but also by what would have been received from like employment that was available and would have been obtained had the employee exercised reasonable diligence to seek and obtain employment.[42] Mitigation of damages through the employee's efforts is often spoken of as a "duty." However, the *Restatement of Contracts* points out that legally there is no such duty but rather that the plaintiff simply cannot recover avoidable damages.[43]

Consistent with the point of view of the *Restatement of Contracts*, mitigation is an affirmative defense to be asserted by the employer who is sued for wrongful discharge. It is the burden of the employer to show that the employee received compensation or by the exercise of reasonable diligence would have received compensation and thus have reduced the amount of damages.[44] There are cases holding that employees who are fired arbitrarily or maliciously have no duty to

---

[41]*Bramhall v. ICN Medical Laboratories, Inc.*, 284 Ore. 279, 586 P.2d 113 (1978); *Franklin v. Texas Int'l Petroleum Corp.*, 324 F. Supp. 808 (W.D. La. 1971).

[42]*Southern Keswick, Inc. v. Whetherholt*, 293 So.2d 109 (Fla. Dist. Ct. App. 1974); *Patrick v. McAleenan Boiler Co.*, 136 Ill. App. 536 (1907); *Miller v. Community Discount Centers, Inc.*, 83 Ill. App.2d 439, 228 N.E.2d 113 (1967); *Seco Chems., Inc. v. Stewart*, 169 Ind. App. 624, 349 N.E.2d 733 (1976); *Indiana State Symphony Soc'y v. Ziedonis*, 171 Ind. App. 292, 359 N.E.2d 253 (1976); *Rimedio v. Revlon, Inc.*, 528 F. Supp. 1380 (S.D. Ohio 1982).

[43]RESTATEMENT OF CONTRACTS §336 (1932) expresses the requirements that a plaintiff act reasonably to mitigate damages as follows:
"Section 336. Avoidable Harm; Losses Incurred In Efforts To Avoid Harm. (1) Damages are not recoverable for harm that plaintiff should have foreseen and could have avoided by reasonable effort without undue risk, expense or humiliation. (2) Damages are recoverable for special losses incurred in a reasonable effort, whether successful or not, to avoid harm that the defendant had reason to foresee as a probable result of his breach when the contract was made."
Comment d to section 336 states:
"d. It is not infrequently said that it is the 'duty' of the injured party to mitigate damages so far as that can be done by reasonable effort on his part. Since his legal position is in no way affected by his failure to make this effort, however, it is not desirable to say that he is under a 'duty.' His remedy will be exactly the same, whether he makes the effort and avoids harm or not. But if he fails to make the reasonable effort with the result that his harm is greater than it would otherwise have been, he cannot get judgment for the amount of this avoidable and unnecessary increase. The law does not penalize his inaction; it merely does nothing to compensate him for the harm that a reasonable man in his place would have avoided."

[44]*Fulton v. Tennessee Walking Horse Breeders*, 63 Tenn. App. 569, 476 S.W.2d 644 (1971); *Savitz v. Gallaccio*, 179 Pa. Super. 589, 118 A.2d 282 (1955); *Grauer v. Valve and Primer Corp.*, 47 Ill. App.3d 152, 361 N.E.2d 863 (1977); *Hudson v. Yeoman of Am.*, 176 Ill. App. 445 (1912); *Currieri v. City of Roseville*, 50 Cal. App.3d 499, 123 Cal. Rptr. 314 (1975); *Rosenberger v. Pacific Coast R.R.*, 111 Cal. 313, 43 P. 963 (1896). But cf. *Goodwyn v. Sencore, Inc.*, 389 F. Supp. 824 (D.S.D. 1975); and *Bornstein v. Neuman*, 92 A.D.2d 578, 459 N.Y.S.2d 462 (1983).

mitigate,[45] that part-time workers are not subject to the mitigation rule,[46] and that public employees are not obliged to mitigate.[47] There is no duty to mitigate liquidated damages.[48] There are numerous authorities that touch on the subject of mitigation, but only a few need be outlined here to describe the practical importance of the doctrine.[49]

The employee seeking damages for wrongful discharge must obtain work, if it is available, similar to the work he had before discharge. In some cases, the definition of similar work is enlarged if the employee has several skills or trades. For example, where the discharged employee had been a police officer and also had extensive experience and skill in roof repair, he had a duty to find work in roof repair or in police work if that were available.[50] Even where similar work is available, the employee need not leave his family to qualify for the work.[51] Likewise, the employee need not accept work at a substantial distance from his home or look beyond the immediate community, neighborhood, or locality for work.[52]

The employer is not entitled to create a "catch 22" situation for the employee by offering the same or similar work after a wrongful discharge on the condition that the employee give up his claim.[53] Employers have likewise been unsuccessful in attempting to create setoffs by offering menial employment[54] or the old job but at a reduced salary.[55] Even where the employer offers the same or similar work at the same salary, the employee is not required to take it if reassociation with the employer would be offensive or unpleasant to either of them.[56]

Setoff of the estimated value of the employee's work done on his own home after a wrongful discharge has not been required.[57] Money from collateral sources such as unemployment and social security[58] or compensation from a part-time or full-time job held concurrently

---

[45]*Steranko v. Inforex, Inc.*, 5 Mass. App. 253, 362 N.E.2d 222 (1977); *Mason County Bd. of Educ. v. State Superintendent of Schools*, 295 S.E.2d 719 (W. Va. 1982).

[46]*People ex rel. Burne v. Johnson*, 32 Ill.2d 322, 205 N.E.2d 470 (1965).

[47]*Gunsolley v. Bushby*, 19 Ore. App. 884, 529 P.2d 950 (1974).

[48]*Wassenaar v. Panos*, 111 Wis.2d 518, 331 N.W.2d 357 (1983); *Salvatori Corp. v. Rubin*, 159 Ga. App. 369, 283 S.E.2d 326 (1981); *Fletcher v. Amax, Inc.*, 160 Ga. App. 692, 288 S.E.2d 49 (1981) (severance pay policy).

[49]See generally Annot., 44 A.L.R.3d 629 (1972), for an exhaustive treatment of mitigation.

[50]*State ex rel. Schilling & Klinger v. Baird*, 65 Wis.2d 394, 222 N.W.2d 666 (1974).

[51]*State ex rel. Martin v. City of Columbus*, 58 Ohio St.2d 261, 389 N.E.2d 1123 (1979).

[52]*Smith v. Concordia Parish School Bd.*, 387 F. Supp. 887 (W.D. La. 1975); *Punkar v. King Plastics Corp.*, 290 So.2d 505 (Fla. Dist. Ct. App. 1974).

[53]*Billetter v. Possell*, 94 Cal. App.2d 858, 211 P.2d 621 (1949); *Schwarze v. Solo Cup Co.*, 112 Ill. App.3d 632, 445 N.E.2d 872 (1983).

[54]*Williams v. Robinson*, 158 Ark. 327, 250 S.W. 14 (1923).

[55]*Farmers' Coop. Ass'n v. Shaw*, 171 Okla. 358, 42 P.2d 887 (1935).

[56]*Smith v. Beloit Corp.*, 40 Wis.2d 550, 162 N.W.2d 585 (1968); *Schisler v. Perfection Minker Co.*, 193 Minn. 160, 258 N.W. 17 (1934).

[57]*Mixson v. Rossiter*, 223 S.C. 47, 74 S.E.2d 46 (1953).

[58]*Rabago-Alvarez v. Dart Indus., Inc.*, 55 Cal. App.3d 91, 127 Cal. Rptr. 222 (1976); *Traighten v. Miller Bros. Indus., Inc.*, 80 A.D.2d 802, 437 N.Y.S.2d 101 (1981) (not deducted as mitigation unless improperly received); *Schwarze v. Solo Cup Co.*, 112 Ill. App.3d 632, 445 N.E.2d 872 (1983).

with the former employment[59] may not be applied in mitigation of damages. However, it has been held that if the former employee leases a farm, he must set off as reasonable mitigation the estimated return from leasing and working the farm that represents reasonable wages for such service.[60] If the employee sets up his own corporation and pays himself a salary, the salary is a setoff for purposes of mitigation even though the employee invested all of his own capital into the new company and owns all the stock.[61]

Nullification of Covenant Not To Compete

A wrongful discharge can serve as a shield for an employee as well as a sword. If there was between employer and employee a covenant not to compete which would otherwise be enforceable by the employer to prevent the employee from taking advantage of confidential business information, the employer will be unable to enforce that covenant after wrongfully discharging the employee. This is in effect, a form of relief for the employee.

The governing principle of contract law is that any material failure of performance by one party that is not justified by the conduct of the other discharges the latter's duty to perform under the contract. Accordingly, if an employer wrongfully discharges the employee prior to expiration of the contract, the employee is relieved from honoring a covenant not to compete. Any other outcome would strip the employee of his ability to earn a livelihood.[62]

Employer's Rights to Defense and Indemnity Under Insurance Policies

The employer must not overlook the possibility that employee claims of wrongful discharge or alternative claims such as defamation or negligent performance of the employment contract are covered by the employer's general liability or workers' compensation policies. Determining whether they are requires a close examination of the employee's claim, the language of the policy, and the judicial au-

---

[59]*Albert Johann & Sons v. Echols*, 143 Ind. App. 122, 238 N.E.2d 685 (1968).
[60]*Lee v. Hampton*, 79 Miss. 321, 30 S. 721 (1901); *Mason County Bd. of Educ. v. State Superintendent of Schools*, 295 S.E.2d 719 (W. Va. 1982); *In re KDI Corp.*, 21 Bankr. 652 (S.D. Ohio 1982).
[61]*Stevenson v. ITT Harper, Inc.*, 51 Ill. App.3d 568, 366 N.E.2d 561 (1977).
[62]*Ritz v. Music, Inc.*, 189 Pa. Super. 106, 150 A.2d 160 (1959); *Aristocrat Window Co. v. Randall*, 56 Ill. App.2d 413, 206 N.E.2d 545 (1965); *Economy Grocery Stores Corp. v. McMenamy*, 290 Mass. 549, 195 N.E. 747 (1935); *Cornell v. T.V. Dev. Corp.*, 17 N.Y.2d 69, 215 N.E.2d 349, 268 N.Y.S.2d 29 (1966); *Millet v. Slocum*, 4 A.D.2d 528, 167 N.Y.S.2d 136 (1957), *aff'd*, 5 N.Y.2d 734, 152 N.E.2d 672, 177 N.Y.S.2d 716 (1958); *Post v. Merrill, Lynch, Pierce, Fenner & Smith, Inc.*, 48 N.Y.2d 84, 397 N.E.2d 358, 421 N.Y.S.2d 847 (1979). See also American Bar Association, Section of Litigation, WHEN CAN YOU TAKE IT WITH YOU—TRADE SECRET AND NON-COMPETITION CLAUSES IN EMPLOYEE AGREEMENTS (1982).

thorities in the particular jurisdiction governing the circumstances that trigger the insurer's duty to defend and to indemnify.

It is beyond the scope of this text to discuss in detail the standard forms of policies and exclusions that may afford protection to the employer. However, *Solo Cup Co. v. Federal Insurance Co.*[63] provides an example of the analysis and issues involved in insurance coverage cases. In *Solo Cup Co.*, it was held that an "umbrella excess liability policy" issued to the company provided coverage for the defense of an employee's Title VII sex discrimination suit. The court reasoned that the policy definition of an insured occurrence would extend only to a liability incurred by reason of Solo's unintentionally exposing women to discriminatory conditions. Nevertheless, the complaint against Solo was so general that it could conceivably embrace the disparate impact theory, which concerns employment practices fair and neutral in form but discriminatory in operation.

If the policy or policies in question provide defense or indemnity coverage or both for the unintended consequences of intended acts, a significant number of wrongful discharge claims may be covered. For example, an employer's discharge of an employee is certainly intentional and may be well justified in terms of the existence of just cause for discharge. However, if an employee rule book or personnel policy requires notice, hearing, or a graduated disciplinary procedure that inadvertently is not followed, the employer's jeopardy to a judgment is an unanticipated consequence of an intentional act. But insurance coverage of these claims or the lack of it cannot be taken for granted without careful study of the claim, the coverages and exclusions, and the governing judicial standards for coverage.

Reinstatement or Injunction Against Discharge in Private Employment

There is an almost universally recognized bar to the exercise of a court's equitable powers to reinstate an employee or enjoin discharge if the purpose is solely to provide monetary relief.[64] The denial of these remedies rests on several grounds. Monetary relief can be given in the form of a money judgment, which is an adequate remedy at law. In addition, the rule at common law long has been that one cannot be compelled to retain another in his service, because the employer does not have a comparable remedy against the employee

---

[63]619 F.2d 1178 (7th Cir.), *cert. denied*, 449 U.S. 1033 (1980). See also *Union Camp Corp. v. Continental Casualty Co.*, 452 F. Supp. 565 (S.D. Ga. 1978); *Transport Ins. Co. v. Lee Way Motor Freight, Inc.*, 487 F. Supp. 1325 (N.D. Tex. 1980); *Community Unit School Dist. No. 5 v. Country Mut. Ins. Co.*, 95 Ill. App.3d 272, 419 N.E.2d 1257 (1981); *School Dist. No. 1 v. Mission Ins. Co.*, 58 Ore. App. 692, 650 P.2d 929 (1982).

[64]*Brockmeyer v. Dun & Bradstreet*, 113 Wis.2d 561, 335 N.W.2d 834 (1983), by analogy to antidiscrimination statutes, holds that reinstatement and back pay are the most appropriate remedies for public policy exception wrongful discharges. This case is unique insofar as it approves reinstatement as a remedy for a common law wrongful discharge claim.

and because the courts cannot provide the continual supervision necessary for specific enforcement of personal service contracts. Finally, forcing an employee upon the employer may create needless friction and lead to further injuries.

Kurle v. Evangelical Hospital Association[65] reversed an order of reinstatement of a nurse to a private hospital. The opinion covers all the usual grounds for denial of equitable relief.

> "Plaintiff sought a preliminary injunction restraining and enjoining defendant from preventing her entering defendant's premises or from interfering with her work on its premises as a nurse, with pay and other benefits. But the trial court's order does not so enjoin or restrain defendant from preventing plaintiff from entering the premises of defendant hospital or resuming her work. The trial court's order required that plaintiff's employment be reinstated, and that she be granted the back pay and benefits she enjoyed prior to her May 28, 1980, suspension. The comments of the trial judge in the record make clear that, by his order, he intended that plaintiff be reinstated for the single purpose of receiving back pay and benefits. Such relief is purely economic for which plaintiff has an adequate remedy at law; such limited reinstatement, as ordered by the trial court, provides no protection for plaintiff's good name and reputation, but provides her only monetary relief. (See *Bromberg v. Whitler*, 57 Ill.App.3d 152, 156 (1977).) The presence of an adequate remedy at law is an additional basis for our finding that the trial court erred in granting the preliminary injunction.
>
> "There is yet another reason why the trial court should have granted the motion to dismiss Count I of the complaint and should have denied injunctive relief, both temporary and permanent. It seeks to have the court order defendant employer to continue to employ the plaintiff. At common law it was recognized that a person cannot, by decree of court, be compelled to retain another in his service. (*Reid Ice Cream Co. v. Stephens*, 62 Ill.App. 334, 339 (1895).) The policy underlying this principle arose from the reluctance of courts to interfere with and enforce any type of personal relationship. *Wollensak v. Briggs*, 119 Ill. 453 (1887); *Cowen v. McNealy*, 342 Ill.App. 197 (1950); *Rabinovich v. Reith*, 120 Ill.App. 409 (1905).
>
> "This rule of law has recently been applied with continued vigor. In *Zannis v. Lake Shore Radiologists, Ltd.*, 73 Ill.App.3d 901 (1979), plaintiff doctor brought an action for wrongful termination of his employment contract with defendant. He prayed for reinstatement, back pay and benefits. (73 Ill.App.3d 901, 903.) The sole issue on appeal was whether plaintiff's complaint stated a cause of action for equitable relief. The Appellate Court for the First District found that plaintiff was not entitled to equitable relief, stating:
>
>> '* * * Plaintiff's contract with defendant * * * was a personal service contract. It is well settled that, with reference to such contracts, * * * a court should not compel an employee to work for his employer, nor compel an employer to retain an employee in his service. * * *' (73 Ill.App.3d 901, 904.)
>
> "The court reasoned that it would be impractical, if not impossible, for a court to provide the continuous supervision necessary to enforce

[65]89 Ill. App.3d 45, 411 N.E.2d 326 (1980). See also *Theodore v. Elmhurst College*, 421 F. Supp. 355 (N.D. Ill. 1976); *Witt v. Forest Hosp., Inc.* 115 Ill. App.3d 481, 450 N.E.2d 811 (1983); *Zannis v. Lake Shore Radiologists, Ltd.*, 73 Ill. App.3d 901, 392 N.E.2d 126 (1979).

a personal service contract, especially where such services required special skill, knowledge, judgment or discretion (73 Ill.App.3d 901, 904). As further support for its finding, the court stated that, since personal service contracts often require a relationship of cooperation and trust between the parties, as a matter of public policy, courts avoid the friction that would develop by compelling an employee to work, or an employer to hire or retain someone against their wishes (73 Ill.App.3d 901, 905).

"An examination of the cases cited by plaintiff in support of her contention that, today, Illinois courts have the equitable power to reinstate an employee who has been wrongfully discharged, reveals that they are distinguishable from the present case. *People ex rel. Jaworski v. Jenkins*, 56 Ill.App.3d 1028 (1978), *Sola v. Clifford*, 29 Ill.App.3d 233 (1975) and *Corbett v. City of Chicago*, 323 Ill.App.3d 429 (1944), all involve actions by public bodies or public officials in wrongfully discharging public employees. The authority of a court to order public bodies or public officials to carry out their public or statutory duty is no support for the contention that a private employer can be compelled to do so.

"We recognize, however, that there are certain areas of the law where the legislature has required reinstatement of an employee by a private employer, *e.g.*, when an employee is discriminated against because of race, color, creed or sex. (See, *e.g.*, Equal Employment Opportunity Act of 1972, U.S.C. §2000e-5(g) (1974).) But absent the presence of a duty imposed by statute, we find no authority enabling us to depart from the policy expressed by Justice Harlan many years ago in *Arthur v. Oakes*, 63 Fed. 310 (1894):

> 'The rule, we think, is without exception that equity will not compel the actual, affirmative performance by an employee of merely personal services, any more than it will compel an employer to retain in his personal service one who, no matter for what cause, is not acceptable to him for service of that character.' 63 Fed. 310, 318."

In *Sampson v. Murray*,[66] the U.S. Supreme Court in a footnote commented that in "extraordinary cases" irreparable injury might be found in discharge cases so as to warrant preliminary injunctive relief. A separate concurring opinion in the *Kurle* case cited *Sampson* and argued that if reputational injury warranted reinstatement of public employees, the same injury justified reinstatement of private employees. Moreover, the opinion argued, the widespread use of reinstatement in public employment, in statutes prohibiting sex, race, and handicap discrimination in employment, and in collective bargaining have "swallowed the rule" against reinstatement in private employment.[67] At least one commentator has come to the same conclusion.[68]

Plainly, if equitable relief in the form of reinstatement or injunction against discharge is claimed, justification must be more than continuing the stream of income. Special grounds, if they exist at all, will be factors other than general job market conditions that make reemployment in similar work and pay very unlikely. More often

---

[66]415 U.S. 61 n.68 (1974).
[67]*Kurle v. Evangelical Hosp. Ass'n*, 89 Ill. App.3d 45, 55, 411 N.E.2d 326, 333 (1980).
[68]D. Dobbs, REMEDIES §12.25 (1980).

than not, it will be true that a discharge for poor performance itself cripples the employee's ability to find another employment. Justice Douglas observed that "we live in an Orwellian age in which the computer has become 'the heart of a surveillance system that will turn society into a transparent world.'"[69] It is worth quoting at length a portion of Justice Douglas' dissent in *Sampson* which develops his view of the employee's reputational injury and its impact in our "transparent world":

"A point is made that respondent has not shown irreparable injury. That misstates the issue. The District Court issued a stay pending a hearing on whether a temporary injunction should issue. The hearing, if held, would encompass two issues: (1) whether the grounds for respondent's discharge antedated her present employment (see, 149 U.S. App. D.C. 256, 269, 462 F.2d 871, 884) and were not restricted to her record as a probationary employee; and (2) whether she would suffer irreparable injury. As stated by the Court of Appeals, respondent 'may show * * * irreparable damage if the hearing before Judge Gasch is allowed to proceed to a decision.' *Id.*, 269, 462 F.2d at 884. The stay was issued by the District Court only because the federal agency involved refused to produce as a witness the officer who had decided to discharge respondent. Both the District Court and the Court of Appeals were alert to the necessity to show irreparable injury before an injunction issues.

"On that issue there is more than meets the eye. Employability is the greatest asset most people have. Once there is a discharge from a prestigious federal agency, dismissal may be a badge that bars the employee from other federal employment. The shadow of that discharge is cast over the area where private employment may be available. And the harm is not eliminated by the possibility of reinstatement, for in many cases the ultimate absolution never catches up with the stigma of the accusation. Thus, the court in *Schwartz v. Covington*, 341 F.2d 537, 538, issued a stay upon a finding of irreparable injury where a serviceman was to be discharged for alleged homosexual activity: '[A]ppellee has shown that he will suffer irreparable damage if the stay is not granted. Irrespective of the government's recent assurance that the appellee would be reinstated if he prevails upon review of his discharge, the injury and the stigma attached to an undesirable discharge are clear.' Unlike a layoff or discharge due to fortuitous circumstances such as the so-called energy crisis, a discharge on the basis of an employee's lifetime record or on the basis of captious or discriminatory attitudes of a superior may be a cross to carry the rest of an employee's life. And we cannot denigrate the importance of one's social standing or the status of social stigma as legally recognized harm. In *Ah Kow v. Nunan*, 5 Sawy 522, the Circuit Court, speaking through Mr. Justice Field, held that a Chinese prisoner could recover damages from the sheriff who cut off his queue, the injury causing great mental anguish, disgrace in the eyes of friends and relatives, and ostracism from association with members of his own race.

"There is no frontier where the employee may go to get a new start. We live today in a society that is closely monitored. All of our important acts, our setbacks, the accusations made against us go into data banks,

---

[69]*Sampson v. Murray* 415 U.S. 61, 96 n.2 (1974), (Douglas, J., dissenting). See also Miller, *Computers, Data Banks and Individual Privacy: An Overview*, 4 COLUM. HUMAN RIGHTS L. REV. 1 (1972).

instantly retrieved by the computer. * * * Moreover, this generation grew up in the age where millions of people were screened for 'loyalty' and 'security'; and many were discharged from the federal service; many resigned rather than face the ordeal of the 'witch hunt' that was laid upon us. Discharge from the federal service or resignation under fire became telltale signs of undesirability. Therefore, the case of irreparable injury for an unexplained discharge from federal employment may be plain enough on a hearing."[70]

Analysis of reputational injury as a premise for reinstatement shows that the question is not whether the remedy at law is inadequate. It plainly is. The problem is that once the damage is done, it cannot be undone by reinstatement or injunction. Reinstatement to the former job, like retraction of a libelous statement, still leaves the employee with the reputational injury. This is a situation where both the remedy at law and the equitable remedy are inadequate. The question was addressed in *Dos Santos v. Columbus-Cuneo-Cabrini Medical Center*.[71] A physician employed by a corporation providing anesthesiology services to a hospital under an oral contract terminable at will was discharged by the corporation. She was not permitted to offer the same services as a hospital staff physician because the corporation had an exclusive contract with the hospital. Upon her petition, the district court preliminarily enjoined enforcement of the exclusive contract. Although reinstatement was not sought or granted by the court, the relief that was granted was based on many factors typically argued to justify reinstatement:

> "We note initially that a temporary loss of income does not usually constitute irreparable injury because this deprivation can be fully redressed by an award of monetary damages. *Sampson v. Murray*, 415 U.S. 61, 90 (1974). In the instant case, any loss of income inflicted on plaintiff by the defendants' actions will be temporary and can be compensated fully should she prevail on her claim that the exclusive contract in question is unlawful. If she succeeds, plaintiff will be entitled to an order removing the exclusive contract as an obstacle to her practice of anesthesiology at Columbus Hospital and she will receive (treble) damages compensating her for any loss of income she suffers during the period of her exclusion. Under these circumstances it is irrelevant that plaintiff claims she may be unable to find other employment as an anesthesiologist in the Chicago area. *Sampson, supra*, 415 U.S. at 92 n.68; *Ekanem v. Health & Hospital Corp.*, 589 F.2d 316, 321 (7th Cir. 1978) (per curiam) ('Inability to obtain other employment is not considered irreparable harm because a terminated employee has an adequate remedy at law by obtaining a judgment in his favor.'). Thus, plaintiff has an adequate remedy at law for any temporary loss of income resulting from the operation of the allegedly unlawful exclusive contract.
> "The district court also found that plaintiff would suffer injury to her professional reputation as a result of her exclusion from Columbus Hospital, thus impairing her prospects for future employment. In *Sampson, supra*, 415 U.S. at 89, the Supreme Court expressly

---

[70]*Sampson v. Murray*, 415 U.S. at 96.
[71]684 F.2d 1346 (7th Cir. 1982).

rejected the proposition that 'either loss of earnings or damage to reputation might afford a basis for a finding of irreparable injury and provide a basis for temporary injunctive relief.' (Footnote omitted.) We need not decide whether plaintiff's claim of injury to reputation is controlled by *Sampson*, however, because even if this injury is irreparable it does not support the preliminary injunction issued by the district court.

"Plaintiff sought and obtained a preliminary injunction invalidating the exclusive contract, which was the sole basis on which she was denied access to Columbus Hospital. But this injunction cannot redress the claimed injury to her professional standing because the exclusive contract is not the source of that injury. Plaintiff has suffered an injury to reputation not because of the operation of the exclusive contract (such arrangements are, as noted, prevalent among hospitals in the Chicago area) but rather because of the decision by the plaintiff's employer, Associates, to terminate her employment summarily. The relief awarded by the district court is simply incapable of erasing the fact that plaintiff was fired by her employer and it cannot remove the stigma and damage to reputation that often accompanies such a termination of employment. Thus, even if plaintiff's injury to reputation is both real and irreparable, it does not support the preliminary injunction that was granted.

"The district court in its decision also found that plaintiff had suffered irreparable injury in that she had been deprived of valuable experience in the practice of anesthesiology. This finding is somewhat ambiguous. If it refers to the loss of experience pending trial or to plaintiff's inability to secure alternative employment in her specialty, temporary relief is precluded by the *Sampson* and *Ekanem* cases previously noted. If the finding refers instead to diminished prospects for future employment because of impaired reputation, preliminary relief from the operation of the exclusive contract is unwarranted because such relief is ineffective. If the finding referred to a deterioration in professional skills pending the outcome of the litigation, however, there might be some basis for a finding of irreparable injury, see *Equal Employment Opportunity Commission v. City of Janesville*, 630 F.2d 1254, 1259 (7th Cir. 1980), but plaintiff has neither alleged nor proven an atrophy in her skills. There is consequently no basis for concluding that loss of experience in the practice of anesthesiology constitutes irreparable injury.

"For these reasons, we hold that plaintiff has failed to demonstrate that she was threatened with irreparable injury as a result of the operation of the exclusive dealing contract she challenges as unlawful."[72] (Footnotes omitted.)

Careful analysis of the facts in a specific case and comparison to

---

[72]*Id.* at 1349. Note 3 of the opinion cited cases relied upon by plaintiff which affirmed reinstatement where that remedy would prevent impairment of plaintiff's professional reputation:

"3. Plaintiff relies on several cases holding that a termination of employment can cause an irreparable damage to reputation sufficient to warrant preliminary relief. *Fitzgerald v. Mountain Laurel Racing, Inc.*, 607 F.2d 589 (3d Cir. 1979), *cert. denied*, 446 U.S. 956 (1980); *Thompson v. Southwest School District*, 483 F. Supp. 1170 (W.D. Mo. 1980); *Assaf v. University of Texas System*, 399 F. Supp. 1245 (S.D. Tex. 1975). In each of these cases, however, the requested relief (usually reinstatement) effectively redressed the threatened injury to reputation. In the instant case, by contrast, the relief awarded by the district court cannot prevent the impairment of plaintiff's professional reputation caused by her termination by Associates."
Id. at 1350.

authorities granting reinstatement is essential if the plaintiff is to obtain equitable relief from the trial and reviewing courts. With respect to irreparable injury and inadequate remedy at law, the following cases merit consideration.

In *Ezekial v. Winkley*,[73] a physician employed by a hospital won reinstatement because he stressed the difficulty of estimating money damages. Though he performed services for the hospital, his employment also qualified as a surgical internship which, if satisfactorily completed in three years, led to professional recognition as a surgeon. After more than a year in the program, he was discharged. His suit for an order compelling the hospital to conduct a hearing to review the merits of the discharge was denied by the trial court and the intermediate appellate court. The California Supreme Court reversed and ordered the hospital to conduct a hearing. This unusual equitable remedy was warranted not because the physician had suffered reputational injury, for he had this in common with other discharged employees. However, money damages for his injury would have been more difficult to estimate than in the typical discharge situation because the amount of his lifetime income, but for the hospital's discharge, depended upon successful completion of the remainder of the work/study program and ultimately whether he was successful and well recognized as a surgeon. His job was plainly a stepping stone in a long course of professional education.

Superficially, the question of reinstatement of a self-employed physician to all or part of the privileges he enjoyed as a member of a hospital medical staff closely resembles the question of reinstatement of a physician-employee to the hospital. However, there is a significant difference between an employee and a staff physician: the former is subject to the supervision of the hospital's senior employees and staff members, while the latter gives orders and directions to the hospital employees—including nurses, radiologists, anesthesiologists, laboratory personnel, and many other highly specialized medical personnel—who care for his patients. Thus, while court-ordered reinstatement of an employee leaves the reinstated employee subject to the orders and direction of the employer, reinstatement of a physician to medical staff privileges is in reality an open-ended court order that requires the hospital personnel to be the subordinates of the reinstated physician and subject to his orders.[74]

Reinstatement of a former member to another kind of voluntary professional organization such as a medical society, or a court order that requires a voluntary association to accept a certain applicant for membership, may be of doubtful value to the prevailing applicant or member. Ordinarily, membership in the society or association is desired because membership is a "seal of approval" on the member's

---

[73]20 Cal.3d 267, 142 Cal. Rptr. 418, 572 P.2d 32 (1977).
[74]Although there are injunction appeals pending, no opinions on point have come to light as of this writing.

professional qualifications or stature. But if a court requires an association to include the name of a particular individual on its membership roster, it does not follow that third parties will credit the individual with the same stature accorded to persons who achieved membership through normal channels.

In *Duval v. Sevrson*,[75] reinstatement was justified because the plaintiff had been part owner of the bicycle repair business where he worked before his co-owners fired him. The court recognized that the employee's co-owners had separated him not only from his job but also from money he had invested in the business to foster his permanent employment. Reinstatement was the appropriate remedy.

Where an executive's written employment contract called for arbitration of disputes and the arbitrator ordered reinstatement after a discharge, the court held that the arbitrator's award could be specifically enforced. There were, however, strong dissents.[76]

Need for Judicial Supervision

The reluctance or, more accurately, the general refusal of courts to order reinstatement stems from a general objection to ordering specific performance of contracts that will require judicial supervision. The court is aware that if it orders reinstatement it is not equipped to monitor continued performance of the contract. But the analogy to specific performance of contracts may be exaggerated. Once the court has ordered reinstatement, it would need to intervene only in the event the employee subsequently complained of discharge or unfair treatment in the work place.[77] Monitoring performance, in any event, should not invariably loom as an obstacle to reinstatement. The burden is far less onerous than supervision of businesses in bankruptcy, schools in school desegregation, legislative reapportionment, hiring and promotion using nondiscriminatory criteria, supervision of prisons and jails, and location of public housing to promote desegregation—all of which are familiar subjects of equity jurisdiction. The common law tradition of avoiding remedies that require some measure of continuing judicial control has been steadily eroded.

Forced Association

The problem of forced association perhaps presents the strongest objection to the remedy of reinstatement. A forced relationship, particularly where close personal contact, intellectual skill, and profes-

---

[75]15 Ill. App.3d 634, 304 N.E.2d 747 (1973).

[76]*In re Staklinski*, 6 N.Y.2d 159, 160 N.E.2d 78, 188 N.Y.S.2d 541 (1959); *Rentar Indus., Inc. v. Rubenstein*, 118 Ill. App.3d 1, 454 N.E.2d 752 (1983) (arbitration ordered where employee's written contract provided that remedy).

[77]If grounds for discharge arose after reinstatement, the employer could discharge under its usual procedures. The fact that the employee would likely contest the second discharge as a breach of the reinstatement decree need not require denial of reinstatement.

sional judgment are required, may be undesirable especially after a dispute has arisen.[78]

The right to associate with only certain persons has been recognized as constitutionally significant only in cases involving membership in political[79] or social[80] organizations. Membership in such groups is itself a form of protected expression.[81] While the U.S. Supreme Court has denied a law firm's claims that the First Amendment privacy and associational rights could be invoked by a commercial, profit-making business organization in a discrimination case,[82] no case has been located in which an employer has made these claims.

Beyond constitutional concerns, the weight that should be given by the court to associational problems depends on the facts of the case. Such problems should be examined in the context of the probable relations within the group of colleagues with whom the plaintiff would work most closely if reinstated. The group's size, the nature of its working relationship, and its support of the employee are among the relevant considerations. In a large group, the sheer number of employees may minimize forced interaction and maximize the choice of associates. A court should examine the extent to which functions may be carried out without excessive interaction with or dependence upon senior executives or fellow employees in the working group.[83]

Like the problem of judicial supervision, the problem of forced association may be exaggerated. Courts have ordered the hiring of lawyers[84] and professors.[85] The forced association objection would seem to be at least as great when a university or firm is ordered to hire someone with whom it has not had experience, as when an organization is forced to retain an individual it has already seen fit to employ for several years. These circumstances should be assessed by the court and preclude an award of reinstatement where a hostile

---

[78]See 5.A.A. CORBIN ON CONTRACTS §1204 n.59 (1964).

[79]See, e.g., *Branti v. Finkel*, 445 U.S. 507 (1980) (First and Fourteenth Amendments protected two Republican county assistant public defenders from discharge by newly appointed Democratic public defender solely on basis of their political beliefs); *NAACP v. Alabama ex rel. Patterson*, 357 U.S. 449 (1958) (NAACP not required to disclose its membership list).

[80]See *Lucido v. Cravath, Swaine & Moore*, 425 F. Supp. 123, 129 (S.D.N.Y. 1977). Title VII exempts bona fide private membership clubs from the definition of employers covered by the Act. 42 U.S.C. §2000-e(b) (1976). But see *Mills v. Fox*, 421 F. Supp. 519, 13 FEP Cases 1009 (E.D.N.Y. 1976) (private club cannot be used as cover for operation of business that would otherwise be covered by Title VII).

[81]See L. Tribe, AMERICAN CONSTITUTIONAL LAW §12-23, at 702 (1979), and Gavison, *Privacy and the Limits of Law*, 89 YALE L.J. 421, 456 (1980).

[82]*Hishon v. King & Spaulding*, __U.S.__, 52 U.S.L.W. 4627, May 22, 1984; see also *Lucido v. Cravath, Swaine & Moore*, 425 F. Supp. 123, 129 (S.D.N.Y. 1977).

[83]*Francoeur v. Corroon & Black Co.*, 552 F. Supp. 403 (S.D.N.Y. 1982) (reinstatement refused in Title VII case because of acrimony between parties); *Witt v. Forest Hosp., Inc.*, 115 Ill. App.3d 481, 450 N.E.2d 811 (1983) (reinstatement refused because of hostile environment).

[84]E.g., *Kamberos v. GTE Automatic Elec., Inc.*, No. 74 C 151 (N.D. Ill. 1978) (corporate law department ordered to hire woman attorney), *rev'd in part*, 603 F.2d 598 (7th Cir. 1979) (plaintiff not qualified).

[85]E.g., *Schwartz v. Florida*, 494 F. Supp. 574 (N.D. Fla. 1980) (rejected white female applicant entitled to post as assistant professor); cf. *McConnell v. Anderson*, 316 F. Supp. 809 (D. Minn. 1970) (librarian awarded job denied him in violation of constitutional rights), *rev'd on other grounds*, 451 F.2d 193 (8th Cir. 1971), *cert. denied*, 405 U.S. 1046 (1972).

relationship between the parties will adversely influence efficiency and the safety of others.

Employer's Public Safety Responsibility

Reinstatement may be inappropriate if the employee individually can have a direct impact upon health and safety in the work place or the health and safety of outsiders. A few examples of such employees will make the point: a nurse with an unexplained involvement in an insulin overdose of a patient; an airline pilot dismissed for lack of self-control in stress situations; a truck driver whose cargo included explosives dismissed for careless driving; a physician who deviated too frequently and too far from norms of practice accepted by peers or the employer.

The *court* may well be convinced that the employer breached a statutory duty or its contract of employment with the dismissed employee and that reinstatement would not create an association problem or increase the risk to the health or safety of co-workers or the public. But if the employee seeking reinstatement was terminated because the employer perceived that he presented a threat to the safety of co-workers, patients, passengers, or the public, the question arises whether the court is entitled to discount entirely the employer's judgment. When reinstatement raises questions of public health and safety, all doubts should be resolved in favor of the safety of the public and co-workers. The brief encounter that a judge has with employer and employee in the course of a lawsuit is not enough to permit the court to make the kind of decisions entrusted to arbitrators, who generally have a wealth of experience in the particular industry and perhaps with the particular employer. A court does not have that special background. Moreover, some employers are licensed by the state or federal government to conduct their business or perform special services. A license does not permit the employer to act arbitrarily to abuse employees. However, as long as the employer qualifies for the license or privilege to conduct the business, public policy, if not common sense, should bar the court from substituting its own judgment for the employer's respecting public health and safety questions.

Discovery Privileges Based Upon Confidentiality of Subject Matter

Whether the employee seeks a remedy at law or in equity or both, the outcome of the case and its threat to the employer may be influenced as much by what the employee can reach in the discovery process than the ultimate judgment. Employment litigation often embraces within its subject matter performance evaluations that were prepared under the assumption that they would remain confidential.

If it is relevant to the merit of the claims and defenses to compare the performance appraisals of other employees or compare appraisals done by several supervisors of one employee, disclosure will discourage candor in the future. This same sensitive problem arises when former members of and applicants to voluntary associations such as hospital medical staffs challenge membership decisions. It occurs when the employer or voluntary association has made a confidential self-critical analysis of its practices with the intention of improving future performance. *Marrese v. American Academy of Orthopedic Surgeons*[86] concerned a professional association's refusal to turn over all correspondence and related documents concerning a denial of the plaintiffs' applications for membership and documents that concerned all other denials of membership applications between 1970 and 1980. The discovery issues reached the appellate court after a contempt judgment was entered against the association. The court held that there was no First Amendment privilege against the disclosure of this material, but did recognize and protect the association's interest in the confidentiality of its membership files:[87]

> "Yet there is in this case, if not a First Amendment right, at least a First Amendment interest—maybe two First Amendment interests—which the discovery sought by the plaintiffs would impair and which differentiates this from the usual antitrust case, where discovery is sought of invoices or salesmen's report or the minutes of a corporation's board of directors. The Academy is a forum for exchanges of information about surgical techniques and related matters of substantial public interest. These exchanges may be inhibited if the Academy has to disclose its membership files. The protective order that the district judge entered is not a complete answer, not only because it is the kind of lawyer's arrangement that laymen instinctively distrust, but also because the particular order allows the plaintiffs themselves, and not just their counsel—allows, in other words, two disappointed applicants for memberships—to get hold of their files. If the Academy complies with the discovery order, its members may be reluctant to offer candid evaluations of applicants in the future, and the atmosphere of mutual confidence that encourages a free exchange of ideas will be eroded. Cf. *NAACP v. Alabama, ex rel. Patterson*, 357 U.S. 449 (1958), where in a case involving resistance to disclosure of membership information in discovery proceedings the Supreme Court recognized a First Amendment right of association for the purpose of expression and advocacy of ideas. In setting aside constitutional considerations, one should not have to raise the ghosts of Aristotle and of deTocqueville to be reminded that voluntary associations are important to many people, Americans in particular, that voluntary professional associations are important to American professionals (a proposition that is the premise of the plaintiffs' antitrust suit as it was of their Illinois suit), that confidentiality of deliberations and membership applications is essential to the voluntary character of an association, and therefore that the involuntary disclosure of the membership files of a voluntary association may harm worthy private interests.
> * * *

---

[86]706 F.2d 1488 (7th Cir. 1983), *on rehearing*, 726 F.2d 1150 (7th Cir. 1984).
[87]706 F.2d at 1495.

"Discovery of sensitive documents is sometimes sought not in a sincere effort to gather evidence for use in a lawsuit, but in an effort to coerce the adverse party, regardless of the merits of the suit, to settle it in order not to have to disclose sensitive materials. The use of the liberal discovery provisions of the Federal Rules of Civil Procedure to harass opponents is common, and requires the vigilance of the district judges to prevent. The power granted by Rule 26(d) to control the sequence and timing of discovery is one of the district courts' too little used tools for preventing the predatory abuse of discovery and we are at a loss to understand why the power was not used here."

The confidentiality consideration and the potential abuse for discovery noted by the court in *Marrese* can arise in many employment controversies.[88] A state constitutional guarantee of privacy has been invoked to bar discovery of an employee evaluation made under a guarantee of confidentiality.[89] Nevertheless, as noted in Chapter 7, the legislatures of a growing number of states are opening up employee evaluations to discovery by statute, even in the absence of a litigated dispute. These statutes are based on the notion that evaluations may be more accurate if open to dispute by the employee and on the instinctive belief that individuals should be entitled to know the reasons for actions taken by others which vitally affect their interests.

---

[88]For recent scholarly treatment of the subject, see Steinman, *Privacy of Association: A Burgeoning Privilege in Civil Discovery*, 17 HARV. C.R.-C.L. L. REV. 355 (1982); Duffy, *Privacy vs. Disclosure: Balancing Employee and Employer Rights*, 7 EMPLOYEE RELATIONS L.J. 594 (1982); Note, *The Privilege of Self-Critical Analysis*, 96 HARV. L. REV. 1083 (1983).

[89]*Johnson v. Winter*, 127 Cal. App.3d 435, 179 Cal. Rptr. 585 (1982); *Board of Trustees v. Superior Court*, 119 Cal. App.3d 516, 174 Cal. Rptr. 160 (1981); *Gray v. Board of Higher Educ.*, 692 F.2d 901 (2d Cir. 1982).

Appendix A

Federal and State Statutes*

Federal Statutes

Statute	Prohibited practice	Protected conduct or status	Citation
Age Discrimination in Employment Act	discharging, discriminating	age[1]	29 U.S.C. §623(a)(1) (1982)
Asbestos School Hazard Detection & Control Act	discharging, discriminating	bringing asbestos problem in school building to public attention[2]	20 U.S.C. §3608 (1982)
Bankruptcy Code	discharging	filing for bankruptcy[3]	11 U.S.C. §525 (1982)
Black Lung Benefits Act	discharging, discriminating	suffering from pneumoconiosis (Black Lung disease)[4]	30 U.S.C. §938(a) (1976)
Civil Rights Acts of 1866 & 1871	discriminating	nonwhite	42 U.S.C. §1981 (1976)
Clean Air Act	discharging, discriminating	commencing proceedings; testifying at, assisting, participating in proceedings	42 U.S.C. §7622(a) (Supp. V 1981)

[1]Ages 40–69.
[2]Employees of agencies receiving assistance under statute.
[3]Public employees only.
[4]Miners protected; mine operators prohibited.

Statute	Prohibited practice	Protected conduct or status	Citation
Coal Mine Health & Safety Act	discharging, discriminating	reporting violations, filing charges, testifying	30 U.S.C. §815(c) (Supp. V 1981)
Consumer Credit Protection Act	discharging	garnishment for one indebtedness	15 U.S.C. §1674(a) (1982)
Employee Retirement Income Security Act	discharging, discriminating, interfering with attaining ERISA right	exercising ERISA right, providing information, testifying	29 U.S.C. §1140 (1982)
Energy Reorganization Act (Nuclear Regulatory Commission)	discharging, discriminating	commencing proceedings; testifying at, assisting, participating in proceedings	42 U.S.C. §5851(a) (Supp. V 1981)
Equal Employment Opportunity Act (Title VII)	discharging, discriminating	race, color, religion, sex, national origin	42 U.S.C. §2000e-2(a)(1) (1976 & Supp. V 1981)
	discharging, discriminating	pregnancy	42 U.S.C. §2000e(k) (1976 & Supp. V 1981)
	discharging, discriminating	sexual harassment	29 C.F.R. §1604.11 (1983)
	discharging, discriminating	opposing unlawful practice; testifying at, assisting, participating in proceedings	42 U.S.C. §2000e-3(a) (1983)
Fair Labor Standards Act	discharging, discriminating	(minimum wage, equal pay, age discrimination) instituting proceedings, testifying	29 U.S.C. §215 (a)(3) (1982)

Statute	*Prohibited practice*	*Protected conduct or status*	*Citation*
Federal Employers' Liability Act	discharging, discriminating	providing voluntary information to person in interest as to facts incident to injury or death of covered employee	45 U.S.C. §60 (1976)
Hazardous Substances Release Act (Superfund)	firing, discriminating	providing information to government; filing proceedings; testifying	42 U.S.C. §9610(a) (Supp. V 1981)
Jurors' Employment Protection Act	discharging, threatening, coercing	jury service[5]	28 U.S.C. §1875 (1982)
Longshoremen's & Harbor Workers' Compensation Act	discharging, discriminating	claiming compensation, testifying	33 U.S.C. §948a (1976)
National Labor Relations Act	discriminating	encouraging or discouraging labor organization membership; filing charges, testifying	29 U.S.C. §§158(a)(3), 158(a)(4) (1982)
Occupational Safety & Health Act	discharging, discriminating	instituting proceedings, testifying, refusing to work under hazardous conditions with no alternatives available	29 U.S.C. §660(c) (1982); 29 C.F.R. §1977.12(b)(2) (1983)

---

[5]"Permanent" employees protected.

Statute	Prohibited practice	Protected conduct or status	Citation
Public Health Service Act	discriminating in employment or staff privileges	performing or assisting or refusing to participate in sterilization, abortion, or research activity on religious or moral grounds[6]	42 U.S.C. §300a-7(b) (1976 & Supp. V 1981)
Railroad Safety Authorization Act of 1978	discharging, discriminating	instituting proceedings; testifying; refusing to work under hazardous conditions with no alternatives available	45 U.S.C. §441(a) (Supp. V 1981)
Railway Labor Act	interfering, influencing, coercing	employee organizing; membership in labor organization	45 U.S.C. §152 Fourth (1976)
Rehabilitation Act of 1973	failing to take affirmative action to employ and advance	handicap[7]	29 U.S.C. §793(a) (1982)
Safe Containers for International Cargo Act	discharging, discriminating	reporting existence of unsafe container; reporting violation to Labor Department	46 U.S.C. §1506(a) (Supp. V 1981)

---

[6]Recipients of federal public health financial assistance.
[7]Employer must do over $2,500 per year in business with the federal government.

Statute	Prohibited practice	Protected conduct or status	Citation
Safe Drinking Water Act	discharging, discriminating	commencing proceedings; testifying at, assisting, participating in proceedings	42 U.S.C. §300j-9(i)(1) (1976)
Solid Waste Disposal Act	firing, discriminating	instituting proceedings, testifying	42 U.S.C. §6971(a) (1976)
	laying off	employer compliance with statute[8]	42 U.S.C. §6971(e) (1976)
Surface Mining Control & Reclamation Act	discharging, discriminating	instituting proceedings, testifying	30 U.S.C. §1293(a) (Supp. V 1981)
Toxic Substances Control Act	discharging, discriminating	commencing proceedings; testifying, assisting, participating in proceedings	15 U.S.C. §2622 (1982)
Vietnam Veterans Readjustment Act	failing to reemploy for one year	service in armed forces	38 U.S.C. §§2021, 2024(a) (1976)
	failing to permit leave of absence and reemploy for six months	active duty or training by reservists	38 U.S.C. §§2024(b), 2024(c), 2024(d) (1976) & Supp. V 1981)
Water Pollution Prevention & Control Act	firing, discriminating	instituting proceedings, testifying	33 U.S.C. §1367(a) (1976)

---

[8]Employer forbidden to lay off workers because required to comply with statute.

State Statutes*

Subject	Citation
ALABAMA	(ALA. CODE)
Blacklist	§13A-11-123 (1982)
Day of rest	§13A-12-1 (1982)
Extortion of job applicants (coal mines)	§25-9-28 (1975)
Jury service	§§12-16-8 (1975 & Supp. 1983), 12-16-8.1 (Supp. 1983)
Labor union	§§25-7-6 (1975 & Supp. 1983), 25-7-33 (1975)
—right to work (no union shop)	§25-7-31 (1975)
Safety in the work place	§25-1-1 (1975)
—coal mine	§25-9-29 (1975)
Voting—intimidation	§§17-23-10, 17-23-11 (1975)
ALASKA	(ALASKA STAT.)
Discrimination—race, religion, color, national origin, age, handicap, sex, marital status, parenthood	§18.80.220(1) (1981 & Supp. 1983)
—pregnancy	§18.80.220(1) (1981)
—retaliation	§18.80.220(4) (1981)
Fraud	§§23.10.015, 23.10.030 (1981)
Labor union (public employees)	§23.40.080 (1981)
Lie detector	§23.10.037 (1981)
Return transportation from job	§§23.10.380, 23.10.385 (1981)
Safety in the work place	§18.60.075(4) (1981)

---

*The nature of state statute indexes, which resemble one another only generally, makes it possible that this compilation does not include all of the statutes that might be applicable. We invite readers who are aware of statutes that are not included to suggest them to us.

Subject	*Citation*
—complaint, testimony	§18.60.089 (1981)
Toxic substances—right to know	§18.60.067 (Supp. 1983)
Voting—time off	§15.15.100 (1982)
Wage & hour—complaint testimony	§23.10.135 (1981)

ARIZONA   (ARIZ. REV. STAT. ANN.)

Subject	Citation
Abortion—refusal to perform	§36-2151 (1974 & Supp. 1983–84)
Air pollution—reduction in pay for use of pollution control equipment	§36-1718 (1974 & Supp. 1983–84)
Blacklist	§23-1361 (1983); ARIZ. CONST. art. 18, §9
Discrimination—race, color, religion, sex, age, national origin	§41-1463 (1974 & Supp. 1983–84)
—retaliation	§41-1464(A) (1974 & Supp. 1983–84)
Extortion of job applicants	§23-202 (1983)
Fraud	§23-201 (1983)
Jury service	§21-236 (1975 & Supp. 1983–84)
Labor union	§23-1341 (1983)
—right to work (no union shop)	§23-1302 (1983)
Military service	§§26-167, 26-168 (1976 & Supp. 1983–84)
Safety in the work place	§23-403 (1983)
—complaint, testimony	§23-425 (1983)
Sales to employees	§23-203 (1983)
Voting—intimidation	§16-1012 (Supp. 1983–84)

ARKANSAS   (ARK. STAT. ANN.)

Subject	Citation
Abortion—refusal to perform or undergo	§41-2560 (1977 & Supp. 1983)
Blacklist	§81-211 (1976)
Discrimination—race, color, creed, national origin, ancestry (state contractors)	§6-1506 (Supp. 1983)
—sexual harassment	§81-405 (1976)
Jury service (public employees)	§12-2371 (1979)
Labor union	§81-201 (1976)

Subject	Citation
—right to work (no union shop)	§81-202 (1976 & Supp. 1983); ARK. CONST. amend. 34, §1
Medical examination— payment for	§81-212 (1976)
Military service (public employees)	§12-2370 (1979)
Safety in the work place	§81-108 (1976 & Supp. 1983)
Sales to employees	§§81-306, 81-307 (1976)
Voting—intimidation	§3-1105(o) (1976 & Supp. 1983)
—time off	§3-1306 (1976)
Witnesses—general (public employees	§12-2371 (1979)
Workers' compensation	§81-1335 (1976 & Supp. 1983)

CALIFORNIA

Subject	Citation
Abortion—refusal or willingness to perform	CAL. HEALTH & SAFETY CODE §25955 (West Supp. 1984)
—requiring employee to be sterilized	CAL. GOV'T CODE §12945.5 (West 1980)
Arrest record	CAL. LAB. CODE §432.7 (West Supp. 1984)
—marijuana conviction	CAL. LAB. CODE §432.8 (West Supp. 1984)
Blacklist	CAL. LAB. CODE §1050 (West 1971 & Supp. 1984)
Day of rest	CAL. LAB. CODE §551 (West 1971 & Supp. 1984)
Discrimination—race, religious creed, color, national origin, ancestry, handicap, marital status, sex	CAL. GOV'T CODE §12940(a) (West 1980 & Supp. 1984)
—age	CAL. GOV'T CODE §12941(a) (West 1980 & Supp. 1984)
—pregnancy	CAL. GOV'T CODE §§12943, 12945 (West 1980 & Supp. 1984)
—sexual harassment	CAL. GOV'T CODE §12940(i) (West Supp. 1984)
—retaliation	CAL. GOV'T CODE §§12940(e), 12940(f) (West 1980 & Supp. 1984)
Dishonesty—report to employer	CAL. LAB. CODE §2930 (West Supp. 1984)
Fraud	CAL. LAB. CODE §972 (West 1971 & Supp. 1984)

Subject	*Citation*
Garnishment	CAL. LAB. CODE §2924 (West 1971 & Supp. 1984)
Jury service	CAL. LAB. CODE §230 (West 1971 & Supp. 1984)
Labor union	CAL. LAB. CODE §§921 (West 1971), 922 (West 1971 & Supp. 1984)
Lie detector	CAL. LAB. CODE §432.2 (West 1971 & Supp. 1984)
Medical examination— payment for	CAL. LAB. CODE §222.5 (West 1971)
Military service	CAL. MIL. & VET. CODE §§394 (West 1955), 394.5 (West Supp. 1984)
Politics—activity, candidacy, public office	CAL. LAB. CODE §§1101, 1102 (West 1971 & Supp. 1984)
Safety in the work place	CAL. LAB. CODE §6400 (West 1971 & Supp. 1984)
—complaint, testimony	CAL. LAB. CODE §6399.7, 6310, 6312 (West Supp. 1984)
—refusal to work	CAL. LAB. CODE §6311 (West 1971 & Supp. 1984)
Service letter (public utility)	CAL. LAB. CODE §1055 (West 1971)
Term—terminable-at-will if not for specified period ...	CAL. LAB. CODE §2922 (West 1971 & Supp. 1984)
—no enforcement against employee beyond 7 years	CAL. LAB. CODE §2855 (West 1971 & Supp. 1984)
Toxic substances—right to know	CAL. LAB. CODE §§6399, 6399.7 (West Supp. 1984)
Unlawful order	CAL. LAB. CODE §2856 (West 1971 & Supp. 1984)
Voting—time off	CAL. ELEC. CODE §14350 (West 1977)
Wage & hour—testimony	CAL. LAB. CODE §1196 (West 1971 & Supp. 1984)
Whistleblowing (public employee)	CAL. GOV'T CODE §10545 (West 1980 & Supp. 1984)
—report of patient neglect	CAL. PENAL CODE §11161.8 (West 1982 & Supp. 1984); CAL. GOV'T CODE §12940(e) (West Supp. 1984)
Witnesses—general	CAL. LAB. CODE §230 (West 1971 & Supp. 1984)
Workers' compensation	CAL. LAB. CODE §132a (West 1971 & Supp. 1984)
COLORADO	(COLO. REV. STAT.)
Abortion	§18-6-104 (1978 & Supp. 1983)
Blacklist	§8-2-111 (1973)

Subject	Citation
Discrimination—race, color, creed, handicap, sex, national origin, ancestry	§24-34-402 (1982)
—age	§8-2-116 (1973)
Fraud	§8-2-107 (1973)
Garnishment	§5-5-106 (1973)
Jury service	§13-71-118 (1974)
Labor union	§8-3-106 (1974)
—right to work (no union shop)	§8-3-108(1)(c)(I) (1974 & Supp. 1982)
Medical examination— payment for	§8-2-118 (1973)
Military service	§18-6-104 (1978)
Politics—engage or participate	§§8-2-102, 8-2-108 (1973)
—run for office	§8-2-108 (1973)
—serve in public office	§8-2-108 (1973)
Safety in the work place	§8-1-107(2)(b) (Supp. 1982)
Voting—intimidation	§1-13-719 (1980)
—time off	§1-7-102 (1980)
Wage & hour—assist or testify at proceedings	§8-6-115 (1973)
CONNECTICUT	(CONN. GEN. STAT. ANN.)
Arrest record	§§31-51(i) (West 1972), 46a-80 (West Supp. 1984)
Benefits (group insurance cancellations)	§31-51h (West 1972 & Supp. 1984)
Blacklist	§31-51, (West 1972 & Supp. 1983–84)
Day of rest	§§53-302, 303 (West 1960), 53-302a, 303e (West Supp. 1984)
Discrimination—race, color, creed, age, sex, ancestry, marital status, family, national origin	§46a-60(a)(1) (West Supp. 1984)
—handicap	§§46a-60(a)(1), 17-137k(c) (West Supp. 1984)
—sexual harassment	§46a-60(a)(8) (West Supp. 1984)
—pregnancy	§46(a)-60(a)(7) (West Supp. 1984)
—retaliation	§46(a)-60(a)(4) (West Supp. 1984)
Electronic surveillance	§31-48(b) (West 1972 & Supp. 1984)
Garnishment	§52-361(h) (West 1960 & Supp. 1984)
Jury service	§51-247(a) (West Supp. 1984)

Subject	Citation
Labor union	§31-105 (West 1972 & Supp. 1984)
Lie detector	§31-51g (West 1972 & Supp. 1984)
Military service	§§27-33, 27-33a, (West 1975), 52-571 (West 1960)
Personnel file—access	§31-128a (West Supp. 1984)
Politics—candidate or official	§§2-3a (West 1969 & Supp. 1984), 31-511 (West Supp. 1984)
Sales to employees	§31-48 (West 1972)
Safety in the work place	§§31-49 (West 1972), 31-370(a) (West Supp. 1984)
—complaint, testimony	§31-379 (West Supp. 1984)
Toxic substances—right to know	§§31-40K, 31-370(b) (West Supp. 1984)
Voting—influence	§9-365 (West 1967)
Whistleblowing	§31-51m (West Supp. 1984)
Witnesses—general	§54-85b (West Supp. 1984)

DELAWARE (DEL. CODE ANN.)

Abortion—refusal to participate	tit. 24, §1791(a) (1974)
Discrimination—race, color, age, religion, sex, national origin	tit. 19, §711 (1979 & Supp. 1982)
Garnishment	tit. 10, §3509 (1974)
Lie detector	tit. 19, §704 (1979)
Military service (public employees)	tit. 29, §5105 (1983)
Safety in the work place	tit. 19, §106 (1979 & Supp. 1982)
Voting—intimidation	tit. 15, §5162 (1974)

DISTRICT OF COLUMBIA (D.C. CODE ANN.)

Discrimination—race, color, religion, national origin, sex, age, marital status, handicap, family responsibilities, personal appearance, student status & sexual orientation	§1-2512 (1981)
—pregnancy	§§1-2502(17), 1-2512 (1981)
—retaliation	§1-2525(b) (1981)
Garnishment	§16-584 (1981)
Lie detector	§§36-801, 36-802 (1981)
Politics (discrimination for political affiliation)	§1-2512 (1981)

Subject	*Citation*
Safety in the work place	§36-228 (1981)
Voting—intimidation	§1-1318(a)(3) (1981 & Supp. 1983)
Workers' compensation	§36-316 (1981)

FLORIDA (FLA. STAT. ANN.)

Subject	Citation
Abortion—refusal to participate	§390.001(8) (West Supp. 1984)
Blacklist (railroad)	§351.20 (West 1968)
Conspiracy to procure discharge	§448.045 (West 1981)
Discrimination—race, color, religion, sex, national origin, age, handicap, marital status	§23.167 (West Supp. 1984)
—sickle cell trait	§448.075 (West 1981 & Supp. 1984)
—retaliation	§23.167(7) (West Supp. 1983)
Jury service	§40.271 (West Supp. 1984)
Labor union	FLA. CONST. art. 1, §6
—right to work (no union shop)	FLA. CONST. art. 1, §6
Military service (state & county employees)	§§250.48 (West 1975), 715.01 (West 1982)
Safety in the work place	§440.56 (West 1981)
Sales to employees	§448.03 (West 1981)
Voting—intimidation	§104.081 (West 1982)
Workers' compensation	§440.205 (West 1981)

GEORGIA (GA. CODE.)

Subject	Citation
Abortion—refusal to participate	§16-12-142 (1982)
Day of rest	§10-1-573 (1982)
Discrimination—age	§34-1-2 (1982)
—handicap/retaliation	§§34-6A-4, 34-6A-5 (1982)
Garnishment	§18-4-7 (1982)
Labor—right-to work (no union shop)	§34-6-23 (1982)
Safety in the work place	§§34-2-2, 34-2-10(a) (1982)
Term-salary period presumed term	§34-7-1 (1982)
Voting—time off	§21-2-404 (1982)

HAWAII (HAWAII REV. STAT.)

Subject	Citation
Arrest or court record	§378-2(1) (1976 & Supp. 1983)
Bankruptcy (wage earner plan)	§378-32(1) (1976 & Supp. 1983)

Subject	Citation
Discrimination—race, sex, age, religion, color, ancestry, handicap, marital status	§378-2(1) (1976 & Supp. 1983)
—pregnancy	§378-1 (Supp. 1983), 378-2(1) (1976 & Supp. 1983)
—retaliation	§378-2(5) (1976 & Supp. 1983)
Garnishment	§378-32(1) (1976 & Supp. 1983)
Jury service	§§79-14, 612-25 (1976)
Labor union	§377-4 (1976)
Lie detector	§378-21 (1976)
Military service (public employee)	§79-23 (1976)
Politics—state legislature	§79-19 (1976)
Safety in the work place	§396-6 (1976)
—complaint, testimony	§396-8 (1976 & Supp. 1983)
Toxic substances—right to know	§396-7 (1976)
Voting—time off	§11-95 (1976 & Supp. 1983)
Witnesses—workers' compensation or garnishment discharge	§378-32(3) (Supp. 1983)
—general	§§79-14, 621-10.5 (Supp. 1983)
Workers' compensation	§378-32(2) (1976 & Supp. 1983)

IDAHO (IDAHO CODE)

Subject	Citation
Abortion—refusal to participate	§18-612 (1979)
Day of rest	§18-6202 (1979)
Discrimination—race, color, religion, sex, national origin, age	§67-5909 (1980 & Supp. 1983)
—retaliation	§67-5911 (Supp. 1983)
Farm labor sanitation proceedings—institute or testify	§44-1904 (Supp. 1983)
Garnishment	§28-35-106 (1980)
Jury service	§2-218 (1979)
Labor union	§44-901 (1977)
Lie detector	§44-903 (1977)
Military service (state employees)	§46-216 (1977)
Safety in the work place	§§44-104, 72-720 (1977)
Sales to employees	§44-902 (1977)

Subject	**Citation**
Wage & hour—complaint or testimony	§44-1509 (1977)

ILLINOIS   (ILL. REV. STAT.)

Subject	Citation
Abortion—refusal to perform or undergo	ch. 111½ §5201 (1983)
Arrest record (inquiry prohibited)	ch 68, §2-103 (1983)
Day of rest	ch. 48, §8b (1983)
Discrimination—race, color, religion, national origin, ancestry, age, sex, marital status, handicap	ch. 68, §§1-103(Q), 2-102(A) (1983)
—retaliation	ch. 68, §6-101(A) (1983)
Electronic Funds Transfer accounts—requiring employees to use	ch. 17, §1352(2) (1983)
Garnishment	ch. 48, §39.11; ch. 62, §88 (1983)
Jury service	ch. 78, §4.1 (1983)
Labor union	ch. 48, §2b (1983)
Medical care—refusal to perform or undergo	ch. 111½, §5307 (1983)
Medical examination— payment for	ch. 48, §172d (1983)
Military service	ch. 126½, §§32, 33, 34 (1983)
Personnel file—access, correction, collection of irrelevant materials, notice of disclosure	Act 83-1104, 1983 Ill. Leg. Serv. 7290 (West), to be codified at ILL. REV. STAT. ch. 48, §2001 *et seq.*
Safety in the work place	ch. 48, §137.3(a) (1983)
Sales to employees	ch. 121½, §205 (1983)
Toxic substances—right to know	ch. 48, §1402 *et seq.* (1983)
Voting—time off	ch. 46, §§7-42, 17-15 (1983)
Whistleblowing (state employees only)	ch. 127, §63b119c.1 (1983)
—mental health patient abuse	ch. 91½, §734 (1983)
Witnesses—general (criminal)	ch. 38, §155-3 (1983)
Workers' compensation	ch. 48, §138.4(h) (1983)

INDIANA   (IND. CODE ANN.)

Subject	Citation
Abortion—refusal to participate	§16-10-3-2 (West 1984)
Blacklist	§22-5-3-1 (West 1981)

Subject	*Citation*
Discrimination—race, religion, color, sex, national origin, ancestry	§22-9-1-2 (West 1981)
—age	§22-9-2-1 (West 1981)
—handicap	§§22-9-1-2, 22-9-1-13 (West 1981)
—retaliation	§§22-9-1-6(i), 22-9-2-8 (West 1981)
Fraud	§35-43-5-3(1) (West 1978 & Supp. 1983–84)
Garnishment	§24-4.5-5-106 (West 1980)
Jury service	§35-44-3-10 (West 1978)
Labor union	§§22-6-1-2, 22-6-1-3 (West 1981)
Military service	§§10-2-4-2 *et seq.*, 10-5-8-1 *et seq.*, 10-5-9-1 *et seq.* (West 1982)
Politics—legislative office	§2-3-3-1 (West 1981)
Safety in the work place	§§22-1-1-10 (West 1981 & Supp. 1983–84), 22-8-1.1-1 (West 1981)
—complaint, testimony	§22-8-1.1-38.1 (West 1981)
Sales to employees	§22-2-4-3 (West 1981)
Service letter	§22-6-3-1 (West 1981)
Voting—intimidation	§3-4-7-3 (West 1981)
—time off	§3-1-21-7 (West 1981)
Workers' compensation ("device")	§22-2-2-12 (West 1981)
IOWA	(IOWA CODE ANN.)
Abortion—refusal to participate	§146.1 (West Supp. 1983–84)
Blacklist	§730.2 (West 1979)
Discrimination—race, religion, color, national origin, sex, creed, age, handicap	§601A.6 (West 1975 & Supp. 1983–84)
—retaliation	§601A.11 (West Supp. 1983–84)
Dishonesty (false charge to employer of employee crime)	§730.3 (West 1979)
DWI (driving while intoxicated) course (absence for)	§321.283 (West 1966 & Supp. 1983–84)
Garnishment	§§642.21(2)(c), 537.5201(5) (West Supp. 1983–84)
Labor union	§731.2 (West 1979)
—right to work (no union shop)	§731.3 (West 1979)

Subject	Citation
Safety in the work place	§88.4 (West 1972 & Supp. 1983–84)
—complaint, testimony	§88.9(3) (West 1972 & Supp. 1983–84)
Voting—intimidation	§49.110 (West 1973 & Supp. 1983–84)
—time off	§49.109 (West 1973 & Supp. 1983–84)
Wage & hour—complaint, testimony	§91A.10(5) (West Supp. 1983–84)

KANSAS (KAN. STAT. ANN.)

Subject	Citation
Abortion—refusal to participate	§65-443 (1980)
Bankruptcy (public employees)	§75-4316 (1977)
Blacklist	§44-117 (1981)
Discrimination—race, religion, color, sex, handicap, national origin, ancestry	§44-1009 (1981 & Supp. 1983)
—retaliation	§44-1009(a)(4) (1981)
Garnishment	§60-2311 (1983)
Labor union	§§44-809, 44-813 (1981)
—right to work (no union shop)	§§44-802, 44-809(4) (1981)
—testimony	§44-809(1) (1981)
Military service	§48-222 (1983)
Safety in the work place	§§44-609, 44-636 (1981)
—testimony	§44-615 (1981)
Voting—time off	§25-418 (1981)
Wage & hour—testimony	§44-615 (1981)

KENTUCKY (KY. REV. STAT. ANN.)

Subject	Citation
Abortion—refusal or willingness to participate	§311.800(5) (Bobbs-Merrill 1983)
—refusal to undergo	§311.810 (Bobbs-Merrill 1983)
Day of rest	§§436.165(3)(a) (Bobbs-Merrill 1975), 436.165(4)(a) (Bobbs-Merrill Supp. 1982)
Discrimination—race, color, religion, national origin, sex, age	§344.040 (Bobbs-Merrill 1983)
—handicap	§207.130 (Bobbs-Merrill 1982 & Supp. 1982)
—retaliation (conspiracy)	§344.280(1) (Bobbs-Merrill, 1983)
Garnishment	§427.140 (Bobbs-Merrill 1972 & Supp. 1982)

Subject	Citation
Jury service	§§29A.160 (Bobbs-Merrill 1980), 337.415 (Bobbs-Merrill 1983)
Labor union	§336.130 (Bobbs-Merrill 1983)
Military	§38.460 (Bobbs-Merrill 1980)
Safety in the work place	§338.031 (Bobbs-Merrill 1983)
—complaint, testimony	§338.121 (Bobbs-Merrill 1983)
Voting	
—intimidation	§121.310 (Bobbs-Merrill 1982)
—time off	§118.035 (Bobbs-Merrill 1982); KY. CONST. §148
Witnesses—general	§337.415 (Bobbs-Merrill 1983)

LOUISIANA

Subject	Citation
Abortion—refusal to participate	LA. REV. STAT. ANN. §40:1299.31 (West 1977)
Blacklist	LA. REV. STAT. ANN. §23:963 (West 1964)
Day of rest	LA. REV. STAT. ANN. §51:191 (West 1965)
Discrimination—age/ retaliation	LA. REV. STAT. ANN. §§23:972 (West Supp. 1984), 23:893 (West 1964)
—handicap	LA. REV. STAT. ANN. §46:2254 (West 1982 & Supp. 1984)
—sickle cell trait	LA. REV. STAT. ANN. §23-1002 (West Supp. 1984)
Fines against employees prohibited	LA. REV. STAT. ANN. §23:635 (West 1964 & Supp. 1984)
Garnishment	LA. REV. STAT. ANN. §23:731 (West Supp. 1984)
Jury service	LA. REV. STAT. ANN. §23:965 (West Supp. 1984)
Labor union	LA. REV. STAT. ANN. §§23:823; 23:824 (West 1964)
—right to work (no union shop)	LA. REV. STAT. ANN. §§23:983, 23:984 (West Supp. 1984)
Medical exam—payment for	LA. REV. STAT. ANN. §23:897 (West 1964)
Military service	LA. REV. STAT. ANN. §29:38 (West 1975)
Politics—activity, candidacy, affiliation	LA. REV. STAT. ANN. §23:961 (West 1964 & Supp. 1984)
Safety in the work place	LA. REV. STAT. ANN. §23:13 (West 1964 & Supp. 1984)

Subject	*Citation*
Sales from particular seller ...	LA. REV. STAT. ANN. §23:963 (West 1964)
Terminable-at-will except for term or project	LA. CIV. CODE ANN. arts. 164, 2746, 2747, 2748 (West 1952)
—not over ten years	LA. CIV. CODE ANN. art. 167 (West 1952 & Supp. 1984)
Voting—intimidation	LA. REV. STAT. ANN. §23:962 (West 1964)
Wage & hour—labor investigation testimony ..	LA. REV. STAT. ANN. §23:964 (West 1964)
Whistleblowing (environmental)	LA. REV. STAT. ANN. §30:1074 (West Supp. 1984)
Witnesses—general, labor	LA. REV. STAT. ANN. §23:964 (West 1964)
Workers' compensation	LA. REV. STAT. ANN. §23:1361 (West Supp. 1984)

MAINE   (ME. REV. STAT. ANN.)

Abortion—refusal to participate	tit. 22, §1592 (1980)
Blacklist	tit. 17, §401 (1983)
Day of rest	tit. 17, §3201 (1983)
Discrimination—race, color, sex, handicap, national origin, ancestry, religion, age	tit. 5, §4572 (1979 & Supp. 1983–84)
—pregnancy	tit. 5, §4572-A (1979 & Supp. 1983–84)
—retaliation	tit. 5, §4572-E (1979)
Garnishment	tit. 9A, §5-106 (1980)
Jury service	tit. 14, §1218 (1980 & Supp. 1983–84)
Lie detector	tit. 32, §7166 (Supp. 1983–84)
Medical examination— employer payment	tit. 26, §592 (1974)
Military service	tit. 26, §811 (1974)
Personnel file access	tit. 26, §631 (Supp. 1983–84)
Political office	tit. 26, §821 (Supp. 1983–84)
Safety in the work place	tit. 26, §561 (1974)
—complaint, testimony	tit. 26, §570 (Supp. 1983–84)
Service letter	tit. 26, §630 (Supp. 1983–84)
Toxic substances—right to know	tit. 26, §1701 *et seq.* (Supp. 1983–84)
Unlawful order—endangering health or safety	tit. 26, §833 (Supp. 1983–84)

Subject	Citation
Whistleblowing	tit. 26, §833 (Supp. 1983–84)
Workers' compensation	tit. 39, §111 (1978 & Supp. 1983–84)

MARYLAND

Abortion—refusal to participate	MD. HEALTH-GEN. CODE ANN. §20-214(a)(2)(ii) (1982)
—refusal to undergo	MD. HEALTH-GEN. CODE ANN. §20-214(c)(1) (1982)
Day of rest	MD. ANN. CODE art. 27, §492 (1982)
Discrimination—race, color, religion, sex, age, national origin, marital status	MD. ANN. CODE art. 49B, §16 (1979 & Supp. 1983)
—pregnancy	MD. ANN. CODE art. 49B §17 (1979 & Supp. 1983)
—handicap	MD. ANN. CODE art. 30, §§2A, 33(a) (1983), art. 49B §16 (1979 & Supp. 1983)
—retaliation	MD. ANN. CODE art. 49B, §16(2)(f) (1979)
Jury service	MD. CTS. & JUD. PROC. CODE ANN. §8-105 (1984)
Labor union	MD. ANN. CODE art. 100, §64 (1979)
Lie detector	MD. ANN. CODE art. 100, §95 (1979 & Supp. 1983)
Privacy—handicap inquiries not directly material to fitness for job	MD. ANN. CODE art. 100, §95A (1979 & Supp. 1983)
Safety in the work place	MD. ANN. CODE art. 89, §32 (1979 & Supp. 1983)
—complaint of testimony	MD. ANN. CODE art. 89, §43 (1979 & Supp. 1983)
Voting—time off	MD. ANN. CODE art. 33, §§24–26 (1983)
Workers' compensation	MD. ANN. CODE art. 101, §39A (1979 & Supp. 1983)

MASSACHUSETTS   MASS. GEN. LAWS ANN.)

Abortion—refusal to participate	ch. 112, §12(I) (West 1983)
Day of rest	ch. 136, §5 (West 1974 & Supp. 1984–85); ch. 149, §47-51A (West 1976)
Discrimination—race, color, creed, national origin, sex, age	ch. 151B, §4(1) (West 1982)

Subject	Citation
—age	ch. 149, §24A (West 1982)
—handicap	ch. 149, §24K (West 1982 & Supp. 1984–85)
—pregnancy (maternity leave)	ch. 149, §105D (West 1982 & Supp. 1983)
—retaliation	ch. 149, §24G (West 1982)
Fraud	ch. 149, §21 (West 1982)
Jury service	ch. 234A, §61 (West Supp. 1984–85)
Labor union	ch. 149, §§20, 20A, 20D (West 1982)
Lie detector	ch. 149, §19B (West 1982)
Medical examination— employer payment	ch. 149, §159B (West 1982)
Military service	ch. 149, §52A (West 1982)
Notice—reciprocal if forfeiture	ch. 149, §159 (West 1982 & Supp. 1984–85)
Personnel files (medical)— access	ch. 149, §19A (West 1982)
Safety in the work place	ch. 149, §6 *et seq.* (West 1982)
Toxic substances—right to know	1983 Mass. Leg. Serv. ch. 470, at 942 (West), to be codified at MASS. GEN. LAWS ANN. ch. 111F, §1 *et seq.*
Voting—intimidation	ch. 56, §33 (West 1975)
—time off	ch. 149, §178 (West 1982)
Wage & hour—complaint, testimony	ch. 149, §§105B (West 1982), 148A (West Supp. 1983)
Workers' compensation (rehire preference)	ch. 149, §51B (West 1982)
MICHIGAN	(MICH. STAT. ANN.)
Abortion (nondiscrimination)	§3.548 (201d) (Callaghan Supp. 1984–85)
Arrest record (record may be concealed by employee)	§3.548 (205a) (Callaghan 1978 & Supp. 1984–85)
Day of rest (police)	§5.3321 (Callaghan 1982)
Discrimination—race, religion, color, national origin, age, sex, marital status, height, weight	§3.548 (202(1)a) (Callaghan 1978 & Supp. 1984–85)
—handicap	§3.550 (202b) (Callaghan 1978)
—pregnancy	§3.548 (201d) (Callaghan Supp. 1984–85)
—sexual harassment	§§3.548 (201(1)a), 3.548 (103h) (Callaghan Supp. 1984–85)

Subject	Citation
—retaliation	§3.548 (202) (Callaghan 1978 & Supp. 1984–85)
Extortion of job applicants	§§28.583, 28.587(1) (Callaghan 1982)
Fingerprints and photographs—payment for	§28.586(1) (Callaghan 1982)
Fraud	§17.421 (Callaghan 1982)
Garnishment	§§27A.4015 (Callaghan 1980 & Supp. 1984–85), 27A.8307 (Callaghan 1977)
Jury service	§27A.1348 (Callaghan 1976)
Labor union	§17.454(8) (Callaghan 1982)
Lie detector	§18.186(26) (Callaghan 1980 & Supp. 1983–84)
Medical examination—payment for	§28.586(1) (Callaghan 1982)
Military service	§§4.1487(1), 4.1487(3) (Callaghan 1977)
Personnel file access	§17.62(1) (Callaghan 1982)
Safety in the work place	§17.50(11)(a) (Callaghan 1982 & Supp. 1984–85)
—complaint, testimony	§17.50(29)(10) (Callaghan 1982)
Toxic substances—right to know	§17.50(61)(2) (Callaghan 1982)
Whistleblowing	§17.428(9) (Callaghan 1982)
Workers' compensation—consistent discharge to prevent coverage by statute	§17.237 (125) (Callaghan 1982 & Supp. 1983–84)

MINNESOTA (MINN. STAT. ANN.)

Subject	Citation
Abortion—refusal to participate	§145.42(2) (West Supp. 1984)
Benefits—protection from discharge	§181.82 (West Supp. 1984)
Blacklist	§§179.12(6) (West 1966 & Supp. 1984), 179.60 (West 1966)
Day of rest	§624.02 (West 1964)
Discrimination—race, color, creed, religion, national origin, sex, marital status, handicap, public assistance, membership on local commission, age	§363.03(1)(2) (West 1966 & Supp. 1984)

Subject	Citation
—age	§§181.81 (West Supp. 1984), 363.03(1)(2) (West 1966 & Supp. 1984)
—pregnancy	§363.01(29), 363.03(1)(2) (West Supp. 1984)
—retaliation	§363.03(7) (West 1966 & Supp. 1984)
Fraud	§181.64 (West 1966)
Garnishment	§571.61 (West Supp. 1984)
Jury service	§593.50 (West Supp. 1984)
Labor union	§179.10 (West 1966 & Supp. 1984)
Lie detector	§181.75 (West Supp. 1984)
Medical examination— payment for	§181.61 (West 1966)
Military service	§§192.34 (West 1962 & Supp. 1984), 192.265 (West Supp. 1984)
Politics—time off to attend meetings	§202A.135 (West Supp. 1984)
—public officials and legislators	§§210A.09 (West Supp. 1984), 3.082 (West 1977), 3.083 (West 1977 & Supp. 1984)
Safety in the work place	§182.653 (West Supp. 1984)
—complaint, testimony	§182.654(9) (West Supp. 1984)
Toxic substances—right to know	§182.65 *et seq.* (West Supp. 1984)
Voting—intimidation	§211.24 (West 1962)
—time off	§204c.04 (West Supp. 1984)
Wage & hour—complaint, testimony	§179.12(4) (West 1966 & Supp. 1984)
Workers' compensation	§176.82 (West Supp. 1984)
MISSISSIPPI	(MISS. CODE ANN.)
Blacklist (telegraph employees for union membership)	§§77-9-725, 77-9-729 (1972)
Civil rights	§79-1-9 (1972 & Supp. 1983); MISS. CONST. art. 7, §191
Day of rest	§97-23-63 (1972 & Supp. 1983)
Jury service	§13-5-23 (1972 & Supp. 1983)
Labor union	§71-1-47 (1972 & Supp. 1983)
—right to work (no union shop)	§71-1-47 (1972 & Supp. 1983); MISS. CONST. art. 7, §198-A
Military service	§§33-1-15, 33-1-19 (1972 & Supp. 1983)

Subject	Citation
Political rights	§79-1-9 (1972); Miss. Const. art. 7, §191
Social rights	§79-1-9 (1972); Miss. Const. art. 7, §191
Voting—intimidation	§23-3-29 (1972)

MISSOURI (Mo. Ann. Stat.)

Subject	Citation
Abortion—refusal to perform or undergo	§197.032 (Vernon 1983)
Day of rest	§578.115 (Vernon 1979)
Discrimination—race, creed, color, religion, national origin, sex, ancestry, handicap	§296.020(1) (Vernon 1965 & Supp. 1984)
—retaliation	§296.020(4) (Vernon 1965 & Supp. 1984)
Garnishment	§§525.030 (Vernon 1953), 525.030(5) (Supp. 1984)
Labor union	Mo. Const. art. 1 §29
Military service	§41.730 (Vernon 1969)
Politics—candidacy for office, political position, engaging in political activity	§115.637(6) (Vernon 1980 & Supp. 1984)
Safety in the work place	§§282.180 et seq., 292.010 et seq. (Vernon 1965), 292.300 et seq. (Vernon 1965 & Supp. 1984)
Service letter	§290.140 (Vernon 1965 & Supp. 1984)
Voting—intimidation	§§115.635(6), 115.635(8) (Vernon 1980)
—time off	§115.639 (Vernon (1980)
Workers' compensation	§287.780 (Vernon 1965 & Supp. 1984)

MONTANA (Mont. Code Ann.)

Subject	Citation
Abortion—refusal to participate	§50-20-111(3) (1983)
Blacklist	§§39-2-802, 39-2-803 (1983)
Discrimination—race, creed, religion, color, sex, national origin, age, handicap	§§49-1-102, 49-2-303(1)(a) (1983)
—marital status	§49-2-303(1)(a) (1983)
—pregnancy & maternity leave	§§49-2-310, 49-2-311 (1983)
—retaliation	§49-2-301 (1983)

Subject	Citation
Fraud	§39-2-303 (1983)
Garnishment	§39-2-302 (1983)
Lie detector	§39-2-304 (1983)
Medical examination— payment for	§39-2-301 (1983)
Military service	§§10-1-604, 10-2-211 (1983)
Safety in the work place	§50-71-202 (1983)
Service letter	§39-2-801 (1983)
Term—salary period presumed term	§39-2-602 (1983)
Unlawful order	§39-2-404 (1983)
Voting—intimidation	§§13-35-214(2), 13-35-226 (1983)

NEBRASKA (NEB. REV. STAT.)

Subject	Citation
Abortion—refusal to perform	§§28-339, 28-340 (1979)
Discrimination—race, color, religion, sex, disability, marital status, national origin	§48-1104(1) (1978)
—age	§48-1004(1)(a) (1978)
—retaliation	§48-1114 (1978)
Garnishment	§25-1558(c) (1979)
Jury service	§25-1640 (1979 & Supp. 1982)
Labor union	§48-217 (1978); NEB. CONST. art. XV, §13
—right to work (no union shop)	§48-217 (1978); NEB. CONST. art. XV, §13
Medical examination— payment for	§48-221 (1978)
Military service	§§55-161, 55-166 (1978)
Politics (election judge)	§32-1050 (1978)
Safety in the work place	§48-401 *et seq.* (1978)
Service letter	§§48-209, 48-210, 48-211 (1978)
Voting—intimidation	§32-1223 (1978)
—time off	§32-1046 (1978)

NEVADA (NEV. REV. STAT.)

Subject	Citation
Blacklist	§§613.200, 613.210 (1979 & Supp. 1981)
Discrimination—race, color, religion, sex, age, handicap, national origin	§613.330 (1981)
—retaliation	§613.340 (1981)

Subject	Citation
Dishonesty—report to employer	§613.160 (1979)
Extortion of job applicants	§613.120 (1979 & Supp. 1981)
Fraud	§§613.010, 613.030 (1979 & Supp. 1981)
Labor union	§613.130 (1979 & Supp. 1981)
—right to work (no union shop)	§613.250 (1979 & Supp. 1981)
Military service	§412.606 (1979 & Supp. 1981)
Politics—candidate or political activity	§§613.040, 613.070c (1979)
—legislature	§218.044 (1983)
Safety in the work place	§618.375 (1983)
—complaint, testimony	§618.445 (1983)
Sale to employees	§613.140 (1979)
Service letter	§613.210(4) (1979)
Toxic substances—right to know	§613.380 (1983)
Voting—intimidation	§293.585 (1979)
—time off	§293.463 (1983)
Wage & hour—testimony	§608.015 (1983)
Witnesses—general	§50.070 (1981)

Subject	Citation
NEW HAMPSHIRE	(N.H. REV. STAT. ANN.)
Day of rest	§275:32 (1977)
Discrimination—race, color, religion, creed, sex, marital status, age, handicap, national origin	§§354-A:2 (1966 & Supp. 1981), 354-A:8(I) (1966 & Supp. 1981 & 1983)
—retaliation	§354-A:8(VII) (1966)
Extortion of job applicants	§275:6 (1977)
Fraud	§637:8 (1974 & Supp. 1983)
Jury service	§500-A:14 (1983)
Labor union	§275:1 (1977)
Medical examination— payment for	§275:3 (1977)
Military service (not mandatory)	§112:12 (1977)
Personnel files	§275:56 (Supp. 1983)
Safety in the work place	§277:1 *et seq.* (1977)
Toxic substances—right to know	§§277-A:6, 277-A:7 (Supp. 1983)

Subject	*Citation*
NEW JERSEY	(N.J. STAT. ANN.)
Abortion—refusal to perform	§2A:65A-3 (West Supp. 1983–84)
Discrimination—race, creed, color, national origin, ancestry, age, marital status, sex, handicap, draft status, atypical blood trait, religion	§10:5-12(a) (West 1976 & Supp. 1983–84)
—retaliation	§10.5-12(d) (West 1976 & Supp. 1983–84)
Garnishment	§27A:170-90.4 (West Supp. 1983–84)
Jury service (public employees)	§2A:69-5 (West 1976)
Labor union	§§34:12-2, 34:12-3 (West 1965); N.J. CONST. art. 1, §19
Lie detector	§2C:40A-1 (West 1982)
Medical examination— payment for	§34:11-24.1 (West 1965)
Military service	§§10:5-5(g), 10:5-12 (West 1976 & Supp. 1983–84)
Safety in the work place	§34:6A-3 (West Supp. 1983–84)
Sales to employees (control of)	§34-11-21 (West 1965)
Voting—intimidation	§§19:34-27, 19:34-30, 19:34-31 (West 1964)
Wage & hour—complaint, testimony	§34:11-56(a)24 (West Supp. 1983–84)
Workers' compensation	§34:15-39.1 (West Supp. 1983–84)
NEW MEXICO	(N.M. STAT. ANN.)
Blacklist	§30-13-3 (1978)
Discrimination—race, color, religion, sex, age, handicap, national origin, ancestry	§28-1-7A (1983 & Supp. 1984)
—retaliation	§28-1-7I(2) (1978)
Jury service	§38-5-18 (Supp. 1983)
Labor union	§50-2-1(B) (1978 & Supp. 1983)
Military service	§§28-15-1, 28-15-2 (1978)
Safety in the work place	§50-9-5 (1978 & Supp. 1983)
—complaint, testimony	§50-9-25 (1978 & Supp. 1983)
Sales to employees	§30-13-5 (1978)
Voting—intimidation	§1-20-13 (Supp. 1978)
—time off	§1-12-42 (Supp. 1978)

Subject	*Citation*
NEW YORK	
Abortion—refusal to participate	N.Y. CIV. RIGHTS LAW §79(i) (Consol. 1982)
Arrest or irrelevant criminal record	N.Y. EXEC. LAW §296(16) (Consol. 1983); N.Y. CORRECT. LAW §752 (Consol. 1977 & Supp. 1983); N.Y. EXEC. LAW §296(15) (Consol. 1983)
Day of rest	N.Y. LAB. LAW §160 *et seq.* (Consol. 1983 & Supp. 1983); N.Y. EXEC. LAW §296(10) (Consol. 1983)
Discrimination—race, creed, color, national origin, sex, marital status, handicap	N.Y. EXEC. LAW §296(1)(a) (Consol. 1983)
—age	N.Y. EXEC. LAW §§296(1)(a), 296(3a)(a) (Consol. 1983)
—retaliation	N.Y. EXEC. LAW §§296(1)(e), 296(3)(a)(c) (Consol. 1983)
Eavesdropping (organized labor activity)	N.Y. LAB. LAW §704(1) (Consol. 1983)
Extortion of job applicants	N.Y. LAB. LAW §198b (Consol. 1983)
Fingerprints prohibited	N.Y. LAB. LAW §201a (Consol. 1983)
Garnishment	N.Y. CIV. PRAC. LAW §5252 (Consol. 1978)
Jury service	N.Y. JUD. LAW §519 (Consol. 1983)
Labor union	N.Y. LAB. LAW §703 (Consol. 1983); N.Y. CONST. art. 1, §17
Lie detector	N.Y. LAB. LAW §§736, 739 (Consol. 1983)
Medical examination— payment for	N.Y. LAB. LAW §201b (Consol. 1983)
Military service	N.Y. MIL. LAW §§251, 252 (Consol. 1979)
Retaliation—exercise of rights under labor code ..	N.Y. LAB. LAW §§1, 215 (Consol. 1983)
Safety in the work place	N.Y. LAB. LAW §200 (Consol. 1983 & Supp. 1983)
—complaint, testimony	N.Y. LAB. LAW §215 (Consol. 1983)
Sales to employees	N.Y. GEN. BUS. §396(i) (Consol. 1980)
Toxic substances—right to know	N.Y. LAB. LAW §880 (Consol. 1983)
Voting—intimidation	N.Y. ELEC. LAW §§17-150(3), 17-154(3) (Consol. 1978)

Subject	*Citation*
—time off	N.Y. ELEC. LAW §§3-110, 17-118 (Consol. 1978)
Wage & hour—complaint, testimony	N.Y. LAB. LAW §215 (Consol. 1983)
Workers' compensation	N.Y. WORK. COMP. LAW §120 (Consol. 1982 & Supp. 1983)

NORTH CAROLINA   (N.C. GEN. STAT.)

Abortion—refusal to perform	§14-45.1(e) (1981 & Supp. 1983)
Blacklist	§14-355 (1981 & Supp. 1983)
Discrimination—race, religion, color, national origin, age, sex	§143-422.1 (1983)
—handicap	§§143-422.1 (1983), 168-6 (1982)
—sickle cell trait	§95-28.1 (1981)
Labor union	§95-81 (1981 & Supp. 1983)
—right to work (no union shop)	§95-80 (1981)
Medical examination— payment for	§14-357.1 (1981)
Military service	§127A-20 (1981)
Safety in the work place	§95-129(1) (1981)
—complaint, testimony	§95-130(8) (1981)
Workers' compensation	§97-6.1 (1979 & Supp. 1983)

NORTH DAKOTA   (N.D. CENT. CODE)

Abortion—refusal to participate	§23-16-14 (1978)
Blacklist	N.D. CONST. art. XII, §17
Day of rest	§12.1-30-01 (1976)
Discrimination—race, color, religion, sex, marital status, national origin, handicap, public assistance	§14-02.4-03 (Supp. 1983)
—age	§§14-02.4-03 (Supp. 1983), 34-01-17 (1980)
—pregnancy	§§14-02.4-02 (14), 14-02.4-03 (Supp. 1983)
—"moral" work place	§36-06-05(2) (1980)
—retaliation	§14-02.4-18 (Supp. 1983)
Garnishment	§32-09.1-18 (Supp. 1983)
Jury service	§27.09.1-17 (1974 & Supp. 1983)

Subject	*Citation*
Labor—right to work (no union shop)	§34-01-14 (1980 & Supp. 1983)
Medical examination—payment for	§34-01-15 (1980)
Military service (public employees)	§37-01-25 (1980)
Safety in the work place	§34-06-05(2) (1980)
Term—at-will rule	§34-03-01 (1980)
—unenforceable against employees beyond 2 years	§34-03-01 (1980)
Unlawful order	§34-02-08 (1980)
Wage & hour—complaint, testimony	§34-06-18 (1980)

OHIO (OHIO REV. CODE ANN.)

Abortion—refusal to participate	§4731.91(D) (Baldwin 1979)
Blacklist	§1331.03 (Page 1979)
Discrimination—race, color, religion, sex, national origin, handicap, ancestry, age	§4112.02 (Baldwin 1983 & Supp. 1983)
—age	§§4101.17, 4112.02 (Baldwin 1983)
—pregnancy	§§4101.01(B), 4112.02 (Baldwin 1983)
—retaliation	§4112.02(I) (Baldwin 1983)
Garnishment —general	§2715.01 (Page 1981)
—for marital support	§2301.39 (Page 1981)
Jury service	§2313.18 (Baldwin Supp. 1982)
Labor union	§4113.02 (Baldwin 1983)
Medical examination—payment for	§4113.21 (Baldwin 1983)
Safety in the work place	§4101.12 (Baldwin 1983)
Sales to employees	§4113.18 (Baldwin 1983)
Voting—intimidation	§3599.05 (Baldwin 1982)
—time off	§3599.06 (Baldwin 1982)
Wage & hour—complaint, testimony	§4111.13 (Baldwin 1983)
Workers' compensation	§4123.90 (Baldwin 1983)

OKLAHOMA (OKLA. STAT. ANN.)

Abortion	tit. 63, §1-741(B) (West Supp. 1983–84)

Subject	Citation
Jury service	§10.090 (1983)
Labor union	§661.010 (1981)
Lie detector/breathalyzer	§§659.225, 659.227 (1983)
Medical examination— payment for	§659.330 (1983)
Military service (public employee)	§408.240 (1983)
Safety in the work place	§654.010 (1981)
—complaint, testimony	§654.062 (1981)
Wage & hour—complaint, testimony	§653.060 (1983)
Witnesses—legislative	§659.270 (1983)
Workers' compensation	§659.410 (1983)

PENNSYLVANIA (PA. STAT. ANN.)

Subject	Citation
Abortion—refusal to participate	tit. 18, §3213(d) (Purdon 1983)
Arrest record and misdemeanors	tit. 18, §9125 (1979)
Day of rest (theater employees)	tit. 43, §481 (Purdon 1964)
Discrimination—race, color, religious creed, ancestry, age, sex, national origin, handicap	tit. 43, §955(a) (Purdon 1964 & Supp. 1983–84)
—high school certificate in lieu of high school degree	tit. 43, §955(k) (Purdon Supp. 1983–84)
—retaliation	tit. 43, §955(d) (Purdon 1964)
Extortion of job applicants	tit. 18, §7322 (Purdon 1983)
Jury service	tit. 45, §4563 (Purdon 1981 & Supp. 1983–84)
Labor union	tit. 43, §206(e) (Purdon 1964)
Lie detector	tit. 18, §7321 (Purdon 1983)
Medical examination— payment for	tit. 43, §1002 (Purdon 1964)
Military service	tit. 51, §§7304, 7309 (Purdon 1976)
Personnel files	tit. 43, §1322 (Purdon Supp. 1983–84)
Safety in the work place	tit. 43, §25-2 (Purdon 1964 & Supp. 1983–84)

RHODE ISLAND (R.I. GEN. LAWS)

Subject	Citation
Abortion—refusal to participate	§23-17-11 (1979)
Blacklist	§28-7-13(9) (1979)

Subject	Citation
Day of rest	§§25-3-3, 25-3-9 (1979)
Discrimination—race, color, religion, sex, age, national origin	§28-5-7(A)(1) (1979 & Supp. 1983)
—handicap	§§28-5-7(A)(2), 42-87-3 (Supp. 1983)
—retaliation	§28-5-7(E) (1979 & Supp. 1983)
Jury service	§9-9-28 (Supp. 1983)
Labor union	§28-7-12 (1979)
Lie detector	§28-6.1-1 (1979)
Medical examination— payment for	§28-6.2-1 (1979)
Military service	§30-11-2 *et seq.* (1982)
Safety in the work place	§28-20-8 (1979)
—complaint, testimony	§28-20-21 (1979)
Toxic substances—right to know	§28-21-1 *et seq.* (Supp. 1983)
Voting—influence	§17-23-6 (1981)

SOUTH CAROLINA	(S.C. CODE ANN.)
Abortion—refusal to participate	§44-41-50(c) (Law. Co-op. 1976)
Day of rest	§53-1-40 (Law. Co-op. 1976 & Supp. 1983)
Discrimination—race, color, creed, sex, age, national origin	§1-13-80(a)(1) (Law. Co-op. 1976 & Supp. 1983)
—pregnancy	§§1-13-30, 1-13-80(a)(1) (Law. Co-op. 1976 & Supp. 1983)
—retaliation	§1-13-80(b)(2) (Law. Co-op. 1976 & Supp. 1983)
Labor union	§§41-1-20, 41-7-10 (Law. Co-op. 1976 & Supp. 1983)
—right to work (no union shop)	§41-7-20 (Law. Co-op. 1976)
Military service	§§25-1-2310, 25-1-2330 (Law. Co-op. Supp. 1983)
Politics—political opinions or exercise of political rights	§16-17-560 (Law. Co-op. 1976)
Safety in the work place	§41-15-80(1) (Law. Co-op. 1976)
—complaint, testimony	§§41-15-510, 41-15-520 (Law. Co-op. 1976 & Supp. 1983)
Voting—influence	§17-23-6 (Law. Co-op. 1981)

Subject	Citation
SOUTH DAKOTA	(S.D. CODIFIED LAWS ANN.)
Abortion—refusal to participate	§34-23A-13 (1977)
Discrimination—race, color, creed, religion, sex, ancestry, national origin	§20-13-11 (1979)
—retaliation	§20-13-26 (1979 & Supp. 1983)
Jury service	§16-13-41.1 (1979)
Labor union	§60-9A-2 (1978)
—right to work (no union shop)	§60-8-3 (1978 & Supp. 1983)
Medical examination—payment for	§60-11-2 (1978)
Military service	§33-17-15 (1977)
Term—salary period presumed	§60-1-3 (1978 & Supp. 1983)
—monthly period secondary presumption	§60-1-4 (1978)
—no enforcement against employee beyond 2 years	§60-2-6 (1978)
Unlawful order	§60-2-7 (1978)
Voting—time off	§12-3-5 (1982)
Wage & hour—complaint testimony	§60-11-17.1 (1978)
TENNESSEE	(TENN. CODE ANN.)
Abortion—refusal to perform	§39-4-204 (1982)
Blacklist	§50-1-202 (1983)
Discrimination—race, creed, color, religion, sex, national origin, age	§4-21-105 (1979 & Supp. 1983)
—handicap	§8-50-103 (1980 & Supp. 1983)
—retaliation	§4-21-114 (1979)
Fraud	§50-1-102 (1983)
Jury service	§§22-4-108 (1980 & Supp. 1983), 39-5-523 (1982 & Supp. 1983)
Labor union	§§50-1-201, 50-1-202 (1983)
—right to work (no union shop)	§50-1-203 (1983)
Medical examination—payment for	§50-1-302 (1983)
Military service	§58-1-604 (1980)
Personnel files (public employees)	§8-50-108 (1980)

Subject	*Citation*
Safety in the work place	§50-3-105 (1983)
—complaint, testimony	§§50-3-106(7), 50-3-409 (1983)
Sales to employees	§50-2-106 (1983)
—dictate choice of physician	§50-1-302 (1983)
Voting—intimidation	§§2-19-134, 2-19-135 (1979)
—time off	§2-1-106 (1979)

TEXAS

Abortion—refusal or willingness to participate	TEX. REV. CIV. STAT. ANN. art. 4512.7 (Vernon Supp. 1982–83)
Blacklist	TEX. REV. CIV. STAT. ANN. art. 5196(1) (Vernon 1971 & Supp. 1982–83)
Discrimination—race, color, handicap, religion, sex, national origin, age	H.B. No. 14, 1983 Tex. Sess. Law Serv. ch. 7, at 45 (Vernon), to be codified at TEX. REV. CIV. STAT. ANN. art. 5221K, §5.01(1)
—pregnancy	H.B. No. 14, 1983 Tex. Sess. Law Serv. ch. 7, at 38, 45 (Vernon), to be codified at TEX. REV. CIV. STAT. ANN. art. 5221.K, §§1.04(c), 5.01(1)
—retaliation	H.B. No. 14, 1983 Tex. Sess. Law Serv. ch. 7, at p. 46 (Vernon), to be codified at TEX. REV. CIV. STAT. ANN. art. 5221K, §5.05(a)(1)
Jury service	TEX. REV. CIV. STAT. ANN. art. 5207b (Vernon Supp. 1982–83)
Labor union	TEX. REV. CIV. STAT. ANN. arts. 5196a, 5207a (Vernon 1971 & Supp. 1982–83)
—right to work (no union shop)	TEX. REV. CIV. STAT. ANN. art. 5154g (Vernon 1971 & Supp. 1982–83)
Military service	TEX. REV. CIV. STAT. ANN. art. 5765, §§7, 7(a) (Vernon Supp. 1984)
Politics—attend precinct convention	TEX. ELEC. CODE art. 13.34a (Vernon 1967 & Supp. 1982–83)
Safety in the work place	TEX. REV. CIV. STAT. ANN. art. 5182a §3(a) (Vernon 1971 & Supp. 1982–83)
Service letter	TEX. REV. CIV. STAT. ANN. art. 5196 (Vernon 1971 & Supp. 1982–83)*
Voting—time off	TEX. ELEC. CODE art. 15.14 (Vernon Supp. 1984)

---

*Held unconstitutional in *St. Louis S. Ry. v. Griffin*, 106 Tex. 477, 171 S.W. 703 (1914).

Subject	Citation
Workers' compensation	TEX. REV. CIV. STAT. ANN. art. 8307c (Vernon Supp. 1984)

UTAH (UTAH CODE ANN.)

Subject	Citation
Abortion—refusal to participate	§76-7-306(1) (1978)
Blacklist	§§34-24-1, 34-24-2 (1974), UTAH CONST. art. XII §19, art. XVI §4 (1971)
Discrimination—race, color, age, sex, religion, ancestry, national origin, handicap	§34-35-6 (1974 & Supp. 1983)
Garnishment	§70B-5-106 (1981)
Jury service	§78-46-21 (Supp. 1983)
Labor union	§§34-19-1 (1974 & Supp. 1983), 34-19-13, 34-20-7 (1974)
—right to work (no union shop).......................	§34-34-4 (1974)
Lie detector	§34-37-16(2) (Supp. 1983)
Medical examination— payment for	§34-33-1 (1974)
Safety in the work place	§35-9-5 (1974)
—complaint, testimony	§35-9-11(2)(a) (1974)
Voting—intimidation	UTAH CONST. art. XVI, §3 (1971)*
—time off	§20-13-18 (1976)
Wage & hour—testimony	§34-22-12 (1974)

VERMONT (VT. STAT. ANN.)

Subject	Citation
Discrimination—race, color, ancestry, national origin, sex, birthplace, age, handicap	tit. 21, §495(1) (1978 & Supp. 1983)
—retaliation	tit. 21, §495(5) (1978 & Supp. 1983)
Garnishment	tit. 12, §3172 (Supp. 1983)
Jury service	tit. 21, §499 (1978)
Labor union	tit. 21, §1503 (1978 & Supp. 1983)
Medical examination— payment for	tit. 21, §301 (1978)
Military service	tit. 21, §§491, 492 (1978)
Politics—public office	tit. 21, §496 (Supp. 1983)
Safety in the work place	tit. 21, §223 (1978 & Supp. 1983)

---

*"Legislature shall prohibit political control of employees."

Subject	*Citation*
—complaint, testimony	tit. 21, §231 (1978)
Voting—intimidation	tit. 17, §2017 (1982)
Witnesses—general	tit. 21, §499 (1978)

VIRGINIA (VA. CODE)

Subject	Citation
Abortion—refusal to participate	§18.2-75 (1982)
Arrest or juvenile record	§19.2-392.1 *et seq.* (1983)
Blacklist	§40.1-27 (1981)
Day of rest	§40.1-28.1 (1981)
Discrimination—race, religion, color, sex, national origin, (state contractors)	§2.1-374 (1979)
—handicap	§40.1-28.7 (1981 & Supp. 1983)
Garnishment	§34-29(f) (1976 & Supp. 1983)
Jury service	§18.2-465.1 (1982)
Labor union	§40.1-58 (1981)
—right to work (no union shop)	§40.1-61 (1981)
Lie detector	§40.1-51.4:3 (1981)
Medical examination— payment for	§40.1-28 (1981 & Supp. 1983)
Military service	§44-98 (1981)
Safety in the work place	§40.1-51.1 (1981)
—complaint, testimony	§40.1-51.2:1 (1981)
Workers' compensation	§65.1-40.1 (Supp. 1983)

WASHINGTON (WASH. REV. CODE ANN.)

Subject	Citation
Abortion—refusal to participate	§9.02.080 (West 1977)
Blacklist	§49.44.010 (West 1962 & Supp. 1984–85)
Discrimination—sex, marital status, race, creed, color, national origin, handicap	§49.60.180(2) (West 1962 & Supp. 1984–85)
—age	§§49.44.090, 49.60.180(2) (West 1962 & Supp. 1984–85)
—retaliation	§49.60.210 (West 1962 & Supp. 1984–85)
Garnishment	§7.33.160 (West Supp. 1984–85)
Labor union	§§49.32.030, 49.36.010 (West 1962 & Supp. 1984–85)
Lie detector	§49.44.120 (West Supp. 1984–85)

Subject	Citation
Military service	§§38.40.040 (West 1964), 38.24.060 (West Supp. 1984–85)
Safety in the work place	§49.16.030 (West 1962 & Supp. 1984–85)
—testimony	§49.12.100 (West 1962 & Supp. 1984–85)
Wage & hour—complaint or testimony	§49.46.100 (West 1962)

WEST VIRGINIA   (W. Va. Code)

Subject	Citation
Arrest record—see juvenile record	
Benefits—reduction while disabled	§23-5A-2 (Supp. 1983)
Day of rest	§61-10-25 (1977)
Discrimination—race, religion, color, national origin, ancestry, sex, age, handicap	§§5-11-3(h), 5-11-9(a) (1979 & Supp. 1983)
—retaliation	§5-11-9(i)(3) (1979 & Supp. 1983)
Jury service	§52-3-1 (1981)
Juvenile record	§49-5-17 (1980 & Supp. 1983)
Labor union	§21-1A-4 (1981)
Lie detector	§21-5-5b (Supp. 1983)
Medical examination— payment for	§21-3-17 (1981)
Military service	§15-1F-8 (1979)
Politics—legislators	§6-5-11 (1979)
Safety in the work place	§21-3-1 (1981 & Supp. 1983)
Sales to employees	§21-5-5 (1981)
Toxic substances—right to know	§21-3-18 (1981 & Supp. 1983)
Voting—time off	§3-1-42 (1979)
Workers' compensation	§23-5A-1 (1981)

WISCONSIN   (Wis. Stat.)

Subject	Citation
Abortion—refusal to participate	§140.42 (1981)
Arrest or criminal record	§111.321 (1981)
Blacklist	§134.02 (1981)
Day of rest	§103.85 (1981)
Discrimination—race, creed, color, handicap, marital status, sex, national origin, ancestry, age	§§111.321, 111.322(1) (1981)

Subject	Citation
—sexual orientation	§111.36(1)(d)(1) (1981)
—sexual harassment	§111.36(b) (1981)
—pregnancy	§111.36(a) (1981)
—retaliation	§111.322(3) (1981)
Garnishment	§812.235 (1981)
Grooming—notice of requirement	§103.14 (1981)
Jury service	§756.25(1) (1981)
Labor union	§§103.46, 103.52 (1981)
Lie detector	§111.37 (1981)
Medical examination— payment for	§103.37 (1981)
Military service	§21.145 (1981)
Notice—reciprocal if forfeiture	§103.17 (1981)
Personnel records—access	§103.13 (1981)
Safety in the work place	§101.11 (1981)
—complaint, testimony	§101.595 (1981)
Toxic substances—right to know	§101.58 *et seq.* (1981)
Voting—intimidation	§103.18 (1981)
—time off	§6.76 (1981)
Witnesses—general (criminal)	§103.87 (1981)
Workers' compensation—loss of insurance exemption ..	§102.31 (4) (1981)
WYOMING	(WYO. STAT.)
Abortion—refusal to participate	§35-6-106 (1977)
Discrimination—sex, race, creed, color, national origin, ancestry	§27-9-105 (1983)
Jury service	§1-11-401 (Supp. 1983)
Labor union	§27-7-110 (1983)
—right to work (no union shop)	§§27-7-109, 27-7-111 (1983)
Military service	§19-2-505 (1977)
Safety in the work place	§27-11-105(a)(xiv) (1983)
—complaint, testimony	§27-11-109(e) (1983)
Voting—intimidation	§22-26-116 (1977)
—time off	§22-2-111 (1977)
Wage & hour—equal pay retaliation	§27-4-304 (1983)

Appendix B

Three State Whistleblowers' Protection Acts

MICHIGAN'S WHISTLEBLOWERS' PROTECTION ACT

MICH. STAT. ANN.:

§ 17.428(1) Definitions

As used in this act:

(a) "Employee" means a person who performs a service for wages or other remuneration under a contract of hire, written or oral, express or implied. Employee includes a person employed by the state or a political subdivision of the state except state classified civil service.

(b) "Employer" means a person who has 1 or more employees. Employer includes an agent of an employer and the state or a political subdivision of the state.

(c) "Person" means an individual, sole proprietorship, partnership, corporation, association, or any other legal entity.

(d) "Public body" means all of the following:

(i) A state officer, employee, agency, department, division, bureau, board, commission, council, authority, or other body in the executive branch of state government.

(ii) An agency, board, commission, council, member, or employee of the legislative branch of state government.

(iii) A county, city, township, village, intercounty, intercity, or regional governing body, a council, school district, special district, or municipal corporation, or a board, department, commission, council, agency, or any member or employee thereof.

(iv) Any other body which is created by state or local authority or which is primarily funded by or through state or local authority, or any member or employee of that body.

(v) A law enforcement agency or any member or employee of a law enforcement agency.

(vi) The judiciary and any member or employee of the judiciary.

§ 17.428(2) Report of violation of law; prohibited conduct on part of employer

An employer shall not discharge, threaten, or otherwise discriminate against an employee regarding the employee's compensation, terms, conditions, location, or privileges of employment because the employee, or a person acting on behalf of the employee, reports or is about to report, verbally or in writing, a violation or a suspected violation of a law or regulation or rule promulgated pursuant to law of this state, a political subdivision of this state, or the United States to a public body, unless the employee knows that the report is false, or because an employee is requested by a public body to participate in an investigation, hearing, or inquiry held by that public body, or a court action.

§ 17.428(3) Civil action, alleged violation

(1) A person who alleges a violation of this act may bring a civil action for appropriate injunctive relief, or actual damages, or both within 90 days after the occurrence of the alleged violation of this act.

Commencement of action, county. (2) An action commenced pursuant to subsection (1) may be brought in the circuit court for the county where the alleged violation occurred, the county where the complainant resides, or the county where the person against whom the civil complaint is filed resides or has his or her principal place of business.

Damages, definition. (3) As used in subsection (1), "damages" means damages for injury or loss caused by each violation of this act, including reasonable attorney fees.

Necessary showing. (4) An employee shall show by clear and convincing evidence that he or she or a person acting on his or her behalf was about to report, verbally or in writing, a violation or a suspected violation of a law of this state, a political subdivision of this state, or the United States to a public body.

§ 17.428(4) Judgment order, contents; award

A court, in rendering a judgment in an action brought pursuant to this act, shall order, as the court considers appropriate, reinstatement of the employee, the payment of back wages, full reinstatement of fringe benefits and seniority rights, actual damages, or any combination of these remedies. A court may also award the complainant all or a portion of the costs of litigation, including reasonable attorney fees and witness fees, if the court determines that the award is appropriate.

§ 17.428(5) Civil fine, disposition

(1) A person who violates this act shall be liable for a civil fine of not more than $500.00.

(2) A civil fine which is ordered pursuant to this act shall be submitted to the state treasurer for deposit in the general fund.

§ 17.428(6) Construction of act, collective bargaining agreement; disclosures affecting confidentiality of communications

This act shall not be construed to diminish or impair the rights of a person under any collective bargaining agreement nor to permit disclosures which would diminish or impair the rights of any person to the continued protection of confidentiality of communications where statute or common law provides such protection.

§ 17.428(7) Construction of act, compensation for participation in investigation

This act shall not be construed to require an employer to compensate an employee for participation in an investigation, hearing or inquiry held by a public body in accordance with section 2 of this act.

§ 17.428(8) Posting notices, protections and obligations of act

An employer shall post notices and use other appropriate means to keep his or her employees informed of their protections and obligations under this act.

§ 17.428(9) Short title

This act shall be known and may be cited as "the whistleblowers' protection act".

Connecticut's Whistleblowers' Protection Act

Conn. Gen. Stat. Ann.:

§ 31-51m. Protection of employee who discloses employer's illegal activities. Civil action

(a) As used in this section and section 31-278:

(1) "Person" means one or more individuals, partnerships, associations, corporations, business trusts, legal representatives or any organized group of persons;

(2) "Employer" means a person engaged in business who has employees, including any political subdivision of the state but excluding the state; (3) "Employee" means any person engaged in service to an employer in a business of his employer;

(4) "Public body" means any public agency, as defined in subsection (a) of section 1-18a, or any employee, member or officer thereof.

(b) No employer shall discharge, discipline or otherwise penalize any employee because the employee, or a person acting on behalf of the employee, reports, verbally or in writing, a violation or a suspected violation of any state or federal law or regulation or any municipal ordinance or regulation to a public body, or because an employee is requested by a public body to participate in an investigation, hearing or inquiry held by that public body, or a court action. The provisions of this subsection shall not be applicable when the employee knows that such report is false.

(c) Any employee who is discharged, disciplined or otherwise penalized by his employer in violation of the provisions of subsection (b) may, after exhausting all available administrative remedies, bring a civil action, within ninety days of the date of the final administrative determination or within ninety days of such violation, whichever is later, in the superior court for the judicial district where the violation is alleged to have occurred or where the employer has its principal office, for the reinstatement of his previous job, payment of back wages and reestablishment of employee benefits to which he would have otherwise been entitled if such violation had not occurred. An employee's recovery from any such action shall be limited to such items, provided the court may allow to the prevailing party his costs, together with reasonable attorney's fees to be taxed by the court. Any employee found to have knowingly made a false report shall be subject to disciplinary action by his employer up to and including dismissal.

(d) This section shall not be construed to diminish or impair the rights of a person under any collective bargaining agreement.

MAINE'S WHISTLEBLOWERS' PROTECTION ACT

ME. REV. STAT. ANN., TIT. 26:

§ 831. Short title

This subchapter may be cited as the "Whistleblowers' Protection Act."

§ 832. Definitions

As used in this subchapter, unless the context indicates otherwise, the following terms have the following meanings.

1. Employee. "Employee" means a person who performs a service for wages or other remuneration under a contract of hire, written or oral, expressed or implied, but does not include an independent contractor. Employee includes a person employed by the State or a political subdivision of the State.

2. Employer. "Employer" means a person who has one or more employees. Employer includes an agent of an employer and the State, or a political subdivision of the State.

3. Person. "Person" means an individual, sole proprietorship, partnership, corporation, association or any other legal entity.

4. Public body. "Public body" means all of the following:

A. A state officer, employee, agency, department, division, bureau, board, commission, council, authority or other body in the executive branch of State Government;

B. An agency, board, commission, council, member or employee of the legislative branch of State Government;

C. A county, municipal, village, intercounty, intercity or regional governing body, a council, school district or municipal corporation, or a board, department, commission, council, agency or any member or employee thereof;

D. Any other body which is created by state or local authority or which is primarily funded by or through state or local authority, or any member or employee of that body;

E. A law enforcement agency or any member or employee of a law enforcement agency; and

F. The judiciary and any member or employee of the judiciary.

§ 833. Discharge of, threats to or discrimination against employee for reporting violations of law or refusing to carry out illegal directives

An employer shall not discharge, threaten or otherwise discriminate against an employee regarding the employee's compensation, terms, conditions, location or privileges of employment because the employee, acting in good faith, or a person acting on behalf of the employee, reports verbally or in writing, what the employee has reasonable cause to believe to be a violation of a law or rule promulgated pursuant to the laws of this State, a political subdivision of this State or the United States to his employer or a public body, or because an employee is requested by a public body to participate in an investigation, hearing or inquiry held by that public body, or a court action. This paragraph does not apply to an employee who has reported or caused to be reported what he has reasonable cause to believe to be a violation to a public body, unless the employee has first brought the alleged violation to the attention of a person having supervisory authority with the employer, and has allowed the employer a reasonable opportunity to correct that violation. The requirements of the foregoing sentence do not apply when the employee has specific reason to believe that reports of violation to his employer will not result in promptly remedying the violation.

An employee mandated to report suspected abuse, neglect or exploitation under Title 22, section 3477 or 4011 shall follow the requirements set forth in those sections for those circumstances. An employer shall not discharge, threaten or otherwise discriminate against an employee regarding the employee's compensation, terms, conditions, location or privileges of employment because the employee followed the requirements of those sections.

An employer shall not discharge, threaten or otherwise discriminate against an employee regarding the employee's compensation, terms, conditions, location or privileges of employment because the employee has refused to carry out a directive which in fact violates a law or rule promulgated pursuant to the laws of this State, a political subdivision of this State or the United States, when that violation would put at risk the health or safety of that employee or any other individual.

§ 834. Civil actions for injunctive relief or other remedies

An employee who alleges a violation of his rights under section 823 and who has first made a reasonable effort to maintain or restore his rights through any grievance procedure or similar process which may be available at his place of employment may bring a civil action for appropriate injunctive relief and other remedies provided in section 825 within 90 days after the occurrence of that alleged violation or, if a grievance procedure or similar process is used, within 60 days after the grievance procedure or similar process terminates without resolution. The action may be brought in the Superior Court for the county where the alleged violation occurred, the county where the complainant resides or the county where the person against whom the civil complaint is filed resides or has his principal place of business.

An employee shall establish each and every element of his case, as set out in section 823, by a preponderance of the evidence.

§ 835. Remedies ordered by court

A court, in rendering a judgment in an action brought pursuant to this subchapter, shall order, as the court considers appropriate, reinstatement of the employee, the payment of back wages, full reinstatement of fringe benefits and seniority rights or any combination of these remedies. A court may also award the prevailing party all or a portion of the costs of litigation, including reasonable attorneys' fees and witness fees, if the court determines that the award is appropriate.

§ 836. Penalties for violation

A person who violates section 829 is liable for a civil fine of $10 for each day of willful violation which shall not be suspended. Any civil fine imposed under this section shall be submitted to the Treasurer of State for deposit to the General Fund.

§ 837. Collective bargaining rights

This subchapter shall not be construed to diminish or impair the rights of a person under any collective bargaining agreement.

§ 838. Compensation for employee participation in investigation, hearing or inquiry

This subchapter shall not be construed to require an employer to compensate an employee for participation in an investigation, hearing or inquiry held by a public body in accordance with section 823.

§ 839. Notices of employee protections and obligations

An employer shall post such notices as are prescribed by the Department of Labor as a means of keeping his employees informed of their protections and obligations under this subchapter.

§ 840. Jury trial; common law rights

Any action brought under this subchapter may be heard by a jury. Nothing in this subchapter may be construed to derogate any common-law rights of an employee.

Appendix C

Measuring Pecuniary Damages in Employment Actions*

The use of economists to value pecuniary damages in personal injury and death actions has become commonplace during the past two decades. Before that, economic testimony was confined largely to antitrust and business law suits. When brought to bear in personal injury and death actions, economic testimony often concerns the pecuniary value of human capital. That is, the economist estimates the present value of the money and non-money (fringe benefit) earnings a worker would have been expected to enjoy had his working life not ended prematurely.

The economist plays a similar role in employment actions. Specifically, the economist presents evidence regarding two sets of estimated present values. One set relates to what the present value of the pecuniary potential of the worker in question would be if the actionable event had not occurred. The second set relates to the pecuniary potential of the worker given that the event did occur. The difference between the two present value estimates is the measure of pecuniary damages associated with the occurrence of the actionable event.

The following discussion examines how the lawyer for the defendant or the plaintiff can utilize economic analysis to obtain a useful appraisal of the pecuniary losses that properly may be associated with an employment action. The first section introduces a general principle for quantifying pecuniary damages in employment actions and outlines its implementation. The second section explores the issues involved in estimating the present value of a worker's future earnings. The third section illustrates how the techniques of measurement are applied in a concrete case. The final section considers the limitations upon the economist—what he can do and what he cannot do.

---

*This section was contributed by William R. Bryan and Charles M. Linke, Professors of Finance, University of Illinois (Urbana-Champaign).

General Theory of Loss and Its Implementation

Employment actions are not fundamentally different from other cases involving damage issues. As a first step, a theory of loss must be articulated. While legal guidelines may conflict with economic reasoning, generally both legal and economic logic suggest the "with and without" theory of damages for employment actions. The "with and without" principle is a shorthand expression referring to comparative cost-benefit analysis. The power of this principle emerges from its straightforward statement of the problem, namely, how does the compensation that could reasonably have been expected without the occurrence of the event in dispute compare to the compensation that can reasonably be expected with the occurrence of the event? As stated above, it is the difference between the present values of these two pecuniary values that is the measure of pecuniary damages in an employment action.

Stating the with-and-without principle of cost-benefit analysis is not difficult. Implementation, however, is a challenging three-stage process. First, the elements of compensation associated with an individual's employment on both a pre-event and post-event basis must be identified. Second, the pecuniary value of these elements of compensation must be estimated. Finally, the pecuniary value estimates must be converted to their present-day values. The second and third stages are discussed in the next main section. The following subsection discusses the first stage.

Elements of Compensation

A worker's earnings are composed of two elements, money earnings and nonmoney earnings. Money earnings are simply the gross dollar earnings a worker sees on his paycheck, corresponding to the W-2 form(s) he files each year with the Internal Revenue Service. Nonmoney earnings consist of the value of the payments an employer makes to an employee in the form of employer-provided (or employer-subsidized) health insurance, retirement plan, savings plan, stock option plan, and the like.

An appraisal of a worker's earnings potential would be incomplete if the value of nonmoney earnings or fringe benefits were ignored. Some fringe benefit values are already reflected in a worker's money earnings record. Such benefits would include paid vacations and holidays, sick leave, overtime or shift premium payments, and performance bonuses. Other fringe benefits such as medical care and other insurance coverages for the worker and his eligible dependents, pension or retirement plans, savings and stock option plans, and personal use of an employer-provided automobile are not reflected in a worker's money earnings record. Nor are these benefits considered in occupational earnings data published by such authoritative sources as the U.S. Department of Commerce or the Bureau of Labor Statistics of the U.S. Department of Labor.

The value of a worker's employer-provided fringe benefits can be estimated in several ways: (a) by employer cost, (b) by replacement cost if the worker were to buy the same benefits elsewhere, or (c) by the value of the actual benefits that would have been realized by the worker over time. A good valuation guideline for younger workers is to value insurance and retirement plans at employer cost expressed as a percentage of the present value of expected future money earnings. For younger workers such fringe benefits display a reasonably stable percentage relationship to wages, and the pecuniary value of these benefits may be expected to rise in line with money earnings over time. In the case of older workers, however, the value of replacement costs or the present value of the actual benefits provides a more useful approach. This is because the present value of future money earnings diminishes, whereas the present value of retirement benefits increases, as an older worker nears retirement.

Estimating the Present Value of a Worker's Future Earnings

This section explores the issues involved in estimating the present (trial date) value of a stream of periodic payments consisting of a worker's expected future earnings. These issues are faced in evaluating both the pre-event and the post-event compensation streams. That is, we estimate the pecuniary value of the pre-event and post-event compensation streams and convert those future values into their present (trial date) values.

Present Value of an Income Stream

As a first step, it may be useful to explain what is meant by the idea that an income stream (a series of amounts) can be converted into an equivalent present value (a single amount). The easiest way to introduce the concept is to present a numerical example.

For simplicity, imagine that we are interested in determining the amount of money required today to replace an individual's earnings over the next three years. Assume this worker earned $10,000 last year, and that his earnings are expected to grow, or increase 8 percent each year. This means that the worker's earnings will be

$10,800 in year 1 [$10,000 + .08 ($10,000)]
$11,664 in year 2 [$10,800 + .08 ($10,800)]
$12,597 in year 3 [$11,664 + .08 ($11,664)]
$35,061

If money can be invested to earn 9 percent per annum, then

$ 9,908 invested today at 9 percent will amount to $10,800 in one year,
$ 9,817 invested today at 9 percent will amount to $11,664 in two years, and
$ 9,727 invested today at 9 percent will amount to $12,597 in three years.
$29,452

Thus, only $29,452 is needed today to replace the $35,061 of expected earnings. We refer to the $29,452 amount needed today as the "present value." As illustrated in Table 1, the $29,452 present value plus all the interest it will earn (including the interest on reinvested interest) will be completely used up through time in replacing the $35,061 expected earnings. It is clear that the critical variables in estimating the present value of a worker's expected future earnings are (a) the loss period, (b) the starting earnings level, (c) the growth rate of money earnings, and (d) the interest rate or time-value-of-money discount rate. In the example, the loss period was three years; the starting earnings level was $10,000; the growth rate

TABLE 1
Replacement of Expected Earnings by their Present Value
Plus Interest Earned

Value	Year 1 +	Year 2 +	Year 3 =	Total
Present value today	$ 9,908	$ 9,817	$ 9,727	$29,452
Plus Year 1 interest	892	884	875	2,651
Plus Year 2 interest				
on principal		884	875	1,759
on Year 1 interest		79	79	158
Plus Year 3 interest				
on principal			875	875
on Year 1 interest			79	79
on Year 2 interest			87	87
	$10,800	$11,664	$12,597	$35,061
Required withdrawal	$10,800	$11,664	$12,597	$35,061
Balance after withdrawal	$ 0	0	0	0

of money earnings was 8 percent; and the rate of interest (the discount rate) was 9 percent.

Selecting the Appropriate Wage Growth and Investment (Discount) Rate

Initial salary and projected loss periods are often readily quantifiable. The remaining issues relate to the wage growth rate and the investment or discount rate. In the example developed above, an 8 percent growth in income was assumed along with a 9 percent rate of discount. That example involved only a three-year time period. Typically, it is necessary to make projections over long time periods. It is important to understand how that can be done, in view of the fact that economists cannot predict what the actual level of interest rates and the actual wage growth rates will be over an extended future period.

What an economist *can* assert is that interest rates reflecting the time value of money and wage growth rates will covary closely over extended periods of time. In addition, he can offer credible evidence regarding persisting *differentials* between the rate of growth in wages and such interest rates.

The growth rate in the average worker's money wages has been approximately equal to the yield on three-year U.S. Treasury securities during the past 30 years. This fact permits estimation of the present value of a worker's future earnings with a reasonable degree of certainty. For, given the initial level of income and the length of the time period, all that is necessary in order to estimate the present value of a worker's anticipated future income stream is knowledge of the *differential*. That is, knowledge of the differential between the wage growth rate and interest rates reflecting the time value of money is sufficient to estimate any income stream. If, for example, a 1 percent differential were appropriate (with the discount rate higher than the growth rate), it makes virtually no difference whether the actual combination is 5 percent *vs.* 4 percent, or 9 percent *vs.* 8 percent. In contrast, an increase in the absolute size of the differential has a major impact. A 2 percent differential results, for example, in a reduction in present value of approximately 11 percent.

Hence, a critical issue in addressing a wage evaluation problem is the determination of the appropriate differential. The selection of an appropriate differential must be based upon wage growth and investment (discount) rates that are economically consistent. To meet this criterion they must be consistent with theoretical considerations and must bear some relation to experience.

Which Interest Rate?

In the foregoing material we side-stepped a central issue: discount rates (or, alternatively, interest rates and investment rates). We indicated that the present value of an income stream is the amount we would need to set aside today in order to meet specified payments in the future. We observed that it is not really necessary to know the actual growth rates and discount rates, but only the differential between them.

In the discussion above we used three-year U.S. Treasury securities to determine this differential. But why not use long-term Treasury securities? Why not use corporate bonds? Why not evaluate the loss with the prospective yield from a well-designed stock investment strategy? In part, the reasons lie in considerations relating to the trade-off between risk and return in the capital markets. Another consideration supporting the use of short-term U.S. Treasury securities relates to the covariance of short-term interest rates and the growth in wages. The following two subsections discuss these factors.

Risk Return Trade-Off

The adage "You get what you pay for" applies to all markets. In the capital markets, you get higher expected investment returns only by paying for these *prospective* higher returns through the assumption of greater risk. In other words, all investment vehicles offer an expected investment return that is the sum of the time value of money (here represented by the default-free yield on shorter term U.S. securities) plus a return premium for the additional risk assumed.

Capital market prices (or returns) are efficient in the sense that they provide the investor or purchaser with the appropriate risk-adjusted return on the investment in question. But the risk return logic of the capital markets would be turned upside down if any investment rate other than the time value of money were employed in evaluating pecuniary damages in a lawsuit.

The flip-flop in logic is illustrated by reference to the example discussed above. Using a 9 percent time value of money rate in the example, it was found that the worker would need $29,452 today to replace his earnings over the next three years. If a riskier investment yield of 15 percent were used to calculate the present value of the lost earnings over the next three years, the present value would fall to $26,494. Consider what this would have meant. The worker would have been forced to invest in a riskier, higher-yielding asset, but would have been entitled to *less* money ($29,452 minus $26,494 = $2,958, or about 10 percent less) to replace his earnings over the next three years. Thus, the risk premium earned by investing in a riskier, higher-yielding asset would have been realized by the payor and not the investor-worker who would be taking the risk leading to the higher return. This outcome would be exactly opposite to the risk return logic of the capital markets. According to that logic, the investor taking the risk gets the risk premium.

The risk return trade-off in the capital markets requires that an economist make a careful distinction between the concepts of valuation strategy on the one hand and investment strategy on the other. Valuation strategy relates to the determination of the time-value-of-money rate of return used to discount the expected future earnings to their present value. It is to be distinguished from investment strategy or the actual portfolio or combination of investment vehicles (i.e., government securities, corporate bonds, common stocks, annuities, real estate, etc.) in which the calculated present value amount will be invested. The investment strategy actually followed by the recipient of an award is independent of the valuation procedure employed in estimating the required award. As discussed earlier, the discount rate used in determining the size of the award should not be based on the potential return from a portfolio of risky assets. As indicated, use of this return to calculate the present value of the award would cause the recipient to bear the prospective additional risk, while the payor of the award would receive the immediate benefits related to the higher expected return. This outcome makes no economic sense, and is inconsistent with the risk return trade-off logic of the capital markets.

Moreover, to move away from the time value of money as a valuation technique would place the expert witness in the position of advising the court regarding the appropriate risk return trade-off for a specific individual. The expert witness cannot offer such testimony with a reasonable degree of economic certainty. The acceptable risk return trade-off is, finally, a matter of personal preference.

Covariance of Short-Term Interest and Wage Rates

If we set aside issues relating to risk return trade-off, that is, assume that the return indicated is the return achieved, there is still another consideration that supports use of the interest rate on short-term securities for valuation purposes. This consideration relates to the adaptability of the investment medium to variations in growth rates in wages.

Wage growth rates and the time value of money can be expected to covary closely over an extended period. Without stopping to develop this observation in detail, it is sufficient to state that economists often summarize the determinants of wage growth and interest rates as follows:

Annual wage rate growth	=	Annual rate of increase in labor productivity	+	Annual rate of change in the price level
Annual time value of money	=	Annual real rate of interest or productivity of capital	+	Annual rate of change in the price level

The longer-run annual increase in labor productivity has averaged 2.5-3 percent in this country, and empirical studies have estimated the real rate of interest to be in the 2.5-4 percent range. Thus, over protracted stretches of time the growth in money earnings and the time value of money will covary closely. This, of course, is to be expected since at the margin employers equate the productivity of their capital and labor inputs.

It is the theoretically expected and empirically observed covariance of the time value of money and wage growth rates that permits an economist to make estimates of the present value of a worker's future earning capacity with a reasonable degree of economic certainty. As discussed above, an economist can make such an estimate even though he cannot determine the particular levels and time configurations of wage growth rates and interest rates in the future.

Guidelines for Selecting Rates

The preceding discussion suggests two guidelines an economist may employ in selecting appropriate wage growth and investment (discount) rates in analyzing the present value of a worker's future earnings:

(1) The analyst should employ the current market-determined time value of money yields. This follows from the fact that capital markets are efficient. That is, capital market prices/yields reflect the expectations of all transactors investing their wealth. Specifically, a three-year U.S. Treasury security yield may appropriately be taken as the time value of money. The yields on shorter maturities are too susceptible to transitory money market pressures; the yields on longer-term bonds embody a premium for interest rate risk. The three-year Treasury security possesses important advantages: Its yield varies with changes in the price level, and its duration is consistent with the time horizon of worker's compensation adjustments or raises.

(2) The growth rate of workers' money earnings should be consistent with the time-value-of-money discount rate. That is, the wage rate coupled with the discount rate needs to produce an appropriate differential.

The economic setting in the 1980s has been unusual in that the spread between three-year Treasury yields and wage growth rates has been atypical. To implement the valuation guidelines, the analyst should take the market-determined yield on three-year Treasury securities and then move to the theoretically expected and historically observable 0–1 percent differential between three-year Treasury yields and wage growth rates. For example, an analyst might calculate the present value of a worker's future earnings using a wage growth of 6 percent and a three-year Treasury security valuation strategy in which reinvestment occurs at rates declining linearly from the current 11 percent market yield to 7 percent over a three-year period. The longer-run 7 percent investment return and 6 percent wage growth rate is a conservative estimate of the expected and observable relationship between the yields on three-year Treasury securities and the wage growth rates of the average worker.

Estimating Pecuniary Damages: An Example

As discussed earlier, the with-and-without principle poses two questions that must be answered in estimating pecuniary damages in an employment action: First, what pecuniary values in the form of money earnings and nonmoney earnings could the worker reasonably have been expected to realize without the actionable event? Second, what pecuniary values in the form of money earnings and nonmoney earnings can the worker reasonably expect to realize with—or given the occurrence of—the actionable event? The difference between these two values, year by year, is the measure of pecuniary damages associated with the actionable event.

Below is shown an example calculation for a 50-year-old male lawyer whose discharge is being contested. Imagine the facts are as follows:

> The hypothetical worker, C.B., was discharged December 31, 1982, when he was 60 years old. C.B. had been the legal counsel for a major corporation prior to his discharge. His responsibilities were comparable to those of an Attorney VI position as defined by the Bureau of Labor Statistics of the U.S. Department of Labor in its annual publication *National Survey of Professional, Administrative, Technical, and Clerical Pay*. During the five years preceding termination (1978–82), C.B. had received annual money compensation equal to that received by the average lawyer holding an Attorney VI position (see Table 2).
>
> At the time of his discharge, C.B. had an expected working life of five years (1983–87) and an expected retirement period of 10 years (1988–97). His wife was expected to live an additional five years (1998–2002). (The work life and life expectancy periods are assumed certain for expository convenience. However, the U.S. National Center for Health Statistics and the Bureau of Labor Statistics publish data that allow the economist to adjust his analysis for the uncertainty regarding an individual's expected working life and life expectancy.)
>
> At the date of discharge, C.B.'s annual money earnings rate was $76,202. He could reasonably have expected that his future money earnings would grow in line with the earnings of the average lawyer holding an Attorney VI position.* (Without stopping to develop the logic for the wage growth assumption to be used in this analysis, it is sufficient to state that the wage growth rate is envisioned to decline linearly over a three-year period from the 11 percent trial date (December 31, 1983) rate to a historically consistent and economically sustainable growth rate of 6 percent.)
>
> C.B. had also received employer-provided nonmoney wages in the form of health care insurance coverages for him and his wife and a noncontributory pension plan. The value of the health care insurance

Table 2
Annual Money Income of Average Attorney VI

Year	Money Income
1961	$15,336
1971	33,375
1978	51,798
1979	56,964
1980	60,641
1981	66,958
1982	76,202
1983	84,917

---

*C.B.'s 1983 money income would have risen to $84,917, as used in Table 3.

was equal to 4 percent of C.B.'s money earnings. C.B. and his wife would have received a joint survivors' pension at C.B.'s retirement at age 65 equal to 50 percent of the average earnings during his last five years of employment. His wife would have received a survivor's retirement payment equal to one-half the pension amount prior to C.B.'s death. C.B. had also received a fringe benefit in the form of the use of a company car for which he had paid $30 a month. The monthly lease payment for the car was $530, which leaves a net value of $500 a month or $6,000 a year. The car value is assumed to increase at a 6 percent yearly rate.

C.B. took an early retirement pension with no survivor benefit of $500 a month or $6,000 a year at the time of his December 31, 1982, discharge. He was unable to find a legal position and did not work during 1983, the first year following his termination. At the time of the December 31, 1983, trial, C.B. had agreed to take a position effective January 1, 1984, as a lawyer with a small firm. His salary in his new position was to be only about 60 percent of that of a lawyer holding an Attorney VI position. In addition, he was to receive no car, and the health insurance coverages provided by his new employer would have a cost equal to approximately 5 percent of his salary. The new employer had no pension plan.

The pretax estimate of the pecuniary damages C.B. suffered as a result of his termination is shown in Table 3. The pecuniary loss emerges directly from an analysis that follows the with-and-without principle of cost-benefit analysis:

Earnings that could reasonably have been expected without the termination occurrence	$1,203,554
Less the earnings that can reasonably be expected given the termination occurrence	268,307
	$ 935,247
Less the early retirement pension value	90,000
Equals the pecuniary loss	$ 845,247

The December 31, 1983, present value of the $845,247 pecuniary loss is $499,086. This present value is based upon (a) midyear flows; (b) pretrial losses brought to a December 31, 1983, present value using the 9.5 percent yield available on one-year Treasury bills; and (c) post-trial present values calculated using a valuation strategy employing three-year U.S. Treasury securities yielding 11 percent. The 1 percent differential between the longer-run 6 percent earnings growth rate and the discount rate is achieved by having the reinvestment of interim interest and principal cash flows occur at rates that decline linearly from the current 11 percent to 7 percent over a three-year period.

The logic of the with-and-without principle of cost-benefit analysis has the twin advantages of being theoretically correct and making common sense. The hypothetical case of C.B. was a straightforward application of this principle. Most actual cases, however, will not be amenable to so straightforward an analysis. Fortunately, there are a number of sophisticated econometric techniques available to the economist for extracting measures of pecuniary loss from earnings data. The authors have used one of these techniques, a dummy variable regression procedure, to estimate the

TABLE 3
Present Value of the Pecuniary Loss Resulting from C.B.'s Termination

| | Pre-Termination Position | | | Post-Termination Position | | | | | |
	Money Earnings (1)	+ Fringe Benefits (2)	= Total Earnings (3)	Money Earnings (4)	+ Fringe Benefits (5)	= Total Earnings (6)	Loss [(3)–(6)] (7)	− Adjustment for Early Retirement Pension (8)	= Net Pecuniary Loss [(7)–(8)] (9)
Pre-Trial Period									
1983	$ 84,917	$ 9,397	$ 94,314	$ 0	$ 0	$ 0	$ 94,314	$ 6,000	$ 88,314
Post-Trial Expected Working Life									
1984	94,258	10,130	104,388	56,555	2,828	59,383	45,005	6,000	39,005
1985	103,055	10,864	113,919	61,833	3,092	64,925	48,994	6,000	42,994
1986	110,956	11,584	122,540	66,574	3,329	69,903	52,637	6,000	46,637
1987	117,614	12,279	129,893	70,568	3,528	74,096	55,797	6,000	49,797
Retirement Period									
1988			51,080				51,080	6,000	45,080
1989			51,080				51,080	6,000	45,080
1990			51,080				51,080	6,000	45,080
1991			51,080				51,080	6,000	45,080
1992			51,080				51,080	6,000	45,080
1993			51,080				51,080	6,000	45,080
1994			51,080				51,080	6,000	45,080
1995			51,080				51,080	6,000	45,080
1996			51,080				51,080	6,000	45,080
1997			51,080				51,080	6,000	45,080
Survivor Period of Wife									
1998			25,540				25,540		25,540
1999			25,540				25,540		25,540
2000			25,540				25,540		25,540
2001			25,540				25,540		25,540
2002			25,540				25,540		25,540
			$1,203,554			$268,307	$935,247	$90,000	$845,247

impact of a qualitative event—termination—upon a time series of earnings data.

The Limits of the Economist's Role

Both lawyers and economists must be mindful of just what it is that the economist can and cannot do. The economist cannot predict the economic future of a specific individual; his interest in specific socioeconomic data about a worker should not be interpreted to mean he is prepared to forecast what would have happened to a particular individual whose expected working life ended prematurely.

What the economist can do is predict with reasonable certainty the most likely economic future of the average or representative person in the statistical peer group (or statistical cohort) of individuals having socioeconomic characteristics similar to the terminated worker. And it is this prediction that remains the best estimate of the economic future of any actual individual belonging to that peer group or cohort.

Of course, the economist is prepared to "individualize" his data as much as possible; but he has no special competency to consider any issue that depends more upon the specific or personal characteristics of a worker than upon general socioeconomic characteristics. In the final analysis, the economist's appraisal is for the average person in the worker's statistical cohort. The concept of the statistical cohort is one of the techniques used by the Social Security Administration and other federal agencies, insurance companies, and other organizations in making projections into the future.

The contribution of the economist to the presentation of a persuasive appraisal of pecuniary loss revolves around the application of his econometric skills to the quantification of four critical variables: (a) the loss period, (b) the starting earnings level, (c) the growth rate of money earnings, and (d) the interest rate or time-value-of-money discount rate. It is in the quantification of the expected growth rates of money earnings and the anticipated rates of interest that the economist makes his contribution. Specifically, it is the economist's knowledge of the differential between the wage growth rates and interest rates reflecting the time value of money that permits him to estimate the present value of a worker's anticipated income stream with a reasonable degree of economic certainty.

Estimation Methodology

The following formula describes the basic methods used to estimate the present value of a worker's earnings:

$$PV_{A,t_0} = [\sum_{N=A}^{R} [Y_{N,t_0} \cdot P_{N,t_0} \cdot \prod_{\alpha=A}^{N} (1 + G_{\alpha,t_0})]/ \prod_{\alpha=A}^{N} (1 + D_{\alpha,t_0})]$$

where PV_{A,t_0} = the present value today (t_0) of the total sum of earnings received between a starting age (A) and the retirement age (R);

Y_{N,t_0} = the current (t_0) annual earnings at age N of the average worker with the same socio-economic characteristics;

P_{N,t_0} = the probability the worker will survive to work during year N based upon current (t_0) mortality data;

G_{α,t_0} = the current (t_0) expected annual increase in this average worker's earnings in year α as a result of the growth in productivity and the price level;

D_{α,t_0} = the current (t_0) expected discount rate in year α.

The Y_{N,t_0} income variable is developed using the age-education-occupation-income life cycle contained in publications of the U.S. Bureau of the Census (EARNINGS BY OCCUPATION AND EDUCATION, OCCUPATIONAL CHARACTERISTICS, and the P-60 CONSUMER INCOME series). Specifically, the reporting of income data cross-classified by occupation, education, and age categories (i.e., ages 18–24, 25–29, 30–34, 35–39, 40–44, 45–49, 50–54, 55–59, 60–64, and 65 and over) requires Y_{N,t_0} to be proxied as $Y_{N,t_0} = (Y_{A,t_0})(LCC_N)$, where Y_{A,t_0} is the current (t_0) income level and LCC_N is the life cycle coefficient. The LCC_Ns are calculated by first relating the earnings in time t of the average worker in age category N to the earnings in time t of the average worker of all ages, and then standardizing the LCC_Ns to the LCC_A value.

The U.S. Department of Commerce employs a comparable methodology to estimate the present value of a worker's anticipated earnings during his expected working life (see, for example, U.S. BUREAU OF THE CENSUS, CURRENT POPULATION REPORTS, SERIES P-60, NO. 139, LIFETIME EARNINGS ESTIMATES FOR MEN AND WOMEN IN THE UNITED STATES: 1979, U.S. Government Printing Office, Washington, D.C., 1983).

Master Table of Cases

A

A.B. Mach. Works, Inc. v. Brissimitzakis, 51 A.D.2d 915, 381 N.Y.S.2d 77 (1976) 162

AFSCME v. Shapp, 443 Pa. 527, 280 A.2d 375 (1971) 170, 171

Abendpost Co. v. Hertzel, 67 Ill. App. 501 (1896) 126

Accountants v. City of Detroit, 399 Mich. 449, 249 N.W.2d 121 (1976) 159

Adair v. United States, 208 U.S. 161 (1908) 37, 40

Adams v. Federal Express Corp., 547 F.2d 319 (6th Cir. 1976) 280

Adams v. Fitzpatrick, 125 N.Y. 124, 26 N.E. 143 (1891) 29, 31

Adams v. Walker, 492 F.2d 1003 (7th Cir. 1972) 174

Adams-Riker, Inc. v. Nightingale, 119 R.I. 862, 383 A.2d 1042 (1978) 60

Adkins v. Kelly's Creek R.R., 458 F.2d 26 (4th Cir. 1972) 48

Adler v. American Standard Corp., 291 Md. 31, 432 A.2d 464, 115 LRRM Pt. 2 4130 (1981), *subsequent opinion*, 538 F. Supp. 572 (D. Md. 1982) 254, 258, 262, 264, 267, 292

Adolph v. Cookware Co. of Am., 283 Mich. 561, 278 N.W. 687 (1938) 57

Advance Ross Elec. Corp. v. Green, 624 S.W.2d 316 (Tex. Cir. App. 1981) 112, 123

Agarwal v. Johnson, 25 Cal.3d 932, 603 P.2d 58, 160 Cal. Rptr. 141 (1979) 212, 216

Agis v. Howard Johnson Co., 371 Mass. 140, 355 N.E.2d 315 (1976) 216, 217

Agostini v. Strycula, 231 Cal. App.2d 804, 42 Cal. Rptr. 314 (1965) 216

Aikens v. United States Postal Serv., 460 U.S. 711 (1983) 263, 302

Akers v. Sedberry, 39 Tenn. App. 633 (1955) 108

Alamar v. Dwyer, 447 F.2d 482 (2d Cir. 1971), *cert. denied*, 404 U.S. 1020 (1972) 170

Albers v. Wilson & Co., 184 F. Supp. 812 (D. Minn. 1960) 50

Alcorn v. Ambro Eng'rs, Inc., 2 Cal.3d 493, 468 P.2d 216, 86 Cal. Rptr. 88 (1970) 212

Alessi v. Raybestos-Manhattan, Inc., 451 U.S. 504 (1981) 147

Alexander v. Gardner-Denver Co., 415 U.S. 36 (1974) 142, 151, 162

Alexander v. Potts, 151 Ill. App. 587 (1909) 126

Alexander v. Standard Oil Co., 97 Ill. App.3d 809, 423 N.E.2d 578 (1981) 94

Alexis Stoneware Mfg. Co. v. Young, 59 Ill. App. 226 (1894) 19, 33

Alfaro de Quevedo v. De Jesus Schuck, 556 F.2d 591 (1st Cir. 1977) 174, 175, 176

Alford v. Georgia-Pacific Corp., 331 So.2d 558 (La. Ct. App. 1976) 321

Alkire v. Alkire Orchid Co., 79 W. Va. 526, 91 S.E. 384 (1917) 59

Allen v. Flood, A.C. 1 (1898) 16

Allen-Bradley Local 1111 v. Wisconsin Employment Relations Bd., 315 U.S. 740 (1942) 139

Allison v. American Airlines, 112 F. Supp. 37 (D. Okla. 1953) 209

Alpern v. Hurwitz, 644 F.2d 943 (2d Cir. 1981) 112

Alterman Foods, Inc. v. Ingram, 158 Ga. App. 715, 282 S.E.2d 186, 115 LRRM Pt. 2 4647 (1981) 85

Aluminum Workers v. Chromalloy Am. Corp., 489 F. Supp. 536 (N.D. Miss. 1980) 150

American Nat'l Ins. Co. v. Jackson, 12 Tenn. App. 305 (1930) 107, 109

American Pet Motels, Inc. v. Chicago Veterinary Medical Ass'n, 106 Ill. App.3d 626, 435 N.E.2d 1297 (1982) 196, 326

American Road Serv. Co. v. Inmon, 394 So.2d 361 (Ala. 1980) 214, 218

American Standard, Inc. v. Jessee, 150 Ga. App. 663, 258 S.E.2d 240 (1979) 206, 209

American Surety Co. v. Schottenbauer, 257 F.2d 6 (8th Cir. 1958) 194, 195, 200

Ammons v. Bodish, 308 F. Supp. 1149 (S.D. Ohio 1970) 316

Anderson v. Board of Trustees, 10 Mich. App. 348, 159 N.W.2d 347 (1968) 341

Anderson v. Kammeier, 262 N.W.2d 366 (Minn. 1978) 310

Anderson v. Seaton, 14 Ill. App.2d 53, 143 N.E.2d 59 (1957) 92

Anderson v. Shipowners, 272 U.S. 359 (1926) 236, 239

B

Christy v. Petrus, 365 Mo. 1187, 295 S.W.2d 122 (1956) 285

Chuy v. Philadelphia Eagles Football Team, 431 F. Supp. 254 (E.D. Pa. 1977), *aff'd*, 595 F.2d 1265 (3d Cir. 1979) 216

Circle Security Agency, Inc. v. Ross, 107 Ill. App.3d 195, 437 N.E.2d 667 (1982) 127

Cisco v. United Parcel Servs., Inc., 476 A.2d 1340, 116 LRRM 2514 (Pa. Super. 1984) 277

City of, *see* name of city

Clark; Commonwealth v., 14 Pa. Sup. Ct. 435 (1900) 37

Clark v. McGee, 49 N.Y.2d 613, 404 N.E.2d 1283, 427 N.Y.S.2d 740 (1980) 317

Clark v. Waterman, 7 Vt. 76 (1835) 10

Clarke v. Brunswick Corp., 48 Mich. App. 667, 211 N.W.2d 101 (1973) 88

Clarkson v. Liablan, 202 Mo. App. 682, 216 S.W. 1029 (1919) 203

Clayton v. Automobile Workers, 451 U.S. 679 (1981) 151

Cleary v. American Airlines, 111 Cal. App.3d 443, 168 Cal. Rptr. 722, 115 LRRM 3030 (1980) 46, 49, 68, 70, 71, 72, 98

Clem v. Bowman Lumber Co., 83 N.M. 659, 495 P.2d 1106 (1972) 121, 130, 131

Cleveland, Cincinnati, Chicago & St. Louis Ry. v. Jenkins, 174 Ill. 398, 51 N.E. 811 (1898) 38, 247

Clifford v. Cactus Drilling Corp., 109 Mich. App. 776, 312 N.W.2d 380 (1981) 288

Cloutier v. Great Atl. & Pac. Tea Co., 121 N.H. 915, 436 A.2d 1140, 115 LRRM Pt. 2 4329 (1981) 266, 282, 284, 296, 297, 299, 301

Coffeyville Brick & Tile Co. v. Perry, 69 Kan. 297 (1904) 37

Coffin v. Landis, 46 Pa. 426 (1864) 21, 24, 27

Cohen v. Lion Prods. Co., 177 F. Supp. 486 (D. Mass. 1959) 149

Coker v. Wesco Materials Corp., 368 S.W.2d 883 (Tex. Civ. App. 1963) 131

Colaizzi v. Walker, 542 F.2d 969 (7th Cir. 1976) 317

Cole v. Dow Chem. Co., 112 Mich. App. 198, 315 N.W.2d 565 (1982) 225

Coleman v. Department of Labor, 288 A.2d 285 (Del. 1972) 125

Collins v. Industrial Bearing Trans. Co., 575 S.W.2d 875 (Mo. App. 1978) 248

Collins v. Mainline Bd. of Realtors, 452 Pa. 342, 304 A.2d 493 (1973) 384

Collins v. New England Iron Co., 115 Mass. 23 (1874) 23

Collins v. Parsons College, 203 N.W.2d 594 (Iowa 1973) 48

Collins v. Thomas, 649 F.2d 1203 (1981) 180

Colorado Anti-Discrimination Comm'n v. Continental Air Lines, 372 U.S. 714 (1963) 139, 144

Colorado Springs Coach Co. v. State of Colo. Civil Rights Comm'n, 35 Colo. App. 378, 536 P.2d 837 (1975) 162

Colson v. Steig, 89 Ill.2d 205, 433 N.E.2d 246

(1982) 326

Comby v. Farmland Indus., Inc., 524 S.W.2d 132 (Mo. App. 1975) 248

Comerford v. International Harvester Co., 235 Ala. 376, 178 So. 894 (1937) 253

Commercial Union Assurance Cos. v. Safeway Stores, Inc., 26 Cal.3d 912, 610 P.2d 1038, 164 Cal. Rptr. 709 (1980) 64, 67

Committee to Protect First Amendment v. Bergland, 626 F.2d 875 (D.C. Cir. 1979) 176

Commonwealth v., *see* name of opposing party

Communale v. Traders & Gen. Ins. Co., 50 Cal.2d 654, 328 P.2d 198 (1958) 62

Community Unit School Dist. No. 5 v. Country Mut. Ins. Co., 95 Ill. App.3d 272, 419 N.E.2d 1257 (1981) 410

Conley v. Board of Trustees, 707 F.2d 175, 115 LRRM Pt. 2 4260 (5th Cir. 1983) 90, 168

Connell v. Higgenbotham, 403 U.S. 207 (1971) 166

Connell v. Stalker, 20 Misc. 423, 45 N.Y.S. 1048 (City Ct.), *aff'd*, 21 Misc. 609, 48 N.Y.S. 77 (Sup. Ct. 1897) 209

Conner v. Dart Transp. Serv., 65 Cal. App.3d 320, 135 Cal. Rptr. 259 (1976) 162

Conners v. Connolly, 86 Conn. 641, 86 A. 600 (1913) 202

Connick v. Myers, 461 U.S. 138 (1983) 124

Connor v. Phoenix Steel Corp., 249 A.2d 866 (Del. 1969) 73, 104

Conrad v. Delta Air Lines, 494 F.2d 914 (7th Cir. 1974) 145

Conrad v. Ellison-Harvey Co., 120 Va. 458, 91 S.E. 763 (1917) 61

Construction Workers v. Laburnum Constr. Corp., 347 U.S. 656 (1954) 139

Contreras v. Crown Zellerbach Corp., 88 Wash.2d 735, 565 P.2d 1173 (1977) 212, 213

Conway, Inc. v. Ross, 627 P.2d 1029 (Alaska 1981) 126

Cook v. East Shore Newspapers, Inc., 327 Ill. App. 559, 64 N.E.2d 751 (1945) 309, 328

Cook v. Safeway Stores, 266 Ore. 77, 511 P.2d 375 (1973) 309, 328

Coombe v. Penegar, 348 Mich. 635, 83 N.W.2d 603 (1957) 210

Cooper v. Yellow Freight Sys., 589 S.W.2d 643 (Mo. App. 1979) 162

Copp v. Colorado Coal and Iron Co., 46 N.Y.S. 542 (1897) 30

Coppage v. Kansas, 136 U.S. 1 (1915) 37

Corbeil v. Canestari, 57 A.D.2d 153, 393 N.Y.S.2d 796 (1977) 174

Corbin v. Madison, 12 Wash. App. 318, 529 P.2d 1145 (1974) 328

Corby v. 7100 Jeffrey Ave. Bldg. Corp., 325 Ill. App. 442, 60 N.E.2d 236 (1945) 121

Cordle v. General Hugh Mercer Corp., 116 LRRM 3447 (W. Va. 1984) 275

Cordova v. Bache & Co., 321 F. Supp. 600 (S.D.N.Y. 1970) 233, 235, 241

Corenswet, Inc. v. Amana Refrigeration, Inc., 594 F.2d 129 (5th Cir. 1979) 74

E

F

Feeley v. McAuliffe, 335 Ill. App. 126, 80 N.E.2d 376 (1948) 207

Feinberg v. Pfeiffer Co., 322 S.W.2d 163 (Mo. Ct. App. 1959) 51, 52

Fekete v. United States Steel Corp., 424 F.2d 331 (3d Cir. 1970) 162

Feldman v. Houle, 400 So.2d 180 (Fla. Dist. Ct. App. 1981) 381

Feola v. Valmont Indus., Inc., 208 Neb. 527, 304 N.W.2d 377 (1981) 102

Ferreyra v. E. & J. Gallo Winery, 231 Cal. App.2d 426, 41 Cal. Rptr. 819 (1964) 49

Ferris v. Hawkins, 135 Ariz. 329, 660 P.2d 1256 (1983) 159, 161

Fields v. Dinkins, 156 Ill. App. 528 (1910) 130

Fincke v. Phoenix Mut. Life Ins. Co., 448 F. Supp. 187 (W.D. Pa. 1978) 207, 406

Finger v. Koch and Schilling Brewing Co., 13 Mo. App. 114 (1883) 30

Finkel v. Branti, 457 F. Supp. 1284 (S.D.N.Y. 1978), *aff'd*, 598 F.2d 609 (2d Cir. 1979) 177 (*see also* Branti v. Finkel)

Fireboard Prods. v. Townsend, 202 F.2d 180 (9th Cir. 1953) 49, 57, 58, 60, 61, 85

Firestone Textile Co. Div., Firestone Tire & Rubber Co. v. Meadows, 666 S.W.2d 730, 114 LRRM 3559 (Ky. 1983) 264, 286

Fish v. Marzluff, 128 Ill. App. 549 (1906) 104

Fisher v. Carrousel Motor Hotel, Inc., 424 S.W.2d 627 (Tex. 1967) 212

Fisher v. Church of St. Mary, 497 P.2d 882 (Wyo. 1972) 121

Fisher v. J.C. Penney Co., 135 Ga. App. 913, 219 S.E.2d 626 (1975) 207

Fisher v. John L. Roper Lumber Co., 183 N.C. 485, 111 S.E. 857 (1922) 48, 85, 110

Fiske v. Lockheed-Georgia Co., 568 F. Supp. 590 (N.D. Ga. 1983) 125

Fitzgerald v. McCutcheon, 270 Pa. Super. 102, 410 A.2d 1270 (1979) 218

Fitzgerald v. Mountain Laurel Racing, Inc., 607 F.2d 589 (3d Cir. 1979), *cert. denied*, 446 U.S. 956 (1980) 415

Flager Museum v. Lee, 268 So.2d 434 (Fla. Dist. Ct. App. 1972) 404

Flannery v. Allyn, 47 Ill. App.2d 308, 198 N.E.2d 563 (1964) 309

Fletcher v. Agar Mfg. Corp., 45 F. Supp. 650 (W.D. Mo. 1942) 48

Fletcher v. Amax, Inc., 160 Ga. App. 682, 288 S.E.2d 49 (1981) 408

Fletcher v. Crichton, 183 La. 551, 164 So. 411 (1935) 97

Flowers v. Crouch-Walker, 552 F.2d 1277 (7th Cir. 1977) 301

Floyd v. Lamar Ferrell Chevrolet, Inc., 159 Ga. App. 756, 285 S.E.2d 218 (1981) 79, 281

Flying Tiger Line v. U.S. Air Coach, 51 Cal.2d 199, 331 P.2d 37 (1958) 62

Fogelman v. Peruvian Assoc., 127 Ariz. 504, 622 P.2d 63 (Ct. App. 1980) 401

Foley v. Community Oil Co., Inc., 64 F.R.D. 561, 115 LRRM Pt. 2 4582 (D.N.H. 1974) 99

Foley v. U.S. Paving Co., 262 Cal.2d 499, 68 Cal. Rptr. 780 (1968) 62

Food Fair, Inc. v. Anderson, 382 So.2d 150 (Fla. Dist. Ct. App. 1980) 217

Food Fair Stores, Inc. v. Commonwealth, 11 Pa. Commw. Ct. 535, 314 A.2d 528 (1974) 126

Fortune v. National Cash Register Co., 373 Mass. 96, 364 N.E.2d 1251, 115 LRRM Pt. 2 4658 (1977) 63, 64, 65, 67, 154, 261, 301

Foster v. Mobile County Hosp. Bd., 398 F.2d 227 (5th Cir. 1968) 334

Foster Wheeler Corp. v. Zell, 250 Ala. 146, 33 So.2d 255 (1947) 72

Foxall v. International Land Credit Co., 16 L.T. 637 (1867) 17

Foyt, A.J., Chevrolet, Inc. v. Jacobs, 578 S.W.2d 445 (Tex. Civ. App. 1979) 288

Frachtman v. Fox, 156 N.Y.S. 313 (Sup. Ct. 1915) 126

Frampton v. Central Ind. Gas Co., 260 Ind. 249, 297 N.E.2d 425, 115 LRRM Pt. 2 4611 (1973) 156, 250, 258, 286, 295

Francia v. White, 594 F.2d 778 (10th Cir. 1979) 180

Franco v. Long Island R.R., 94 A.D.2d 756, 462 N.Y.S.2d 697 (1983) 145

Francoeur v. Corroon & Black Co., 552 F. Supp. 403 (S.D.N.Y. 1982) 418

Franklin v. Texas Int'l Petroleum Corp., 324 F. Supp. 808 (W.D. La. 1971) 123, 407

Franklin Mining Co. v. Harris, 24 Mich. 115 (1871) 21, 28

Frary v. American Rubber Co., 52 Minn. 264, 53 N.W. 1156 (1893) 130, 131, 132

Frazer & Torbett, CPA's v. Kunkel, 401 P.2d 476 (Okla. 1965) 101

Fredricks v. Georgia-Pacific Corp., 331 F. Supp. 422 (E.D. Pa. 1971) 108

Freeman v. Eastman-Whipstock, Inc., 390 F. Supp. 685 (S.D. Tex. 1975) 237, 239, 240

Freeman v. Kelvinator, Inc., 469 F. Supp. 999 (E.D. Mich. 1979) 149

Freight Drivers, Local 208 v. Braswell Motor Freight Lines, 422 F.2d 109 (9th Cir. 1970) 159

Fried v. Straussman, 82 Misc.2d 121, 369 N.Y.S.2d 591 (Sup. Ct. 1975) 365

Fries v. Mine Workers, 30 Ill. App.3d 575, 333 N.E.2d 600 (1975) 45, 49, 83

Fritz v. Huntington Hosp., 48 A.D.2d 684, 367 N.Y.S.2d 847 (1975) 364

Fulton v. Tennessee Walking Horse Breeders, 63 Tenn. App. 569, 476 S.W.2d 644 (1971) 49, 401, 407

G

Gabriel v. Bank of Suisun, 145 Cal. 266 (1904) 26, 29

Gabriel v. Opoznauer, 153 N.Y. Supp. 999 (1915) 29

Gray v. Allison Div., Gen. Motors Corp., 52 Ohio App.2d 348, 370 N.E.2d 747 (1977) 319, 323

Gray v. Board of Higher Educ., 692 F.2d 901 (2d Cir. 1982) 421

Greater Fort Worth and Tarrant County Community Action Agency v. Mims, 627 S.W.2d 149 (Tex. 1982) 404

Great Northern Hotel Co. v. Leopold, 72 Ill. App. 1108 (1897) 29

Green v. Kinsella, 36 A.D.2d 617, 319 N.Y.S.2d 780 (1971) 319

Green v. Lundquist Agency, Inc., 2 Mich. App. 488, 140 N.W.2d 575 (1966) 195, 199

Green v. Medford Knitwear Mills, Inc., 408 F. Supp. 577 (E.D. Pa. 1976) 85

Greenberg v. Hollywood Turf Club, 7 Cal. App.3d 968, 86 Cal. Rptr. (1970) 376

Greene v. Howard Univ., 412 F.2d 1128 (D.C. Cir. 1969) 90

Greenwood v. Atchison, Topeka & Santa Fe Ry., 129 F. Supp. 165 (S.D. Cal. 1955) 286

Greenya v. George Washington Univ., 512 F.2d 556 (D.C. Cir. 1975) 320

Greer v. Arlington Mills Mfg. Co., 1 Penn. (Del.) 581 (1899) 27, 30

Greer v. People's T. & T. Co., 18 Jones & S. 517 (1884) 19, 33

Gregg v. Atlantic Coastline R.R., 143 F. Supp. 677 (E.D.S.C. 1956) 127

Gregg v. Georgia, 428 U.S. 153 (1976) 172

Greisman v. Newcomb Hosp., 76 N.J. Super. 149, 183 A.2d 878 (1962), *aff'd*, 40 N.J. 389, 192 A.2d 817 (1963) 355, 356

Gressing v. Musical Instrument Sales Co., 222 N.Y. 215, 118 N.E. 627 (1918) 85

Griffin v. Eastman Kodak Co., 80 A.D.2d 689, 436 N.Y.S.2d 441 (1981) 288

Griffin v. Piedmont Aviation, Inc., 384 F. Supp. 1070 (N.D. Ga. 1974) 145

Grillo v. Board of Realtors, 91 N.J. Super. 202, 219 A.2d 635 (1966) 361

Grillo v. Sidney Wanzer & Sons, 26 Ill. App.3d 1007, 326 N.E.2d 180 (1975) 345

Grinnell Corp.; United States v., 384 U.S. 563 (1966) 231

Griswold v. Connecticut, 381 U.S. 479 (1965) 224, 276

Grodjest v. Jersey City Medical Center, 135 N.J. Super. 393, 343 A.2d 489 (1975) 358

Gronlund v. Church & Dwight Co., 514 F. Supp. 1304 (S.D.N.Y. 1981) 102

Gross v. Abernathy, 47 Mich. App. 703, 209 N.W.2d 813 (1973) 321

Grouse v. Group Health Plan, Inc., 306 N.W.2d 114, 115 LRRM Pt. 2 4438 (Minn. 1981) 79, 82, 193

Grubb v. Leroy L. Wade & Son, 384 S.W.2d 528 (Mo. 1964) 159

Guererro v. Burlington City Memorial Hosp., 70 N.J. 344, 360 A.2d 334 (1976) 359

Guillery v. Godfrey, 134 Cal. App.3d 628, 286 P.2d 474 (1955) 212

Gunsolley v. Bushby, 19 Ore. App. 884, 529 P.2d 950 (1974) 88, 404, 408

Guyette v. Stauffer Chem. Co., 518 F. Supp. 521 (D.N.J. 1981) 218

H

Haag v. International Tel. & Tel. Corp., 342 F.2d 566 (7th Cir. 1965) 66

Haag v. Revell, 28 Wash.2d 883, 184 P.2d 442 (1947) 121

Hackethal v. Loma Linda Community Hosp., 91 Cal. App.3d 59, 153 Cal. Rptr. 783 (1979) 379

Hackett v. Food Maker, Inc., 69 Mich. App. 591, 245 N.W.2d 140 (1976) 49, 403

Hadley v. Baxendale, 9 Ex. 341, 156 Eng. Rep. 145 (1854) 398

Hahn v. Kotten, 43 Ohio St.2d 237, 331 N.E.2d 713 (1975) 321

Haight v. Badgeley, 15 Barb. 499 (1853) 20

Haines v. M.S. Welker & Co., 182 Iowa 431, 165 N.W. 1027 (1918) 200

Halcombe v. Leavitt, 124 N.Y.S. 980 (Sup. Ct. 1910) 347

Hale Hardware Co. v. Ragland, 165 Ark. 258, 263 S.W. 962 (1924) 125

Hall v. Hercules, Inc., 494 F.2d 420 (10th Cir. 1974) 320

Hall-Moody Inst. v. Copass, 108 Tenn. 582, 69 S.W. 327 (1902) 128

Hamby Co. v. Palmer, 631 S.W.2d 589 (Tex. Civ. App. 1982) 405

Hamilton v. Stockton Unified School Dist., 245 Cal. App.2d 944, 54 Cal. Rptr. 463 (1966) 65

Hamilton v. U.S. Pipe & Foundry Co., 213 F.2d 861 (5th Cir. 1954) 319

Hamilton County Hosp. v. Andrews, 227 Ind. 217, 84 N.E.2d 469, *cert. denied*, 338 U.S. 831 (1949) 384

Hamilton Depositors Corp. v. Browne, 199 Ark. 953, 136 S.W.2d 1031 (1940) 129

Hamlen v. Fairchild Indus., Inc., 413 So.2d 800 (Fla. Dist. Ct. App. 1982) 190

Hanaford v. Stevens & Co., 39 R.I. 182, 98 A. 209 (1916) 108, 122, 132

Hansen v. Harrah's, 115 LRRM 3024 (Nev. 1984) 286

Hansome v. Northwestern Cooperage Co., 115 LRRM 3027 (Mo. Ct. App. 1984) 288, 302

Hanson v. Ford Motor Co., 278 F.2d 586 (8th Cir. 1980) 188, 192

Hanson v. Innis, 211 Mass. 301, 97 N.E. 756 (1912) 203

Hanzimanolis v. City of New York, 88 Misc.2d 681, 388 N.Y.S.2d 826 (Sup. Ct. 1976) 315

Harbridge v. Greyhound Lines, 294 F. Supp. 1059 (E.D. Pa. 1969) 313

Harger v. Jenkins, 17 Pa. Super. 615 (1901) 110

Harless v. First Nat'l Bank, 246 S.E.2d 270,

I

K

KDI Corp., In re, 21 Bankr. 652 (S.D. Ohio 1982) 114, 409

Kahn v. Suburban Community Hosp., 45 Ohio St.2d 39, 340 N.E.2d 398 (1976) 335

Kaiser Found. Hosps. v. North Star Reinsurance Corp., 90 Cal. App.3d 786, 153 Cal. Rptr. 678 (1979) 64

Kamberos v. GTE Automatic Elec., Inc., No. 74 C 151 (N.D. Ill. 1978), *rev'd in part*, 603 F.2d 598 (7th Cir. 1979) 418

Kamberos v. Schuster, 132 Ill. App.2d 392, 270 N.E.2d 182 (1971) 320

Kamiar Corp. v. Haley, 224 Va. 699, 299 S.E.2d 514 (1983) 406

Kansas City College v. Employer's Surplus Line Ins. Co., 581 F.2d 299 (1st Cir. 1978) 67

Kansas Pac. Ry. v. Roberson, 3 Colo. 142 (1876) 24

Kaplank v. Carney, 404 F. Supp. 161 (E.D. Mo. 1975) 338, 339, 340

Kapp v. National Football League, 390 F. Supp. 73 (N.D. Cal. 1974), *aff'd*, 586 F.2d 644 (9th Cir. 1975) 235, 241

Katz v. Goodman, 176 N.Y.S. 488 (Sup. Ct. 1919) 129

Kaufman v. Grant-Crawford Co-op Oil Co., 106 Wis.2d 771, 318 N.W.2d 26 (Ct. App. 1982) 155

Kellogg v. Citizens Ins. Co. of Pittsburgh, 94 Wis. 554 (1896) 19, 29

Kelly v. Carthage Wheel Co., 62 Ohio St. 598 (1900) 29

Kelly v. IBM, 573 F. Supp. 366 (E.D. Pa. 1983) 147

Kelly v. Mississippi Valley Gas Co., 397 So.2d 874, 115 LRRM Pt. 2 4631 (Miss. 1981) 279, 286

Kelly Tire Serv., Inc. v. Kelly Springfield Tire, 338 F.2d 248 (8th Cir. 1964) 188

Kelsay v. Motorola, Inc., 74 Ill.2d, 172, 384 N.E.2d 353, 115 LRRM Pt. 2 4371 (1978) 148, 156, 286, 301, 406

Kemp v. Street & Elec. Ry. Employees, 255 Ill. 213, 99 N.E. 389 (1912), *rev'g* 153 Ill. App. 344 (1910) 202, 207

Keneally v. Orgain, 186 Mont. 1, 606 P.2d 127, 115 LRRM Pt. 2 4576 (1979) 262, 286

Kennedy v. Hub Mfg. Co., 221 Mass. 136, 108 N.E. 932 (1915) 201, 209

Kent v. Fugere, 438 F. Supp. 560 (D. Conn. 1977) 145

Kepper v. School Directors, 26 Ill. App.3d 372, 325 N.E.2d 91 (1975) 93

Keserich v. Carnegie-Illinois Steel Corp., 163 F.2d 889 (7th Cir. 1947) 120, 127

Ketchum v. Green, 557 F.2d 1022 (3d Cir. 1977) 193

Kevil v. Standard Oil Co., 8 Ohio N.P. 311 (1901) 50

Keyishian v. Board of Regents, 385 U.S. 589 (1967) 171, 172

Kiefer; United States v., 228 F.2d 448 (D.C. Cir. 1955) 187

Kiely v. St. Germain, 670 P.2d 764 (Colo. 1983) 52

King v. Regents of Univ. of Cal., 138 Cal. App.3d 812, 189 Cal. Rptr. 189 (1982) 393

King v. Steiren, 44 Pa. St. 99 (1862) 19

King Sales Co. v. McKey, 104 Ga. App. 63, 121 S.E.2d 48 (1961) 192

Kinzler v. NYSE, 62 F.R.D. 196 (S.D.N.Y. 1974) 241, 242

Kippen v. American Automatic Typewriter Co., 324 F.2d 742 (9th Cir. 1963) 126

Kirk v. Hartman & Co., 63 Pa. 97 (1869) 21

Kitsos v. Mobile Gas Serv. Corp., 404 So.2d 40, 117 LRRM 2336 (Ala. 1981) 57

Klekamp v. Blaw-Knox Co., 179 F. Supp. 328 (S.D. Cal. 1959) 91

Klinge v. Lutheran Charities Ass'n, 523 F.2d 56 (8th Cir. 1975) 338

Klor's Inc. v. Broadway-Hale Stores, Inc., 359 U.S. 207 (1959) 231

Klug v. Flambeau Plastics Corp., 62 Wis.2d 141, 214 N.W.2d 281 (1974) 50

Knapp v. Palos Community Hosp., _____ Ill. App.3d _____, 465 N.E.2d 554 (1984) 335, 337, 339, 347, 366, 368

Knowles v. Unity College, 429 A.2d 220 (Me. 1981) 98

Kobeck v. Nabisco, 166 Ga. App. 652, 305 S.E.2d 183 (1983) 224

Koehler v. Buhl, 94 Mich. 496, 54 N.W. 157 (1893) 29, 130, 131

Koelling v. Board of Trustees, 259 Iowa 1185, 146 N.W.2d 284 (1966) 337

Kollman v. McGreggor, 240 Iowa 1331, 39 N.W.2d 302 (1949) 66

Konowitz v. Archway School, Inc., 65 A.D.2d 752, 409 N.Y.S.2d 757 (1978) 321, 323

Kosloski v. Kelly, 122 Wis. 365 (1904) 30

Kotteman v. Gross, 184 So. 380 (La. Ct. App. 1938) 110

Kouff v. Bethlehem Alameda Shipyard, Inc., 90 Cal. App.2d 322, 202 P.2d 1059 (1949) 272

Kozlodsky v. Westminster Nat'l Bank, 6 Cal. App.3d 593, 86 Cal. Rptr. 52 (1970) 195, 206

Kraftco Corp. v. Koblus, 1 Ill. App.3d 634, 274 N.E.2d 153 (1971) 53

Kramer v. Philadelphia Leather Goods Corp., 364 Pa. 531, 73 A.2d 385 (1950) 130, 131

Kramer v. Wien, 92 Misc. 159, 155 N.Y.S. 193 (App. Term. 1915) 131

Krause v. Bell Potato Chip Co., 149 Ore. 388, 39 P.2d 363 (1935) 401

Kravetz v. Merchants Distribs., Inc., 387 Mass. 457, 440 N.E.2d 1278 (1982) 62, 110

Kremer v. Chemical Constr. Corp., 456 U.S. 461 (1982) 151, 162

Krenek v. Abel & Abel Air Conditioning, 594 S.W.2d 821 (Tex. Civ. App. 1980) 317

Kreutzberg; State v., 114 Wis. 530 (1903) 37

Kreutzer v. Clark, 271 Ark. 243, 607 S.W.2d 670 (1980) 343

Krizan v. Storz Broadcasting Co., 145 So.2d

M

McGowan v. Maryland, 366 U.S. 420 (1961) 282

McGrath v. Zenith Radio Corp., 651 F.2d 458 (7th Cir. 1981) x, 80, 189, 191, 192, 193, 403, 406

McGraw v. Bill Hodges Truck Co., 629 P.2d 792 (Okla. Ct. App. 1981) 101

McGraw v. Hash, 132 W. Va. 127, 51 S.E.2d 774 (1949) 195

McGuire v. Jankiewicz, 8 Ill. App.3d 319, 290 N.E.2d 675 (1972) 310, 312

McIntyre v. Smith-Bridgman & Co., 301 Mich. 629, 4 N.W.2d 36 (1942) 61, 104

McKelvy v. Choctaw Cotton Oil Co., 52 Okla. 81, 152 P. 414 (1915) 85

McKinley v. Eloy, 705 F.2d 1110 (9th Cir. 1983) 125

McKinney v. National Dairy Council, 491 F. Supp. 1108, 115 LRRM Pt. 2 4861 (D. Mass. 1980) 57, 99, 155, 256

McKinney v. Statesmen Publishing Co., 36 Ore. 509, 56 P. 651 (1899) 85

McLaughlin v. Ford Motor Co., 269 F.2d 120 (6th Cir. 1959) 49, 61

McLaughlin v. Union-Leader Corp., 100 N.H. 367, 127 A.2d 269 (1956) 405

McLean v. News Publishers Co., 21 N.D. 89, 129 N.W. 93 (1910) 403

McLellan v. Mississippi Power & Light Co., 545 F.2d 919 (5th Cir. 1977) 275

McMath v. Ford Motor Co., 77 Mich. App. 721, 259 N.W.2d 140 (1977) 61

McMillan v. Vanderlip, 12 Johns. 165 (1815) 11

McMullan v. Dickenson Co., 63 Minn. 405, 65 N.W. 661 (1896) 50

McMullan v. Thornburgh, 508 F. Supp. 1044 (E.D. Pa. 1981) 180, 181

McNulty v. Borden, Inc., 474 F. Supp. 1111, 115 LRRM Pt. 2 4563 (E.D. Pa. 1979), *modified*, 542 F. Supp. 655 (E.D. Pa. 1982) 49, 99, 237, 243, 244, 267, 291

Mead Johnson & Co. v. Oppenheimer, 458 N.E.2d 668, 115 LRRM 3684 (Ind. App. 1984) 263

Meadows v. Radio Indus., Inc., 222 F.2d 347 (7th Cir. 1955) 53

Meadows v. South Carolina Medical Ass'n, 266 S.C. 391, 223 S.E.2d 600 (1976) 203

Mears v. O'Donoghue, 58 Ill. App. 345 (1895) 104

Meat Cutters v. Jewel Tea Co., 381 U.S. 676 (1965) 235

Medical Soc'y v. Walker, 245 Ala. 135, 16 So.2d 321 (1944) 384

Mee v. Bowder Gold Mining Co., 47 Ore. 143, 81 P. 980 (1905) 108

Mellen v. Industrial Comm'n, 19 Utah 2d 373, 431 P.2d 798 (1967) 210

Melton v. Bow, 241 Ga. 629, 247 S.E.2d 100 (1978) 322

Menefee v. CBS, Inc., 458 Pa. 46, 329 A.2d 216 (1974) 207, 209

Meredith v. C.E. Walther, Inc., 422 So.2d 761, 115 LRRM Pt. 2 4341 (Ala. 1982) 271

Merkel v. Carter Carburetor Corp., 175 F.2d 323 (5th Cir. 1949) 320

Messina v. Continental Purchasing Co., 272 N.Y. 175, 5 N.E.2d 62 (1937) 195, 200

Metzner v. Bolton, 9 Ex. 518 (1854) 17

Meurer Steel Barrel Co. v. Martin, 1 F.2d 687 (3d Cir. 1924) 54, 55

Meyer v. Byron Jackson, Inc., 120 Cal. App.3d 59, 174 Cal. Rptr. 428, 115 LRRM Pt. 2 4295 (1981) 148, 155, 156

Midgett v. Sackett-Chicago, Inc., 118 Ill. App.3d 7, 454 N.E.2d 1092, 114 LRRM 3089 (1983), *aff'd*, No. 59341, 117 LRRM 2807 (Ill. 1984) 152, 259

Midwest Chevrolet Corp. v. Noah, 173 Okla. 198, 48 P.2d 283 (1935) 188, 192

Midwest Micromedia, Inc. v. Machotka, 76 Ill. App.3d 698, 395 N.E.2d 188 (1979) 343

Miller v. Board of Educ., 450 F. Supp. 116 (S.D. W. Va. 1978) 180

Miller v. Community Discount Centers, Inc., 83 Ill. App.2d 439, 228 N.E.2d 113 (1967) 49, 95, 407

Miller v. Dictaphone Corp., 334 F. Supp. 840 (D. Ore. 1971) 91

Miller v. Eisenhower Medical Center, 27 Cal. 3d 614, 614 P.2d 258, 166 Cal. Rptr. 826 (1980) 340, 379

Miller v. Indiana Hosp., 277 Pa. Super. 370, 419 A.2d 1191 (1980) 341

Miller v. Lawlor, 245 Iowa 1144, 66 N.W.2d 267 (1954) 51

Miller v. Missouri Pac. Transp. Co., 225 Ark. 475, 283 S.W.2d 158 (1955) 98

Miller v. Riata Cadillac Co., 517 S.W.2d 773 (Tex. 1974) 57

Miller v. United States Rubber Co., 137 N.J. 682, 61 A.2d 241 (1948) 203

Millet v. Slocum, 4 A.D.2d 528, 167 N.Y.S.2d 136 (1957), *aff'd*, 5 N.Y.2d 734, 152 N.E.2d 672, 177 N.Y.S.2d 716 (1958) 409

Millett, J.C. Co. v. Park & Tilford Distillers Corp., 123 F. Supp. 484 (N.D. Cal. 1954) 54

Milligan v. Union Corp., 87 Mich. App. 179, 274 N.W.2d 10 (1978) 49

Mills v. Fox, 421 F. Supp. 519, 13 FEP Cases 1009 (E.D.N.Y. 1976) 418

Millsap v. National Funding Corp., 57 Cal. App.2d 72, 135 P.2d 407 (1943) 48

Milton v. County of Oakland, 50 Mich. App. 279, 213 N.W.2d 250 (1973) 148

Milton v. Illinois Bell Tel. Co., 101 Ill. App.3d 75, 427 N.E.2d 829, 115 LRRM Pt. 2 4428 (1981) 214

Mims v. Metropolitan Life Ins. Co., 200 F.2d 800 (5th Cir.), *cert. denied*, 345 U.S. 940 (1952) 314

Minyard v. Daking Mill, Inc., 599 S.W.2d 742 (Ark. 1980) 49

Mississippi Employment Sec. Comm'n v. Philadelphia Mun. Separate School Dist., 437

N

115 LRRM Pt. 2 4571 (1975) 264, 271

Nekolny v. Painter, 653 F.2d 1164 (7th Cir. 1981) 175, 180, 181

Nemitz v. Norfolk & W.R.R., 436 F.2d 841 (6th Cir. 1971), *aff'd on other grounds*, 404 U.S. 37 (1971) 145

Nesbit v. Giblin, 96 Neb. 369, 148 N.W. 138 (1914) 108

Newburger, Loeb & Co. v. Gross, 563 F.2d 1057 (2d Cir. 1977) 237, 241

Newcomb v. Brennan, 558 F.2d 825 (7th Cir.), *cert. denied*, 430 U.S. 968 (1977) 174, 176

Newman v. Greater Kansas City Baptist & Community Hosp. Ass'n, 604 S.W.2d 619 (Mo. Ct. App. 1980) 248, 258

Newport, City of, v. Fact Concerts, Inc., 453 U.S. 247 (1981) 180

Newsday, Inc. v. Ross, 80 A.D.2d 1, 437 N.Y.S.2d 376 (1981) 160, 162

Newton v. Brown & Root, 280 Ark. 337, 658 S.W.2d 370, 115 LRRM 2041 (1983) 263, 284

Newton v. Johnson Organ & Piano Co., 180 Cal. 185, 180 P. 7 (1919) 77

Newton v. State Farm Mut. Auto Ins. Co., 700 F.2d 419 (8th Cir. 1983) 248

Newton Toney; Rex v., 2 T.R. 453 (1788) 14

New York Times v. Sullivan, 376 U.S. 254 (1964) 140, 324

Nichols v. Coolahan, 51 Mass. 449 (1845) 23, 24

Nichols v. National Tube Co., 122 F. Supp. 726 (N.D. Ohio 1954) 91, 109, 402

Nichols v. Spencer Int'l Press, Inc., 371 F.2d 332 (7th Cir. 1967) 236, 237, 239, 241

Nilsson v. Cherokee Candy & Tobacco Co., 639 S.W.2d 226 (Mo. Ct. App. 1982) 100, 101

Nixon; United States v., 418 U.S. 683 (1974) 342

Nizinski v. Currington, 517 P.2d 754 (Alaska 1974) 315

Nogee v. Neisner Bros., 351 Ill. App. 166, 114 N.E.2d 463 (1953) 64

Norton v. Cowell, 65 Md. 359 (1886) 29, 30

Notzke v. Art Gallery, Inc., 84 Ill. App.3d 294, 405 N.E.2d 839 (1980) 114

Novosel v. Nationwide Ins. Co., 721 F.2d 894, 114 LRRM 3105 (3rd Cir. 1983) 273

Novosel v. Sears, Roebuck & Co., 495 F. Supp. 344, 117 LRRM 2702 (E.D. Mich. 1980) 86, 215, 218

Nunn v. City of Paducah, 367 F. Supp. 957 (W.D. Ky. 1973) 275

Nunnery v. Barber, 503 F.2d 1349 (4th Cir. 1974), *cert. denied*, 420 U.S. 1005 (1975) 170

Nye v. Department of Livestock, 639 P.2d 498 (Mont. 1982) 260

O

Oakes v. Chicago Fire Brick Co., 388 Ill. 474, 58 N.E.2d 460 (1945) 56

Oates v. Eastern Bergen Co. Multiple Listing Serv. Inc., 113 N.J. Super. 371, 273 A.2d 795 (1971) 362

Obde v. Schlemeyer, 56 Wash.2d 449, 353 P.2d 672 (1960) 79

O'Bier v. Safe Buy Real Estate Agency, 256 Ark. 574, 509 S.W.2d 292 (1974) 64

O'Brien v. Matual, 14 Ill. App.2d 173, 144 N.E.2d 446 (1957) 347

O'Brien v. Pappas, 49 N.Y.S.2d 521 (1944) 203

O'Brien v. Western Union Tel. Co., 62 Wash. 598, 114 P. 441 (1911) 203

Odell v. Humble Oil Ref. Co., 201 F.2d 123 (10th Cir. 1963) 253

Odell v. Village of Hoffman Estates, 110 Ill. App.3d 947, 443 N.E.2d 247 (1982) 338

Odom v. Bush, 125 Ga. 184 (1906) 30, 31

Odom v. East Avenue Corp., 178 Misc. 363, 34 N.Y.S.2d 312 (1942) 212

Ohio Ferro-Alloys Corp. v. Tichnor, 83 Ohio L. Abstracts 254, 168 N.E.2d 334 (Common Pleas Ct., Muskingum County 1959) 127

Ohio Table Pad Co. v. Hogan, 424 N.E.2d 144 (Ind. Ct. App. 1981) 85

Ohlsen v. DST Indus., Inc., 111 Mich. App. 580, 314 N.W.2d 699 (1981) 156

O'Keefe v. Associated Grocers, 120 N.H. 834, 424 A.2d 199 (1980) 148

Oklahoma Portland Cement Co. v. Pollock, 181 Okla. 266, 73 P.2d 427 (1937) 48

O'Leary v. Sterling Extruder Corp., 533 F. Supp. 1205, 115 LRRM Pt. 2 4160 (E.D. Wis. 1982) 404

Olson v. Naymark, 177 Minn. 383, 225 N.W. 275 (1929) 401

Oltersdorf v. Chesapeake & Ohio R.R., 83 Ill. App.3d 457, 404 N.E.2d 320 (1980) 405

O'Neill v. ARA Servs., Inc., 457 F. Supp. 182, 115 LRRM Pt. 2 4846 (E.D. Pa. 1978) 291

Operating Eng'rs, Local 926 v. Jones, 460 U.S. 669 (1983) 139, 141, 203

Ornatek v. Nevada State Bank, 93 Nev. 17, 558 P.2d 1145 (1977) 312

Orr v. Ward, 73 Ill. 318 (1874) 24

Orsini v. Trojan Steel Corp., 219 S.C. 272, 64 S.E.2d 878 (1951) 49

Osborn v. Review Bd., 178 Ind. App. 22, 381 N.E.2d 495 (1978) 123

Osburn v. DeForce, 122 Ore. 360, 257 P. 685 (1927) 124

Osterkamp v. Alkota Mfg., Inc., 332 N.W.2d 275, 115 LRRM 2824 (S.D. 1983) 90

Ostrofe v. H.S. Crocker Co., 670 F.2d 1378, 117 LRRM 2105 (9th Cir. 1982), *vacated*, 460 U.S. 1007 (1983) 239, 240, 242, 243, 244

O'Sullivan v. Mallon, 160 N.J. Super. 416, 390 A.2d 149, 115 LRRM Pt. 2 5064 (1978) 267, 269

Ott v. Gandy, 66 Ga. App. 684, 195 S.E.2d 180 (1942) 195

Ozier v. Haines, 411 Ill. 160, 103 N.E.2d 485 (1952) 60

P

Roe v. Wade, 410 U.S. 113, *rehearing denied*, 410 U.S. 959 (1973) 224

Rogeau v. Firestone Tire & Rubber Co., 274 So.2d 454 (La. Ct. App. 1973) 320

Rogers v. International Business Machs. Corp., 500 F. Supp. 867, 115 LRRM Pt. 2 4608 (W.D. Pa. 1980) 98

Rogers v. Loews L'Enfant Plaza Hotel, 526 F. Supp. 523 (D.D.C. 1981) 213

Rogozinski v. Air Stream by Angell, 152 N.J. Super. 133, 377 A.2d 807 (1977) 309, 310, 317, 318

Rolfs v. Pooley Furniture Co., 176 Ill. App. 93 (1912) 123

Rollinger v. Dairyland Creamery Co., 66 S.D. 592, 287 N.W. 333 (1939) 107

Rookard v. Health and Hospital Corp., 710 F.2d 41, 115 LRRM Pt. 2 4089 (2d Cir. 1983) 124

Rosales v. City of Eloy, 122 Ariz. 134, 593 P.2d 688 (App. 1979) 216, 217

Rosaly v. Ignacio, 593 F.2d 145 (1st Cir. 1979) 178

Roseland v. Phister Mfg. Co., 125 F.2d 417 (7th Cir. 1942) 236, 237, 245

Rosen v. Druss, 178 N.Y.S. 259 (App. Term. 1919) 132

Rosenberg v. Redevelopment Auth., 428 F. Supp. 498 (E.D. Pa. 1977) 176

Rosenberger v. Pacific Coast R.R., 111 Cal. 313, 43 P. 963 (1896) 26, 29, 407

Rosenbloom v. Metro Media, 403 U.S. 29 (1971) 326

Rosenthal v. Rizzo, 555 F.2d 390 (3d Cir. 1977) 174, 177

Ross v. Duke, 116 Ariz. 298, 569 P.2d 240 (Ct. App. 1977) 320

Rotermund v. Basic Materials Co., 558 S.W.2d 688 (Mo. App. 1977) 248

Roundtree v. Board of Review, 4 Ill. App.3d 695, 281 N.E.2d 360 (1972) 123

Rowe v. Noren Pattern & Foundry Co., 91 Mich. App. 254, 283 N.W.2d 713 (1979) 48, 57, 99

Rowe v. Pierce, 467 F. Supp. 14 (E.D. Tenn. 1979) 316

Roxana Petroleum Co. v. Rice, 109 Okla. 161, 235 P. 502 (1924) 57, 130

Royster Guano Co. v. Hall, 68 F.2d 533 (4th Cir. 1934) 48, 402

Rua v. Bowyer Smokeless Coal Co., 84 W. Va. 47, 99 S.E. 213 (1919) 59

Rucker v. Higher Educ. Aids Bd., 669 F.2d 1179 (7th Cir. 1982) 161

Ruddy v. Journeymen Plumbers, 79 N.J.L. 467, 75 A. 742 (1911) 195

Rudman v. Cowles Communications, Inc., 30 N.Y.2d 1, 280 N.E.2d 867, 330 N.Y.S.2d 33 (1972) 129

Ruiz v. Bertolotti, 37 Misc.2d 1067, 236 N.Y.S.2d 854 (Sup. Ct. 1962) 212

Russell v. Princeton Laboratories, Inc., 50 N.J. 30, 231 A.2d 800 (1967) 104

Russell v. Variety Artists, 53 Hawaii 456, 497

P.2d 40 (1972) 321

Rutherford v. American Bank of Commerce, 565 F.2d 1162 (10th Cir. 1977) 201

Rutledge v. St. Vincent Memorial Hosp., 67 Ill. App.2d 156, 214 N.E.2d 131 (1966) 343

S

STP Corp. v. United States Auto Club, Inc., 286 F. Supp. 146 (S.D. Ind. 1968) 384

Salanger v. U.S. Air, 560 F. Supp. 202, 115 LRRM Pt. 2 4545 (N.D.N.Y. 1983) 277

Salerno v. O'Rourke, 555 F. Supp. 750 (D.N.J. 1983) 125

Salt Creek Freightways v. Wyoming Fair Employment Practices Comm'n, 598 P.2d 435 (Wyo. 1979) 159, 161

Salter v. New York State Psychological Ass'n, 14 N.Y.2d 100, 198 N.E.2d 250, 248 N.Y.S.2d 867 (1964) 362

Salvage v. Spur Distrib. Co., 33 Tenn. App. 20, 228 S.W.2d 122 (1949) 49

Salvatori Corp. v. Rubin, 159 Ga. App. 369, 283 S.E.2d 326 (1981) 108, 408

Sampson v. Murray, 415 U.S. 61 (1974) 412, 413, 414

San Antonio & A.P. Ry. v. Sale, 31 S.W. 325 (1895) 29

Sanders v. Arkansas-Missouri Power Co., 593 S.W.2d 56 (Ark. Ct. App. 1980) 52

Sanders v. Stewart, 157 Ind. App. 74, 298 N.E.2d 509 (1973) 317

San Diego Bldg. Trades Council v. Garmon, 359 U.S. 236 (1959) 138

Sands v. Potter, 165 Ill. 397, 46 N.E. 282 (1896) 107

Sanis v. Duncan & Copeland, Inc., 153 Ga. App. 765, 266 S.E.2d 546 (1980) 193

Santa Fe Indus., Inc. v. Green, 430 U.S. 462 (1977) 193

Santex, Inc. v. Cunningham, 618 S.W.2d 557 (Tex. Civ. App. 1981) 288, 404

Sarasota County Pub. Hosp. Bd. v. El Shahawy, 408 So.2d 644 (Fla. Dist. Ct. App. 1982) 340

Sargent v. Illinois Inst. of Technology, 78 Ill. App.3d 117, 397 N.E.2d 443 (1979) 93

Sargent v. Johnson, 551 F.2d 221 (8th Cir. 1977) 64

Sarusal v. Seung, 96 Wash. 295, 165 P. 116 (1917) 97

Saunders v. Big Bros., Inc., 115 Misc.2d 845, 454 N.Y.S.2d 787 (Civ. Ct. 1982) 90

Savage v. Seed, 81 Ill. App.3d 744, 401 N.E.2d 984 (1980) 310

Savard v. Industrial Trades Union, 76 R.I. 496, 72 A.2d 660 (1950) 203

Savitz v. Gallaccio, 179 Pa. Super. 589, 118 A.2d 282 (1955) 407

Savodnik v. Korvettes, Inc., 488 F. Supp. 822, 115 LRRM Pt. 2 4601 (E.D.N.Y. 1980) 66

Sax v. Detroit, Grand Haven & Milwaukee

Sherman v. Mutual Benefit Life Ins. Co., 633 F.2d 782 (9th Cir. 1980) 191, 193

Sherman v. St. Barnabas Hosp., 535 F. Supp. 564, 115 LRRM Pt. 2 5133 (S.D.N.Y. 1982) 209

Sheshunoff & Co. v. Scholl, 564 S.W.2d 697 (Tex. 1978) 401

Shewmaker v. Minchew, 504 F. Supp. 156 (D.D.C. 1980), *aff'd*, 666 F.2d 616 (D.C. Cir. 1981) 215

Shipp v. Waller, 391 F. Supp. 283 (D.C. Cir. 1975) 316

Shorr Paper Prods., Inc. v. Frary, 74 Ill. App.3d 498, 292 N.E.2d 1148 (1979) 343

Shuler v. Corl, 39 Cal. App. 195, 178 P. 535 (1918) 26, 32, 85

Shumzte v. Sohon, 12 F.2d 825 (D.C. Cir. 1926) 107

Siefert v. Arnold Bros., 138 Cal. App. 324, 39 P.2d 1059 (1934) 85

Sigmon v. Goldstone, 116 A.D. 490, 101 N.Y.S. 984 (1906) 111

Signorelli v. Morice, 174 So. 124 (La. Ct. App. 1937) 108

Silberg v. California Life Ins. Co., 11 Cal.3d 452, 521 P.2d 1103, 113 Cal. Rptr. 711 (1974) 64

Silberman v. Penn Gen. Agencies, Inc., 63 A.D.2d 929, 406 N.Y.S.2d 93 (1978) 162

Siles v. Travenol Laboratories, Inc., 13 Mass. App. 354, 433 N.E.2d 103, 115 LRRM Pt. 2 4178 (1982) 263

Silkwood v. Kerr McGee Corp., 667 F.2d 908 (10th Cir. 1981) 147

Silveira v. Aircraft Casting Co., 291 So.2d 19 (Fla. Dist. Ct. App. 1974) 320

Silver v. Mohasco Corp., 94 A.D.2d 820, 462 N.Y.S.2d 917 (1983) 186, 190

Silver v. Queen's Hosp., 63 Hawaii 430, 629 P.2d 1116 (1981) 340, 341

Simmons v. Stanton, 502 F. Supp. 932 (W.D. Miss. 1980) 179, 180

Simpson v. Sperry Rand Corp., 350 F. Supp. 1057 (W.D. La. 1972) 275

Simpson v. Western Graphics Corp., 53 Ore. App. 205, 631 P.2d 805, 115 LRRM Pt. 2 4605 (1981), *aff'd*, 293 Ore. 96, 643 P.2d 1276 (1982) 90, 112

Sinclair v. Sullivan Chevrolet Co., 31 Ill.2d 507, 202 N.E.2d 516 (1964) 57, 60

Sinclair Ref. Co. v. McCullom, 107 Ind. App. 356, 24 N.E.2d 784 (1940) 406

Sines v. Wayne County Superintendent of the Poor, 58 Mich. 503, 25 N.W. 485 (1885) 61

Sinnett v. Hie Food Prods., Inc., 185 Neb. 221, 174 N.W.2d 720 (1970) 66

Skagerberg v. Blandin Paper Co., 197 Minn. 291, 266 N.W. 872 (1936) 49, 50

Skagway City School Bd. v. Davis, 543 P.2d 218 (Alaska 1975) 404

Skolnick v. Nudelman, 95 Ill. App.2d 293, 237 N.E.2d 804 (1968) 312

Slabon v. St. Louis Car Co., 138 S.W.2d 673 (Mo. 1940) 48, 83, 85

Slavodnick v. Korvette's Inc., 488 F. Supp. 822 (E.D.N.Y. 1980) 147

Slevin v. City of New York, 551 F. Supp. 917 (S.D.N.Y. 1982), *rev'd in part sub nom.* Barry v. City of New York, 712 F.2d 1554 (2d Cir. 1983) 224

Slochower v. Board of Educ., 350 U.S. 551 (1956) 163, 166

Smelter Workers v. Kyrk, 199 Okla. 464, 187 P.2d 239 (1947) 203

Smetherton v. Laundry Workers, 44 Cal. App.2d 131, 111 P.2d 948 (1941) 202

Smith v. American Cast Iron Pipe Co., 370 So.2d 283 (Ala. 1979) 275

Smith v. Anheuser Busch Brewing Co., 346 So.2d 125 (Fla. Dist. Ct. App. 1977) 322

Smith v. Atlas Off-Shore Boat Serv., Inc., 653 F.2d 1057, 117 LRRM 2414 (5th Cir. 1981) 286

Smith v. Beloit Corp., 40 Wis.2d 550, 162 N.W.2d 585 (1968) 49, 408

Smith v. Concordia Parish School Bd., 387 F. Supp. 887 (W.D. La. 1975) 408

Smith v. Cotton Bros. Baking Co., 609 F.2d 738 (5th Cir. 1980) 275

Smith v. Department of Human Resources, Greenwell Springs Hosp., 408 So.2d 411 (La. Ct. App. 1981) 122

Smith v. District of Columbia, 399 A.2d 213 (D.C. 1979) 320

Smith v. Evening Star News Ass'n, 371 U.S. 195 (1962) 150

Smith v. Ford Motor Co., 289 N.C. 71, 221 S.E.2d 282 (1976) 194, 195, 204, 207

Smith v. Hayward, 7 Ald. & El. 544 (1837) 11

Smith v. Kerrville Bus Co., 709 F.2d 914, 114 LRRM 2911 (5th Cir. 1983) 90

Smith v. Montgomery Ward & Co., 567 F. Supp. 1331, 115 LRRM Pt. 2 4283 (D. Colo. 1983) 215, 217

Smith v. Pallay, 130 Ore. 282, 279 P. 279 (1929) 401

Smith v. Pollack Co., 9 La. App. 432, 121 So. 240 (1928) 79, 403

Smith v. Pro Football, Inc., 593 F.2d 1173 (D.C. Cir. 1978) 241

Smith v. Sohio Petroleum Co., 163 So.2d 124 (La. Ct. App. 1964) 48

Smith v. Theobald, 86 Ky. 141 (1887) 29

Smithers v. Metro-Goldwyn-Mayer Studios, Inc., 139 Cal. App.3d 643, 189 Cal. Rptr. 20 (1983) 247

Smyth v. Fleischmann, 214 S.C. 263, 52 S.E.2d 199 (1949) 192

Sniadach v. Family Fin. Corp., 395 U.S. 337 (1969) 386

Snurf v. DiCara, 42 A.D.2d 791, 346 N.Y.S.2d 546 (1973) 316

Socony-Vacuum Oil Co.; United States v., 310 U.S. 150 (1940) 231

Soley v. Ampudia, 183 F.2d 277 (5th Cir. 1950) 310

Solo Cup v. Federal Ins. Co., 619 F.2d 1178 (7th Cir.), *cert. denied*, 449 U.S. 1033

Y

State-by-State Table of Cases

COLORADO

Dist. Ct. App. 1978) 316

Densmore v. City of Boca Raton, 368 So.2d 945 (Fla. Dist. Ct. App. 1979) 316

Dickinson v. Auto Center Mfg. Co., 639 F.2d 250, 115 LRRM Pt.2 5100 (5th Cir. 1981) 45

Dowling v. Blue Cross, 338 So.2d 88 (Fla. Dist. Ct. App. 1976) 216

Drennen v. Westinghouse Elec. Corp., 328 So.2d 52 (Fla. Dist. Ct. App. 1976) 311, 320

Edgewater Beach Corp. v. Sugarman, 153 Fla. 555, 15 So.2d 260 (1943) 79

Edwards v. Doherty, 74 So.2d 686 (Fla. 1954) 130

Feldman v. Houle, 400 So.2d 180 (Fla. Dist. Ct. App. 1981) 381

Flager Museum v. Lee, 268 So.2d 434 (Fla. Dist. Ct. App. 1972) 404

Food Fair, Inc. v. Anderson, 382 So.2d 150 (Fla. Dist. Ct. App. 1980) 217

Gellert v. Eastern Airlines, 370 So.2d 802 (Fla. Dist. Ct. App. 1979) 214

Glynn v. City of Kissimmee, 383 So.2d 774 (Fla. Dist. Ct. App. 1980) 310, 319

Goodman v. Winn-Dixie Stores, Inc., 240 So.2d 496 (Fla. Dist. Ct. App. 1970) 73, 109

Good Samaritan Hosp. v. Bishop, 413 So.2d 158 (Fla. Dist. Ct. App. 1982) 286

Hamlen v. Fairchild Indus., Inc., 413 So.2d 800 (Fla. Dist. Ct. App. 1982) 190

Hazen v. Cobb, 96 Fla. 151, 117 So. 853 (1928) 130, 131

Hope v. National Airlines, 99 So.2d 244, 115 LRRM Pt. 2 4580 (Fla. Dist. Ct. App. 1958) 50, 57

Jorgensen, Roy, Assocs., Inc. v. Deschenes, 409 So.2d 1188, 115 LRRM Pt. 2 4917 (Fla. Dist. Ct. App. 1982) 96

Lay v. Roux Laboratories, Inc., 379 So.2d 451 (Fla. Dist. Ct. App. 1980) 212

Marion County School Bd. v. Clark, 378 So.2d 831 (Fla. Dist. Ct. App. 1979) 154, 159

Muller v. Stromberg Carlson Corp., 427 So.2d 266, 115 LRRM Pt. 2 3447 (Fla. Dist. Ct. App. 1983) 91, 194, 195

Paddock v. Bay Concrete Indus., Inc., 154 So.2d 313 (Fla. 1963) 130

Piezo Technology v. Smith, 413 So.2d 121 (Fla. Dist. Ct. App. 1982), *aff'd*, 427 So.2d 182, 117 LRRM 3378 (1983) 286

Punkar v. King Plastics Corp., 290 So.2d 505 (Fla. Dist. Ct. App. 1974) 408

Sarasota County Pub. Hosp. Bd. v. El Shahawy, 408 So.2d 644 (Fla. Dist. Ct. App. 1982) 340

Silveira v. Aircraft Casting Co., 291 So.2d 19 (Fla. Dist. Ct. App. 1974) 320

Smith v. Anheuser Busch Brewing Co., 346 So.2d 125 (Fla. Dist. Ct. App. 1977) 322

Southern Keswick, Inc. v. Whetherholt, 293 So.2d 109 (Fla. Dist. Ct. App. 1974) 407

Wardlow v. City of Miami, 372 So.2d 976 (Fla. Dist. Ct. App. 1979) 317

West v. Troelstrup, 367 So.2d 253 (Fla. Dist. Ct. App. 1979) 206, 209

GEORGIA

Alterman Foods, Inc. v. Ingram, 158 Ga. App. 715, 282 S.E.2d 186, 115 LRRM Pt. 2 4647 (1981) 85

American Standard, Inc. v. Jessee, 150 Ga. App. 663, 258 S.E.2d 240 (1979) 206, 209

Barrett v. Thomas, 649 F.2d 1193 (5th Cir. 1980) 193

Basic Four Corp. v. Parker, 158 Ga. App. 117, 279 S.E.2d 241 (1981) 400

Beavers v. Johnson, 112 Ga. App. 677, 145 S.E.2d 776 (1976) 217

Cummings v. Walsh Constr. Co., 561 F. Supp. 872, 115 LRRM Pt. 2 4070 (S.D. Ga. 1983) 195, 206, 213, 215, 224

Electrical Workers (IBEW) v. Briscoe, 143 Ga. App. 417, 239 S.E.2d 38 (1977) 203

Ely v. Stratoflex, 132 Ga. App. 569, 208 S.E.2d 583 (1974) 193

Fisher v. J.C. Penney Co., 135 Ga. App. 913, 219 S.E.2d 626 (1975) 207

Fletcher v. Amax, Inc., 160 Ga. App. 682, 288 S.E.2d 49 (1981) 408

Floyd v. Lamar Ferrell Chevrolet, Inc., 159 Ga. App. 756, 285 S.E.2d 218 (1981) 79, 281

Gardner v. Celanese Corp., 88 Ga. App. 642, 76 S.E.2d 817 (1953) 186

Georgia Power Co. v. Busbin, 242 Ga. 612, 250 S.E.2d 442, 115 LRRM Pt. 2 4310 (1978), *aff'g in part and rev'g in part* 145 Ga. App. 438, 244 S.E.2d 26, *appeal following remand*, 149 Ga. App. 274, 254 S.E.2d 146 (1979) 195, 206, 209

Godwin v. Westberry, 231 Ga. 492, 202 S.E.2d 402 (1973) 208

Goodroe v. Georgia Power Co., 148 Ga. App. 193, 251 S.E.2d 51, 115 LRRM Pt. 2 4303 (1978) 291

Hobbs v. Davis, 30 Ga. 423 (1860) 21

Hudson v. Venture Indus., Inc., 147 Ga. App. 31, 248 S.E.2d 9 (1978) 190

Jones v. Operating Eng'rs, Local 926, 159 Ga. App. 693, 285 S.E.2d 30 (1981) 209

King Sales Co. v. McKey, 104 Ga. App. 63, 121 S.E.2d 48 (1961) 192

Kobeck v. Nabisco, 166 Ga. App. 652, 305 S.E.2d 183 (1983) 224

Land v. Delta Airlines, 147 Ga. App. 738, 250 S.E.2d 188 (1978) 317, 320

Lanham v. Mr. B's Oil Co., 166 Ga. App. 372, 304 S.E.2d 738 (1983) 190

Magarahan v. Wright, 83 Ga. 773 (1889) 29

Melton v. Bow, 241 Ga. 629, 247 S.E.2d 100 (1978) 322

Mondon v. Western Union Tel. Co., 96 Ga. 499 (1895) 31

Odom v. Bush, 125 Ga. 184 (1906) 30, 31

Ott v. Gandy, 66 Ga. App. 684, 195 S.E.2d 180 (1942) 195

Phillips v. Goodyear Tire & Rubber Co., 651 F.2d 1051, 115 LRRM Pt.2 4173 (5th Cir. 1981) 270

Spencer v. Community Hosp., 87 Ill. App.3d 214, 408 N.E.2d 981 (1980) 339, 340, 367

Staton v. Amax Coal Co., 122 Ill. App.3d 631, 461 N.E.2d 612, 116 LRRM 2517 (1984) 112, 113, 114, 120

Steinberg v. Chicago Medical School, 69 Ill.2d 320, 371 N.E.2d 634 (1977) 87

Sterba, People ex rel., v. Blaser, 33 Ill. App.3d 1, 337 N.E.2d 410 (1975) 92

Stevenson v. ITT Harper, Inc., 51 Ill. App.3d 568, 366 N.E.2d 561, 115 LRRM Pt. 2 5053 (1977) 62, 66, 98, 208, 409

Sutton v. Workmeister, 164 Ill. App. 105 (1911) 202

Technical Representatives, Inc. v. Richardson-Merrell, Inc., 107 Ill. App.3d 830, 438 N.E.2d 599 (1982) 400

Treister v. American Academy of Orthopaedic Surgeons, 78 Ill. App.3d 746, 396 N.E.2d 1225 (1979) 335, 347, 367

Trustees of Soldiers' Orphan Home v. Shaffer, 63 Ill. 243 (1872) 19

Van Daele v. Vinci, 51 Ill.2d 389, 282 N.E.2d 728, *cert. denied*, 409 U.S. 1007 (1972) 335, 338, 339, 365

Van Norman v. Peoria Journal Star, 31 Ill. App.2d 314, 175 N.E.2d 805 (1961) 328

Vincent v. Maeras, 447 F. Supp. 775 (S.D. Ill. 1978) 174, 180

Virgin v. American College of Surgeons, 42 Ill. App.2d 352, 192 N.E.2d 414 (1963) 338, 354

Vogel v. Pekoc, 157 Ill. 339, 42 N.E. 386 (1895) 53

Ward v. Howard P. Foley Co., 119 Ill. App.3d 894, 457 N.E.2d 155, 115 LRRM 2404 (1983) 152

Washingtonian Home v. City of Chicago, 281 Ill. 110, 117 N.E. 737 (1917) 343

Welch v. Chicago Tribune Co., 34 Ill. App.3d 1046, 340 N.E.2d 539 (1976) 310, 320

Whitaker v. Pierce, 44 Ill. App.3d 148, 358 N.E.2d 61 (1976) 345

Wilhoute v. Fastenware, Inc., 354 F. Supp. 856 (N.D. Ill. 1973) 192

Witkowski v. St. Anne's Hosp., Inc., 113 Ill. App.3d 745, 447 N.E.2d 1016 (1983) 147, 283

Witt v. Forest Hosp., Inc., 115 Ill. App.3d 481, 450 N.E.2d 811, 115 LRRM Pt. 2 4345 (1983) 269, 291, 292, 411, 418

World Columbian Exposition v. Richards, 57 Ill. App. 601 (1894) 97

Worrick v. Flora, 133 Ill. App.2d 755, 272 N.E.2d 708 (1971) 208

Wyatt v. Jewel Cos., 108 Ill. App.3d 840, 439 N.E.2d 1053, 115 LRRM Pt. 2 4811 (1982) 152

Zagar v. Field Enters. Educ. Corp., 58 Ill. App.3d 750, 374 N.E.2d 897 (1978) 82

Zannis v. Lake Shore Radiologists, Ltd., 73 Ill. App.3d 901, 392 N.E.2d 126 (1979) 411

Zeinfeld v. Hayes Freight Lines, 41 Ill.2d 345, 243 N.E.2d 217 (1969) 309

INDIANA

Batts v. Review Bd., 179 Ind. App. 405, 385 N.E.2d 1174 (1979) 108

Bendix Corp. v. Radecki, 158 Ind. App. 370, 302 N.E.2d 847 (1973) 159

Brockman v. Detroit Diesel Allison Div. of Gen. Motors Corp., 174 Ind. App. 240, 366 N.E.2d 1201 (1977) 318

Campbell v. Eli Lilly & Co., 413 N.E.2d 1054, 115 LRRM Pt. 2 4417 (Ind. App. 1980) 53, 291

Cox v. Baltimore & O.S.W. Ry., 180 Ind. 495, 103 N.E. 337 (1913) 83

Cox v. Guy F. Atkinson Co., 468 F. Supp. 677 (N.D. Ind. 1979) 121, 406

Dove v. Rose Acre Farms, Inc., 434 N.E.2d 931 (Ind. Ct. App. 1982) 102

Eby v. York-Division, Borg-Warner, 455 N.E.2d 623 (Ind. App. 1983) 52, 79

Frampton v. Central Ind. Gas Co., 260 Ind. 249, 297 N.E.2d 425, 115 LRRM Pt. 2 4611 (1973) 156, 250, 258, 286, 295

Hamilton County Hosp. v. Andrews, 227 Ind. 217, 84 N.E.2d 469, *cert. denied*, 338 U.S. 831 (1949) 384

Hillenbrand v. Evansville, 457 N.E.2d 236, 115 LRRM 2219 (Ind. App. 1983) 263

Holcomb & Hoke Mfg. Co. v. Younge, 103 Ind. App. 439, 8 N.E.2d 426 (1937) 29, 30, 59

Indiana Civil Rights Comm'n v. Sutherland Lumber, 394 N.E.2d 949 (Ind. Ct. App. 1979) 128

Indiana State Employees v. Negley, 357 F. Supp. 38 (S.D. Ind. 1973) 170

—365 F. Supp. 225 (S.D. Ind. 1973), *aff'd*, 501 F.2d 1239 (7th Cir. 1974) 174, 175, 176

Indiana State Symphony Soc'y v. Ziedonis, 171 Ind. App. 292, 359 N.E.2d 253 (1976) 407

Johann, Albert, & Sons v. Echols, 143 Ind. App. 122, 238 N.E.2d 685 (1968) 409

Jones v. Review Bd., 399 N.E.2d 844 (Ind. Ct. App. 1980) 127

Lawson v. Howmet Aluminum Corp., 449 N.E.2d 1172 (Ind. App. 1983) 222

Martin v. Platt, 179 Ind. App. 688, 386 N.E.2d 1026, 115 LRRM Pt. 2 4782 (1979) 267, 291

Mead Johnson & Co. v. Oppenheimer, 458 N.E.2d 668, 115 LRRM 3684 (Ind. App. 1984) 263

Montgomery Ward & Co. v. Guignet, 112 Ind. App. 661, 45 N.E.2d 337 (1942) 91

Morris v. City of Kokomo, 178 Ind. App. 56, 381 N.E.2d 510 (1978) 179

Ohio Table Pad Co. v. Hogan, 424 N.E.2d 144 (Ind. Ct. App. 1981) 85

Osborn v. Review Bd., 178 Ind. App. 22, 381 N.E.2d 495 (1978) 123

Pearson v. Youngstown Sheet & Tube Co., 332 F.2d 439 (7th Cir. 1964) 98

Pennsylvania Co. v. Dolan, 6 Ind. App. 109, 32 N.E. 802 (1892) 32, 48, 85

Pepsi-Cola Gen. Bottlers, Inc. v. Woods, 440

561, 278 N.W. 687 (1938) 57

Anderson v. Board of Trustees, 10 Mich. App. 348, 159 N.W.2d 347 (1968) 341

Butler v. Wayne County Sheriff's Dep't, 75 Mich. App. 202, 255 N.W.2d 7 (1977) 317

Cain v. Allen Elec. & Equip. Co., 346 Mich. 568, 78 N.W.2d 296 (1956) 88

Chamberlain v. Bissel, Inc., 547 F. Supp. 1067, 115 LRRM Pt. 2 4137 (W.D. Mich. 1982) 218

Chamberlain v. Detroit Stove Works, 103 Mich. 124 (1894) 29

Clarke v. Brunswick Corp., 48 Mich. App. 667, 211 N.W.2d 101 (1973) 88

Clifford v. Cactus Drilling Corp., 109 Mich. App. 776, 312 N.W.2d 380 (1981) 288

Cole v. Dow Chem. Co., 112 Mich. App. 198, 315 N.W.2d 565 (1982) 225

Coombe v. Penegar, 348 Mich. 635, 83 N.W.2d 603 (1957) 210

Couch v. Administrative Comm. of the Difco Laboratories, Inc., 44 Mich. App. 44, 205 N.W.2d 24 (1972) 88

Davis v. Scher, 356 Mich. 291, 97 N.W.2d 137 (1959) 346

Dietz v. American Dental Ass'n, 479 F. Supp. 554 (E.D. Mich. 1979) 382

Ebling v. Masco Corp., 79 Mich. App. 531, 261 N.W.2d 74 (1978) 405

Franklin Mining Co. v. Harris, 24 Mich. 115 (1871) 21, 28

Freeman v. Kelvinator, Inc., 469 F. Supp. 999 (E.D. Mich. 1979) 149

Gaydos v. White Motor Corp., 54 Mich. App. 143, 220 N.W.2d 697 (1974) 88

Green v. Lundquist Agency, Inc., 2 Mich. App. 488, 140 N.W.2d 575 (1966) 195, 199

Gross v. Abernathy, 47 Mich. App. 703, 209 N.W.2d 813 (1973) 321

Hackett v. Food Maker, Inc., 69 Mich. App. 591, 245 N.W.2d 140 (1976) 49, 403

Hersh v. Kentfield Builders, Inc., 385 Mich. 410, 189 N.W.2d 286 (1971) 199

Hoffman v. Garden City Hosp.-Osteopathic, 115 Mich. App. 773, 321 N.W.2d 810 (1982) 335

Hrab v. Hayes-Albion Corp., 103 Mich. App. 90, 302 N.W.2d 606 (1981) 286, 299

Jamison v. Storer Broadcasting Co., 511 F. Supp. 1286 (E.D. Mich. 1981) 148

Koehler v. Buhl, 94 Mich. 496, 54 N.W. 157 (1893) 29, 130, 131

Lynas v. Maxwell Farm, 279 Mich. 684, 273 N.W. 315 (1937) 50

Mallory v. Jack, 281 Mich. 156, 274 N.W. 746 (1937) 86

Marwill v. Baker, 499 F. Supp. 560 (E.D. Mich. 1980) 90

McIntyre v. Smith-Bridgman & Co., 301 Mich. 629, 4 N.W.2d 36 (1942) 61, 104

McLaughlin v. Ford Motor Co., 269 F.2d 120 (6th Cir. 1959) 49, 61

McMath v. Ford Motor Co., 77 Mich. App. 721, 259 N.W.2d 140 (1977) 61

Milligan v. Union Corp., 87 Mich. App. 179, 274 N.W.2d 10 (1978) 49

Milton v. County of Oakland, 50 Mich. App. 279, 213 N.W.2d 250 (1973) 148

Moll v. Parkside Livonia Credit Union, 525 F. Supp. 786 (E.D. Mich. 1981) 149

Morris v. Chem-Lawn Corp., 541 F. Supp. 479 (E.D. Mich. 1982) 90, 142

Novosel v. Sears, Roebuck & Co., 495 F. Supp. 344, 117 LRRM 2702 (E.D. Mich. 1980) 86, 215, 218

Ohlsen v. DST Indus., Inc., 111 Mich. App. 580, 314 N.W.2d 699 (1981) 156

Pacheco v. Clifton, 109 Mich. App. 563, 311 N.W.2d 801 (1981) 149

Parets v. Eaton Corp., 479 F. Supp. 512 (E.D. Mich. 1979) 49

Paxson v. Cass County Road Comm'n, 325 Mich. 276, 38 N.W.2d 315 (1949) 105

Pilarowski v. Brown, 76 Mich. App. 666, 257 N.W.2d 211 (1977) 174

Psutka v. Michigan Alkali Co., 274 Mich. 318, 264 N.W. 385 (1936) 88

Pursell v. Wolverine-Pentronix, Inc., 91 Mich. App. 700, 283 N.W.2d 833 (1979) 48, 61

Rowe v. Noren Pattern & Foundry Co., 91 Mich. App. 254, 283 N.W.2d 713 (1979) 48, 57, 99

Sax v. Detroit, Grand Haven & Milwaukee Ry., 125 Mich. 252, 84 N.W. 314 (1900) 32, 48, 57, 130

Schipani v. Ford Motor Co., 102 Mich. App. 606, 302 N.W.2d 307 (1981) 90, 155, 218

Schroeder v. Dayton-Hudson Corp., 448 F. Supp. 910, 115 LRRM Pt. 2 4365 (E.D. Mich. 1977) 93

—456 F. Supp 652 (E.D. Mich. 1978) 149

Schwartz v. Michigan Sugar Co., 106 Mich. App. 471, 308 N.W.2d 459, 115 LRRM Pt. 2 4535 (1981) 156

Sines v. Wayne County Superintendent of the Poor, 58 Mich. 503, 25 N.W. 485 (1885) 61

Southwell v. Parker Plow Co., 234 Mich. 292, 207 N.W. 872 (1926) 57, 59

Stearns v. Lake Shore & Michigan S. Ry., 112 Mich. 651, 71 N.W. 148 (1897) 48

Stimson v. Michigan Bell Tel. Co., 77 Mich. App. 361, 258 N.W.2d 227 (1977) 148, 149

Suchodolski v. Michigan Consol. Gas Co., 412 Mich. 692, 316 N.W.2d 710, 115 LRRM Pt. 2 4449 (1982) 268, 292

Sullivan v. Detroit, Ypsilanti & Ann Arbor Ry., 135 Mich. 661, 98 N.W. 756 (1904) 32, 85

Sventko v. Kroger Co., 69 Mich. App. 644, 245 N.W.2d 151, 115 LRRM Pt. 2 4613 (1976) 286, 288

Tash v. Houston, 74 Mich. App. 566, 254 N.W.2d 579 (1977) 194, 195

Toussaint v. Blue Cross & Blue Shield, 408 Mich. 579, 292 N.W.2d 880, 115 LRRM Pt. 2 4708 (1980) 49, 87, 88, 89, 90, 93, 163

Trombetta v. Detroit, Toledo & Ironton R.R., 81 Mich. App. 489, 265 N.W.2d 385, 115 LRRM Pt. 2 4361 (1978) 145, 152, 262, 269

Clarkson v. Liablan, 202 Mo. App. 682, 216 S.W. 1029 (1919) 203

Collins v. Industrial Bearing Trans. Co., 575 S.W.2d 875 (Mo. App. 1978) 248

Comby v. Farmland Indus., Inc., 524 S.W.2d 132 (Mo. App. 1975) 248

Cooper v. Yellow Freight Sys., 589 S.W.2d 643 (Mo. App. 1979) 162

Eil v. Federal Reserve Bank, 633 S.W.2d 432 (Mo. Ct. App. 1982) 206

Embry v. Hargadine, McKittrick Dry Goods Co., 127 Mo. App. 383, 105 S.W. 777 (1907) 128

Evans v. St. Louis etc. Ry., 24 Mo. App. 114 (1887) 30

Feinberg v. Pfeiffer Co., 322 S.W.2d 163 (Mo. Ct. App. 1959) 51, 52

Finger v. Koch and Schilling Brewing Co., 13 Mo. App. 114 (1883) 30

Fletcher v. Agar Mfg. Corp., 45 F. Supp. 650 (W.D. Mo. 1942) 48

Gambrell v. Kansas City Chiefs Football Club, 621 S.W.2d 382 (Mo. Ct. App. 1981) 123

Goodwin v. Dinkler St. Louis Management Corp., 419 S.W.2d 70 (Mo. 1967) 190

Grubb v. Leroy L. Wade & Son, 384 S.W.2d 528 (Mo. 1964) 159

Hansome v. Northwestern Cooperage Co., 115 LRRM 3027 (Mo. Ct. App. 1984) 288, 302

Harrington v. Kansas City Cable R. Co., 60 Mo. App. 223 (1895) 32

Henderson v. St. Louis Housing Auth., 605 S.W.2d 800, 115 LRRM Pt. 2 5070 (Mo. 1979) 285

Herberholt v. dePaul Community Health Center, 625 S.W.2d 617 (Mo. 1981), *appeal following remand*, 648 S.W.2d 160 (Mo. App. 1983) 248

Hinkeldey v. Cities Serv. Oil Co., 470 S.W.2d 494 (Mo. 1971) 88

Hughes v. Whitmer, 714 F.2d 1407 (8th Cir. 1983) 124

Joslin v. Chicago, Milwaukee, St. Paul & Pac. Ry., 319 Mo. 250, 3 S.W. 352 (1928) 209

Julow; State v., 129 Mo. 163 (1895) 37

Kansas City College v. Employer's Surplus Line Ins. Co., 581 F.2d 299 (1st Cir. 1978) 67

Kaplank v. Carney, 404 F. Supp. 161 (E.D. Mo. 1975) 338, 339, 340

Labrier v. Anheuser Food, Inc., 621 S.W.2d 51 (Mo. 1981) 248

Leftwich v. Harris-Stowe State College, 540 F. Supp. 37 (E.D. Mo. 1982) 160

Logue v. City of Carthage, 612 S.W.2d 148 (Mo. Ct. App. 1981) 405

Mitchell v. St. Louis Co., 575 S.W.2d 813 (Mo. App. 1978) 288

Morsinkhoff v. Deluxe Laundry & Dry Cleaning Co., 344 S.W.2d 639 (Mo. App. 1961) 193

Narens v. Campbell Sixty-Six Express, Inc., 347 S.W.2d 204 (Mo. 1961) 285

Newman v. Greater Kansas City Baptist & Community Hosp. Ass'n, 604 S.W.2d 619 (Mo. Ct. App. 1980) 248, 258

Nilsson v. Cherokee Candy & Tobacco Co., 639 S.W.2d 226 (Mo. Ct. App. 1982) 100, 101

Percival v. General Motors Corp., 400 F. Supp. 1322 (E.D. Mo. 1975), *aff'd*, 539 F.2d 1126 (8th Cir. 1976) 208, 267, 292

Porterfield v. Burger King Corp., 540 F.2d 398 (8th Cir. 1976) 319

Ramacciotti v. Zinn, 550 S.W.2d 217 (Mo. 1977) 313

Riddle v. Trans World Airlines, 512 F. Supp. 75 (W.D. Mo. 1981) 143

Rimmer v. Colt Indus. Operating Corp., 656 F.2d 323 (8th Cir. 1981) 248

Riss v. Anderson, 304 F.2d 188 (8th Cir. 1962) 328

Roberts v. Emerson Elec. Mfg. Co., 338 S.W.2d 62 (Mo. 1962) 248

Rotermund v. Basic Materials Co., 558 S.W.2d 688 (Mo. App. 1977) 248

Slabon v. St. Louis Car Co., 138 S.W.2d 673 (Mo. 1940) 48, 83, 85

Stark v. American Bakeries Co., 647 S.W.2d 119 (Mo. 1983) 248

Stokes v. Enmark Collaborative, Inc., 634 S.W.2d 571 (Mo. Ct. App. 1982) 127

Thompson v. Southwest School District, 483 F. Supp. 1170 (W.D. Mo. 1980) 415

Turner v. Gateway Trans. Co., 569 S.W.2d 358 (Mo. 1978) 318

Westbrook v. Mack, 575 S.W.2d 921 (Mo. 1978) 318

White v. Postal Workers, 579 S.W.2d 671 (Mo. Ct. App. 1979) 310, 319

Williams v. School Dist., 447 S.W.2d 256 (Mo. 1969) 216

MONTANA

Gates v. Life of Mont. Ins. Co., 638 P.2d 1063 (Mont. 1982), *appeal following remand*, 668 P.2d 213, 115 LRRM Pt. 2 4350 (Mont. 1983) 67, 68, 91, 261

Keneally v. Orgain, 186 Mont. 1, 606 P.2d 127, 115 LRRM Pt. 2 4576 (1979) 262, 286

Lovell v. Wolf, 643 P.2d 569 (Mont. 1982) 260

Nye v. Department of Livestock, 639 P.2d 498 (Mont. 1982) 260

Reiter v. Yellowstone Co., 627 P.2d 845 (Mont. 1981) 260

Wainman v. Bowler, 176 Mont. 91, 576 P.2d 268 (1978) 312

NEBRASKA

Farrakhan v. Sears, Roebuck & Co., 511 F. Supp. 893 (D. Neb. 1980) 126

Feola v. Valmont Indus., Inc., 208 Neb. 527, 304 N.W.2d 377 (1981) 102

Nesbit v. Giblin, 96 Neb. 369, 148 N.W. 138 (1914) 108

Russell v. Princeton Laboratories, Inc., 50 N.J. 30, 231 A.2d 800 (1967) 104

Salerno v. O'Rourke, 555 F. Supp. 750 (D.N.J. 1983) 125

Schneir v. Englewood Hosp. Ass'n, 91 N.J. Super. 527, 221 A.2d 530 (1966) 356

Schwankert v. New Jersey State Patrolman's Benevolent Ass'n, 77 N.J. Super. 224, 185 A.2d 877 (1962) 360

Sussman v. Overlook Hosp. Ass'n, 92 N.J. Super. 163, 222 A.2d 530 (1966) 356

Trautwein v. Harbourt, 40 N.J. Super. 247, 123 A.2d 30, *cert. denied*, 22 N.J. 220, 125 A.2d 233 (1956) 346, 350

Valle v. North Jersey Automobile Club, 125 N.J. Super. 302, 310 A.2d 518 (1973) 362

NEW MEXICO

Andrews v. Stearns-Roger, Inc., 93 N.M. 527, 602 P.2d 624 (1979) 246

Bottijliso v. Hutchinson Fruit Co., 96 N.M. App. 189, 635 P.2d 992 (1981) 285, 286

Childers v. Talbott, 4 N.M. 168, 16 P. 275 (1888) 55

Clem v. Bowman Lumber Co., 83 N.M. 659, 495 P.2d 1106 (1972) 121, 130, 131

Gengler v. Phelps, 92 N.M. 465, 589 P.2d 1056 (1979) 318, 321

Hernandez v. Home Educ. Livelihood Program Inc., 98 N.M. 125, 645 P.2d 1381, 115 LRRM Pt. 2 5142 (Ct. App. 1982) 90, 148

Yunkers v. Whitcraft, 57 N.M. 642, 261 P.2d 829 (1953) 190

Zuniga v. Sears, Roebuck & Co., 671 P.2d 662, 115 LRRM 3189 (N.M. Ct. App. 1983) 263

NEW YORK

A.B. Mach. Works, Inc. v. Brissimitzakis, 51 A.D.2d 915, 381 N.Y.S.2d 77 (1976) 162

Adams v. Fitzpatrick, 125 N.Y. 124, 26 N.E. 143 (1891) 29, 31

Aquinto v. Clifford C. Fisher, Inc., 165 N.Y.S. 369 (Sup. Ct. 1917) 130

Ashland Clothes, Inc. v. Cummings, 35 Misc.2d 871, 231 N.Y.S.2d 509 (Sup. Ct. 1962) 162

Ause v. Regan, 59 A.D.2d 317, 399 N.Y.S.2d 526 (1977) 174, 176

Baldwin v. Shell Oil Co., 71 A.D.2d 907, 419 N.Y.S.2d 752 (1979) 319, 322

Barile v. Fisher, 197 Misc. 493, 94 N.Y.S.2d 346 (Sup. Ct. 1949) 203

Barnett v. Cohen, 110 N.Y.S. 835 (Sup. Ct. 1908) 110

Beck v. Only Skirt Co., 176 A.D. 867, 163 N.Y.S. 786 (1917) 130, 131, 132

Beggs v. Dougherty Overseas, Inc., 287 F.2d 80 (2d Cir. 1961) 404

Beiner v. Goetz, 81 Misc. 244, 142 N.Y.S. 244 (1913) 132

Bergamini v. Manhattan & Bronx Surface Transit Operating Auth., 94 A.D.2d 441, 463 N.Y.S.2d 777, 115 LRRM Pt. 2 4094 (1983) 260

Bernstein v. Birch Wathen School, 71 A.D.2d 129, 421 N.Y.S.2d 574 (1979), *aff'd*, 51 N.Y.2d 932, 415 N.E.2d 982, 434 N.Y.S.2d 994 (1980) 159, 160, 161

Bird v. Meadow Gold Prods. Corp., 60 Misc.2d 212, 302 N.Y.S.2d 701 (Sup. Ct. 1969) 162

Book v. Severino, 51 A.D.2d 911, 380 N.Y.S.2d 692 (1976) 310

Borne Chem. Co. v. Dictrow, 85 A.D.2d 646, 445 N.Y.S.2d 406 (1981) 62

Bornstein v. Neuman, 92 A.D.2d 578 459 N.Y.S.2d 462 (1983) 407

Bradford v. Soret, 64 N.Y.S.2d 876 (Sup. Ct. 1946) 195

Brill v. Brenner, 62 Misc.2d 102, 308 N.Y.S.2d 218 (Civ. Ct. 1970) 130, 132

Brinkman v. Buffalo Bills Football Club, 433 F. Supp. 699 (W.D.N.Y. 1977) 147

British Am. & E. Co. v. Wirth Ltd., 592 F.2d 75 (2d Cir. 1979) 320

Brown v. Safeway Stores, Inc., 190 F. Supp. 295 (E.D.N.Y. 1960) 82, 83

Brownell v. Ehrich, 43 A.D. 369, 60 N.Y.S. 112 (1899) 123

Burns v. Smith Corona Marchant, Inc., 36 A.D.2d 400, 320 N.Y.S.2d 869 (1971) 319

Carter v. Brodlee, 245 A.D. 49, 280 N.Y.S. 368 (1935) 83

Catterson v. Caso, 472 F. Supp. 833 (E.D.N.Y. 1979) 175

Chin v. American Tel. & Tel. Co., 96 Misc.2d 1070, 410 N.Y.S.2d 737, 115 LRRM Pt. 2 5066 (Sup. Ct. 1978), *aff'd without opinion*, 70 A.D.2d 791, 416 N.Y.S.2d 160, 115 LRRM Pt. 2 5069 (1979) 94

Clark v. McGee, 49 N.Y.2d 613, 404 N.E.2d 1283, 427 N.Y.S.2d 740 (1980) 317

Connell v. Stalker, 20 Misc. 423, 45 N.Y.S. 1048 (City Ct.), *aff'd*, 21 Misc. 609, 48 N.Y.S. 77 (Sup. Ct. 1897) 209

Copp v. Colorado Coal and Iron Co., 46 N.Y.S. 542 (1897) 30

Corbeil v. Canestari, 57 A.D.2d 153, 393 N.Y.S.2d 796 (1977) 174

Cornell v. T.V. Dev. Corp., 17 N.Y.2d 69, 215 N.E.2d 349, 268 N.Y.S.2d 29 (1966) 409

Corrigan v. E.M.P. Producing Corp., 179 A.D. 810, 167 N.Y.S. 206 (1917) 110

Crawford v. Mail & Express Publishing Co., 163 N.Y. 404, 57 N.E. 616 (1900) 131

Croon v. Breitfellers Sales, Inc., 63 A.D.2d 1108, 406 N.Y.S.2d 390 (1978) 162

Crotty v. Erie Ry., 133 N.Y.S. 697 (1912) 39

Cullen v. New York State Civil Serv. Comm'n, 435 F. Supp. 546 (E.D.N.Y. 1977) 179

Cuppy v. Stollwerck Bros., 216 N.Y. 591, 111 N.E. 249 (1916) 84

Cusumano v. Schlessinger, 90 Misc. 287, 152 N.Y.S. 1081 (Sup. Ct. 1915) 203

Daversa v. William H. Davidow's Sons Co., 89

NORTH DAKOTA

OHIO

Harris v. Trader's & Gen. Ins. Co., 82 S.W.2d 750 (Tex. Civ. App. 1935) 199

Hatley v. American Quarter Horse Ass'n, 552 F.2d 646 (5th Cir. 1977) 384

Hughes Tool Co. v. Richards, 610 S.W.2d 232 (Tex. Civ. App. 1980) 152

Ingram v. Dallas County Water Control & Improvement Dist., 425 S.W.2d 366 (Tex. Civ. App. 1968) 121

James v. Vernan Calhoun Packing Co., 498 S.W.2d 160 (Tex. 1973) 48

Krenek v. Abel & Abel Air Conditioning, 594 S.W.2d 821 (Tex. Civ. App. 1980) 317

Lone Star Gas Co. v. Pippin, 620 S.W.2d 922 (Tex. Civ. App. 1981) 130

Maus v. National Living Centers, Inc., 633 S.W.2d 674, 115 LRRM Pt. 2 4205 (Tex. Civ. App. 1982) 269

Miller v. Riata Cadillac Co., 517 S.W.2d 773 (Tex. 1974) 57

Mr. Eddie, Inc. v. Ginsberg, 430 S.W.2d 5 (Tex. Civ. App. 1968) 121

Murray Corp. v. Brooks, 600 S.W.2d 897, 115 LRRM Pt. 2 4786 (Tex. Civ. App. 1980) 288

NHA, Inc. v. Jones, 500 S.W.2d 940 (Tex. Civ. App. 1973) 109, 399

Phillips v. Goodyear Tire & Rubber Co., 651 F.2d 1051, 115 LRRM Pt.2 4173 (5th Cir. 1981) 270

Reyna v. Gonzales, 630 S.W.2d 439 (Tex. Civ. App. 1982) 400

Reynolds Mfg. Co. v. Mendoza, 644 S.W.2d 536 (Tex. Civ. App. 1982) 90, 127

Roe v. Wade, 410 U.S. 113, *rehearing denied*, 410 U.S. 959 (1973) 224

Santex, Inc. v. Cunningham, 618 S.W.2d 557 (Tex. Civ. App. 1981) 288, 404

Scheps v. Giles, 222 S.W. 348 (Tex. Civ. App. 1920) 406

Schooler v. Tarrant County Medical Soc'y, 457 S.W.2d 644 (Tex. Civ. App. 1970) 333, 384

Schrader v. Artco Bell Corp., 579 S.W.2d 534 (Tex. Civ. App. 1979) 288

Sheshunoff & Co. v. Scholl, 564 S.W.2d 697 (Tex. 1978) 401

Sosa v. Board of Managers, 437 F.2d 173 (5th Cir. 1971) 339, 340

Spainhouer v. Western Elec. Co., 592 S.W.2d 662 (Tex. Civ. App. 1979) 152

St. Louis Southwestern Ry. v. Griffin, 106 Tex. 477, 171 S.W. 703 (1914) 38, 247

Suarez v. McFall Bros., 87 S.W. 744 (Tex. Civ. App. 1905) 201

Swanson v. American Mfg. Co., 511 S.W.2d 561 (Tex. 1974) 123

Texas Employment Comm'n v. Ryan, 481 S.W.2d 172 (Tex. Civ. App. 1972) 121

Texas Steel Co. v. Douglas, 533 S.W.2d 111 (Tex. Civ. App. 1976) 128, 299

Thompson v. Monsanto Co., 559 S.W.2d 873 (Tex. Civ. App. 1977) 152

Tigua v. General Hosp., Inc. v. Feuerberg, 645 S.W.2d 575 (Tex. Civ. App. 1982) 335

Transport Ins. Co. v. Lee Way Motor Freight, Inc., 487 F. Supp. 1325 (N.D. Tex. 1980) 410

Turner v. Byers, 562 S.W.2d 507 (Tex. Civ. App. 1978) 123

Ward v. Consolidated Foods Corp., 480 S.W.2d 483 (Tex. Civ. App. 1972) 48, 49, 86, 121

Warner v. Texas & Pac. Ry., 164 U.S. 418 (1896) 57

Young v. Lewis, 9 Tex. 73 (1852) 24

Zimmerman v. Gianelloni, 206 S.W.2d 843 (Tex. Civ. App. 1947) 195, 199, 209

UTAH

Crane Co. v. Dahle, 576 P.2d 870 (Utah 1978) 129

Mellen v. Industrial Comm'n, 19 Utah 2d 373, 431 P.2d 798 (1967) 210

Polyglycoat Corp. v. Holcomb, 591 P.2d 449 (Utah 1979) 64

Sowell v. IML Freight, Inc., 30 Utah 2d 446, 519 P.2d 884 (1974) 320

VERMONT

Burkhart v. Mobil Oil Corp., 143 Vt. 123, 463 A.2d 226, 114 LRRM 2671 (1983) 152

Clark v. Waterman, 7 Vt. 76 (1835) 10

Jones v. Keogh, 137 Vt. 562, 409 A.2d 581, 115 LRRM Pt. 2 4193 (1979) 289

Raycroft v. Tayntor, 68 Vt. 219, 35 A. 53 (1896) 195

VIRGINIA

Conrad v. Ellison-Harvey Co., 120 Va. 458, 91 S.E. 763 (1917) 61

Crescent Horseshoe & Iron Co. v. Eynon, 95 Va. 151, 27 S.E. 935 (1897) 121

Hatton v. Mountford, 105 Va. 96, 52 S.E. 847 (1906) 123

Kamiar Corp. v. Haley, 224 Va. 699, 299 S.E.2d 514 (1983) 406

Moore v. Plumbers, Local 10, 211 Va. 520, 179 S.E.2d 15 (1971) 246, 281

Raynor v. Burroughs Corp., 294 F. Supp. 238 (E.D. Va. 1968) 400

Sea-Land Serv., Inc. v. O'Neal, 224 Va. 343, 297 S.E.2d 647, 115 LRRM Pt. 2 4242 (1982) 190, 404

Spotswood Arms Corp. v. Este, 147 Va. 1047, 133 S.E. 570 (1926) 128

Terry, In re, 7 Bankr. L. Rep. 800 (E.D. Va. 1980) 275

Tiedman v. American Pigment Corp., 253 F.2d 803 (4th Cir. 1958) 123

Twohy v. Harris, 194 Va. 69, 72 S.E.2d 329 (1952) 50

Jackowski v. Illinois Steel Co., 103 Wis. 448, 79 N.W. 314 (1899) 48

Johnson v. Aetna Life Ins. Co., 158 Wis. 56, 147 N.W. 32 (1914) 199

Kaufman v. Grant-Crawford Co-op Oil Co., 106 Wis.2d 771, 318 N.W.2d 26 (Ct. App. 1982) 155

Kellogg v. Citizens Ins. Co. of Pittsburgh, 94 Wis. 554 (1896) 19, 29

Klug v. Flambeau Plastics Corp., 62 Wis.2d 141, 214 N.W.2d 281 (1974) 50

Kosloski v. Kelly, 122 Wis. 365 (1904) 30

Kreutzberg; State v., 114 Wis. 530 (1903) 37

Loos v. George Walter Brewing Co., 145 Wis. 1, 129 N.W. 645 (1911) 121, 128

Marek v. Knab Co., 10 Wis.2d 390, 103 N.W.2d 31 (1960) 57, 60

McCluney v. Jos. Schlitz Brewing Co., 489 F. Supp. 24, 115 LRRM Pt. 2 4227 (E.D. Wis. 1980) 155

Moody v. Streissguth Clothing Co., 96 Wis. 202, 71 N.W. 99 (1897) 127

O'Leary v. Sterling Extruder Corp., 533 F. Supp. 1205, 115 LRRM Pt. 2 4160 (E.D. Wis. 1982) 404

Prahl v. Brosamle, 98 Wis.2d 130, 295 N.W.2d 768 (1980) 309

Prentiss v. Ledyard, 28 Wis. 131 (1871) 24

Saylor v. Marshall & Isley Bank, 224 Wis. 511, 272 N.W. 369 (1937) 49, 85

Scarpace v. Sears, Roebuck & Co., 113 Wis. 2d 608, 335 N.W.2d 844, 115 LRRM Pt. 2 4491 (1983) 262

Schilling & Klinger, State ex rel., v. Baird, 65 Wis.2d 394, 222 N.W.2d 666 (1974) 408

Schumaker v. Heinemann, 99 Wis. 251, 74 N.W. 785 (1898) 128

Smith v. Beloit Corp., 40 Wis.2d 550, 162 N.W.2d 585 (1968) 49, 408

Sniadach v. Family Fin. Corp., 395 U.S. 337 (1969) 386

Thomas v. Beaver Dam Mfg. Co., 157 Wis. 427, 147 N.W. 364 (1914) 121

Tollesson v. Green Bay Packers, Inc., 256 Wis. 318, 431 N.W.2d 201 (1950) 401

Ward v. Frito-Lay, Inc., 95 Wis.2d 372, 290 N.W.2d 536, 115 LRRM Pt. 2 4320 (1980) 276

Wassenaar v. Panos, 111 Wis.2d 518, 331 N.W.2d 357 (1983) 408

WYOMING

Basin Elec. Power Co-op.—Missouri Basin Power Project v. Howton, 603 P.2d 402 (Wyo. 1979) 196, 203, 206

Fisher v. Church of St. Mary, 497 P.2d 882 (Wyo. 1972) 121

Salt Creek Freightways v. Wyoming Fair Employment Practices Comm'n, 598 P.2d 435 (Wyo. 1979) 159, 161

CANAL ZONE

Soley v. Ampudia, 183 F.2d 277 (5th Cir. 1950) 310

FEDERAL CASES DEALING WITH FEDERAL LAW

Adair v. United States, 208 U.S. 161 (1908) 37, 40

Adams v. Federal Express Corp., 547 F.2d 319 (6th Cir. 1976) 280

Adams v. Walker, 492 F.2d 1003 (7th Cir. 1972) 174

Adkins v. Kelly's Creek R.R., 458 F.2d 26 (4th Cir. 1972) 48

Aikens v. United States Postal Serv., 460 U.S. 711 (1983) 263, 302

Alamar v. Dwyer, 447 F.2d 482 (2d Cir. 1971), *cert. denied*, 404 U.S. 1020 (1972) 170

Alessi v. Raybestos-Manhattan, Inc., 451 U.S. 504 (1981) 147

Alexander v. Gardner-Denver Co., 415 U.S. 36 (1974) 142, 151, 162

Alfaro de Quevedo v. De Jesus Schuck, 556 F.2d 591 (1st Cir. 1977) 174, 175, 176

Allen v. Flood, A.C. 1 (1898) 16

Allen-Bradley Local 1111 v. Wisconsin Employment Relations Bd., 315 U.S. 740 (1942) 139

Alpern v. Hurwitz, 644 F.2d 943 (2d Cir. 1981) 112

Aluminum Workers v. Chromalloy Am. Corp., 489 F. Supp. 536 (N.D. Miss. (1980) 150

Ammons v. Bodish, 308 F. Supp. 1149 (S.D. Ohio 1970) 316

Anderson v. Shipowners, 272 U.S. 359 (1926) 236, 239

Andrews v. Louisville & Nashville R.R., 406 U.S. 320 (1972) 144

Aponte v. National Steel Serv. Center, 500 F. Supp. 198 (N.D. Ill. 1980) x

Armano v. Federal Reserve Bank, 468 F. Supp. 674 (D. Mass. 1979) 214, 215, 216

Armstrong v. Manzo, 380 U.S. 543 (1965) 335

Arnett v. Kennedy, 416 U.S. 134 (1974) 71, 165, 166

Arthur v. Oakes, 63 F. 310 (1894) 40

Assaf v. University of Texas System, 399 F. Supp. 1245 (S.D. Tex. 1975) 415

Associated Builders & Contractors, Inc. v. Irving, 610 F.2d 1221 (4th Cir. 1979) 257

Associated Gen. Contractors v. California State Council of Carpenters, 459 U.S. 519 (1983) 238, 240, 244

Atkinson v. Equitable Life Assurance Soc'y of

Index

About the Authors

William Holloway is a partner in the Chicago law firm of Hinshaw, Culbertson, Moelmann, Hoban & Fuller. He is a graduate of Northwestern University Law School and holds a Master of Science in Taxation from DePaul University. He has tried employment cases on behalf of both employers and employees that concerned wrongful discharge, trade secrets, race discrimination, oppression of minority shareholders, and medical staff credentials. He is a member of the Illinois Society of Trial Lawyers and the Illinois State and American Bar Associations.

Michael Leech is a partner in the law firm of Hinshaw, Culbertson, Moelmann, Hoban & Fuller in Chicago. He is a graduate of the University of Virginia (*magna cum laude*) and the University of Virginia Law School. He is a trial attorney handling business litigation and has represented both employers and employees in many disputes involving employee discharge and equal employment opportunity issues, in addition to lecturing and writing articles in these fields.